Methodological School of Management

Methodological School of Management

V. B. Khristenko
A. G. Reus
A. P. Zinchenko
et al.

B L O O M S B U R Y

LONDON · NEW DELHI · NEW YORK · SYDNEY

First published in Great Britain 2014

Copyright © V. B. Khristenko, A. G. Reus, A. P. Zinchenko et al., 2014

Bloomsbury Publishing Plc
50 Bedford Square
London
WC1B 3DP

www.bloomsbury.com

Bloomsbury Publishing
London, New Delhi, New York and Sydney

A CIP record for this book is available from the British Library.

ISBN: 9781472910295

10 9 8 7 6 5 4 3 2 1

Design by Curran Publishing Services Ltd, Norwich, UK
Typeset by Curran Publishing Services Ltd
Printed In Barcelona, Spain by Tallers Gràfics Soler

Contents

Figures and tables

Figures[1]

---

1 Note: this list does not include 32 uncaptioned figures in Part I, or photographs throughout the book.

Tables

Acronyms and abbreviations

APR	annual percentage rate (of interest)
BOTS	big organisational and technical systems
BPS	Baltic Pipeline System
CAU	components and assembly units
CC	competence centre
CEES	Common European Economic Space
CIL	Central Institute of Labour
CIS	Commonwealth of Independent States
CNC	computer numerically controlled
COMECON	Council for Mutual Economic Assistance
CPC	Caspian Pipeline Consortium
CTN	Corporate Training Network
DB	design bureau
DM	decision makers
EBRD	European Bank for Reconstruction and Development
ECA	Export Credit Agency
EDB	experimental design bureau
ESPO	Eastern Siberian–Pacific Ocean pipeline
EU	European Union
EurAsEC	Eurasian Economic Community
FFSR	Fund for Financial Support of the Regions
FMBA	Federal Medico-Biological Agency
FOREM	Federal Wholesale Market in Electricity and Capacity
FSB	Federal Security Service
FTP	Federal Targeted Programme
GDP	gross domestic product
GECF	Gas Exporting Countries Forum
GMP	Good Manufacturing Practice
Gosstroi	State Committee of the Russian Federation on Construction, Housing and Utilities
GUUAM	Georgia, Ukraine, Uzbekistan, Azerbaijan, Moldova Organisation for Democracy and Economic Development
HR	human resources
IAF	International Accreditation Forum

IBRD	International Bank for Reconstruction and Development
IEA	International Energy Agency
IEF	International Energy Forum
ILAC	International Laboratory Accreditation Co-operation
IMF	International Monetary Fund
IPO	initial public offering
KM	knowledge management
LNG	liquefied natural gas
MC	management company
MCO	Master of Command Organization
MET	Minerals Extraction Tax
MIC	military-industrial complex
MMC	Moscow Methodological Circle
MRO	maintenance, repair and operations/overhaul
MTC	military-technical co-operation
OA	organisational activity
OAG	organisational activity game
OECD	Organization For Economic Co-operation and Development
OLM	organisation, leadership and management
OPEC	Organization of Petroleum Exporting Countries
OREI	Organisation of Regional Economic Integration
PAK FA	Prospective Airborne Complex of Frontline Aviation
PAS	project analytical session
Quartet	Russia, Belorussia, Ukraine and Kazakhstan
R&D	research and development
RF	Russian Federation
RJSC UES	Russian Joint Stock Company Unified Energy System
RSFSR	Russian Soviet Federated Socialist Republic (renamed the Russian Federation in 1991)
SCA	Sukhoi Civil Aircraft
SES	session of experience sharing
SKBM	Samara Design and Machine Engineering Centre
SKD	semi-knocked down assembly
SOL	scientific organisation of labour
TAS	thinking-action systemisation/system
TCC	technology competence centre
TOC	theory of constraints
TPS	Toyota Production System

UAC	United Aircraft Corporation
UEC	United Engine(-Building) Corporation
UNECE	United Nations Economic Commission for Europe
USC	United Shipbuilding Corporation
USSR	Union of Soviet Socialist Republics
VAT	value-added tax
WTO	World Trade Organization

Foreword

Some may ask, why would Lord Bell write the foreword to a book on a subject that seems so distant from his immediate interests? I asked this question myself and quickly found the answer: passion and flair. I recognise them in life immediately and have a great regard for both. The best results in what we do, as professionals, are achieved when we work with passion and flair. Without these qualities the process as well as the outcome is that much more tedious and laboured.

When I first met Andrei Reus, one of the authors of this weighty volume, I sensed this passion when he was telling me about the book and what he believed it would bring to the English-speaking world. I also recall the admiration and respect showed to his teacher, Georgy Shchedrovitsky, and this further stirred my curiosity about the project. All the authors are extremely successful in their careers, and this is a clear testimony to the value of Shchedrovitsky's research, ideas and the body of knowledge he left behind.

In my line of work, in order to convince, persuade or alter people's perceptions and attitudes, I often need to present the best argument possible. Clarity of thinking about a problem will usually be reflected in the clarity of the solution. The readers of this book are presented with ways of tackling various problems, resolving tricky managerial situations and achieving organisational targets. The techniques of thinking offered here will be useful for professionals working in various fields – government administration, management of individual companies and state-run corporations, corporate governance and general decision-making practices.

But this book is not just about theoretical approaches to methodology of management, it raises the curtain on a host of practical issues and offers tremendous and exciting insights into modern Russian history and realities. The *Methodological School of Management* will be met with interest by a wide range of specialists – historians, political commentators, industrialists – but most of all, it would be invaluable for those who are learning how to manage people and issues alike.

So, read it, enjoy it, use it!

Lord Bell

Preface

Dear Reader,

Our publishing house is pleased to present a unique monograph containing key results of work by Russia's Methodological School of Management.

This school is not well known to Western specialists in systems engineering methodology and management. But we believe that its long history and the achievements of its proponents merit close attention, and that the school deserves a place in the global systems engineering landscape. We have therefore undertaken the translation and publication of this book.

The school was created by the pupils of Georgy Shchedrovitsky (1929–1994). Important Russian predecessors of the school include Alexander Bogdanov, the author of *Tectology: Or a Universal Organisational Science*, Alexei Gastev, who wrote *How to Work*, Platon Kerzhentsev and his *Principles of Organisation*, as well as several other Russian specialists in matters of work organisation.

The school and its pupils were grounded in the rich intellectual environment of Soviet Russia's rapid industrialisation (Shchedrovitsky's father was a key figure in the creation of the Soviet aviation industry). The school also gained much from the analysis and development of work by the best foreign thinkers in the field of management expertise and methodology.

The Methodological School of Management sees itself as a part – justifiably, in our view – of what has been called the 'systems movement', which evolved during the second half of the twentieth century in the works of such well-known Western thinkers as Ludwig von Bertalanffy, Russell Ackoff, Ross Ashby, Stafford Beer, Jay Forrester, West Churchman and many others. This movement forged tools for complex intellectual work and a language for systemic thinking and management organisation. Its ideas have entered the tool kits of most major control systems and corporations in the world's leading economies, from NASA and Toyota to retail chains.

Management science in Russia developed for a long time along its own trajectory, but always taking account of the international systems mainstream. Numerous programmes and projects were implemented in Russia for the creation of large organisational and technical systems (the term comes from Ackoff). The best-known among them are probably GOELRO (the programme for electrification of the Soviet economy), industrialisation (the creation of heavy industry, machine building and the Soviet aircraft industry), the evacuation and reassembly of a huge number of enterprises from western to eastern parts of the country at the beginning of the Second World War, and of course creation of the Soviet nuclear weapons programme and the missile and space industry. The list might be continued. The preparation and implementation of these programmes created a wealth of organisational and management experience. Unfortunately, the transmission of this expertise to new situations and to new generations of managers was on a person-to-person basis, without the systematic planning that could have ensured the best results.

We are not aware of any deep analysis or major publications of a theoretical and methodological nature that illuminate the Soviet systems experience. This is partly the fault of the extreme closedness and secrecy that attached to programmes and projects in the defence industry during the Soviet period, and the resulting shortage of opportunities for communication and discussion between leading experts, engineers and organisers in the USSR. It also reflects the climate of suspicion and distrust, which existed in the USSR towards all new trends in managerial and scientific thought that were not sanctioned by Marxist-Leninist theory (cybernetics was branded a 'bourgeois pseudoscience', genetics came in for criticism as the 'a handmaid of capital', and so on). Georgy Shchedrovitsky's *Methodological Problems of Systems Research* was only published in 1964 (see page xxix) and a first omnibus entitled *Systems Research* came out in 1969.

Such was the context – alongside the global mainstream and sometimes in advance of it – in which Shchedrovitsky's systems methodology took shape and was developed by the Moscow Methodological Circle (see the list of publications in English on page xxix).

Leading Western systems analysts have noted and continue to note the significant contribution of Shchedrovitsky's ideas to systems science and to the approach championed by this science.[1]

---

1   See, for example, Harold Bud Lawson's *A Journey through the Systems*

For various reasons – historical and other – the advances made by the Methodological School of Management were not widely propagated, and did not generate a major flow of publications or the creation of university departments. But the basic concepts, tools and methodologies of systems thinking and systems engineering developed by the Moscow Methodological Circle have been transmitted and used by numerous groups of Shchedrovitsky's pupils in various spheres of engineering and management science. These groups have continued their teacher's work on the formation of systems thinking and systems language in Russia. The Methodological School of Management is one such group.

The first part of this volume presents excerpts from the works of Georgy Shchedrovitsky, while the following parts (II to VII) contain works by the present leaders of the school: Viktor Khristenko, who has more than 15 years' experience in senior posts in the Russian Government; Andrei Reus, who has headed some of Russia's largest machinery-building enterprises; and Alexander Zinchenko, who has set up a number of innovative educational institutions. Works by other proponents of the School are also presented.

The works of these authors add up to a substantial body of methodological literature. The products and results of their reflexive thinking and the conversion of their experience into knowledge that is capable of transmission are made accessible by the texts and diagrams brought together in this monograph.

To conclude this introduction, it is worth formulating a few points that might summarise the place of the Methodological School in international management science and organisational technologies.

◆ The Methodological School is not an educational institution, but a range of tools – capable of transmission – which are used by its leaders in their current managerial practice. And this practice extends to a number of fields: government administration, management of economic sectors, corporate governance and the management of individual corporations. These tools require constant updating and extension to reflect new developments and new fields of activity.
◆ The Methodological School is a mechanism for knowledge

Landscape, translated into Russian and published by MQM Press, Moscow, 2013, p. 21.

management (the project and programme approach, the phase-gate system, 'lean thinking' and life-cycle management) in order to achieve new standards of management theory and practice.

◆ The Methodological School is a method for the creation of a communication space in large organisational systems in order to achieve product goals.

We wish you enjoyable reading and proper understanding of the management situations in which the decision-making practice of the Methodological School of Management has taken shape. And we hope that you will be able to make useful application of its concepts, knowledge and schemata in your own work.

Works by Georgy Shchedrovitsky published in English

1   G. P. Shchedrovitsky, 'Methodological problems of system research', *General Systems*, Vol. XI (1966) (translation by A. Rapoport of *Problemy metodologii sistemnogo issledovaniya*, Moscow, 1964).

2   G. P. Shchedrovitsky, 'Concerning the analysis of initial principles and conceptions of formal logic', *Systematics*, Vol. V, No. 2 (1967) (translation of 'Kanalizu iskhodnykh printsipov i ponyatiy formal'noy logiki', *Philosophical Research: Proceedings of the Bulgarian Academy of Sciences*, 1966) (also published in *General Systems*, Vol. XIII, 1968).

3   G. P. Shchedrovitsky, 'Configuration as a method of construction of complex knowledge', *Systematics*, Vol. VIII, No. 4 (1971) (not published in Russian).

4   G. P. Shchedrovitsky, 'Problems in the development of planning activity', *General Systems*, Vol. XXII (1977) (translation of 'Avtomatizatsiya proyektirovaniya i zadachi razvitiya proyektirovochnoy deyatel'nosti' [*Design and Implementation of Automated Systems in Design (Theory and Methodology)*], Moscow, 1975).

5   G. P. Shchedrovitsky, 'Methodological organization of systems-structural research and development: principles and general framework', *General Systems* Vol. XXVII (1982) (translation by A. Rapoport of 'Printsipy i obshchaya skhema metodologicheskoy organizatsii sistemno-strukturnykh issledovaniy i razrabotok' [Systems research: methodological problems], *Yearbook 1981*, Moscow, 1981) (also published in *Systems Research, Vol. II: Methodological Problems*, ed. J. M. Gvishiani, Pergamon Press, 1985).

6   G. P. Shchedrovitsky, 'Basic principles in analyzing instruction and development from the perspective of the theory of activity', *Soviet Psychology*, Vol. XXVI (Summer 1988), pp. 5–41 (translation of 'Ob iskhodnykh printsipakh analiza problemy obucheniya i razvitiya v ramkakh teorii deyatel'nosti', *Education and Development: Proceedings of the Symposium*, Moscow, 1966).

7   G. P. Shchedrovitsky, 'Two concepts of system' in J. Willby (ed.), *Proceedings of the 46th Annual Conference of the International Society for the Systems Sciences*, Asilomar, Calif., July 2002 (Translation of 'Dva ponyatiya sistemy', in *Proceedings of the 13th International*

Congress on the History of Science and Technology, Vol. Ia , Moscow, 1974).

8   G. P. Shchedrovitsky and S. I. Kotel'nikov, 'Organisational activity games – a new way of organising and a method for developing collective thinking activity', *Soviet Psychology*, Vol. XXVI (Summer 1988) (translation of 'Organizatsionno-deyatel'nostnaya igra kak novaya forma organizatsii i metod razvitiya kollektivnoy mysled-eyatel'nosti', *Innovation in Organizations: Proceedings of the Institute of Systems Research Seminar*, Moscow, 1983).

9   G. P. Shchedrovitsky and R. G. Nadezhina, 'Two types of leadership relations in children's group activity', *Soviet Psychology*, Vol. 26 (Summer 1988) (translation of 'O dvukh tipakh otnosheniy rukovodstva v gruppovoy deyatel'nosti detey', *Questions of Psychology*, No. 5, 1973).

Introduction to the English edition of the Methodological School of Management series

Dear Reader,

The weighty volume that you are now holding consists of seven sections, bringing together texts and documents created in the course of a decade. They were all previously published as separate monographs, and were republished in 2012 by Alpina Publishers as a series of books in a single package. Each of these books was prepared for publication as a separate work devoted to management analysis of a particular group of situations in the working careers of the authors. Each is preceded by an introduction and ends with conclusions from the analytical work which was carried out in that situation. We can say that each book belongs to a particular stage of recent Russian history, and this fact defines the differences between their subject matter and structure.

However, these texts and documents have a common idea and common historical logic, which justifies their treatment as an integrated whole. All of them present the theoretical basis and practical application of the concepts, schemata and knowledge of Russia's Methodological School of Management.

This is why we have decided to prepare the English edition as a single volume, consisting of seven parts that reflect the current state of development of the school, to which we all belong, in the most comprehensive manner possible.

The purpose and objective of the authors is to acquaint an English-speaking audience – businesspeople, government administrators and specialists in management methodology – with the original and applied thinking, methods and approaches used by the Methodological School of Management, which was established in the Soviet era and still operates successfully in modern Russia.

The first part of this volume stands apart. It is an anthology of works by our teacher, Georgy Petrovich Shchedrovitsky

(1929–1994), under whose leadership a body of knowledge – the 'starting capital' of the Methodological School of Management – took shape. So the first part of the volume acquaints readers with the basic principles and ideas of organisation, leadership and management methodology, and sets a benchmark for understanding the spirit and meaning of the management work that we have carried out.

This part contains only a few of the principles of this methodology and examples of their use. For a fuller acquaintance with the legacy of Georgy Shchedrovitsky, we invite readers to visit the websites ww.fondgp. ru and www.mmk-documentum.ru

Several important texts by Shchedrovitsky have been published in English in their full versions. They can be found at http://www. fondgp.ru/gp/biblio.

The origin and content of the ideas of the Russian Methodological School of Management might be better understood if we precede them with a few words about the difficult historical and social context in which the school took root and evolved.

The long-term goal or horizon, which Shchedrovitsky resolved to work towards in 1952, was to restore Russia's professional classes after many decades of devastation, and thereby to enable our country to regain its rightful place in the world (Georgy Shchedrovitsky, *I Have Always Been An Idealist*, Moscow, 2001, p. 301). Shchedrovitsky made his resolution shortly before the death of Joseph Stalin (in March 1953) and the decline of Soviet totalitarianism. The ending of Stalin's oppressive regime and the subsequent thaw led to an unprecedented surge of energy among young and talented people. Shchedrovitsky was a student at the time: he was enrolled first at the faculty of physics and then at the philosophy faculty of Moscow State University, where many of those who would go on to become the best minds of post-war Russia and leading lights in various fields first met and communicated. This was the intellectual melting pot in which what would later be called the Moscow Methodological Circle first took shape.

In this environment tasks were formulated in order to achieve progress toward the long-term horizon described above. We can reconstruct these tasks as follows.

To create a technology of thinking based on study of the works of prominent thinkers from all times and peoples, and extraction from them of methods, operations and procedures for efficient thought (Shchedrovitsky, 'The technology of thinking', *Izvestiya* no. 234, 1961). This involved study of the works of Plato, Aristotle, de Cusa, Descartes, Locke, Bacon, Condillac, Hegel, Kant, Marx, de Saussure, Popper, Lakatos, Toynbee, Ackoff and many other thinkers.

To equip the vanguard of Soviet (Russian) society – managers and engineers, people who create the future and are responsible for the consequences of their actions – with this technology of thought, and primarily with a capacity for systemic thinking. This, in essence, is what Shchedrovitsky believed to be necessary for a methodology of organisation, leadership and management (see particularly his 'Methodological organisation of systems-structural research and development: principles and general framework', *General Systems*, Vol. XXVII, 1982, trans. A. Rapoport).

To enable the reproduction and transmission of a technology of thinking to new generations of managers and engineers, not in the form of theoretical knowledge, but through solution of the current practical problems of specific enterprises, organisations and economic sectors. Shchedrovitsky created what he called 'organisational and activity games' for this purpose (see Shchedrovitsky and S. I. Kotel'nikov, 'Organisational activity games – a new way of organising and a method for developing collective thinking activity', *Soviet Psychology*, Vol. XXVI, Summer 1988).

This manner of setting objectives was unique in world history, because it was based on the special features of the social and cultural situation in Russia at the time.

It is interesting to make a comparison with how management methodology evolved in the West. The 'managerial revolution' in the twentieth century had led captains of industry and finance to understand that an arm-wrestling contest between the 'visible hand' (the term belongs to Alfred Chandler) of organisers, managers, analysts, planners and decision-makers, on one side, and the 'invisible hand' of the market (as formulated by Adam Smith and classical economic theory) on the other side, ends in the victory of the former. Economics with its 'signals' is only one of the many tools used by a manager, and the 'laws of the market' are adjusted at the right time and in the right place by competent people to support and implement their management decisions.

Frederick Winslow Taylor, the first person to work seriously on the description, standardisation and rationalisation of management, devised simple and clear rules which could teach workers the best way to load sand, transport iron and so on, and workers who used the system improved their productivity exponentially. The figure of the manager who rationalises and organises the work process gained credibility worldwide. Taylor presented his results as the scientific organisation of work, but in fact he produced what would today be called work methodology and technologisation.

The summit of achievement in the tradition issuing from Taylor is the Toyota production system, in which the Japanese united the best international practices for maximising productivity.

We, the authors of the present monograph, consider ourselves to be Shchedrovitsky's pupils. We studied the art and science of management under his leadership for several decades, in which time we tested his methodological principles in practice, incorporated the best international experience as part of the resources of the Moscow Methodological School, and nurtured Shchedrovitsky's legacy. We continue to train new students and to work on our own self-improvement, and we want to see the diffusion and expansion of interest in the Methodological School of Management. Therefore, as we emphasise once again, the later parts of the of this monograph (Parts II to VII) have been prepared with one simple goal, which is to make the main body of knowledge in management methodology and our accumulated experience accessible to an English-speaking audience worldwide.

The largest portion of the present monograph – Parts II to VII – consists of books that are already in the public domain. These are three books by Viktor Khristenko: *Rails, Pipes and Cables* (Part II), *Energy for Industrial Growth* (Part III) and *Airplanes Come First* (Part IV), followed by three books that have been prepared by a team led by Andrei Reus: *Knowledge in Management and the Management of Knowledge* (Part V), *On the Knowledge Management Method: Integration processes for a mechanical engineering corporation* (together with A. P. Zinchenko, S. B. Kraychinskaya and D. S. Talyansky) (Part VI) and *Knowledge Management in Working with Corporate Personnel (Corporate Anthropotechnics) at OAO UIC Oboronprom* (together with A. P. Zinchenko and S. B. Kraychinskaya) (Part VII).

In our management projects we have mainly applied three groups of ideas (approaches, schemata and techniques) which were developed by members of Shchedrovitsky's Moscow Methodological Circle. We should emphasise that this represents only one small fragment of the legacy of this remarkable man, and of his colleagues and students in the Circle. These approaches have helped us to address the tasks and challenges that we have had to face in our own work as managers.

The three groups of ideas are:

◆ a systematic approach and a methodology for systematic thinking, which we have used to make schematic models of public and corporate governance structures (see Parts II to V);
◆ a concept of knowledge, which we have developed into an original method of knowledge management (see Part VI);
◆ a method for designing and conducting organisational activity games, which we have used and continue to use in project-analytical sessions as a tool of personnel management (or human resource management) in order to develop the next generation of managers at large corporations (see Part VII).

Our primary audience for these works is people training to become managers. But we are also keen to reach the (almost unlimited) audience of anyone who is interested in what can be achieved by the application of intellect to the organisation of work. We want to show how this is being done today in Russia.

We invite all of our readers to ask us questions and make criticisms. We are keen to engage in dialogue and to participate in discussions via the Internet.

Part I
Selected Works

A Guide to the Methodology of Organisation, Leadership and Management

G .P. Shchedrovitsky

Preface: how to use this book

The Russian title of the material reproduced in translation here is *Khrestomatia*, which means an anthology of selected works by a single author or on a single topic. The word has Greek roots that mean 'a book useful for teaching'. Such a book contains materials systematised in accordance with a plan for the teaching of a certain subject in an educational institution, or for self-instruction in that subject. In the manner of a guidebook, the text helps us to understand how to use the sorts of instrument that are usually transferred from generation to generation. The contents of the present 'guidebook' are methodological and theoretical resources that support and enable the activity of organisers, leaders or managers (OLM activity).

The audience for this book has a clear focus. It consists of specialists working in various systems of management, whose objectives are to rationalise processes and to apply technology in their thinking and their activity in order to make efficiency gains. The anthology will also be of use to people who are learning such skills.

The author of this material is Georgy Petrovich Shchedrovitsky. Shchedrovitsky did not leave a consistent, complete exposition of the fundamentals of OLM methodology. As the head of a team of co-workers and students he practised that methodology, and up to the last days of his life he was developing a range of tools, principles and concepts. He left behind him numerous publications, unpublished works (lecture notes, various reports and presentations), project designs and consultations for organisational activity games.

I could name a dozen of Shchedrovitsky's best-known co-workers and try to identify their specific contribution to the common cause. Several interesting texts by them could have been added to the anthology. However, none of them achieved such clarity of exposition and depth of understanding as Shchedrovitsky himself. My colleagues and I would therefore prefer to wait until these specialists have worked for a couple of decades more and have made their names through future anthologies of OLM methodology and in other spheres.

We have taken as the basis for this material the text of lectures delivered by Shchedrovitsky in 1981 as part of further learning courses for senior managers and specialists at the Soviet Ministry of Energy. These lectures present basic ideas, schemes and constructions simply and clearly, making them easily understandable, in the manner of a textbook – as if tailor-made for inclusion in an anthology. The texts have no need for commentary, which would inevitably fail to do justice to the author's own thought and would only be an annoying hindrance to the reader.

The lectures use a precise scheme – almost a technology for organising communication with a large audience of people interested in the theme. Each topic is presented in a definite sequence, and several dozen topics are dissected in the course of the 12 lectures.

The lecturer starts by explicitly or implicitly *formulating a question*, which has no direct and unambiguous answer. If the question is understood (that is, it is meaningful to the audience), then work begins on the construction of a method which can either give an answer to the question or make it possible to work around it. (If such a method has already been developed, details are given.) This stage of the process uses references to earlier workers and authorities, anecdotes and specific cases, which offer a pattern or a concept-tool for the movement of thought. After the audience has witnessed the construction taking shape, the next step is to apply it to specific and real management situations and to show its instrumental capabilities. The lecturer knows the specifics of his listeners' work responsibilities, so he has no hesitation in telling them how to think and work. The audience listens, understands and discusses what it has heard. In effect, they actively assimilate the content.

The editors decided that as far as possible they would not interfere with this scheme, and would let the text move from issue to issue in a way that is consistent with the author's own logic. For this reason one and the same topic may recur in the text on several occasions, but on each occasion it displays a different aspect and is an element in another solution for another situation.

We have not hesitated to shorten the texts, taking out fragments that only make sense by reference to a specific time and event. These excisions do not detract from the thread of the exposition, and numerous repeats and restatements can be excused by the Russian proverb which tells us that 'repetition is the mother of learning'. In the opinion of colleagues who also specialise in matters of methodology, we have successfully avoided reduction to a 'dry residue' (the kind of reduction that Shchedrovitsky adamantly opposed) and have created a basic toolbox, ready for use.

We have divided up the text with headings that indicate the subject (the principal content) of each section.

A. G. Reus

G. P. Shchedrovitsky

Workshop and toolkit for organisers, leaders and managers

Purpose of this collection

I want to give you the resources – the word does work here – for self-organisation. So that you have a specific working technique at your disposal: a 'technique' in the sense of a set of resources. Nowadays we often use the term 'office equipment', by which we mean real articles used in the office (typewriters and so on), but I would like to requisition the word to mean techniques, methods of work, rules of self-organisation.

What I am writing about is a totality of complex knowledge that can be taught to professional organisers, leaders and managers. It is not knowledge from a particular field of technology, but knowledge about how to lead and to manage.

The engineering nature of organisation, leadership and management work

Everything starts with engineers who master the principles. They do not discover what was already in nature, but create a structure, something fundamentally new, something that was not there in nature. They collect the elements and create – by assembling, joining together, 'bootstrapping' – completely new things not made by nature, and in doing this they are supported by creative – bold, 'crazy' – thought. All this is bound together in a unity, which does not follow the laws of nature, discovered by science: there was nothing to 'discover' until an engineer created something.

The work of organisers, leaders and managers has the character of engineering work: it is structural and technical.

Organisers, leaders or managers must always be one step ahead; they have to come up with something new.

Technical knowledge

Suppose that you have to lead or manage people. You must determine their future actions, make a decision concerning their actions.

As a result you have a goal in advance, and you consider this person as a means or tool to achieve this goal. This how things always are if you are an organiser, leader or manager. But people might resist, 'break loose', or act in some unforeseen way. You say one thing to them, and they – perhaps they are creative individuals – do something else. And you do not know whether you need to regulate their manner of execution or if you only need to set the goal. In short, each time you need to have knowledge about the individuals and their actions, but this knowledge must be oriented from the very outset to your goals. You have to achieve a certain goal through these people. And so your knowledge answers the question: how can you achieve your goal through these people, and adjust their actions and your relations with them as a function of your goals? Such knowledge is what we call *technical knowledge.*

Technical knowledge gives us the answer to a question about an object, its mechanism and its action. However, this knowledge does not have a general nature: it is specifically geared to the achievement by us of our goals. It shows how adequate the object is for achieving these goals, and what we must do with it, how we must act on it in order to achieve our goals.

Technical knowledge is very complex. It is actually much harder than scientific knowledge. And the work of an engineer is actually much more difficult than the work of a scientist. The work of a practical worker is even more complex.

Technical and scientific knowledge

What is scientific knowledge? Imagine that you are once again dealing with these people. But you have no goals in relation to their transformation, the passage to another situation, or forcing them to act in a certain way. You are interested in what sort of a people they are in general. You want to 'take a snapshot' of them for purely cognitive purposes. You ask what they are like. You have no goal-related attitude towards them. You start to 'play' with them carefully in order to see how they behave. Then you are obtaining scientific knowledge. Scientific knowledge is always a 'snapshot' of an object, or a fixing of the laws that govern it – regardless of our goals and our ways of influencing it.

Technical knowledge is not just a matter of goals, it is also about your means of influence. You are not interested in the object in itself, but in the achievement of the goal using your existing tools and methods of action. And you see this object in this context. But in the case of scientific knowledge you pretend that you do not have goals. Hence the idea of a multilateral, multidimensional description of the object. The more you know about it, I believe, the better. For the purposes of technology, on the contrary, too much information is always a drawback.

Necessary and sufficient information is needed. You need to have adequate knowledge.

The concept of organisational management activity

Organisation, leadership and management activity is activity over and above other activity. And this differs fundamentally from, say, practical activity with natural material.

Here I have to introduce ideas of different types of activity and acts in order, first to indicate the object with which the organiser, leader and manager is concerned, and second to explain the characteristics of the activity of the organiser, leader and manager.

The act of activity

Just as we present the world in the form of atomic structures, molecules, in exactly the same way the world of work consists of elementary acts, which are organised in complex chains rather like molecules. There is activity caused by links of co-operation, communication, caused by the introduction of particular technologies, and so on. And I will represent this elementary unit of activity, what we might call an act, using the schema shown in Figure 1.1.

What you see is a person portrayed as a bundle of material, with certain skills and constantly using what a psychologist might call internalised tools. For example, language is an internalised tool. If someone has mastered algebra, its language and all its transformations, this is an internalised tool they possess.

In addition, the person has what we might call the 'control panel' of consciousness. In Figure 1.1 this is represented by the arrows.

What I want to emphasise by this is that what we always have are not relations of perception, but intentional relations. What does this mean? You see me here. But where do you see me – in your eye, or standing in front of you? Consciousness always works using efferent relations, or in other words, relationships that move outwards. The world is organised by our consciousness as something external to us. Consciousness is always active, and not passive.

9

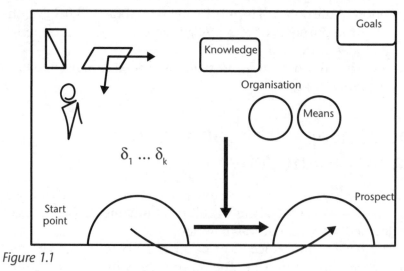

Figure 1.1

The activity of transformation

This schema is what operates when I move my chair, work on some technical process, or do some calculations. We obtain some source material, capture it and apply to it certain actions, tools or equipment, in order to transform it into a particular product, meeting a goal. This product emerges from the act of activity. We use tools and equipment.

If we connect tools and equipment with actions, we get machinery, mechanisms. Consider the actions of an excavator operator. Is the operator digging a ditch or operating the excavator? This is a multilayered, complex activity. In exactly the same way, when you are learning to drive a car, you are operating the car, and in some sense the borders of the car are your borders. Similarly the excavator operator, when they have learned how to work the machine, is not operating the excavator, but digging the ditch.

Organisational management as a sociotechnical activity

We can compose complex mosaics of relations between activities. We can construct links of co-operation, for example when the product of the work of one person becomes the source material for another person. We can construct links of support when, for example, the product of the work of one person becomes a tool, equipment for another person. Or the product of the work of one person – methodological or structural knowledge – becomes knowledge, a knowledge tool for another.

And finally, we can obtain complex sociotechnical links when all this structure of activity of one person becomes source material for the activity of another person (see Figure 1.2).

We need to trace this 'strange' event, where the activity of a person is aimed not at the transformation of natural material, but

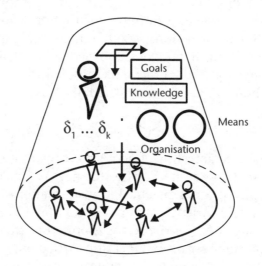

Figure 1.2

at the organisation of the activities of other people, at leadership of such activities or at management.

Here is one activity, that of the leader or manager, with all these elements, and below, as its object, is the activity of another person or other people. We can now ask, what is influenced in the process of organisation, leadership and management? What can we influence? We can influence goals. We can influence knowledge: to give other knowledge and thereby to manage. We can add other source material. For example, we can influence operations or actions by introducing new technology. We can change tools and equipment, introduce new machinery, and this will amount to putting new organisations and management in place. We can change capabilities. Here we arrive at what is sometimes known as psychotechnics, anthropotechnics, group technics (you can create groups and influence group organisation), culturetechnics or the laying down of standards. All these are different methods of organisation, leadership and management.

Scientific-methodological support

No matter what the activity people build, they need scientific-methodological support. I am introducing such a concept here.

This scientific-methodological support, on the one hand, speaks through methodological knowledge, what and how people should do something, or what actions they should accomplish. (In methodological knowledge everything is focused on actions. Often we call such actions instructions, regulations, algorithms and so on.) On the other hand, it provides knowledge about an object that gives us a snapshot of the object, its presentation and image. This knowledge should always be connected in a special way.

Knowledge of the objects of sociotechnical work

When we have sociotechnical activity – organisation, leadership and management – the need arises for new knowledge about the object. In conventional practical transformational activity, this knowledge was knowledge about nature, and in the eighteenth century the huge cycle of the sciences of nature arose as a support for traditional engineering, engineering carried out on the material of nature. The development of sociotechnical activity, or in other words the transformation of organisational management activity into mass and conventional activity, creates the need for a new type of knowledge – knowledge about the objects of sociotechnical work and related sciences. In other words, it calls for sciences concerning activity.

Historical and theoretical reconstruction of the origin of scientific and technical knowledge

There was a teacher, who was also a scientist.

And they passed on knowledge that can be applied to certain situations.

And their pupil acted in these situations (see Figure 1.3).

What happens next? Scientists and teachers become different people, and scientists busy themselves in scientific research institutes. And there they begin to produce knowledge, but not

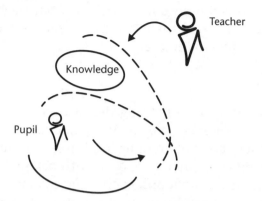

Figure 1.3

knowledge for learning, but knowledge in and of itself. Science becomes separated from the kind of subjects that are taught.

Further, the scientist produces knowledge not for the situation in which the teacher teaches, and not for the situations in which pupils apply their knowledge. They begin to produce 'knowledge in general' (see Figure 1.4).

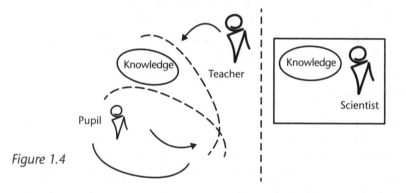

Figure 1.4

Science

What is science in contrast to methodology? Science works on the assumption that – roughly speaking – all future situations are the same as the past. Why is it based on such a strange principle? Because science will always seek to define invariants. It deals with an unchanging situation and formulates laws for it – laws that nature obeys.

Knowledge accumulates, grows, and the objective world and nature are treated as unchanging. The same laws apply throughout this world. Sometimes we do not know what they are, but essentially, if we discovered them, then we would see that everything behaves according to these laws.

Practice

How do practitioners work? They deal with different situations and accumulate experience. They move on and know that every future situation they face will be different. These new situations will be different from those they have dealt with before. So they must act differently in these situations. Everything changes.

Imagine that a practitioner wants to rely on science in their work. Science seeks universal laws. It finds certain invariants in all situations, and says that if on one occasion, an object fell according to the law $gt_2/2$, in another situation it will fall in exactly the same way. In the original situation the action was equal to the reaction, and in the next situation it will be the same. Whatever the scientific law, whatever position you take, it is always indifferent to the diversity of situations. But then, if you base yourself on science, you will never be able to use it to take variations between situations into account. You will never be able to predict how the situation will change and evolve because science from the beginning, in all situations, seeks the identical, the invariant, the unchanging.

Science and practice

Let me go back to the situation outlined in Figure 1.4. We focused on the scientist who produces on the principle of invariance. They pass on the knowledge to the teacher. The teacher, creating certain learning situations, embeds this knowledge into pupils and shapes their abilities based once again on the idea that situations are unchanging, because the scientist indicated that this was the case. And so engineers (or other people) who have learned this way, with their entire stock of the scientific knowledge they have been taught – all conveyed as universal principles – begin to work in practice. They deal with ever-changing situations, with different circumstances, and must somehow muddle through. And this proves that science is inadequate from the outset for the situational nature of real practice. That applies to any practice, including that of the organiser, leader and manager.

The question is, can the skills of an organiser, leader and manager be built on scientific knowledge?

Taking up a new post: a means of organising ideas

The process of taking up a new post is very complicated and, I would say, not trivial. Today each person organises this work themselves, individually, on the principle of accumulation of individual experience. However, since this procedure is standard, it should, as far as possible, be comprehended in general terms and given a technical vocabulary. It is an incredibly complex process, and involves many different relations. We must first disentangle all the strands, then learn how to reassemble them.

In order to disassemble these relationships, as a first approximation, I will introduce an 11-column table and offer 11 planes of analysis. Each column will be subdivided into many others and developed in a complex fashion. All these columns are closely linked with each other – there are dependencies between them. For example, origin and layers – the first and sixth columns – are closely linked. In what sense? A layer or layers are the term I use for where a person lives, where they belong, and the origin is the layer from which they originate.

Table 1.1 Plans of analysis

1	2	3	4	5	6	7	8	9	10	11
Origin	Educational background	Culture	Family	Individual identity	Layers	Groups	Organisation	Behaviour, thinking, mental activity	Communication	Self-consciousness

Being included in a place and the attitude of inclusion

We start with a certain type of person with certain character traits determined by their family, their general culture, educational background and origin, who comes to a particular place. I shall draw this, placing the figure of a person in a circular place. With one hand they hold fast to the place, while with their other hand they make nonchalant gestures, pretending they do not give a damn about the place and can come and go as they please (see Figure 1.5).

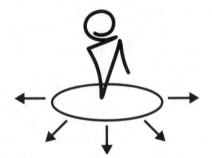

Figure 1.5

On the one hand, the person comes to this place and must live according to the laws of the place, and on the other hand they have their individual traits, their family and so on, either as shackles or as something that protects and supports their independence. They also have a certain culture, a certain origin and so on. The person splits into two or three. They must live a kind of double, triple life, and somehow put everything in order.

There is a formal procedure of inclusion of the content of certain columns into others. On the one hand they vary in historical terms, in terms of development, genesis and so on, but on the other hand, one is embedded in the other.

Joining the group

At first our person comes into contact with a group and must join this group, establish group relationships, join the organisation, take their place there and put their stamp on the organisation. This depends largely on their behaviour, thinking, mental activity, reflections and understanding – in short, on the techniques of their individual performance or behaviour. They must be included in the organisation's system of communication, and much will depend on their self-awareness and on how that awareness will change.

There are various sorts of group. In the army there are platoons and companies. There are research units and training groups. All these are organisations and groups at the same time. Sometimes a group arises and then it is formed into an organisation. Sometimes an organisation is defined at first, externally, and then it subdivides into groups. Sociologists distinguish between formal organisations – an institution, laboratory, workshop, section, whatever – and informal organisations or groups.

By a 'collective' I mean people united by the frameworks of a formal organisation. Many people define a collective in terms of goal-setting, and believe that if there is a single goal, then there is a single collective. But I do not agree, and I think it is in the interests of the organisational management of work to see things otherwise, because our research shows that such collectives – with a common goal – do not in fact exist. It is in groups, in a club (in a broad sense[1]), that we enter into a relationship with each other – discussion groups, political groups, groups of agreement or non-agreement – with respect to the structures of production.

The organisation

Two columns, the eighth and the ninth (that is, organisation, and behaviour/thinking/mental activity), always exist together, and can never really be taken in and of themselves. But in this existence together there is something fundamentally heterogeneous, as if they live under different laws. This is worth looking at.

The organisation collects people together and forces them to work in a single system. It provides co-operative structures, defines subordinates and superiors, co-ordinates activity and so on. However, people as individuals have their own interests, individual goals and attitudes, orientations and culture. They belong to a family (to a greater or lesser extent), they originate from different strata of society and have different educational backgrounds. And what is more, these people are organised into groups, from which it follows that the organisation 'lives' (I would say that it acts as a parasite, but this word is harsh and might have negative connotations, and

---

1   Clubs is not an ideal English term; the general meaning here is a collaborative group. It is discussed further on page 57.

therefore I say that the organisation lives) in groups and in individual personalities, or in collectives divided into groups, and in individual personalities.

Marx believed that group attitudes create the human essence. And labour – these are his words – 'consumes man, but never creates anything in man'. But people's essential powers are created by the activities of politics, art and science – although I do not mean science in our modern sense, when it is a form of manufacturing, but science as a free pastime.

Group and organisation

An organisation does not have the power of self-development. Only people can develop organisations. Organisations ossify, come to a standstill; situations become inadequate. People need to get out of them and start to rebuild them. Therefore, the most important thing determining the path of development is group relations. And organisations – industrial, manufacturing and other types – have only one purpose: to provide the best possible organisation of production. But not of life. A person cannot have a goal that is simply: to work. I say that point blank. A person cannot have such a goal by definition. Because it is meaningless.

What is the beauty of the organisational management of work today? The fact that personal actions, group action and work can practically coincide. I am not saying they always do, but they can coincide. There is today such a place and such a way of life and work of people, where they actually act as carriers of public consciousness, where they can think, set goals and objectives, and implement them. And therefore their professional and their personal lives may coincide.

Individuality and organisation

We have an individual, a personality. They begin by joining a group. And now they are in contact with the organisation and start to relate to it in very complex ways. The problem of individuality and the organisation, the organisation and individuality, arises here in an acute form. The person must occupy a certain place and become a 'cog' in this organisation, but not simply a cog. After all, we intend to consider what happens when someone takes up the position of a boss – a principal. As such they have the right to, and they need to, resist the organisation. And in this sense the place of principal is in a very special place and a very special position.

That person must resist the organisation, even if they created it.

In a general sense, this opposition – between individuality and the organisation – is one of the main sociocultural conflicts of our time. In and of itself it developed some time in the thirteenth or fourteenth centuries. The modern concept of individuality developed precisely at this time, in certain Italian cities. It is closely associated with the battle of the parties in Florence and with the existence of the prince as a formal power (since princes had no real power).

Individuality only starts to take shape in opposition to the organisation. This is a paradoxical thing. You can be an individual if you resist the organisation, if you separate it from yourself. And conversely, to be a person of the organisation you must dispense with your individual qualities, even with individuality. So people in an organisation, pursuing the interests of the organisation, should all be the same; they should be indistinguishable.

The most important problem in the twentieth century was how to save the individuality of the person despite the loss of many factors of individuality that goes with the further development of the organisation. We come to a completely new relationship between the organisation and individuality as such. Not between the organisation and the person, but between the organisation and individuality, because the person always lives in the organisation and the person cannot exist outside the organisation. Human society cannot exist outside it. Without organisation we could not have production, we could not have clubs; nothing. So the discord, the conflict, is not between the person and the organisation, but between individuality and the organisation. Moreover, individuality develops only as resistance to the organisation, as the right and opportunity of the person to get out of the organisation into a club and there to resist the organisation in search of their own free decisions. It is the person's right to locate their life in this resistance. Because whoever resists organisations should always be fully aware that they will beat and kick them without mercy.

A historical example of individuality is Giordano Bruno. The cardinal who questioned him on charges of heresy said, 'Acknowledge only that you might not be right. You do not have to say that you are not right, just say that you might not be right!' But Bruno refused. And because he and the cardinal were friends (they had studied together), the cardinal said to him, 'What are you doing? They are asking such a small thing from you – and if you do it, you will stay alive.' Bruno said, 'No, I will go to the stake to prove I am right.' What kind of dogmatism is that? What does it mean, that he is right? That is not the point. Bruno was showing his qualities of individuality.

Another example is Socrates. He had irked the Athenians with his questions to such an extent that they sentenced him to commit suicide by drinking a cup of hemlock. His students collected 30 talents of gold so that he could flee. But he said, 'I'm not a fool, I'm a philosopher. I do not seek rewards, but the truth. I will drink this hemlock so that these Athenians will always be remembered as bad people, who committed a crime against individuality.'

The activity of organisation, leadership and management

Organisation, leadership and management occur in human society inherently, and are not possible outside this human society. However they do not immediately become the subject of special, much less scientific, study: organisers, leaders and managers have accumulated their experiences individually. And the study of organisation, leadership and management only began some time in the 1860s, when the class of organisers, leaders and managers became a mass phenomenon. The class emerged as a profession, and the work of organisers, leaders and managers became the subject of special study.

This study has followed two paths. The first is management theory, as it is most often called in the United States. The second is cybernetics, which took shape in 1948 as a natural science discipline concerning management. What distinguishes and contrasts these two paths?

Management

Management theory was focused from the very beginning on the activities of managers – of leaders, organisers and managers. So all studies from the very outset were of an openly pragmatic nature, pragmatic and technical. The methodology and theory of management constantly put the question of how to act correctly. What should (precisely this form is intended, *should*) managers do in order to achieve their goals, to make the work of their company effective? The result of such an analysis should be rules of effective work – rules of effective organisation, or effective management.

Cybernetics

In cybernetics, by contrast, the natural aspect is predominant. In 1948, Norbert Wiener wrote *Cybernetics, or Control and Communication in the Animal and the Machine*. He sought to identify the processes of management, and he contrasted this procedural approach with the pragmatic approach. In cybernetics the activity of management is not discussed and analysed, but precisely its processes are analysed, and it is assumed that these processes exist in and of themselves without regard to human activity.

A simple representation of management was introduced in cybernetics. There is the management system, there is the managed system, there is what is seen as a direct link – in other words, management as such – and there is 'feedback' (see Figure 1.6).

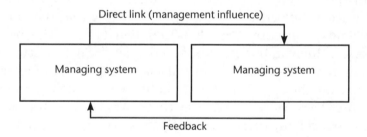

Figure 1.6

Goals are not fixed in this schema. Try to work out who is the manager and who is managed, just by looking at it. We cannot, because the direct and feedback links are symmetrical, and the difference between the managing and the managed systems is not fixed in the structure of the object.

Moreover, it is assumed here that the managed object always gives feedback to the managing system. The idea was born from the regulator circuit – a simple electrical system. But when this system began to be applied to all objects, there developed the idea that the managed object always sends feedback. The manager influences it, and it sends feedback. But it is possible to ask, based on ordinary experience: is it always the case that when you manage an object, it sends a signal back to you?

Natural and artificial

And a third point. The differences between the natural and the artificial, the natural and the technical, were not taken into account.

The concepts and categories of the natural and the artificial are essential for the twentieth century. They were also important before, but today a mass of complex upheavals is based on these concepts.

Take this example. A piece of chalk is lying on the table. Now I pick it up, I can throw it out of the open window, I can unclench my fingers and it will start to fall. How will a practical person and a scientific person describe these processes? They will describe them in fundamentally different ways.

The practical person will say, 'The chalk was lying on the table, then I picked it up and threw it. The chalk flew through the air because I threw it,' or, 'The chalk started to fall because I was holding it at first and then I unclenched my fingers and stopped holding it.' The scientific person would say, 'Everything that the practical person said is nonsense. If the chalk flies then it is not flying because the person threw it, but according to the laws of nature. There is a law of inertia, a law of attraction and a law of resistance of material, and therefore the entire curve of its flight is determined by applying these three laws. Moreover, you say that it was lying on the table. It was not in fact lying there, but was flying at a constant speed.'

Scientific person are not generally interested in what we do. They build their picture of the world in abstraction from human activity. They see nature in which all subjects or objects act according to natural laws.

But what happens in our real world? In our real world there are never any objects of nature, but there are objects of our practical activity. We take a piece of chalk to write with , we process timber, or we plant a forest, construct a dam. We reprocess one into the other, one material into another material.

Any object is always at the same time an object of our human activity and an object of nature. And in this sense it is not a natural, not an artificial object, but a hybrid object, artificially natural. It is technical – it realises human thought, it is created by human art, and therefore it is artificial – and at the same time it is natural.

Thus, the traditional scientific point of view of the outside world as acting according to the laws of nature is a one-sided abstraction. But a purely technical approach, when we view all objects as created, perpetrated by us, is a one-sided approach in exactly the same way. We need to take a combination of both, by 'gluing' one to the other.

Objects of management activity

The very idea of management is based on this two-sidedness of an object. If the object was acting only according to natural laws, without regard to human activity, management would be impossible. If objects were only artificial and we could move them like chairs, then management would not be necessary. The very idea of management, as we shall see a little further on, arises from the fact that objects are dual in nature.

During the Renaissance, the world was viewed as a world of technical objects, objects of our activity. Leonardo da Vinci clearly realised this position; he was a design engineer to the core. Then, from the seventeenth century onwards science blossomed, and we began to look at everything as 'nature'.

It is an amusing thing. People needed science and the laws of nature in order to replace God and appeals to God. We appeal to science now in exactly the same way as we used to appeal to God. God gave, God took away. Now science has defined its own laws, and we perceive that everything happens according to the laws – so we have no control over anything and we are not to blame for anything; everything happens according to science. This is the principal role of science.

This means that every object is an object of activity. Generally, when we say 'object' we mean that something belongs to an activity, that an activity sets the boundaries of the object. In and of itself the object has no boundaries. You walk into a forest – it is infinite. Hence the abstraction that matter is infinite in space and in time. This means that it has no boundaries as such. But where do the boundaries arise from? The boundaries arise when people carve out a plot and plough it so they can plant wheat or potatoes. Or when they dig a well or design a house. Practice 'cuts out' objects; in nature itself there are no objects. An object is the object of our action.

But what is inside the object is matter, material. And this material 'lives' – note the word – not only according to the laws of activity, but also by its own material laws. And hence the need arises for two viewpoints.

Artificial-natural and natural-artificial objects

This chalk is a typical natural-artificial object. It is an object of our activity, and therefore I can follow a well-known psychologist by saying that the chalk wants you to write with it. It has a purpose. And it is specially made, by the way, so that it is convenient to hold. The chair wants you to sit on it, the cigarette wants you to smoke it, the cake wants you to eat it. But at the same time, these objects consist of material, and this material may rot, may collapse, explode and so on – there are processes going on in there.

So when I say that these are artificial-natural objects, I mean that they act according to laws of two types. On the one hand, the object acts according to the laws of human activity. Here the object may be a material (this is a functional definition) or a product (also a functional definition), a tool, an object of study or whatever. When we pronounce these words, we pin down the function of this bunch of material in our activity.

And on the other hand, it acts according to its own laws, according to the laws of nature.

And between the laws of nature and the laws of activity into which we 'insert' it, there should be certain consistencies and inconsistencies, certain relations. So the problem each time is to 'capture' the relevant material, to insert it into a certain functional place in the structure of the activity.

The category of nature

The category of nature was developed in the seventeenth century. Three people in particular were responsible for this: Francis Bacon, writing the landmark work *The New Organon* in 1620; Galileo Galilei, constructing the new science of mechanics; and René Descartes who constructed a new methodology of scientific research and as a supplement to it defined three sciences, including analytical geometry.

Bacon constructed the concept of nature and Galilei gave paradigms of law-governed description. They, as it were, extracted this 'piece', which I outlined, put it on one side separately and looked for its laws.

Only objects of nature have laws. That is a very important point.

And objects of nature, as we now well know, are always ideal objects: mass at a point, absolutely rigid construction, absolutely solid body, motion in a vacuum – that is, abstract motion. And science only describes ideal objects, which it takes to be objects of nature. We then use this in practice as the laws of the life of our material. And we create objects through structures.

The question was posed: do objects of activity have laws?

They have no laws. Activity may have laws – of change, development and so on – but objects of activity are not subject to laws, because we construct or define these objects.

Types of object

And that is why from the nineteenth century we began to divide all objects into two types: target or teleological objects, and objects that are causally determined. And we began to distinguish clearly two questions: the 'why' and the 'what for'. Here, for example, is a house. Does it have laws? Why are the windows rectangular, not round? Or why does the car have such a shape? Because they were designed that way!

If we ask why a vacuum cleaner looks like it does, the answer is that it is like that because we have a goal: we use the vacuum cleaner for a particular purpose. How do designers work? They begin with the functions, purposes, and then for these functions they create a structure that provides those functions.

There are no sciences today that would help engineers to connect their structural, technical point of view with the natural. It is always a matter of their talent and intuition. The plane of connection between the artificial and the natural remains open.

Typological characteristics of organisation, leadership and management

When we begin to consider human activity, the first thing we note is the variety of types of human activity. This variety of types is determined by the typology of activity, and it is reflected in the nature of our professions: an engineer does engineering work, a builder builds, a teacher teaches and so on. And there is a typology of various types of activity. The typology may be built for various reasons, but what is important for us now is only the idea of types.

Other things that must interest us are, first, the comparative characteristics of organisation, leadership and management, and second, their distinctive characteristics with respect to a variety of other activities.

Organisation

Organisation is for all intents and purposes structural work, whose material is people. In this case, the word 'organisation' is used in two senses: organisation as the activity of organising and the organisation as the result of this work.

When we organise we collect something. Let us take a look at design. We need some structural elements, so there is a designer with a set of elements. We must collect these elements in a particular way, and we must establish some kind of connection and relations between them. When we are doing this sort of work we must impose some organisational form on these elements. We can produce organisation through interfacing them with each other, or we can bind them specially in some way. And when we have done such work on the integration of the elements and the establishment between them of certain relations and connections, we stop this work, and then the whole, which we have organised, can begin to operate according to its laws. But its action according to its laws no longer belongs to organisational work. Organisational work consists only in the fact that we bring together the particular elements, collect them and establish certain relations and connections between them.

Organisers deal with a particular set of elements, collect elements of a certain type and form in particular quantities, combine them and set certain relations and connections between them. When they have done this and have thus created the structure of the organisation – and the structure is defined by the location of the elements and the type of connections and relations – they recede into the background, and this thing either remains dead or begins to operate according to its laws. This always happens, whether we are designing a machine, a car or a nuclear power station. When you design a machine, it either works, or as often happens, does not work. The same is true of organisation.

Subsequently the organisation will continue to function regardless of the purposes of the organiser, regardless of what they put into it and provided for, or according to their goals.

Will the organiser 'own' its continued functioning, or will its activity be irrespective of them, of their plans? This question does not immediately concern organisational work. Organisational work is restricted by the choice of elements, their assembly and the determination of certain relations and connections.

Management

What is management and in what instances do we carry out management? Is it possible, let's say, to manage a chair? It can be delivered, you can move it, you can break it, refashion it. This will be a certain practical, transformational activity. But this is not management. Now a more complex case – a car. Here stands the car, you have not yet pressed the accelerator – can you manage it? You cannot. And when does it become possible to manage the car? When it has started moving. Management is only possible in relation to objects that have self-propulsion.

Imagine a situation when you can control the flight of a chair. Imagine yourself in a brawl from *The Three Musketeers*: someone throws a chair, and instead of defending yourself from it, you send it flying the other way. You have performed a one-off, momentary act of management – you changed the direction of the flight of the chair. In this sense, you performed management of this process. But what were you managing? You were managing the flight of the chair, but not the chair.

Leadership

Leadership is only possible within an organisation, within the framework of special organisational connections. What is the essence of leadership? It is the setting of goals and objectives for other elements. But in order for you to set goals and objectives for other elements – in other words, people – they have to reject their own goals and objectives and undertake to accept your goals and objectives. And that is precisely what happens in the framework of the organisation.

The organisation of people always happens like this. The person who occupies a certain position gives up their own goals and objectives, their own self-propulsion (by the fact of occupying that position), and is obliged to move only in accordance with this position and with the goals and objectives that will be assigned to them through the channels of the organisation by higher authorities.

But since people are not always aware that they must surrender their own goals and objectives in carrying out their duties, and in addition, because people who have surrendered their own goals and objectives are usually not much use for anything, the reality is that they do not reject their own goals and objectives, or only reject them within certain limits. Such is the game. They pretend that they are ready to give up some of their goals and accept other people's goals and objectives, and what they really mean to do is another question. They may temporarily conceal their own goals, but they may use the performance of their official tasks to achieve their own goals.

When self-propulsion begins, leadership either becomes impossible or can only be carried out within a very narrow range, and the need for management appears. Leaders not only lead, but also need to manage, because their subordinates do not always entirely surrender their own goals, their self-propulsion. But when self-propulsion begins, it will not be possible to lead them. We have to use a different technique – the technique of management.

Organisation, management and leadership

Organisation is collecting elements, combining them into a whole, establishing relations and connections – and that is all. Management is influencing the motion of objects, changing the trajectory of this motion. Management is only possible if the object we manage is in motion, self-propulsion. Management is the use of this self-propulsion by managers for their own purposes.

Leadership necessarily involves organisation – in modern sociology they usually say 'formal organisation'. This is only possible within the framework of an organisational structure, and as long as people accept this organisational structure. That is, they give up their own goals and objectives, and undertake to carry out the goals and objectives set by the higher authorities. Very often we lead in order to manage, or manage to provide leadership: in other words, the acceptance of a goal.

All this is connected in the reality of work.

I always contrast organisation, leadership and management with other activities. How? For example, we could say that organisation is the same as design, but design only relates to non-human elements, while organisation is design applied to people.

We could say that organisational work is the design of an organisation. But why is it design? What if you start work at the level of design? And what if you first create a project (a draft) of the organisation, and then implement it? This is also quite possible, and we shall later see how gradually, with the development of organisational management, other activities (design, planning, prediction) are drawn into it.

Management turns out to be a complex, integrated and systemic (these are different things) activity, which draws all the other activities into itself, subordinates them to its own logic and organises them in an integrated and systemic fashion.

Further, I contrasted structural organisation, management and leadership with practical transformational activity. I have always emphasised that management is not practical transformation, although it brings in practical activity.

The organisation as the result and the means of organisational work

Look now at the organisation as the result of organisational work. It is important for me to say that the organisation can be regarded as both an artificial entity and as naturally living thing. Who takes an artificial view of organisations? Organisers themselves. And those who design and create organisations always looks at them as their own creations.

The organiser makes it, and in this sense organisations can be of any kind depending on the goals and objectives of the organiser. The main question is: why does the organiser create a particular organisation? And on this basis organisational work can be included in management activity, by (let's say) considering the organisation as a means to resolve management objectives. Consequently, the organisation acts here as an artificial entity. It has a purpose and can be considered, as can any structure, in terms of the functions that it, the organisation, must provide. So we are talking about the functions of the organisation, about the purpose of the organisation. These are all characteristics that are seen from an artificial point of view.

As a tool, as a means, as an artificial entity, the organisation does not and cannot have goals. Organisers can have goals. But for their goals, in relation to their goals, the organisations they create are a means, a means for them to achieve their goals.

The organisation as a form of the life of the collective

The organisation has been created. And the organiser – a pure organiser, not a manager – has gone. The organisation has been created, and it has begun to live its own life. And then it turns out that, from a natural point of view, other goals may appear in this organisation – the goals of the collective, which was organised. There might be a strike, for example. And, generally, something quite different begins, inasmuch as this organisation begins to live its own life. Then we go back to the previous columns and must seek forms, methods, laws of the life of the groups and the collectives within organisations.

When the organisation is seen from a natural viewpoint, it is not yet the means, but the form, the condition of the life of the collective (the people) who work in it.

And it is even possible to see the organisation in the same way as we see the sunrise and sunset: the people working in it completely forget that the organisation was created by some other person to resolve particular objectives, achieve particular goals, for a particular purpose. It, this organisation, will be perceived by them like the movement of the heavenly bodies, as a natural condition of life.

The system–object management scheme

A number of things are needed in order to carry out management.

There must be some object that has self-propulsion, that is on a certain trajectory, and that passes into another state – which we can call state (2) – after some time which we shall call $\mathbf{T}$ (see Figure 1.7).

There must be another object acting in the role of managing system and seeing itself as the managing system, which – this is a very important point – associates its existence with the states of the first object. For example, the first object may be material that is needed for the activity of this system. But it is needed in this

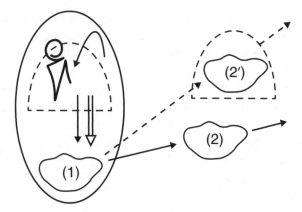

Figure 1.7

state (2). The system assimilates it. Or it may be that this system considers the object as a condition of its existence. Hence there must necessarily be a relationship of interdependence running from top to bottom. The system that we have called the managing system believes that its existence somehow depends on the object, on its states. This happens in living, pragmatic systems; but such a thing cannot be in inorganic nature: there, the hill cannot believe that its existence is connected with the existence of another hill. But for animals it is a basic principle, and it also transfers into our activity. So, in fact, the managing system does not need the object to pass into the state into which it passes naturally, but into another state, state (2'), which is located on another trajectory.

Because the natural motion of the object does not suit the managing system – and the system has already fixed this motion in some way – then, in order to change the trajectory of the motion of the object, to move it to another, it is necessary for the managing system to produce some kind of influence on the object – either a one-off, or a permanent influence throughout the whole life of the object. And due to these influences the original trajectory of the object's motion will be transferred to a second, which will already be an artificial-natural trajectory: that is, a trajectory arising due to the managing influences.

What is needed for this? The system has to have a goal, which corresponds to state (2'), and the managing system has to represents the first system, the first object, in a certain ideal state. Why 'ideal'? We might put it another way: 'desired' or 'needed'. In addition, the managing system needs particular knowledge about the trajectory of the real motion of the object. It needs to know where it is going.

Managing without prediction is essentially impossible. Whoever refuses to predict , refuses to manage. But certain knowledge is also needed regarding the desired state, or the project for achieving the desired state. And in addition, the managing system must know its capabilities, its resources, its means – know whether it can exercise such managing influences in order to change the natural trajectory to an artificial one. It also needs to know whether it can construct such influences, a plan of such influences, and so on.

The managed system is as it were inside the managing system; it is 'captured', assimilated by the managing system. Incidentally, therefore, the managing system is always aggressive, parasitical. There can be no other relationship.

Management thinking

This capture is very interesting – it is capture by thought. A training system is necessarily aggressive. In order to teach someone, we have to capture them. Not only that, we have to handle them so that they are no longer self-propelled, and begin to 'move' them . Otherwise, there will be no training.

Politics

Running a little ahead of myself, I might ask: do you know what politics is? It is when two systems try to mutually control each other, when both grab each other with claims to control and neither is in a position to do this, and a conflict unfolds between them. And when they mutually understand that each wants to control and neither can, they switch to political activity, and other work begins. This is the next, more complex type of action.

Knowledge in management

But (going back) in order to exercise this capture, it is necessary to develop predictive tools, design tools, means of investigating possible trajectories. And then it turns out that the whole mystery and specificity of management activity lies in our knowledge. Only someone who has particular knowledge about the managed object can manage. The success of management depends on knowledge.

As it turns out, we can manage if we have the relevant knowledge and understanding. And the possibility of managing does not depend on official position. It is leadership that depends on official position. Therefore the leader can be one person, and the manager, the actual manager, might be another. It all depends on what systems of knowledge and what techniques of management of people they include in their work. You perhaps know the famous play in which the slave Aesop controls his master because he knows more, understands more. This is the strength of management: it can be exercised contrary to the structures of leadership.

Mental activity and pure thought

The work of an organiser, leader, manager is not so much mental activity as pure thought. A leader or organiser must be constantly thinking.

Genuine organisational and leadership work happens when leaders sit down in their office and think how to act. I would even propose the following: the real leaders and organisers are people who keep their encounters with people to a minimum, who sit in their office and think. When this happens, organisation at the enterprise is on a good footing.

This is why we need to discuss what distinguishes pure thought from mental activity, how they occur and – most importantly – how they are connected with each other. I shall draw a diagram, which captures the essence of the matter.

The situation of collective action

People always live and act in a team: they work in specific groups of people, enter into specific interactions. And these interactions unfold in certain situations. Situations are always made by interactions between people.

In practice this is self-evident, but for theory it is a sealed book. When pre-Marxist science described human work, what it described was a 'Robinson Crusoe', a single person, and it stated that this person carries out actions, relates to nature around him, gains knowledge of the world and so on. Just one person. Marx caricatured this approach: he called previous studies 'Robinsonadas', referring to the situation where Robinson finds himself on a desert island and interacts with nature.

But even though Marx gave this approach short shrift as early as in the 1850s, the greater part of the sciences still take the one person who acts, sets goals, knows the world and so on as their basic model. The fact that people always act in a team, in a specific and complex organisation, has not really penetrated scientific thinking, or is only just beginning to be acknowledged.

I make the following thesis the starting point for our work: people always act in a group, in a collective, in a situation of collective interactions.

Let's draw this in a diagram that marks the boundaries of a situation defined by certain connections between certain places. The minimum number of participants is three, not two. There might be more, but there must be at least three (as shown in Figure 1.8).

Figure 1.8

But at the same time, and this is the second key point, these people are assuredly in relationships with people who are in another situation. This is very important. So, for each person, there are people who are in the same situation as themselves. and there are people who are in a different situation (see Figure 1.9).

It turns out that deciding who is in the first situation and who is in the other situation is not initially possible. This leads to all sorts

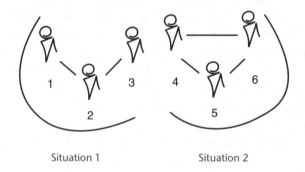

Situation 1   Situation 2

Figure 1.9

of problems. We cannot tell whether we are in the same situation or whether I am in one situation and you are in another.

The boundaries between situations are very complex; they cannot easily be drawn. And a considerable amount of time is needed before it starts to become clear what gives a situation its unity. Space and time can never define the unity of the situation, because the situation is a function of human consciousness, of how people are self-aware, who they take themselves to be and where they takes themselves to be. Highly complex mechanisms are always at work that make a situation into a fusion of the real and the ideal.

Types of situation

This is beautifully described by the image of the 'rookery' in Ilf and Petrov's *The Little Golden Calf*[2] – a communal apartment where a group of completely different people live together: a polar explorer, a former prince who is now a labourer in the Soviet Far East, the janitor Pryakhin, Mrs Pferd and so on. In their communal apartment they have to address various problems: for instance, they have to decide whether to give one of the tenants, Lokhankin, a whipping for constantly forgetting to switch off the light in the toilet. All these people are spatially connected, but they all live in completely different situations. A situation takes shape nevertheless. A situation is always a unity of the subjective and the objective, circumstances, and our attitude toward them. We can live in a situation that belongs to today, and in a situation that is defined in terms of centuries and millennia. If any of you were given the task of designing a programme of development for 20 years into the future, you would thereby be inserted into a situation that lasts for 20 years from now. And the moment you accept the task and start thinking about it, you have expanded the boundaries of your own situation.

When we read American books about their experience of organisational and managerial work, we again expand the spatial boundaries of our situation: we take hold of American experience (or German, French, Japanese experience). The boundaries between situations are highly complex and cannot easily be drawn. And a considerable amount of time is needed for the crystallisation of whatever makes a situation the situation it is.

---

2 This is a well-known Russian satirical novel.

Reflexiveness

Suppose – here I am taking the third step – that someone from the second situation poses a question to someone in the first situation. Suppose we have six people, and the sixth is posing a question to the first.

Let's say, keeping things simple, that they ask, 'You were doing something just now; tell me what you were doing.' What do you have to do in order to answer this question? You have to step outside the position where some mental activity was going on just previously into a reflexive position, to look at yourself in action from outside yourself, to represent to yourself what you were doing (see Figure 1.10).

Figure 1.10

There is a subtlety that we have to bear in mind here. We can each represent to ourselves what we were doing, but the question might be: what was being done in that situation? And that will be a different question. People often see clearly and know what they were doing, but they do not see and know what was going on around them. And sometimes they see what was going on around them, but have no idea what they were doing themselves. There are complex oscillations of consciousness here. Sometimes people know how badly others did, but have no idea that they did badly themselves.

What we call people's intelligence, their subtlety, is not defined by the structure of their thought, but by this reflexiveness. We say of one person that they are obtuse and of another that they are subtle and cunning. The ancient Greeks called Odysseus 'the man full of resource'. The resourceful Odysseus stood out from others by having excellent powers of reflexiveness.

Generally speaking, this is one of the most powerful individual psychological measures of human beings – what in any person is the relationship between consciousness of mental activity, that is, consciousness directed onto the objects of their action, and their reflexive consciousness – that is, how they see and comprehend themselves.

Now, as I work, my consciousness is constantly bifurcating or undergoing a certain interference. First of all, I have a content that I must explain to you. Next, I constantly watch the audience, and I choose a few people and try to look them in the eye. And I use some part of my consciousness to observe myself, to monitor what I am doing, to try to imagine how this looks from your point of view, from your position. So there are several modes of operation, which are functioning simultaneously, including a reflexive monitoring. We usually call someone subtle and sensitive if this reflexive component is strongly developed in them, if they can see themselves from outside, and can clearly understand and know what they are doing.

A lot of surprising things start from here. For example, a person can ask themselves, how does another person see me, what is their attitude towards me? Many human activities and games, in such realms as war and sport, are based on this possibility.

What happens when a footballer find himself in a one-on-one situation with the goalkeeper? The footballer says to himself, 'He thinks I am going to shoot for the bottom right corner, so I will shoot for the left.' At one more remove, 'He thinks that I think that he thinks I'm going to shoot for the right corner. But I'm going to shoot for the left.' The footballer has not only thought about what the goalkeeper thinks, but also about what the goalkeeper thinks about what the footballer thinks. This is a real factor in the actual situation. This is the origin of reflexive games, reflexive management, reflexive politics. We introduce the concept of tiers of reflexivity: the number of these 'I think of what he thinks I am thinking.'

This component, which takes account of tiers of reflexivity, defines what we call subtlety of the human mind as opposed to obtuseness. There are people – great scientists, inventors – who have done great things, but who are very obtuse. Such people work like steam engines. They do not have a situation, but they have a programme, which they follow. Events along the way, negative reactions from other people, matter nothing to them – their wheels keep turning. The other extreme is someone who is always worried about what somebody else or some group of people think of them, about how they will appear to them. All their actions are a function of these representations. And as a result they do nothing.

Types of reflexiveness

Reflexiveness is the ability to see all the wealth of content in retrospect (in other words, looking over your shoulder and asking, what did I do?) and also to an extent in prospect. Projects and planning arise from prospective, forward-directed reflexiveness, when a person begins to think, not 'What did I do?' but 'What will happen if I do this?' This forward play, prospective reflexiveness, is what enables planning, the making of projects, the design of programmes and so on.

Reflexiveness takes different forms. For example, I am telling you something here and now, but at the same time the fringe of my consciousness is constantly following how you are receiving this, how you react to it. This reflexive plane goes in parallel. But it might be left out, and later, when I go into the other room, I ask other people, who were observing me, 'What did I do?' And they start telling me what I did and said. Sometimes I am surprised, and I say that they cannot be right – 'Was that really what happened?' Because sometimes the entirety of consciousness is focused on the direct plane and the reflexive component goes away. When a person experiences something emotionally, the reflexive component narrows. Later they will emerge from the situation, take stock and say, 'What did I do then? I acted wrongly!' But at the time when they did it, they were so emotionally charged with the event that they were entirely contained in the situation.

So reflexiveness is the representation in consciousness of what we are doing and how we are doing it.

In this sense, reflexiveness is the contrary of abstract thought because reflexiveness is entirely focused on the content of action. Reflexiveness is highly concrete.

The criterion of correct or incorrect is not applicable to reflexiveness. It is worth noting that reflexiveness is what is at stake when we say that this is my view and that is yours. Everyone has their take on matters, their point of view. Reflexiveness is closely dependent on a person's experience and the angle from which they view each situation. Reflexiveness is highly subjective. It is subjective and experientially rich.

Another important point is this: the way we live and act is determined by reflexiveness. It organises our space and time. I can watch my own life – for example, my relationships with people who are important to me – like a movie. The episodes that make up my life can be ranged one by one, they shape the meaningful series of my relationships, and what happened when I was 18 is before my eyes as if it happened yesterday. Reflexiveness is what ultimately organises our vision of our own life, it fashions the structure of our lived activity. It makes large omissions, connects important moments, gives them emotional colour, ties certain 'ribbons' to others and so on.

People know themselves and their actions through reflexiveness, in reflexive awareness. From this it follows that the wealth of human experience is determined by reflexiveness, by the extent to which people think through what has happened to them. This is the basic unit . The unit is not the action, but the action plus the subsequent reflexive thinking through: how did I act and what happened?

We know today what a huge role is played in this by dreaming. When people dream they travel the same road again and again. When we sleep we take no action, but, as many psychological studies have shown, reflexiveness continues to operate. Recurring dreams are reflexiveness at work.

Communication

I now move on to the next step. The example above had the sixth person asking the question, and I have to respond by telling them what I did. What is expressed in our text? We express in it what was registered by our reflexiveness. Initially reflexiveness proceeded without a text – I simply saw what I did, represented the situation to myself. The question was, 'What are you doing? Why are you doing it like this and not some other way?' And to answer this question people enter the reflexive position and express their reflexive take on what occurred in the form of a text (see Figure 1.11).

At this point very strange things start to happen. The person has constructed a text. Roughly speaking, it includes a block of language and other resources, concepts that we use. The reflexiveness has been given shape through the use of words, concepts, knowledge and representations. It has acquired a particular appearance – by the mediation of the words of a language and the meanings that those words contain. This is a new complex process, the process of expression of our ideas in the text of speech.

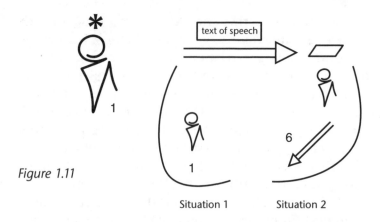

Figure 1.11

Situation 1   Situation 2

So there is a text. What must our sixth person do now? They must understand this text. But what do we mean by 'understand'?

Understanding

At the simplest level to understand is to apply a text, which we have received, to our action in a situation, or to construct a new action in accordance with this text.

Imagine the following situation. A master of sport performs some action – it might be a score through the ring in basketball or a shot in football or something else. And a young sports player asks them how they do it. And the master starts to tell them – not by showing, but by saying: 'I do it in this way.'

In the case of a throw in basketball, the master says, for example, that the wrist has to be soft and relaxed, the elbow drawn forward, and so on. What does it mean to understand this text? As the young sports player listens to this text, they also articulate it, 'mark it up', and begin, as it were, to reproduce this action in their own situation.

This is most easily represented in algorithms and instructions. They are constructed in a way that enables us to perform an action that exactly corresponds to them: 'Do this (say, move the switch to a certain position), then do this, this and this.' And what is the meaning of the sentence 'The area of a triangle is equal to half the product of the base and the height ($S = 1/2ah$)'? If you want to obtain the area of a triangle, you must measure the base, measure the height, multiply one by the other and divide by two. This is a detailed instruction-sequence. This is the simplest possible example. How do we understand it? We say, S is the area of a triangle. We understood what was at issue, and we applied it to the object. And what is *h*? It is the height. In other words, if the triangle is given to us, if it is located in the situation, then factually, what someone does when they understand the algorithm is simply to start applying the text to the object (see Figure 1.11).

So understanding is recreation in the situation of what was discussed in the text. And if we can move from the text of the message to the situation, we say that we understand. If we cannot do this, we say that we have not understood. And our understanding may be both correct and proper or incorrect and improper. But 'correct' and 'incorrect' are very contingent expressions here because, in a sense, understanding is always right. The boundaries are better expressed by saying 'they have got it' or 'they haven't got it'. I have got it if I am able to create the situation, to construct it and start to act in it. But it might then turn out that I understood in my own way, not as intended by the person who gave the explanation. But still, I have got it.

So we have understanding, as opposed to 'I haven't got it.' I haven't got it if I heard the text, even took note of it, but cannot make the step to the situation. I cannot see or imagine what is at stake. There is also proper and improper understanding.

In our example the question was posed from another situation. That situation is different from the first, so the text introduced that other situation into the first. And in each text, each communication, we have a struggle between the situations. The person who receives the text begins to adapt it to their situation, understand it from the viewpoint of their situation and to assess it in terms of their situation. They might say, 'I don't need all this, I don't know what you are talking about, this doesn't fit with my situation.'

Each person understands in terms of how the situation in which they are located affects them. So everyone understands their situation. We usually express this understanding with the word 'meaning'.

Meaning

What is 'meaning'? It is a tricky question. Really, there isn't any meaning. Meaning is a phantom. But here's the trick. I can say a sentence, like 'The clock has fallen off the wall', in two situations with two completely different meanings: 'The *clock* fell' and 'The clock *fell*.' The change of accent corresponds to two fundamentally different situations. Imagine this: when I am lecturing, I have got used to the fact that there is a clock here on the wall. At some point, I turn, I see an empty space, and someone in the audience says, 'The clock fell off the wall.' They might simply have said 'it fell' because, in this instance, the word 'clock' carries no new information. I look at the clock, I have got used to it and everyone in the lecture hall has got used to it. We look at that place and someone says 'it fell off the wall', and that phrase provides new information.

But now imagine a different situation. I am giving a lecture and all of a sudden there is a crash behind me. What has made it? I am told, 'The clock fell off the wall.' The situation is entirely different because what is new in this instance is the message about the clock. I heard something fall – that is a given – and I am told that it is the clock that fell. We pin this down in terms of 'subject' and 'predicate' in their functional relationships: in the first case, the clock is the subject, and in the second case the subject is the falling. We carry out syntactical analysis and highlight a difference between the two oppositions 'noun–adjective' and 'subject–predicate'. The distinction between subject and predicate is this: when we have a text, the subject is what we are talking about and the predicate is the characteristic that we ascribe to it. So when I hear any text, I understand it though an analysis: I work out what is the subject. Why do I work it out? I relate it to the situation.

The subject might be an action. In an algorithm I always treat actions as items, to which characteristics are ascribed. So I am always doing a particular sort of work: I parse the text syntactically, identify its syntactical organisation, its predicate structure, and map this onto the situation. This is a process of scanning, of relating the text to the situation. When you understand my text now, you carry out this complex relational work. You are constantly identifying what is being talked about and what I am saying about it. This is the standard work that goes on automatically, you understand what is being said to the extent that you can find these objects and relate the text to them.

The structure of meaning

Now imagine the following device. I project a ray of light from my consciousness as I compare things – first, second, third thing – all the time extracting information and drawing it to myself. And there is a little paint brush with black paint attached to this ray and every time I send out the ray the brush leaves a mark. When I jump to something else the brush leaves a mark again; when I go back it makes another mark. In this way the brush leaves a kind of grid behind it. Then we look at the grid and we say that it is *meaning*. So meaning is a particular structural representation – a sort of freeze-frame – of the process of understanding.

We can look at this another way, by asking a trick question: does movement have parts or not? I make a movement – what parts can there be in it? And, generally, how can you stop it and capture it temporally? You cannot do any such thing because in order to obtain parts, you have to cut it up. But my movement isn't capable of being cut up!

But see what we actually do. Here is a movement. For example, something falls. It leaves a trail. Now we begin to slice this trail into sections, we get parts of the trail and we transfer it to the movement. So the movement obtains parts secondarily, by transfer onto it of the parts of its trail. Otherwise, we cannot work with movements in thought. In order to cut them up, transform them, or do something else with them, we have to stop them – to represent some 'frozen' part of the movement structurally. This is how we work with any process – whether of understanding, work or something else. We divide it into stages and phases, but in order to do this we have to find and register the traces (the trail) of this process.

We ought to speak in such a way that those listening cannot fail to understand. How they understand is a very complex question. We all understand through the prism of our own peculiarities. And very often understanding is richer than what the speaker or writer of the text intended. The text always contains much that the speaker, the author of the text, did not personally put into it. This is due, first of all, to the fact that the author uses the tools of language. It is fair to say that language is always smarter than us, because all the experience of humankind is stored and accumulated in it. Language is the principal battery for storing experience. Second, the person who understands carries their own situation with them and always understands in the light of that situation, and often sees something more or something else in the text than its author.

Reflexive and active understanding

We can stop at understanding: I have represented a situation to myself and left the situation, as it were, inactive, in pure reflexiveness. There can be a reflexive understanding, and there can be an active understanding. We are now struggling to change our education system, because, as a rule, it is limited to reflexive understanding. We garner a lot of knowledge and 'store it away' without any idea of why we need it. A part of our studying amounts to this: I read a lecture, give seminars, and the student gives back what I said, with some omissions, and that is supposed to be sufficient. But in reality the transmission of knowledge is not an end in itself. Knowledge is transmitted so that people know how to act, and know how to act in changing, practical situations. There is often a huge barrier, produced by our system of upper secondary and higher education, between reflexive understanding and active understanding. This, as we usually say, is verbal learning: we are teaching people how to gabble, but not how to act, to convert understanding into action.

In order to really understand something we need to constantly translate it into action. People only find out whether they have understood rightly or wrongly when they begin to act. Because there is no difference between getting it right and wrong in understanding as such – the difference is determined by action. The action is the criterion of correct understanding.

Understanding and thinking

Understanding is a basic human function, but thinking is a very refined function. The prominent Scandinavian linguist H. J. Uldall said that thinking is like horses that dance, it is very rare and plays the same role in the lives of people as dancing for horses – a person has to learn specially how to do it, and even people who have been through a good school of thought and have done some thinking on a couple of occasions cannot always repeat it a third or fourth time.

Why do we need this blackboard, why do we draw these schemata? What are we doing here? What does all this have to do with the real world of our lives? I will put it very bluntly. Thinking only happens on the blackboard, and with the help of the blackboard. When we have a board, then we have thinking. Without it there is no thinking.

The reality of thinking

This world, drawn on the blackboard, on paper or on a drawing board, forms the reality of thinking.

This reality of thinking in our European civilization was created some time around the sixth century BC and was called *logos*. Hence the word 'logical'.

What do we have on the board? On the board we have certain signs and symbolic forms –diagrams, graphs, tables – which, and this is the most important thing, live their own lives. According to the laws of logic, as we say. And this rule-governed – not random! – life forms the work of *logos*.

These symbolic forms are fundamentally different from artworks. We can draw artworks how we want. But if we have written down, for example, a system of algebraic equations, differentials or the like, then at each step there are strictly defined laws of transformation of these equations. You cannot write an equation and then create any other equation instead of it – you must perform strictly prescribed transformations. Similarly in analytic geometry – two-dimensional or three-dimensional – there are highly rigid laws that are taught by rote in any university that specialises in technical science, mathematics or physics. And the numbers, whether in the decimal, binary or ternary system, follow strictly defined rules of transformation. In each case, there are rules that are always built on two bases. There is mathematics, which prescribes the rules in pure form, and there is, putting it contingently, 'physics', which concerns the world of objects. These objects are invariably not real, but ideal.

Take the simplest example. If I write Ohm's law for a circuit in its simplest form, $I = U/R$, then I am saying that I is the current, U is the voltage (electromotive force) and R is the resistance. And now I separate two planes: the mathematical meaning and the physical meaning of this expression, of this formula. Let's remember what meaning is.

The mathematical sense has a particular mathematical understanding behind it and the physical sense has a physical understanding. How do they differ from each other? In the mathematical sense, I can make any transformations. For example, $U = IR$. In a mathematical sense, that is correct. Or like this: $R = U / I$. From a mathematical point of view, that is also correct. And this is a classic example, because from the physical viewpoint the transformations are meaningless – in reality the resistance R is always given by itself. So in the mathematical sense these expressions are correct and transform into each other. But for physics meaning only attaches to the first, because in reality, physically, strength of current is determined by the ratio of the difference in potential between the beginning and end of the conductor (i.e. the voltage) to its resistance.

Logical rules and ideal objects

So all these diagrams on the board live by the laws of *logos*, and *logos* divide into logical rules (including the whole of mathematics, since mathematics is an aspect of logic and logic is an aspect of mathematics) and physical rules, or as we can now say in order to achieve greater generality, ontological rules or 'laws of nature'.

But the reference to 'nature' is out of place, because these are always laws of ideal objects. Whether we take Newton's laws or Descartes' laws governing the collision of spheres, the conservation of momentum, or any similar physical law, these laws are always valid only for ideal objects: for heavy points, absolutely rigid bodies, absolutely elastic bodies and so on, which do not in fact exist and never can exist. That is what *logos* comes down to: logical rules and laws of nature, or ontological rules. But what are ontological rules or laws? They are the laws of ideal objects.

And now let's wrap up these illustrations. Imagine that I have never in my life seen any construction site, never felt one with my hands, worked on one. I take your text about a construction site and make sense of it not in relation to the real work situation, but in relation to the blackboard: that is, I translate it into the reality of thought and assess it using logical and ontological rules. We are used to working with models. But this is a special case, perhaps involving mathematical correspondences or other schemata instead of models. There may be some organisational charts, flow charts (in this sense, flow charts are not models), or some specific organisational charts, which I asked you to give me, showing systems of organisation, systems of subordination, systems of personal and group relationships. I get my grasp of your text by relating it to these schemes. What then happens to our understanding of one another? It disintegrates and becomes disordered.

On the other hand, here I am telling you something. I am not basing myself on a situation, but I have certain little models: let's say, I have read various books about the theory of organisation, management and similar topics. And I draw diagrams, write something on the board. Factually, I am in a special position – I have exited from the situation. And I translate what I have on the blackboard and the little notes I have written in an exercise notebook from the world of *logos* into a text, and what I tell you is not about actual management, but about these diagrams – models of organisation, management and leadership in companies or elsewhere. And what do you do? You naturally begin to apply all this to what you have registered in your reflexiveness, in your experience. And by doing this we are doing something that is crucial for human thought: we are imposing our mental schemes of ideal objects onto reality.

The reality of mental activity and the reality of thinking

The world of mental activity, of our practical activity, is our reality, the real world of what we do, our work, our relationships. And the world of thought is the ideal world, an ideal reality. Through communication, and then – in reduced form – through the unification of pure thought with mental activity, a person always lives in these two worlds: the real world and the ideal world.

The ideal world is the world of science and, vice versa, the world of science is the ideal world. Science has taken shape in the ideal world, it lives by it and develops it. And there is nothing wrong with that – on the contrary, it gives us a powerful means of analysis. This is analysis of reality. Because it is one and the same reality that is captured in different ideal mental schemes, depending on what language we use and what system of knowledge and concepts we apply. So we begin, as it were, to look at reality from different angles. Figure 1.12 should help to make this clear.

Imagine that this circle is the real world and we are standing around it. One of us has one projection, another has a different one and a third has yet another – because of our different goals and tasks. In each instance the projection is a different language, and for specific goals and objectives. So there is a set of projections, each

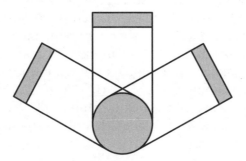

Figure 1.12

of which is 'applied' in the reality of thought. Scientists deploy all this using their own laws – of mechanics, thermodynamics, electrodynamics, the theory of gravity and so on. Organisational theorists deploy it in terms of organisation, leadership and management.

They mark everything up: they introduce these funny little figures, which they manipulate, rather like the ones I draw – positional people – or some mathematical equations come into play, the laws of thermodynamics, or some other laws. And so unfolds the world of *logos*, which we need in order to take all these schemes and begin to impose them in a certain order on reality and to see reality through these schemes and with their help. In this way we combine the ideal world with the real world . And when we do that, we think. And we only think when we are doing this.

When I am communicating with people and I start to build speech texts, focusing on the blackboard – that is, on the ideal reality of thought, describing what happens in this ideal reality, according to logical rules and so-called 'laws of nature' – that is when I am thinking. And that is pure thought. We can now say that what is ideal is one thing, but what is real is something quite different. But this has to be properly understood. Science does not give us laws by which real things exist. In general, science does not have anything to do with real things. Science begins from a certain idealisation. To carry out an idealisation is to be able to pull something out of reality and transfer it to the reality of thought.

Connections and the elimination of connections

But there is a difficulty here. We need a mathematical description – but of what? What was Michael Faraday's method when he was just beginning to study the first laws of electromagnetism? He did not know what depends on what. Faraday was a dedicated and diligent worker and kept a diary of his work. When he began work on these laws, he was dealing with observations in real situations – Volta's and Galvani's effects and the experiments carried out by Oersted. When Oersted closed a circuit, there just happened to be a compass nearby, which was brought into motion. It had previously been thought that magnetic phenomena were one thing and electricity was something different and that they were not related to each other. Oersted discovered the relationship in 1820, and study of this phenomenon began. And Faraday describes which wire he put in place, whether it was copper or brass or zinc, its exact position – his notes map out the entire circuit, one for one.

We know now that electromagnetic phenomena do not depend on the material or the type of wire, but he did not know that. So it was important for him to identify what is relevant to the ideal life of electromagnetism, and what is not relevant, and to discard a huge number of factors. He had to do this, because the real world is poly-systemic: everything is connected with everything else. But that is not the case in the world of science – in science we always have to decide what things are not connected, what can be discarded as irrelevant. And a process of abstraction occurs, identifying the factors that can be associated using simple, homogeneous math-ematical relations. So the lift from the reality of mental activity to the realm of pure thought is incredibly difficult and complex, and consists of discarding everything that cannot be expressed by homogeneous mathematical or analogous structural dependencies. Michelangelo said, very beautifully, that the talent of the sculptor is to take the stone, see a future sculpture in it and remove what is superfluous. Similarly here: the work of the scientist is to see what is really connected with what in the complexity of reality, where there are many different dependencies. And the reality of thought has to show the connection of what is 'really' connected.

Idealisation

Now I shall use an example to show you how this lift occurs and how it is achieved. I already started telling you this story in a different context. Aristotle began to study free fall in the fourth century BC. He attached various philosophical fantasies to it: he thought that there was something that exercises an attraction, that all natural movements tend towards the centre of the Earth because of some unknown entities. He began to study this. And after him all researchers up to and including Leonardo da Vinci – who had a highly refined experimental technique – found the same thing. If we take three or four bodies of different mass and see how fast the bodies fall, it turns out that the greater the mass, the greater the speed. This is a hard and fast law. You can verify it again and again: climb a tower and throw down objects and you will see that a heavy object falls faster and a lighter one reaches the ground later. Aristotle formulated a law, that the speed of fall depends on the mass.

But what does Galileo's law say? That any body falls with the same acceleration: in other words, at the same rate regardless of its weight, whether it is heavy or light. Experiment shows us, though, that the heavier the body, the faster it falls. Why? As Galileo teaches us, there is no direct connection between mass and velocity, but there is a connection between them via the level of resistance of the medium: the heavier the body, the less will be the impact resistance of the medium. This is an extra link, which confuses the whole picture. Empirically, the greater the mass, the greater the speed, but this relationship is not valid, it does not exist, and what are effective are indirect, 'additional' connections, which explain everything. It took 2,000 years of investigation before the real laws could be found.

We are lucky enough to stand on the shoulders of Galileo and know that all we need to do is to take away the atmosphere. But how did he know it? Before him, no one knew. The next interesting thing to ask is: do we use the Galileo's law in a vacuum or in air? We use it in air.

The vacuum equipment we are shown in school, in which a pen, a stone and a piece of paper all fall in the same way, came later. Torricelli did that after Galileo had formulated the law. But Galileo had to reach his conclusion by the power of thought alone, when real practice – the whole of empiricism – told him the opposite. Leonardo da Vinci, for all his experiments, could not find the law: he was too focused on reality. There are various 'games' that operate in reality. One 'game' is that a body is attracted by the Earth and falls at constant acceleration. But the body interacts with the environment, and the environment slows down the speed of the fall – this is a different 'game' that is superimposed on the first. So really we are dealing with two or three different 'games' in this movement and with their combined result. And we need to free them from one other. How was Galileo able to do this? He said:, 'If the facts do not fit my scheme, then so much the worse for the facts.' He was a bold man, and his boldness nearly led to him being burned at the stake.

I say that in all seriousness. He was led that way by his manner of thinking. That is relevant to what we were talking about yesterday, when you asked me whether it would be possible to draw a fantasised organisational scheme. What I would say is that it is not only possible, but necessary. Because if the facts do not fit our schemes, then we must say to hell with the facts if we want to rise to the reality of thought. This lift, from reality to the reality of thought, always requires great courage. We have to free ourselves from a mass of things and write a law.

I have said so much in praise of science – now let me make a criticism of it. Science is an excellent thing if properly applied. But practitioners quickly run into trouble if they take science at face value and start to use its specific projections in their incredibly complex practice, and to believe that their object – the object that they as practitioners have to deal with – is one and the same with the object portrayed by the theorist. Far from it.

Theory and practice

Practice is always much more complex and richer than any theory. The theory gives only one-sided, abstract projections. The practitioner's work, particularly that of the organiser, is much more complex than that of the scientist, and requires much more sophistication and understanding.

The most important thing for the practitioner and the organiser is understanding. To make the point more clearly, what is important for them is not thinking, but understanding. Pure thought is just one of their tools, and has a strictly limited role in their action.

Imagine that you have called on the assistance of one scientist, and of a second, third and fourth. Each of them has offered you a scheme and says that your practice is consistent with this scheme. And you have four schemes, in which each of the scientists sees the object from a different angle, from where they stand. You have to deal with the real object, and you have to work out how to use all these schemes. You need to discover where to apply one and disregard the others, on the grounds that they do not correspond to the situation, where to use the second and where the third. And maybe in some instances you will use them all together. But you are not Caesar, so you have to use them in a certain order or to find a way of combining them. And there will be no one at hand to give you assistance.

The problem of the reality of these schemes, of their connection, is a highly delicate problem related to human understanding. Scientists can be dogmatic, they can wear blinkers. But leaders cannot permit themselves to do that, because they are dealing with a complex practice, where all of these planes are interconnected and subtly interact. And theory has no answer to the question of how they are interconnected. Only practitioners can find the answer, and they can only do so at the cost of cuts and bruises endured and through the reflexiveness that they maintain when enduring those cuts and bruises.

A leader who deals with practice in the real world has to feel that practice and see it in all its complexities, and to be able through reflexiveness and the use of scientists – note the word 'use' – to rise to the level of expressing them in their purely intellectual, theoretical construction. At the same time they must be able to assess the potential of each science, and this is a higher function than actual scientific research. There is nobody but them to carry out this assessment. All scientists say that their own science is the most important and that it provides keys that can solve all problems. Such is the professional point of view of any scientist. If they thought otherwise, they could not work in their field.

The leader has to do the theoretical work of many schemes, combine them and apply them in practice. This is the hardest task.

The practice of thought

Practitioners, when they are in a situation, remember all the time that they will have to go into thought mode, so they are already thinking when they are in the real situation. They are oriented towards thought. Whether with the assistance of scientists or alone, they make sense of the situation in the reality of thought. They start to bring schemes together and, moving down into the situation, they take schemes of thought as their point of departure. As they immerse themselves in practice, they are again thinking. The poles they start out from are practical mental activity, reflexiveness and understanding, but understanding that is penetrated by schemes of thought.

The orthogonality of mental activity and reality

We live all the time as if in a system of mirrors: what happens in our real interactions is displayed in a particular way on the orthogonal surface of the reality of thought and is somehow represented there.

Why do I call this mental activity 'orthogonal'? A projection from an orthogonal plane is always equal to zero. This means that we cannot project mental activity into reality directly and without mediation. Or, to put it simply, everything in our thinking is fiction.

Nothing in reality corresponds to it if we carry out a procedure of direct projection. So we need very complex mediated procedures for making the transfer from the reality of thought to reality as such. And what we have become accustomed to call 'design' consists of just such procedures.

First systematic presentation of the leadership apparatus

Let us take it that a certain Mr Ivanov is appointed to the principal position. We can use our usual drawings to show the 'instrument panel' of his consciousness, where his ideas about the world are registered, where he makes circuits and draws things together, links things with each other, equates them with each other and so on. He has his own blackboard or drawing board, or set of blackboards and drawing boards, on which he sets out various schemes. He has certain abilities to act, internalised resources, goals, objectives, a prospective line of action, an education, an origin, membership of certain groups. He has a specific place, and this place is associated in a particular way with four other places that are closest at hand (see Figure 1.13).

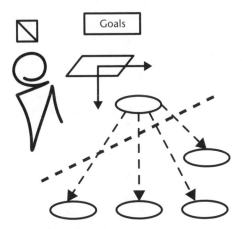

Figure 1.13

Rules for dealing with empty spaces

Twenty-two years ago I was doing research into issues of child education. I shall describe one of the issues we looked at. There are direct arithmetical problems: there were five birds sitting in the tree, six more arrive, how many are there now? Children solve these problems quickly and easily. But they find indirect tasks harder: some birds were sitting in a tree, six more arrived and then there were 11, so how many were there before?

Educationalists, teachers and psychologists were puzzled why children found this difficult, but the answer turned out to be very simple. The children had been taught: if more birds arrive, you have to add, and if some of them fly away, you have to subtract. The children are taught like that and then they are given an indirect problem. The children have a rule that they trust: if birds arrive, then add. So they try 6 + 11 and get 17.

Pre-school children cannot add and subtract in their head, but use sticks instead. The direct problem is easy to solve: they put down as many sticks as there are birds sitting in the tree, then they add the number of birds that arrived, and do a recount.

Pre-school children approach the indirect problem in the same way. The adult tells them that some birds were sitting in a tree, and the child puts down four sticks. They are told that we do not know how many birds were sitting in the tree, but they say, 'It doesn't matter, we'll leave these sticks for now and see how many we really need later.' So, in effect, the child is expressing x – an unknown quantity. They put down four sticks, but they know that it is an indefinite quantity. This is what small children do, who have not yet been taught this in school. And I do the same. I do not know how it all works, but for the moment I draw it like this. Here is someone – the chief engineer who is also the first deputy principal, and then another four places (one deputy for each production segment), there is a person in each place and each of them has a mental instrument panel and a blackboard or drawing board (Figure 1.14).

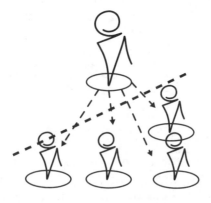

Figure 1.14

Next we shall assume that they all have whatever the principal has. In this sense, they are indistinguishable from him. I draw the possible positions of the principal. There are three positions in the diagram. But we have only one chief, not three, and what I have registered is his triple existence. He exists once as a place – as the chief of construction management. The second time he exists as the person who fills this place. And the third time he exists without a place. Let's say, for example, that the work has come to an end and he has gone on holiday (Figure 1.15).

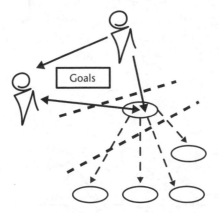

Figure 1.15

Finally he has a fourth position, with the asterisk, where he is reflexive, analysing and representing himself in all his instantiations and forms of existence. On the blackboard he can be represented as an object: he sees himself from the outside. If he is very sophisticated, he can represent himself being reflexive; if he is not very sophisticated he can only represent himself in the other positions (Figure 1.16).

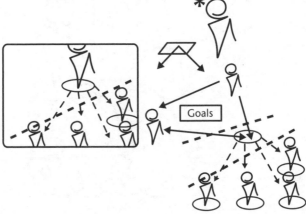

Figure 1.16

55

Systemic organisation in a group of managers

I shall distinguish different systems of formation. The five officials I have marked are linked by specific relationships of leadership and subordination. There is a connection between the principal and the chief engineer, between the chief engineer and the other deputies, and between the principal and the deputies. I emphasise again that these are not connections between people as such, but are connections of leadership and subordination, which arise from their position at work – they are official relationships.

At this stage I am still only defining a possible type of connection. I need to do that in order to say that certain connections exist. Let's say, to begin with, there are the connections shown in Figure 1.17.

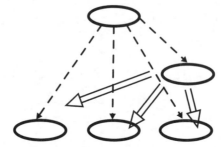

Figure 1.17

In addition, there are connections between them as people. For example, do you or do you not respect me? Do you think that I am a strong person or not? These are different relationships. And I do not attach them to the signs for places, but directly to people (Figure 1.18).

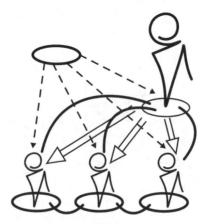

Figure 1.18

What we have done thereby is to take the first step in systematic analysis of apparatus management. What are the principles of this analysis? What did I start out from?

I posited a system of places linked by relationships of command and subordination. In modern sociological literature, these structures, as I said, are called 'formal structures'. 'Formal structures', roughly speaking, are the structures of places or of relationships between places, as fixed in some regulatory documents – they might be statutes concerning official posts, divisions, services or the like – which clearly and strictly list the rights and responsibilities of every place. They do not say what Ivanov, Petrova or Sidorova must do, but what the chief technologist, chief engineer, head of personnel and so on must do.

Workplace and club

The next thing we need to do is to distinguish two important concepts, the 'workplace' and the 'club'. 'Club' is not meant here in the sense of a place where people dance, sing and drink, but more broadly to include, for example, the Jacobin Club. The club, in essence, is a place where politics happen (Figure 1.19).

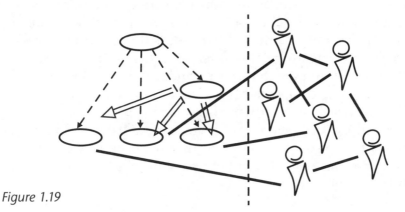

Figure 1.19

What makes the club different from the workplace? The difference is that in the workplace there is a totality of formal positions, formal structures. In the army this is embodied in ranks and epaulettes. And there is also another formal structure – that of jobs. So there is a double formal nomenclature. But at the club a person is not the bearer of any place, but is simply a person. Correspondingly, at work a person is a human unit (in brackets I would write 'a cog in the machine'), while at the club they are an individual.

But the idea of informal structures leads to various difficulties. The point is that informal structures exist in the club, but we are also positing the existence of informal structures in the workplace. So I could talk about informal structures in the club and about 'pseudo-workplace' informal structures.

The human unit and the individual

What is important here is the distinction made between the workplace (formal structures) and the club (informal structures). Someone is a human unit when they are the ideal performer in their job, when they have no emotions, no dividedness, when they know what they have to do and get on with it. And that is all there is to them. That is why I call them a 'cog': they are the ideal performer of their task, the perfect choice for the job. But an individual is someone who has emotions, drinks, suffers, uses stratagems and enters into specific relationships, feels an affinity with some people and not with others, has hates and loves and even secret loves.

If each person was divided down the middle and operated as a 'cog' when at work and as an individual after work, things would be simple and we would not be drawing informal structures in the workplace, but what in fact happens is that the club makes an impression on the workplace. As a result, these two things start to exist in parallel and simultaneously, since a person is always both a cog and an individual, and this is as true in the workplace as everywhere else, which leads to major dissonances. So we have a place, a functional place in a certain structure, and we have the individual who fills that place. The place together with the person filling it gives us an element: an element of a structure or system (depending on how we look at it).

Formal and informal organisational structures

However, the overlap of formal and informal structures is not limited to the workplace. The same happens in the club. In the way I presented things, when people leave work they become pure individuals, unrelated to the position they occupy in the workplace. But this never happens in reality. What are the insignia on epaulettes? They are a status symbol, regardless of where the person is located. A colonel is still a colonel when he is walking down Gorky Street and when he is relaxing at his dacha, and not just when he is with his division. The fact is that if you take a small group of people, these marks of distinction are always present in their minds.

First, I have outlined a set of places and defined the structure that is formed by these places. Then I have taken the people who occupy these places and included them in a group, and I treat the group as an informal structure. I initially introduced a collective, a set of people. Now I posit that they form a group, and I also trace their informal, 'club' existence. So their existence as a collective and as a group is, so to speak, broader than their formal existence. They function both in their places and outside those places.

What is important here is that I have distinguished not just one structure, but three structures based on one material: the formal structure, the informal structure, and the latter divided into two or having two planes of existence – the informal structure in the workplace and the informal structure at the club. I have distinguished several structures and several different types of connections using one material: there are official connections based on places, formal connections of command and subordination, and there are informal, personal connections and relationships.

Problems and problematisation

A problem does not arise when one person expresses a correct thought and somebody else a false thought. If one person expresses a correct thought and somebody else expresses a false thought, there is no problem. It is just that one person is wrong, and we have to carry out an examination to figure out who is right. A problem arises when two people say contrary things, and both are right. That is where a problem initially arises.

This nature of the problem as paradox is seen at the origin of modern mechanics. What did Galileo show in 1632? He studied the free fall of bodies, and he had the concept of velocity defined as distance divided by time – there was no other concept of velocity then. And he saw that if you drop a ball in a vertical and in an inclined plane, you obtain two mutually exclusive and equally correct results: that the velocities of these balls are different and that their velocities are the same.

His reasoning was as follows. When the ball that was dropped vertically has completed its trajectory and reached a point below its starting point, the ball that was allowed to descend on an inclined plane has gone a shorter way than the first ball, so the velocity of the second ball is less. So the balls move at different velocities. Galileo then took the ratio between the distances travelled by each ball and the ratio between the times they took to travel those distances, and it turned out that their velocities were equal. And when he had shown that, he had created a problem situation.

Galileo was not differentiating between average and instantaneous velocities. He only introduced this distinction later on the basis of the paradox he had found. Because the explanation of what happens in the experiment is that the concept of average velocity is not suitable for the comparison of accelerated movements. The concept of velocity is invariable for uniform movements. But if you take accelerated movements, you cannot compare them using the concept of velocity: you need to introduce some derivative, depending on the structure of the movements. But that came later.

The transition from object analysis to the design of analytical tools

Let's see what it is that we do here. When we have registered two mutually exclusive judgements and shown that both are right, we have a paradox, or what the ancients used to call an *aporia* or antinomy: in other words, two statements that exclude one another. Then we have to stop looking at and studying the object, and look instead at the tools of our analysis, to modify and transform concepts. And only by changing our concepts can we arrive at correct characterisations and assessments of the object, eliminate the paradox and solve the problem.

The solution is obtained by designing new, more accurate and more appropriate concepts. But this can only happen if we identify the problem. So the problem does not arise when one person is right and another is wrong, but when two mutually exclusive propositions are correct, forcing us to look for new ways of representing the object.

Consider another interesting paradox. There is the a series of the natural numbers: 1 2 3 4 5 6 7 8 9 ... You will of course say that the number of these numbers that are squares of other numbers is less than the number of all the numbers: after all the squares are 1, then 4, 9 and so on, while 2, 3 and many other numbers are not included. But now look at a different procedure. When we square 1 we get 1,

2 squared is 4, 3 squared is 9, and so on. Tell me, will I eventually get to a situation where I cannot attach a number to its square? No. So I say that the number of squares is exactly the same as the number of numbers (the first sequence starts, 1 2 3 4 5 6 7 8 9 ... and the second starts 1 4 9 16 25 36 49 64 81 ...). In 1889 Cantor introduced the concept of cardinality of the set, and said that 'equal to or not equal to' is not applicable in principle to infinite quantities. You cannot work with the concept of equality and inequality in this sphere.

Here we have one procedure being applied to objects and another procedure being applied to the same objects. And the one procedure gives one result, and the other gives a different result. But the object is one and the same. In Galileo's case we compare two movements, vertical fall and inclined fall, and in Cantor's case we take the series of squares and the series of natural numbers. And there are two procedures of comparison. On the one hand, we take out a part, we break down sets into subsets, and on the hand case we establish mutually equivalent correspondences and create two equinumerous sets.

The secret is that if you have succeeded in arriving at a paradox, then you have discovered a problem; you have found the weak spot in the conceptual system.

Systems analysis

I am gradually bringing our discussion round to the issue of systems analysis. Consider this: on the one hand, every deputy principal belongs directly to the system of first-level management, but on the other they belong to their own system of management, with themselves as the principal. The question is how these two systems are interlinked. It turns out that they are not directly connected and coupled together, but are both tied to one and the same person. Their connection is provided by this person.

See how it works: both systems function using this person, and that person is a kind of mechanism for transmission and harmonisation. And this transmission and harmonisation happens by virtue of their functioning in the two systems. Factually, we are all such 'transmission rods'. If we remove the people who occupy these places, everything stops.

We need to be able to dismantle systems into complex units, into subsystems, and to put them together again. And this brings us to a surprising paradox: a system is by definition something that cannot be divided into parts.

If we split the system into two, we have two systems. What makes us say that we have just one system? If we use the word 'system', we effectively imply that it, this whole, cannot be divided into parts.

We cannot make sense of this at the level of our everyday common sense and everyday notions. We are used to drawing boundaries around things. This is a crane, this is the construction site, this is a plot of land. These are all things, and not systems.

When we look at tables, chairs and the like we do not apply systemic concepts to them. But when we are dealing with such items as a construction site, do we need to use the concept of a system, the category of systems? The category of systems carries with it a different, nonsubstantial principle of drawing boundaries. Let me say for the moment that we need the concept of a system here at the level of representation. We previously worked in the category of the thing and we knew what the boundaries of things were, because there were spatial volumes, which we could not enter, they set limits to our movement. But this is not true of systems.

Systems, in this sense, are nonsubstantial formations. They consist of connections, of processes, and processes define their boundaries. But what are procedural boundaries or process boundaries? What are the boundaries of connections? Or there is the question I always pose to you: can connections be broken or not? If we break them, do we divide the system into parts or destroy the system? It turns out that the connections cannot be broken. So what is to be done? After all we have to make divisions, we cannot take everything at once.

Where is the boundary of the system?

The problem arises of where to draw the boundaries of systems and of how many systems there are. What is the coupling between the system of the principal, which includes their deputies, and the deputies' own systems, in so far as each of them is the head of a particular system, its principal? How are they coupled together and how should they be coupled together? I shall translate this into an artificial, technical mode and ask, when you come to this place, how will you organise the interface of these systems? How will you organise the collective and relationships within the collective? What has to be done is first, to solve real situational problems, depending on who is in which place, which group they belong to, where they are included, what external connections they have. Then second, we need a technology for our work (we have not got to this yet); we need methods of situational analysis. We have seen that systems do not unfold into subsystems and that the very expression 'division of systems into subsystems' contains a paradox. It cannot be done: the system cannot be divided into subsystems, and that is part and parcel of the definition of a system, of a structure.

So we have two sets of problems: real situational problems, and generalised problems of system analysis. We now have to move in these two planes, and then pull them together.

Entering the place of the leader

The first question that arises is this: should a newly appointed principal occupy their position at once, or should they wait a month or two?

A new principal makes a strategic mistake if they leap into their new position and start to function as an element of the administrative-leadership system. Why? Because, by so doing, they have accepted that system. More than that: they have already sold their freedom. They have surrendered their prerogative as principal to no advantage.

The question is this: do you leap into the boss's armchair, or do you just maintain your right to the chair without insisting that it is the source of your authority and that it is yours? It is of course yours, you have a right to it, nobody else will try to sit down there. But you can use this chair as a tool in your work.

If you sit down in the chair, connections are immediately activated – the connections implied by the management system, as well as a lot of others from outside. Tell me, once you have entered this place, and these connections have been activated, will you have time to think and act?

You will not.

That is right: you will have no time.

What does it mean if a principal has sat down in their armchair? It means they have started to function in the system of connections. Then I ask, from what moment should a principal start to function within an organisational-administrative system? And should they function within such a system? That is the question. Perhaps they should not function within it at all?

Where is the boundary of the system? Perhaps the leader should never enter this system? Should they adapt themselves to a place in the structure, or should they adjust the place in the structure to fit them?

It all depends on how principals view themselves – as organisers, leaders or managers. Or (the fourth option) as functionaries within this system. And a parallel question arises: what is to be the object of this activity? These are, as it were, two sides of the same question. What does the boss make into an object of their activity, first and foremost?

The administrative-organisational structure of places

Let me begin to transfer all this to the level of theory. What do principals have to do with? They have to do with the administrative-organisational structure of places. This is one system. They have to do with people who constitute an informally organised group, with human attitudes, relationships of sympathy, antipathy, entrenched hostility and so on. They have to enter this group and occupy a certain place in respect of it. They have to do with complicated strata systems, in which these people are inserted, and with administrative-organisational systems, which close their circuits via these people.

But if they want to harness this system to their needs, they must perform a particular kind of work – that of an organiser or designer – with respect to this structure. And this work is not carried out within the system, but outside it. In order to rebuild it, they must stay outside the structure (or exit from it).

Now consider this: whether they want to or not, a principal will enter the group and make big waves in it, like a stone thrown into water. They come there as a person with new qualities, new attitudes, strength of will, and they hold this place in their hand – it is their place, that of the principal. So they will restructure all the groups of people in this collective, whether they want to or not. It is inevitable. And they will either crash into it head first and come away with bumps and bruises, or approach it with proper awareness and assess themselves in relation to the collective.

Self-determination

The first thing the principal must do is to carry out the task of self-determination. What exactly is that? They must assess the whole situation, including formal-administrative structures, the informal group (to keep things simple I shall take only the first layer, but there are depths here), external structures, strata structures, and they must assess how these aspects fit with their own individuality. That means that they also have to assess their individuality relative to this place, this structure, this group, and the entirety of the structures and systems that are generated there. A bilateral process of self-determination takes place: in a reflexive position, principals both assess structures in relation to themselves as individuals, and assess their individuality in relation to these structures and systems (including the people they contain).

Now you might ask me, how is this done? Your first question might concern the technique of this action. I respond with another question – what exactly do you mean? What makes you think that you will find my technique useful? Look, I may be good at wittering away about all sorts of things, and not everyone can do that. But the question is – do we need the same technique or different techniques? For example, I may have powerful connections high up, I might be a protégé of the first deputy minister because we studied together at university, and that is one structure of behaviour.

Let me tell you what I would do if I was appointed principal. For the first few days, I would not take part in the life of the collective. I would just sit in my office and keep quiet, and leave everything that needs doing to the chief engineer.[3] This chimes with my basic idea that a principal should not be involved in actual functioning. That is what I think. So I would entrust all of the direct management work to the chief engineer and keep out of it myself, as a matter of principle. I would use the excuse of being new in the job and ask the engineer to deal with all of the day-to-day management while I sit and watch them do it. I would keep things like this later on too, when I had carried out a thorough reorganisation – I would take no part in ordinary functioning, but keep right out of it. This way, I would leave myself time to think, so that no one could report that I 'consistently fail to carry out my responsibilities'.

If principals stop involving themselves in functioning, they have time to work on organisation.

---

3 Although chief engineer would be the title in Russian, the English equivalent might be a production controller or manager.

Schematisation

What is important is not so much where we sit and think or even how we think. What is important (this is a crucial point) is what we take as the object of our analysis, and our actions when we start setting out our thoughts on the blackboard or the drawing board. The important thing is what schema we draw on our board, what we represent as our object, what the schema of it is. If we draw an organisational structure, then that will be the object of our action. If we draw the interface of group administrative-managerial structures, they will be the object of our analysis and later of our action. If we draw production lines, they will be the object of our action. Do you see my point?

The actions of an organiser, leader and manager consist in applying specific schemata to reality. The object structure that results will depend on which schemata the individual applies.

Designing a development programme

Two perfectly real situations develop: that of taking up the new post and that of designing a programme. Both cases present the real conditions of activity of a principal. In the first case, they must do work associated with taking up the post, analysing the situation and defining their position. The design of a development programme is the main aspect of a managerial approach.

Programme design is what management is all about. Someone who cannot design development programmes cannot manage people. And leaders are the only people who can do this work. There is no one else to whom it can be delegated.

So a principal does not get involved in day-to-day operations?

Absolutely right. How can we call them a principal if they are carrying out day-to-day business? That is why we do not have real principals – they are all too busy carrying out dispatcher functions instead of doing what they ought to be doing.

Management

When does management first appear? It first appears when a rigid pattern of organisation is embedded into the system. And it shows, second, when deviations and breaches of the pattern become a regular occurrence. When these conditions are present at once, you have two things that are, as it were, mutually exclusive: first, there is a formal organisation, and second, regulatory documents are failing to be observed as they should be observed in real situations. This is when the need for management arises.

Management is needed when you are building a system out of unreliable elements, when the reliability of the whole has to be ensured despite the unreliability of the elements. Do I make myself clear? It is only then that we need management.

This is management in the sense of work techniques that you apply in real situations and that always enable you to compensate for the deviations that inevitably appear every hour, every day, every month. You do not correct deviations using a predetermined standard, but you compensate for deviations. If things have become unsynchronised, you do not attempt to reverse the situation, but compensate for deviations in one system by contributions to another system.

If you have a rule, a schedule, and departures from the schedule are prohibited, you no longer need management. But this never happens – there are always breakdowns in the schedule.

It is important to have a large range of comparisons, so consider an example from the game of ice hockey. There is a simple principle for team strategy: at every point of the field there must be two of our players for every opposing player. It is a simple principle and it was applied. The Soviet school of ice hockey began from here: from a strategic concept about how to manage the game of hockey. Then there was a second idea. How were teams selected in the early days of the game? The strongest player was assigned to the first team, the second best player to the second team, the third best to the third, and so on. Then, one day, a famous coach decided to do it differently. He thought, I have three strong forwards, so I shall put them all in the first team and the others in the second team. And he created three teams of greatly differing strength, and set different strategic goals for each of them: the first team (which became the best in the country) was to score the maximum possible number of goals, the second team had to prevent the opponents from scoring any goals, and the objective of the third group was to concede as few goals as possible. Do you see the principle? Thanks to this distribution of forces the team with the three strongest players always scored more goals than the third team conceded, because defending is easier than attacking. And the coach made the club the best in the country.

This is the application of a management system. Let me say once again: management is the art of keeping the whole unit together when its elements are various. When there is no variation, there is no management.

The object-theme and the object of analysis

The object of our action is always a sociotechnical object. We give it certain boundaries as a function of our goals, and then we transform this highly complex reality into a specific schema. We create a link between this schema and reality, and at the same time we draw the boundaries of this reality. This gives us the theme and the object (see Figure 1.20).

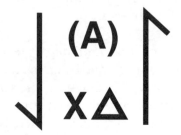

Figure 1.20

What is the object-theme?[4] The object-theme is a complex structure, linking our schemata, knowledge and ideas with what exists in reality, towards which our actions are directed. This structure includes the application of a schema and the knowledge corresponding to that application, as well as the part of reality on which we act – other people, technology, whatever – and connections of substitution, presentation or reference.

What then is the object? It is what we 'cut out' in reality using the procedure just described.

Let us look at this step by step, because it is very important. I have drawn a diagram here.[5] It is a mass of marks in different

---

4   Translator's note: the Russian term is *predmet*. The word's derivation is from from Latin: *pred-* = ob-; *-met* = -ject. It can mean object, subject or theme. 'Object-theme' has been used here, since the author is making a contrast between *predmet* and *ob'yekt* as two kinds of object.

5   Figure 1.20, shown here in black and white and not the different colours mentioned.

colours, arranged in a certain way. What do you see when you trace the connections in this schema? Do you see the reality of administrative-organisational relationships?

I hope the answer is yes.

How did you understand it? By applying it in your thought to the object.

Any sign, any schema is a kind of gateway, through which we pass in order to arrive somewhere. The object is what we are making for. The thing with the help of which we make for the object is a form, a sign form. A schema is an example of a sign form. In order to understand what is at issue, you have to refer this schema to the object we are talking about.

Object-theme structure

In Figure 1.20 there is a sign form (A), which we have substituted for an object (the arrows denote the substitution). We can look at the sign form (or pronounce words), but we mean a certain object that we have delineated and distinguished. This structure as a whole is called an object-theme or object-theme structure.

When children are born, become included in the human world and begin to be socialised, they never deal with objects, but always with object-themes. This is to say that all the things in our world are denoted by words, and words carry meaning. A sofa is something to lie on; a table is for eating or writing at, but not for sitting on. A chair is what you can sit on.

Let me put it like this: people never have to do with what we call 'reality'. Never in their lives. People never reach objects. People always have to do with the world of human culture (see Figure 1.21).

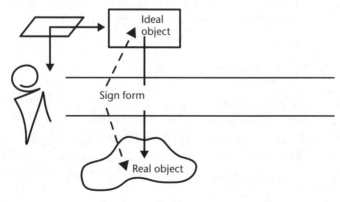

Figure 1.21

The 'object-theme' environment of humanity

At some point in the seventeenth or eighteenth centuries the idea took shape (and was developed by naturalist philosophers) that a person is a certain subject: a distinct individual, who interacts with the world of nature, with objects. Interacting with objects, through their perception and senses, people perceive and represent these objects, and form concepts about them.

You are firmly convinced, as are millions of other people, probably – I shall explain in a minute why I say 'millions' and why I say 'probably' – that we have to do with the world of objects and somehow interact with it. Such is the legacy of this philosophical tradition (often referred to as 'sensualism').

What do I say? That individual people never have to do with the world of objects. From the moment they are born they enter the world of object-theme structures or object-themes, the world of culture and meanings. It is interesting how Nicholas Mikloukho-Maklay describes the perception of objects that are unnamed. When he was working with the Papuans of New Guinea, he took out a mirror for the first time, and they all gathered round him and cried, 'Water! Water!' Why water? Because they saw their reflections in it. Then someone poked the mirror with their finger and said, 'solid water'. That is why I say that there are no unnamed things, and there cannot be any. If you come across something that has not yet been named, of for which do not know the name, you will initially call it by a word you know ('water', said the Papuans, pointing to the mirror). With the name, we ascribe to this something a use in our culture.

The world of people consists of their activities: that is, of what is included in this activity, what is generated by this activity and denoted accordingly by words. These words, which we attach to the object, capture the experience of human action.

An action plan

Arriving at their new place of work, the principal has to decide their action plan for the immediate future. For this purpose, they need to single out the sequence of objects for their action within the complex unity which we call 'management of an organisation'. Much depends on their strategic goals and how they define them. Will they maintain the stance of a researcher for a month or two or will they start to act at once? Will they act as an organiser or as a manager? Their goals and strategic plans are important, because they define how the principal sees their work unfolding in the future.

How do the plans take shape? They take shape when the principal draws certain schemata on a drawing board or blackboard using what they have learned previously. By doing this they create object-theme structures.

Now let me answer the question of what comes first. Do principals first get acquainted with the available information and then start drawing schemata? No. They start the drawing work first, and then get acquainted with the information.

Here is a humorous example. If I ask someone to go out on the street and observe, they will not go before they have asked me what I want them to observe. The same is true for principals. They must have a plan of self-organisation, for example, 'First, get to know my deputies.' They must have a system of test assignments for the deputies. The next step in their plan might be to get acquainted with the system of organisation at this level of the administration: to grasp what formal relationships exist between the deputies, and so on.

All this time their interest must spread over several planes simultaneously: formal structure, group relations and personality. For this purpose they need to have schemata prepared in advance for each instance on the blackboard or drawing board. Information only becomes information when it is assigned to certain cells. The question is not whether they will ask certain things and find certain things out. The question is what exactly they want to know and in what order they want to know it. For this purpose, they need the relevant object-theme structures, and not object structures. The object they have to deal with will become apparent secondarily, thanks to the object-theme form, which they choose in advance as their pattern.

If they see themselves as organisers and want to rebuild the administrative and organisational structure, they must focus their attention on this, and know how to portray it all. If they are interested in informal groups, they must have the relevant patterns and a set of procedures for measurement (tests again). If they are interested in personality, they should have other patterns with a list of questions to ask. And principals must always know the complete list of structures that directly interest them and which they need to master.

What is the special feature of the principal's position? They should be equally interested in real and naturally existing positions, on the one hand, and in systems, which they need to introduce through their organisational work (in other words, technical systems created by themselves or someone else), on the other hand. So systems analysis divides into two aspects: the technical (artificial) and the natural. The principal will be working in these two modalities all the time – the modality of the actual and the modality of what is needed or what is efficient.

That is why I have told you about object-theme structures. The principal, like everyone else, has to do with object-theme structures and not with objects.

Self-organisation

A principal has been appointed. They have a certain set of capacities by virtue of all their previous experience. They know how to use the blackboard or the drawing board to draw schemata. They have a body of knowledge that determines their thinking. And they have to deal with a certain world, which is the world of people's mental activity. This world is both social and natural. But the natural world is given to them through the social world.

There are no objects in this world. There is only substance, which is not cut into parts, delineated, or represented as a thing.

Take the example of a forest. We enter a 'forest', and our ability to distinguish glades, clearings and separate groups of trees depends on our subsequent analytical work. All this is the result of our organising, cognitive work.

This is how it is for every person separately and this is how it has been historically for humanity. Humanity gradually distinguished itself from the world of nature and opposed itself to it. The things we speak of are always the product of our social and culturally organised activity. And in this sense, each thing accumulates previous human labour, holds that labour within itself. Then another activity begins – that of using or applying this object-theme.

Making activity into an object-theme

Every such object-theme marks a break in processes of activity. For example, an activity took place and produced a certain object-theme. This object-theme has appeared – here is the desk with a microphone, you are holding pens, wearing watches, whatever – and all of this absorbed previous processes of activity, thanks to which it was 'objectivised'.

It is as if activity perishes in the object-theme and becomes embodied in it at the same time. Then another activity begins – that of application. The application is directed towards the same object-theme. But we could say that it is work with an earlier activity, which now exists as object-theme. What is important here is the heterogeneity of the process. First there is a process of labour which is objectified in some object-theme, as it were, creamed off and congealed in it, and then this past, objectivised labour becomes the object-theme of the next activity – that of application. So object-themes are only a differential instantiation of activity; they are that in which activity exists in frozen, embalmed form.

And what does the process of activity mean? Processes of human activity are inseparable from processes of communication, or in other words from speech, and the words of speech constantly depict and accompany activity. The process I was just speaking about is not a single homogenous process, but many different processes taking place at the same time. It is not merely a practical activity for the transformation of material, but is also necessarily thought fixed in words. So an object-theme does not merely have the form of natural material – polished, varnished and so on – but is also necessarily a structure of such a type: there is natural material, onto which we impose a form, and in addition each action, each thing in the world around us, has a word attached to it, which means that thing and which is substituted for it.

So the object-theme exists in dual form, as a thing and as a word. An object-theme is always a historically and culturally determined link between a word and a thing, a thing and a word. Why do I say this twice? Because there are two connections, the connection of substitution – from the thing to the word, and the connection of reference – from the word to the thing.

Processes and layers of mental activity

What happens in processes of mental activity? They always take place in two parallel planes. In one plane, we as it were change the material of things, and in the other plane, in a parallel process, we work with words or signs. Between the two, there are constant processes of bonding between our work with things and our work with words. Between words and things there is a space of meanings – meanings unfold, which we disclose through processes of understanding.

The process of mental activity consists of several parallel processes. We could put it differently: mental activity unfolds as several inter-connected, multi-plane processes. This is always something akin to a shelf unit. And the tasks differ in their degrees of complexity and the number of languages involved. People are always striving to reduce the number of piled-up planes, but their number is constantly growing as new opportunities for solving problems are provided by new languages that are brought into the process.

For example, algebra differs from geometry, because the latter has four languages, one above the other (fields; the language of geomet-rical drawings and figures, which we substitute for the fields; the language of algebraic symbols such as 'section AB'; and the language of logical relations expressed in axioms or rules, the language of proportions, without which geometry would be completely unthinkable). Euclid's *Elements* has a rigid division between its books: there is a book on work with figures and drawings, and there is another book on the theory of proportions, which later led to the language of theoretical arithmetic. Meanwhile algebra has only one language, so algebra is much simpler than geometry.

Relations of substitution and reference cannot be formalised, they always go by intuition. But work in a single language, on a single plane, is always formalised and subordinated to certain rules. If you have learned the rules for transformation of algebraic relations or rules for differentiation and integration, the work will proceed in a formal manner.

What does it mean to solve a geometrical problem? You need to know what kind of drawing should be used to initially represent this problem, and there are not, and cannot be, any formal rules for this.

Ways of solving problems

The object-theme is always the linkage between the thing and the word. This is a double linkage, consisting of the movement from the thing to the word (linkage of substitution) and from the word to the thing (linkage of reference). That is, there has to be a direct transition and a reverse transition. Thinking itself necessarily unfolds as a multi-plane movement: first movement within a thing, then movement within the substituting words, then in the words substituting for the first words, and so on. And always in parallel.

This is what problem solving is built upon. We work, we run up against an insuperable barrier, we switch to the level of substituting words, then to the next level until we find a solution. Then we move back to the thing. The meaning of problem solving is finding a language in which the solution is evident. As soon as we find such a language, we find the solution.

Now let us see how this works in arithmetic problems with trains, such as we solve at school. A train departed from point *A* to go to point *B* at a certain time and travelling at a certain speed, and another train departed from point *B* to go to point *A* at a certain time and travelling at a certain speed. When do they pass each other on the track? How do we solve this problem of arithmetic?

We need to have a language in which the solution is trivial. Once such a language was found, the solution became trivial. The language used is that of sections: the section is *AB*, so the meeting point is somewhere in this section at point *C*. The solution is trivial. However in truth this is not yet a solution, since we need to know the distance from *C* to each of the departure points, and the time when the trains meet. Still, the power of the descriptive language consists in our having found the solution that they will meet at point *C*; that is given. Now we can start moving backwards, looking for numerical expressions of time, distance and so on. But we have found the solution in one language, and now we can transform it into a numerical solution.

Archimedes solved problems of this type. He had to define the area of figures outlined by certain curves. Highly complex methods of differential and integral calculus are required for this task. But he found the relation of these areas in a very simple way – he took pieces of thick bull's skin, cut them into the relevant figures, weighed them, and found the solution like that. Having found the answer, he looked for a formula to express the proportions that he had found.

So what does finding a solution to a problem consist of? I repeat once again: it consists of finding a language where this solution is evident. Having found this language, we translate it into another language, into the different linguistic form in which we need the answer. We can do this because thinking consists of many parallel processes, some of which unfold in things and others in the signs that substitute for these things. That is why looking for a solution is always a sort of volatilisation process between languages until we get to the language where the solution is evident, and then we make the journey back the way we came.

We see the schema and we can see what is in it, but there is no transition to the plane of the thing. As soon as we find it, we can read the schema easily, which is to say that we immediately see, automatically and easily, what world of things and actions with things is hidden behind it. All the richest abilities of mental activity are given to us by the fact that objects are such multi-plane structures of things, actions with things, signs substituted for things, actions with signs, actions with things again, and so on.

Actuality of the principal's thought

You should only step into the job of principal when it becomes your personal job, when you begin to see your personal goals and tasks. I do not mean those of a mercenary nature, and suchlike, although these also exist, and that has to be acknowledged and is permissible.

Imagine the case where a principal does not see themselves as an organiser and reorganiser of an administrative structure, but simply takes up the place of principal as a place in a ready-made structure. How should we assess their idea of the thing now? As inadequate and inconsistent with their position. It will be ridiculous if now, in this position, the principal takes this structure as the thing in the actuality of their thinking on the blackboard. There will be an immediate rupture between what is represented as the thing in the actuality of their thinking, and that upon which they have to act in reality. Because now, in this position, they have to act on a quite different thing. The thing they now have to act on, as a rule, is technology. When principals start to hold staff conferences and planning meetings, they generally discuss how work is proceeding, how construction of the canteen is getting on, whether the plan is being fulfilled and so on. What they then write on their blackboard should relate to these themes – fulfilment of the plan, relevant operational tasks and so on.

This idea of the thing will correspond to the position that has been occupied, and the thing will be cut out in the appropriate way. What about the management mechanism? In this case, the principal simply fails to notice it. They know nothing of the existence of such a mechanism. They are interested in keeping to the construction work schedule, ensuring that workers turn up on site, receiving reports from section managers and suchlike. Different goals entail different ideas of the thing.

We are working at the junction of three positions. One position is the inner position, when we view ourselves as occupying a certain position within a structure – that of principal, for example. The second position is external, when we oppose ourselves to the thing, saying that this is our thing, all this is a unity. The third position is the reflexive position. We carry out some work and then we ask ourselves, what did I do and how did I do it? In this, we are exiting to a reflexive position and can start to describe what we did. Then, if we have the language, and can portray it all, we go to the external position and present a schema on the blackboard – the schema of the thing, inside which we were previously located.

Only then do we oppose ourselves to the object for the first time. When we work within a structure, this structure is not an object for us, but a condition for our action. We do not record and describe the structures of social activity in which we are included, just as we do not describe the air we breathe (a fish does not register water as a condition of its existence, it simply lives in it).

Reflexive position and goals

People are usually genuinely unaware of what they are doing; they do not give themselves an account of how they behave and act. For this, they need to exit into the reflexive position. This reflexive position is then shaped as an external attitude towards themselves, their action, and the fragment of the social world they inhabit. This fragment then emerges as object.

Human activity does not always imply an object. When someone gets up in the morning, goes to the toilet, has breakfast and hurries off to work, they have no object. When they start performing their usual functions at work in accordance with the regulations, there is also no object and no task of transforming something or doing something. They simply work, carry out their functions. This is what we all do.

There is an interesting question we might ask: are there any goals to be seen here? No, there are no goals.

People run around without goals. Hence the difference between behaviour and activity. People are always behaving. I will speak for myself, to avoid giving offence. Every morning I wake up, I rub my eyes, I tell myself that it is time to get up. I get up, though reluctantly. I stumble about, gradually coming to my senses. Is there a goal for me?

Not to be late for work.

What sort of a goal is that? I move about with my eyes half-closed, wash, have breakfast – no goal here. I walk out of the door and get into a bus – no goal. I get on the local train (I have a season ticket) – still no goal. I get off, find myself on Komsomolskaya Square, I walk – no goal yet. In the metro, I look at my watch and see that I am four minutes late. And I have a lecture to give. This is when a goal appears for the first time – I think that if I push my way through from the middle of the carriage, where I am now, towards the exit, make the change of trains quickly and run up the stairs, I will gain two minutes. Then I begin to think which carriage I should get into when I make the change. Now I have a goal.

When does the goal appear? It appears when there is a failure, breakdown or disruption in the course of customary behaviour. That is when I begin setting goals.

Activity-based approach

What is a naturalistic approach? There are objects of nature; they are outside us. We stand opposite them and they stand opposite us. The world of objects creates situations, and we see these objects as given.

An activity-based approach contrasts with the naturalistic approach. How does a proponent of the former work? They have no objects. They say – there is me, I act, and by this action I accumulate experience. There are no objects here. They perform certain customary actions, sometimes successfully, sometimes not. When something goes wrong, they exit to a reflexive position, assess the situation, and look for the reasons and causes of what has happened. This gives the first outline of a situation, but there are no objects so far. Then they enter a particular position, which is specifically the thinking position. And at this point they complete the cycle, as it were. They set out the results of their reflection, of their analysis of the situation, including the delineation of the borders of a certain object, upon which they now have to act, which they want to change in some way.

So, for an activity-based person, there is no world of objects standing opposite them, but a world of activity, which includes their own self. This is the first position.

The second position is the reflexive position, when the person must become aware of and make sense of their activity and the structures around them, in which they are included. And only at the third stage do they arrive at the contrast between their self and this world, and only then do they give shape to what they previously acted on, which they interpreted in their reflexiveness as the object that stands opposite them.

Formation and self-awareness of the individual

So people come into this world, function in it, and only later begin to perceive themselves and distinguish themselves as individuals. Personality and individuality are always gained through struggle, they are not given to us from the outset. Not every person 'has' individuality. There were times in history when people did not have individualities at all. A slave does not have any individuality. It has to be worked for and obtained through the realisation of a personal attitude towards action, and specifically, through awareness of ourself as an individual.

So what is the essence of the activity-based approach? People are viewed not as Robinson Crusoes standing opposed to the world of nature (such was the view from the late sixteenth to the middle of the nineteenth or early twentieth centuries), but as included in the world of activity, in activity-based structures, where they have a place and fill this place.

After a historically mediated and complex struggle, people may assert themselves to be personalities and individuals. They do this, first by awareness of themselves and of their role, and second by exiting to an external position and contrasting themselves as individuals with the rest of the world.

The subject–object relation

This relation is the relation of subject and object. People now see themselves as subjects, they are distinguished from the objects of nature, and this relation enables them to place themselves in opposition to nature and to theorise it.

All this is nothing other than the external, fully delineated, final form. If anyone thinks that things were this way from the start, they are greatly mistaken, they are prey to prejudices and illusions, they do not understand the real structure of the world, and therefore they can be manipulated. We can do anything we like with them, because they have an inadequate understanding, from the outset, of their own situation and of the overall situation.

Today is the time of large activity-based organisations that use people as resources. So the struggle for human rights in opposition to the organisation is moving to a new stage – it is one of the main issues of the twentieth century, and will probably continue to be so in the twenty-first and twenty-second centuries. The question is this: can individuals have the power and might to resist the pressure of the organisation and thereby to enable the proper development of human society? Will they find the strength in themselves to remain as individuals in the context of these very powerful structures? The issue here is of the techniques that people must acquire in order to protect themselves against organisations, to keep their reason, responsibility, the sense of being their own masters: in other words to maintain an active philosophy of life.

The struggle for an active philosophy of life is the struggle to preserve individuality – individuality, which is bloody-minded enough to judge itself equal to any organisation. It says, 'I am a system, equal in power to them.' When asked, sarcastically, what power that is supposed to be, the individual answers that they are intelligent, can think and that this is their power. Organisations cannot think.

Elements of systems analysis

Historical preconditions

The prehistory of systems analysis extends to infinity, so that any search for its beginnings would be endless. The conventional starting point is taken to be the first well-known work in the tradition – the *Treatise on Systems* by Condillac. In effect two thinkers from the turn of the seventeenth and eighteenth centuries began the construction of a line of thought that extends to the present and looks set to continue into the future. The first was Leibniz, most of whose works remain little known, despite his eminence in his own day, and the second was Condillac, who was not only an outstanding philosopher, but also laid the foundations of semiotics or the theory of signs. In effect, he founded the science of chemistry by creating a language for it. Lavoisier, the author of the first textbook on chemistry, acknowledged Condillac's role when he wrote, 'The works of Abbé Condillac have shown that everything depends on a well-constructed language. The language must be able to represent relations between things in a clear and simple way. When we have such a language, we can know what happens in the world. We have therefore decided to denote every part of substance with a particular name, to give it a corresponding symbol.'

Formulae of composition

Lavoisier, Berthollet and Fourcroy introduced the formulae of composition that we know well from standard chemistry textbooks. This is not yet a structural language of chemistry, but a language of composition. They took this idea from Condillac, who drafted the plan for the construction of chemistry as a science.

The systemic character of knowledge

In his *Treatise on Systems* Condillac discussed the problem of the consistency of knowledge. He showed that knowledge always forms a system. We cannot point to some area of knowledge and say, 'there it is and there are its boundaries'; we cannot treat it as a thing. Consequently, as Condillac stated in his *Treatise,* knowledge does not consist of things, but of systems. If it seems to us that we have to do with some specific knowledge, which is singular, separate, without a context, then our conception is mistaken, because factually, in all such cases we have to restore multiple connections with other fields of knowledge.

Initially, when scientists spoke of systems they only meant knowledge, and not things or objects. Later, when Bernoulli viewed some quantity of gas under a piston as a multitude of small parts, he never viewed their totality as a system, because there was no concept of connection. A multitude is not a system, and the mechanics of those days were the mechanics of a point – the kinematics of a point and the dynamics of a point. Later, at the turn of the eighteenth and nineteenth centuries, scientists who worked in mechanics began to discuss systems of points, having taken the idea from Condillac, and began to transfer the ideas of knowledge systems to objects.

Object and thing

Here, the distinction of object and thing becomes relevant. We had a sign form – and Condillac was the first to draw attention to the systemic nature of the sign form – and now we have begun to discuss what the nature of the thing is and to project onto the thing the segmentations obtained from knowledge and its sign forms. There has been a transference from the world of language to the world of the object.

The engineering approach

This is a universal approach. We always start from our technical constructions, which we know, which we created, and transfer the schemata of these constructions to things. Hence begins the permanent dependence of natural science on technology and engineering in a broad sense. An engineer always has the advantage of knowing the construction of a machine or mechanism they created, or a building they built. But for a scientist the object of nature is always a black box. That is why when a modern physiologist begins discussing how the human brain operates and its structure, a cybernetician says, 'There is no mystery about it – the brain is a highly complex computer.' This transition from the computer built by us to an object of nature is a basic principle. It is why engineering constructions are often taken as models of objects in nature.

From parts to unity

The transfer of the systemic concept of knowledge to objects was therefore perfectly natural. Initially, there were two concepts: the multiplicity of parts and the existence of connections between them. The third and very important aspect was the delimitation of this multiplicity, or the assignment of these parts to a unity. But the connections proved intractable at the outset, because Condillac died without inventing a language for the representation of connections. He invented a language for the parts, but not for the connections.

Structure

The next very important step is the emergence of the idea of structure, which took place in the 1840s. An important part was played by the works of the French chemist Jean-Baptiste Dumas, who discovered the paradoxical fact that substances with the same set of elements can have completely different qualities.

Before that, chemistry had said that the properties of a whole were determined by the properties of the parts that constitute it, and there was a large class of phenomena that tended to confirm this. But Dumas showed that the properties of the whole are not determined by the properties of its parts. So a classic paradox was obtained and there was a problem to be solved. This is to say that there was a need to go back to basic notions, to the means of analysis, and to find the inadequacy in them.

Let us see how the main categories were ordered. There is the world of things with their qualities. There is the world of multitudes, or complexes. There were already certain ideas about process. Condillac introduced the notion of a system, implying connection between parts. In parallel, there emerged the notion of the constitution of a whole. And when Dumas presented his facts, it turned out that all those categories simply did not work.

The category

We give the name of category to a certain linkage, with four focus points. It is usually said that categories are the most general concepts. That is so, but it is only half of the matter. The other half consists of the fact that categories are concepts with a particular logical content and meaning, namely concepts in which we fix a linkage between languages and concepts that are applicable to the object – a proper representation of the object – and the operation or our action (see Figure 1.22).

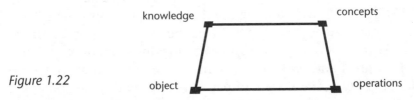

Figure 1.22

Such linkage is in fact a category. So a category is a concept (a categorical concept), which pins down in our mental activity the connections and correspondences between operations, which we perform, the object to which these operations are applied, the language in which all this is expressed, and our concepts.

If we work in categories and evaluate all phenomena – operations that are carried out, language, representation of the object and concepts – by means of categories, we give ourselves a highly powerful, unrivalled tool for analysis and problem solving. The person who works in categories and analyses in categories works better than any computer, and finds and locates errors quickly and easily.

It is true that certain classes of tasks are incapable of solution by means of categories. But a skilled user of the mechanism of categories can immediately give a general assessment of a situation and find their orientation in it.

The category of structure

When Dumas discovered the strange fact that substances made from one and the same element-parts (I use a compound word for a special reason, which will soon become clear) have different features, he called the set of categories into question. The set ceased to function for these cases, and a new category was needed. This category was that of structure, which was proposed almost simultaneously by two chemists, Butlerov and Kekulé.

All of the formulae that we know so well began to appear from that time, including signs for bonds, and the language of bonds. The important thing was that these bonds have a definite configuration. By removing the elements – by, as it were, folding them away into points – we obtain pure structure. The structure is an integrity of bonds, a configuration of bonds.

The notion of bonds

But there were problems with Butlerov's idea. Mendeleyev and the elder Menshutkin were among the first scientists to see them. They asked Butlerov what the nature of his bonds was supposed to be. Their reasoning was roughly as follows: imagine that I have a mirror, and I dropped and broke it, but I need it very much as I have no other one. I can take a sheet of paper, cover it with glue and apply the small parts of the mirror to it, or I can make thin pins and use them to pin the parts together. But in both cases the links are artificial additions to join a broken unity.

Mendeleyev argued like this: very well, you have collected the parts of the mirror and bonded them together, but where were the bonds before you broke the mirror? How can we distinguish a bond from a nonbond? If there is a complex mechanism with some transmission device, we can say this device is a bond. But this will be stretching a point. Or we can take a chair and say that it consists of wooden sections fixed together with screws, and these screws are bonds. However, it means that every time we need to artificially impose the distinction between elements and bonds.

They drove Butlerov into a corner, and he had to acknowledge in the mid-1880s that there are no bonds in nature, but we use the concept in our language to denote processes that unfold inside the objects.

I do not know what does more credit to Butlerov – that he invented these bonds, or that he renounced their existence, because the second thing is also a great thought. He was the first person in the world to do it, and we are now moving increasingly in that direction. Later I shall show you systematically how that happened.

As a result of further work in this direction, somewhere around 1908–11, the schema we all know from school textbooks appeared, where an electron revolves around atoms and thereby binds them. Hence it became possible to determine valence, change of bonds and other issues.

The structure of bonds

So Dumas's results were presented as the concept of structure, and then everything fell into place. It is clear that there can be a difference in properties when composition is the same, because properties of the unity are not determined by the elements, but by the structure of bonds within this unity. Bonds and structure became the leading factor constituting properties. Scientists began to deduce properties of the unity from bonds and the structure of bonds. The unity was now defined by its inner structure – not only and not so much by what was bonded, but by the structure as such.

Processes

So the concept of structure had appeared, but there was one more difficulty. There was no place in this way of looking at things for processes: structure had become almost the most important point of the systemic conception, but the concept of process was absent. Processes were not taken into account at all in late nineteenth and early twentieth-century chemistry, and this is a very important point.

In the first textbook of chemistry, Lavoisier had written, 'A chemist who analyses and then synthesises substances does with his own hands what nature should have done, but for some reason did not do.' Chemists believed that they only do and could only do what nature does: they believed that they were imitating, repeating natural processes. Nature initially established that an object can be broken down to these or other parts and can be put together from these or other parts, and the chemist divines this fact in the same way as a sculptor divines the shape of their future work of art in a block of stone. The chemist only reproduces, through the procedures of analysis and synthesis, what was already built in by nature at the level of structure.

That is why chemistry, unlike physics, has never taken an interest in processes within the object. It was and remains a technical science; it shows how to take things apart and put them together, how to analyse and synthesise. It does not say how things 'really' happen. For some reason, it is physics that knows the answers to how everything happens in nature. Physics gives us the idea of molecular structure, atomic structure and so on: it describes natural processes. That is why this whole development in chemistry occurred without any attention to the idea of the process.

So for a long time processes were excluded from the structure-and-system representations, which became the mainstream thanks to the developments described above.

Matters took a new turn after the Second World War, or to be exact, in the course of it. During the war, as you know, American and British scientists were not recruited to physically defend their country, but to intelligence and counter-intelligence, where they were put to work on tasks of organisation and management.

British and American intelligence, counter-intelligence and their system of military management were created by chemists and mathematicians. The British and Americans view this as their greatest attainment in the war, and believe that this approach is what gave them the crucial advantage.

Some of the scientists who had been put to work in this way noticed a surprising significance of structural features. It turned out that when convoys were crossing the Atlantic Ocean and were attacked by German submarines and bombers, everything depended on how the ships were positioned. They could be positioned in such a way that every vessel reached its destination, or in such a way that every vessel was destroyed.

On one occasion a British admiral demanded to know how many German planes were brought down by anti-aircraft guns on convoy ships. It turned out that the number was very low. So he ordered the guns to be dismantled, but that only made things worse – ships were lost wholesale. It became clear that what was important was not only the number of kills, but the preventive effect achieved by the presence of guns. So the number zero came to be viewed as having a definite significance, and from here there is a direct road to organisation. This is the starting point for the analysis of operations, the making of charts and so on. But that should be a topic for separate discussion. Initially, these charts were of a merely technical and military nature, and they were only declassified (in the United States) in 1956.

The systems movement

In 1949, the Austrian (by birth, but by then already Canadian) biologist Ludwig von Bertalanffy put forward a completely new idea. He said that all objects are nothing other than systems. The category of the system, which Condillac had related to knowledge, Bertalanffy related in a generalised form to objects. He formulated the idea that living organisms, human society and everything else are nothing other than systems, and should be viewed from a completely new, systemic point of view. But he himself did not understand well what could be meant by considering things from a systemic viewpoint.

The cybernetics movement

The ground-breaking book by Norbert Wiener, *Cybernetics*, was published at almost the same time as Bertalanffy put forward his idea and – unexpectedly even to Wiener – led to the appearance of a new movement: the cybernetics movement. A mass of people from various fields, professions and branches of science seized on this book as their bible, and the cybernetics movement began erasing borders between specialisations.

It was not important for cyberneticians whether you were a physicist, mathematician, biologist or engineer by profession. It was only important that you viewed the world in a special way, as containing systems of control. This was not yet the systems movement as such, but the cybernetics movement. It treated everything in the world as control systems.

Bertalanffy watched all this and was surprised as anyone by the unexpected success of Wiener's ideas. He decided to take the same road, and in 1954–5 he set up an organisation called 'General Systems' and an annual publication by the same name. Affiliates appeared all over the world, and the systems movement emerged.

The history of the systems approach

The idea came from philosophy, at the level of category analysis – the idea of organisation of knowledge and language, just as Condillac had described it. Then this idea is transferred to objects. But it is important to note that it is not objects themselves that are systemic or nonsystemic. The systematicity is in a certain way of viewing them. If we view something systematically, it is systemic, and if we view it in another way, let us say as a point, it is nonsystemic.

If I just want to count how many of you there are (in my lecture audience), why should I say that every one of you is a system? I turn everyone into a point, use a counting stick, and I do not have to use systemic ideas. But if someone falls ill because of a malfunction of their central nervous system, a physiologist must treat them as a system.

Objects as such are not systems or nonsystems. Everything depends on our purpose when we look at them. If we think of the object in a systemic way, it appears to us as a system. But in other instances we do not have to do this.

At first the development of these ideas was limited to a small group of people. They developed principles and concepts and gradually pinned them down in categories. A new language of systemic representation took shape, objects were represented as systems, and operations – systems analysis and synthesis – were created. The new grows from the old: the old has to be transformed to obtain something new. And a general category-based concept of a system gradually formed.

Much time passed, and when the need arose – in the Second World War – these ideas, which had been developed some time earlier, suddenly found a wide and powerful application. There was an explosion. What had been developing slowly and almost unnoticed was suddenly seen to be vitally important. And all those who wanted to survive – survive and win – started to use this resource. The urgency of the situation made them apply it widely and indiscriminately. When the urgency was overcome, people started to take stock, reflect and see that a host of new tasks can be resolved in the same way. The movement quickly gained numerous followers.

To begin with, most of them were enthusiasts with limited understanding of the field. The size of the movement undermined the quality of its ideas. But the creation of a new social base is important.

Systems ideas became technical ideas, and won over huge numbers of people, including those working in the sphere of organisation and management.

The first concept of a system

Measuring and articulation of parts

There is an object upon which we act, to which we can apply certain operations. We take two groups of operations. The first group consists of measurement operations, through which we can discover certain qualities of the object, (a), (b), (c) ... and record them in our knowledge as properties of this object. The second group of operations consists of decomposition, breaking into parts. It is interesting to note that our procedures will be completely random until we know the inner structure of the object – it is as if a doctor cut up a person like a butcher cuts beef. The lines of fracture do not correspond in any way with the inner structure, they are applied to the object from without. So we end up with four objects instead of

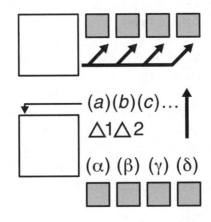

Figure 1.23

one. But because we obtained them by breaking the first object into parts, we can now introduce the category of unity and parts. We say that these objects are parts, and what we had before was the whole (see Figure 1.23).

This part–whole relation is a kind of reverse procedure. I say 'kind of' because the very operation of division produces a qualitative boundary of the object's existence. There was one object, now it is gone, and instead of it there are parts. That is why I say that the category of whole and part is a kind of reverse operation.

The part–whole category

Supposing that these are the parts of a whole that existed before, we interconnect two chronotopes, or in other words two space–time entities. The first is the whole that existed before, and the second is the entity incorporating the parts. In our thought, we can break through this space–time barrier. When we have the whole, we can imagine how we break it into parts, since this is an action in the category of whole and part. When we have the parts, we can imagine how we put them together into a whole.

The parts have properties, which we can designate as (α), (β), (χ), (δ) and so on. This is when the objective duality, which I have been discussing from the very outset, appears. Operations of division and imaginable procedures of assembly are what we do to objects. But what are we do to with properties? We now have to identify properties with each other. At the same time, relations between the properties are also important. The properties can be divided into properties that are common to the whole and the parts, and properties that are different for the whole and the parts. Common properties in turn can be divided into additive and nonadditive properties.

That is why, if we break the object into parts, it is not clear in principle whether the parts will keep any of the properties of the whole or not; and if they keep them, whether the sum of the properties of the parts will correspond to any of the properties of the whole. If the sum does correspond, we say that these are additive properties. For example, weight and mass are additive properties. If we weigh an object, then break it into parts and weigh the parts, we will obtain the same weight, only in a different distribution. Other properties will be nonadditive. It might turn out that a property is preserved, but that its quantity in the parts is less or more than that in the whole.

It might also turn out that the parts do not have a quality that the whole had. Hegel put this very clearly when he said that a living being has no parts; only a dead body has parts. If we cut a unitary living body into parts, what we obtain are parts of a dead body instead of parts of the living body.

Having divided the object up, we now have to correlate the properties of the parts with the properties of the whole. If we divide an object up, we want to know in advance what properties the parts will have, and putting an object together, we want to know what properties the whole will have. Today, as a rule and for most objects, we do not know these things and cannot do this. When a radio engineer assembles a circuit from known structural components, they do not know in principle what they will end up with. There will be many resonance phenomena and other things of a purely systemic nature.

But this is not the case for all objects, and this is why objects are divided into those that can be split into parts, and those that cannot. A living body cannot be split into parts, but a carcass can. Surgeons used to work like butchers, without following the inner structure of the object; they did not think, as Lavoisier did, that there are partitions established by nature which should be followed. In the early days of surgery the surgeons made cuts at random. In fact, surgeons still cut people in a hit-or-miss way even now, when they are dealing with the lymphatic system or systems of biochemical regulation. We know that these systems exist and that they are very important, but we still cannot localise them.

We can see, therefore, that there is a certain procedure for objects and that relations between properties fixed in signs must correspond to it. And we must know how to carry out these actions in such a way that they correspond with the partition and the reverse procedure of assembly. This is now the main challenge for all sciences that have to do with complex objects, including the theory of organisation and management.

To recap, a part or parts is what we obtain as a result of cutting something up.

Connecting parts into a whole

Now we come to the reverse procedure. What do we need to do to get back to the whole? We need to take our four parts and connect them with each other, impose connections which will keep them together. We could do it by fastening a hoop around them. That would work just as well as a connection. Then we would have a dual structure of connection, inner and outer. But these are still connections (see Figure 1.24).

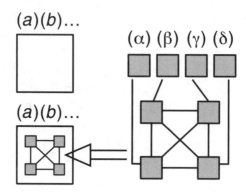

Figure 1.24

So the procedure of linkage begins. First we had the procedure of partition, and now we have that of linkage. But what is interesting is that we do not see the linkage as the opposite of the procedure of partition, because we have not yet got back to the whole. It is not clear what has happened here. Only a corpse has parts, so if we cut the organism into parts, and then put these parts together into a whole, we will not obtain a living organism. When this was acknowledged, it was understood that such a partition, even if it takes account of the inner structure, is a special procedure resulting in something different from the initial unity. Systems thinkers asked, how does what we end up with relate to the initial unity? Then they performed what is essentially an operation of insertion. They inserted what had been obtained into the original thing – inside it, so to speak – and began speaking of the whole. I am not interested for the moment whether this procedure is realisable or not; I am talking about what they did in thought. The properties (α), (β), (χ), (δ) belong to the parts – I say 'parts', though that is not quite exact and I shall correct myself in a moment. The whole is the initial unity with the properties (α), (β), (χ). We have obtained properties of the parts and properties of the whole, and we need to somehow distinguish them.

This was first done in thermodynamics, where a distinction was made between the macroscopic and microscopic planes, the inner and the outer. This is where we can talk about inner structure, or composition. The whole remains as the frame, into which we insert this structured unity.

Elements

What is important is that while we are cutting, we deal with parts, and when we link them together, the parts turn into *elements.* The concept of an element is inseparable from the concept of linkage. Elements are just like parts, but after we put them together into a unity, they become that which is connected. Elements are what is connected, what is included in a structure and organised by a structure.

The concept of an element was introduced by Lavoisier and Fourcroy. Elements are what are unified into a whole. But then the famous paradox appears, on which scientists spent a hundred years: is there a difference between an element and a simple body? This remains confused in Mendeleyev's table of the elements. The table is called a table of the elements, but it gives the properties of elements as simple bodies, as substances. How does a simple body differ from an element? An element is a chemical unit, and a simple body is a physical unit. A simple body always occurs as a molecule. An element is, for example, H, but a simple body is H_2, where there are always two atoms in the molecule.

Mendeleyev himself did a lot of work on this. He insisted on the distinction between elements and simple bodies, emphasising that elements are a concept of microscopic, 'inner' analysis. Elements are what a unity is made up of, so an element is a part inside the whole, which functions inside the unity, without as it were being torn out of it. A simple body, a part, is what we have when everything has been disassembled and is laid out separately. But elements only exist within the structure of connections. So an element implies two principally different types of properties: its properties as material, and its functional property derived from connections.

In other words, an element is not a part. A part exists when we mechanically divide something up, so that each part exists on its own as a simple body. An element is what exists in connections within the structure of the whole and functions there.

An element has properties of two kinds, attributive properties and functional properties. *Functional* properties are those that emerge in a part when we include it in a structure and disappear when we exclude it. For example, if I was a husband, I might quarrel with my wife, go to a registrar's office and get a divorce, so I lose the functional property of being a husband. I cease to be a husband, because being a husband means to be in a certain relation, to have a wife and be registered as such, with a corresponding note in my passport. If this connection is broken, this functional property disappears. *Attributive* properties are those that an element preserves regardless of whether it is inside this system or outside it. The word 'this' is highly important here, because it might turn out that a property that seems to be attributive is simply a functional property from another system.

Functional properties belong to an element to the extent that it belongs to the structure with connections, while other properties belong to the element itself. If I take out this piece of material, it preserves its attributive properties. They do not depend on whether I take it out of the system or put it into the system. But functional properties depend on whether or not there are connections. They belong to the element, but they are created by a connection; they are brought to the element by connections.

This brings us back to the issue of individuality. Attributive properties belong to the individuality of the principal, and functional properties are those that the person acquires when they sit down in the boss's chair. At this point they acquire a whole pile of functional properties. If we take the principal out of this place, they lose these qualities. These functional properties appear to be incredibly powerful, and the system of the organisation 'steamrolls' people to such an extent that they are left almost bereft of attributive properties.

Place and content

The next important step for us is to stratify the element. Let us say there are three connections from the element. There might also be a connection with the whole, which would be another type of connection, which science is still feeling its way towards. We can gather together functional properties that correspond to connections and take stock of them.

Doing that, we introduce the concepts of 'place' and 'content'. An element is a unity of a place and its content – the unity of a functional place, or a place in the structure, and what fills this place.

A *place* is something that possesses functional properties. If we take away the content, take it out of the structure, the place will remain in the structure (assuming that the structure has a conservative and rigid nature), held there by connections. The place bears the totality of functional properties.

The *content* by contrast is something that has attributive functions. Attributive functions are those that are retained by the content of a place, when this content is taken out of the given structure (we can now express it in this way). We never know whether these are its properties from another system or not. Now we might take something out as content, but it is in fact tied to another system, which, as it were, extends through this place.

Systems are more complex than anything thought up by science-fiction writers. Systems can extend through other systems. And it can turn out that functional properties from other systems look like attributive properties of this structure, although in the other system they are functional properties.

So we have a place and its content. An interesting question arises: what is the correlation between attributive properties and functional properties, or in other words, between properties of place and properties of content? They exert pressure upon each other and mutually support one another. Properties of contents must correspond to functional properties.

Self-organisation by place and breaking out of the system

Do we mould ourselves to a place or is the place moulded to us? It is a bilateral process, because every person must take a place, without which they would not be a person. But they have a way out – they can 'furnish' the place to suit themselves, create a place for themselves. Many people have done this. You ask, what does a certain man do? The answer is: he is Ivanov. His name is his place; he is his place. When we say Leo Tolstoy, Lenin or Marx, we do not ask about their job. So there are strictly individualised places.

There can be a job called 'village school teacher' or a place called 'Makarenko'.

A person works for 15 years to earn their status and their name, and then their name works for them for another 20 years. Once they have earned themselves a name, people can permit themselves some flourishes. But, really, people can always permit themselves some flourishes. For every individual the problem of their individual existence is that of finding the limits of what they can disobey without self-destruction, to see to what extent they can break out of the system. Existence as an individual is always a breaking-out of the system. But at every stage of their development, people can only break out within certain limits, to the degree of their attributive properties, because only people with sufficiently well-developed attributive – not merely functional – properties can dare to break out of the system. To do this they must be people who do not depend on the place they occupy.

Functional property

We have a structure. We put it inside the unity and receive an inner structure. What is that unity? Again, we apply the same principle and ask – how do we now represent such a system? We can now represent it twice, at two different levels.

The first level contains the position with connections. The second level is the inner structure, consisting of attributive properties and functional properties. Notice that we can measure attributive properties, but can we measure functional properties? It turns out that we do not know today how to measure functional properties, and that their measure is the structure.

Structure is the measure of functional properties, and is always singular.

So we obtain external connections, functions – but what is a functional property? We obtain a functional property when we break a connection, take out an element, but want to preserve the representation of connection as a property of this element.

Let me repeat this, since it is a very important point. If we want to analyse elements, we must analyse functional properties, because if there are no functional properties, there are no elements either.

Now imagine we need to take out functional elements. Now we work not as a butcher, but as a surgeon who knows how the human body is arranged. We begin cutting in such a way that our scalpel should not cut elements, but should sever connections and enable us to take out functional organs. We take them out, and what do we obtain? If we did not take account of functional properties, then there would be no element left there, but only the content.

What else do we need to do to in order take out elements as elements? We need to keep the connections. We cut them, but these broken-off connections remain there and we now call them functional properties. Functional properties are a way of fixing and keeping the broken connections of an element as belonging to that element.

So when we have a system, we obtain connections that include it in a much broader unity. Now we have to tear all of that out. And we tear out a set of connections in the form of functional properties. As well as that, we have a totality of elements and connections between them, or the structure. We assign certain attributive properties to this unity.

Properties of function, or functional properties, belong to an element only. Not to a simple body, but to an element. This is because functional properties arise on account of connections. When we say of someone that he is a husband or a father, we fix his manner of functioning within a certain unity. This is not a property that belongs to him as such, but it is determined by his relation to another person, or in other words by a connection. But I do not need to talk about the person as an element in the 'husband–wife' relation, I can just say he is a husband. And I do not speak about his properties as a substance, but of his properties as an element.

Properties are properties and connections are connections, and we have a special language to denote them. Connections have the peculiarity that they create properties of elements. The element, situated in connections, receives properties from each connection. Factually, there are no such properties: they are fictitious, and there are only connections or even processes.

We have torn this element out, excised it from life. But we need to preserve this life. Then we start talking about functions of the element. We ask, what are the functions of a principal? We speak of the connections in which that person lives, about the process of their work, about how they live and act, but thereby we have transferred them into the form of their properties. We ask about the properties they need to have, referring to these properties as 'functions', though we mean connections and processes. When we talk about functions or functional properties, we are talking about connections and processes in a special language – the language of properties.

As Condillac said, when we have a thing, we view it in the totality of connections in which it exists, and the thing is nothing other than the reflection of these connections.

The second concept of a system

I have told you about the first concept of a system, which coincides in many ways with structure. (People worked on this concept until 1969. In its refined form, the concept was developed in 1963. But the work had been in progress since the twelfth century.)

I want to remind you of the general definition. A complex object is represented as a system in the first place, when we have distinguished it from its surroundings by either completely breaking all of its connections or by preserving them in the form of functional properties; in the second place, when we have divided it into parts (mechanically or according to its inner structure) and thus obtained a totality of parts; in the third place, we have connected the parts and turned them into elements; in the fourth place, when we have organised the connections into a unified structure; and when, in the fifth place, we have put this structure back in its previous place, thus delineating this system as a unity.

What is insufficient in this first concept of a system? To ask what is insufficient about it is not to say that we cannot work with it. On the contrary, we cannot work without it. But that is not enough. It is only the first moment in systems analysis. The point is that there are only connections and no processes here. It is easy for us to say, in the light of Butlerov's works, that there are processes standing behind the connections. But there are no processes here in patent form. This systemic-structural approach does not capture process as such. The second defect is that systems always turn out to be subsystems. There are no criteria for pinpointing the unity of a system.

When this point was understood, the second concept of a system was born. It takes on the first concept in full, but refers it to the structural plane. From the viewpoint of the second concept, to represent something as a simple system is to describe it in four planes as follows:

1 process
2 functional structure
3 organisation of material
4 material alone.

In other words, if we have an object, then to represent this object as a simple system or monosystem is to describe this object first as a process, then as a functional structure, then as an organisation of material, and in fourth place as mere material. And these four descriptions should refer to the same object and be interconnected.

What does it mean to represent an object as a polysystem, or a complex system? It means to describe it many times in such a way and to establish connections between these representations on four planes.

The simplest instance can be presented like this. I take a material and again describe it as a process, as a functional structure, as morphology or the way the material is organised, and as a new material. Then it appears that the first representation, given by the first process, the functional structure and the morphology, is parasitic on the material, which itself represents another system with its own process, functional structure and organisation of the material. And all this can, in turn, be seen as the parasite of another system. So we imagine some systems being parasitic on other systems, creating a kind of a symbiosis of systems.

But there are instances where systems concepts need to be unfolded in a different way.

Systems analysis

Other problems of a special kind appear here, and I need to tell you a separate story about how this second concept took shape and how it joined up with the first concept in 1969, and about the opportunities that it opens up for us today.

A set of operations or procedures that we apply to an object make this object systemic. I have drawn this this object schematically, and it has been included from the outset in certain thematic operations; $\delta 1$, $\delta 2$ are the signs of procedures that have enabled us to pin down its properties (a), (b) and (c). I use the round brackets to emphasise that these are sign forms in which we pin down these properties. We assign these properties to the object.

So every object is situated in a certain thematic structure, as if in a frame. This thematic structure is extremely important. If it was not there, we would not be able to transfer the experience of our activity from one object to another. If we have found out something about one object, for example that it has the properties (a), (b) and (c), then we can only refer the knowledge we have acquired to a similar object, and not to any other object. How do we get this idea of similarity? The other object must also have at least these properties (a), (*b*) and (*c*). This procedure of juxtaposition, which we call comparison, always enables us to transfer our experience from one case to another.

Remember Mikloukho-Maklay's Papuans: when a mirror was shown to them, they shouted that it was water. This is a transition: they can see their reflection in the water as well as in the mirror, so the mirror is water. Subsequently, they noted a distinguishing feature – they called the mirror 'solid water' to distinguish it from the usual liquid water.

But such procedures of juxtaposition, which set a frame for an object, are not specific to systemic representation. And it is not the presence of many features or factors that makes the object into a system. We apply procedures of division to it, and that is what makes it into a system for the first time: a systemic object is an object that we split into part-elements. The possibility of its division is the necessary, though not sufficient, condition for its being a system. Then we connect the parts we have distinguished into a unity in some internal way, establish the structure of connections and simultaneously turn parts into elements. If parts are not interconnected, they are not elements. Elements are those parts that are already included in the structure of connections and therefore make the unity. Then we perform a procedure that effects a reverse movement: we put back the inner structure and elements and connections, thus closing this cycle (note the word 'cycle', we shall need it later); so we put everything back, and having completed this entire move, we obtain a systemic presentation of the object. If we have managed to do this, we say that our object is a system. Success is achieved both in practice and in thought.

What is a 'systemic presentation of the object' from the viewpoint of its graphics, or the construction of the presentation itself? It is nothing other than the form in which the procedures we have completed are recorded.

If I draw some object as consisting of many elements, it means that I can divide it, split it into parts; if I apply these procedures to it I will obtain the results I need. If I draw here the signs of connections, it only means that I can connect these elements with each other to obtain a certain living unity. This is symbolized by the external outline, the sign of a whole, a unity having these properties (*a*), (*b*), (*c*) and so on. So I answer the question 'What is that scheme?' by saying that it is precisely the traces of actions that

I have performed, a way of recording the procedures that have been applied to the object.

The object as a schema of procedures for working with it

I repeat once more, as this is very important – whatever category we take, the depiction of the object is always the schema of the procedures that we apply to it. Any schema, any image of the object is nothing but the scheme of procedures that we apply to the object.

In this regard, Einstein discovered the dialectic method over again when he said that we do not need to ask what time is, but to disclose the procedures we perform when we obtain the idea of time, or putting it simply, to see how we measure time. If we know this set of procedures, we have the operational, procedural content of our concept, our idea of time.

Well, but what if our operations do not correspond with the arrangement of the object? I say that the schema of the object is always only the traces of the procedures that we perform, like a network of these procedures that have been given a graphic, significant expression, and been imposed on the object. But the partitions may be mechanical if they are carried out by a 'butcher'. Good surgeons work differently, as they know the structure of the object. They cut in a goal-directed way, taking account of all the nuances of the inner structure. Hence the difficulty inherent in such cutting, that it must correspond to the object itself.

So this concept of a system has a technical character (remember what Lavoisier said). What does we mean by a 'technical nature'? Our word 'technology' originates from the Greek word *techne*, meaning art or skill, and 'technical' means 'depending on human skill'. Not on science, therefore. When science and technology (or skill) are united, they create engineering. Engineering differs from technology in its groundedness. We might say that technology is a pure skill while engineering is skill founded on strict knowledge.

The art of schematisation

The application of the network of systemic and structural representation to the object is the exercise of skill.

Now that we have obtained an image, we approach it with two requirements. The first requirement concerns the extent to which we can use the image for constructions, and the second concerns its operability.

We need images to work with. The image does not have to correspond exactly to the object. A model of an object does not correspond with the object for a simple reason: if the image was fully identical to the object, we would not need it at all. This is the whole point of a model – by definition, a model differs from the object. The same goes for an image. This is the most important point. Having obtained an image of the object, we must work with it. The image must be adjusted to make it suitable for work; it must correspond to the nature of this work. Hence the requirements about its suitability for constructions and its operability.

Let's see how this happened in the history of the development of numbers. Among nearly all peoples, the figure 10 was initially represented by 10 sticks. This is a model in its pure form – for one sheep we lay down one stick, for two sheep two sticks, and so on to 10, 100 and so on. But now think how we can work with this 100. How can we multiply it or do something else with it? The structure of these images (models) limited our operational and constructive abilities. That is why, when people reached the number 10, they began to denote this number with a sign. So they moved from a sign-model to a sign-symbol.

Further, see what an interesting thing happens to numbers at school. Imagine that you are learning to count. When you have one object, you say one; when you have a second, you say two, when you have a third you say three, and so on. When a child has learned to count, it is time to start adding. They say 'four plus ...', but then they stop, unlike adults typically do addition, and they say there is something wrong. One is this, two is that, four is something else: every symbol denotes its own object. And when we say 'four plus five' how much will it be?

Two.

Of course. Children work with the object content, because they understand clearly the meaning assigned to the symbols. However, you have skipped ahead and say that 'four' is not the fourth object but the totality of everything that you have counted before. You know that we use numbers in two meanings: after 1,500 years of work philosophers and mathematicians twigged that there are cardinal and ordinal meanings of numbers. The important thing here is that we substitute one for the other. When we add things, 'four' acts as a sign for a totality and not as a sign for a fourth object. We have moved from a modelling value to a symbolising value. We have begun to add totals.

Operational systems

Here we approach the concept of a mathematical operating system. What is our system of numbers? It consists of at least three operational structures tied to one type of material. The first structure is counting, where every number has a particular meaning. For as long as people counted, but did not add, they were limited to objects, and in this perspective the numerical form of 10 or 30 sticks was the best. Yet when they began adding and subtracting, it turned out that such a number form was not suited to these procedures. What is more, it turned out that some figures were lacking. For example, when we deduct five from five, what do we get? Zero. What object corresponds to zero – an object that has been destroyed, or one that never existed? There was no way of obtaining zero by any counting in this operating system. The zero is introduced to keep this procedure within the operative system of signs: in other words, so that no procedure with signs takes us outside the system of signs.

OK, but what if we subtract seven from five? Then we need minus numbers. Then there are multiplication, roots and all the rest. We have imaginary numbers and complex numbers. Where did such sign forms come from? They came from the needs of the operating system.

The problem of the sign–object correspondence

Bertrand Russell tells this story from the time when the British were conquering Africa. They found a minor local chief, who seemed to them a promising candidate to become an emperor. They sent him weapons (Winchester rifles and gunpowder), but he could not understand why he should conquer and control other people's land. They sent advisers to work on him, but he maintained that all this made his head spin. He said 'I do not know where I should send my emissaries and where I should not', and similar things. Then they built a shack for him and made a model of all his territory, with model villages, toy soldiers and so on. The advisers told him: you should send a detachment to this place. Get together soldiers, count them off, give them orders and deploy them in such and such a place. The chief mastered all this, he liked the game, and he began moving soldiers around the model and asked the advisers to expand its territory. He annexed the neighbouring area on the model, captured some more land, and so on. He began to wage mock wars, and there came a day when he lost all interest in what was happening in reality in his own land. He won battles and conquered lands, but only in his hut. When the advisers became angry, he said that he liked this game best of all and told them to go and manage everything else themselves.

There is always a problem of correspondence. When we work with diagrams, algebraic expressions, differential calculus, or create mathematical and economic models, or draw schemata, there is often no reality to match them.

What I am saying is quite simple. There is no such object as 'zero' – the object supposed to match the symbol '0'. Humanity quickly reached a point where there were more nondenoting than denoting signs. According to a count at the turn of the century there are about 400 nondenoting signs for every sign that refers to something. Hence the extreme difficulty of reaching the object, of descending to it.

The multitude of signs created by our operations with signs, created by our construction procedures applied to signs, are significant, but they denote ideal objects, as we might put it. When we are working with operating systems, we never know whether we are working with reality or with ideal objects.

Ideal objects

Signs appear as a direct and unmediated image or denotation of the objects that we work with. But subsequently we have to include these significant images in new operating systems. All significant systems are adjusted to these purely symbolic significant operative systems. Such operations give rise to new objects, including ideal objects. Nearly everything we are talking about – nearly everything! – is primarily an ideal object, and in rare cases it is also a real object corresponding to this ideal one.

Yet the problem of the ideal object always remains, and a person who fails to understand that the level of signification alone is important cannot live and work to modern standards.

Take a simple situation. The task is to lay the table for dolls at a kindergarten: go to the next room and fetch a plate, knife, fork and spoon for each doll. What does a child who cannot count do? They go to the next room, and bring a pile of dishes, spoons, forks and knives, then they either go back to get some more, or take back the ones left over once the table has been laid. What does someone who can count do? They start with something that seems pointless for the job they have been asked to do – they count the dolls. They count them and take the number they have arrived at to the next room, where they count out the number of plates, spoons and forks and knives that they need. After they have got as many as they need, they throw away the number, as it has done its work, and bring the things back, confident of having as many plates, spoons, forks and knives as are necessary. People who do not know or represent to themselves the rules of organisation and transformation of the symbolic world cannot live in modern society.

Technical, target, nominal, naturalised and natural objects

I have already described to you how chemistry worked with technical and constructive ideas. Today this problem is highly relevant and much discussed in geology and geography. The concepts of target and nominal objects are the main issue for people whose job is to find subsurface mineral deposits. Imagine that you need to find an oil deposit or a system of oil and gas-bearing minerals. A region is chosen and prospecting begins. Sections are examined, seismic work is carried out, samples are tested and so on. In the course of this work the prospectors sometimes wonder: is what we call a gas or oil deposit a natural object, with boundaries that correspond to how the earth is structured, or is it correlated to our means of prospecting? Do you see the point? A large number of thoughtful geochemists and geologists say that oil and gas fields are nominal and verbal, and we draw their boundaries by looking for the forms we need for our purposes.

'Nominalists' think like this: if you draw the boundaries of an oil and gas field according to your goals, your technical goals, you can draw them in any way you like and say that such is your goal; that is why your target fields are nothing but nominal objects.

Another group of geologists take a naturalistic point of view and speak about a natural object, understanding that for a geologist (as opposed to a geotechnologist) what is important is to know to what extent the boundaries they draw, the structures they discover, correspond to – but what should they correspond to? The first simple attempt at an answer is to say that they should correspond to the real structure of the field. The problem arises of the extent to which these schemes, created in the signifying, symbolic plane, can be naturalised. In other words, can we say that the partition we have made accords with the initial structure of the object – the thing that existed in nature?

The idea of a jet engine was developed back in 1925. So why could it not be put into practice until 1945? Because it was not clear how various types of metal would behave at high temperatures. For 20 years, it was impossible to create such an engine, because whatever metal the designers tried, it failed to withstand the temperatures generated.

Here is another good example, which should makes things quite clear. Construction of a large hydroelectric power station begins. Everything seems fairly simple: the designers need to keep the level of the water above the station as high as they can and then let it pour down through the turbines. But what kind of dam should they build? There are masses of simple processes to be carried out, but what should the dam be like to withstand the water pressure? What inclination should it have? First the designers do calculations, then they produce a model. A small model is built, and water is sent through it. The model is an exact copy of the power station to be built, only 20 or 40 times smaller. Then Academician Kirpichev, who supervised this work on a hydro project, faced the difficult problem of deciding, if everything in the model was multiplied by 40 – the water flow, the pressure – what would happen then?

Do you know what happened when the full-sized dam was built? It collapsed because, as it turned out, with the increased size all the ratios in the equations ceased to operate. There are certain equations for a small dam and different equations for a big dam – not different coefficients, but different equations. Work then began on a highly complex theory of modelling and theory of likenesses. The relevant criteria were developed, and the man who calculated them came to be considered a great scientist.

A project has to be capable of implementation, it must be capable of being imposed on reality in a one-to-one relation. That is what you say. But I say – let's think for a second, what is meant by imposing a project on reality? What could this be?

Design and implementation

What is included in the project and what happens in reality when activity is organised? The project has to be implemented! But what does that mean? The project is not applied to the object, because we have no object, it has yet to be built. We say: in accordance with the project. That means, in accordance with the technical project, with the construction project, with the project for management of the works, and so on. There is a mass of subdivisions, and I am not going to enumerate them all now. What does it mean, though?

You open up all the blueprints and begin reading. When you have finished reading, you must give orders where to send people, how many of them to send, where to position cranes and so on, and organise the work. What is the application of a project to the object? What is implementation?

There are operations with signs. We read schemes, understand them, transform them, compose them with each other, transform them into others and so on. This is the world of real practical work. And signs, significant schemes, created and transformed by us, somehow organise our practical activity. That is why we need them, and that is why we use them.

But we are starting out from a very simple idea: there must be a relation of correspondence between signs and the reality of our practical activities. And yet I say that this contradicts the concept of a sign function. There is no such relation and never can be.

What am I constantly trying to show? We have one layer, that of pure thought (schemes on the blackboard), and another layer, that of practical activity. And the transition from the world of practical activity to the world of thinking is very complex and confused, as is the transition from the world of thinking to the world of practical activity.

So there are two layers that still need to be coupled together in a particular way. Construction in Finland is done differently, not because projects there are applied directly to reality – that is never the case for projects. Projects there fall into a different organisational structure of activity. That is what makes them capable of being implemented. It is organisational work – organisational and management work – that ensures the implementation of a project. The project is a prescription for the principal on how and in what sequence they must act. But the burden of action is borne by the individual person. They must know how to perform actions and they must have the relevant experience.

So the principal reads the project plan and analyses it. After that, they act as a kind of interpreter, translating the contents, which are set out in the project, and for that they need to know how to read it. We can say that not everyone can read a project plan and tell us what it contains. Let me show you how one and the same schema can be read in different ways.

Transition from the schema to activity

So not everyone can read a project plan. The principal reads it. But what does it mean to say that they read it? They must now transform it into something else, acting as a translator. They read it, and then tell Ivanov to take ten workers, go to such and such a place and do 'you know what'. Ivanov knows what the principal means, although the others do not, because Ivanov is qualified. We do not call upon any old Ivanov, but the Ivanov who knows how to do the job. Then the principal calls on Petrov and tells him to take a crane and do 'you know what'. This is the idea: there must be qualified people carrying out certain procedures and operations, and the principal has to arrange their action in a certain way in accordance with the project plan.

The project plan is one of the documents – I emphasise 'one of' – ensuring the proper arrangement of the works (and indirectly, the proper arrangement of people as those carrying out these works). However, it is not the project plan as such that ensures the proper arrangement, but only the project plan as transformed into the organisation of work by the relevant principal.

Here is the project. It is cut into parts, or transformed into a sequence of other projects. And then, further along, it is transformed into another sequence. Finally, it reaches the people who turn it all into a 'living activity', organised in a certain way. And activity gives rise to objects.

All the time we are moving forward, from the past to the future. And from the start, we divide all cases into those where the future will be just like the past, and those where the future will differ from the past, perhaps markedly. So every project is a transfer of the experience that was accumulated in previous situations to other, future situations.

Principles of project implementation

So a project plan is a special sign form. Let us say it is to be implemented in the shape of an atomic power station. What mediates the connection between the project plan and the product (building or construction)? The mental activity of people. Sign schemata are not applied to the object, and the very concept of their correspondence is meaningless without due consideration of the activity they organise. The schema does not correspond to an atom. The schema organises our activity with the atom and in accordance with the atom, both our thought and our technical actions. But this activity has yet to be organised. It is carried out by certain people using machines (whether the latter are cranes, measuring devices or something else does not change anything, because cognitive activity is one and the same).

But in order to arrive at action, we need to travel down a long road along which we divide up the project and transform it into a multitude of project documents. Every working team must receive its own project document. The transition from the initial schema to the object is always via a multitude of other schemata. We transform the initial schema into other schemata, and the schemata are incarnated in a certain way of acting. There is no direct access to the object from the sign schema. Everything is mediated by activity. The schema organises activity, sets it, and we capture the object through activity.

What is characteristic of a project? The fact that it sets certain paradigms of activity: brigades, liaison groups, separate people, professionals and specialists.

Schema projects and schema models

Now let us imagine that we are dealing with pure enquiry, with science, where what we construct are schema models and not schema projects. Schema projects are the thing in accordance with which an object is to be created through activity. A schema model is also an instruction for action – for action, through which an object is to be discovered. And this is always a new object, because science never repeats its search for objects, but always goes further and further, and scientists always have to overturn their previous ideas, as they continue to look for something new.

How do they pursue their search? They put forward a hypothesis, a supposition about the structure of an object. Now, why do I always say that the object is given to us through a schema of action, that a systematic representation is the traces of actions that we must perform?

What is a hypothesis? It is a supposition about the structure of the object. But what is this structure of the object in this and other cases? It is a schema of actions, which we have to carry out in order to identify this new object, to discover it. So we are constantly connecting the action and the object through this schema.

The dual content of the schema

A schema is on the one hand an expression of operational active content, a prescription for action, and on the other hand it is the object, which is discovered through these actions. We must then verify whether such an object exists, or whether it does not exist and never can exist.

Ways of reading schemata: processes

So we have a structural schema, and the first way of reading it is through processes. But we only seem to see processes here. A schema does not portray processes (see Figure 1.25).

You probably know the joke: a student is taking an oral exam and they give the right answers, and at the end the professor asks them whether they have any questions, and the student replies, 'I understand everything, except why the wire is straight, but the electric current is sinusoidal ....' This is the point: we do not know whether the schema imitates processes. What happens when we

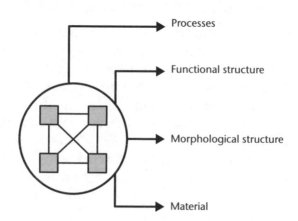

Figure 1.25

read it? After all, if we apply it straight to the object, omitting the mediating role of activity, we will not get any result.

Ways of reading schemata: functional structures

That is why I say that we read this schema on another plane as well – as a functional structure, a set of functionally important elements and connections, which create these functions.

Ways of reading schemata: morphology

And what else can this schema pin down? The difficulty in power engineering is that we have the main schema, a flow schema and an assembly schema. And the installation engineers are dealing with assembly units. And it is impossible to understand one schema in the same way as another: there are lamps there too, so there are not only functional units, but also installation units. So there is also morphology.

Ways of reading schemata: the material

Further on I shall write down the fourth plane – the material. It is now only implicit, but I shall reveal it as I go back.

Now, can you tell me, with regard to all these phenomena, processes, functional structures, organisations of material and the material itself – do they exist in accordance with similar laws or different laws?

Each has its own law.

Yes, they have different laws. And yet we have only one schema. Now look how we represent the object to ourselves. We draw a schema and we say that there must be an object beyond it. We have to carry out the procedure of naturalisation. We have already understood that we still have work to do in order to reach the object, through activity. What object do we need to reach? We are saying now that the object has processes, a functional structure, morphology and material. So our object turns out to exist on several planes.

Now let me ask a trick question: do we have a single object or different ones? Is there one object or are there already four objects?

Is it right that, on a systemic interpretation, there are four objects and not just one object behind this schema? Four ideal objects. Four completely different essences.

So there is a process and there is material, and everything that happens is an interaction between this process and the material. In the course of this interaction, on the one hand (on the side of the material), an organisation of this material emerges – it adjusts to the process, as it were – and on the other hand, the material influences the process, it functionally organises it.

Functional organisation is that whereby the material is reflected in the process. The process is statically captured by organisation as a functional structure. What is the organisation of material or morphology? It is the reflection of the process on the material. Whenever we deal with such process objects, we must always represent them in these four planes. Only thus can we see them as a system (see Figure 1.26).

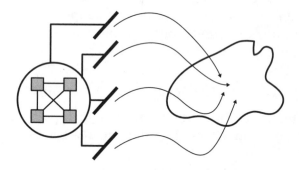

Figure 1.26

But as has been rightly pointed out, for this to be a single object we need all these planes to be connected with each other. We say that they correspond to one very complex systemic object. Here let me draw this systemic object and gather all these presentations together.

Capacities of the second concept of a system

Accounting for natural processes in an object

So the second concept of a system differs from the first by taking account of natural processes in an object. In the first concept of a system, we only had to do with our own procedures. But here, we begin from the categories of process and material, and say that both processes and materials exist in the natural and in the social world. Processes always take place in a certain material. So the material is organised by the processes and the process is organised by the material. A city is a totality of the processes that unfold between people, it is the life of people in the city, it is their telephone calls, their conversation in a room, a restaurant, at the theatre or wherever else. The urban space is organised in a certain way for this purpose.

Setting boundaries to the object

The most important thing is that we can now answer the question where the natural boundaries of the object are. They coincide with that to which a certain process has extended. Naturalisation has taken place. Previously we had technical objects, or target objects. Russell Ackoff's definition is that the system is where my arm reaches to. This is how a technician thinks – the system is in the space over which your power extends. A natural scientist says, differently, that the boundaries of the system are set and defined by the natural process they study. This process forms the boundaries of this systemic object there, where the process has extended to.

Principals have no right to the second approach. They are pure sociotechnologists. Principals, leaders, are people who act in accordance with the first approach. By contrast, a manager must also take account of the natural state of the object through processes.

Principles of self-organisation in an activity-based approach

Engaging with the world

Why do we say 'engaging with' instead of, perhaps, 'cognising'? Because cognising is only one part, and a small part, of engaging with the world.

We engage with the world mainly by drawing to ourselves a certain totality of things as samples or reference points. We take them physically and make them ours. For example, we all wear watches. Watches add a certain standard, reference motion to our natural abilities. We put them on our wrists.

Everyone has a watch, and there is a speaking clock, against which we can check our watches. This is a reference motion. All of us have a representation of one and the same world motion. And all watches are co-ordinated with one another, they are synchronised. This attaches us to our world.

What happens if we come across another motion? We convert it to our reference motion. We either say that this is another motion similar to the reference motion, or we acknowledge the difference and put a formula in place for translation. And this translation formula is nothing else than knowledge. This is how the second moment of engagement with the world appears, through knowledge. The first moment we shall call 'assimilation'.

Cognition

So how do we engage with the world? We take up or assimilate a certain totality of references, and this is a direct engagement. Then we begin to express all other objects of the world through this small group of objects that we have taken up or assimilated. This procedure of expressing other objects through reference objects provides the mechanism of cognition. Cognition is nothing other than the expression of the relations of the whole world of objects to those objects that we take as references.

At first these references were objects and processes in nature. For example, the first clock, the sundial, was formed by the natural motion of shadows. The movement of the sun was seen as a reference motion. Then the hourglass appeared. So we begin by making some objects of nature into our references, and we reach a certain agreement on this. This is a kind of a state committee for standards. Nowadays this service has taken shape institutionally in the form of a committee, but the service always existed. Then these reference points become constructive: in other words, people begin to construct them. Often, constructed machines or tools become reference points. Our engagement with the world leads, primarily, to the expansion of our world of reference points.

But I need to emphasise that the part that we call cognition is secondary. It consists of a reduction of the limitless world of objects to a small group of samples. Knowledge is nothing other than trans-lation formulae, an expression of the world of objects through a set of samples.

In this regard, it is interesting to see how Euclid's geometry is built up. Its first procedure is the construction of an equilateral triangle with the help of a ruler and a pair of compasses. The evidence of its existence is given through the procedure of drawing it. Then the whole world of geometrical figures including circles is reduced to this triangle. Hence the well-known problem of the squaring of a circle: how to express the perimeter of a circle, the area of a circle and so on via a square, or in other words via two equilateral triangles.

Transferring experience

There is a series of previous situations. There is a future situation, which must be constructed. We preserve the experience of the previous situations through reflexiveness as a certain knowledge or totality of knowledge, and then transfer it to the new situation. But this mechanism only enables transfer of knowledge to similar situations. If the situations change, a more complicated structure is formed, which we began discussing last time when we touched on the issue of a project. Past experience is translated into knowledge, then knowledge is transformed into a project, and the project is transferred to the future situation. At this transition from knowledge – which is the recording of a past situation, as if taking a picture of it and portraying it – to the project, which is the plane of the future situation, the future is being formed. It is as if we anticipate the future, as if we actually design it (see Figure 1.27).

Everything in human mental activity is built on transfer from the past to the future. The meaning of cognition and knowledge is ensuring work in the future based on what has been done in the past. How does it happen?

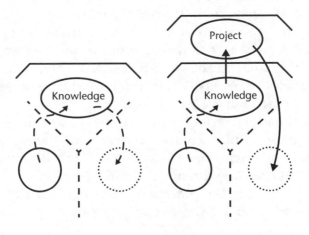

Figure 1.27

First of all, the principle of standardisation operates. As a general rule, the next situation in human activity should be similar to the previous one. And the more similarity there is, the more effective human activity is. Everything would be fine if nothing ever changed in the world. The success of our actions would be guaranteed.

On the value of development

It is very interesting to ask: who needs progress and why? If you feel that are about to fall over, you move your feet and run forward to stop yourself falling. But if you are not going to fall, if you are just standing still, why do you need progress? Why should we run? Progress is nothing other than our attempt to save ourselves from falling.

Since Hegel, we have got used to the idea that progress is good. Why is it good? Why do we need to develop? Just like you, I believe in development and think that to develop is the best thing in the world. However, that is because I am a sportsman in spirit, I have got used to running, and I get the most enjoyment from winning. So I put myself into difficult positions and then get out of them at the cost of great effort. There are people around me who wonder why I keep running about like this: 'Instead of living a quiet, ordinary life, like other people do, he has to be doing tricks, running somewhere.'

Communication and understanding

I am in a state of activity, I am doing something, and then I exit to a reflexive position and express it in the text of a communication. And we have already discussed a variant where we had a blackboard and I first expressed the reflexive position on the blackboard, then expressed what was on the blackboard in the text of a communication. The person who receives the text must understand it. When we receive a message, or any sign forms, we must understand that, and that means moving downwards to activity and embodying this text in our actions. We arrived at it this idea when we were discussing the nature of the project.

So the experience of activity is expressed through reflexiveness in sign texts, and these texts travel to another person, who has to deploy these schemata in action. And this deployment in action happens primarily through understanding.

See how I use the concept of thinking: I say that sometimes we might even do a little thinking, and that is very useful. Do you remember our argument about whether what a leader does is thinking or mental activity? What I state is this: thinking is always written into a system of understanding, and understanding gives sense to any of our actions, including thought actions. So the heart of the matter is never as much to do with thinking as it might seem.

Let me remind you of Uldall's thesis: thinking for people is like dancing for horses, and it plays the same role in the life of people as dancing in that of horses.

But we cannot say the same about understanding. Understanding is what gives meaning to our actions and signs, and what makes our activity meaningful.

Knowledge in actions

We have already covered this issue, and there is only one thing I want to remind you of now. There is the original material and the product, there is transformation through certain actions, tools and means, there are certain goals, and there is knowledge. I am driving at a single point here: knowledge enters activity 'from outside', through communication. It records past experience and ensures the transmission of experience. Knowledge records all the moments of an action. Knowledge records them all, and having obtained knowledge, we have to translate it into living activity. So knowledge – let us remember what Condillac said – is always systemic, because it enables all the elements of action. Knowledge does not correlate with the object directly. Knowledge unfolds as activity with all the elements of the action.

Further on, this principle expanded for us into two other princi-ples. We have singled out one part of the schema of the act: the basic material, and partially the tools and product. This part is presented as an object in a special package. We have also singled out an oper-ational, or operational activity, part. Sometimes it concerns actions only, and sometimes it also includes tools and resources. And I have fixed all this in a principle of the duality of any knowledge and of any sign form.

Signs and schemata

Any sign form has a dual content: first it is operational and active, and second it is object-oriented. And most importantly, it assures the co-ordination of one and the other, the proportionality between actions and the object, and the object and the action. It does not matter which sign form we take, whether a calendar schedule, or a critical path, or a totality of schedules, there are always these two contents – the operational that is read as a totality of actions, and the object-oriented, when you see a certain structure of the object behind the first. This kind of knowledge is structured in such a way that it correlates the action with the object, and the object with the action in advance, making them commensurable to each other.

The schema of the category

Any knowledge has four aspects to its content. Let me remind you of the schema of the category: in one aggregate it has the object, in another it has actions or operations, in a third it has signs or languages, and in the fourth it has concepts.

When we say 'system', 'multitude', 'process', 'relation', we are identifying so-called categorical concepts, or concepts expressing categories. Any knowledge belongs to one or another category, and that is to say that knowledge always carries four characteristics of its content. We have already discussed two of them – the object and the action-operation. Now we can concentrate on the last two characteristics.

First, any knowledge exists in a particular language, particular graphics, and a particular structure, and second, it exists in particular concepts.

Whatever knowledge we take, it lies at the intersection of these four indicators. Knowledge points to action-operations, to the object, and at the same time it shows us its significant, linguistic form and points to concepts, in which it exists.

Let us take the schema of the category entitled 'system'. What is given there? In the first place, I can draw it in a strictly defined and specific language. In the second place, I have a number of concepts standing behind it – the concepts of parts and whole, of elements and connections, and of structure.

When I introduced the first concept of a system, I gathered concepts belonging to the first type of systemic thinking. In effect, I introduced this thinking through these concepts. Besides that, there is a certain presentation of the object standing behind this. We say that the object consists of parts and elements, it has connections, it has a 'hoop' fastening it together – it has integrity. Finally, we need to see operation-actions behind it.

The understanding of any text is always connected with processing the text in these four planes.

The schema of dual knowledge

We have effectively been working in it all the time, but although I already discussed it earlier, this is the first time I am discussing it explicitly. So here is the schema of dual, or multiple, knowledge.

Let us imagine that we have a schema of our object. We have drawn it and now we begin to understand it as a schema of the object. Every knowledge carries four types of content – it shows its language or form, points to an object, to operations and concepts. This means that we have to understand the system in these four planes and know what refers to what. Now let me ask a question. Here is this schema given to us, and we know that this schema represents the object, but I want to ask: what is this object? We ask this question all the time when knowledge is transferred. The person who hears and must understand the message asks all the time, what is the object – the object that they will have to deal with in a practical situation?

There are two strategies we can apply in answering this question, a formal and a substantive strategy.

Formal ontologisation

How would a formalist answer the question, what object do we have here? They would point to the form and say, this kind of object. We have already received its photograph or picture. They would say that the object is such as it is depicted there. Consequently, they will interpret the sign form and related concepts as the object. We can say that they perform a formal ontologisation – they take the picture, project it onto the world of objects, and say that objects are such as we have depicted them in this schema (see Figure 1.28).

Searching for the object in concepts

How do substantive analysts reason? They say, this is nothing other than a picture of the object. What is a picture then? We have already found out that we apply the schema of our actions or operations

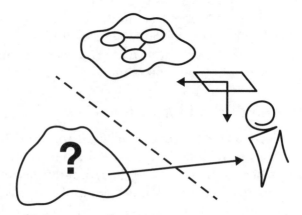

Figure 1.28

to the object. So it is not the object, but only a picture of it, and the object is in fact different. Analysts draw the object and ask the question, what is it, this object, independently and separately from the form of our knowledge, what is this object 'really' – leaving aside the knowledge and sign form in which it is given to us?

The pertinent remark has already been made that formalists see the object in the concept and substantive analysts search for the object in concepts. So the first believe that the concept is an object, while the second want to extract the object itself from the concept, to see something new.

The very pertinence of the expression already shows that these two planes are easily mixed, and that is why the condition for operating with them is the schema of dual knowledge. Dual knowledge gives us a space for representing the object and a special space for the object itself. In this people impinge on the prerogatives of God, take themselves as equal to God. They do not only have knowledge about the object, they also want to see the 'object itself' as it is – leaving knowledge aside. They want to view the object directly. A phrase has even appeared: to know the truth at first hand. This is really the prerogative of God, since only God can see the object as it really is.

The object 'itself': an ontological picture

Indeed this is the axis on which all our scientific and technical thinking turns today, and you will quickly understand why this is so. I want to go through this point again. By introducing the schema of dual knowledge and drawing a place for the object apart from knowledge, human beings impinge on the prerogatives of God: they want to know more than their natural limits allow. We all know objects only via knowledge. But now, humans in their insolence say that it is not enough for them to know objects through knowledge, they want to know the object itself, not as it is represented in knowledge. This is the beginning of philosophy and science.

See what we do. We record a sign form, expressing our knowledge of the object, and then we build another image of the object 'itself' separate from this knowledge. We obtain two (or three, four, whatever) images and begin to correlate them with each other. The point here is not that we will find out what the object 'itself' is, but it is important for us to ask the question and thereby obtain another image, different from the first one. Then we will have the opportunity to work with a connectedness. Let us imagine that the object is a complex process and that today we can picture it in static structures only. The questions are, what have we lost in the object, what limitations have we acquired on our activity with the object, and so on?

Besides that, people, as it were, establish an immanent contradiction, and a never-ending forward rush begins – this is the start of criticism. They say, today science has shown us objects in this way, but this is only another image, because all we ever make are pictures. That is why we know nothing but our limited ideas. This does not imply that we are always mistaken. Probably it would be better to say that our truths are always specifically limited. But we constantly ask, what is the object itself, and by doing we constantly create a new, empty functional place and move forward, setting ourselves the task of filling this place. This is like the motion of any developing body. As soon as we give an answer, we immediately apply this device and say that we have built an image of the object 'itself', but this is only our limited knowledge once again. So what is the object 'itself'? In other words, on each occasion we put an empty place in front of us, only to fill it with the next image. We have literally leaned forward and begun to fall, so we need to move our feet in order not to fall.

This is the device of dual knowledge: we separate the functional place of the object from our knowledge and put it in front of us as an empty space. This is a device. We are always dissatisfied. People can be divided into 'satisfied' and 'dissatisfied'. Some are always satisfied, and others are always dissatisfied. This does not have anything to do with the quality of their knowledge. Some are satisfied with any knowledge, good or bad, while others are never satisfied with knowledge, whatever its quality.

Notice that all methodological work is built on this device of much knowledge. There could not be any methodological work at all without it. The knowledge that we create about the object as such has the special name of ontological pictures, or ontological presentations.

Ontological work is necessary when you want to develop. If you do not want to develop, you never need ontological work. This work is the vital condition of design planning. Design can only be carried out on the basis of ontology, and not on the basis of knowledge, because knowledge is always knowledge about an object that already exists. If you need a project, you need ontology, or some supposition about how the object 'itself' is structured.

Let me try to show you that human activity excludes development as a matter of principle. All mental activity is arranged in order to prevent any development from taking place. Development only begins at rare moments when systems of activity become unbalanced.

Scientific knowledge

Meanwhile, let me say the following. There is the world of knowledge. There is an intention to enquire what the object is in itself. At first, an empty place is identified – a place as empty, something unknowable. This is the main point. When we do this, a permanent mechanism of development is established. People who do not want to develop do a simple thing, they disconnect this part. Hence the paradoxical conclusion: the person who appeals to science resists development. The person who does everything in accordance with science is the person who resists science, who makes it impossible.

Science is necessary in order to preserve the established state of affairs, because scientific knowledge is always a justification, an underpinning of the structures that have taken shape; it is their legitimisation.

Science appears as a social institution, replacing religious beliefs. Previously, people deferred to God and divine ordinance, and then science deferred to the laws of nature, but the function remained the same. That is why science stood in opposition to religion. While religion explained everything that happened by divine ordinance, science explained it as ordained by nature.

Social sciences

The social sciences are a complex area, because mental activity is a self-developing and self-projecting system. Hence the question which has arisen today, whether the social studies are sciences in the precise meaning of the word. The answer to this question is negative. Not because these sciences are pseudo-scientific babble, but because they have a different function. Their primary mission is to support design planning and constructive work.

Formal thinking

What is formal thinking? We have a prism, which is knowledge. We do not want to look behind it. We see what we see in our prism. That is a formal approach. We start from a form and project it into content. Let me say: if there is a distinction between form and content, the content is already captured by the form, and it is of the same kind as the form. This is a formal approach. We see the world as it is given to us in our sign forms and our constructive forms.

But content is when we apply the method of dual knowledge and say, the object is never such as we know it. That is, we adopt a position where we are always wanting to look behind the form and see what is there, or in other words, to see content as content, and not through a form. Technically, what happens is that we 'extract' this unknowable, this unknown, because we only know through a form, and this is the only way that we can know, and the object remains unknown. Content differs from form, it is other and we have to find it in some way. This is the content-based approach, the approach that operates using the schema of dual, triple and nth degree knowledge.

It is oriented to constant transgression of its own limits. The progress to the unknowable is what differentiates the content-based approach from the formal approach, as the latter always preserves that which is known, it always wants to stop at what has already been achieved.

Content-based thinking

Hence the problem of the technique of content-based thinking. The technique of the formal approach is clear, but the content approach uses a completely different technique, which has to be mastered.

The idea I am steering you towards is that the work of an organiser and a manager is always content-based work, hence the problem of development.

There is the concept and there is the object. Formalists see a concept instead of an object; they think that their concepts are the objects. But content-based analysts see an object beyond the concept – as something else – and they try to prise out the object through the concept.

The principle of the artificial and the natural

We use this principle all the time. It can be deduced directly from the principle of dual knowledge. What happens in this 'dual' principle, in a content-based approach? We have mastered something, so we have brought it into relation with some example that we know, perhaps an engineering example, and now we see the object through another object, the reference object. Then we say – this object is the same as the reference object, but it is a different object, not the same one. We have already mastered it artificially, technically, but it still exists as a natural object. Now we can make the next step, to take out its 'natural' content. This is the principle of the artificial and the natural.

Human beings have made their active mark on all the material surrounding them. Everything we do is the realisation of this ideology.

Structure and organisation

Let's sort out what structure and organisation are. Imagine that we have a wooden frame and three balls joined together with springs, and they are also drawn apart by other springs fastened to the frame. Why do I call such a thing a 'structure'? If we take away one of the balls, the previous dynamic equilibrium is immediately destroyed. As soon as we take out a ball, the other balls shift and we have a quite different structure, corresponding to a different dynamic equilibrium.

Here is another example. Imagine a piece of wood with three holes that have been hollowed out for balls, and the balls are in the holes. I take out one of the balls. The unity has changed because I took out one ball. But will there be a change in the position of other balls? No, their position does not change.

The first example is an example of structure, the second is an example of organisation. But now we need to extract features or characteristics. Let me say: both organisation and structure are certain unities. I used examples with three balls in order to make the structural and organisational examples the same in character and number of elements. How did they differ from each other?

In the first case, there was a certain configuration of connections, a structure. That means that if we break one of the connections, all the rest change automatically. So structure is a unity of itself – the structure itself is the unity and it is unique. A structure cannot be broken into parts, the procedure of splitting cannot be applied to it at all. It would amount to 'killing' or destroying the structure.

Now consider organisation. Here also there is unity, but this unity has little to do with connections. So here the interesting question arises of what sort of unity we are talking about. In the first case, integrity belonged to connections and to structure. In the second case, it does not belong to connections and structure. I would say that there are no connections in an organisation. Can we split it into parts? Yes, we can. An organisation can be divided into parts. It can be cut up, and put back together. But the balls in the organised layout are in strictly determined places. So there are places in the organised nature, but these places, as it were, do not 'reach as far as' the elements them- selves – the balls, in our case. They are indifferent about their filling. So an organisational nature is indifferent to the filling of its places. We obtain a concretisation of division: an organisation can be simply cut into parts, or can be taken apart in a special way.

Two important concepts follow: those of connection and of relation. For example I might say that Peter the Great was taller than Napoleon. Tell me, were there any connections between Peter the Great and Napoleon? There were none. So when I say taller, it is not a connection, but a relation. Relations are used in inferences and are characterised by transitivity. Peter the Great was taller than Napoleon, Napoleon is taller than a dwarf, so Peter the Great is taller than a dwarf. But if I say that I like Peter, and Peter likes Sidor, it does not follow at all that I like Sidor. Connections are not transitive.

In the organisation with balls, there are clear relations – relations of arrangement and positioning. In this regard positioning is not a connection or a structure, a structure of connections. It is a certain totality of relations. Now I can put it more strongly: organisation fixes relations between elements. Structure, on the contrary, is a structure of connections.

Let me introduce two more concepts – 'organised structure' and 'structured organisation'. I shall start with the latter. Imagine that in a plank there are hollows, and there are balls connected with springs. If I take out a ball now, it is not clear what will happen. The organisation will hold the balls in place, but the springs will pull them in various directions, pull the balls from their places. Whichever is strongest will win out. We could also imagine that instead of cells there are grooves in the plank, so the organisation not only holds the balls, but also gives different variants for relations between the balls. And the structure holds them in a certain situation. It is difficult to say whether this is an organised structure or a structured organisation. But it is important that a divergence is beginning to appear between them.

In reality, we always have to do with organised structures and structured organisations. The difference between the two is in the order in which one thing is applied to another. We can organise existing, established structures: in reality, structures correspond to processes, and we also can also structure existing organisations.

The main task of an organiser and a manager – one of their main tasks – is just this. They organise and organisationally reinforce existing structures through the totality of relations, or introduce new structures to the existing organisations. And on each such occasion their intention is to enable some processes. They need to project both structures and organisations onto processes.

Category analysis

If you want to find out what a system is, start by analysing the sign form, reinstate the object to which it refers, the operations, and then go to the set of concepts that serve this category.

Exit to content: systems mathematics

So the schema brings us not to one object, as happened in the case of formal work and formal ontologisation, but to four types with various contents, to each of which we apply an objective status. We say that processes, functional structures, organisations of material and material itself all exist objectively.

Once we understand that, we register the circumstance, which initially appeared strange, that these four different contents are expressed in a single schema. But in fact this is understandable. I told you about functions of sign expressions in general, and said that sign forms are what fasten together our operations and actions to draw the object into a unity. So it is no coincidence that we express four different contents in one sign form. By so doing we draw them together as a unity and, as it were, obtain one object. This corresponds with the practice of our work.

All the objects we deal with in organisational and managerial work are complex objects with a process plane, a plane of functional structures, a plane of organisation of the material and a plane of the material as such. Each of them needs its own language and schemata, because they are different types of content. There must be a Language 1 for processes, in which schemata of processes will be built; there must be a Language 2 for constructing schemata of functional structures; a Language 3 for schemata of organisation of the material, and finally a Language 4 to record schemata of the material itself as object. And we have registered the important point that our object will only be presented systematically when all these schemata are interlinked and correlated with each other in a certain way.

Only then will we be dealing with a real objective system where processes correspond to a functional structure, the functional structure to the organisation of the material, and the material itself to all of these. Then we will have a living, real object – and it is not important whether it is natural or activity-based, organisational and managerial.

Conjunctive tables of meaning

I have highlighted these two important concepts, functional structures and organisations of material. I began the discussion by reference to models. This is important, because later I shall apply another method, involving conjunctive tables of meaning. But so far I have started working with models and showing the difference between functional structures and organisations of material. While doing that, I also employed a special device: I asked the question, how are functional structures organised, and how are organisations structured functionally?

Meanwhile I am addressing the main problem. We have already noted that the system will be an object when all of the layers are connected to each other, when we correlate processes with functional structures, and functional structures with organisations. If we do that, we will have a systemic representation of the object. Otherwise, we will only have a heap of disparate projections and planes. We need to bring them together, to understand how one thing correlates with another.

So we begin to link things. Let us take processes: what can be done with them? They can be structured, organised or materialised. What can be done with substance or material? It can be organised, structured and made into a process. How does this happen? Let me give a series of examples to explain these distinctions.

Organisation of the process

The first example is the organisation of a process. Every day where I live, on Obruchev Street, I see the same thing: what might be called a war with architects and the district administration on one side, and local residents on the other side. There is a shopping centre close to the apartment block where I live. Naturally, all the residents of the apartment block take the shortest route to the shopping centre. But for some unknown reason, there is a lawn in their way. A tarred path has been put down around the lawn, but you cannot go straight across it. People trample their own path across the lawn. The trampled path gets dug over, replanted, and cordoned off with wire.

It is interesting to observe how space is organised. When we make tarred paths, we are organising processes in a certain way, providing a direction, a channel for them. The British do it like this: first they plant lawns in parks, people walk there and create natural paths where they walk, and then after a while the authorities turn these paths into genuine tarred paths. What is happening in this case? I would describe it this way. First, people are given the opportunity to turn the material into a process, so that natural paths appear, and only afterwards are the paths organised (by being tarred). In our country we first organise the space, based on ideas about symmetry and some other abstract principles, and then a struggle begins between this organisation and the related process.

Functional structuring

Here is another example. Imagine that I see a multitude of dots. What are they – a structure or an organisation of material? It is not clear. Now, imagine that I give someone the task of counting the number of dots. The counter has to perform a certain process, and functionally structures this 'something', thereby showing that this is a certain organisation of the material.

The material here is the dots, and they are arranged or organised in a certain way. But people create various functional organisations depending on how they count them. Let us see what organisations there can be. If you count the dots in a tedious way, one by one, do you need any functional organisation? I would say that you do need it, but it is unnoticeable (see Figure 1.29). But you can use different ways of counting, by which you begin to structure this multitude. Smarter people work like this: they single out one square here, another square there, and then count six by six and five by five. A functional structuring has taken place. Two squares have been singled out from among the multitude (Figure 1.30).

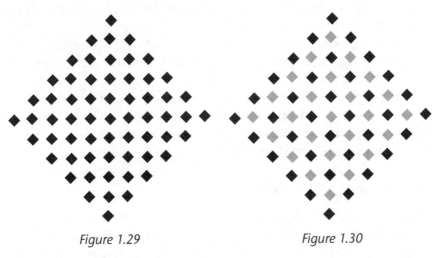

Figure 1.29   Figure 1.30

But students at the mechanics and mathematics faculty do it differently. They know formulae that are more complicated, and they apply progressions.

What we find each time is that the method of our movement *performs* a functional structuring, but it also *assumes* a functional structuring. So we go from the process towards the functional structure, and the functional structure performs a grouping of various elements of the material.

Let's try to transfer these ideas to some real-life instances. What sets a good chess player apart from a mediocre one? Both of them are in front of a chessboard with a certain configuration of chess-pieces. But the good chess player sees a mass of functional structures among the chesspieces, while the mediocre player sees only a few of them, only the most trivial.

What distinguishes a good military commander from a bad one? The fact that the first can see more functional structures based on the way his detachments are now deployed. What distinguishes a good construction manager from a bad one? The fact that, given the same resources and mechanisms on the construction site, the good manager can immediately see numerous functional structures and construct a variety of work plans.

I draw the following conclusion: functional structuring is one of the most important aspects of organisational and managerial work, particularly when we are dealing with situations that are changing.

Similarly, the skill of correct functional structuring is the main quality required for solving problems and tasks. What distinguishes a person who knows how to solve complex geometrical problems? It is how the person sees the initial material of the problem – as a complex of triangles, or as a set of internal framework constructions, or in some other way. Each operation they carry out is a certain functional structuring, taking out and inserting elements.

Pursuing the same thought, I would say that knowing how to solve complicated problems depends first and foremost on being able to apply functional structuring.

The concept of a polysystem

When we reach the level of the polysystem, the range of method-ological problems becomes much more complex, because we have to deal with a large number of processes, and processes of a strange nature.

Imagine life on an iceberg. People put up tents on it, and start carrying out meteorological research. Meanwhile, the iceberg drifts and undergoes various internal processes: it begins to melt, crack, some pieces of it ride up over others, and so on. We have an incredible number of little four-plane systems, coupled together in a surprising way and constantly influencing each other. Let me analyse some varieties of this coupling.

We have two processes, two functional structures in one material. This presupposes the insertion of organisations into each other. Now imagine that the organisation that I have introduced begins to live, and a new process appears – its own process. So the two coupled monosystems are drawn into a third, systemic existence. For example, the human material ages. And the whole highly complex organisation that we have represented systematically now becomes involved in the process. Now both linear and functional processes (speaking in the terms of the example) begin to 'grow old'. They fade in importance.

A new principal arrives, they make an acerbic comment and tell somebody off. This is of great importance. Suppose they go on in the same way, using the same technique – they tell people off, one after the other. What happens? Their strictures lose their meaning: the process of ageing takes place.

Now I want to present my main thought. Please prepare to grasp it. Until now, I have been discussing what a system is as such – a monosystem – what the alternatives are and so on. Now I am going to turn all that around.

We apply alternatives, we set out instances and choose between them – all that is well and good, and I shall leave it on one side. But the secret of systems analysis is not to have all these alternatives of systemic representation, but to answer the question: if this is our construction, then in the form of what polysystem – with what ties and interlacing of systems with each other – can we represent it?

Imagine that I ask you to draw a systemic image of your construction, to tell me how many monosystems there are. Which of them do you take into account? How are these monosystems joined to each other? To put it differently, how many basic processes will you take into account?

'Naturalisation' of organisation and leadership

We have got used to seeing our organisational and managerial work as a way of supporting a stable process. But if we stop looking at organisational and managerial work as a standard working process then there are no well-balanced, standard mechanisms. As organisers, managers and leaders we have to support this balance all the time through our organisational and managerial work. We have no time to rest. As we discussed before, nearly all of us work in this mode, although we should probably work in a different mode, where we have arranged the process in such a way that all that's left for us to do is to sit and twiddle our thumbs. But these are completely different strategies.

There are two processes: one of them is technological, and the other is the work process. We have set up a system to manage these processes. We have created a system of leadership, and management appears through leadership. We have put our natural life and our discordances into it. Now our system is not a technological system and is not a system of works, but it is all that plus, in addition, a naturalised system of organisation that has begun to live its own life.

We set up the system as a tool, but now the tool begins to live its own life. The tool turned out to be complex and contradictory, with its own processes. Now we are no longer engaged in ensuring the functioning of the basic technological process. Now all our efforts go into managing a system of organisation and leadership, which lives its own life and therefore does unpredictable things.

The purpose of methodological self-organization

A method is needed to solve a new class of problems. This is how I shall try to explain it.

We are told how the introduction of computers will make problem solving easier and reduce the number of people who need to be employed. This is nonsense. The introduction of computers increases the number of people employed, but in the course of time it will enable us to solve problems that we have never solved before. When differential and integral calculus were introduced, people could calculate areas bounded by curves. But what is interesting is that people also had to deal with such areas before then, and they managed to do it somehow. For example, take a barrel at the market. People measure its depth with a stick and say that it contains about a hundred litres. It's that simple: no differential and integral calculation is required. If you told me that doing the measurements with differential and integral calculus is easier than doing it with the stick, I would not agree, refined though the mathematical approach might be.

Let's imagine that an organiser and manager has to deal with complex objects. They deal with these objects within their personal limitations, so management and leadership at this initial stage is superficial, and everything that does not receive the attention of their leadership and management lives its own natural life. There is a borderline between what is managed and lives an artificial life, and what is not managed and therefore lives a natural life.

When the manager obtains new resources and methods, they may be able to engage at a new level and make their management more efficient. Then they will go on to the next level. Nevertheless, from my point of view they are still managing the same object, except that at first they do it using one set of parameters, which are on the surface, and leave everything else to take its natural course; and then later they use a broader range of parameters. The application of new methods, including methods of systems analysis, enables us to manage and organise in a more specific way, using a larger number of parameters.

The use of new methods always means further complication of the managerial system. What does it give us? It gives us the chance to do what we did not do before, and to avoid doing what we did before.

As I see it, new methods are always introduced by a small group of enthusiasts, who want to do something more than they did before. For some reason they need to do this: I do not know their personal reasons for it and I am not going to discuss them. But the new method soon becomes a paradigm, and competition leads to its propagation, because the old working methods are uncompetitive and cannot be continued.

I had a chat once with a famous film director, who had a reputation for putting things bluntly, and he gave me a formula that I like to repeat: he said that the attempt to solve complicated problems in a simple way is what we call fascism.

Let me extrapolate: as I see it, there are no simple solutions to complex problems. This is very important to me. The only way of solving complex problems is by using complex methods. Whenever we try to solve complex problems using simple methods, we destroy a living unity. I think that was his point.

Functions of knowledge

Knowledge does not necessarily involve tools or instruments. Rather, it is in principle something that is more important and more significant than tools or instruments. What is more, those who see knowledge as an instrument or tool for work reduce themselves as individuals to a simple appendage of these tools. They say, give me a hammer and a nail and tell me what to knock in and where. Give me an assault rifle, make it simple and reliable, and I will shoot.

Regardless whether the tool is military or industrial equipment, people see themselves in this case as mere workers. That is also to say, whether we like it or not, that they see themselves as hirelings. They are appendages of their tools, and other people treat them together as a single unit.

Knowledge appears to bear with it certain methods of action. Every such method of action is manifested in two capacities – the capacity to act and the capacity to understand. And these functions are characteristic of any knowledge. Knowledge contains in itself certain methods of action and human capacities: the capacity to act and the capacity to understand.

The vast majority of actions in co-operative organised structures are actions without understanding. And when one person becomes a bearer of a goal, and others are organised at a lower level, these others not only can, but must act without understanding.

This is the meaning of organisation. Organisation is a form of structuring human labour where – whether we want it or not – the right and ability to set goals and understand the meaning of their activity is taken away from the vast majority of participants and is usurped by the leader and managers.

You know that many war criminals had to be acquitted at the Nuremberg trials, because they said that they had been performing their duties, that they had been only a cog in the machine and had sworn to obey orders from their superiors.

That is why I say that, seen from one perspective, people in an organisation do not have to understand what they are doing (I shall talk about the other perspective shortly). They have to act in a certain way regardless of whether or not they understand what they are doing.

Let me distinguish four embodiments of knowledge. Let me say that it is quite possible to use knowledge as a tool; it is possible and necessary, and is a proper way of applying knowledge. But this is not what makes knowledge special. The relation of knowledge towards people is different from this. Knowledge changes people, transforms them, makes them different and stronger. I would say that knowledge should be considered less as a tool or instrument, but rather in relation to a person's abilities. A knowledgeable person does not only have a tool or an instrument, although they have that too. But what a person with knowledge has principally (through this knowledge) is a method of action, which becomes their capacity.

Next let me distinguish between the capacity to act and the capacity to understand: they are different things.

This might prompt a clear and justified question: does it not follow from what I have said that people can have a strong capacity for action without having a capacity for understanding? Would that not be strange? I say no, it is not strange. It does not mean a person does not think: even to perform an action without understanding, you have to think how to structure and execute this action.

We perform actions, and then we begin to understand their meaning, their immediate and long-term effects. A person is always included in a highly complex situation and the effects of their actions spread out from them like waves. That is why we say that the effects of our actions await us further along the road along which we travel.

I would assert that the use of knowledge as a method of action, as an ability to act and understand, sets contradictory or at least different requirements for the organisation of knowledge in comparison with the use of knowledge as a tool or instrument. While we can say with a certain degree of accuracy that a tool or an instrument should be easy to use, we set quite contrary requirements for knowledge as a capacity. We say that this knowledge should be sufficiently complex to make us more complex and equal to the needs of the time and the complexity of the problems we face.

Now consider the history of humankind. In order to put the production of knowledge on a firm footing in any of these functions – that of a tool, the capacity to act, or the capacity to understand – people must always pull something onto themselves. Doing this, they take on the role of many specialists. Someone else invented the tool, the knowledge, the means. There is the practician who uses tools, and above them there is the technician who creates those tools. But the technician is not the last in this chain: further up, we find the scientist who gives them knowledge, a teacher who shapes the knowledge, and a philosopher at the service of the teacher.

The engineering approach

This co-operation becomes more complicated as we proceed. An engineer, in the best sense of the word, appears: someone who can do anything. Engineer Smith in *The Mysterious Island* (by Jules Verne) had only one coffee bean, but managed to grow a plantation. Engineers can do anything. They are autonomous, because they are engineers. They are autonomous, and they do not need other people who create tools. As scientists, they can also create knowledge, and they can create tools and techniques: they unite everything in themselves.

So we arrive at the methodologist. The methodologist today is someone who is autonomous and gathers all these functions in themselves. We are moving constantly towards the microcosm, and the issue of human individuality as opposed to a complex organisation is highly relevant for us. There is always a struggle between them, because people are always grappling with one and the same problem: are they cogs in this machine, this organisation, its small and partial appendages, or can they do something on their own?

The choice of position – self-determination

People are constantly being polarised. They cause themselves to be polarised because of their attitudes.

One person says, I want to have simple means, simple tools; I will take what humanity has made, give me simple tools and I will learn how to use them.

Another says: humanity is developing, and I must always run to keep up with it, adopt new knowledge, get involved in this process of creating the new, and contribute to developing what I have acquired. A person is born, and they have before them all the mass of culture accumulated previously. They can relate themselves to it. They have to relate to this culture, to take it all, rise to its level, absorb this knowledge and become involved in the process of producing new methods of action, the formation of new human capacities (they are the bearers of these), and the production of tools and instruments.

And this, I say, always involves a choice. People have to make their own decision on each occasion. They could have either of two positions in relation to this knowledge. In the first case, they say it should be simple and convenient to use. In the second case they say, I must master – albeit in a reduced and compact form – the whole world of culture. These two points of view are in polar opposition. And, like it or not, we must constantly choose between them. Perhaps our choice will not be of an extreme position, but it must be somewhere between the two positions, between one extreme and the other.

Position and self-organisation

The main problem for us in our action is always how to organise ourselves, how to begin our action in order to achieve the goal, the result we need. So the first problem is that of organising our own actions.

I shall make a bold statement. There are many situations in which a person acts. They cannot all be predicted or described in advance. So the organisation of our own actions has to be largely independent of the specific features of any particular situation. The organisation of our own actions must be autonomous with respect to the conditions of the situation, as if separated from it. So far as possible we need universal forms for the organisation of our actions, forms that can operate everywhere, or at least in a wide range of situations. So an approach for organising our actions which is more universal and generalised is thereby more effective. Generalised approaches are more effective because they cover a larger number of situations.

But generalised approaches have the inconvenience of failing to cover the specific details of a situation. Here let me offer an important conclusion: approaches or methods (methods are smaller units, from which approaches are made up) and human capacities (as I have said, these are mostly built from a reflexive attitude to our own experience) are always correlative. The application of a specific approach or method requires certain capacities, and the reverse is also true. We could say that the more specific the capacities are, the more generalised an approach can be.

But the principle remains the same: any person with any capacities needs, first and foremost, to self-organise, to determine what they should do and how, including the case of an unusual, uncertain or partially described situation. For that purpose, they need methods and approaches.

What are methods and approaches expressed in, primarily? Often, they are expressed in principles. *Principles are what define actions, telling us how to act.*

Part II
Rails, Pipes and Cables

Experience of Managing
Infrastructure Complexes

V. B. Khristenko

V. B. Khristenko

Foreword

A *Khrestomatia*[1]

This Part of the volume continues the series of publications devoted to the Russian Methodological School of Management. We have chosen to collect excerpts illustrating the methodological approach and its categories, schemes and concepts as exemplified in the work of Viktor Borisovich Khristenko, vice prime minister of the Russian Federation in 1998 and 1999/2004.

Lifting the curtain

This is a collection of excerpts – some successful schemes, reports, accounts, interviews and statements. They do not claim to be a complete or profound account. Rather, they highlight important parts of a system of management which is fast-moving and subject to political pressures and economic risks.

Continuity

Our goal is not just to record a certain period of life with a collection of texts and schemes. This book aims to identify how the ideas, theories and experimental constructs developed in laboratory conditions by our teachers and predecessors have been used in management practice at a high level.

The methodology of organisation, leadership and management (OLM) has an exotic past. It is one of many examples of 'intellectual high technology' developed in this country. It was not the product of some secret state-funded research institute. Rather, it was developed by groups of enthusiasts with an inspired leader. Their wish was that OLM methodology should make the USSR and Russia stronger, and their Russian management methodology was oriented towards the Russian management model.

The historian L. N. Gumilev once proposed the following way of looking at the position of the state. The state views the situation from the perspective of an eagle in flight. The regions' position is that of a watcher on a hill. The individual citizens see their interests from rabbit holes at the foot of the hill. The government must have an abstract, generalised picture of the situation. It must not be

---

1   The Russian for a collection of selected writings by a single author.

distracted by details but must also understand, identify and evaluate details in the context of the overall picture.

Method must be transmitted

Inspired by Michael Milken, major financier and massive crook, the following slogan become a commonplace among managers of large transnational corporations: 'Think global, act local.' Applied to the state's management systems, that principle gives rise to 'super-powers' and 'global police officers' whose national interests are almost contiguous with the activities of transnational corporations.

Hence a huge number of 'insoluble' international conflicts – ideological, religious, ethnic or racial – evolve from the same financial and economic background. But that principle does not, in our view, apply to the state. The state's system of executive power operates in a territory delimited by borders. Its purpose is to resolve internal conflicts and prevent external ones. Therefore it must think systemically.

This collection of texts is intended to elucidate that simple thesis. It is structured so as to enable the reader to reconstruct each method step by step.

Management practice during the reform of the Russian economy

More than five years in the post of vice prime minister of the Russian Federation is long enough to draw conclusions on how the Russian Methodological School's conceptual apparatus of concepts of schemes works in the system of public administration. You would get nowhere without proper, disciplined thinking and effective tools. In those five years Viktor Khristenko had to develop planning charts for many situations, infrastructures and corporate conflicts. He then used them to disentangle many national economic crises. The thorough grounding in methodology he had received in the 1990s served him well there.

I was fortunate to participate in some events of the methodological movement – a wide variety of works, seminars and games. I was honoured to make the acquaintance of Georgy Petrovich Shchedrovitsky and to work closely with his followers.

I was fortunate also to find myself alongside Viktor Khristenko at the start of his work at the pinnacle of the federal government in difficult times for Russia. I am sure he was able to make good use of the things he had trained in and practised so hard out of sheer curiosity. He chose the methods and techniques that his position demanded. Not only that, but he knew how to apply them in the right proportions.

Georgy Petrovich used to insist that to learn how to do conceptual work and to acquire real experience of working with schemes took five years as either the secretary of a regional committee of the Party or as a senior manager in industry. Khristenko was never a Party regional secretary, but he did have great experience of managing a city and region. That was how his career as a leader began.

In 1998 as vice prime minister he worked with a corpus of schemes that provided a systematic representation of the financial and economic structure of the country. They identified the main work processes, functional structures and organisations with which the executive had to deal. He had to make a stand against vulgar economism by deploying the 'visible hand' of the executive against the 'invisible hand' of the untamed Russian market. That helped him appreciate the federal nature of the Russian Federation and the structure of various spheres of activity and 'inter-budgetary relations'.[2] These last were to receive his particular attention.

That work was resumed in early 2000 in a new context – the reforms of President Putin. It focused on the concept of the 'managed budget'. There followed schemes covering the activities of the fuel and energy complex and the nation's vital infrastructures – the housing and public utilities complex, transport and other elements. Particular stress was laid on the 'infrastructures ensuring the integrity of the state' and the enterprise and business zones from which the state derives finance. Khristenko said that:

◆ Pipeline networks, electricity transmission lines and railways are vital to the integrity of the state and must be controlled, in one form or another, by the executive.
◆ The national infrastructures created in Soviet times were by many criteria ahead of their time, and must be preserved wherever possible. The fact that no town planning, engineering, technological or

---

2   Translator's note: 'Inter-budgetary relations' is an approximate translation of the Russian term *mezhbyudzhetnye otnosheniya*: 'Mutual relations of organs of state power and local self-government on matters of the redistribution of funds between budgets'.

Figure 2.1 What is a 'managed budget'?

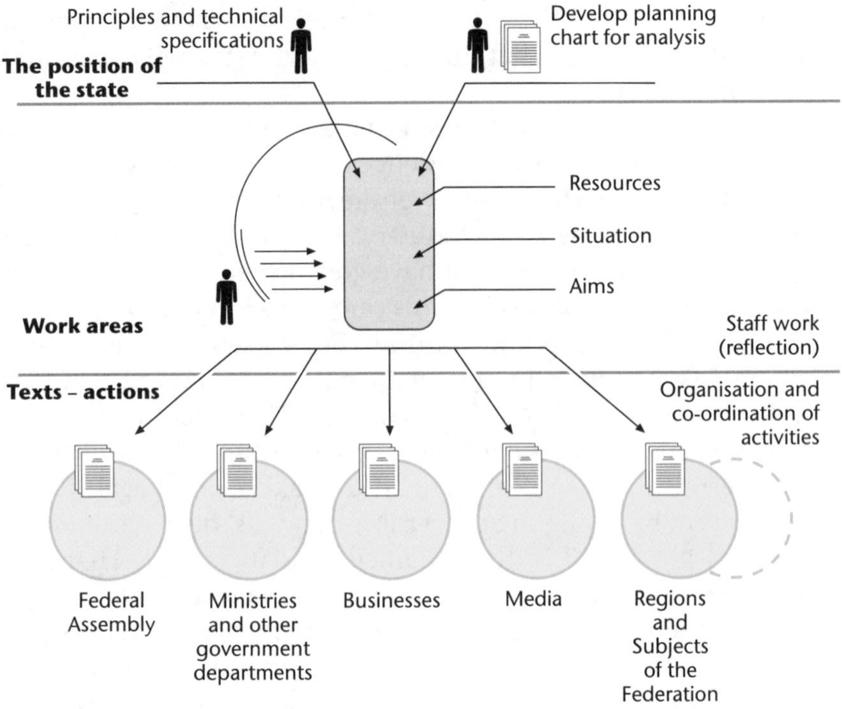

economic analyses were performed before privatisation in order to determine the state's economic priorities has endless unforeseen consequences today.

◆ The main thing when working with any large system is: don't wreck it.

Those conclusions, elevated to the status of principles, then determined his actions as vice prime minister.

In each situation Khristenko addresses the question of when and how principles, schemes and planning charts can be used in a landscape that is continually changing. So many failures of public policy have occurred because of exclusive reliance on system schemes that make no allowance for the shenanigans of business. Standards and laws are based on the assumption that the state will act entirely according to declared principles and business will act rationally. In fact, neither acts rationally and neither follows prescribed rules.

The vice prime minister's responsibilities extend to another area also covered by schemes and theses. That is foreign trade. Anyone in this post must spend a lot of time on economic integration in the post-Soviet space (the CIS) and with Europe and the countries of the Asia-Pacific region. To that end special effort is devoted to the concepts of the 'single economic space', the 'common economic space' and so on. These topics will form the background and the evidence for further work.

Let me end with a few words on how this book is meant to be read and worked with. It is structured like a workbook. The diagrams and texts are meant to be interactive. They demand critical engagement and a willingness to think. So, reader, take up your pencil; read, mark, learn and inwardly digest. That's what page margins are for.

A. G. Reus

V. I. Khristenko in discussion with G. Gref

Rails, pipes and cables

The frame of pipes, rails and cables helped save Russia from collapse; it became the country's skeleton.

As I worked my way up through the levels of the administrative hierarchy, the frame on which I built management solutions was, from very early on, the methodological theory of the school of G. P. Shchedrovitsky. I came to fully appreciate the correctness of many of his observations and conclusions when I found myself confronted by tasks on the scale of the entire system. That is the same social and management system that G. P. taught me to understand in the distant 1980s. The point is that, once you are armed with methodological theory, you cannot go back to demonstrably primitive approaches to super-complex problems.

Work in government

From Izvestiya, *8 June 2001:*

I am not a lone wolf. I always work in a team. I can claim that my team is fairly well established, even though I am not from Moscow. It includes some people from Chelyabinsk, though we do not recruit on geographical grounds. Of course the team are close to me: I trust them; we have worked together in the past; they really know how to make themselves useful.

The government could do without vice prime ministers, but on one condition: that the objects managed by government remain stable. The decision-making procedures and rules applying to them must also be stable and enshrined in law. In our case none of that is so. The objects of management – the various branches of the economy – are undergoing transformation, and what form they should ultimately take is a matter of continual discussion among different government departments. The rules of decision making are in the earliest stages of legislative regulation. In the circumstances there is more than enough work.

From Argumenty i fakty, *29 July 1999:*

You can cut a loaf of bread into slices, but you cannot put the slices back together to make a loaf. It is more or less the same with the economy. Just putting together the steel, electricity and oil and gas industries doesn't give a unified national economy. You only get the loaf if there is a integrated system that includes credit, monetary, fiscal, tax and tariff policy. My job is to make an integrated economy.

From Kommersant, *16 June 1999:*

Were you not something of an orphan when you joined the government? When they offered you the post, everything had already been decided and the portfolios and duties had already been allocated.

Quite the opposite, I was in a better position from the outset than anyone else. By the time Stepashin invited me to join the government, all the arguments about whether a special vice prime minister post to take charge of financial and economic affairs was necessary, and if so whether it should be *first* deputy or just *a* vice prime minister, were over. The president and prime minister had decided they needed a first vice prime minister for macro-economics. People who disagree can think what they like, but do not talk to me about it.

Any discussion of who got what portfolio should be left to observers of the political – or possibly leather goods – scene.[3] I

---

3   Translator's note: a portfolio can be either conceptual or a physical briefcase.

Figure 2.2 The position of the state

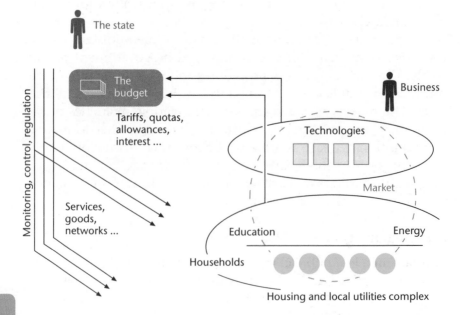

Figure 2.3 Organisation of staff work

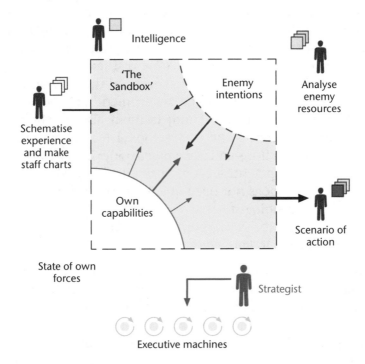

hold the same portfolio now [1999] as I did a year ago when I was in a similar job. If you remember, Sergei Kiriyenko's government contained no first deputy prime ministers. From the point of view of formal political analysis, my new appointment is a promotion. But these are just formalities. There is work to do. Let's not waste time on endlessly and pointlessly trying to work out who's climbed furthest up the greasy pole.

It is strange for me to hear people saying I am unlikely to provide a counterweight to someone or other. I am a counterweight to myself. I have come through the school of hard knocks. [Apart from me] only Chubais[4] has ever come back to government in the financial and economic affairs brief, and no one would call him a lightweight. I do not want to compare myself with anyone else or give offence but if they had wanted to appoint someone weaker or more biddable, they could have gone looking among the other managers at deputy minister level.

---

4   Editor's note: Anatoly Borisovich Chubais has held a number of political and business positions since the 1990s.

As for the tag 'provincial finance expert', regional finance is not the worst starting point for understanding a financial macrosystem like Russia. The interactions of budgets at different levels are at least as important in national politics as the energy complex from which prime ministers have also come (some of them even having two goes at it). I am certain that the recovery of the Russian financial system depends not only on the government's relationship with the [International Monetary Fund] IMF but also on the relationship between the centre and the regions. I may be a specialist in inter-budgetary relations and not a practitioner of general medicine – but then general practitioners in Russia usually get called quacks. Macro-economics does not need quacks, and if it gets them it will soon need the pathologist.

From Kommersant, *16 June 1999:*

It is not for me to judge how well I am coping with my duties. The country's leaders who appointed me will do that. I have some difficult problems to solve. They include the public revenues, regulation of foreign trade and negotiations with international financial organisations. New ones are always being added. There is the problem of the fuel and energy complex, for example. No one, I think, can say I am a lobbyist for the energy industry. In dealing with its problems I will have to harmonise my actions with the interests of the economy as a whole. I must consider the needs of not only the energy industry. Time will tell whether I cope with these duties. Other people will judge.

From Komsomolskaya pravda, *24 June 1999:*

My post originally meant taking oversight of financial and economic affairs. Beyond that the usual questions arose. What government departments was I in charge of? What did it all mean? If I didn't control the ministries of finance, economics and taxation or the tax police, the job didn't amount to anything. Macro-economics cannot be considered separately from foreign trade. If it had turned out they'd put me in charge of two men and a dog, I simply wouldn't have bothered staying in the White House.[5]

---

5   Editor's note: White House is a common term for government buildings in Russia.

From Kommersant, *16 June 1999:*

In terms of capability we've got a normal working team. There's nothing wrong with it. In terms of the political facts, we shall see. I don't do futurology. My sacking was predicted almost every week last summer. In the end it so happened, of course, that I was the last one to leave the Kiriyenko government. It wasn't that I hung on; it just happened like that. Both those who'd supported me and those who'd been angling for my job ended up going before me. Perhaps it's because I was last out then that I am first back in now.

We've tortured ourselves in masochistic experiments long enough. The harder the blow, the louder the cheers. I want to prove by doing it that it is time to do politics in a positive way.

Do you like winning?'

Yes, I do like winning.

In economics, miracles never happen

From Argumenty i fakty, *22 March 2000.*

> The rational reform of the economy must continue, calmly and without hysteria. It will create positive momentum to solve economic problems

The main thing is to establish priorities. There are over 200 federal special-purpose programmes, but by spreading scarce resources thinly over such a wide area we are not achieving worthwhile results. It would be better to keep ten programmes and say that for the next five years they have priority. Trying to please everyone means people stop trusting the government. It is better to say: 'This is what we promised and we will deliver it 100 per cent.'

Economic transformations cannot succeed without reform of public administration (though it has been tried) because there is no mechanism that can make them work. There have been thousands of examples. Take bankruptcy procedure. It seems straightforward and the legislation looks pretty sound. But narrow parochial interests collide with those of the state and the result is a sort of hall of mirrors. What we want is enterprises restored to health and solvency. What we see is privatisation.

The problem is not only that funds fail to reach the intended targets. We lack any system to monitor the implementation of major decisions at any level. And that is so even though we have hundreds

Figure 2.4 The field of activity

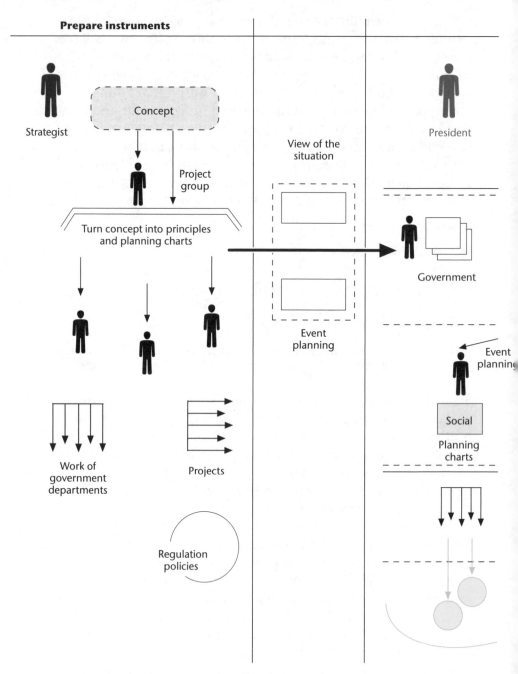

Co-ordination and control of works

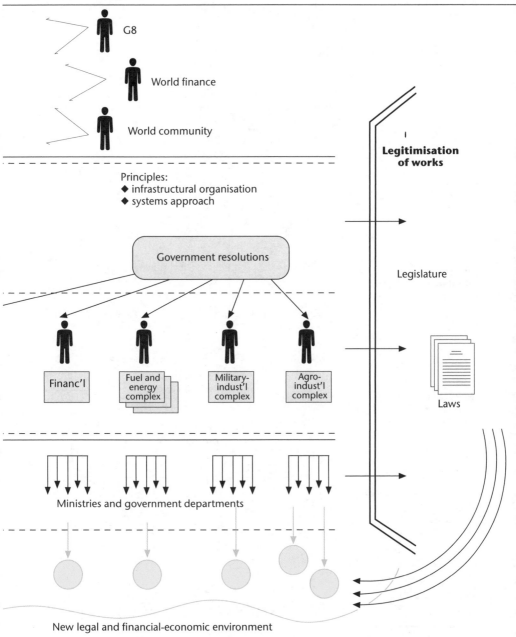

Figure 2.5 Co-ordination of reforms starting from the position of the executive

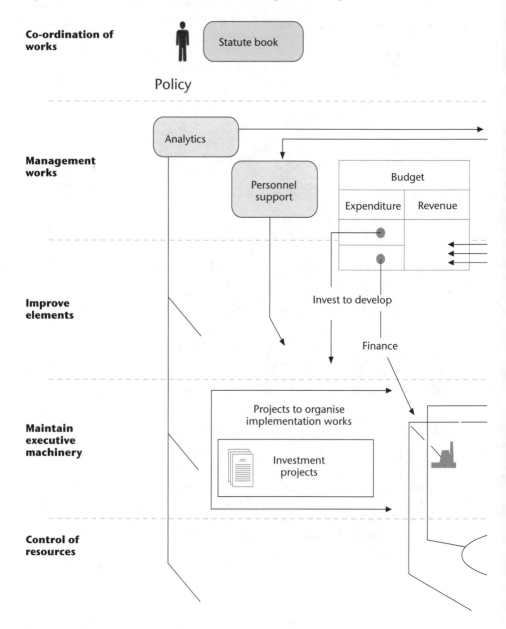

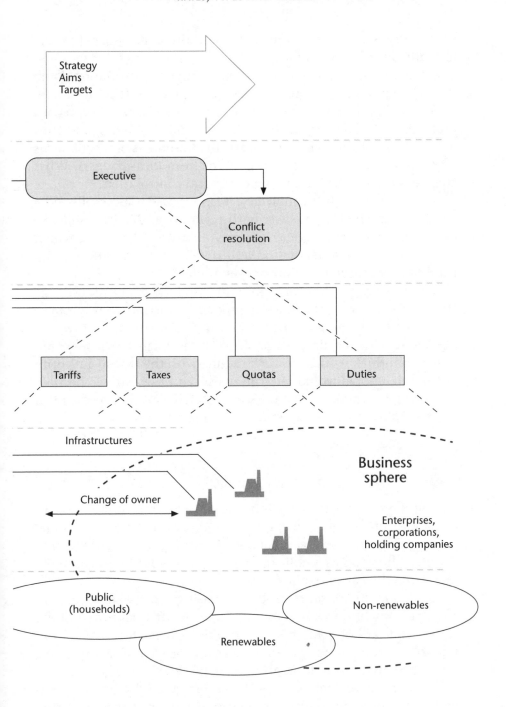

of thousands of federal officials working in local offices that are formally directly subordinated to Moscow. The idea is that all those at the centre have to do is meet their financial, organisational and staffing requirements in full. If they don't, local authorities themselves will tackle the everyday problems, even housing problems, that should be the responsibility of the federal officials, and they will get by perfectly well. There are infinite numbers of mechanisms – benefits and allowances – all paid for from local budgets. What chance is there of separation of powers and control then?

It is the same with the judiciary. It is supposed to be a fully independent branch of state power both vertically and horizontally. So how come every year we get thousands of local legislative acts which conflict with federal legislation and the Constitution and no one thinks to cancel them in time or even protest?

Everyone knows that something must be done. But no one sets about dealing with the known problems. Instead they propose targets and approaches which are in my view completely wrong, like the scheme for directly appointed governors. Now if we could restore a normal, vertical power structure with the federal authority at the top, people would feel the power and the care of the state regardless of whether governors are elected or appointed and of whatever slogans are written on their campaign posters.

Sources of growth

From Rossiyskaya gazeta, *2 February 2000:*

New sources of growth need to be found today. Increasing effective demand is one such source, but the national finances need to be put in order before that can happen. A recent government meeting discussed how to save public money, in an attempt to find a way of increasing the pay of public-sector workers at least.

Yet we should not suppose that increasing personal incomes will automatically bring growth in output. Look what happened in the second half of last year [1999]. Personal incomes rose, but so did imports. As soon as we started to clear the backlog of salaries there was a surge in demand for higher-quality foreign-made goods.

Rising effective demand must be accompanied by rising investment. Enterprises must invest money in new equipment and making more competitive products. That is the chief problem – and we are already on the way to solving it. That can also be demonstrated

Figure 2.6 Overall competitive equilibrium (the 'unseen hand'). The economic life-cycle

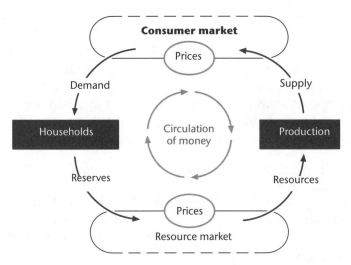

in the example of last year. The rise in demand for investment in 1999 was crucial to the increase in output. Admittedly most of the investment was not borrowing but from organisations' own funds. To think that you can keep devaluing the rouble, as in 1998, to help production grow is illogical. It is simply wrong. The government has no such intention.

We must start by distinguishing between short-term and long-term measures. Clearly, the need to stick strictly to the budget this year constrains the opportunities for tax reform. But such reform is crucial for stimulating investment demand in the long term. We will be able to do a lot in 2000, however.

First it must be borne in mind that monetary and credit policy, particularly if it affects the money supply, has a significant effect on investment demand. I have already mentioned that capital investment in industry increased last year. That means that most of the 1999 increase in the money supply was successfully employed by enterprises to bolster their working capital and for cash settlements among themselves.

Second, the most acute problem, that of enterprises' debts, needs to be resolved. Here we cannot do without both administrative pressure on debtors and purely economic solutions. In very general terms, we want businesses to stop trying to solve their problems by ratcheting up debt and persisting with non-cash settlements, so we will make that more bother than it is worth.

Third, we must look closely at not only tax rates but also the types of expenditure that can be counted against production costs to reduce liability for tax, especially in the case of the capital spending, which determines investment demand. Another point worth considering is accelerated capital allowances, particularly for accumulated fixed assets. One more area, finally, is the gradual restoration of the financial and, particularly, credit market. If industry is to be able to attract investment, investors and banks need to have some objective guidance on returns. All this together will make it possible to improve the financial situation of enterprises.

From Ekonomika, *January 2001:*

Improving the climate for investment is one of our strategic tasks. I would point to three main preconditions for increasing investment: reduce the tax burden, make enterprises more efficient, and reduce capital flight.

We continue to work on the legal regulation of all aspects of business and, it goes without saying, ensuring the law is complied with absolutely. Laws should in general have a direct effect. That reduces the risks and costs of leaving it to officials to make up rules as they go along – although that, it should be said, can happen in any country.

The system of governance

From Obshchaya gazeta, *2 March 2000:*

Some of the media, quoting you, have said that the federal government is setting up representative offices in Federal Districts. Won't they just duplicate the work of presidential representatives?'

To start with, the reports are distortions. Perhaps it's just that the media always wants intrigue and where there is none they have to invent it. There are going to be no offices of the government in federal districts. That is quite plain.

Second, there is the president's decree on plenipotentiary presidential representatives. It contains some remarkable stuff that the government really needs. It says that the role of plenipotentiary representative includes monitoring the implementation not only of laws and presidential decrees but also of resolutions and orders of the government. That means that the government will have allies in the Subjects of the Federation.[6] That will be helpful to both the government and our territorial local offices.

The task is to establish a scheme of co-operation between the central part of the government, government structures' local offices and the plenipotentiary representatives. This subject was discussed with the ministries for some weeks and I gave a report at the president's daily briefing. By the end of this week we will put out a resolution which will set out the starting position for co-operation. As for the local offices, we are considering three models for co-operation at local level.

The local offices will co-operate effectively with the presidential representatives, and so also with the president's Control Directorate. We also need to break the tie binding the territorial branches of federal government departments to the territories. When federal local offices cannot keep going without extra help, nothing good comes of it. Local branches of our government departments sometimes receive allowances from local budgets because we do not fund them adequately to pay for local utility services, and so they are at the mercy of local authorities.

In the upshot, instead of a continuous line of government servants from top to bottom we have a broken, bent and dotted line representing the path by which somehow decisions are supposed to flow downwards and accounts of their implementation are supposed to flow up.

But let us return to models of co-operation. The first model – structures at federal district level – is not of course suitable for all government departments. It would be ridiculous if, say, the Fisheries Committee or the Ministry of Railways had local offices in all seven federal districts. Both are extra-territorial structures defined by the activity they are responsible for, not by a particular political or politico-military structure. The second model of co-operation will be more common, whereby one territorial branch of a federal government department in the centre of a federal district will be endowed with additional information and analysis functions. It will also co-operate with the president's plenipotentiary representatives. This model applies to a good half of all ministries and government departments.

---

6   Editor's note: Russia is divided into seven federal districts, which are made up of 89 Subjects of the Federation. Thus the Volga Federal District, for example, comprises 20 Subjects of the Federation.

Figure 2.7 Planning chart showing separation of functions and powers of the government and presidential plenipotentiary representatives in federal districts

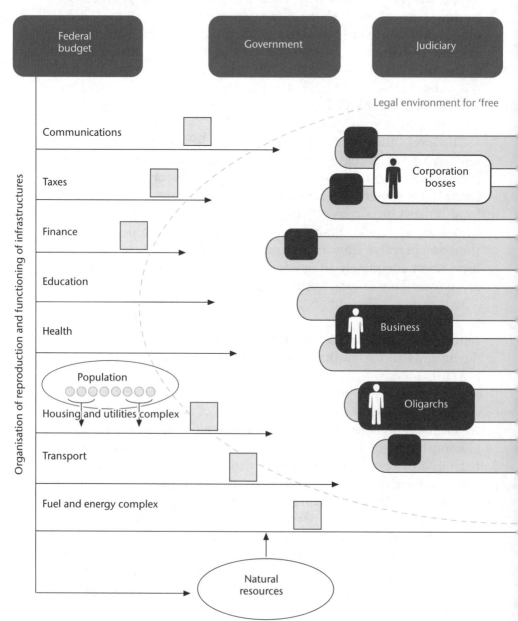

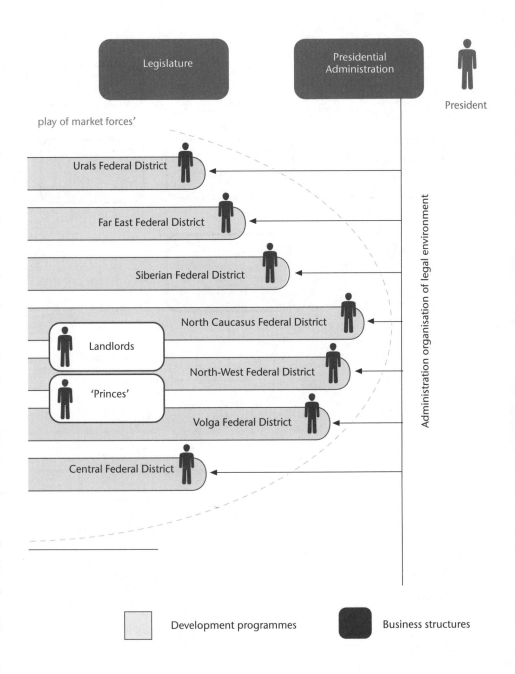

play of market forces'

Figure 2.8 Functions of the government in the system of governance of the Russian Federation

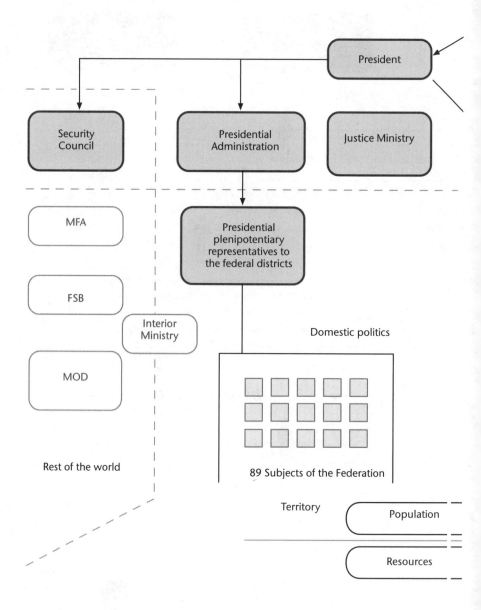

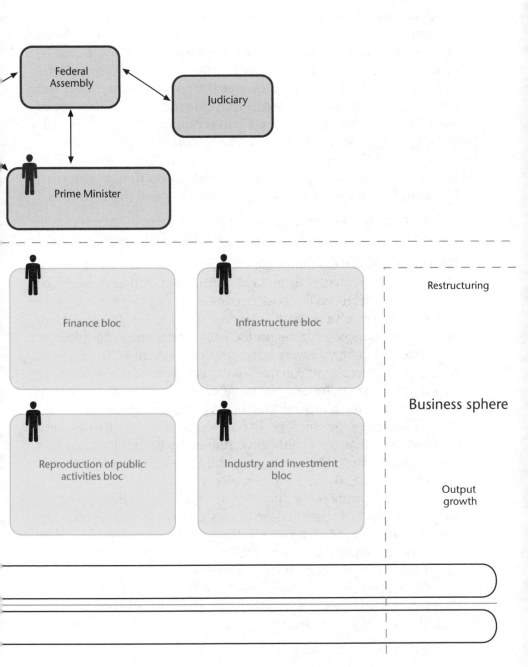

Let us take for example the Volga Federal District. It comprises 20 Subjects of the Federation, and the Ministry of Taxation has a branch in each. The ministry is all-pervasive, in the sense that its three-tiered system comprising the centre, regional inspectorates and city or district inspectorates over the entire country. That will not change. What will happen is that one territorial office, say in Nizhniy Novgorod, will acquire a composite function and the role of co-operating with the presidential plenipotentiary representative. Also each deputy minister is assigned a federal district so that they can sort out any problems of co-operation that might arise. The same goes for the Anti-Monopoly Ministry and several others.

The first model decouples government departments' branches from territories whereas the second model doesn't. So what is the point of it?

The problems of decoupling are different and more global. Public officials' independence from local authorities can ultimately be achieved only if the civil service becomes like military service: once you're in and you've worked your way up to a certain rank, then every three years you can be posted somewhere else. Your place of residence or where you were born count for nothing. That system can be made to work, but you need to pay good salaries. People whose contracts take them to new places must be able to rent somewhere to live, or be offered official lodgings. Living arrangements should be the concern of the employer of public officials. Only then will we be able to say that the federal government bodies are independent of local authorities. The rest of the world does it that way. We will begin introducing those principles next year.

The third option is for those government departments which have no network of territorial structures and where there is no point creating one. The Ministry of Health and the Ministry of Culture would be examples. In their case the task of co-operation with plenipotentiary presidential representatives is left with the centre.

Defence and security answer directly to the president. We here are concerned with economic matters. The economy cannot be made to fit the structure of Federal Districts.

Why not? What if there were federal district budgets?

Yes, but then we wake up in a different country with a different name and a different constitution. It would be a country of seven states. It is my deep conviction that if power were concentrated in that way at the level of the federal districts, the resulting centrifugal

Figure 2.9 Planning principles

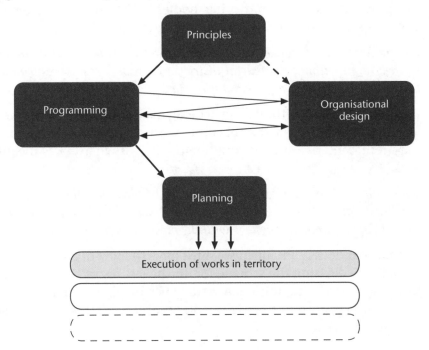

forces would be stronger than they are with 89 Subjects. I am certain the country cannot be split into 89 pieces, but dividing it into seven districts would be much less difficult.

A programme of economic development cannot be created within a single district. A district is not an entity that has development potential. The most we could say is that by concentrating power we can ensure the bottom-up implementation of all decisions relating to, in particular, the reform of the economy. There must be some kind of filter to prevent local authorities making any decisions which contradicts laws or decisions of the government or the president. That does allow reform to progress.

For example, suppose the government at federal level decides to put an end to cross-subsidies. That decision then has to be implemented on the ground. We sign agreements with the regions to put their finances back on a sound footing, which include a paragraph on ending cross-subsidies. The question is then how to ensure compliance. In the past, when the Ministry of Finance or the Ministry of Energy attempted to enforce agreements, governors could just swat them away like flies. Now there are the president's plenipotentiary representatives who have direct contacts with the prosecutor's office and other bodies and they can challenge governors' decisions. They can't just be brushed aside.

But the vertical component of government departments could be made stronger even without the federal districts. There is already presidential power, government power and a unified state.

It could be done without the federal districts, but it is simpler and more likely to get the job done with them. The plenipotentiary representative system could help – that is what it was meant to do.

But plenipotentiary representatives can also give government departments the brush-off. What if government departments' territorial branches cannot find a common language with the president's representative?

So that that does not happen we must have the sort of co-operation we are now devising the scheme for. In the last resort the president would step in and adjudicate. Anyway I personally have hardly ever been in the position of being unable to find a common language with someone.

Budget revenues

From Obshchaya gazeta, *2 March 2000:*

The results for the first two months of the year – which are generally thought to be the most difficult because they contain so many public holidays – showed that the budget is entirely balanced and realistic. Judge for yourself: customs and the Ministry of Taxation were due to collect RUB 49.6 billion in January. In fact they took RUB 58 billion. Their February target was RUB 50.3 billion and the actual result will be RUB 53–55 billion.

These are heartening figures, but they do not mean that the whole year will be so easy and straightforward. The greatest risk is that world prices of the commodities on which our export earnings depend – crude oil and refined products, gas, iron and steel and other metals – will change in the second half. At the moment the market favours this country more than ever. The oil price on exchanges is going through the $30 per barrel barrier and palladium is $700 an ounce. Such unbounded joy cannot last for ever.

And so you are making the most of it by raising export duties on oil?

You have to agree that's only logical. Export duties make a major contribution to the budget. They make up RUB 87 billion of the total revenue (which is RUB 797 billion). The rates of duty naturally vary according to commodity prices, in this case the oil price. If the price rises, so does the duty. One difficulty arises because, under part one of the tax code which came into force on 1 January this year, new tax rates do not take effect until at least one month after publication. Thus the government cannot react quickly to any change in the world market. Taxpayers always have a month's notice and the budget loses out as a result.

What is the answer?'

I am a great advocate of setting scales of rates of export duty once and for all. Then there is no argument about whether the rate is €20 or €25 a tonne effective on 1 March or 1 April. Everyone can just look it up in a table: as soon as the average price reaches a given level, the duty payable is such and such. That would stop people getting so upset as they do now. The government hopes to get just such an arrangement included in part two of the tax code which is currently before the State Duma.

Are you not afraid that the major Russian oil companies, which form a powerful lobby, will get their act together and force the government not to raise export duty?

They have no grounds, either political or financial, to revert to the status quo ante. Last year the oil companies tried to fend off an increase in export duty by saying their enormous income was being invested in capacity. Very well, we told them, show us the investment programmes in your company accounts. Whereupon they went rather quiet. Export duties are not an attack on oil companies' revenue. They are what the companies are asked to pay for using a national resource. The rise in the world oil price was not their doing. It was bestowed on this country by an act of God. It must be paid for.

From Rossiyskaya gazeta, 24 December 1999:

It is not the government that needs additional revenue. Additional revenue is needed by the state to meet its spending commitments. Ultimately it is needed by each and every citizen. The state's prime purpose is to maintain the integrity of the country, public order, security and the most important social guarantees.

Clearly, given the financial and other difficulties in which the country finds itself, everyone must bear some part of the burden. That goes not only for private citizens but also for Russia's largest enterprises, the oil companies and Gazprom. Social justice demands that if big exporters make additional profits due to increases in the world oil price, then the burden of the problems the country has to bear as a whole should fall on their shoulders first. The oil companies and Gazprom are, after all, Russian companies with predominantly Russian employees. Take Chechnya. The uncompromising war against terrorism is being waged in the interests of the whole of Russian society.

As for export duties themselves, they are being introduced in conditions which are relatively favourable to exporters. The decisions were taken after due consideration and with great caution and applied to Gazprom after all others. The government is committed to the development of the oil and gas complex and the improvement of its capacities, but it expects the same commitment and determination to be shown by the companies themselves in their everyday operations and to be shown by specific indicators (like volume of investment, production and sales).

Will the new duties reduce Gazprom's ability to invest? The government is ready to support Gazprom's strategic Blue Stream project. We plan to raise RUB 10 billion (around $370 million) from the new duties on gas, whereas the total amount of support for Blue Stream is, on Gazprom's own figures, over $4 billion, almost half of which is being given by Russia.

Here is another not inconsiderable thing. The new export duties will have no impact on the 1999 budget. They will take effect in 2000. You know how much argument there was over the adoption of the 2000 budget. The government had to fight hard to defend essential items and parameters. Now is not too soon to create the right conditions so that the funding is available in good time to cover the expenditure in next year's budget.

Why did the government decide to start by raising export duties? Are there really no other means of raising additional revenue?

Tax administration aims to increase the rate of tax collection. It is an everyday task. Ensuring that due taxes are paid must not be confused with raising additional revenue. If a tax is demanded by law, it must be paid. The fact that now we might almost view collecting due tax as providing a revenue reserve is nothing to be proud of. In societies where obedience to the law is a rule that everyone accepts, not much extra revenue results from extra efforts spent on tax collection. In this country some people do not pay their taxes in full, or at all. I must admit that one reason may be that enterprises are, let's say it outright, quite heavily taxed. The relationship between collection rates and the amount of tax is, like tax reform itself, an important subject in its own right.

The government proposed to reduce some taxes in the draft budget for 2000, which was put to the State Duma but did not have enough support. It intends to return to the matter as a matter of priority soon.

As for tax collection rates, much has already been achieved. The actual collection rate was 67 per cent in 1998. The 1999 budget assumed an average tax collection rate of 70 per cent and the actual figure will be a bit higher. The 2000 target is at least 74 per cent.

It is customs policy that creates flexibility in the state's economic policy. It is particularly useful for protecting the interests of Russian producers and consumers. Foreign trade duties are a way of balancing revenue and influencing demand and supply, depending on the state of the economy.

At the moment the government can do such things quickly. The last State Duma, however, wanted to bring in a law fixing customs duties. Really! Those deputies must be especially clairvoyant if they can predetermine fluctuations in world market prices just by writing them into law.

Moreover, in our specific conditions customs duties compensate for the ineffectiveness of other taxes, such as the excise duties which large companies have long since found ways of avoiding. Customs (not only export) duties enable the state to control the real volume of goods flows. There is, so to speak, no hiding place. Yet customs policy, even though it involves a certain amount of economic coercion, relies on market economic principles and can only be effective in a market economy. That the government increasingly resorts to the customs as an instrument of policy shows, first, its commitment to more robust markets in Russia and, second, that markets in this country are already mature enough to allow economic levers to be used to influence them and their participants.

Attempts to counter what the government is doing with customs policy are a throwback to the sort of thinking that characterised the command economy. The government used to pick and choose enterprises, affording some a special market position. As a side-effect, it ended up weakening itself. If the government takes stronger economic measures, such as a stronger customs and tariff policy, that means the state is stronger and so is the executive's vertical chain of command, and consequently all market participants bear more equal economic responsibility to the state.

Whenever we talk about export duties, the main argument is about rising world oil and gas prices and the increasing profits of the exporters. But though external conditions are favourable, exporters remain hostages to the internal problems of the Russian economy. It is the old problem of non-payment. Perhaps it would have been sensible to start by doing something about non-payment and clearing the debts owed to enterprises from the budget. Then the oil companies and Gazprom could pay extra taxes.

We can agree with the argument that both the oil companies and Gazprom suffer because energy consumers do not pay up. The economy owes money to Gazprom. However, let us not forget that the government itself is in the same position. Sometimes even oil and gas producers owe money to the government, especially if you consider all the tax liabilities of enterprises in Russia.

From Rossiyskaya gazeta, *2 February 2000:*

This time round I am again absolutely certain that everyone on the federal payroll will get their pay plus 20 per cent. But things in the regions are more difficult. Not all Subjects of the Federation are able to do the same.

In several regions the fiscal position is, to put it bluntly, unsatisfactory. As a result they still cannot clear their salary arrears. They would need RUB 1.5–2 billion to pay off all their accumulated debts.

How they pay is as important as what they pay with. This is about the battle against non-payment and non-cash settlements. It about the distribution of the available resources. Our condition is that 40 per cent of the regions' own funds must go on paying salary arrears.

With that proviso, each region will determine its own financial scheme to increase the salaries of its public-sector employees. Events last year [1999] showed that each Subject of the Federation can devise its own schemes to increase pay in stages.

Much depends on how people choose to spend their income. Last year we made great efforts to pay pension arrears and salaries. And what happened? At a particular moment demand for imported goods began to increase. Imports reached almost 17 per cent of total effective demand, having averaged under 5 per cent during 1998.

People have freedom of choice. Until the quality of Russian-made goods is improved to at least match the average of the rest of the world, Russian consumers will vote with their wallets for foreign industry as soon as they can afford to. The government and business itself still have a lot to do to change that.

How do you account for Russians' undeclared income, those cash-in-hand earnings on which no tax is paid?

It is true that in many enterprises the employees' salaries are not their main source of income. They also make money from illicitly selling unaccounted-for goods, on deposit accounts or in other ways. That is why it is so important that our estimates of the capacity for economic growth take account of hidden demand, which does not necessarily favour Russian producers. Dragging the money out of the shadows is both difficult and necessary. I think we must divert both consumer and investment demand to the domestic market. But that will only happen once people stop being afraid to keep their money in Russian banks, and start to buy shares in Russian businesses and buy Russian-made goods instead of imports. If people vote with their wallets for their country, it gets richer. And so do its citizens. In this country the process is still at the stage of sloganeering and exhortation.

We must finally carry out a thorough reform of personal taxation. I do not mean only reducing rates of income tax. Any money people put into building or buying a home or property or spend on their children's education and so on should be taken out of tax altogether. I am absolutely convinced of that and am prepared to defend my point of view.

House building, for example, is at the moment perhaps the only area where there is a direct relationship between rising incomes and rising output. There is enormous potential there. Everybody wants to buy their own flat. That means we connect our lives and the lives of our children to Russia. Investment in housing is the best indicator of people's attitude to their country.

In fact, Russia is building more and more housing. But everyone knows that when you buy a flat the actual price you pay is not what it says in the contract, but higher. We, thank God, turn a blind eye. And quite right too. We are leaving one little corner of the market where people can invest their savings in a house or flat and can't take them out again. It does not matter where the money comes from. It might be an insurance scheme or something else. If we were to attempt to insist on proper valuations, people would lose any remaining desire to buy property and start looking for ways to hide their money elsewhere.

It is important to get the point across clearly: a country is rich if its citizens are well off and aware of their responsibilities to the country. I am sure that today the political will exists to turn that idea into specific government decisions.

From Obshchaya gazeta, *11 November 1999:*

What do you think of the idea of having two budgets? Would they be a temporary measure or for the long term?'

We can discuss having two budgets, but that's really a political proposition. We can discuss having a budget surplus, which is a financial proposition. The issue is whether we need a source of funds which

Figure 2.10 Public finances

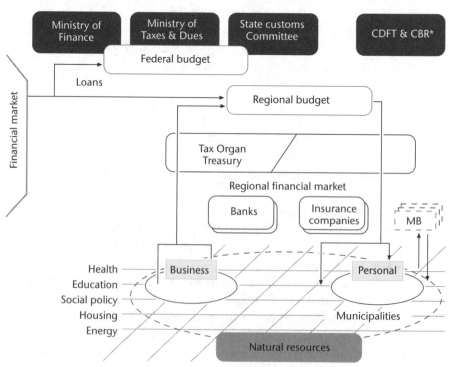

* Chief Directorate of the Federal Treasury and Central Bank of Russia

is built up to spend on problems in the future. In the immediate future the problem is the debt. Later it might be problems of development. I think we should be guided by that thought. Otherwise a mass of little problems that any state has will just get swept under the carpet.

Budgetary federalism

From Komsomolskaya pravda, *24 June 1999:*

When people tell me I am an expert in inter-budgetary relations, I feel proud. Honestly. You have the relations among the 89 Subjects of the Federation plus the federation centre, all fighting their own corner. That is a big battlefield. I can't think of a more interesting job than trying to keep on top of it. On the other hand it is not realistic to expect someone to be absolutely professional at everything. It just needs someone who is able to empathise with the people in charge of particular areas and for those people to be in place.

From Obshchaya gazeta, *11 November 1999:*

What we have adopted in the government is the next link in the chain of the relationship between the centre and the Subjects of the Federation. The previous three-year period went under the title of Reform of Inter-budgetary Relations and had more to do with procedures for ensuring that federal resources were distributed to the regions in a reasonable and justified way. Now that task is complete. But it leaves unaddressed the wider issues of delineating budgetary authority, bringing order to matters of shared competence, defining revenue sources and, the main thing, establishing a stable tax and hence revenue base. Bringing stability to budgetary relations between the centre and the Subjects (revenue sources plus transfers) even for a three-year period is a sacred task. It means we incentivise the regions to boost their economic potential.

From Ekonomika i zhizn, *20 October 2000:*

A new stage in the reform of inter-budgetary relations is beginning. It aims to make regional and local authorities more accountable for the effective use of budget resources and to ensure equal access for all citizens to budget-funded services and social guarantees. Let me pick out three main things that we intend to do next year:

◆ First, complete the process begun in 1999 of adopting a new method of distributing the Fund for Financial Support to Subjects of the Federation based on an objective assessment of their budgetary needs and tax potential.

◆ Second, clearly define the scope of financial accountability of the Subjects of the Federation for the implementation of federal laws relating to social matters, such as the Law on Veterans, the Law on the Social Protection of Invalids and the Law on State Benefits for Citizens with Children.

◆ Third, support budgetary reform at regional and local level.

In the 2001 draft budget the allocation of federal budget funding under 'Financial aid to lower-level budgets' was based wholly on the above-mentioned principles.

The development of budgetary federalism in Russia: from dividing up money to separation of powers

From Rossiyskaya gazeta, *17 February 2001:*

The growing pains of Russian budgetary federalism

In 1991 the Russian Federation inherited the budgetary system of a highly centralised state that was formally a federation but essentially unitary, and where the regional and local authorities possessed no significant budgetary autonomy whatever. All lower-level budgets were set by higher-level government bodies or agencies, which also made those budgets balance by specifying individual standard amounts for revenue generation and providing centralised subsidies to cover 'plan deficits'. Only in a system of central planning and direct administrative subordination of regional and local authorities could such a system be made to work. What it did not do was ensure that budget-funded services were provided efficiently or that the budgetary system as a whole was balanced. Regional and local levels lacked any incentive to use budget funds efficiently, as budget deficits and the responsibility for covering them were effectively handed back to higher levels.

Given that inheritance, it is not surprising that in the 1990s Russian budgetary federalism should have had to suffer serious but apparently inevitable growing pains, some of which threaten to turn into chronic conditions.

Let us start with the asymmetry of the budget structure. It is a deformity dating back to the nation and territory-based state structure which Russia inherited. The spate of Soviet republics asserting their sovereignty in the early 1990s only aggravated it. First came special budgetary status for the republics of Tatarstan, Bashkortostan and Sakha (Yakutiya), which was established in fact before being enshrined in bilateral agreements with the federal centre. Second, the republics were on average better financed because of cash injections from the federal budget. Third, *oblasts* and *krais* attempted to gain parity of budgetary status by way of individual agreements with the federal centre.[7]

Fortunately the 'political' budgetary asymmetry has gradually disappeared in recent years. The Republic of Sakha (Yakutiya) reverted to the common budgetary space in 1996. The unified rules of inter-budgetary relations have for the most part applied to the republics of Tatarstan and Bashkortostan since 2001. Whereas the republics used, for some unknown reason, to have much better-funded budgets than the *oblasts*, the budget statistics clearly show that the gap has narrowed. Since 1998 no more bilateral agreements have been made to delineate taxation and budgetary powers and the existing agreements, most of which expire in 2001/02, are being applied only in so far as they do not conflict with federal legislation. Of course inter-budgetary relations continue to be affected by political considerations, but overall Russia's official budgetary structure has become far more symmetrical and transparent than it was in the mid-1990s.

Only two or three years ago some quite serious attempts were made to introduce 'economic asymmetry' into the budget structure. Ten to 15 Subjects of the Federation, calling themselves 'the donor regions', laid claim to some kind of special budgetary status. But the whole proposition was obviously dubious from the outset. The fact that a region is not in receipt of federal transfers shows only that its budget is fully funded internally. That is something to be proud of only if you ignore the fact that a region's tax potential is built up over decades by the efforts of the country as a whole. Anyway, no *region* pays taxes to the federal budget. Taxpayers pay tax. The taxes that are paid into the federal budget come from the territories of all the

---

7   Editor's note: *Krais* (border or edge) and *oblasts* (area or zone) are administrative divisions. Under the Russian Constitution, *oblasts* are considered to be Subjects of the Federation. Nine of the Subjects are classified as *krais*.

Subjects of the Federation, so in that sense they are all donors. And all are recipients because all regions receive funding from the federal budget, whether it be financial aid or federal government departments' direct spending. With the creation of the Federal Treasury it became possible to track federal expenditure with considerable geographical precision. According to estimates by the East–West Institute, between 35 and 40 regions, with two-thirds of the population of Russia, contribute more to the federal budget than they get back from the federal budget in total via all channels. That alters the traditional picture of 10 or 15 'donor regions' supposedly keeping the rest of the country going.

Another idea that was madly popular at one time but seems to have quietly disappeared is that of the 'single channel' of inter-budgetary relations. It supposed that all taxes would in the first instance go to the budgets of the regions, which would then make fixed contributions to the federal budget. Such systems are the privilege of confederations, which are all but extinct in the world of today. They depend on the erroneous view that the regions pay their own money into the federal budget. The true state of affairs is the exact opposite: the federal centre gives regional and local budgets a share of the receipts from federal taxes. If there is to be any question of a 'single channel', it could only mean replacing the multiplicity of standard contributions from federal taxes to regional budgets by a single standard amount or payment. What emerges ever more clearly here are the flaws in the ideology of 'dividing up money without separating powers', irrespective of whether budget funds are being made to flow from the bottom up or the top down.

That the fight continues, for some reason, against 'financial counter-flows' is another manifestation of the same ideology. There are no such flows in the Russian budget system. As has been said already, the federal budget runs on taxes paid not by the regions, and still less by regional authorities, but by taxpayers – individuals and businesses. Ultimately regional government is also the target of funds from the federal budget or budget-funded public services, although a proportion of federal revenues does go into regional budgets in the form of financial aid. From time to time it is proposed to solve this entirely fictitious problem by requiring different regions to make different standard contributions from so-called 'regulating taxes'.[8] That would in essence be a form of financial aid

---

8 A form of payment used to balance contributions.

which could be provided far more simply and effectively to Subjects of the Federation directly from the federal budget using objective, transparent criteria.

'Regulating taxes' are inseparable from the myth that the dreaded 50–50 proportion, with which every discussion of the federal budget for the last three years has kicked off, in some way serves the regions' interests. Over 50 per cent of all tax is taken from the territory of only ten Subjects of the Federation with 22 per cent of its population. They stand to gain most from decentralisation of tax receipts. Most Subjects and most of the population, on the other hand, have a clear interest in partial redistribution of funds among the regions and hence in increasing the federal budget's share of tax revenues. According to estimates by the Centre for Fiscal Policy, in order to ensure the budgets of all the Subjects of the Federation are funded to an equal extent it would be necessary for 85 per cent of all tax revenue to be concentrated in the federal budget and then about half of it to be redistributed to the regions as financial aid. Now clearly that is only a theoretical calculation, but it vividly demonstrates the direct dependence between centralisation of revenue and the ability of the federal budget to carry out one of its principal functions, that of providing equal levels of funding to regional budgets and hence equal access to the main public services and guarantees for all citizens.

The 'separation of money' ideology reaches its height with the continual appeals about Subjects' budget deficits which, it is claimed, the federal centre must cover. In the public mind, regional and local budgets are still thought of as simply territorial subsets of one big state budget. Even though the money is actually spent by regional and local authorities, most complaints about territorial budgets' failure to meet their obligations, from salaries to winter preparations, are as before addressed to the federal government. To some extent that is only fair. Both the revenues and the expenditures of territorial budgets are formally regulated from the top. By dividing up the money by such means as the notorious 'regulating taxes' without also separating powers, we shall never be able to bring territorial budgets into balance or achieve the effective management of regional finances, simply because no one is truly accountable for them. That growing pain has persisted too long and had a dreadful effect on the whole budget system.

Conclusions and lessons from the reforms of the 1990s

In the course of the 1990s the system of inter-budgetary relations underwent three reforms: in 1991, 1994 and 1999/2000.

The foundations of a new Russian tax system were laid in 1991. As regards inter-budgetary relations, one concept that was carried over from the old system was that of 'regulating taxes' whereby receipts from the main taxes were broken down across budgets at different levels. There was thus an opportunity to proceed to separating powers and not just apportioning money, but it was missed. Uncontrolled decentralisation means that territorial budgets now make up a larger proportion of all revenues and expenditures of the budget system. But a clear legislative basis is lacking. Instead matters proceeded by way of individual agreements and political horse-trading.

In late 1993 and early 1994 the first systematic reform of inter-budgetary relations was carried out. It set uniform standards for the amount of the main federal taxes diverted to regional budgets, expanded the taxation powers of Subjects of the Federation (imposing, in effect, a regional profits tax in particular) and created the Fund for Financial Support to the Regions with funds (transfers) distributed, for the first time, according to a formula.

The system of inter-budgetary relations established in the mid-1990s had, ostensibly at least, some of the hallmarks of budgetary federalism. But still it lacked a firm legislative footing as it was mainly concerned with dividing budget resources (by way of the annual law on the federal budget) between the various levels of the budget system and regions. In 1996/98 there was a new upsurge of subjectivism in inter-budgetary relations. The regional finances were in a state of profound crisis. The practice of meeting budget obligations in non-cash forms became widespread and public-sector salaries went massively into arrears. There was an abrupt rise in the debts of regional and local budgets.

In 1998 the government of the Russian Federation devised the first ever medium-term reform programme in this field. It was discussed and agreed by a tripartite working group including representatives of the government, the State Duma and the Federation Council. It was entitled Concept for the Reform of Inter-Budgetary Relations in the Russian Federation 1999/2001. Its aims were, in general, met.

The main aim was to create a new system of financial support for the Subjects of the Federation. In 1999/2001 the Fund for Financial Support of the Regions (FFSR) was thoroughly reformed. An entirely new, far more transparent and objective method of distributing transfers was introduced with a view to ensuring the regions' budgets were more equally supported. At the same time incentives were created to encourage rational and responsible budgetary policies at the local level.

The new method relies on assessing the real level of funding of regional budgets, taking into account objective expenditure demands (budgetary expenditure indices) and tax resources (tax potential indices). FFSR transfers are distributed so as to increase the level of funding for regions with per capita tax resources below the Russian average, thus guaranteeing the least-developed territories a minimum level of budget funding. However a subsidy-receiving region cannot have a level of budgetary funding after receipt of transfers that is higher than or even equal to any region not in receipt of transfers, and most recipient regions still have an incentive to increase their own revenues.

Another point of principle is that budget funding is assessed without regard to regions' actual expenditures and revenues. All calculations are based on data from federal government ministries and departments (principally the Federal State Statistics Service, Goskomstat) describing the economy, population and geography of the regions. If, as happened in 1994/98, transfers are distributed according to budget report figures, then the biggest recipient will be whoever can conceal most revenues, boast most expenditure and otherwise massage the input data.

It is worth adding that both the method and the calculations for the next budget year are thoroughly verified and re-verified by the tripartite working group on the improvement of inter-budgetary relations before going before the State Duma. All input data and inter-mediate and final results are officially promulgated by the Russian Federation's Ministry of Finance. Therefore when each of the last three years' draft transfer distributions were presented to the State Duma during consideration of that year's law on the federal budget, no amendments were necessary. In 1996/98 reallocations of transfers between regions were seen as part of the natural order of things.

From 2001 on the mechanism of financial support to the Subjects of the Federation acquired a completely new element, the Compensation Fund. Unlike the FFSR, which serves to equalise overall budget funding levels, it is designed to finance so-called 'federal mandates', that is, obligations imposed on regional budgets by federal laws. In 2001 Compensation Fund subventions and subsidies were distributed to all Subjects of the Federation, irrespective of their financial situation, to finance the federal laws 'On state benefits for citizens with children' and 'On the social protection of invalids in the Russian Federation'. In addition, the federal budget now contained the Regional Development Fund (support to investment in public infrastructure) and the Regional Finance Development Fund (support to budgetary reform, awarded on a competitive basis).

Other noteworthy achievements of the Concept are a complete inventory of federal mandates and the legislation governing:

◆ budgetary expenditure at all levels;
◆ amendments to the Budgetary Code;
◆ measures requiring taxes to be paid at companies' actual place of business;
◆ the drafting of Interim Recommendations to Subjects of the Russian Federation on the regulation of inter-budgetary relations;
◆ starting to implement a programme of technical support for reforming the budget system at regional level with the aid of a loan from the International Bank for Reconstruction and Development.

The drift towards increasing individualisation of inter-budgetary relations was reversed. Instead of individual agreements on allowances and privileges, now there were model agreements defining the obligations of Subjects of the Federation in the process of restoring the public finances to health.

The overall success of the Concept can be explained by three factors. First, it was not a one-off intervention, but a three-year programme which had undergone a lengthy period of preparation and discussion among both experts and politicians. Second, it had the approval of not only the government but also the State Duma and the Federation Council and so served, despite various remaining differences, as a general political mandate for reform. Third and most important, its preparation and implementation entailed the creation of a new organisational mechanism to monitor and 'quality test' the results and to produce and implement agreed decisions – the tripartite working group on improving inter-budgetary relations, which included representatives of the various branches and levels of government. These lessons must be learned and applied to subsequent stages of the reform of inter-budgetary relations.

Reform alternatives in the 2000s

There can be no doubt that the reform of inter-budgetary relations must continue. The only questions are in what direction and with what aim.

The system that was created in the course of the 1990s was perfectly workable in terms of the division of money. With the adoption of a new method of distributing FFSR transfers we learned to make fairly accurate and objective estimates of the normal spending and revenues of the Subjects of the Federation. Of course our methods can and must still be improved, but on the whole they now enable us to use uniform, formal criteria to sort out the distribution of budgetary resources both between levels of the budget system and between regions. Reform in this area would certainly have positive results but it would at the same time set in stone the system of 'dividing up money without separating powers'.

There is an alternative: seize the momentum of reform and within three or four years move to an entirely new system which separates powers without dividing up money. This would have all the advantages of the first approach but at the same time would increase – several times over, not just by a few per cent – the effectiveness of the system of inter-budgetary relations and the management of regional finances.

In our opinion, the existing system of inter-budgetary relations does not fit with either modern principles of budgetary federalism or Russia's medium-term development strategy.

The concept of 'market-preserving federalism' developed from international experience in the second half of the 1990s proves that an effective system of budgetary federalism which supports sustainable economic growth must meet five main criteria:

◆ The powers of different levels of government must be clearly defined.
◆ The regional authorities must possess sufficient autonomy within their territories and powers to conduct financial and economic policy.

- ◆ The federal centre must have effective powers to maintain a single economic and legal space and to mobilise economic resources flexibly.
- ◆ Regional authorities must be subject to rigid budgetary constraints.
- ◆ All these conditions must be stable and not up for negotiation.

However, as OECD research in Russia has shown, the Russian system of inter-budgetary relations meets none these criteria.

At the moment around half of all tax revenues and expenditures of the Russian Federation's consolidated budget are concentrated at the level of regional and local budgets. On that criterion Russia is in practice no worse off and, in terms of local budgets, actually better off than other federal states. In fact, however, the Russian budget structure remains highly centralised even by comparison with unitary states. The expenditures of regional, and particularly of local, budgets are over-burdened with 'federal mandates' (salaries, social security payments and benefits, and a variety of routine payments) while most of their revenue comes from deductions from federal taxes and financial aid. There is a marked imbalance between the spending obligations imposed from above and the revenue sources bestowed from above to finance them.

The regions can therefore lay political and financial responsibility for the state of the budget and social affairs at the door of the federal centre while keeping for themselves an almost free hand to conduct 'informal' budget policy (by way of selective sequestration, use of alternative forms of money, and offsets, diversion of resources into extra-budgetary funds and accounts, individual tax privileges, covert subsidies, reckless borrowing from lenders – including financial structures under the control of the borrower – and so on). The inevitable consequence of inadequate statutory regulation of the power to manage public finances is inadequate accountability for how they are managed.

There is a pervasive contradiction at the heart of the system of 'dividing the money'. Decentralisation of budgetary resources means centralisation of 'official' budgetary powers, which in turn means decentralisation of 'unofficial' ones. From the outset that creates distorted conditions and perverse incentives for the conduct of economic and budgetary policy at local level. As a result, the regional and local authorities' main effort is not devoted to economic growth, structural reform, improving the climate for investment and business, or a rational and responsible tax and budget policy that makes sense to the public, investors and lenders. Instead they concentrate on horse-trading with higher levels of government to obtain additional resources, benefits or privileges, look for ways to evade federal constraints and demands and strive to maintain administrative control over financial flows.

In order to eliminate this contradiction, there must be legislation to establish the taxation and budgetary autonomy of regional and local authorities: that is, their right and duty within the framework of federal legislation to make independent revenue and expenditure decisions in their budgets and to take political, financial and legal responsibility for the results. Until such time as regional and local authorities hold officially recognised powers to devise and conduct their own taxation and budgetary policy, they will not be fully accountable to the public, investors and lenders for the state of the public finances, social affairs and the conditions for economic development in their territories.

Along with decentralised taxation and budgetary powers and enhanced accountability for their use, a competitive environment must be created and maintained for regional and local authorities. It must be both economic (a single economic space with no restrictions on the movement of goods, workers or capital) and political (democratic institutions and civil society). Competition among products and businesses must be complemented by competition among regions and economic policies. That depends on one essential condition: regional and local authorities must be under rigid budgetary constraints so that their budgets depend not on some higher authority but on the results of their own financial and economic policies. In other words, if regional and local budgets collect extra revenue or cut back wasteful spending the proceeds should not be confiscated by a higher-level budget. Neither should deficits and debts be covered by additional financial aid and/or individual allowances and privileges.

Meanwhile the enormous overburden of social liabilities and the drastic differences in budget funding levels between regions may demand short and medium-term increases in the proportion of budgetary revenue that goes to the federal budget. Regional and local authorities may be responsible for a smaller proportion of the total resources in the national budget system, but they will have much more real taxation and budgetary autonomy and accountability for how budget resources are used. In the longer term the proportion of resources concentrated at regional and local level is expected to rise.

In our opinion, only a system which separates powers instead of just dividing up money will do for Russia's development strategy. That will provide:

- *economic efficiency*: creating long-term institutional incentives for regional and local authorities and agencies to undertake structural reform and maintain a competitive environment and a favourable investment and business climate;
- *budgetary accountability*: management of public finances in the name and on behalf of the public, with territories' tax and other resources used with maximum efficiency to provide public services, along with transparency and accountability of tax and budget policy;
- *territorial fairness*: equal access to the main public services and social guarantees for all citizens irrespective of their place of residence;
- *political consolidation*: achieving public consent about the way taxation and budgetary powers are distributed among authorities at different levels, creating conditions for the effective exercise of regional and local authorities' functions, facilitating the development of civil society and reinforcing the territorial integrity of the country.

Real powers, real accountability

To get from dividing up money to separation of powers requires all parts of the system of inter-budgetary relations (spending powers, tax-raising powers, budget equalisation, regulation of the management of regional finances) to undergo co-ordinated reforms informed by the single common principle that *only where there are real powers can there be real accountability and a real stake in the results of actions*.

As regards spending powers it is necessary to minimise the scope of jointly financed expenditure and delineate as precisely as possible the different levels' rights and responsibilities for:

- legislative regulation;
- financial provision;
- their own financing of specific types of public service.

Figure 2.11 The state as 'single factory'

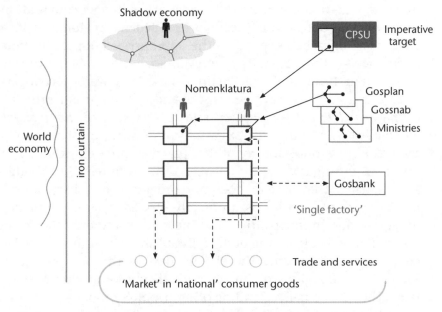

The principles of that delineation should be enshrined in the Budgetary Code. Implementation should then be prescribed in industry-specific legislation (not individual bilateral agreements). The principles will include:

◆ *Subsidiarity*: Spending powers should be held as close as possible to the consumer of budget-funded services.
◆ *Territoriality*: Non-mobile public goods and services used predominantly by the population of a defined territory should be paid for from the regional or local budget.
◆ *Economy of scale*: Purchasing in bulk is often more efficient.
◆ *External effect*: The greater the interest society as a whole has in the individual regions or municipalities performing their functions properly, or the greater the general harm from them not doing so, the greater grounds for centralisation and vice versa.

We must aim to ensure that all three types of power are allocated to the same level. That automatically solves the problem of federal mandates. We must ban outright any laws or other normative legal acts which impose additional expenditure on lower-level budgets without giving them sources of finance, as well as any exception-creating rules whereby such expenditures are accounted for by way of inter-budgetary relations and/or budget equalisation. Any financial obligations specified by a federal, regional or local enactment must be assigned to the appropriate budget and must be financed entirely from its own revenues, either directly from the budget or in the form of targeted financial aid to lower-level budgets.

To put it another way, we must abandon the current principle of *'my mandate but your budget'* and replace it with *'my mandate and my budget'*. As regards tax-raising powers, we must for several reasons forsake once and for all the practice inherited from Soviet times of splitting tax receipts between different levels of the budget system. First, that system does not provide a link between the taxing authority (which is ultimately elected by the population of regions and municipalities) and the quality and quantity of the services provided from the budget. Establishing that link is the key condition for increasing the effectiveness of the budget system. Second, if the regions obtain most of their revenue from federal taxes, they are actually spending other people's money and, as ever in such circumstances, not doing it responsibly. Third, the federal level can always change the standard deductions by regulating taxes or the way they are collected (the tax base, rates or allowances). So regions and municipalities are shorn of any long-term incentive to maintain a favourable investment climate or build up (and show in their accounts) their own tax base. Fourth, there is surreptitious competition with the federal government for the same tax base (one reason alternatives to cash are so prevalent at the regional level is that all are striving to maximise their share of regulating taxes). Fifth, regional and local authorities with limited opportunities to pursue their own taxation and budgetary policies resort to 'semi-legal' measures against taxpayers, which undermines the purpose of tax reform. Finally, if the people paid taxes at the rates specified by the regional and local authorities, the accountability and transparency of the latter would increase significantly.

The end result of the reform will be a complete abandonment of the idea of dividing taxes and tax revenues into *own*, *allocated* or *regulating*. All taxes and tax revenues should be somebody's own. There is no point even discussing the standard deductions from federal taxes which go into lower-level budgets – whether they should be for one or three years, uniform or differentiated, high or low. They should be eternal, unchanging and equal to zero. The federal budget should receive federal taxes in full with no 'splitting off'. Regional taxes should go into regional budgets and local taxes to local budgets.

The Tax Code must specify both the taxation powers (the taxes) belonging to each level and the overall proportions in which tax resources are to be divided among them. As the tax receipts at each level of the budget system will be determined by the tax policy (tax rates) and taxation efforts of the authorities at that level, the imperative for them to defend their revenues by passing budgetary laws to divide up tax receipts simply evaporates. That such legislation exists is a sign of a transitional period. The centralised system did not need any because there was no one to talk to, and a truly federal system will not need it because there will be nothing to talk about.

The general principles for dividing taxes include the following rules:

◆ The tax-raising powers of the federal authorities must be sufficient to regulate the national economy and maintain a nationwide single economic and tax space.
◆ If revenues are generated by the national economy as a whole, they should be subject to federal taxes.
◆ The more mobile and unevenly distributed territorially the tax base is, the higher up the budget system it must be taxed.
◆ The harder it is to enforce payment of tax where the taxable activity actually takes place, the higher up the tax system the tax must be applied.
◆ Regional and local taxes must not impede the movement of capital, workers, goods or services.
◆ Regional and local taxes must not permit tax burdens to be exported to other regions or municipalities.

Hence the federal budget could be allocated indirect taxes (customs duties, VAT, excise duties), taxes on profits (capital) and personal incomes, and charges for natural resources which are unevenly distributed. Most suitable for the regional level are add-ons to profits and personal income taxes, and taxes on small business and natural resources. Funding of local budgets could be based on property taxes and charges for utilities. That, however, is merely a very broad-brush picture. The scheme would need to be adapted to Russian conditions and implemented gradually.

Stage one should be to move away from the current system of *one tax, three budgets* to a system of *one tax, one budget* whereby 100 per cent of the money raised from any particular tax imposed by budgetary legislation is allocated to a single budget level. The principle of splitting tax receipts remains for the moment but the groundwork is being done to replace it by separate taxes.

Stage two will implement the principle *'my income, my tax'*. That is, any tax which is 100 per cent allocated to regional budgets becomes a regional tax, not a federal one. In the first instance the Tax Code may impose regional or local taxes at a uniform rate across the whole country. Although the taxation powers of the regional and local powers will be purely symbolic, the fact that a particular tax is specifically regional or local will sharply increase authorities' interest in building up their tax base.

Stage three will be *'my tax, my tax rate'*. Regional and local authorities will be allowed to set the rates of their taxes subject, possibly, to federal constraints (the tax base will have to be specified by the Tax Code, which simplifies tax administration).

Finally, the concluding stage will remove the restrictions on regions' and municipalities' ability to determine the rates and base of their taxes (rates will be contained at sensible levels and the tax base will be the same everywhere because of the competitive forces which by that time will have taken effect).

Different taxes, one imagines, will pass through these stages at different speeds. The tax on profits, for example, was divided, for all practical purposes, into federal and regional taxes in 1994/98. Thus it would be only logical to fix that division in the Tax Code straight away, giving Subjects of the Federation the right to set tax rates independently anywhere between specified minimum and maximum levels. Personal income tax, small-business taxes and charges for common natural resources will probably have to be allocated 100 per cent to budgets of the Subjects of the Federation at first and only then converted into properly regional taxes. Whereas in respect of the last two taxes the tax powers of the Subjects of the Federation should be gradually expanded, the tax base and a 'flat' uniform rate of regional personal income tax for all regions must be fixed by the Tax Code for a considerable time.

But the general direction of travel must be consistently, and as clearly as possible, away from the 'regulation' of territorial budgets' tax revenues under budget legislation and towards separation of taxes and greater tax autonomy for regional and local authorities under tax legislation.

As regards budget equalisation, most of the work has already been done under the Concept 1999/2001. The Fund for Financial Support of the Regions will continue in the long run to do the heavy lifting of financial aid to Subjects of the Federation, in terms of both volume of funding and the creation and development of a methodological base, basic data and calculation techniques. The main points of the transfer distribution method introduced in 2001 and the procedure for determining the main parameters for calculations must be enshrined in legislation. It may even be appropriate to fix the basic proportions of the distribution of transfers for the next three years, making annual adjustments as required by changes in the economy by distributing a small amount from the Fund by the same method.

The second fundamental element of the system of financial support to the regions is the Compensation Fund. This will probably have to be made bigger in order to take in any remaining 'unfinanced federal mandates' (most of which are to be abolished). At the same time the powers of the Subjects of the Federation must be expanded to determine the level and types of social security provision so that regional authorities are able to balance their obligations by using the funds provided by the Compensation Fund. Moreover, there must be changes to the method of distributing subventions so as to make regions keener to use the funds provided efficiently and to minimise the scramble for subventions. As reform of social security proceeds (with allowances being replaced by targeted benefits based on need), the Compensation Fund should provide money in the form of a single block subvention for all social security purposes (under a framework federal law) to be distributed among the regions in proportion to their population adjusted for average income.

The lack of co-ordination between the FFSR (equalisation of funding to meet the regions' 'own' expenditure) and the Compensation Fund (finance for federal mandates) could be bridged by a co-funding mechanism for social expenditure. Its aim would be to incentivise the regions to maintain a given level of funding for the most significant types of expenditure (i.e. those with substantial external effects – education, health and culture). Matching federal subsidies could be distributed among all Subjects of the

Federation, but the amount of co-funding should depend (under a formula) on the funding level of the regions' budgets (the least well-funded receiving 80 per cent, say, and the best-funded 20 per cent). Provision of subsidies must be conditional on Subjects of the Federation putting up their share of the relevant expenditure and, in the longer term, improving the quality of the services provided, undertaking structural reforms in appropriate areas and so on.

The system of financial aid to Subjects of the Federation is to acquire additional elements, such as the Fund for Regional Development and the Fund for the Development (a more exact term would be Reform) of Regional Finances. Both were in the federal budget in 2000/01, but are not yet operational in fact [as of February 2001]. The Fund for Regional Development is designed to bring together funding which is dispersed among many federal and regional investment programmes. The aim is to provide (on a competitive basis) investment grants for the development of regional industrial and social infrastructure. The Fund for the Development (or Reform) of Regional Finances, set up with a loan from the International Bank for Reconstruction and Development (IBRD), is designed to promote reform at the regional level. Its funds will be available to implement budgetary reform in around five or ten regions selected by competition each year. In 2001 it is planned to complete the selection of regions to receive the first tranche (the preliminary selection comprised St Petersburg, Belgorod, Vologda, Samara and Chelyabinsk *oblasts*, Khabarovsk *krai* and the Chuvash republic) and announce the competition for the second tranche of the planned IBRD loan.

This suite of instruments makes it possible to pursue any policy of financial support to the regions and at the same time enables the Subjects of the Federation to calculate the bulk of financial aid for themselves. The greater the autonomy of the regional authorities (brought about by, among other things, the reduction, if not complete abolition, of federal mandates), the more grounds there are to redistribute funds towards the FFSR. Retaining onerous federal mandates requires a large Compensation Fund, and maintaining nationwide standards for the provision of budget-funded services requires them to be co-financed, at least, from the federal budget. As the Regional Development Fund mechanism gets into its stride, there should also be an increase in the investment component of financial support to the regions. As for the Fund for Development (Reform) of Regional Finances, its effectiveness depends not so much on its size (it could be comparatively small) as on the overall duration of the programme, the criteria by which regions are selected and the mechanism for checking up on the implementation of regional reform plans.

One general and crucial requirement is that the system of financial support to Subjects of the Federation should be subject to rigid budgetary constraints. As was said earlier, any revenue that local authorities can raise by their own efforts or save from their budgets must not be confiscated by higher-level budgets, and neither should losses or debts be compensated by additional financial aid. The first point can be met by separating taxation powers and distributing financial aid not according to the actual tax take but on the basis of the tax potential (which lags two to three years behind the current budget year). To meet the second point it is necessary to gradually reduce, if not abolish outright, the funding provided to budgets of the Subjects of the Federation for reciprocal settlements, and all budgetary loans. The former can be replaced by specific types of targeted financial aid (via the Compensation Fund, for example) approved under formulas for the coming budget year. The latter can be replaced by non-returnable financial aid and/or long-term loans from the contingency fund in the event a Subject suffers a financial emergency or is declared to be in financial crisis (according to objective criteria of what constitutes an emergency or a crisis); in such a case, temporary restrictions on the budgetary powers of the regional administration will also be introduced. As long as there is still even a theoretical possibility of gaining anything like substantial funding from additional aid from the federal budget, the authorities in many regions will not make the effort needed to manage their budgets efficiently and responsibly.

The final set of reforms will regulate the management of regional finances. Federal legislation must clearly set out common minimum requirements for territorial budgets, the budget process and, in a number of cases, budgetary policy. At the same time we must be careful to avoid excessive regulation and legislation which either is unenforceable (or where compliance cannot be monitored) or has no significant effect on the overall state of the budget system.

All budget levels must adopt treasury-based execution. However, hurrying all transfer-recipient regions into reliance on the services of the Federal Treasury might only delay the creation of a common treasury system of budgetary execution, because it would require an enormous one-off investment, increase the risks of sub-optimal solutions and lead to an increase in 'informal' regional budgets. Subjects of the Federation (unless highly subsidised or in financial crisis) must be given the right to choose between using the services of the Federal Treasury or setting up, within a given time limit, their own treasuries in accordance with common federal standards.

Federal legislation must pay particular attention to ensuring that regional and local authorities meet their obligations to public, budget-funded organisations and lenders. Therefore legislative regulation of the deficit and debt levels of regional and local budgets must be retained. However, it must be appreciated that investment in public infrastructure must be funded by borrowing and not from current revenues. Public infrastructure is generally designed to serve several generations of taxpayers, and borrowing to invest brings in future consumers of those services to help pay for them. That being so, the existing quantitative restrictions on regional borrowing policy, which are not nearly always helpful to the investment process, must be replaced with qualitative requirements.

In addition to minimum federal requirements, the federal government must support the voluntary compliance of regional and local authorities with higher standards of quality in management and budgetary policy. The federal level must devise and maintain a Code of Practice which runs ahead of what legislation demands. Subjects of the Federation and municipalities that comply with the Code must have access to additional funds provided from the federal budget (the Fund for the Development of Regional Finances), international financial organisations (IBRD and European Bank for Reconstruction and Development (EBRD) investment loans), private investors and lenders (as they gain an official credit rating) and so on. To that end the federal level must create a system to monitor the creditworthiness and quality of management of regional finances.

Regional or local authorities that fail to discharge their financial obligations or comply with the demands of federal legislation in relation to budgetary management should, and in certain prescribed cases must, be subjected by the federal government to a regime of outside financial management.

Local and municipal budgets

The proposed reform must extend to all levels of the budget system, including local budgets. But doing so requires a solution to a very serious problem.

The Budget and Tax Codes specify a three-tier tax system. The tiers are the Federation, the regions (meaning the Subjects of the Federation) and the local level (meaning municipalities, in accordance with the law on the general principles of organisation of local self-government). In fact, we have two levels of local public authority and consequently two levels of local budget, one of which is 'outside the law'. That does not mean it should not exist, just that it is not provided for in federal legislation. In most Subjects of the Federation, municipality status is given to towns and cities that were formerly subordinate to the *oblast* and to administrative districts. The latter contain smaller administrative units – district towns, villages and rural administrations – that have appointed or elected authorities and quasi-budgets (spending estimates). In certain Subjects of the Federation, and entirely in accordance with federal legislation and the nature of local self-government, municipal status is enjoyed by hundreds of population centres, above which are territorial entities (like the old districts), usually with chiefs appointed from above and quasi-budgets of their own. There are some even more complicated schemes comprising two levels of municipality, one of which has lost some of its powers.

In whatever way Subjects of the Federation may have tried to adapt to the clashes with federal legislation, the results are wretched. First, citizens' rights to local self-government are infringed. This may be because at 'village' level (which includes some fairly large district towns with populations as large as *oblast* towns) no full-fledged budget exists; or it may be because there are several hundred local budgets that cannot be accommodated in any remotely unified system of separation of taxation and budgetary powers and budget equalisation as they are totally dependent on the regional authority. Second, constitutional principle notwithstanding, local self-government (at the district level particularly) is overwhelmed with state functions that it should not properly have. That, on the one hand, blurs responsibility for implementation and, on the other, undermines the whole idea of self-government. Third, when an entire level of the budget system is 'invisible' to the law, that is hugely damaging for the management of the public finances as it forces regional and local authorities to manage their budgets by a variety of ruses and contrivances. Fourth, the established and generally perfectly sensible two-tier territorial organisation of social infrastructure is left in suspended animation. Finally, it is impossible to arrive at even a framework decision for top-to-bottom decentralisation of the budget system because the 'municipal level' is too high in some regions and too low (or simply undefined) in others for the same tax and budget powers.

So what is the solution? In our view there is no reason why one level of the budget system should be kept hidden. It exists. It is necessary. It should be properly captured in the Budgetary Code. At the very minimum the Subjects of the Federation should be given the right to decide for themselves how many levels their budget systems should comprise. The Constitutional Court has repeatedly ruled that Subjects of the Federation may create a third ('local') level of state power with elected representatives and executive organs. In accordance with the generally recognised principles of the budget structure the local level must have independent budgets, and tax and budget powers including power to regulate the relationship with municipal-level budgets. In those places where local self-government is already organised on a communal basis, this local level will resurrect the district level of the budget system. In Subjects of the Federation where local self-government is organised on the territorial principle, it suffices to give the current large municipalities the tax and budget powers of the territorial organs of state power and permit the creation of municipalities (with full-fledged local budgets) at the level of individual settlements. Once all the powers of local self-government have passed to the lowest level of the budget system, the territorial municipalities will carry out only local government functions and could if necessary be transformed into administrative-territorial entities with 'state' status.

In this way a new intermediate level of the budget system will appear between the regional and the municipal ('settlement') levels. For convenience it would be helpful to call this *local* (budgets, taxes and property), retaining the term *municipal* for local self-government.

Territorially, this local level would comprise administrative-territorial entities directly belonging to a Subject of the Federation and named in its constitution or charter. They would be the same as the old districts and, probably, *oblast*-subordinated towns. They would have the status of either 'state' administrative-territorial entities or 'large' municipal entities (either way, their authorities would be elected and not appointed). Their tax and budget powers and functions would be either those of the state (at the third, local level) only or simultaneously 'local' state and municipal (local self-government) powers, in the transitional period. In the longer term they would have mainly state powers, although large cities could retain dual status or even have two elected organs of power and two budgets, one local and one municipal.

There are two ways such a system could be developed. In one, tax and budget legislation would allow the delegation of the expenditure and tax powers of Subjects of the Federation to the executive organs of administrative-territorial entities which belong directly to the Subject (irrespective of their status; the sole requirement would be the existence of elected organs of public power). In the other, the Tax and Budget Codes would set out minimum taxation and spending powers for administrative-territorial entities belonging to Subjects of the Federation. Just as in the first option, these might be organs of local self-government or the 'local' organs of the state. Additional powers could be delegated to them by the regional authorities, but the de facto creation of a sub-regional level of the budget system with its own powers and autonomy guaranteed by federal legislation is something that absolutely must happen.

Each option has advantages and disadvantages. Option one enables Subjects of the Federation to determine their own degree of budgetary decentralisation in the light of local circumstances and requires no fundamental amendments to tax or budgetary legislation; however, it does not guarantee the autonomy of the local level of the budget system. Option two does provide autonomy but may not be entirely suitable for local circumstances and a number of legal difficulties will have to be resolved, including changing the structure of the Budgetary and Tax Codes.

Which is chosen will have a significant effect on how, and how fast, inter-budgetary relations can be reformed. For instance, under option one all taxation and spending powers not allocated to the federal or municipal level must be regional powers. Common sense suggests that sooner or later Subjects of the Federation will delegate purely local expenditure (on schools, primary medical care, etc.) and taxation powers (in respect of corporate tax, for example) to the local level. But the transitional period is likely to take too long. As things stand there are more arguments in favour of option two. If it is adopted, the spending powers of the local (sub-regional) level must be clearly spelled out in the Budgetary Code and industry-specific legislation, and adequate tax and taxation powers must be spelled out in the Tax Code.

Quite possibly there are other approaches too. But in any event this is a problem and it needs addressing. Otherwise reform will again be stymied by relations between the Federation and the Subjects. The problem is not so much a lack of attention to local budgets as the indeterminacy of the current budget structure at sub-regional level.

Many of the problems and solutions we consider above were outlined in the Strategy for the Development of Russia to 2010. It is expected that the detail will be filled in by the relevant section of the government programme for the socio-economic development of Russia 2002/04 which is now [2001] in preparation. However, the matter is so significant, complex and, without exaggeration, crucial to the development of the country that a special programme for the development of budgetary federalism in Russia in the period to 2005 is, in our opinion, imperative. Such a programme would be a follow-on to the Concept for the Reform of Inter-Budgetary Relations 1999/2001, which demonstrated that consensus and co-ordinated action among different branches and levels of power were a vital condition of successful reform. The tripartite Working Group on Improvement of Inter-Budgetary Relations has worked hard on these problems for three years and dealt with its tasks well. That unique experience must not be lost. Newer, larger problems should be addressed now by turning the tripartite Working Group into a commission made up of representatives of the government, the administration of the President of the Russian Federation, the State Duma, the Subjects of the Federation and municipalities. Its principal task should be to devise and implement a programme for the development of budgetary federalism in the period to 2005.

The fuel and energy complex

From Vedomosti, *22 March 2000:*

The fuel and energy complex is a vital reserve of national wealth, but also one reason we are so poor. This paradox has arisen because Russia's natural resources are so in demand from the rest of the world that the poor Russian economy can no longer afford them. Make them cheaper at home and the lower price will mean other countries buy them up. Make them more expensive and both industry and the population at large will be ruined. Stop the flow abroad, put up taxes and duties on cheap exports, and the budget becomes a hostage of the energy industry – and if the energy industry sneezes the whole country gets a cold. As long as the fuel and energy complex has only a fiscal function, of providing a third of the revenue of the consolidated budget, there can be no evolution and no progress.

So you deny outright the fiscal role of the fuel and energy complex?

Of course the state of the public treasury cannot be forgotten. But that function cannot be seen as the only possible one. Why, when high energy prices lead to the emergence of new energy-saving technologies everywhere else in the world, do they become a burden on the budget in Russia? Because there is no state-regulated means of compelling businesses to be economical with the national wealth. Maintaining the same level of energy consumption while energy saving stands still and domestic energy prices are kept down is just subsidising stagnation. It would be better to compensate businesses for investing in energy-saving measures than to tolerate their continual profligacy. According to experts, Russia could increase total output by 50 per cent or 100 per cent in ten years. That rise cannot be achieved without a drastic improvement in energy efficiency.

Are you looking for any quick fixes?

The main thing this year is to increase the level of cash settlements among industries in the fuel and energy complex. We can already boast some successes. At the beginning of last year [1999] 15 per cent of goods despatched were paid for by cash settlement at RJSC Unified Energy System (RJSC UES). By the end of the year it was 40 per cent. At Gazprom cash settlements for goods despatched rose from 20 per cent to 32 per cent. At Transneft the proportion of cash settlements is far higher.

Figure 2.12 The energy complex

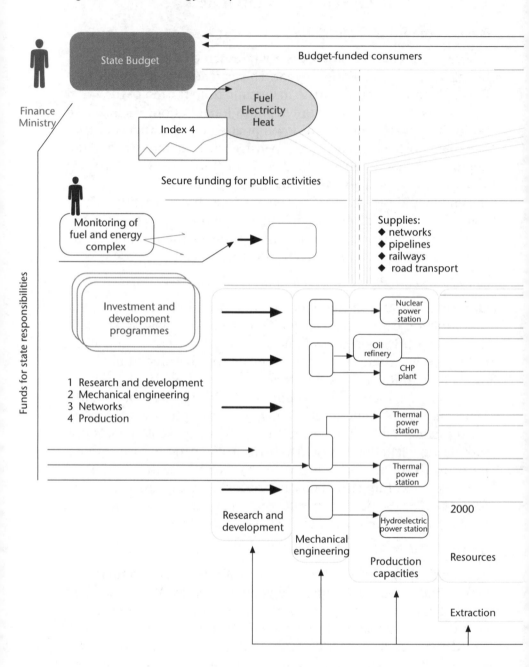

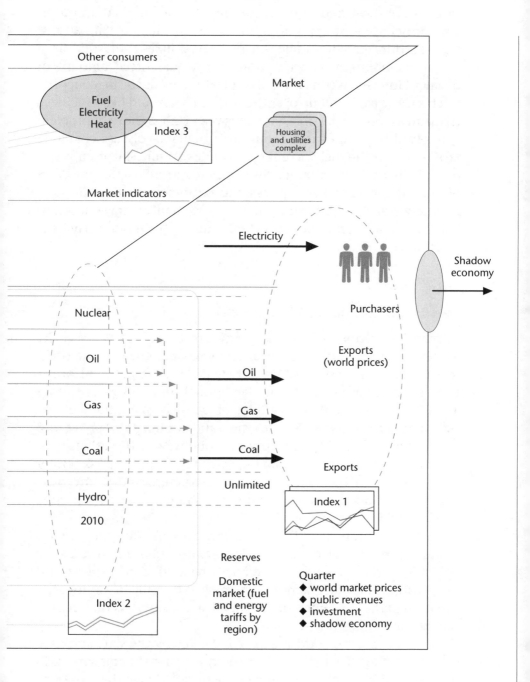

The right not to be disconnected does not give anyone the right to consume heat and light in unlimited, uncontrolled amounts. One principle must apply to all: how much can the state afford? Non-disconnectability must mean two simple things: a fixed physical amount of consumption and a guaranteed amount of payment for what is consumed. The ideal aim would be to reduce the electricity arrears built up over the past years. I would like to achieve that aim as soon as possible, even this year. Unless the debt problem is resolved we cannot talk about tariff policy or discuss changing tariff levels in the fuel and energy complex. While Gazprom is still owed RUB 108 billion by its customers – and RJSC UES has debts of around the same size – prices and tariffs for energy cannot be remotely realistic. All tariffs contain an element to cover accumulated debts, so tariff policy and eliminating debt and non-payment must proceed in parallel.

Tariff policy

Speech to the State Duma, 6 February 2002:

Russian Federation policy on energy tariffs and energy security for the economy and the social sphere is designed to maintain macro-economic and social stability, enable structural transformations in the economy and stimulate growth in industry and other areas of the national economy. Such objectives can be attained only by bringing the interests of consumers and natural monopolies into something like equilibrium. Any bias one way or the other, such as may arise as a result of lobbying by different groups, risks either propping up an ineffective economic structure and disincentivising production or creating resource constraints on both economic growth and social security.

There are some fuels and oil products today which are not products of natural monopolies, so their prices are not subject to direct state regulation. Yet a competitive market, regulation of exports and non-tariff means of regulation have made it possible to improve the situation in the consumer market for oil and oil products and rein in the increase in fuel prices.

Natural gas prices continue to be regulated by the state and were subjected to artificial restraint in the hope that the Russian 'dash for gas' would help the development of other parts of the economy. As a result, gas is currently half the price of coal and four and a half times cheaper than fuel oil. The illusion of unlimited cheap energy keeps business technologically backward, subsidises its often unproductive spending and encourages wasting of energy. That is energy we are, in essence, stealing from future generations. Depressing the price of natural gas has inevitably increased the demand for it.

The structure of fuel and energy consumption for thermal electricity correlates directly with the overall structure of energy consumption in the Russian economy as a whole. You can take different periods and compare the relative changes in gas prices, electricity tariffs and industrial and consumer prices. The numbers come out differently depending on what date you take as the base line, but it is clear what is going on. In the regulated economy the problem of fixed assets getting old and having to be retired is becoming worse and worse. It is not as if energy efficiency has improved either.

At its session of 24 January the government of the Russian Federation considered how and when to vary tariffs on the products and services of natural monopolies. It decided it was possible to raise gas prices and electricity tariffs as follows:

◆ Gas prices will rise from 15 February 2002.
◆ The RJSC UES subscription rate will rise by 20.2 per cent from 1 January.
◆ The tariff for electricity from the Federal Wholesale Market in Electricity and Capacity (FOREM) will rise by 20 per cent from 1 March 2002.

Those are the main price parameters of tariff policy which the Russian Federation government has adopted in relation to energy. Before that the government had considered in general terms the macro-economic constraints associated with the regulation of natural monopolies and specified a maximum increase of 35 per cent. You can see that the government decided to raise prices less than it could have within the declared ceiling.

These are difficult decisions. What principles have we followed?

First, tariff policy must be predictable and transparent. Economic stability is equally necessary for the government – it affects everything from the budget to social obligations and the meeting of economic targets – the population and economic actors because it also makes budgeting more predictable, reduces the risks of running a business and improves the climate for investment. The government takes a fairly cautious approach to increasing prices for the products and services of natural monopolies. Bargaining of any sort in tariff-setting is unacceptable in principle and must never be allowed to happen. Our decisions are in line with the medium-term strategy for the development of the economy within forecast indicators and do not go beyond the parameters underlying the approved federal budget for 2002.

Second, investment programmes must be developed to prevent or remove the resource and structural constraints on economic growth. Genuine economic growth in the country and structural reorganisation are impossible without proper supplies of energy to consumers, particularly if you consider the poor energy efficiency of most of the economy and local public utilities. The natural monopolies justify increased tariffs for their products and services with reference to extreme problems of the obsolescence of fixed assets and the urgent need for modernisation and extra extraction, generation and transportation capacity. That takes money, and the gas and electricity industries can get it from the consumer, or by making substantial savings, or from investors if they can make themselves attractive enough prospects. Progress in this area will be achieved by reforming the natural monopolies, getting rid of non-core assets and optimising and prioritising investment programmes. For the last two months the government has been reviewing the investment programmes of both Gazprom and RAO UES of Russia. We have succeeded, to a certain extent, in moderating their appetites and establishing a system of investment programme priorities – and that was in fact taken into account in our decisions on the parameters of tariff policy.

The third principle underlying tariff policy is its effect on the country's energy balance. The prices of coal, gas and fuel oil, in equivalent terms, stand currently in the ratio $1:0.6:2$, that is, if the price of one unit of coal is 1, gas costs 0.6 and fuel oil costs 2. That constitutes an existential threat to the coal-mining industry.

Fourth, it is necessary to allow for the highly volatile state of world energy markets. Earnings from the sale of energy on the foreign market are an important way of not only raising revenue for the budget but also subsidising energy prices in the domestic market and covering losses on sales there. The government cannot ignore the risk of downward price movements on the world market, no matter what their nature or origins.

Any significant fall in the export price of oil takes the export price of gas with it, albeit with a delay of six to nine months. It is patently obvious even now that the trend in the oil export price in the last few months since October [2001] will produce a fall of at least 30 per cent in the gas export price compared with now [February 2002].

Around the middle of the year the Russian Federation government will consider, as is its normal routine, whether further changes to the gas price or electricity tariffs in 2002 are appropriate. It will take account of its analysis of the macro-economic indicators of the development of the Russian Federation, its assessment of the financial and economic state of the natural monopolies (both on the results of 2001 as recorded in their annual reports and on the basis of the 'quick-look' information for 2002), and its assessment of the state of energy consumers. As well as reviewing the investment programmes of the natural monopolies, the government will take equal care to assess their executive budgets. We will not, however, ignore the situation regarding payments for energy consumption. There is no point increasing tariffs and prices if monopoly holders are unable to collect payment from consumers of all types. Otherwise we re-enter a vicious circle of virtual figures and the shadow economy. Neither will we lose sight of such things as the energy efficiency of both industry and the public utilities sector and, indeed, the gas and energy industries themselves, nor, of course, targeted social subsidies for particular groups and categories of people.

Energy strategy

From Itogi, *10 June 2003:*

Russia's growing GDP is directly linked to the implementation of the Energy Strategy. The fuel and energy complex produces over a quarter of GDP, half of national exports and a good half of budgetary revenue. The Energy Strategy provides for development of the fuel and energy complex in two phases. Up to 2010 it will continue to provide the driving force for the rest of the economy. Thereafter the burden of leadership will fall on the shoulders of the petrochemical and other sectors. The thinking is that the next seven years will see the creation of the conditions for catch-up growth by the non-primary sectors of the economy, with the fuel and energy complex becoming a sort of backstop that lends stability to the economy as a whole. If we can manage to achieve all that, GDP might very well grow at the President's target rate.

Why was there so much such kicking and screaming over the adoption of the Energy Strategy?'

This document has had a long and difficult gestation. Not only has it been under discussion for years but it has been completely rewritten twice. The first version took the Gosplan approach of spelling out in detail every last check and balance. What was actually needed was a document laying down approaches and an overall line of development. Then you would have something on which to base programmes – industry-specific ones (for example in the coal industry or power engineering), corporate ones (for RJSC UES or Gazprom), or ones covering more than one industry (licensing arrangements) and so on. Then on that basis there would be specific projects. The task of strategy is to co-ordinate the two main lines of development – socio-economic processes and the development of the fuel and energy complex itself. Meanwhile, external factors resulted in two basic development scenarios in the strategy, one optimistic and one moderate. The first supposes that by 2020 GDP will be a whopping 3.2 times what it is now and the second, more modestly, 2.4 times. As regards the domestic agenda, the main task is to make the Russian economy more energy efficient. Russia's GDP is still two or three times more energy intensive than that of developed countries with comparable natural and climatic conditions. In that sense the task of doubling energy efficiency by 2020 looks to be no less ambitious than achieving the increase in GDP – and no less difficult.

Why is Russia such a glutton for energy?'

Because we are so resource-rich. That is also why the domestic market is badly priced. The first to break out of this situation was the oil sector in 1992. It was followed by coal, although that admittedly required the whole industry to be profoundly restructured. And the gas sector has hardly changed at all. There is not even a medium-term prospect of Russia managing to have a competitive gas market. That means the state will have to keep a closer eye on it to ensure that, on the one hand, independent gas companies are not discriminated against and, on the other, the appetites of the gas monopoly don't run away with it. The treatment currently prescribed by the government is not just a diet but a starvation diet. We are not meeting the costs of producing and transporting gas within Russia: Gazprom covers them itself from its profits on gas exports. Will that continue indefinitely? Of course not, because the conditions are not being created for the development of independent gas production and distribution networks. As a result, we risk finding ourselves without gas soon. Gas must be used more efficiently, for example by adopting combined-cycle gas turbine electricity-generating technology which is 50 per cent or 100 per cent more efficient than what we have now. But at current raw material prices no one will spend on new equipment if they can help it. Neither is there any sign of a desire to rationalise the structure of fuel consumption by, for example, using more coal. Why should there be, when gas is so cheap? In the strategy, by the way, the gas price trend to 2006 is moving towards $35–39 per cubic metre, reaching $45–49 per cubic metre in 2010, as against $23 per cubic metre today. The state's regulatory function will be extended to gas transmission over the same period.

Let us move on to oil. What have you got to say about the situation on the world oil market since the Iraq war? Has there been any major rearrangement of spheres of influence? What do the changes mean for Russia?

The predictions by some analysts of fantastic oil price rises to $80 a barrel and then a collapse have been proved wrong. That is, the consequences of the Iraq war have so far not been fatal, though they might be in the medium term if Iraq not only recovers but increases its oil output. A return to the previous capacity (1.5 million barrels a day or 75 million tonnes a year) would not in itself cause serious difficulties for the rest of the market. Even that will need more than the restoration of Iraq's oil complex: the whole industry – who produces how, and who trades Iraqi oil and on what terms – needs to be legitimised. It would be a different matter if Iraq seriously upped its production. It could be producing 300 million tonnes a year in 2006/08. That would be serious. As Iraq is a member, OPEC will come under increasing pressure from the US. The pressure on OPEC could affect Russia as well. And all that while the world market demand for crude oil is stagnating.

Perhaps OPEC will simply cease to exist or, conversely, a new global organisation of petroleum-exporting countries will be created that has Russia as a member?

I don't think so. OPEC came through the Iraq crisis by avoiding becoming politicised. Can it resist any possible pressure from, say, Iraq? Time will tell, but the chances are that it can. Will there be a new OPEC? I personally am not a believer in a global cartel. There is no logic: it would have to include the oil consumers as well and the result would be a sort of global Gosplan. I do hope it doesn't come to that. The OPEC of today is necessary to many, including Russia. It is helpful to us to be able to monitor the state of the market via such an organisation. It must also be borne in mind that the global trend towards consolidation of oil companies in turn keeps risks down.

How then can the risks to the Russian economy be minimised?

First, the risks to the oil sector can be covered by the sector's own profitability. The sovereign risks are more difficult. That is also why we set store by structural changes in the economy, so that the fuel and energy complex isn't the only mainstay. Second, the transportation of Russian energy will develop in various directions, for example, to the East (meaning the Asia-Pacific region via the Angarsk–Nakhodka pipeline with an offshoot to Daqing), the Baltic and Europe (the Adriatic and the northern route to the Kola peninsula and a possible route into the northern European and North American markets). Third, we must balance output and reserves. There are two schools of thought. The first says we should cut output because the reserves are not as great as they seem, and 350 million tonnes a year is the right production level (for comparison, this year we produced 400 million tonnes). The other says we should increase output without regulation of any sort. The government shunned extremes and decided output should rise gradually towards 450 million tonnes by 2010. For gas the amount is 680–720 billion cubic metres a year. That level will have to be maintained for 30 to 50 years. That can be done only if we invest in exploring new fields and replenishing the reserves. Fourth, we must increase energy efficiency. We have already spoken about that. All I would add is that special attention must go to developing nuclear energy. Its share will rise from 15 per cent to 20 per cent.

You mentioned the consolidation trend in the petroleum industry. Which companies will merge next?

The trend is associated with the globalisation of all markets, not just the oil market. You see the same thing happening in steel and car making. In a way it is a response to the state of the global economy, which is increasingly operating according to common supra-national rules. There is no doubt that Yukos and Sibneft combined will be much stronger in the foreign market: experts estimate that the merged company has the world's third-largest oil reserves, fourth-largest oil output and seventh-largest market capitalisation. Let me say something about the consequences for the domestic market. The Russian oil market has never been competitive in the full sense of the word. Whether it has ten large companies operating in it or only five is not especially important. At most it creates work for the anti-monopoly authority, which will have to keep a beadier eye on them.

You voiced some doubts about whether the Western Siberia–Murmansk pipeline should be built by Russian companies. What do you think of the idea of non-state-owned trunk pipelines in principle?

About 110,000 km of oil pipeline in Russia belongs to private companies. They are not small pipelines either but up to 700 mm diameter pipes moving oil as required within fields, connecting to trunk pipelines and linking fields. The Transneft pipeline system is about half that size, but it is the trunk network. Still, not all trunk pipelines are controlled by the state: the Caspian Pipeline Consortium, for example, has its own export facilities, but it is something of an exception. The policy of the state is that the state is directly responsible for infrastructure (transport in the widest sense). That is because infrastructure creates the conditions for the activities of all parts of the economy and to a great extent determines the opportunities for business in the country, and even the very integrity of the state. I am convinced that if in 1992, when privatisation was at its height and we were handing out sovereignty to the Subjects of the Russian Federation, we had thrown infrastructure into the melting pot as well, we would now be living in a different country. The frame of pipes, rails and cables helped save Russia from collapse; it became the country's skeleton. State-owned infrastructure is integral to energy, economic and military security. Remember there are different types of infrastructure. It is not just pipelines but roads and so on.

For some reason no one wants to invest money in roads. Even the road tax provokes protests. But everyone's mad keen on pipelines. So the development and management of the trunk pipeline system is something that the state will deal with.

Is there enough money?

Sometimes there isn't. At one time there was even a programme to cannibalise old pumping stations (about a hundred of them) for parts, which reduced the pipeline capacity. But in 1999 we came to our senses, the station closure programme was wound up and we embarked on a process that was the direct opposite. Today the government has plans for a whole range of revenue-raising projects, but it may be that there still isn't enough money. There is a need for private investment. How can it be raised? By enticing potential investors to give some form of syndicated loan or by offering investors oil transport options in return for putting up money. There could be many different forms of co-operation.

What will happen to the project to build an oil pipeline from Angarsk to Nakhodka and Daqing to serve the Japanese and Chinese markets? The route has changed several times.

The overall decision on the project is that it will be built along the Angarsk–Nakhodka route with a separate line off it to Daqing. But both Nakhodka and Daqing can be reached in various ways. Work is now going on to produce feasibility studies and select the route. For Nakhodka we need capacity of at least 50 million tonnes of oil a year. I think that can realistically be achieved in 15 years. Daqing will take around 30 million tonnes a year.

The oil complex

From Vedomosti, *25 March 2002:*

You cannot say there is any universal formula for cuts as if you only had to input a set of parameters, turn a handle and out pops a number, say 144,000 barrels or 82,000 barrels. We analyse trends in the economies of consumer countries and the reserves of oil held in industrialised countries' reservoirs and add in the state of the domestic and CIS markets. Of course world oil prices are an integrated figure. If Brent crude goes above $25 a barrel, that is a reason to think about squeezing the market supply. The Western European and American markets growing consistently with GDP growth over 2 per cent is also a clear signal that demand is on the up. The situation in the domestic market is also important to us: demand for oil products traditionally surges in the sowing season in agriculture and the holiday period in Russia and the CIS. If current trends of industrial and consumer demand continue, then we will be able to make more accurate predictions of export volumes in the third quarter.

From Izvestiya, *8 June 2001*:

The oil companies must rise to the challenges of globalisation. They must consolidate if they want to compete with the largest global companies, so there will be mergers and acquisitions. A second process is rationalisation of refineries. As of today we have only low-level oil refining capacity, which means we cannot truly compete in petrochemicals. Developing better oil refining capabilities will be the way ahead for all oil companies. There is no doubt that as that development proceeds, the oil and gas businesses will separate.

We want to see an end to the existing price discrimination and restricted access to the gas pipeline network. Expanding the petrochemicals end of the oil and gas sector will allow us to replace imports in a very wide range of goods in the domestic market. That process will be accompanied by the expansion of oil and gas companies into petrochemical capacities in neighbouring countries, not least in Europe. That level of ambition is feasible only for large organisations.

Figure 2.13 The place of vertically integrated companies in the oil complex

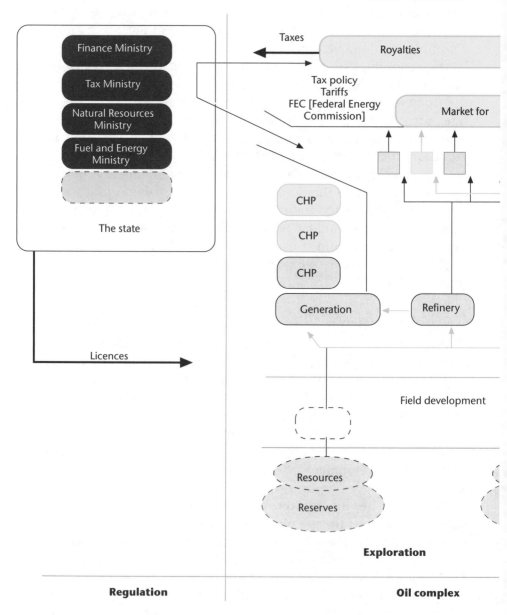

CHP: Combined heat and power.

of the oil complex

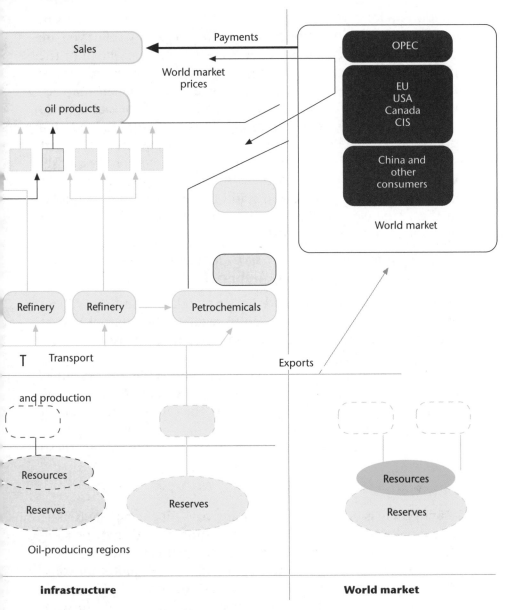

Sales

Payments

World market prices

oil products

OPEC

EU
USA
Canada
CIS

China and
other
consumers

World market

Refinery

Refinery

Petrochemicals

T Transport

Exports

and production

Resources

Reserves

Reserves

Resources

Reserves

Oil-producing regions

infrastructure

World market

213

Oil exports

From Novaya gazeta, *21–27 August 2000:*

Should we perhaps just sell it all? I suppose that will be the first question up for consideration by the new commission on the principles of the distribution of Russia's export capabilities. But you are making a fetish of pipelines. That is not the main problem of the fuel and energy complex. The problem is not the pipeline, but the price differential between the domestic and the foreign markets, which means that everyone tries to send all their oil abroad and none of it remains here. Everyone gains from exports. To fend off a catastrophe in the domestic market, the government has to resort to various regulatory mechanisms. But we cannot afford to quickly bring the domestic price into line with the world price. Neither the people nor the economy could stand it. And as for selling quotas on the exchanges, that is no more than a good anti-corruption mechanism and as such a good PR move.

Our government is in dire need of such PR. Articles on corruption in the Russian oil business appear every week in the West.

Of course this is something we have to work at – and we will. So far, of the three things we can do to regulate the internal market by economic means while it is disconnected from the world market price, we have achieved one and a half.

One achievement is that we have learned to apply export duties to both crude oil and refined products, thus taking some of the excess profits on exports for the budget. The oil industry has fallen into line, though the companies protest out of habit. But export duties are not sufficient to solve the problem, because they are so inelastic.

And second?

Second, there is ensuring the economy pays for the energy it uses. We are halfway to doing that. We must understand that the state has to be absolutely responsible for its budget. Currently the state itself is guilty of non-payment because its budget quotes unrealistically low prices for the energy it intends to consume. Therefore, since the beginning of the current year, we have started to work on a financial process for paying for budget holders' consumption of fuels and energy. That will be complete by the end of the year.

The next step, once that budgetary process is up and running, will be to increase the budget for payments for fuel and energy. If I want, say, three light bulbs for a military unit in Udmurtiya and that is approved, then the budget should provide three roubles for three bulbs, provided that the financial process can guarantee that that sum will be spent on light bulbs and will go to RJSC UES so that it then has real money which it can use to buy petrochemicals.

The boss of RJSC UES, Mr Chubais, told us that at the moment the public sector is paying for only 60 per cent of the electricity it uses. That is shocking.

But true. We create the deficit ourselves and do not balance the budget, which sets off a chain of non-payments in the economy. Well, we are trying to do something about that from the fourth quarter of this year [2000] by providing an extra RUB 6 billion to meet payments for fuel and energy.

So we have tackled the problem of duties and in the budget we have a half-finished job, but the third measure has so far got nowhere. We need a system for stockpiling oil reserves, which does not exist in this country. As a result we are unable to insure against spikes in demand on the domestic market which cause shortages and increase prices. There is always a shortage of diesel fuel. As soon as there's good weather, people go to the seaside and the country runs short of petrol. Such surges in demand lead to shortages and price hikes for petrol and other fuel because the oil companies have no spare output to divert to the domestic market. Everything is committed under long-term contracts. We will have to stockpile oil products so that they can be put onto the market to meet demand peaks. That will certainly need money from the budget – perhaps $200–300 million. We need stockpiles of 300–500,000 tonnes of petrol and around a million tonnes of diesel.

Once all three measures are in place I will be able to rely on a range of levers and can stop worrying about the situation in the domestic market, provided that the system of payments is fully functional. Today we have completed one and a half out of three tasks, so we are stuck with having to deal with the remaining task and a half by administrative interventions. Yes, it's bad. And unbalanced budgets are also bad. But it's the best we can do for the moment. What is important is that people understand that the use of administrative measures is being reduced, and that means there is also less scope for corruption.

Oil transportation

From Vedomosti, 25 March 2002:

As chairman of the board of directors of Transneft you would like tariffs to rise, but as the member of the executive responsible for the fuel and energy complex and the national economy you have to stand for low tariffs.

If you see a contradiction there, there is something to it. That position is what enables me not to get carried to extremes by turning a conflict of interests into a communal conflict. If you represent both sides rather than just one, it is easier to tread the fine line where Transneft has enough resources to improve the efficiency of its pipelines while the burden on the consumer is not made excessive. Therefore I think that combination of roles is justified.

What do you make of the idea of giving Transneft the functions of export co-ordinator?

It is a co-ordinator already by its very existence, because most of the raw material goes by pipeline. But I see co-ordination more widely in terms of where exports go. The Ministry of Energy doesn't have to involve itself in what company is permitted to send how much out through Tuapse or via Ukraine. Exporters just sort themselves out. Public officials or Transneft don't have to go checking up on deliveries at some plant in Germany or the Czech Republic or anywhere else. The oil companies can see for themselves. We need to deal with strategy: should we lock ourselves into the European market or establish another channel to North America? Choosing to expand our markets creates a task for the economy: delivering to America is effective only in 20–300,000-tonne tankers. If we are talking about a through route to the port of Omisalj in Croatia, then we're serious. Say 5 million tonnes in the first instance, and thereafter 15 million isn't beyond the realms of possibility. But then those are completely different geographical possibilities for the country and the companies, and entirely different tanker terminals. If we cut a route to the Baltic, that's another step in a new direction. And what about, say, the South-East Asian market? Can our suppliers get a foothold in Japan, Korea or China? Where are the resources coming from for a new direction? Now that's what I call export co-ordination.

The minister of energy, Igor Yusufov, insists that his department should take over the commission on access to oil export pipelines, which currently you control.

The commission works according to established routines and no question about its terms of reference has arisen in the government. Its purpose when it was created was to work out a normative base and ensure equal access for all companies to Transneft's services. As regards exports outside the CIS, 95 per cent of the tidying up has been done. The remaining 5 per cent relates to companies that want exclusive deals from time to time. It seems that not all companies have got the message that the adopted arrangements are in earnest and meant to last, but there are almost no complaints from the companies. Another problem relates to supplies to the CIS. Some companies are still sorting out their relationships. But I think in the second quarter [of 2002] we will gradually get the design right for the distribution and regulation of supply volumes. Once the rules are clear people won't have to waste any time worrying about how much their company gets. Finally, a third concern is the transit facilities Russia offers other countries. Here there will also be clear regulation underpinned by intergovernmental agreements. On top of all this there needs to be a government order winding up this part of the commission's activity. But the commission will continue to work across a broad front. The oil companies are ever more insistent about their claims to develop gas fields. But rational investment is possible only if there is reliable access to Gazprom's pipeline. I imagine this subject will come up increasingly in the near future.

Transneft has plans to build an oil pipeline in China. Meanwhile Yukos is about to do the same thing. It is a very expensive project. Are you going to build it together? Have you been able to agree a price for oil exports with China? Is the price in line with world market prices?

This is a global project because it affects infrastructure development in Eastern Siberia and the Far East, and Russia's standing in the markets of South-East Asia. We are currently dealing with the feasibility study. We are in dialogue with China to find a workable solution. I think that we will have made a good estimate of our strategic prospects and the prospects for crude exports by the end of the year. As for Yukos's standing in the Chinese market, our efforts there concern not only pipelines but also railways. There are so many bottlenecks in transportation, and at the moment neither side is able to resolve them. Just getting that done could be the springboard to organising exports by pipeline – and finding sources of finance for the project.

217

Transneft and the members of the Caspian Pipeline Consortium have argued over the quality of the oil going into the pipeline. CPC demanded compensation. How was the oil quality bank dispute resolved?'

It was settled by the companies themselves, without government involvement. What compensation, by whom and to whom was decided by agreement. The CPC quality bank is now very attractive to us as a means of managing oil quality everywhere in Russia. Having assessed the sources and balance of sour crude, we must decide how and where it should be refined.

From Gazeta, *17 February 2003*:

Russia will not have the private pipelines that the oil industry would like to build. What it will have is this. In terms of system development, we must change pump technology. There will be a quick decision about this; a government resolution is due in March. It will also call for certain refurbishment works at one oil booster station. That will not take much time, perhaps two or three months, and around $25 million. But even before actual refurbishment we will be able within a year to increase the volume of oil pumped by 10 million tonnes a year. After the refurbishment that can be raised to 16 million tonnes.

That is the first decision currently being considered. Another concerns the investment decision about the second stage of the Baltic Pipeline System (BPS). Currently we have 12 million tonnes in stage one but are aiming at 60. This scheme will take about two years to implement. I think that if all organisational matters can be dealt with soon, then we will get 42 million tonnes out of the BPS by the end of 2004.

A third decision concerns the Far East. The government meets in mid-March to discuss pipeline construction in the light of available resources. I think the eastern segment will involve oil from not only Eastern but also Western Siberia. The fourth priority would be the north and the new projects along the Barents Sea basin to the White Sea.

So far as new pipeline projects are concerned, let me emphasise again that all options emanate from the single simple axiom that the Russian Federation's pipeline system should belong to the Russian Federation.

We have now built up an extraordinarily high rate of oil extraction. All the figures are far in advance of the estimates of a few years ago. Output is some 35–40 million tonnes higher than expected, reaching 380 million tonnes last year [2002]. Plainly at this rate we will reach 440–450 million tonnes in the next two or three years. Then the question arises of whether we want to overtake the Soviet Union and get to 600, or to do something else. My view would be that we want to do something else. Our exports already exceed those of the Soviet Union. Environmental constraints mean we cannot beat the USSR for output, and neither do we need to anyway. Therefore I think that 450 million tonnes looks like some kind of ceiling. The industry could operate pretty sustainably at that level. Then we need to very precisely assess how best to secure the country's future. Whenever we make decisions about the development of transport capacity, terminal complexes or anything else, we must keep our feet firmly on the ground and know what is under the ground. We must think about what will be left for our descendants – our children and our children's children and grandchildren.

From Ekonomika, *July 2002:*

Ensuring that all exporters have equal access to the trunk pipeline network is no easy task. But today's chosen mechanism is such that, ultimately, decisions are arrived at by objective criteria and the scope for subjectivity is minimised. The tensions that still remain can be explained by extraneous constraints, which at least offer a necessary breathing space in which to sort out the situation and start to modify the map of our points of contact with foreign consumers.

It is worth remembering that last year the fuel and energy complex saw a record amount of building and the emergence of greater-than-ever opportunities for the Russian energy industry in the foreign trade area. New transport routes like the Baltic Pipeline System, the Sukhodolnaya–Rodionovskaya pipeline and the Caspian Pipeline Consortium, and agreements to build a new gas pipeline through Poland, open new opportunities for a strong, confident policy in our relations with foreign partners. By actively embracing a new, pragmatic approach we are preparing the ground for negotiations on any number of issues. The state must play the leading role in everything to do with the fuel and energy complex. That means establishing the rules of the game for economic players, strictly in accordance with the law and in line with the national interest. Some great strides were made in 2001; I don't just mean access to the trunk pipeline network but also the export tariff scale and the amount of revenue collected for the budget. Matters of mutual relations with operating companies are always complex. There may be misunderstandings or resistance to any change initiated by the state. But in any event we proceed on the basis of mutual respect for each other's interests. Investment in development and retooling is an interest shared by the government and the companies. So is a fair global oil price. The past year has shown that we can act together.

From Izvestiya, *8 June 2001:*

So far as Transneft is concerned, there is not the slightest point talking about privatisation. Even the decision on privileged shares should be amended. Transneft, in my view, must remain a state-owned company with its own sources of development. The company's monopoly position and political salience are natural. I cannot see any grounds for even partial privatisation or any reasons, even fiscal ones, for taking such a decision.

There are two problems in terms of access to the pipeline network. They are the technical limit on the volume that can be carried and the need to determine who can be allowed access to this limited resource and on what terms. The basic principle is equality of access. The Commission on Access to Export Pipelines will need another two or three months to dot all the i's and cross all the t's.

Thereafter there will no further need for special decisions in individual cases: the system will operate automatically. As for auctions, well, there are things which have to do with certain needs of the state – intergovernmental agreements, special programmes and so on. The question arises of who all that should be entrusted to. According to the letter of the law it has to be decided on a competitive basis.

I think the needs of the state might amount to about 2.5–3 million tonnes of oil per year. Whether the competition should be closed or open will depend on the purpose. We are currently working on a government order that adopts a scale of export duties which the customs authority can then apply automatically.

Six months ago I quoted a figure of 15–20 million tonnes. That has gone down for a number of reasons. First, there are some balances carried forward. The companies determine quarter by quarter how much oil to extract and how much to send for export. Export volumes have a clear linkage to export routes. For various reasons, for example the weather at Novorossiysk or a break in the performance of contracts for financial reasons, a quantity of oil may remain unsold and automatically be carried forward to the next quarter. But why should all the risks of one particular company be borne by all the others? If you want to use Novorossiysk you have to be aware that it might suffer rough weather. By banning carried-forward balances and getting rid of the cause, we have created a more transparent scheme.

There remains the question of above-estimate, above-plan output, which used to be auctioned off. It turns out that we are producing three different balances to account for quarterly oil output. One is submitted by the company and exaggerates output in order to secure additional export rights. The Ministry of Energy produces its own estimate, which is always lower. And there is a third type, the forecast. I proposed to the working group that we should summon the representatives of the oil companies – and now there is a proposal to end the discussion about above-plan output in the second quarter of the year and start using a single balance. It will be based on applications from the companies. It will work like this: they apply, are granted equal access and get on and export. But if they don't produce the stated output or don't put it into the system, then the amount of underproduction is forfeited in the next quarter and a sanction is applied.

The gas complex

From Gazeta, *17 February 2003:*

If we are talking about the prospects for the development – I hesitate to use the word *reform* – of the gas industry in Russia, there are several serious concerns for the country as a whole and the industry in particular. Gas today is a resource belonging not to Gazprom but, given our balance of payments, to the whole country. In essence Gazprom stands not for Gazprom but for the country. That applies to the gas resources of our immediate neighbours and partners in Asian countries. It also applies to the greater European gas market. All these factors go far beyond the parameters of discussion of, for example, public utilities.

These complexities cannot be ignored. Nobody today subscribes to the view that the Russian domestic gas price covers the costs of extraction and transportation and will support development and replenishment. No way. Of course the price today is too low. It must be raised. At least we need to indicate a trend of rising prices up to a certain date so as to achieve a level of prices which will support the normal replenishment cycle.

Why, all over the world, are monopolies being reformed? To stop them blackmailing the country and the consumer. To use competition to force them to do something about costs and price. When a monopoly starts putting up market prices we recognise that monopolies must be fought. Now let's consider our situation. Are our gas prices monopolistic? Yes, they are. If we treat the Russian gas market as a monopoly by any normal market standards and take steps to combat 'this monster', the result will be a fairly rapid and steep increase in prices. Because they have to be set at a level that will support the normal replenishment cycle. Will the consumers thank us? Certainly not. The fight against monopolies is normally fought on behalf of consumers. Our situation is the reverse. We have a monopoly gas price which is too low. And it is regulated by the state.

In this situation, what control do we have over costs? However many controllers we appoint in the shape of the Federal Energy Commission, the Ministry of Economic Development or the government, it is clear that we are not going to get the better of this leviathan around which so much revolves – even though everyone knows that the best controller of any organisation's costs is the competition. It is clear that the structural changes

Figure 2.14 Gas complex infrastructure

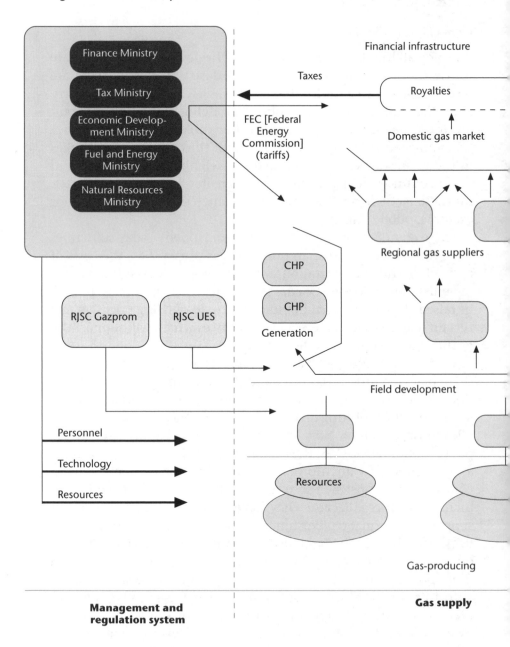

CHP: Combined heat and power.

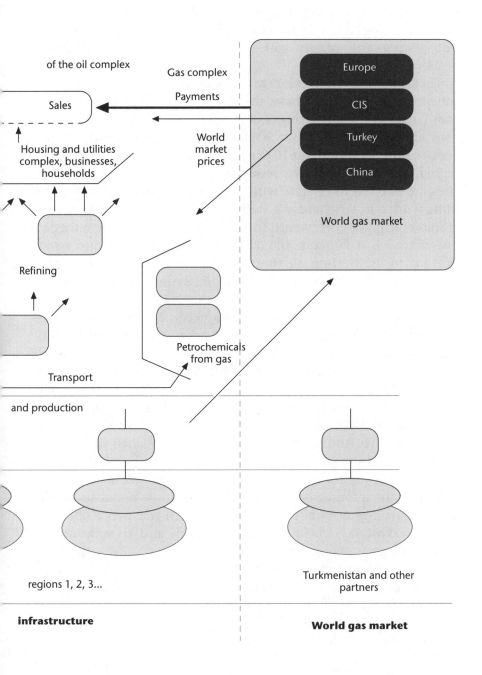

of the oil complex

Gas complex

Payments

Sales

Housing and utilities
complex, businesses,
households

World
market
prices

Europe

CIS

Turkey

China

World gas market

Refining

Petrochemicals
from gas

Transport

and production

regions 1, 2, 3...

Turkmenistan and other
partners

infrastructure

World gas market

will produce something between the two positions I have just described. Some combinations will have to do with sorting out pricing and others will deal with controlling monopoly costs.

There are also alternative gas producers. And moreover these independent producers have their hands on what by European standards are sizeable resources. By Gazprom standards, of course, they are tiny: Gazprom has 90 per cent and the rest have 10 per cent of annual output. But 10 per cent of 600 billion is a lot. Russian legislation places no price restraints on independent producers: they are allowed to operate with unregulated prices. Things don't quite work out like that for a variety of reasons: where 90 per cent is sold cheaply it is very hard to sell 10 per cent dear. Here we can only have gas if someone discovers it, builds the fields and transports it to us. Getting all that done is far more than Gazprom can do alone, so there is a place in the system for independent structures.

Apart from the independent producers, we must also take account of the interests of our Central Asian partners. That particularly concerns the development of the concentration of resources there. Gas is a global topic in the framework of the Eurasian space. Because the industry is so capital-intensive only the combination of independent gas producers on one side and co-ordination between the Russian and Central Asian resource bases on the other can be effective. And relationships must be established with transit countries (Ukraine and Belarus).

There is no question here of imperial ambitions. We do not aim to 'conquer' the resources of Central Asia. It must be understood that we are pursuing normal business interests. In that sense relations with Kazakhstan, Uzbekistan, Turkmenistan and Ukraine are all links in the same chain. We see those countries not only as providers of transit services but as countries with gas reserves of their own. Together we must think up ways of taking account of all interests. The same goes for our independent producers.

From Gazeta, *9 October 2011:*

The answer to the question whether we will or won't give Miller[9] his increases in gas tariffs will emerge in practice. A structure which

---

9   Alexey Miller was head of Gazprom at this time.

is to co-ordinate the tariffs of several monopolies will by definition operate more conservatively and less chaotically.

So Gazprom tariffs will go up, just less often?

The domestic price of gas will go up if the essential elements of Gazprom's business become more expensive, its costs are not met and so on. It would be pointless to hold prices down, if only because those factors are directly damaging to the gas producer. We do after all have to consider more than monopoly costs. We must think how to get more heat and more electricity from the same volume of gas. At present GDP grows but energy consumption grows faster. If everything is given for nothing, no one values anything and no one saves.

So this year tariffs are frozen for everyone?

What does it mean to say tariffs are or aren't frozen? It's more complicated than that. You could think of what's happening as a kind of non-indexation. What do tariffs mean generally? They are intended to let me appraise or enter into the financial position of those I regulate. Their financial position is the result not only of the level at which various tariffs are set, but also of the ways they receive tariff payments, what debts are owed to them and what debts they owe to other people. It is mainly a question of evaluating their financial position. A tariff is needed only for that. It is not some abstract thing. What is the point of increasing it, if no one is going to pay it? None. Is it worth increasing it, and if so by how much, if there are other instruments lying unused which could be used to clear up balance sheets? What in that regard is going on with Gazprom?

First, Gazprom has set about restructuring its debts to the budget, having been ordered to do so by the government. It has a clear scheme for paying its current bills and six years to clear its debts in instalments. Meaning what? Meaning, essentially, a loan from the government and – as all its penalties and fines are written off – at a negative interest rate to boot. The state, therefore, has given Gazprom a financial resource that it could have received in a different way if tariffs had been raised and the whole burden laid on the consumer. Second, the country's gas producers are this year paying off old debts as well as paying for their current supply. The overall level of payments is extremely high. Even the federal budget is trying to clear all of last year's debts this year. Third, there are active efforts, assisted by the government representatives on the board of directors, to clear up Gazprom's mass of inefficient assets.

So all this talk of Gazprom being cast adrift and forgotten about, not having its tariffs increased for years on end and so on is wrong. No one is forgotten and nothing is forgotten. Even so, for all the reasons given, it is likely that discussions on the indexation of gas tariffs could start early next year.

From Vremya MN, *15 August 2000:*

Every month Ukraine helps itself without permission to 1.2–1.5 billion cubic metres of Russian gas from the pipeline through its territory. That is becoming a threat to Russia's fuel balance. That gas is not even being paid for. In essence we are subsidising Ukrainian industry and Ukrainian consumers with Russian money. So the first task in relations with Ukraine is to produce and agree a joint gas balance. It should determine the volume of Russian gas supplied to Ukraine for transit through its territory, and ultimately the volume of commercial gas supplied. Ukraine is not exporting or re-exporting any gas. The second task is to create structures capable of monitoring the transit and gas-distribution stations in Ukraine. They must include representatives of operators operating in Europe, Gazprom's partners, because they have exposure to risks in Ukraine too. Finally we will be forced to appeal to the international financial organisations from which Ukraine receives assistance with its economic programmes.

While we are setting up a proper system to control gas transit through Ukraine, it will be possible to discuss contractual arrangements to fill the gap between how much Ukraine produces and gets paid for transit and how much it needs. Whatever the solution ultimately is, it should be arrived at by diplomacy. As for Ukraine's debt for Russian energy, so far as we are concerned it must be national debt. That is, in essence, what it is, because Gazprom on the one hand gets no money for its gas when Ukraine takes it without permission and, on the other, is itself indebted to the budget. So Ukraine's debt must be recognised as national debt and dealt with by the Paris Club or else by restructuring.

I would like to stress that the situation is teetering on the edge of an emergency and demands an urgent response. This situation must be regularised. We cannot allow our own energy security to become dependent on anything or anyone.

The coal complex

Speech to the State Council, 29 August 2002:

The coal industry is basically the only industry where restructuring has taken place with the active involvement of the state since the very early 1990s. In all that time the state took greater responsibility for the consequences of the transformations in the industry than it did in even those traditional homes of economic paternalism, the agro-industrial complex or the military-industrial complex. Suffice it to say that over $6 billion from the budget has been spent on the reform process in just the last seven years [to 2002]. The figures look impressive, especially if you do not ignore the remaining social security and environmental protection problems.

Quite how positive the results of this process were can be judged by a number of important criteria. Over the seven years, productivity almost doubled and was higher than ever for the Russian coal industry. Following restructuring, over 93 per cent of the most loss-making, worked-out or dangerous mines ceased production and are being closed. By last year it was evident that the industry will be entirely able to operate at a profit in the new economic conditions, although maintaining that level will be more difficult.

The main restructuring effort was designed to create a competitive market in coal in a comparatively short time. The industry comprises mainly private coal companies and they must be able to remain self-financing in the long term.

These objectives have been achieved in part. The coal market currently is free of price controls. Coal-mining concerns have been privatised for cash. Today the coal industry contains about 60 coal-mining joint-stock companies. Private companies produce over 75 per cent of the total coal output. The bulk of the privatisations is planned to finish in 2002, after which private companies will account for 95 per cent of total coal output.

For all the pluses and minuses of the past restructuring, it is clear that it has laid the foundation both to address the industry's current problems and to determine how it develops from now on. Consequently we must pursue the restructuring process to its logical conclusion. That means completing privatisation and ensuring social obligations are met. That, in essence, is the horizon of possibilities which is visible from inside the industry.

Meanwhile it is important to think of strategy. That means the strategy of the state in resolving those issues that primarily and directly concern it and it alone. One current concern is drawing up a new policy for a coal industry whose members are privately owned companies.

To that end it is important to look at the situation from the outside, not through the eyes of the coal producers but through those of coal consumers and the state. There is no point discussing the development of the supply side without understanding the demand side. The market for coal is either the steel industry (48.9 million tonnes) or electrical power generation (162.8 million tonnes, including both industrial and local schemes), plus another 26.7 million tonnes used by local public utilities for domestic purposes excluding power generation. Of all the coal produced last year, almost 40 per cent was supplied to coal-fired power stations, 16 per cent went to the steel industry, 16.5 per cent was exported and 10.5 per cent was burnt by local authorities and individual consumers. It goes without saying that the market for coal can and must be abroad as well as at home.

It should be mentioned in passing, now that we are talking about exports, that state involvement in large infrastructure projects such as Ust-Luga is enormously important to the coal industry. The problems of coal exporters are now due more to infrastructure than to market factors. The greatest problem is transport and the greatest transport problem is ports.

A remarkable feature of recent times has been the emergence of mainly regional markets for coal. Coal sales were worth RUB 113 billion in 2001, of which over 35 per cent came from exports. For comparison, that total is over twice as much in real terms as the coal market was worth in 1999. The increase is mainly the result of higher coal prices.

Coal mining in this country has long since stopped being an end in itself. That can best be seen in the relationship between the coal industry and steelmaking. During the privatisation of the coal industry, steelmakers took over those enterprises which produced coking coal. At the same time, coal-mining companies own large stakes in steelmaking combines. Their interests coincided not merely because of the need to solve problems of guaranteed supply and payment and to clear accumulated debts (which problem remains characteristic of the relationship between the electricity industry and the coal industry to this day) but also because of the inter-penetration and fusion of strategic intentions. The last issue still to be resolved is the privatisation of mines in Vorkuta.

The main function of the state today is becoming not so much solving private problems as reacting to changes in market conditions arising from the terms of the sale of Russian steel, defending the interests of our steelmakers in the international arena, tariff policy and so on.

The development problems of the steel industry were considered at a meeting of the government of the Russian Federation on 16 May 2002. A special resolution on the development strategy of the industry to 2010 is now in preparation. An important component is to ensure that the coal industry meets the requirement of the coke-based chemical industry for the appropriate grades of coking coal. This strategy is as important to the coal industry as the Energy Strategy.

All the positive aspects which have become a fact of life in the relationship between the coal and steel industries are still at the stage of preliminary drafting for reform of the electricity industry. On the other hand there is a great load of current problems which need to be settled. They cannot be solved in one fell swoop. That will not help neutralise risks as such, because the root causes of disruptions to both supply and payment are not being dealt with. Because preparations for reform in the electricity industry are not yet complete, a stable relationship cannot be established between the coal industry and its largest customers, the generating companies.

From Ekonomika, *July 2002:*

The coal industry really does enjoy the support of the state. It is the only industry so far to receive large amounts of direct financial aid from the federal budget. This year its planned allocation is RUB 8 billion, most of which is meant for investment. Whether that is good or bad is another question. To some extent it is a tribute to a particular tradition which emerged in previous years. But in the last two years aid to the industry has been to some extent transformed, becoming more rational and effective. Subsidised interest rates are offered on commercial development loans for terms of up to three years. Second, the signs of overproduction in the industry must cause concern. How has it arisen? The slight rise achieved last year was largely because both the electricity industry and the utilities started to come round to maintaining normal levels of fuel stocks to get them through the autumn and winter heating season. To prevent any repetition of regional energy crises we kept a close eye on this issue at all levels. Headquarters were set up and regular telephone conferences with territory chiefs were held. That massed attack established a rhythm for the build-up of fuel stocks and ensured continuity of supply to the power industry and also led to a substantial increase in coal output.

So you were trying your best, but overdid it?

Not quite. The 'problem' which occurred was that all of a sudden the amount of energy used by the Russian economy, measured against GDP, started to move in the right direction. That is, it fell. At the same time the search for a way to maintain a rational load on existing generating capacity led to the industry adopting more efficient sources of energy, primarily nuclear and hydro. So the demand for steam coal was limited by entirely objective processes and circumstances. Coking coal also experienced a fall in demand because of the situation the steelmaking industry found itself in, i.e. the 'steel war'. As a result, the actual coal output exceeded the demand of the electricity and steel industries. What could we do? For a start we had to find a way to increase coal exports. Today they are unfortunately limited by transport constraints, meaning the railways and the handling capacity of sea terminals. A new terminal is being built at Ust-Luga in Leningrad *oblast*. That process is being kept under close observation by the central authorities.

We are talking about exporting coal that somehow the country has no use for, while at the same time we continue to buy in coal from Kazakhstan.

Using coal from Ekibastuz as a replacement for Russian coal is not a new subject. I would just remind you that a number of large power stations in Sverdlovsk, Chelyabinsk, Omsk and Perm *oblasts* were designed and built during the era of the Soviet planned economy specifically to use coal from Ekibastuz. All their furnace and boiler plant is technically set up to use that type of coal, which has a high ash content. To refit and upgrade them now would take a serious amount of material and financial resources. And then we must allow for geography. The transport costs of bringing coal from the Russian regions could prove unwarrantedly high. Those costs would affect the tariffs by increasing these stations' generating costs, which in turn would affect the prices of the products made by the enterprises that use their energy and so on down the supply chain. These matters are all determined by economic expediency.

From Ogonyok, *May 2001:*

All these years we have been talking only about loss-making mines. Around 150 of the most loss-making have actually closed. For people to say that they were the cause of this year's coal crisis is utter rubbish. For one thing, the coal industry is more than just the loss-making mines. There are also open-cast mines where coal is extracted efficiently. They do not get the attention they deserve. Why not? Partly because we have privatised them. For example, we sold off the Krasnoyarsk coalfield. That brought money into the budget. At that time the coalfield had debts to the budget running into billions. The government could bankrupt the enterprise tomorrow. No problem. Just send the bailiffs in and the enterprise would be no more. What is the name for that? Craftiness. On the other hand, there are examples where the balance sheet is clear, but there is no money for development. The time has come to support the bit that's still alive.

So you might resurrect other mines too?

Not those that have already closed, no.

The electricity complex

From Gazeta, *17 February 2003:*

When you and I speak about the electricity generating industry we mean not only the economic aspects but also the technical side, which today is not in great shape. That has a crucial influence on whether the economic model operates properly or not. That may not make sense. Let me explain. I will start with the network, because much of the industry directly depends on how well developed it is. Take for example the flow from Western Siberia to the Urals and the Centre. There is efficient generating capacity at stations in Surgut, but as the network is not developed, there is no way to get that lovely cheap electricity to market.

So why is everyone saying there is no hurry? Because we all assess particular risks differently. Writing direct contracts into a draft law is a dangerous business. You don't have to be a genius to realise that direct contracts will push the best generating capacity into the arms of the consumers with the highest liquidity. Those left outside the fence will be in a worse position in terms of both price and reliability. The government's task is to minimise those risks.

Some of the other amendments which were adopted at the second reading are a great improvement. The measures dealing with suppliers of last resort are much better drafted. They are clearer and provide better protection to the most vulnerable group of consumers, which is the public – even if they are still open to various interpretations. Our view is that for the time being we will have to keep cross-subsidies on supplies to the public, and only move to charging them the actual cost of electricity at some point in the future when increasing incomes make it possible to do so. At present electricity is cheaper for the consumer than for industry, even though in Europe, for example, the consumer pays three times or at least two and a half times more than industry. That is because electricity reaches the consumer via a system of step-down transformers, substations and local circuits, all of which are expensive. It is the same with the gas we send to Germany: we sell it at \$115, but the German consumer pays \$360, because someone has to pay the costs of getting it to them by building a distribution network, and someone has to meet the surge in demand when everyone gets up in the morning and turns on the gas at the same time. Gas has to be stored somewhere and spikes in demand have to be met. All that costs money. That is why the price paid by the end consumer is so much higher.

In this country the situation is the opposite and we should keep it that way. That is rather different from the radical proposal of some reformers who say we should abandon cross-subsidies immediately and all at once. I think the amendments as drafted create no threat to the reform of the electricity industry. They are an acceptable way of bringing it to a new state of efficiency. Importantly, they also minimise the threats and risks to the public. They spell out fairly precisely the government's responsibility for regulating many nuances of these relationships.

The publication of the documents entitled *Rules for the Operation of the Wholesale Market* will sound the starting gun for reform of the electricity industry. The date the *Rules* become operational will be indicated and there will be 90 or 180 days' notice, as the government sees fit in the circumstances. That is time enough for any unregulated nuances and risks that may exist to be smoothed out in these documents. In principle this approach is absolutely correct. I cannot imagine how we can purport to legislate now to regulate the massively complicated situation of the electricity industry in Russia for five years into the future. You know how hard it is to amend legislation after the event, particularly once relationships among new owners in the power industry have formed.

Ultimately, it doesn't matter who the investors entering the electricity industry are. What is important is that they should have the funds and that legislation should oblige them to accept responsibility for the state of the electrical power system. What has been adopted is the fruit of some serious compromises.

Compromises with whom? I see only the government and deputies. Deputies are the people's chosen representatives and they represent the interests of consumers. The consumers of electricity are the public and industry.

Responsibility is focused on the government, which will have to decide on a specific timetable for reform. It will answer for how it has prepared the ground for normal, fair competition leading to controlled costs and all the rest of it. As for the network complex, that is the direct responsibility of the state. Not only should the state's stake in it not be reduced but, on the contrary, it should be increased. I think, in the end it should really be 100 per cent. My personal view is that anything with an element of natural monopoly – anything that creates conditions for everyone and not just some individuals – must belong to no one but the state. People trying to call themselves investors in the circumstances are liars. They will never invest anything in the network, except for one reason: they just want a piece of the action and guaranteed dividends afterwards, because all dividends will be paid from earnings which are made on tariffs set by the state. That is simply perverse. The network component of the electricity industry is the thing that in reality not only creates the possibility of normal competition but is essential for the integrity of the country.

Legislation in support of reform of the electricity industry of the Russian Federation

Speech to the State Duma, 4 June 2002:

Current Russian Federation legislation does not provide for systematic regulation of legal relations in the electricity complex as it undergoes reform. The Russian Federation Civil Code, chapter 30, section 6, governs a narrow area of relations between energy supply organisations and end consumers of energy. Yet the provisions of that chapter are not applicable in respect of important types of legal relations associated with the buying and selling of electricity in the wholesale market, electricity transmission and system-level services. A number of matters – like price formation, licensing of certain types of activity, details of the bankruptcy procedure in relation to energy companies and details of the trade in shares of electricity industry organisations – are all regulated by separate federal laws governing relations in the electricity industry. But none of them govern the system of economic relations in the electricity market, define the participants in the market, their rights and obligations, or the system of managing the technological infrastructure of the market.

Because of the technological organisation of the energy industry, clear legislative regulation of the system of legal relations in the industry is an indispensable condition if it is to operate reliably and without interruption. The technological features of the industry relate primarily to the physical circulation of electricity and to the common infrastructure necessary for the organisational management of the technological regimes controlling networks and flows of energy (the unified national electricity grid and the system of supervisory control and data acquisition in the electricity industry).

The technological specificity of the industry makes it necessary to have institutions for buying and selling electricity: that is, wholesale and retail markets. A unified system of management of the technological regimes that operate the industry and energy flows is necessary if the electricity industry is to operate reliably and without interruption. That requires common rules for the trading of electricity when companies or individuals make transactions to buy, sell or provide ancillary services.

The draft laws aim to lay the legal basis for economic and industrial relations in the electricity sphere, the powers of government bodies to regulate those relations, and the basic rights and obligations of participants in the process of production, transmission, distribution or consumption of electricity.

The draft laws propose a model for the organisation of relations in the industry. It is based on ensuring that the electricity industry rigorously observes the principles which article 8(1) of the Constitution of the Russian Federation provides for all spheres of economic activity, to support the technological unity of the electricity system of the country and ensure it operates reliably and safely while maintaining the guarantees of a single economic space, free movement of goods, services and finance, and supporting competition and freedom of economic activity.

The draft laws define the electricity industry as a sphere of the economy comprising the totality of:

◆ the industrial and technological objects used directly in the process of producing, transmitting and distributing electricity;
◆ the economic actors engaging in those types of activity;
◆ the complex of economic relationships created in the process of carrying out those types of activity.

The main objectives of the draft laws are as follows:

◆ to meet the energy demands of the national economy, primarily by means of a complex of economic measures, and form an effective system of long-range forecasting of demand and supply in the electricity market;

◆ to ensure electricity market participants fully meet their obligations;
◆ to set transparent and comprehensible rules for economic and industrial relationships in the industry;
◆ to form an exhaustive list of forms and methods of government intervention in the electricity industry (including price regulation, technical supervision, etc.) and restrict administrative rule-making in the form of non-legislative ordinances regulating relations in the electricity industry;
◆ to take steps to protect the rights of citizens and consumers of electricity in retail electricity markets;
◆ to establish rigorous state control and regulation of the technological basis of the electricity industry, the unified national electricity network and the system of supervisory control and data acquisition, in particular by means of securing a state share of at least 51 per cent of the charter capital of any organisation engaging in the stated types of activity.

Institutionally, the technological infrastructure of the electricity industry – comprising the unified national electricity network and the system of supervisory control and data acquisition – is identified as a 'natural monopoly'. That is a defined term connoting a particular legal status and purpose (draft law 'On amendments to the provisions on the Federal Law on natural monopolies'). The right of market participants to discrimination-free access to the infrastructure is expressly guaranteed (i.e. there is a specific provision against granting some participants preference over others as regards use of the infrastructure). There is a prohibition on combining the functions of managing the technological infrastructure of the industry and trading in energy.

Freedom of economic activity in the energy market may be restricted only in order to:

◆ balance the economic interests of all market participants;
◆ defend the strategic interests of the state;
◆ prevent accidents in the process of producing, transmitting and distributing energy.

The system of operational control and data acquisition in the electricity industry will be a natural monopoly and is to be completely removed from any involvement in trading in energy and the economic interests of any other actors. The principle is established that electricity industry actors have an absolute duty to comply with the control commands of the system operator, as is the principle that ensuring the economic effectiveness of decisions taken by the system operator or other operational control bodies has priority.

From Ogonyok, *May 2001:*

The network component must not simply be hived off from RJSC UES. In the end it must be 100 per cent owned by the state.

But RJSC UES say a controlling share is enough.

And I say 100 per cent! The sector is to become a natural monopoly regulated by the state. So you would think that the state would be responsible for its development. Consequently all decisions about sources of finance must be taken by the state. On what basis should the state end up providing capital at an interest rate it has no control over? In the name of what should it spend the state's economic (and political) resources so that some shareholders who have unexpectedly become co-owners become even more gold-plated at the expense of other people and not because of their own contribution to development?

If those are your views, aren't you getting it in the neck from the oligarchs?

I have normal relationships with those who are called oligarchs. The reasons for that are perfectly natural. I am not dependent on any of them and have no trouble keeping up contacts, particularly on a personal level, and maintaining my personal position. I do not come from any oligarch 'family'.

Still, they must try to curry favour with you?

But you yourself say 'they'. That means there are many of them. And if they are not all one person, that means they have separate, conflicting interests. I have, thank goodness, no reason, except purely businesslike and substantive ones, to take the side of anyone in particular.

You must at least have seen oligarchs in the flesh?

I think so.

And you've met Abramovich?

Yes. Last time the governor of Chukotka and I discussed deliveries of supplies to the north and unpaid utility bills.

What happens? Do they give you their requests and you give them what they want, or not, as you see fit?'

They bring arguments which, as they see it, are not about their companies but of significance to the sector as a whole. They have changed. Now they argue in terms of the industry or the economy. All these people who are called oligarchs have, fortunately, come through the early stages when they first made their money and when, as Karl Marx said, there was no crime at which capital would scruple for a profit of 300 per cent. However, it is clear that any regulatory decisions, whether on duties, taxes or access to export pipelines, bear on very specific economic interests of companies. Which is good. Which is as it should be.

Figure 2.15 The concept of the infrastructure complex

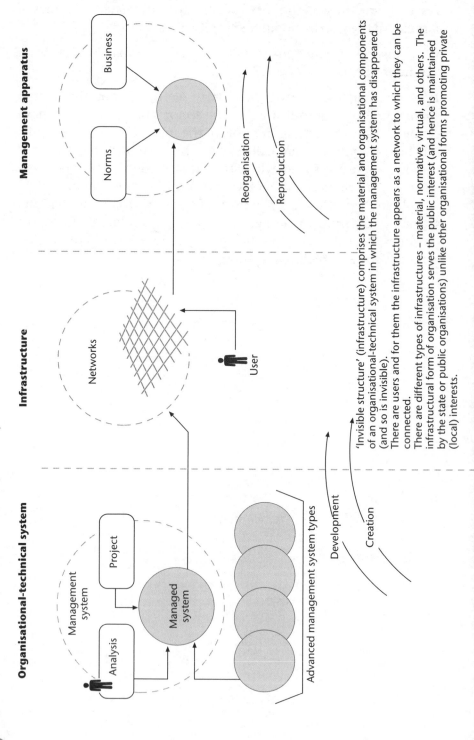

Organisational-technical system

Infrastructure

Management apparatus

Norms

Business

Reorganisation

Reproduction

Networks

User

Management system

Project

Analysis

Managed system

Advanced management system types

Development

Creation

'Invisible structure' (infrastructure) comprises the material and organisational components of an organisational-technical system in which the management system has disappeared (and so is invisible).

There are users and for them the infrastructure appears as a network to which they can be connected.

There are different types of infrastructures – material, normative, virtual, and others. The infrastructural form of organisation serves the public interest (and hence is maintained by the state or public organisations) unlike other organisational forms promoting private (local) interests.

The infrastructure complex

Transport

Speech to the Collegium of the Ministry of Transport, 4 March 2003:

The drag on GDP caused by transport deficiencies is a major influence on the competitiveness of the Russian economy. It is very large by comparison with leading countries – three times worse than the United States and an order of magnitude worse than Germany.

It is not only the obvious effect of geography. It is also that the system of transport nodes and communications that we use now was created in different socio-economic conditions and intended for a different foreign trade structure.

The creation of an open market economy and Russia's active pursuit of integration with the global market have radically changed the nature, volume and directions of export and import cargo traffic. By comparison with 1991, imports have more than halved and exports have trebled. Whereas before the reforms we traded mainly with our nearest neighbours, now most of our trade is with countries outside the CIS.

It is not too soon to draw conclusions from the first year of implementation of the federal special-purpose programme entitled Modernisation of the Transport System of Russia. We have succeeded in consolidating limited resources to focus on the main trade routes. I hope the Russian Ministry of Transport has abandoned once and for all the practice of dissipating money over a large number of building projects.

Infrastructure is one of the most capital-intensive and unresponsive sectors of the economy. Therefore transport problems will continue to preoccupy the government's attention for a long time yet.

Traditionally those problems manifested themselves at the interfaces between different government departments or modes of transport. This year we have experienced certain restrictions on the export of goods like coal, bulk liquids and grain owing to bottlenecks at sea ports and the railways which serve them.

There can be no doubt that it is important to identify and remedy such bottlenecks. However, that must be done not by means of operational traffic management decisions but by forecasting foreign trade and ensuring a balanced development of transport infrastructure, including all modes of transport.

Figure 2.16 The infrastructure complex

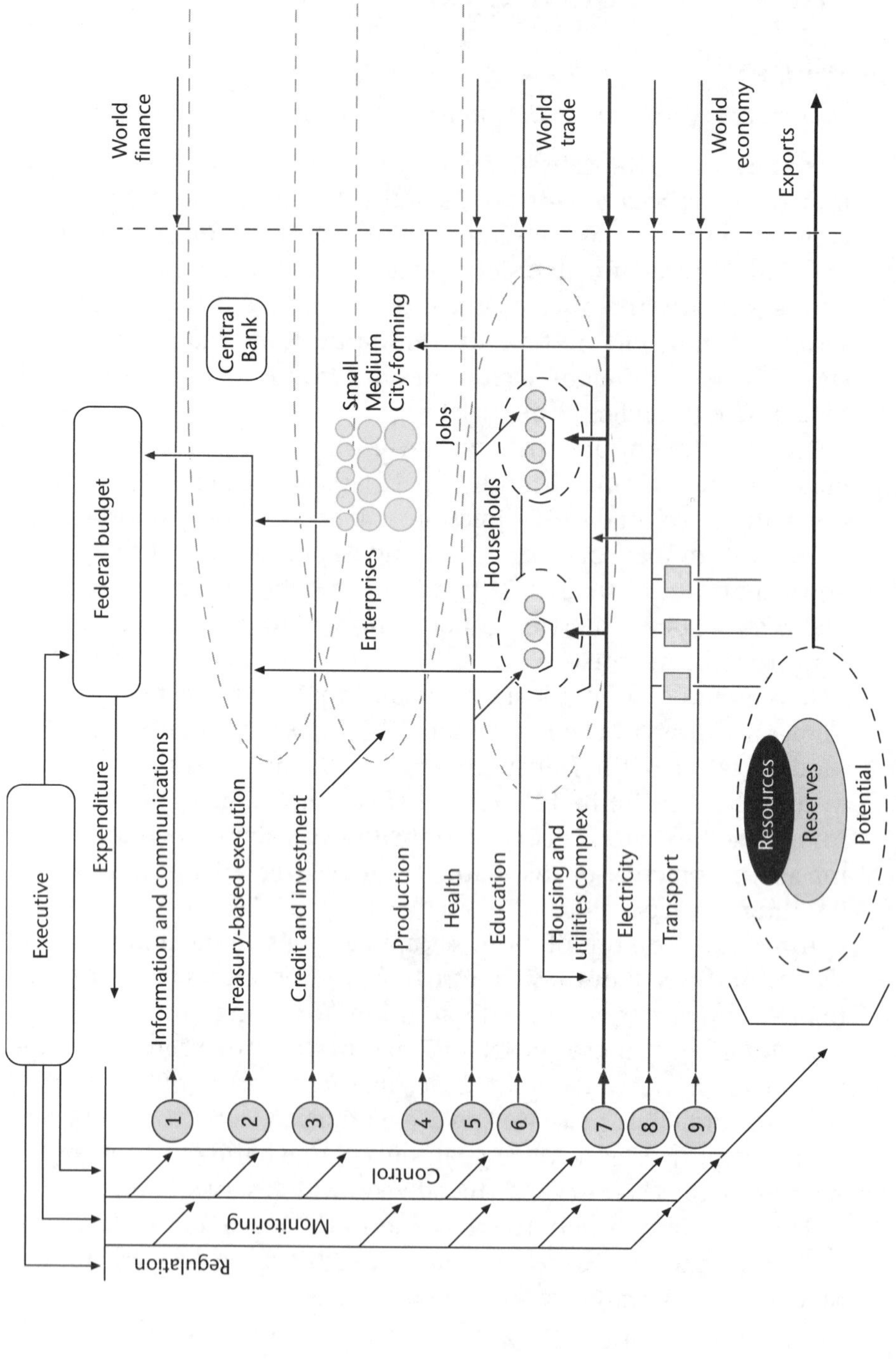

I think it cannot be said often enough that infrastructure development is the one area where state involvement will continue for the foreseeable future. The state will create fair conditions for both equal access to infrastructure and development of the competitive environment. The state will continue to control tariff policy in infrastructural natural monopolies.

Improved efficiency and productivity of transport nodes demands, first of all, highly specialised ports and harmonised design solutions in the development of airports, port facilities and cargo terminals.

Management decisions and investment projects should be evaluated with reference not to corporate, narrow departmental or, as is sometimes the case, overtly factional interests, but to the need to support strategic exports of oil, coal and other commodities.

As you know, in only the past year [2002/03] a number of important decisions have been taken to improve the competitiveness of the transport system.

Procedures have been determined and funds have been made available to subsidise some of the leasing costs and interest on loans from Russian commercial banks to buy Russian-made ships and aircraft.

Merchant ships insured by Russian ship owners under bare-boat charters[10] have been exempted from customs duties and taxes.

Federal budget funding has been provided for modern security screening equipment at airports in Moscow, the south and the north-west. The total funding for modernisation of national airports has been more than doubled.

A mechanism has been found and funding has been provided to refit the nuclear icebreaker *50 Let Pobedy*, which will ensure reliable operation of the northern shipping route.

All necessary decisions have been taken to raise loans from the European Investment Bank for infrastructure projects like the construction of the Chita–Khabarovsk highway, the creation of a movement control system for shipping in the Gulf of Finland and several others.

The government plans to review the whole range of issues relating to the finance of regional road programmes in the light of the first-quarter results [of 2003]. Of course we cannot afford to fail in this area. Nevertheless the time has come to look more closely at how funds are distributed and spent in the road-building industry at

---

10 A system of chartering that does not include the crew or provisions, only the hire of the boat.

both federal and regional level. We need to know what scope there is for competitive tendering, what use is made of modern road-building technology and new materials, and how to keep on top of the notorious repair problems.

There are even more important tasks before us in the immediate future. Once the laws reforming the federal railways come into force, favourable new conditions will arise for Russia to have competitive inter-modal freight operators and develop freight forwarding and container transport. The conditions will be created to create a unified market-oriented transport system which will be competitive in itself and make Russian goods very competitive on the world markets.

Much work is associated with the enterprises that can be privatised. In our view, the Collegium of the Ministry of Transport should get on with it. Reform of urban public transport is going slowly, there are delays with reform of airports, and the basic federal laws and sub-legislative acts will take years in the staffing and redrafting process.

Moreover, questions of principle need to be addressed by making wider use of the Government Commission on Transport Policy. The state transport policy concept adopted by the government in 1997 is largely out of date. The economic situation of the country has changed and there have been profound structural reforms of transport.

In the past two years the government has approved a number of market-oriented concept documents. They are the international transport corridor concept, the shipping policy concept and the concept of state regulation of civil aviation. Currently under consideration by the government is the concept for the development of inland water transport. A batch of laws has been adopted to reform federal railway transport. The policy of the state in each area has largely been defined: in other words, we have a basis for devising a new transport policy and transport strategy for Russia in the long term.

Speech to a joint session of the Collegiums of the Russian Federation and Ukrainian Ministries of Transport, 9 December 2002:

The development of transport infrastructure is becoming a priority for the state. The development of the economy in both Russia and Ukraine is largely predetermined by transport. It is therefore most timely that the ministries of transport of Russia and Ukraine and the Russian Ministry of Railways have decided to co-ordinate a work programme. On that basis we will soon be able to organise passenger transport more effectively, determine strategic routes for freight, including transit, and get export goods to the customer without delays.

The main problems of the transport industry have to do with its inability to complete its transformation to match new demands. In the CIS market there are clear signs of a reconfiguration of freight traffic owing to disparities of economic development. It has become obvious that the traditional logistic transport chains need to be improved.

For example, there is a shortage of port capacity to trans-ship Russian export goods. The problem is most acute in the south of Russia. The connections between modes of transport are becoming weaker. The co-ordination of the railways and the ports needs to be more carefully co-ordinated by means of modern information technology and logistics. These points should be borne in mind in the amendments to the federal special-purpose programme for Modernisation of the Transport System of Russia 2002/10.

One important issue is the further development of the infrastructure at border crossings for road vehicles and railways on the frontier between the Russian Federation and Ukraine.

In developing transport links with Ukraine as one of the Russian Federation's largest economic partners, we have in mind the close interdependence of the industrial complexes of both countries and the further development and exploitation of the extraordinarily large Ukrainian market for sales of Russian-made goods. In turn, Russia stands to gain supplies from Ukrainian industry and agriculture and its unique resources of raw materials. We also stand to gain from mutually advantageous use of Ukraine's transport communications and sea ports for third-party freight.

Work should continue to bring the treaty and legal basis of transport relations between Russia and Ukraine into line with existing realities, international standards and the exigencies of developing trade and economic co-operation.

Closer integration between Russia and Ukraine is envisaged in co-operation between both countries' transport networks, doing everything possible to promote reciprocal investment of Russian and Ukrainian capital in privatised large transport companies, and increased efforts to create transport companies and transnational financial-industrial structures in aircraft and shipbuilding.

Housing and utilities

Speech to the Collegium of the State Committee of the Russian Federation on Construction, Housing and Utilities (Gosstroi), 15 March 2002:

I shall not attempt to cover all the different tasks and trends. Let me concentrate on what is still at the top of Gosstroi's agenda as 2002 begins. Normal human life in the state is not possible without an adequate policy on housing. The old approaches are hopelessly outmoded. However good they were in their time they have become simply impracticable. Almost everything has changed – social policy, the economy, consumer culture and the system of 'distributing' human resources. Let us not spend too long on the whys and wherefores. Instead let us fix on one thing. We urgently need new instruments and mechanisms for attacking the problems in the one area which throughout the years of reform, despite occasional bursts of renewal, has remained a backwater, a dead end where problems were simply parked and have accumulated, partly because of resistance inside the bureaucratic machine at all levels. There have been some breakthroughs, but never where they were needed. The upshot is that the whole area of housing and utilities policy has become like a nature reserve on the map of modern, self-renewing Russia. And what lives in nature reserves? Only rare animals on the point of extinction. People should live in their own houses or flats and not in an allocation of a few square metres of the public housing stock. Natural wastage means public housing is reaching the end of its useful life. An alarming proportion (70–75 per cent) will soon be unfit to live in. You and I are well aware that in that situation maintenance and repair costs double. If they triple, they become unaffordable. That is one argument in favour of not allowing ourselves to be distracted from the current tasks, but of making sure that in the next year [2002/03] we reorientate the entire system towards a new housing policy. Five per cent annual growth in new housing is the least we should aim at.

Just one example of the relation between old and new in our housing policy: futurologists and designers expatiate in magazines about the 'intelligent home' in which all household systems will be remote-controlled via a computer. What do we in fact have? The hammering of worn-out water pipes, for a start. And that is only half the story. Look at our building regulations. Still there is no provision for the sorts of innovation which could improve the lives of disabled

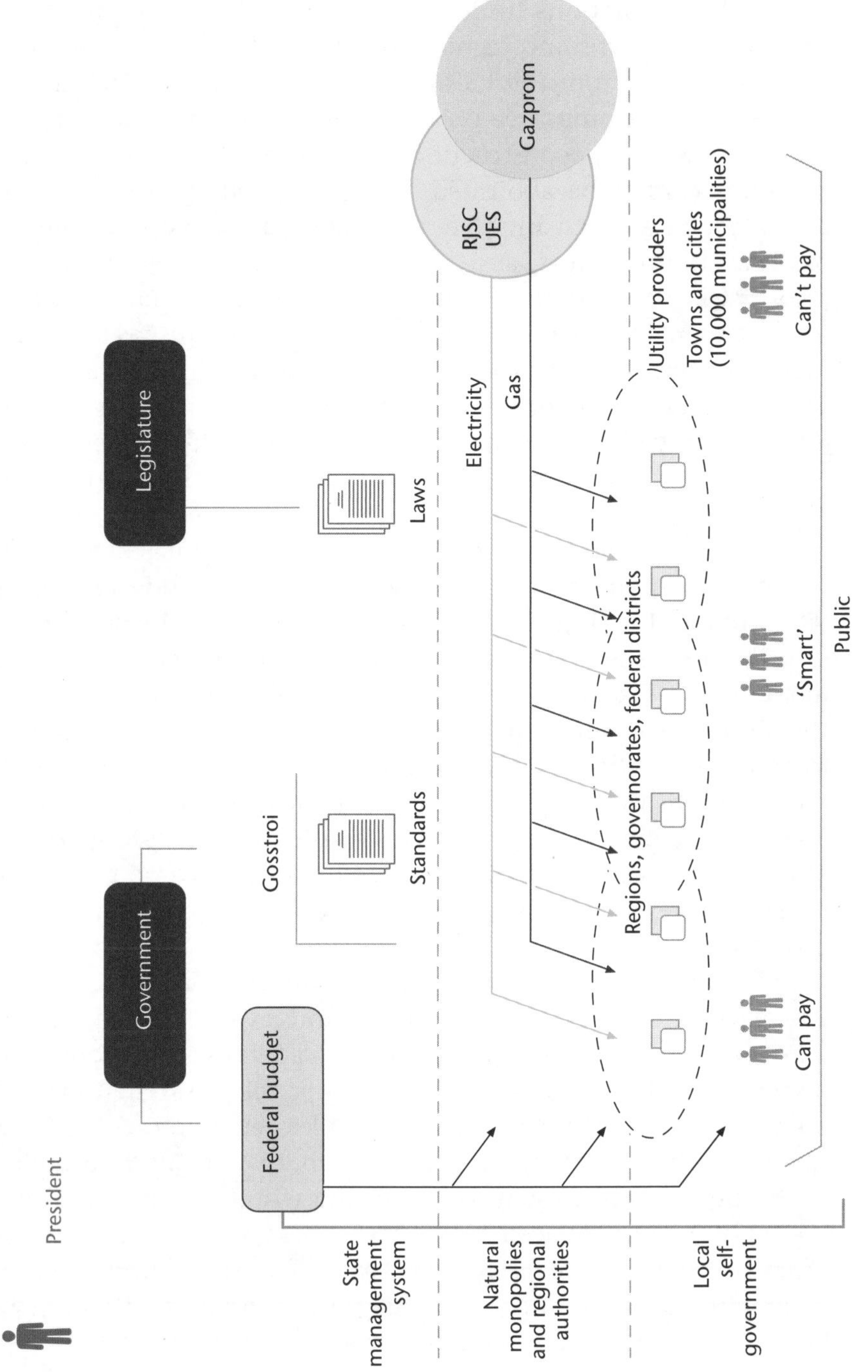

Figure 2.17 Participants in reform of the housing and utility complex

people. What there is still is not just hundreds but thousands of unrepealed regulations from way back. Two hundred chapters of the building norms and regulations, 800 state standards and over 60 publications from the RSFSR State Committee on Architecture or RSFSR State Committee on Construction are still holding back rapidly developing construction firms and organisations. These measures cannot be abolished at a stroke, but they need to be amended. A new licensing system is needed, as it affects the interests of all economic actors, and de-bureaucratising the economy is a priority generally. Some steps have been taken but so far all we have done is open a tiny window to expert assessment, just as an experiment. That won't do. Instead we need to fling open the door and open a wide corridor for anyone who is prepared to work in construction in a modern way. We are taking the initiative here, and this is one area where in a year's time we expect to see a reduction and not an increase of red tape.

There are serious problems associated with the technological foundations of our policy in energy and housing and utilities. We talk often and with good reason about how old and worn out the utilities infrastructure is. In many cases, unfortunately, the replacement process takes over a year and, as a result, everyone from Afoni the plumber to your humble servant still has to be kept on standby to ensure the lights, the heating and the water stay on in our apartments. But as well as worn-out equipment there is a more general problem of what we might call restoring an engineering culture. The extreme case is technicians not checking on time to see that valves are present and correct. Thereafter it all becomes a political problem.

I can say that the administrative demands must and will be strict. The government is making additional funds available to the regions for winter preparations. The task for the leaders of the regions is not just get hold of as much of that money as possible and then spend it, but to use it as a resource to solve a complex set of problems. Money can always be sent to the regions, but what you can't do is build a centralised heating system covering the whole country and have every last washer replaced only if Moscow says so. I went to Turkey recently, where there is a 1,000-year-old underground reservoir which provided water during the siege of Istanbul. But that is good enough for only one city, and only when there's a siege on.

Let us not leave our people languishing in siege conditions. Let us enable them to live normally no matter how low the mercury falls in the thermometer outside. The decline of housing and utilities into mismanagement and neglect in recent years must be stopped.

From Gazeta, *9 October 2001:*

What, ultimately, do people want? It is very simple and banal. They want somewhere to live where there is hot water and heat. Just one problem: all that has to be paid for. The problem of the housing and utilities complex is far larger than all the difficulties of restructuring of RJSC UES, the Ministry of Railways and Gazprom combined. It affects everyone's interests. And in terms of neglect it is deeper. Very many years ago, it seems to me, a great act of sabotage was carried out when the 'centralised' heating system and so on was invented. All our cities are standing on top of these waterpipe-nuclear pipe-tangled bombs.

From Ekonomika, *July 2002:*

If the state has recognised a certain overriding goal of supporting particular industries by subsidising particular costs, then that purpose should be pursued openly, using the budget. That is necessary, it really is. Anything else – what is habitually called cross-subsidy – is a knowingly artificial act directed against a participant in the process.

Do you remember the formula 'consent is the product of the non-resistance of the parties?' Well, cross-subsidies are paid without consent: someone in the economy has to pay extra for some enterprise or to subsidise some category of consumers, but no one asks the people who have to stump up the money whether they consent or not. But there is something else wrong. As a rule, all you can do with any political measure is temporarily hold up some process that is proceeding according to economic necessity. That will work once. It might work twice. The third time you might stand up for someone by following some overriding purpose. Thereafter efforts to use political measures give way to the logic of economic necessity. The thing we kept safe from the laws of the market starts to wear out and die because it has been kept under glass. Because local utilities were a monster we were afraid to touch, nearly 75 per cent of them are now reaching the end of their useful life. In electricity the situation is slightly better, but still bad. If these industries do not reproduce themselves by the natural replacement of capacity, everything will remain cheap, but not for long. It will all come crashing down. Therefore, sooner or later, this 'cautious' approach which says that things are so important that reforming them would be dangerous will have to be abandoned on economic grounds. After political constraints have been applied for long enough, when they are suddenly given up you get a reaction. That was what we saw in Voronezh.[11] A number of new factors suddenly came into play all at once and the consumers on whom the system collapsed had nowhere to turn. They protested; they complained – and, on the whole, quite rightly. Those who up to that point were utterly committed to preserving everything unchanged must answer for their behaviour. It is better to get things done in time than to bury our heads in the sand.

From Gazeta, *17 February 2003:*

Between the boiler operator and me there are a lot of people involved in this business (the reform of the housing and utilities complex). Apart from the federal level there are also the Subjects of the Federation and the municipalities. Each level of power has, or more precisely should have, a clearly defined range of responsibilities in relation to local utilities.

Those responsibilities should be implemented by way of obligations set forth in the budget. What actually happens? Let us start at the bottom. Everything that goes under the title local utilities is currently the property of municipalities. You would have thought that all matters relating to the condition of local utilities would be the concern and responsibility of those owners. The owners who organised the local utilities have to understand that they must, as for any economic structure, have their own plan of revenues and expenditures which is balanced across sources. The expenditure bit is clear enough: everyone rolls up with claims for fuel oil, ducting, insulation or whatever. But the revenue side is not all clear. I cannot now even raise the question of getting the public to pay for the utilities and housing complex because of the strange scare stories built up over 'full payment'.

Full payment. 100 per cent. The figure is eye-catching. But in Russia it is never really going to happen. Our system of social guarantees is designed in such a way that both today and after any

---

11   Voronezh had been the site of well-publicised worker protests.

transformations there may be, it will cover a substantial proportion of the population who will not pay 100 per cent. The expression is used polemically to shut down discussion of anything more serious.

What is to be done? The government gave the answer in the form of a draft law placed before the Duma. It went like this. Today Russian legislation covers many categories of people who receive allowances to pay for housing and utilities. Many recipients are capable, working citizens – service personnel, for example. For them, the proposed transformation amounts to monetising their allowances. These are mainly, I repeat, state servants who will receive an addition to their pay instead of these unpredictable and incomprehensible allowances.

That was the first thing. The second affects citizens receiving allowances either due for past service – having attained a particular military rank, for example – or because of their circumstances, by which I mean on grounds of incapacity. Those are two quite different categories. What was the government's proposal on these two categories? To blow away the clouds and introduce some clarity into Russian legislation about what level of government is responsible for which categories of citizen and, at the same time, to secure financing in the federal budget and the budgets of the Subjects of the Federation for those categories for which each level is responsible.

It might be thought that the federal government had yet again decided to dump everything on the regions. It is doing no such thing. What the Subjects are required to do mirrors exactly what is already in the legislation. Where veterans of labour were the responsibility of the Subjects, that is repeated in this legislation.

That is all very well but it does not address the main issue, which is that local utilities must be of good quality. Homes in winter must be warmer than the streets, especially if you live in Khanty-Mansiysk. That aspect of reform has still to make it into legislation. The most important part of the whole chain is the relationship of the suppliers with the consumers of local utility services: that is, with actual individuals. In the current situation there is a very wide variety of relationships. They are one thing in the mega-cities of Moscow and St Petersburg or the regional centres. They are a different thing in the small towns and different again in the villages. In some places houses now have owners, and their share of housing is pretty big. In some places they have organised themselves into homeowners' associations called *condominiums* (I expect they'll ban that word: it is painfully close to a rude one). And in some places those associations have made arrangements with service providers, the local utility services, for heating, electricity and water. Such arrangements take the normal legal form: they are contracts which if not met can readily give grounds for court action or other means – the usual, legal ones – of settling the matter. Such forms are chiefly adopted in cities, in places where both the residents and the authorities are, as it were, more enlightened and have an interest in so doing. That is a new sort of relationship between local public utilities and the public.

What is to be done about the debts of the housing and utilities complex?

Any debt – in fact, any financial condition – always has two aspects. You can do something about debts if there is no enduring reason why they will not simply recur. Currently the recurring debts of local utilities are an unhealed wound caused by a lack of finance to meet obligations at all levels of power. That is one thing. Second, authorities declare that they have obligations to recipient categories for allowances and for grants to local utilities, but do not make provision for them in their budgets. Only last of all do we come to the debts arising because people don't pay for services. If the first two problems could be solved, the causes of debt recurrence would disappear.

What about the accumulated debts?

There is no doubt that we can and must talk about restructuring the existing debts of local utilities. As with any balance sheet, they include a wide variety of elements. But there are two major items. First there are the debts to the budget from unpaid taxes and so on. Then there are the debts to the energy companies for heat or electricity.

Yes, we could think up mechanisms to restructure both types. By way of illustration I can say that during discussions two years ago of the government decision to restructure the debts to the budget of all enterprises in the national economy, that decision in law went through in the budget. Four special categories were identified whose restructuring was to be different from everybody else's in that they were given additional conditions and a 'holiday' so that businesses could spread out debt repayments over a longer period. The four categories were the coal industry, energy, nuclear power and local utilities.

Having identified them we said, 'Now chaps, we know your industries are all in such a state that you can't pay up like everybody else, so you've got a year's grace. You do not have to pay your debts this year but next year you have got to start.' What do you think happened? The nuclear industry bought into the restructuring scheme completely and has stuck to it. Every one of the companies in RJSC UES bought into the restructuring scheme and have stuck to it. Not all the coal industry did; I cannot boast about the figure, but the bulk of the coal industry did sign up to the agreement and is keeping to it because it understands that it's a normal thing to settle debts. From the local utilities, however, take-up is practically zero. Why? Because they can't even keep up with their current commitments to the budget. The result is that their debts just keep recurring.

The Institute for Urban Economics says condominiums are the most complicated form of self-management: in and of themselves they don't work outside a particular legal and economic context. Suppose, for example, the Moscow water company Mosvodokanal wants me to believe I use 300–400 litres of water a day, but the meter reads only 60. Is it up to me how my use of local utilities is measured? I don't want to go to court with Mosvodokanal. I just want a quiet life without it all being a battle. What I do want is for Vice Prime Minister Viktor Khristenko to ask Mosvodokanal and all the other monopolies where the extra 300 litres went.

Ours is still a young state. Completely establishing the rule of law will take a lot more time. It will take all of us at least as long to become a civil society in which all the things you and I have been talking about, to do with the responsibilities of government and all the other things, are dealt with as a matter of course. In any event anything to do with local utilities must, beyond doubt, be covered by a particular sort of requirement defined at the level of federal law. I mean process audits and a transparent system of costs. All that must be reflected in Russian legislation; of that there is no doubt. But in any event all that will only work if, on the other side, consumers make demands in relation to the provision of services.

But we are only now reaching that stage. We are approaching it with some difficulty for one simple reason. We have changed – we have tried to transform – our legislation on housing issues regularly over the last ten years or so. All such attempts have come crashing down because of an attitude which, although it is correct in some ways, also creates great difficulties. It's what we call the 'complex approach': let's rewrite the entire housing code! Let's put in this, that and the other! When you try to do everything at once and don't feel you can leave anything out, the result is that you achieve nothing. You attempt to reconcile the irreconcilable and foresee the unforeseeable, and the fruits of all the compromising is that in the end no one knows what they are fighting for, and the whole thing quietly dies. Therefore I think there is simply no time now to wipe the slate and start again. We have to proceed by a succession of autonomous, but systematically coherent solutions.

Management staff training

Paper for the All-Russia Conference, 5 November 2002:

Without well-trained modern managers, the effective transformation of the economy is impossible. Because the country's leaders realised the importance of improving the qualifications of business directors and specialists, they decided in 1997 to train at least 5,000 Russian managers each year.

That decision was extraordinary because the Russian Federation government was prepared to invest significant budgetary funds to train young managers irrespective of their companies' form of ownership, size or kind of business.

When this country's leaders approached the leaders of the developed world for support for this initiative, they received it almost unanimously. Abroad, the Russian management staff training programme came to be known as the 'Presidential programme'.

A Commission with 80 regional branches to organise management staff training for organisations of the national economy was created to implement the programme. The legislative basis for implementation was established in the shortest possible time, and the first pilot groups of managers were sent abroad on placements in late 1997 and early 1998.

The success of the programme depended mainly on the support of the regions – the governors and vice-governors who headed the work of the Commission's regional branches. Such support was forthcoming because the programme was seeking to address pressing problems at the local level. It is particularly significant that the selection and subsequent employment of trainees was left to the regions themselves to decide in the light of regional and industrial demands. The Commission devises the programme strategy and performs organisational, methodological and supervisory functions.

It is a cause for satisfaction that in the last few years it has been possible to create an effective infrastructure of regional branches of the Commission in almost all Subjects of the Federation. Nearly 1,500 like-minded staff work in them. The word *work* may not be entirely appropriate: they live with the programme, know all the graduates' problems and support their applications for university training or placements abroad expertly and always with good arguments.

Figure 2.18 Manager training and administrative reform

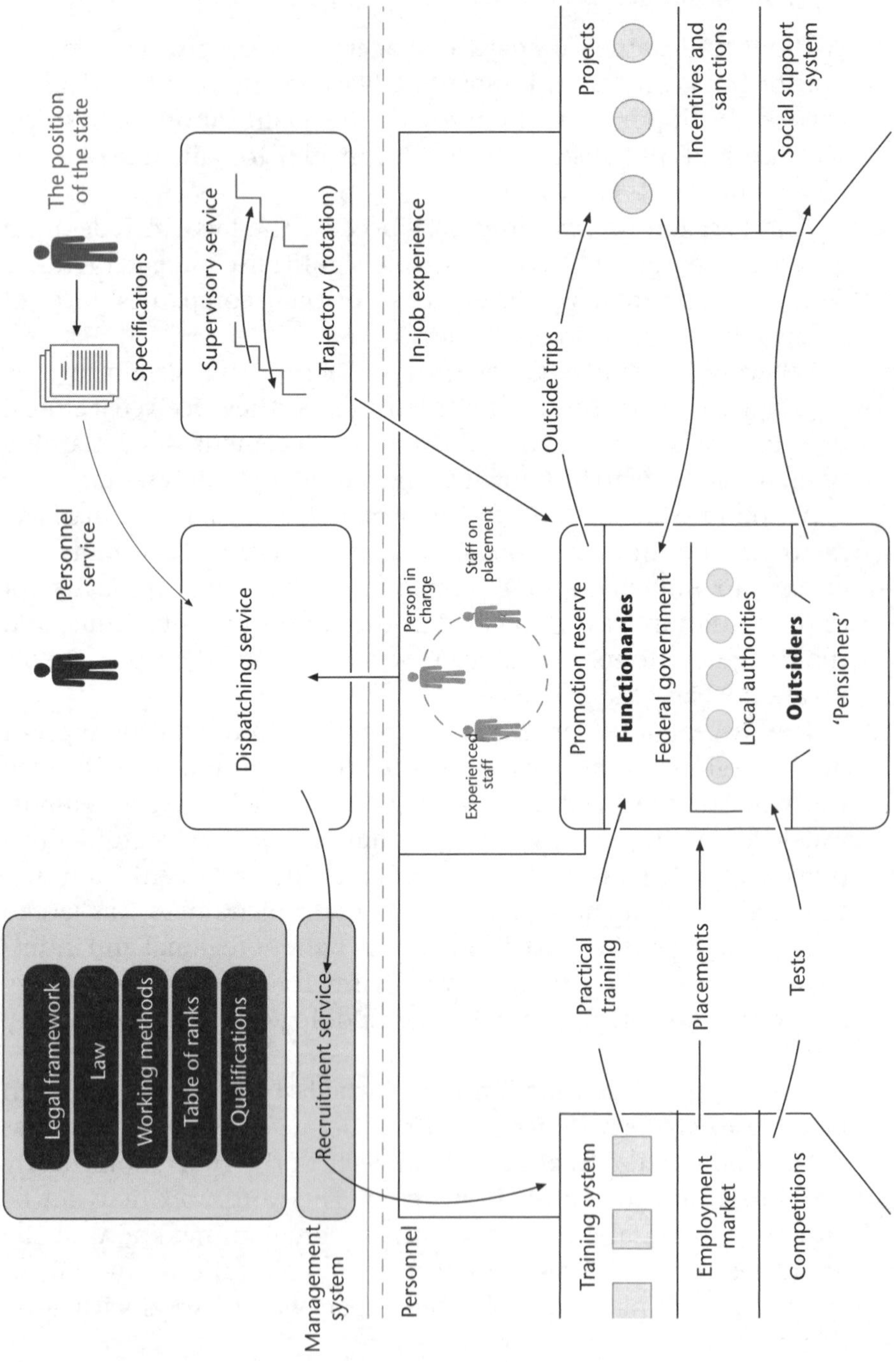

I think only their confidence that they are part of a scheme of national importance producing tangible results can explain the fact that the vast majority of the staff of the Commission's regional branches are still with us, after five years and despite all the political changes. Thanks to their work over the last five years [to 2002], over 26,000 young managers have been sent for training in management, marketing and finance.

The programme is working successfully in the following areas:

◆ Training a new type of manager for real sectors of the economy who know how to work effectively in market conditions. Around 96 per cent of programme graduates, and 80 per cent of the business chiefs who sent employees for training, recognise the value and, more importantly, the applicability of the knowledge and skills gained.
◆ Contributing to the process of reform of Russian businesses and the development of entrepreneurship. Over 65 per cent of programme graduates are actually carrying out programmes of change devised during their studies or placements in their companies or in parts of the business. Most of the projects are designed to improve productivity, reduce production costs and improve the results of financial and economic activities.
◆ Creating conditions to establish and develop international co-operation. I provided the statistics earlier.
◆ Facilitating the professional and career development of young managers. A quarter of specialists report promotions and 40 per cent of participants report substantial pay increases. Over 40 per cent of trainees have received offers of work from Russian or foreign companies and 10 per cent of programme graduates have been invited to work in government bodies at various levels.
◆ Developing entrepreneurship and small businesses. Over 30 per cent of enterprises participating in the programme are small businesses. Furthermore, 8 per cent of programme graduates immediately set up their own companies when their training finished.

Figure 2.19 World economic regions and infrastructures

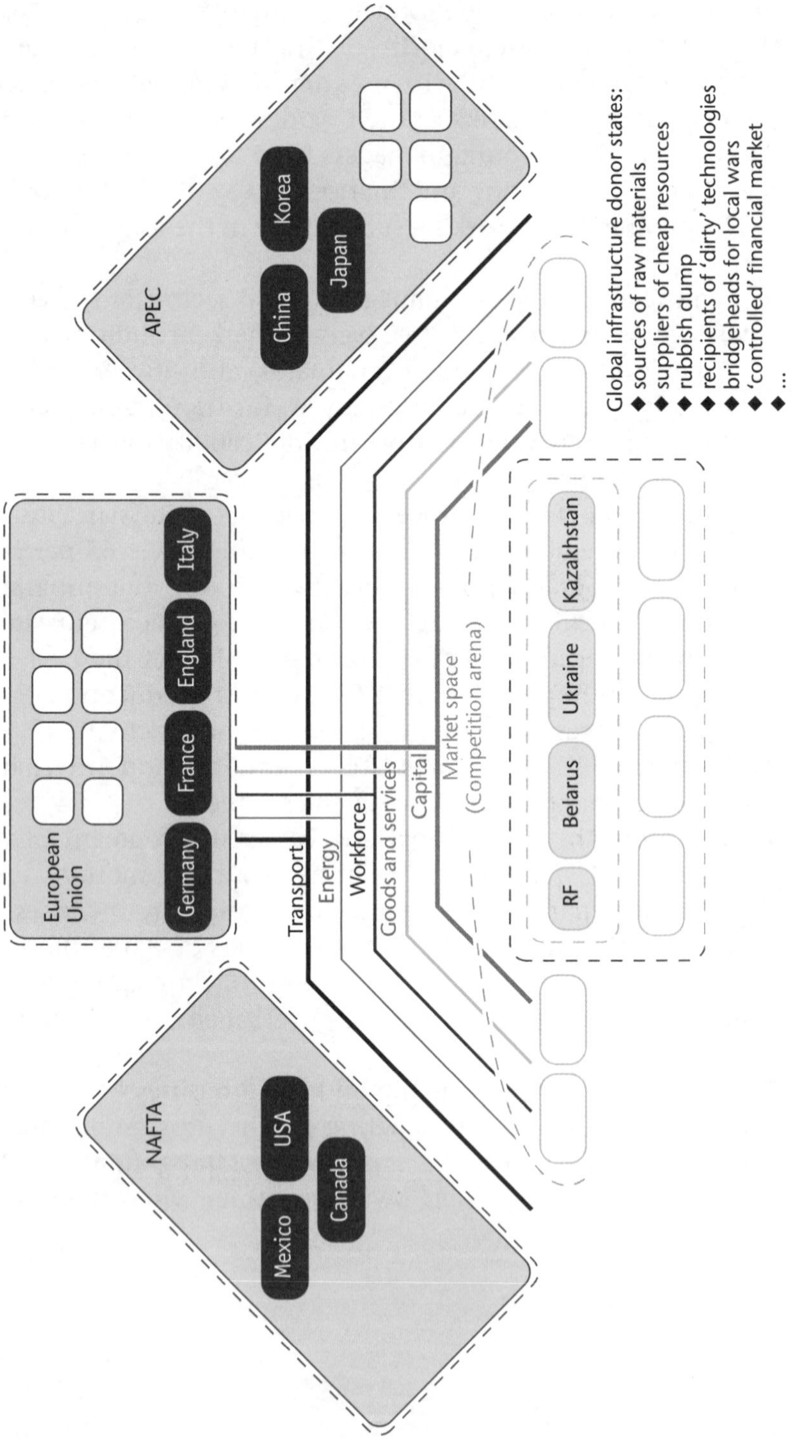

Global infrastructure donor states:
- sources of raw materials
- suppliers of cheap resources
- rubbish dump
- recipients of 'dirty' technologies
- bridgeheads for local wars
- 'controlled' financial market
- ...

APEC

China Korea Japan

European Union

Germany France England Italy

NAFTA

Mexico USA Canada

RF Belarus Ukraine Kazakhstan

Transport
Energy
Workforce
Goods and services
Capital
Market space
(Competition arena)

Integration in the CIS

Approaches to integration

Interview for RIA Novosti, *1 July 2003:*

What will be in the concept for a Russia–EU Common Economic Space?

The concept will be presented at the Russia–EU summit in November. The analytical work in various sectors is just now being completed. On the one hand the work has addressed different spheres of regulation: for example, customs regulations. What would unification or harmonisation of these regulations mean and what would be the consequences for Russia and the European Union? And across sectors – steel, agriculture, car making, aircraft building, etc. – what could be the consequences if regulatory rules were unified and trade relations were liberalised? Those are the sorts of studies we and the European Union commissioned from experts, and their reports are now in.

Overall their general view is positive. Liberalisation and harmonisation of regulations will have a positive effect on the Russian economy. That is the basis for developing this approach. The concept itself is intended to contain some quite precisely defined tasks (what, why and for what), prescribing forms of implementation and means of achieving the aims, along with appropriate milestones and an overall timetable that will allow us to judge whether or not we are moving in the right direction and have achieved what we wanted to achieve. In parallel, we may take this even further for a global industry like energy. By the summit in November we and our EU partners will present the idea of enhanced co-operation, an enhanced energy space between the European Union and Russia. It may be even slightly more enhanced than the common European economic space.

The energy industry in the broad sense always and everywhere – in all countries – has always needed and still needs special regulation. In Russia the Civil Code provides adequate regulation for the trade in everything from peas to steel, for example, but the electricity industry alone required a whole sheaf of laws in order to establish any sort of legal basis for its operation. Any area as important as energy is bound to have special laws and special legislation.

You always stress that Russia and the European Union are building a common economic space, whereas the Quartet of Russia, Belarus, Kazakhstan and Ukraine will have a single economic space. Is the difference more than terminology?

The Single Economic Space being constructed now by the Quartet intends to put out to national regulation some fairly substantial elements of the economy – for a start, anything to do with customs policy and so, presumably, customs tariffs, customs rules and procedures and customs authorities. At the same time, it will at least link policy and domestic competition in a supra-national manner: I mean subsidy policy, tariff policy, technical regulation and so on. That presupposes there will be a supra-national level and means that each country will lose some sovereignty as these matters will be controlled supranationally. The shared space which we are planning with the European Union entails no such loss of sovereignty. It entails co-operation and harmonisation of legislation, but the right of control is retained by both sides. That is the principal difference. So the depth of integration is different.

Will the integration of the Quartet eventually lead to something like the European Union?

The answer is quite simple. The activities of the Quartet were, are and will continue to be based on two things. First, our own experience, because the parties to the Quartet represent different integration models. Russia and Belarus are building a union of their two states. Russia, Belarus and Kazakhstan are members of the Eurasian Economic Community. Russia and Ukraine, Belarus and Ukraine or Kazakhstan and Ukraine are in the CIS. So we have ten years' direct experience of integration processes, which is invaluable and goes to show, at least, that there can be no question of politics winning out over economic pragmatism. Second, there is obviously the experience of the European Union, which is really the only single economic space in existence. It is a single economic-*plus* space, I would say, the plus being the existence of a currency union, the Eurozone, even though it doesn't cover the whole EU area. Those two elements make a single whole in the integration logic of the Quartet.

Is it going to take decades?

For a start, there is no comparison between our experience today and that of the European Union. The European Union was built

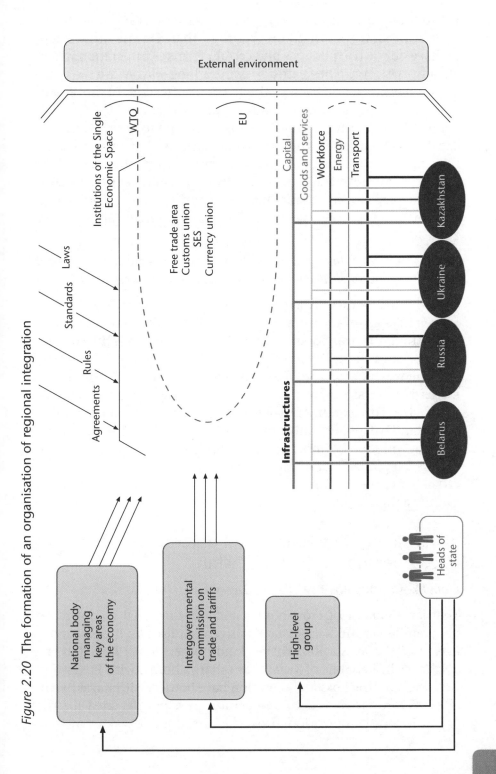

Figure 2.20 The formation of an organisation of regional integration

without any benefit of experience. We have no need to repeat its 40-year history; we can go quicker than that. On the other hand, we have our own experience and certain forms of integration which already exist, so we have already come a long way. As we see it, we do not have to act on each of the freedoms [freedom of movement of goods and services, capital and workers, the aims of the Quartet] separately and in turn, quietly going from one to another, but we can tackle them all at the same time. I think that in fact that is the only way to move forward successfully. Any attempt to draw up a successive timetable will take us nowhere except backwards. In principle, I think, launching these processes and completing them to the extent envisaged at the moment might take us up to 2008/10.

In September the four Heads of State plan to sign the agreement establishing the Single Economic Space. Has it already been drafted?

What is already established is the concept of the Single Economic Space and a set of measures to achieve it. The agreement is a relatively straightforward document which will cover both the concept and the measures. The measures will be set out in a technical document which not only gives a series of milestones and moves forward with the four freedoms but provides a system of agreements to be achieved according to a defined timetable. They will be legal in nature and will require ratification. The technical legal work on each of them will soon be underway. Accomplishing the single space will require a few dozen such agreements.

Therefore the document which kicks off that work can afford to be only a framework.

Advantages of the unrealised potential in co-operation with Kazakhstan

From Ekonomika Rossii, *Vol. XXI (December).*

The development of cross-border and inter-regional co-operation between Russia and Kazakhstan is driven not least by the enormous length of the Russia–Kazakhstan land border: 6,500 km. Half the *oblasts* of the Republic of Kazakhstan share a border with Russia and 12 Subjects of the Russian Federation have borders with Kazakhstan.

We regard cross-border co-operation as a priority area for the expansion of co-operation between Russia and Kazakhstan. The legal basis to do this is already established. It includes bilateral and multilateral agreements. As of today Subjects of the Russian Federation and *oblasts* of Kazakhstan, and also some cities of both countries, have signed 116 agreements on various areas of economic and humanitarian co-operation.

It is Russia's economic relations with Kazakhstan that most clearly show our already active 'assets' and the problematic 'liabilities' and costs. Alongside the achievements, a whole series of problems have arisen in transport and tariffs, technical regulation measures, trade, customs and border processing and so on. The scope for resolving the problems of cross-border territories is really quite limited. Seeking solutions in the mechanisms and institutions of cross-border co-operation will not work. It is necessary to go up a level higher and find answers in the trade and economic co-operation between the Russian Federation and the Republic of Kazakhstan at international level.

The Republic of Kazakhstan has accounted for no more than 3–4 per cent of Russia's total foreign trade volume over recent years. The aggregate for the CIS is 18 per cent of the total. Russia accounts for about a third of Kazakhstan's total foreign trade. In a number of commodities the Kazakhstan market is relevant for both Russian exporters and Russian importers.

The Kazakhstan market is the main foreign market for Russian producers of foodstuffs, railway equipment, automobiles, explosives and so on. Kazakhstan provides a quarter of Russia's imports of ores, over half its fossil fuel and around 50 per cent of its chemicals, metals, etc.

However, it must be noted that in 2002 the volume of trade between our countries in cash terms was 9.4 per cent lower than in 2001 at $4.3 billion. Russian exports were down 13.2 per cent at $2.4 billion and imports from Kazakhstan were down 4 per cent at $1.9 billion.

It is important that we join forces to prevent that decline from becoming a trend. To do so we must understand what is happening and try to devise a set of measures to provide a sort of immunity from it.

First the fall in cash terms was caused by a fall in the prices of energy and a number of raw materials, along with seasonal and market fluctuations. As a result, even an increase in imports of certain products from Russia did not make up for the fall in price.

For example, coke and semi-coke imports to Kazakhstan increased in comparison with the first half of 2001 by 7.5 per cent in volume terms, but in value terms fell by 16 per cent. Oil and gas condensate imports increased by 38 per cent in volume, but fell by 5 per cent in value. The situation is similar for many commodities. At the start of this year deliveries of mineral raw materials increased, but only as a result of a hard winter.

The price arguments look convincing at first glance. However, over a time frame longer than a year – over perhaps three to five years – it emerges that the price fluctuations, like the seasonal fluctuations, cancel out and do not in fact have a significant effect on the state of trade.

Second, the growth of own production in some sectors of the economy of both countries led to increased import replacement, affecting the trade between them.

The third reason concerned certain features of the way indirect taxation in the form of value-added tax (VAT) in Russia and excise duties in Kazakhstan were applied; this created serious barriers. On one hand we are trying to equalise customs tariffs for our countries, but at the same time we impose non-tariff, taxation or technical measures on our bilateral trade.

We could continue with this list of reasons. Unfortunately any such measures only make for more cut-throat competition, thus opening the way for goods from third countries. In particular, as imports of cars from Russia were cut by nearly a third, imports from Japan increased by 50 per cent and imports from the Czech Republic increased by 350 per cent. The same picture is seen in other industrial goods, including vehicles, plant and building structures.

With this understanding of integration processes, we can return to looking at the problems of cross-border co-operation. Administrative measures and barriers must be replaced by economic mechanisms and an entirely different regulatory logic. That must be based on efficiency, cost reduction, proper return on investment and competitiveness in markets outside the Single Economic Space.

Examples of co-operation are the Kuznetsk basin, Ekibastuz, shared arrangements in the energy market, the creation of a single fuel and energy balance, grain, the adoption of a unified tariff policy and policy in the field of technical regulation.

As we solve particular problems of cross-border co-operation it is important to remember the prospects for the future. The end result will be a leap forward in growth for the economies of both countries and in their standard of living.

Speech to economic forum, Alma-Ata, 12 April 2002:

Worth mentioning here are not only the now fashionable globalisation models, but also models of regional and inter-regional integration which can mitigate many negative aspects of the former. For Russia, the possible advantages of such an approach are no longer in doubt. Bilateral and multilateral co-operation in the post-Soviet space (which could also be regarded as an early experiment in globalisation) will develop deeper market-based associations using private financial-industrial and banking capital. The focus of co-operation is naturally on energy, which is equally important for all partners. Whether in oil and gas transport or problems of water use and hydroelectricity, the issue is one of basic infrastructures which could, with little risk of exaggeration, be called vital infrastructures – vital, that is, to living together in a geostrategically important space.

Hence the great store we rightly set by maintaining the general stability of the region. Economic interests demand that we minimise foreign economic risk. A large role here falls to intergovernmental structures whereby contact can be maintained continuously with a view to achieving mutual understanding on all aspects of the life of our countries. We will be guided by the principle of not forcing our partners into any preconceived mould of our own. The existing equilibrium is maintained largely by respecting the uniqueness of each side of the dialogue. Any other approach will do little to accelerate integration and is more likely to do the opposite.

In conclusion I would like to note that though energy is at the front of our minds, we are in no way playing down the importance of other areas of co-operation. In both transport and industry we also feel the vital force which is so necessary to all participants at our summit.

From Evraziya, *October 2001:*

The essence of Russia's policy today towards the countries of the CIS is energetic bilateral co-operation based on pragmatism and mutual respect of interests.

Our multilateral co-operation is built in those areas which enjoy the support of all participants. That approach means we pursue enhanced co-operation primarily with those partners who show the greatest commitment to closer integration.

The building of the union of Russia and Belarus is proceeding according to plan. Belarus, Kazakhstan, Kyrgyzstan, Russia and Tajikistan have combined in the Eurasian Economic Community (EurAsEC), the main goal of which is to complete the creation of a fully fledged customs union and ultimately to create a single economic space. In that connection it is often asked whether co-operation in the CIS format is not at odds with the existence of various other regional associations, EurAsEC, the Collective Security Treaty, GUUAM (the Georgia, Ukraine, Uzbekistan, Azerbaijan, Moldova Organisation for Democracy and Economic Development) and so on.

We believe that it is entirely consistent with the model of multi-speed, multi-level integration of the post-Soviet space. The main thing to emphasise is that such co-operation, in no matter what format, must not and does not cut across the overall aims and interests of the Commonwealth as a whole.

The common interest can be, is and certainly must be served by the unique geostrategic position which the CIS occupies. The territory of the CIS is crossed by the most promising international transport and energy corridors. Expansion of the network will support the operation of both the existing and all planned pipelines, electricity transmission lines and transport communications. That is an advantage which must surely strengthen the position not only of Russia but of the Commonwealth as a whole in the global economy. It is extraordinarily important that these advantages should not be left at the mercy of politics, which, like the Moscow weather, can be pretty changeable. Rather, co-operation should be based on the rigorous logic of economic calculation, on pragmatism. Only then will it be possible to avoid competition, sometimes unjustified, and conflicts, either bilateral or in various multilateral formats of co-operation, in the CIS area.

Then how do you envisage the CIS and EurAsEC? Why create two so similar organisations?

I have tried very hard to answer this question, but I would like to point out to you one thought which seems important to me. The development of integration at regional and sub-regional levels, in particular under the aegis of the CIS, EurAsEC or other organisations, allows us to properly realise the advantages and to eliminate the negative consequences, particularly in the socio-economic sphere, of globalisation.

Contrary to his previous statements, it seems the president of Moldova does not intend either to withdraw his country from GUUAM or to join EurAsEC. What is Russian policy on the enlargement of EurAsEC?

Russia has a clear interest in extending enhanced forms of multi-lateral co-operation to new participants. As the EurAsEC declares itself open to any state which shares its aims, tasks and principles, any country joining, whether as full member or observer, must be prepared to participate in EurAsEC activities. It may be that the transition from observer status to full member status requires a transitional period for harmonisation of the numerous domestic provisions, in particular the nature of the economic legislation, with the level achieved in the multilateral format within EurAsEC. In the economic plane in particular, EurAsEC is the most advanced organi-sation because it has managed to solve the problems of customs-free trade among its members, has substantially solved issues of freedom of movement of goods and has apparently made good progress towards harmonisation of its legislation in that area. Consequently accession to EurAsEC demands analogous procedures on the part of any other state. Nevertheless it is clear that the decision whether to join any international organisation is the sovereign right of each state.

Speech on the occasion of the 10th anniversary of the CIS, 15 March 2002:

Russia's attitude to the CIS is special. For Russians it is a question of maintaining and renewing links formed over decades in economics, culture and education, and by family and personal contacts (among army friends, work colleagues and the like). So much has changed. But in ten years certain fundamental principles of the common-wealth have become manifest, no matter under what cover or abbreviation it exists: they are the interconnectedness and inter-dependence of the elements of previously created economic cycles. These may be weakened or disrupted but they have never ceased to exist. There is the single information space, where one of the languages of the Commonwealth is key. In fact, that is quite enough to establish politico-legal communities, because economic interest and use of a common language as a means of informa-tion exchange are irreversible things. It is another question how uniform the common space is. During the first decade each part made progress on its own at its own rate. Some countries moved ahead. For the Commonwealth it is important that there should not only be a single centre of gravity and progress. The task is to make the Commonwealth a union of equals according to certain key criteria so that the economic space is a single space with unified rules for active economic forces and so that the language – or, more accurately, bilingualism – should become the norm and thus the basis for humanising the life of people in the CIS. Therefore when we speak of the role of the Russian language we mean not only for the protection of the interests of the Russian population but also to protect the interests of the entire Commonwealth as a single whole.

From Rossiyskaya gazeta, *15 July 2002:*

Our high-level group has been working quite hard. The presidents of the Quartet countries have decided to move to the formation of a single economic space which will live by a single set of rules and laws. But today that space is divided by a great many barriers. We erect them ourselves, and absolutely legitimately too. But then we complain to each other because galvanised steel exports have been hit or beer exports have been held up. The presidents have stepped in and ordered there should be no more 'annoying the neighbours'.

We remove all obstacles to the neighbours' beer. But as soon as we deal with beer, up pops the milk problem. It is always like that, because one nation's business complains about competition from neighbouring countries and demands protection. The reason is that our economies have different regulatory regimes. So now we are creating a single space. The concept is being completed now. Moreover at the group's last meeting in Minsk, Russia presented not only a text of the concept, but a mechanism for its implementation. Full implementation will require around 50 international agreements. Getting them will take some years.

The Single Economic Space: political ambition or economic utility?

From Rossiyskaya gazeta, *17 June 2003:*

Vigorous competition is a fact of modern life. The best illustration of that is the events of recent years. Countries with highly developed economies are, wherever they can, driving out less-developed competitors from promising global markets, leaving them only low-tech niches and sectors with low added value. That is how it is now in the world economy into which the CIS countries are trying to integrate. In such an aggressive environment, the quickest way to penetrate the global economy may be to simply dissolve into it leaving no residue. The alternative, which takes more effort and is much harder, is to integrate from a position of if not equality then at least strength. It is accepted I think, by practically all influential political forces in both Russia and every other country in the CIS that making the country competitive should be a major objective of the state. Now we must see to it that that objective is pursued as consistently and effectively as possible. On that will depend the economic stability of our countries and their weight in the world market and in international affairs in general.

In the third millennium, any state's success in economic develop-ment is determined by its ability to exploit internal and, even more importantly, external sources of growth. Russia, like a number of its CIS partners, has in recent years enjoyed a favourable world market situation in energy and has used it to boost its rate of economic growth. However, everyone realises that such a resource has limited potential and large associated risks. No strategy for economic growth can be built upon it.

With the exception of raw materials, the goods and services produced in the 'post-Soviet' space are not yet highly competitive on the world market. That being so, there are various ways for the economy to position itself. One is to maintain or even reinforce the protection of the national market against external competition, thereby stimulating domestic investment in fixed assets, restruc-turing, and flooding the domestic market with products which, as competitiveness increases, will start to find buyers abroad. A serious drawback to this model is the existence of a whole series of almost rhetorical questions: is there enough capital ready to be put to work in such a closed market? What will happen to domestic demand? How able, in these circumstances, are major industries to close the technology gap? And so on.

A possible alternative policy is to liberalise rapidly and open up the market. In that case Russian producers of goods and services can only hope that some of them might survive the competitive onslaught, keep control of their businesses and be able to trade globally. For the foreign markets, as we have seen several times, are not necessarily waiting for us, or even our raw materials, with open arms. I find it hard to imagine that any Russian industrial or business circles could in conscience support such a course. That scenario also brings the threat of the negative social consequences which would appear in the transitional period as the economy adjusted to new conditions of harsh competition.

Practical experience shows that consolidation and integration are important ways of increasing competitiveness. In the context of globalisation, regional and sub-regional integration is becoming the dominant trend at all levels from the corporate to the national level. True enough, the dynamics of such processes are different at different levels. In the European Union, for example, they have been going on for over 40 years and accelerated only in the last decade, when a qualitative breakthrough occurred. The European Coal and Steel Community was formed over 40 years ago, and then there was the Common Market and only after that today's European Union.

The CIS space is the sphere of our strategic interests. For the Commonwealth states Russia, in turn, is a zone of their national interests. The interest of all players in economic progress in all parts of the CIS is natural, because the interdependence of our develop-ment is self-evident. Our infrastructure was originally conceived as a single whole. Across a wide range of goods the neighbouring markets were and remain practically the sole market. While the aim of closer economic ties is official policy in both Russia and the CIS countries, its implementation has run into a number of objective difficulties. For one thing, the consequences of the grave systemic crisis caused by the artificial tearing apart of the economic links forged in the Soviet period have yet to be overcome amidst the rigours of the transition to a market economy.

In the circumstances the CIS states joined forces almost as soon as they regained their independence to at least start creating a new basis for a common space. Their efforts, however, often led nowhere. As a result, there accumulated many overlapping agreements, but they did not produce a new quality of economic co-operation. From the beginning, the documents signed in 1993/94, notably the Treaty on the Creation of the Economic Union, intended that the CIS should develop as a regional integrative association in 'linear' fashion: free trade area, then customs union, then economic and currency union. In the realisation that it was impossible to create a common customs space covering all CIS countries at that time, it was decided in 1995 to create a Customs Union of five Commonwealth states. In 2000 that became the Eurasian Economic Community. That it was right to set up the 'Customs Five' is confirmed by their having higher rates of growth of mutual trade than the other members of the CIS.

There is sometimes criticism or dissatisfaction at the development of economic co-operation in the CIS or even in EurAsEC. Our non-working 'assets' and problematic 'liabilities' and costs are becoming more and more apparent. But self-evidently we are moving towards integration. That is one of the biggest assets of both organisations. They have prevented centrifugal forces from completely tearing us apart and have maintained the vision of future integration.

The overwhelming majority of Russian trade with CIS countries is with Belarus, Ukraine and Kazakhstan. The Quartet makes up 94 per cent of the GDP and 88 per cent of the trade of all the CIS countries combined. It can become the locomotive of integration processes for a very long time into the future.

The narrow path of opportunities

Speaking of the trends in our mutual trade, we can see that we stand on a path of opportunities. It is bounded on one side by the degree of development of each of our economies and on the other by the degree of actual working integration of our economies. Such a path can only lead in one of two ways.

The first is that nations become boxed into their national borders; barriers are erected to the movement of goods, services, capital and workers; and import replacement takes place, but at a loss. I can predict that in such circumstances trade would remain within its present limits: there might be the odd surge for price reasons, but the general trend would be downwards. By taking such measures we would be increasing competition among ourselves and opening the way for goods from third countries. Meanwhile the problems of the market in goods and services would force us to go looking for investors in third countries and via circuitous export routes.

The other prospect is that trans-border costs on the movement of goods, services and capital are minimised and in due course abolished, allowing the whole integrated space to compete as a single entity. If that is the aim, then we must see to it that accession to the World Trade Organization (WTO) does not become an obstacle to continuing the integration process. To that end it is essential that our countries' positions on sensitive parameters are agreed and as close as possible when we join the WTO. Differences in timing over when each country joins are not the determining factor.

The Quartet's integration plans do not break WTO rules, as several facts make clear. First, all the regional economic associations currently in existence operate strictly within the WTO framework. WTO rules clearly state that countries have the right to create regional blocs (free trade areas, customs unions) and pursue agreed foreign trade policies within them.

Second, the point of the WTO is to establish common 'rules of the game' for all participating states. The point of regional blocs is, within those rules, to effectively address practical problems of trade and economic relations between neighbouring countries.

Third, the Quartet is creating a real capability for co-ordinating its members' actions in relation to the WTO, thus greatly simplifying the solution of problems associated with accession.

In forming the Quartet into a Single Economic Space we are saying that the existing free trade area is too small for us. Already we find ourselves in a situation where trade between us is growing more slowly than our separate markets. We must consolidate our potential, harmonise trade rules on goods, services and investment and create a true economic union. The path of opportunity can be made wider by creating the Single Economic Space. Taking that step will increase the competitive potential of our countries' economies in trade with third countries. We must be aware that this will require the creation of supra-national structures for regulation and decision making in a number of areas of economic policy. We should do it with our eyes open. World experience shows that otherwise it is impossible to achieve the level of integration to which we aspire.

The broad path of 'simple' solutions

It is important here not to repeat certain mistakes of the past, not to take the path of 'simple' solutions which cancel out the effects of integration. For example, it is said that we should pick one area – perhaps even a very important one like transport tariffs – and impose a unified policy, then everything would be all right. It will not be all right. There would be a short period of rejoicing brought swiftly to an end by divergences in competition, customs, tariff and other policies, and the return of policies which are if anything worse than before unification. 'Let us proceed from one form of integration to the next, starting with a full-fledged free trade area and then ...' And then nothing. We have been there and done that. As well as the single space for goods we must create a single space for capital, services and workers. That space is currently criss-crossed by barriers. They are barriers we have created with a high degree of sophistication. And we have done so entirely legitimately as each state tries to protect its own businesses.

Progress can only be made by advancing on all fronts at the same time: that is, by creating the conditions to accomplish all four freedoms, thus establishing a single economic space. That is a different logic of regulation. It is based on efficiency, cost reduction, real returns on investment and the ability to compete in foreign (external to the Single Economic Space) markets. The end result is the prospect of an entirely new sort of growth of national economies and living standards.

Now the high-level group which is working on the immediate tasks set by the four presidents has produced a draft concept for the formation of the Single Economic Space. More importantly, we have outlined a series of measures by which the process will be carried out in practice. That means we have arrived at an understanding of an initial list of the international documents that will be required to make the idea of the Single Economic Space a reality.

The European vector

Russia has a stake in integration with its CIS neighbours and the development of relations with the European Union. The two are not alternatives but mutually complementary. The alliance of post-Soviet republics will be in a better position to develop relations with Europe. Objectively, the economic union of the post-Soviet republics will be in a stronger position in foreign markets.

The European Union is also our natural partner in the formation of a common space. The European vector is important to Russia. The European Union must be seen as a community not of the 15 members it has today [2003] but of the 25 states it will comprise from next spring. That makes it a natural partner for joint activities in areas where our competitive advantages can be fully realised – energy, space and other high technologies, chemistry and metallurgy.

At the same time the European Union is far ahead of us, and its experience is very relevant to our aims of creating a supra-national economic space with an integrated system of economic regulation. The current Partnership and Co-operation Agreement between Russia and the European Union declares Russia's intention of gradually harmonising its legislation with that of the European Union. Similar provisions are to be found in bilateral agreements between the European Union and almost all CIS states, many of which have set themselves the aim of further convergence with the European Union, to the point of actually becoming members.

Obviously the creation of economic spaces, whether in the East (the CIS) or West (the European Union), brings advantages to Russia. Both processes can proceed in isolation or may, conversely, be inter-linked, enriching each other and gradually consolidating economic integration over an area with a population three times greater than that of Russia. The latter would appear to be preferable and most realistic for us. That conclusion was reached after discussions in recent years with partners on two projects, the Single Economic Space with Belorussia, Ukraine and Kazakhstan and the Common European Economic Space (CEES).

Will the successful development of the Single Economic Space not impede the economic integration of Russia and the European Union? There are instances where blocs with different levels of inte-gration manage to coexist. The European Union itself is the best example. It has agreements aiming towards integration with dozens of states and pursues greater internal integration at the same time.

Integration processes among CIS states can go faster than the creation of CEES. Our countries are closer together in terms of economic level and competitiveness. Much has already been done to achieve the reciprocal opening of markets. Economic legisla-tion is still in the process of being formed and so can more easily be harmonised. It is therefore all the more important that certain measures we must take now are carefully thought through so that they remain applicable in dialogue with the European Union.

For example, accomplishing the 'four freedoms' involves more than removing border restrictions: in other words, the barriers to entering the market – duties, quotas, investment limits and so on. A completely unified single economic space can be achieved only if all means of economic regulation are harmonised. For example, anti-dumping measures can be done away with only if there is effective common competition legislation. Similarly, common legislation on state aid and a single policy on prices mean that you can do without compensatory duties as an instrument of foreign trade.

The construction of a uniform economic space including Russia and our neighbours east and west is a long-term objective. But some harmonisation measures have immediate effects even in the very earliest stages of the creation of the common space – for example, the unification of product technical requirements, veterinary and plant health standards, customs rules and documents. While the common home is being built, some international segments will be created faster than others, depending on how prepared each country is for deeper integration. Here the analogy with the 'multi-speed Europe' is entirely appropriate. That model has been successfully followed in the last two decades of the evolution of the European Union and has allowed its successful consolidation into a supranational formation that is historically unique in terms of the number of its members and the depth of the integration achieved between them. Continuing the analogy, we may well suppose that as a 'trans-European space' emerges, the centripetal forces attracting new members, such as the CIS and other neighbours of Russia, will grow. The result will be that over the enormous space of Eurasia a new quality of economic co-operation emerges that can be an important engine of growth.

In working towards the Single Economic Space, all our actions are subordinated to the aim that in the not too distant future our countries should take their place among the truly strong, economically advanced and influential states. First of all it must be said clearly – in fact it is obvious – that the creation of such a space cannot be just Russia's business and priority. We cannot and we will not force our plans on anyone. We have no expansionist designs on foreign territories. The single space can only be the product of a conscious shared interest or, more precisely, balance of interests.

It is a qualitatively new step-up that each state participating in integration is endeavouring to take. It will be easiest if we take it together. Now we must mobilise the efforts not only of experts and officials but of business and society too.

The Single Economic Space will be like the European Union before the introduction of the euro

Diversity is wealth. The diversity of structures in the CIS space is the result of an evolution of interests. The states get together and say, for example, 'Let us co-ordinate customs duties in order to protect our markets from encroachment by goods from third countries. All in favour?' And all sign an agreement. In 1995, during the historic process of our integration, unification of duties across the five countries of the customs union was 100 per cent achieved. In other words, five countries had the same external borders so far as customs duties were concerned. It is true that lasted for only a few months and swiftly collapsed. Today about 50 per cent of them remain. Harmonised customs tariffs were maintained only for half a year, then quietly dissolved. No one is to blame for what happened. The system was built not on the basis of supra-national law but on particular agreements.

The four countries which contribute 88 per cent of all the trade and 94 per cent of the GDP of the CIS see integration as the way forward. And we declare that we can create the conditions in which customs regulations, customs tariffs and procedures, anti-monopoly regulations and competition and tariff policies can all be subsumed under supra-national functions. To preserve that unification we are devising a normative base, agreeing starting conditions and dispensing with national regulation in favour of a supra-national body. Of course that will not happen all at once. It takes time and will have to be phased in. The Quartet is not an organisation but a structure for activities. We can be confident that there are good prospects for integration in the post-Soviet space. To take an analogy with Europe, the Single Economic Space will be like the European Union before the introduction of the euro.

All talk of when the Single Economic Space might be formed is best left to the experts. The legal basis is not straightforward. We will have to write dozens of agreements and get them signed and ratified. That is not some random assortment of documents; together they must form a coherent whole. With very hard work, I think it might take five to seven years to get to the Single Economic Space. The first thing to tackle will obviously be customs procedures and tariffs. Our declared principle is 'multi-level and multi-speed' integration in the Single Economic Space. That means that once two or three countries reach a certain level, they sign an agreement, and a fourth and even fifth member can join later.

It took Europe 30 years to create a single economic space and another ten years to get to the Eurozone. The process began with freedom of trade in the limited economic sector of coal and steel.

Moreover only six countries were signed up to free trade, not the current 15. Thereafter European integration began to extend to new sectors and new territories, turning from free trade to customs tariffs and all the rest of it. That is what took 30 years. It took another ten to realise the Eurozone project. Even then not all countries have adopted the euro: only 12 of the 15. Schengen has not been adopted by all either. None of which stops Europe developing and serving as an object lesson for us. When we say that it will take five to seven years to create our Single Economic Space – in other words that we intend to come together five or six times faster than Europe managed – it is because we have 70 years of life together in the Soviet Union behind us and 12 years of integration since its demise. However it is decidedly too early to talk about a currency union for the Quartet.

Also, we must take a rather longer and wider view. We are discussing markets not only in goods but in capital and services. Russia has a direct interest in proper, equal access for our capital to both the services and capital markets. Each of the countries associated with the Single Economic Space has an opportunity to secure mutual respect for its interests. Of that I am certain.

No more economic romanticism for us

From Rossiyskaya gazeta, *15 July 2003:*

No sooner were you off the plane from Vladivostok than you went to see the President of the Russian Federation in Moscow. What had you to report?

My report to the president emphasised particularly that we can be pleased at the way our relations with Japan are developing. Start with the economy. First, it has been decided to launch the second stage of the $10-billion Sakhalin II project, with around $2 billion spent this year. Japanese companies will contribute about $4 billion of the total investment. It is very important that we have agreed on the involvement of Russian contractors in the project. We are not talking about secondary roles either. We shall insist on that. Second, we gave the Japanese side to understand that the Sakhalin I and Sakhalin II projects are to be carried out exactly as stated in the agreements. That is, we have confirmed that the legal arrangements are sound.

In the area of trade, we have seen the first sign of growth in trade between our countries after two years of stagnation. Since the start of the year both exports and imports are already up more than a third.

What is Russia happy with? The structure of our exports to Japan? We sell timber, metals and fish products and buy machinery. Unfortunately, that reflects the structure of our economy generally.

Even when Sakhalin I and Sakhalin II come into force and are producing commercial output of up to $5 billion a year, the overall export structure will not change: we will just be exporting even more raw materials and energy, and nothing else. We harbour no illusions about our road vehicles or domestic appliances becoming competitive on the Japanese market any time soon. But still, we do have space, nuclear and information technologies at a more than viable level, and with them we could well have something to offer Japan on a long-term, mutually advantageous basis.

Another important step has been taken. We have signed an agreement on the disposal of Viktor-3 class nuclear submarines at the end of their service lives. Ms Kawaguchi and I resurrected the system of Japanese centres in Russia where Japanese specialists will train qualified managers, organise cultural exchanges and so on.

What was discussed, but not agreed?

We have not yet got a decision on two major energy projects. One is the construction of the Eastern Siberia–Pacific Ocean pipeline and the other is the Sakhalin–Japan 'power bridge'.

China and Japan have different views on the project. Have we pragmatism enough to do it so that it benefits us and not just them?

There is pragmatism enough. We have the experience. There is no more economic romanticism for us. What does this project mean, if we set aside the details? Russia has the strategic aim of getting the products of its fuel and energy complex (oil, gas and electricity) onto the Asia-Pacific markets. But first Russia has to study the risks, assess them correctly and see how to cover them. The first group of risks has to do with oil production. How much money is needed to make geological surveys, identify more recoverable reserves and ultimately get the oil out of the ground? Well, all that's expensive and that risk must be borne by the oil companies. No madcap schemes, nothing half-baked or otherworldly. This is the business that gave us our largest players. They must prove that they can add up and use some judgement.

The second group of risks has to do with gas production. The problems are the same, but gas extraction is less mature, by some years, than oil in the Eastern Siberian region.

Two other risk groups are the oil and gas pipeline networks. Oil pipelines are Transneft risks, but deploying all the company's resources and capacities to neutralise them would be misguided. Nobody can afford that. It is the same with the gas system, or perhaps that problem is even harder, given that co-ordination with a variety of other structures is required.

There is also a fifth group of risks to do with market risk assessment when we enter the markets of Asia. Certainly the Asia-Pacific market is very promising, though three-quarters of its short-term growth will come from China. Then, while we are thinking about exports, we must not forget our own markets in Eastern Siberia and the Far East. That region has absolutely no gas supply at all.

Does that mean the Russian Federation government will not provide the project finance guarantees the Japanese are asking for?

It won't. First, doing so would contravene the financial policies of the state. Any guarantees must appear in the budget and as such they risk compromising budgetary obligations. Obligations are primarily social and affect specific individuals. Can that principle be sacrificed, even for such serious projects? No, and there's no need for it to be.

The government, as it tries to create a firm financial base, aims to reduce inflation and increase economic growth, which then improves companies' creditworthiness. Let us look at the situation from the point of view of Transneft, for example. The state uses Transneft to implement its pipeline strategy. In particular, it is building the Baltic pipeline system. Phases two and three of the project will cost $1 billion. Where is the money to come from? From the budget? No. We have devised a scheme to raise three, five and seven-year loans, all within Russia. The Russian finance market wants reliable borrowers who can work off large loans and can be trusted to repay them. Moreover it is not going to demand sky-high interest rates, but to offer normal, realistic terms. The country has money. It has lots of money. We are creating a class of creditworthy borrowers and getting finance houses to operate normal long-term lending schemes. Certainly, Transneft will borrow from Sberbank; at the moment only Sberbank is in a position find $350 million for long-term loans. But tomorrow, I hope, there will be other banks. Hence the government does not need to cover those risks using the budget.

The Japanese minister of foreign affairs raised the subject of the Kuril islands in a public speech in Vladivostok. But it is not in the terms of reference of the intergovernmental commission. Why not?

I would not over-dramatise. Ms Kawaguchi gave a lecture setting out her view on certain problems. She said nothing that was not consistent with the spirit of the negotiations on the Kurils. Is there a question over the Kurils? Yes. Should we pretend there isn't? No. Is there a quick and easy solution? No, there isn't, because it affects a mass of vexed issues, not just political ones. It affects people – Japanese people, incidentally, as well as Russians.

Such issues cannot be resolved at the stroke of pen on paper. They are resolved over time, through the establishment of a wide range of mutual relations, not least person to person among the citizens of both countries. That is the way we are going with Japan.

Could you imagine, even theoretically, that we might just sell the Kurils to the Japanese in, say, 20 or 50 years' time? After all we sold Alaska to the Americans.

You might as well ask if I could imagine Russia as an autocracy in 20 or 50 years' time.

Would you go along with the view that Russia should not ratify the Kyoto Protocol? The argument goes that Russia pollutes the environment less than anyone but is expected to pay up in the same way as developed countries.

The whole problem is how fast and how well our economy is going to develop. Let us consider the best case. Say our GDP doubles by 2010 and, as our energy strategy proposes, our energy consumption relative to GDP is halved. Would we be afraid of the Kyoto Protocol then? No. Russia could easily meet its requirements with something to spare. The worst-case scenario is that GDP doubles and we do not save energy. Would we fall under sanctions? Possibly. However, we will *never* double GDP if we do not make the savings. That means the Kyoto Protocol is pushing us towards quality growth. After the final analysis, the experts will give us a forecast and we will determine our policy in accordance with Russia's interests as pragmatically as possible.

Russia is calling on the post-Soviet countries to integrate and at the same time has had some sharp disagreements with Ukraine and Belarus over re-exported meat. Won't the end result be that by making a fuss about meat we damage the process of integration within the Quartet?

Regional integration processes are going on worldwide. Why? Because they are the best response to the challenges thrown up by globalisation. They are begun not on a whim but by necessity. The processes of integration within the Quartet operate at different levels. There is a 'duo' (the union of Russia and Belarus). Three of the Quartet belong to EurAsEC. And Ukraine is in the CIS. Yet none of those blocks achieves the level of 'togetherness' in decision making which would protect the members' shared interests and the particular interests of each at the same time. Without the creation of absolutely homogeneous rules on the inside it is impossible to expect to obtain any of the fruits of integration on the outside.

Your question mentioned meat, but there are also pipelines, steel and a mass of other goods in which trade is occasionally accompanied by conflict. The cause is always the same – unfair competition, whether that means re-exports, dumping or something else. Russia has a set of entirely legitimate means to combat such competition: it can impose tariff quotas or special duties, or it can even resort to fierce protection measures. To do that is to criticise our partners. You, we say to them, are bad people. That is the appropriate, pragmatic response; simple. If anyone then tells us that looks unfriendly, we should not behave so, we are all in it together as we build the Single Economic Space, well: let us not get neurotic over what other people think of us. Instead we should try to understand and remove the causes.

There are several causes. For example, suppose one country has one lot of customs rules and another country has different ones. Or one country gives production subsidies and another one doesn't. Obviously goods which are 'unreasonably cheap' in one country will be exported to the country where they are more expensive and undermine that country's economy. The solution is strict unification of both customs regulations and the rules of internal competition. They must be such that no one country can change anything, even at home, just unilaterally. There must be no 'left opportunism' and no 'right opportunism'. Then there really would be a single economic space.

If we cannot find in ourselves the political will to adopt such a solution, we should go to the people and admit that it's not going to work. But having done so we must immediately establish rigorous customs frontiers and impose all kinds of controls and protection. I think that second route would be a mistake. It would be a mistake, even allowing for the fact that integration stands to cost Russia more than anyone else. What is important is the quality of integration. We are accustomed to talking only about the movement of goods. But there is also a range of services which are up in the air as regards the prospects for developing large-scale industry. There is the sector of capital and workers. Russia's interest is to advance not by little steps but on all four fronts: goods, services, capital and workers. There is no alternative. We have tried everything else. And while we were trying, Europe became a single state.

It is said that Belarus is a model of integration and Ukraine is integration's headache. How so? Is it Lukashenko good guy and Kuchma bad guy? Is it that Ukraine is going to be accepted into the WTO soon and can do without our unions, whereas Belorussia hasn't got a sniff of a chance?

The differences in Russia's relations with Belarus, Ukraine and other states are not 'a headache' but a source of riches. True, our customs duties are 99 per cent unified with Belarus; customs regimes are not yet finally unified, but we are moving in that direction. That is all good, a positive experience. Is everything hunky-dory? No. There are problems, a lot of problems, mainly to do with competition policy. The situation regarding competition policy is actually better

285

in Ukraine than Belarus. But we cannot boast of much unification of customs regimes or rates of duty with Ukraine.

Russia–Japan and Russia–Europe 'power bridges'

Interview for RIA Novosti, *1 July 2003:*

The project has a certain history. Schematically it is fairly simple: use the gas resources of the Sakhalin shelf to generate electricity in south Sakhalin and supply it by underwater cable to Japan. As originally conceived the project was intended to serve the island of Honshu. Today a revised version takes one leg, if not the whole line, as far as the island of Hokkaido.

The project is now attracting more interest. One reason for that is the progress with the Sakhalin shelf projects. Whereas the scheme for the use of gas from Sakhalin II has been decided – a liquefied petroleum gas plant will be built and gas will be supplied in the form of LPG – Sakhalin I is still evaluating its gas capacity and considering the alternatives. One is to use the gas to generate electricity for supply to Japan. In addition, certain changes have taken place over time in Japan affecting the structure of power generation. They mainly affect nuclear energy. Some nuclear stations are being switched off and nuclear energy is becoming smaller as a proportion of the total. Therefore both Japanese business and we have turned back to this project.

Between now [July 2003] and the end of the year, detailed work will be done on the feasibility study for investment in the project.

Another new gas transmission project is the North European Gas Pipeline. There is some interest from European countries but so far they are only talking about investing in a feasibility study.

The European Union will contribute investment to the feasibility study. That was confirmed at recent summits. In the current phase the feasibility study is all there is, because only a feasibility study can identify possible routes, investment volumes and so on. So it is too early to ask for more.

But there are experts who think that Russia only stands to lose money on the project because in the next five to seven years Europe is going to develop other routes and will have an abundance of gas.

First, projects on that scale are not finished in a year. Therefore, as we start working towards the Arctic shelf or building a complex pipeline system we must be aware that there will be at least seven or eight years between the decision and the thing being finished. And the green light to build can only be given after the investment feasibility study at least is ready, and that in itself will take some time. Therefore there is no hurry – but we mustn't delay either. We need to have a portfolio of options to determine the future prospects. Then in due course we can see when to launch.

So the Arctic shelf and the North European route must absolutely be in that portfolio of options for the long term. To put it there and to keep it properly updated we must start work today. When we shall get to the component parts themselves – production or transmission – is a question we can only answer once the feasibility study is done. For experts to speak of current or imminent plans for European directions is not in any way contradictory. Central Asian gas is a resource that must find its place in the general scheme of meeting European demand. Both the agreements that have already been signed and the existing structures are intended to ensure, in fairly quick order, that Central Asian resources can be used in Europe. These things are all mutually complementary. Resolving the apparent contradictions between them is just a matter of being clear about the timetable for their implementation.

Fellow Russians

From Rossiyskaya gazeta, *11 October 2001:*

By hosting this Congress Russia is declaring openly to the world its determination to follow serious policies in relation to Russians living abroad.

Let me emphasise that the new Russian policy in this regard was decided by the president of the Russian Federation, Vladimir Putin, who calls protecting the interests of fellow Russians living abroad one of the state's most important tasks.

From Vek, *11 November 2001:*

We helped our compatriots gather together to see and listen to each other. That is the main thing. I think the time is not too far away when such gatherings will no longer need our support or involvement. That would be the logical culmination of the process begun by this Congress. The start of the next one must be timed to coincide with the founding assembly of a new international organisation of our fellow Russians. It could be the World Organisation of Russians. I think we are right to set that as a goal.

There is another thing, simpler and closer to everyday life. President Putin said that in the last ten years Russia has done little for Russians living abroad. Congress participants appreciated his words and voiced the hope that Russia would do something about them once it was back on its feet. However, even though our state has yet to draw itself up to its full height, the president has today identified work with Russians abroad as a priority of Russian policy. We have tried to be as open as we possibly can with the Russian diaspora. We have told them of our financial capabilities, which are not unlimited. We have explained that Russia has only a limited ability to protect the rights of Russians living abroad because it cannot interfere in the internal affairs of other states. And we have asked Congress participants to say whether they think we are making sensible use of those opportunities we do have. We have received many recommendations and practical suggestions, which will be used to improve the action plan for Russian Federation support to Russians abroad.

As I see it, our homeland is defined for us first by our native language. For me personally that means Russian. Despite my Ukrainian surname I can only think in Russian. We were all brought up on Russian culture and carry that world in us. The concept of *the Russian world* means all those people who carry a tiny part of Russia in them and give it to the world. All our efforts to give people who speak and think the same language an opportunity to gather together and get to know one another are an attempt to maintain and strengthen the Russian world.

Energy dialogue with the European Community

From Evropa, *1 October 2000:*

Structural reform to create effective mechanisms for the functioning of the Russian economy is the core of our economic programme. That is not only important for the internal development of the market but also for Russia's integration in the global economy.

That integration is our main line of co-operation with the European Union in the framework of the Russian Federation's new economic programme. The most important strategic direction of co-operation in this area, in my view, is securing the EU's support for Russia's accession to the WTO and consequently our further integration in the global system of economic relations.

Europe today is Russia's largest trading partner: 35 per cent of our foreign trade is with EU members. Therefore they are our main partners in negotiations on Russia's accession to the WTO. They are the ones with whom we have to settle problems over tariff policy, agriculture and the market in services.

One very substantial issue remains for Russia. Joining the WTO is not an end in itself for us, but a means of furthering the development of the Russian economy. In joining, Russia must maintain both its economic interests and those advantages which it enjoys at the moment. We would like our negotiating partners to take the same attitude.

The Tacis programme is an ancillary – but very important – part of EU support for reform in Russia. It would be useful to have it much more closely oriented to Russia's interests and tailored to the Russian government's reform programme. That aspect of support under the Tacis programme is extremely important to us, as we told our European partners at our last meeting in Brussels. The subject will be raised again at the Paris summit.

Russia is Europe's closest and most suitable partner for strategic co-operation on such matters. Our co-operation on energy cannot be limited to gas only. We are also talking about oil and electricity.

Reliable energy supplies from Russia are a component of Europe's energy security. Russia is an integral part of that. In fact even our own projects to develop the oil and gas sector, electricity and nuclear power go under the title 'The energy security of Europe in the twenty-first century'. I think that the prospects for co-operation with Russia are viewed in the same way by many in Western Europe.

The traditional relationship between Russia and Europe in this area seems to us to provide a good basis for continuing our long-term partnership in the new situation.

However, a fully fledged strategic partnership in energy is unthinkable without increased investment activity in Russia by European capital. In any conversation about a long-term programme it must be understood that to increase energy supplies requires reserves to be increased, so there must be investment in prospecting and exploration. It requires new fields to be developed and constructed, so there must be investment in production. It requires energy to be delivered, so there must be investment in infrastructure.

The dialogue must spark the creation of the conditions needed for European investment in Russia. We understand that it is a two-way process. Success depends not only on European money but on Russia creating certain conditions for Western capital. We would like to see Europe as our main partner not only for trade but also for investment.

The sides are drafting an agreement on mutual promotion of investment. Without that, the dialogue on energy would amount to no more than daydreaming. The starting point is again to be the Paris summit.

Other areas will also be up for discussion at Paris. An important one is co-operation in science and technology, including high-tech space and telecommunications. An RF–EU agreement on science and technology co-operation will be signed in the near future.

EU enlargement will also be well up the agenda in the Russia–EU dialogue. What is the government's position?

Russia never loses sight of this matter. We have long-standing trade contacts with most of the candidates for EU membership. They make up 16 per cent of Russia's foreign trade. Sixteen per cent plus 35 per cent is 51 per cent – as it were, a controlling share of foreign trade – and it is in our interests for it to remain in the hands of the European Union. Therefore the EU enlargement process must not be allowed to damage Russia's trade and economic relationship with either the EU members or the candidate nations.

Both sides are appointing enlargement co-ordinators whose role will include identifying any last hiccup arising between Russia and the European Union in the course of the process, and finding solutions at a working level. We must not allow any concerns that may arise to grow into intractable problems that need the attention of heads of state to resolve.

Because of EU enlargement the question of Kaliningrad has become highly sensitive for Russia. Once Lithuania and Poland join the European Union, Kaliningrad becomes a Russian enclave inside the European Economic Area. Brussels must appreciate the serious-ness of the problem for us. A joint group on Kaliningrad will be formed soon and a joint visit to the region is planned for early next year [2001], with EU commissioners Günter Verheugen and Chris Patten having already expressed a desire to participate.

We expect that the EU member states and the European Union as a whole will act in such a way that Kaliningrad does not become an irritant in our relations but instead serves to expand the sphere of our mutual interests.

Our trade is not limited to energy. In that regard, could you say something about the current difficulties affecting trade between Russia and the European Union?

There are stumbling blocks in our trade relations. Trade in steel and nuclear materials are the two areas which cause the greatest concern to our side. We are aware also of complaints from the European Union.

However, many problems in this area do not derive from Russia's 'transitional' status. Recognition of us as a country with a market economy is overdue. Russia is ready to join the party.

From Delovye lyudi, *1 December 2000:*

Our accession to the WTO must be preceded by a process of multilateral negotiations between Russia and its trading partners which are already WTO members. It is no secret that Europe is our biggest foreign trade partner: 35 per cent of our foreign trade is with EU countries.

Even now we are prepared in the framework of our negotiations for joining the WTO to discuss with our partners who are EU members any problems of tariff policy, agriculture, the market in services and the unification of legislation. Russia and the EU have already reached agreement on the co-ordination of joint work on Russia's accession to the WTO.

Yes, we really are talking about some quite ambitious deadlines to complete the negotiating process, but we do not think that if negotiations stall the only other way to keep on track and on time will be to simply capitulate. In the end the aim is not to stick to deadlines but to do our utmost to preserve Russian interests.

Much depends on our partners. From Europe we expect not tacit support but active assistance and understanding. We also hope for the support of other WTO members. In that regard certain agreements have been achieved with Canada and the United States.

Naturally we realise that joining the WTO will not be all beer and skittles for Russia. More economic openness means less protection for Russian producers, who may not yet be ready to compete with foreigners on equal terms.

There again, it is high time to settle once and for all the matter of

Russia's recognition as a market economy. We have done all we can in order to live up to that status.

Is Russia ready to undertake all the obligations of WTO membership?

You must understand that joining the WTO is not a fetish or an end in itself for us, but a means of economic development. Therefore one precondition of Russia's membership is to maintain its economic interests and to preserve all its advantages. I hope that is understood by our negotiating partners.

The Russia–EU summit in Paris was quite productive. What were the failures?

The political weather at any given moment should not, I think, affect decision making on our strategic co-operation. It is worth remembering that. Especially now the leaders of the European Union have finally got over their obsession with Chechnya.

It is very important that there was a round table of Russian and EU business people in advance of the Paris summit. In essence, that forum had to look at Russia's and the European Union's policies towards each other and vote with its money. Everyone knows politicians vote with their hands. People vote with their feet. Well, business people vote with their money.

The leitmotiv of our recent meetings with EU representatives was this proposition: *We have a great purpose which will take many years to achieve; we will treat any problems or difficulties as just things to be resolved in the course of this work.* That approach informed our recent meetings. I think it allowed us to make a certain breakthrough in our mutual relations. That is of prime importance.

At the moment we are talking about gas supplies to Europe doubling by 2001. That is possible only if there is gas. It must be understood that the long-term programme to increase energy supplies to Europe requires an increase in reserves. That requires investment in exploration and surveying, and in the development and building of new fields. Also, supplying energy requires infrastructure. We should not neglect, either, a guarantee for energy transit to destinations in Europe. So unless there is serious European investment and unless Russia creates favourable conditions to attract capital from EU members, there can be no Energy Dialogue worthy of the name.

There is no doubt that Russia is Europe's closest and most suitable partner for strategic co-operation in the field of the fuel and energy complex. That gives us a sound basis on which to develop a long-term partnership among our nations. Our regular supplies of energy will be the key to energy security in Europe, to which Russia belongs.

We would like Europe to be our main partner not only for trade but also for investment. At the moment it is mainly American and Japanese companies that invest in our energy industry. In due course the RF–EU Energy Dialogue will, I am certain, move us towards concluding an investment promotion agreement with the Europeans.

How will the need for Russia to ratify the European Energy Charter fit in with the strategic energy partnership? Before the real work of the Energy Dialogue can begin, certain normative acts have to be agreed and, in particular, legislation on production-sharing agreements has to be finished.

Russia has signed the European Energy Charter. It is now awaiting ratification by the State Duma and we are applying it provisionally. Still, no one can accuse us today of breaking it. Ratification is on the agenda, but I would not call it a precondition for proceeding rapidly with the Energy Dialogue. It is not as if Europe has been hitherto unable to take around 120 billion cubic metres of our gas a year. Many contracts under which we have been operating up to now were signed back in the time of the Soviet Union. We have long since proved our reliability and do not intend to do anything to spoil our reputation now.

However, it should not be forgotten that countries which should follow not only the spirit but also the letter of the charter do not always observe it.

As regards legislation on production-sharing agreements, the government has produced a definite plan. The processes – first, to establish the Energy Dialogue and develop the specific projects implied in it, and second to deal with the Russian legislation – will run in parallel.

Obviously additional pipelines will still have to be built to send gas to Europe. Through whose territory – Ukraine or Poland – will the new route pass?

Let me start by naming those pipelines that are already operational or ready to commission which could be used to send our energy to Europe. In the middle of next year [2001] Russia and Kazakhstan will commission phase one of the Caspian Pipeline Consortium. Do not forget, either, the additional pipeline from the Caspian to Novorossiysk, which passes nearby the Chechen Republic. Late next year sees the commissioning of the Baltic Pipeline System. Those oil transmission projects are financed by both public and private capital.

There are some opportunities for a direct connection to Europe. There is the Druzhba–Adria pipeline integration project. There are a number of other projects in which European countries might and should have an interest as a reliable source of energy supplies into Europe. One example is the Yamal–Europe gas project which is undergoing technical trials.

All these projects – and, equally, proposals to diversify routes by going through Poland or Ukraine – must be used to support the performance of both existing and future long-term contracts.

So it is quite possible to use either or both of Ukraine and Poland for transit of Russian gas?

Quite possible. A branch of the Yamal–Europe pipeline through Poland has already been commissioned. There is a plan for a second branch with a connection to Slovakia. And that, we think, is generally in line with the spirit of European energy developments. Route diversification is one of the conditions that guarantee security of supply and equal availability.

Hence the construction of a connection through Poland remains a priority for us. That does not mean, however, that we intend to cause difficulties for Ukraine. The problem of delivering gas via that country's territory is already difficult enough. We have only one condition, which is a guarantee that no gas will be taken without authorisation. It would be rash of us not to seek protection against such situations arising.

To what extent is economic growth dependent on high world oil prices? Is the government prepared for any deterioration of the oil market? What would it do in those circumstances?

I would not say that Russia's economic growth depends solely on the favourable state of the oil and energy markets. Far from it. That is proved by, for example, the rising trend in output that we see in steel, other metals and mechanical engineering.

Yet I must admit that the state of the oil market certainly does present certain risks. The question is, to what extent they could affect our economy.

It would seem that stronger economies than ours – the European Union and the United States – ought easily to have been able to withstand a $4 or $5 rise in the price of a barrel of oil. But that little jump caused major difficulties for them too, both economically and politically. It left its mark on Russia also. Such surges have effects on both the domestic market and the budget. Energy prices also rose in Russia but, happily, not to quite the same extent as in foreign markets.

The size of the risks to Russia depends on changes in the oil price. If prices stay between $20 and $22 a barrel, the risks are minimal. If, however, they continue to decline, budget revenues will suffer badly. At least however, events in the oil market give no cause to expect very great price falls.

Some analysts believe that the oil companies are making up for profits lost owing to increased export duties by raising prices on the domestic market. It is quite possible they will lobby for a cut in the rouble/dollar exchange rate or engineer a collapse in the rouble themselves. What is your comment?

It seems to me that such statements are made because oil industry lobbyists want to look important. Of course government does not exist in a vacuum. We are always meeting business representatives and talking to them about problems and how they might be solved. I am sure that the most important thing in our dealings is predictability. Any innovations that are introduced should be stable, long-term and open.

Meanwhile, taxpayers are always likely to find their interests at odds with those of the state. One side wants to pay as little as it can and the other wants to take as much as it can. It is simply not going to happen that their interests coincide. There must be a fair return for taxes, and the boundary of compromise is to tax enough to ensure stable development for the taxpayer. Taxes must not seem like a fate worse than death. If they do then tomorrow there will be simply nobody left to pay them. And in industry, where excess profits are not generated by the hard work of companies or their owners but arise because of the state of the market or from the riches of the earth, they must go to the federal treasury and be spent on improving that same earth.

We are threatened from time to time by apocalyptic predictions of an energy crisis. What in fact are the prospects for keeping the Russian electricity industry and the public supplied with natural gas? Is there any spare capacity to increase gas supplies inside Russia?

You can never have too much gas, just as you can never have too much money. The price difference between gas and fuel oil is quite large and of course the energy companies would prefer gas to be cheap. Still, there is never going to be lots of 'blue fuel'[12] at low prices.

So long as the existing fuel supply and consumption balance is maintained, gas supply problems will not arise. But any alteration of the balance towards larger supplies to Europe is possible only by developing new fields. No other domestic source would make it possible.

Meanwhile the latest conflict between RJSC UES and Gazprom is just another instance of the price disproportion that there is in this country between gas, fuel oil and coal. It is entirely understandable that Gazprom should want to sell gas elsewhere for more money and get paid quicker. It is also understandable that RJSC UES should want to have a cheaper source of electricity. That is a normal conflict of interests which must be fought out in order to find a happy medium. To build it up into a political dispute strikes me as just ridiculous.

From Vremya MN, *23 February 2001:*

The Russia–EU Energy Dialogue was announced by President Putin at the Paris summit [in October 2000]. How far has it got?

The Energy Dialogue, which took place during the Swedish EU presidency, is one of our most important projects with Europe. By the Moscow summit in May [2001] experts are to produce a programme of co-operation in energy so that the leaders of Russia and the European Union can sign a document on the basic principles of the Energy Dialogue. Four expert groups have been set up. The first deals with strategy and balances. Its principal objective is to determine resource capabilities, the likely future evolution of the industry, the structure of the fuel balance in relations between Russia and the European Union and the relation between fuel and final output (meaning electricity, including nuclear power). The second group looks at investment (meaning conditions and the investment climate, including production-sharing agreements). The third considers infrastructure and technology (primarily transport, transit, port facilities and electricity transmission lines). The fourth group deals with energy efficiency and the environment. Between

---

12   Editor's note: 'blue fuel' is a term for natural gas.

now and May the experts will meet at least three times. At this stage, to help the Energy Dialogue, special grants will be available to allow these working groups to set up and hold meetings.

What progress has been made in negotiations to build a gas pipeline to bypass Ukraine and another more westerly pipeline via Finland?

Our Energy Dialogue with the European Union is not only about gas. It is not even just about oil and gas. There is also electricity. Today electricity exports to Europe, though not enormous in volume terms, are no longer some exotic rarity but have become routine. We export to Finland and Ukraine. We plan to supply Turkey via Georgia or Azerbaijan. As for transport by oil pipeline, there is a wider range of both potential and already realised projects – for example, the Caspian Pipeline Consortium (CPC), the Baltic Pipeline System (BPS) and the Omisalj project (the Druzhba–Adria pipeline). So in the long run there is an increasing trend in transport volumes of both Russian and Caspian oil. The CPC will be commissioned on 1 July this year [2001]. The BPS will be completed on 31 December 2001.

As for gas, I would like to note that the intergovernmental agreement between Russia and Ukraine on gas transit guarantees large volumes of gas supply to Europe. However, it is thought that gas exports under existing contracts will rise considerably by 2010 and there is also a need to diversify routes. All of that requires us to build an additional pipeline taking a branch of the Yamal–Europe line to Slovakia. Active negotiations are now underway with Poland and other countries. I am not going to name a date for construction to start, but I do think that the bulk of the negotiations will be complete in the first half of the year [2001].

For the more westerly project, in the Baltic, two versions are being considered: a sea route and a land route. It partly depends on the success of negotiations on the pipeline intended to go through Poland and also on the availability of the raw material. That is, if the amount of potentially available gas increases, and it is Russian gas, the need to build a third pipeline becomes more acute.

Are you expecting a major inflow of investment to the Russian fuel and energy complex? Will investors not be put off by Russia's recent failures in debt renegotiations?

Let us take Blue Stream [the Black Sea pipeline to Turkey]. It required enormous investment – $2 billion – and that money was raised by

Gazprom's foreign partners. The money came from Italy and Japan. Working with investors is nothing new for us. But today we would like to institutionalise our relations with the European Union and be able to resort to such organisations as the European Investment Bank. Clearly we cannot do without private investors and they need a proper investment climate and our good will. We see private investors showing an interest now in Russian projects. An example is the Shtokman field. At the same time we expect to see the maximum concentration of domestic resources on the development not only of the resource base but also of transport. I would not make any direct association between investment and debts. The debts cannot be put off. We could not delay if we wanted to. A solution will be found and so I can see no reason to speculate about how debts might affect investment.

In 2003 the European Union is going to accept new members. Membership is predicted to be 25 by 2010. How will that affect Russia's trade with the European Union?

Russia has always been understanding about EU enlargement and is absolutely not opposed to it. The European Union understands that a greater Europe is impossible without Russia. For its part, Russia considers itself a European power. That is the basis for our dialogue. Of course we do have a degree of concern about EU enlargement. But we will adhere to the WTO rules, which say that the enlargement of customs unions must not reduce but on the contrary increase bilateral trade. The European Union in its present form accounts for 35 per cent of Russia's foreign trade. The candidate countries make up another 16 per cent. The total is 51 per cent, a controlling share of Russia's trade, and it all belongs to Europeans. We hope that the growth of the European Union will not change that ratio. We are engaging in dialogue so as to make sure the enlargement process is mutually beneficial.

Developing the natural gas market

Speech to a Russia–EEC round table, Brussels, 10 December 2002:

The development of the Russian gas industry has largely coincided, in both time and rate, with the development of the EU gas market. The supply of large amounts of Russian gas to the European market did much to maintain high rates of economic growth in the EU member countries in the 1970s and enabled them to establish a rational structure of energy consumption. It also made it possible to reduce the energy vulnerability of Western Europe, which manifested itself most clearly in the acute fuel crises of 1973/74 and 1979/80.

As we developed the gas industry largely in response to Western European demand, we imported large-diameter pipes together with machinery and equipment from Europe, thus creating additional demand for European industry's products and increasing employment.

At present Russian gas is supplied to 20 countries in Western and Central Europe. In 2001 we supplied them with 127 billion cubic metres of gas. The major purchasers are EU members, which last year imported 75.2 billion cubic metres, or three-fifths of our total export volume. Russian gas comprises about 20 per cent of all the gas consumed in Western Europe and about a third of all its gas imports. The region's biggest purchasers of Russian gas are Germany (32.6 billion cubic metres in 2001), Italy (20.2 billion) and France (11.2 billion).

Russian natural gas is supplied to Western Europe under contracts of up to 25 years' duration, most of which were concluded on the basis of intergovernmental agreements. The current long-term contracts with major European purchasers run for another 6–21 years. They contain 'take or pay' clauses, which are a necessary precondition and guarantee that the supplier can recover its considerable investment. At the end of the decade Russian gas supplies to Europe (assuming current contracts are extended) will be at least 160 billion cubic metres and may be as much as 205 billion cubic metres.

Actual exports will depend on the market situation, the demand for gas, the level of prices and, certainly, the size of the risks producers are prepared to take.

The current rate of growth in the demand for gas in Europe is forecast to continue in the future. Gas as a proportion of energy consumption in the region may rise from 22 per cent in 2000 to 29 per cent in 2010. At the same time Europe's dependence on outside sources of natural gas will also grow. In particular it is predicted that by 2020 the EU proportion of gas from outside sources will be 1.7 times higher than it was in 2000 (70 per cent as against 40 per cent).

In the circumstances it would be dangerous to change the rules of the game that have ensured the stability of the European gas market, and especially dangerous to do it without taking account of producer interests. It is entirely self-evident that producers would not be prepared to accept both the price and volume risks that would arise if the gas market were liberalised according to today's scenario. We have no objection to changes as such, but we want to be able to see the logic of them, how long they will take and what market risks they might entail.

Indisputably, new forms and methods of trade – spot transactions, short-term contracts, commodity market trading, electronic trading – have their place. The expansion and integration of the gas transport infrastructure of the region also helps. Nonetheless, spot trades and short-term deals can, it seems to us, only amount to a sort of superficial element, whereas long-term contracts must continue to form the foundation of international gas trading in Europe .

Further evidence is seen in the long-term contracts signed in 2002 for gas supplies to the United Kingdom from the Netherlands and Norway, where the gas market was liberalised even before the adoption of the EU Gas Directive.

It is an absolute precondition for the performance of long-term gas supply contracts that there be an adequate transport infrastructure. Transport capacity is a matter of the utmost complexity, irrespective of whether the commodity to be transported is gas from Russia or from other countries lying to the east of Europe.

Russia's principal gas fields are situated in the north, beyond the Urals or under the Arctic continental shelf. As fields become exhausted, production has to move ever further north or exploit gas-bearing formations at ever greater depths. That naturally increases costs and raises the price of gas for the consumer. Suffice it to say that the costs of developing promising fields like the Shtokman and creating the infrastructure to get the gas to market are $25–30 billion. And the Yamal–Europe project, including the development of the Yamal peninsula, is expected to cost even more.

Suppose that the liberalisation of the European Union's internal market for gas will mean that gas prices suffer a substantial fall and that long-term contracts make up a substantially declining proportion of gas supplies to European countries. In that case gas producers will find it practically impossible to carry out new export projects. That will impede the modernisation and development of the existing pipeline networks which supply Russian gas to the European market.

Now the laws of the market say that if the supply of natural gas declines, the price will inevitably increase, which in turn will make it possible to develop gas exports. That cycle takes five to seven years however, given that it takes a considerable time to make the investment decision and then create new gas production and transport capacities.

Additional risks arise from the European Union's attempts to modify the existing long-term contracts by striking out provisions on territorial limitations as against EU competition law. We have achieved agreement with the European Commission that EU competition laws will be taken account of in any new contracts for exports of gas from Russia to EU members. As for the current contracts, to strike out the territorial limitations, which are a guarantee against unfair competition, would give rise to substantial new risks. Hence it is necessary to find an alternative mechanism to prevent unfair competition and protect our economic interests. That is a complex problem and a solution will take considerable time and effort. The search is currently on for such a mechanism. We maintain that until the matter is resolved the current long-term contracts must be retained without alteration. Given the importance of the issue to gas suppliers, we propose to address the problem in a specially created subgroup in the framework of the Russia–EU energy dialogue.

No less important for Russia are gas transit issues to ensure that Russian gas can be got to market in Europe. Over recent years we have tried to achieve higher gas transit reliability in the framework of a new transit protocol to the Energy Charter. Still, a number of issues of principle remain unsolved. The most acute are the EU-proposed provision on the Organisation of Regional Economic Integration (OREI), on which Russia insists on a 'right of first refusal', and the methods of setting transit tariffs. We are fully convinced that matters of long-term, reliable energy supplies to a Europe that increasingly depends on natural gas imports cannot be satisfactorily resolved without compromises in the field of gas transit.

If we consider the high capital demand of Russian gas export projects, we must note that the predicted expansion of gas consumption in Europe will require the financial involvement of European consumers in the development of the Russian raw material export base and the associated infrastructure.

Also, it is extraordinarily important that Russian companies, and Gazprom in particular, have access to international sources of long-term finance. Russia's poor credit rating and the stiff demands of Western creditors mean that Gazprom finds it very difficult to obtain finance in sufficient quantity and, when it can, it is much more expensive than for Western corporations. When Gazprom seeks finance for its gas transport projects, even though its security is first class, the insurance premiums demanded by European export credit agencies can reach 18 per cent.

There is no ignoring the fact that the high cost of capital inevitably makes investment in developing potential exports less economically attractive and ultimately creates problems for the implementation of new projects to meet the increasing demand.

Another question demanding a solution is the demand of financial institutions – not only the commercial banks but also institutions such as the Export Credit Agency (ECA) and the EBRD – for security in the form of long-term gas supply contracts. Great attention is focused on the quality of the contracts; invariably the presence of 'take or pay' clauses is required, contracts must run for two to three years longer than the loan term and so on. If the long-term contracts are to be modified without altering the European banks' and agencies' lending criteria, the Russian gas industry could be left without sources of long-term debt finance.

In the last third of the twentieth century Russia invested hugely in supplying the gas demand of European countries. Now we must realise that we need a constructive dialogue to balance the interests of gas-producing and gas-consuming countries so as to ensure the energy security of Europe.

While there are long-term contracts, including 'take or pay' obligations in a form acceptable to banks, and a division of the risks between producers and consumers, producers can continue working in the way that has proved effective in the past. In the near future we shall have to undertake a number of major projects to increase the reliability and efficiency of gas supplies to Europe. However, the instability of the gas market means that any substantial investment might prove too great a risk and all talk of large projects will recede into the background.

Organising project finance in the new conditions requires us to find a replacement for the current means of providing guarantees and security. Who could supply such guarantees? The governments of interested importing countries or the European Commission? Or perhaps the European Investment Bank? We have been posing this question for some years now and answer comes there none.

In this way, applying purely administrative remedies in such an important economic sphere without prior discussion and agreement with the main supplier companies and the banks that finance gas projects could lead to serious negative consequences. In its endeavour to improve conditions of price formation in the gas market, the European Union risks destroying the existing, well-established system of sourcing energy from outside, which has been proved reliable over time.

In our opinion, it would be very useful if the European Union were to consider the possibility of setting up a guarantee mechanism for investment in the gas industry, particularly as the main risks associated with gas supply projects to Europe do not, according to some banks, lie outside the borders of the European Union. Devising and introducing such a mechanism would be a great step towards the development of international co-operation in the gas business.

In summary, I would like to stress that the expected growth in imports as a share of EU gas consumption depends upon a stable gas market, and that cannot be achieved by placing nearly all the risks on producers and exporters. Security of energy supplies to Europe can only be achieved by legislation to underpin a system of long-term contracts as the basis of the gas market and by securing producer interests during all subsequent co-operation. We think the European Commission is of the same view.

It must be realised that the European gas market is a practically closed regional market, where hasty or ill-thought-out decisions could have extraordinarily serious repercussions and lead to acute problems in the context of global competition among the world's leading economic centres. These are real risks which must be carefully analysed and taken account of when decisions are made to speed up the process of liberalisation of the gas market.

Russia attaches great importance to its rapidly developing dialogue with the European Union on co-operation in energy. We have for a long time been partners trading in natural gas and are committed to the further strengthening of that partnership. Dialogue between producers and consumers of energy is a necessary element of any policy that aims to maintain the stability of the market in fuel and energy. That dialogue is particularly important for the gas market, where technology means that the bond between the producers and consumers of natural gas is particularly close.

Now seems a good time to expand the scope of the Energy Dialogue to take in the complex problems associated with the changing conditions for participants in the European gas market and consider the economic consequences of those changes for their future business models and how they may be mitigated. To that end we propose to create subgroups of existing working groups of the Energy Dialogue, recruiting financial institutions and consultants as appropriate.

In addition, we think it appropriate to concentrate our Energy Dialogue on the urgent problems of finance for specific projects, without which it will be difficult to secure reliable gas supplies to Europe. The projects which would be in the interests of both Russia and the European Union include the Shtokman field together with a new gas transmission system across the Baltic Sea (the North European Gas Pipeline).

We see the world becoming more interdependent every day. That is the reality. It is therefore in our mutual interest to promote a favourable climate, increase trust between the partners and achieve a fair division of risk.

Part III
Energy for Industrial Growth

V. B. Khristenko

V. B. Khristenko reports about his plans to Vladimir Putin

Foreword

This is one of three sections in which I take stock of a 15-year period of my life: a long and extraordinarily eventful time full of encounters and situations where difficult decisions had to be taken.

Part II, 'Rails, Pipes and Cables', first appeared in 2004 and was essentially a collection of materials illustrating our work from 1998 to 2004, performing many functions within different Russian Government structures. Re-reading this text closely to prepare this edition, I made no changes or additions, and I retract not a single word or statement, although I would probably act differently now in some instances.

Part III is also intended as a form of self-vindication, a section in which the conclusions drawn from a revaluation of our work are supported by a selection of documents, reports, interviews and diagrams.

My aim in this book is to define the specific focus of our endeavours: Russia's energy sector in interdependence with Russian industry – the area for which I was responsible as the director of the Ministry of Industry and Energy from 2004–08. Why a revaluation of what was done in those years now? The straightforward answer is that I was simply unable to set aside enough time until now for the reflection and discussion needed to draw conclusions from our practical experience. As we prepared this series of monographs for publication, it became clear from the scale and significance of the work that we would need to go back to the documents, situations and actions of that period. After the passage of five years, we could see more clearly what was essential and what was secondary. Let me list five of the most significant themes in order of importance.

First – which surprises me now – is the huge amount of work that was done in this period. I shall begin, therefore, with a general description of the measures, documents and decisions that we developed and implemented.

Second is the participation in large-scale projects in energy and industry, which are already being implemented (although I am no longer involved) and will be a focus of great interest for some decades to come for the public, various levels of government and corporate management systems.

Third are the unique managerial decisions that we were able to take and the management schemes that we were able to develop.

Fourth are the forward-looking concepts (such as the Global Sustainable Energy Development project) that were developed and published, but are still awaiting implementation.

Fifth is the development of our managerial competences as we worked towards new objectives: primarily, systems approach tools and ways of organising managerial communication across all platforms of the Ministry of Industry and Energy and the Ministry of Industry and Trade.

So we went back several years, recollected and pondered, identified what was important, formulated the most useful points, selected the most important schemes, and edited the factual material in our reports and interviews. We now present this for your consideration (see Figure 3.1 overleaf).

The objective of the Ministry of Industry and Energy management system

The creation of the Ministry of Industry and Energy in 2004 addressed a specific objective: to organise the transition to programming the development of industries throughout the material sector (with the exception of agriculture, a separate sociopolitical issue) – it being understood that the different sectors brought under one roof had conflicting if not diametrically opposing interests. These sectors formed a loop, in that they were suppliers and consumers for one another (see Figure 3.1, left-hand column), and they were all in a situation where projects that they were hoping to implement depended to a large extent on how others were working.

All these industries – oil, gas, coal, electricity, mechanical engineering and metals – were now in a single administrative system, under the roof of one ministry. The number of conflicts and the responsibilities transferred to this platform were overwhelming.

This framework of the Ministry of Industry and Energy gave its staff the opportunity to acquire unique experience of integration, where we could find ourselves in a very strange position – such as conducting discussions with gas production companies on structuring the gas market, together with chemical and metals companies, as well as electricity and utility providers (who were also under the Ministry of Industry and Energy): and gas consumers also had a direct interest. For the gas sector, the priority was to find a model for liberalising the market while putting the profit on prices for gas exports and domestic gas more in line, to create a level playing field. This would mean a trend towards substantial price rises in the domestic gas market. The electricity sector was also moving towards liberalising the market, not only with respect to pricing, but also delegating responsibility to private investors for developing generating facilities (to be sold into private ownership, naturally). For electricity providers, the priority at that time was to synchronise and harmonise models for reforming the gas and electricity markets. You might think at first glance that low gas prices could only benefit them – but only at first glance. Without realistic market prices for gas, no one will invest in new generating facilities, especially if gas prices remain so low. These investments will never show a return. However, with no investment in energy, there is no need for power plant engineering, and if there is no need to develop power plant

Figure 3.1 Industry policy chart: strategic and programme documents of the Ministry of Industry and Energy

	Strategies and concepts						Action plans, packages of measures			
	Already being implemented			Under development/being finalised			Already being implemented			
	2002–03	2004	2005–06	2006	2007	2008–	2002–03	2004	2005–06	
Energy sector	Energy Strategy of Russia for the Period to 2020			Development of the draft Energy Strategy of Russia for the Period to 2030			Package of Measures to Complete the Restructuring of the Russian Coal Industry in 2006–10 Package of Measures to Stabilise Prices on the Domestic Market for Oil Products Main Areas for Reform of the Electricity Sector of the Russian Federation Russian Government Resolution no. 526 dated 11 July 2011, 'On Reforming the Electricity Sector of the Russian Federation'; Russian Government Order No. 865-r dated 27 June 2003, 'On the Action Plan for Reforming the Electricity Sector'			
Power plant engineering				Power Plant Engineering Development Strategy to 2015						
Aircraft industry	Aircraft Industry Development Strategy for the Period to 2015									
Electronics industry				Electronics Industry Development Strategy for the Period to 2025						
Shipbulding industry				Shipbuilding Industry Development Strategy for the Period to 2020						
Metals industry	Package of Measures to Develop the Russian Metals Industry to 2010						Action Plans for Development of the Metals Industry for 2003–04 and 2004–06			
				Metals Industry Development Strategy for the Period to 2015			Action Plan for Implementation of the Legal, Economic and Organisational Measures to Regulate the Circulation of Scrap Ferrous and Non-Ferrous Metals and Improving Oversight in this Area			
Chemicals & petrochemicals				Chemicals and Petrochemical Industry Development Strategy for the Period to 2015						
Mechanical engineering				Russian Civil Mechanical Engineering Development Strategy to 2015 Russian Machine-Tool Industry Development Strategy for the Period to 2015 Agricultural Mechanical Engineering Development Strategy to 2015 Transport Mechanical Engineering Development Strategy to 2010 and Package of Measures for its Implementation			Action Plan for 2005–06 for the Main Areas for Development of Mechanical Engineering Action Plan for 2006–08 for Development of Russian Agricultural Mechanical Engineering			
Medical & biotechnology industry				Medical Industry Development Strategy to 2020 Pharmaceuticals Industry Development Strategy to 2020						
Timber industry	Main Areas for Development of the Paper and Pulp and Timber Processing Industries						Package of Measures to Increase the Competitiveness of the Russian Timber Industry			
				Timber Industry Development Strategy to 2015			Action Plan for the Implementation in 2005–08 of the Priority Tasks of the Main Areas for Development of the Timber Industry			
Light industry				Light Industry Development Strategy to 2015			Priority Measures for the Main Areas for Development of Light Industry for 2004–05 Action Plan for 2006–08 for the Development of Light Industry			
Car manufacturing	Concept for Development of the Russian Car Manufacturing Industry						Action Plan for Mid-Term Implementation (2005–08) of the Priority Tasks of the Concept for Development of the Russian Car Manufacturing Industry			
Technical regulation										

Orange = strategic documents being implemented; Blue = strategic documents being developed;
Green = strategic documents already implemented.

			Programmes, federal target programmes (FTP), departmental target programmes (DTP), innovation projects					
Under development/being finalised			Already being implemented			Under development/being finalised		
2006	2007		2002–03	2004	2005–06	2006	2007	2008–
Programme for the Future Development of the Electricity Sector of the Russian Federation for the Period to 2020 General Scheme for the Development of Oil Pipeline Transport, Including Oil Product Pipelines, for the Period to 2020 General Scheme for the Development of the Russian Gas Sector for the Period to 2030 General Scheme for the Location of Electric Power Facilities to 2020						FTP Increasing the Efficiency of Energy Consumption in the Russian Federation FTP Development of Atomenergoprom for 2007–10 and to 2015 Programme to set up a unified system for gas production, transportation and supply in Eastern Siberia and the Far East, allowing for possible gas exports to the markets of China and other Asia-Pacific countries		
			FTP Developing Civil Aviation Technology FTP National Technology Base (NTB)					
					FTP NTB			
			FTP Global Ocean FTP NTB					
Action Plan for Development of the Metals Industry for 2007–08					FTP NTB	Development and industrial application of anti-corrosion techniques for components of metal fabrications using chemical thermal modification Development of a DTP		
					FTP NTB	Development of a DTP		
					FTP NTB	Union State Programme 'Setting up and organising mass production of a range of high-efficiency agricultural machines based on a universal, mobile 200–450 hp power unit for 2006–08' Developing and setting up mass production of combine harvesters FTP 'Innovative Mechanical Engineering' in accordance with the Strategy for Developing Russian Civil Mechanical Engineering DTP in accordance with the Machine-Tool Industry Development Strategy to 2015		
					FTP NTB			
						FTP 'Developing Facilities for Value-Added Wood Processing and Developing New Forestland for the Period to 2015'		
						Producing a DTP for 2008–10 for the Development of Light Industry		
					FTP NTB	Union State Programme 'Developing Diesel Automobile Construction for the Period to 2008' Developing a DTP Creating an Engine Family for Heavy Goods Vehicles that Meets the Euro-2, Euro-3 and Euro-4 Standards on Harmful Emissions		
			Programme for the Development of Technical Regulations					

engineering, there is no need to develop special metals. Why go to all that effort and start nit-picking about turbine blades, if all is well as it is? Strange as it may seem, liberalisation of the market was a perfectly acceptable model for the metals industry, giving it an opportunity to operate in two types of market – long-term contracts and the spot market – with clear, predictable parameters for the long-term future.

Everyone understood this situation, but its constituent elements had previously been divided among different structures – the Ministry of Fuel and Energy, the Ministry of Industry, Science and Technology, Gazprom and major specialist corporations – and it was not at all clear where we could discuss this process of liberalising the gas market and develop a systematic approach before meeting with macro-economists.

It was necessary to go to the top person in the country every time in order to talk about this issue. At any other level the tension was explosive. Gas companies wanted one thing, utility providers another, metals companies something else, and electricity companies something else again. It resulted in looking for a scapegoat, which was usually whoever had initiated the discussion with the top person. But there was no systems integrator who could have proposed something in this situation. With the formation of the Ministry of Industry and Energy, all these disputes and conflicts moved to a single platform. Figure 3.2 shows the configuration of this platform and lists the main players.

Figure 3.2 Configuration of the Ministry of Industry and Energy (MIE) and the main players

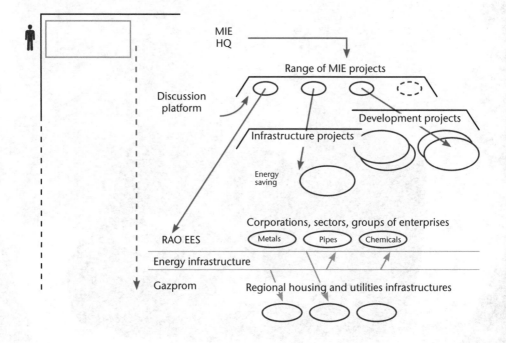

Discussing some questions with members of the government
(A. Gordeev and I. Sechin)

Groundwork: Energy Strategy 2020

> The main aim of this document is to identify pathways to gain a leading edge in the energy sector, make its products and services more competitive on the global market by utilising its potential and establishing priorities for developing the sector, and develop measures and mechanisms for government energy policy that incorporate predictable outcomes for its implementation.
>
> (*The Energy Strategy of Russia for the Period to 2020*)

The first strategic sectoral model prepared with the participation of our team was *The Energy Strategy of Russia for the Period to 2020*, approved in 2003 (see Figure 3.3). Developed at the Ministry of Energy and tabled in the Russian White House during my time as deputy prime minister of the Russian Government, it became the first systematic experiment in industrial policy. Why industrial policy and not just energy policy? The energy sector supports the operation of all sectors of the national economy, and energy is the foundation of the entire economy. Development of such a strategy is the groundwork for building a whole range of strategies for sectoral development. Oil-refining priorities cannot be determined correctly without understanding the specific requirements of the car industry or agricultural machinery. Adequate planning of investments in ferrous metals is impossible without developing infrastructure projects in the oil and gas sectors. We would be unable to decide priorities for shipbuilding without understanding the aims and objectives of development of the Arctic shelf, and so forth. There are many examples. The core focus of the *Strategy* is to harmonise the interests of extraction companies with infrastructures and energy consumers, which are in turn providers and suppliers of materials, equipment or services. During the period of existence of a single Ministry of Industry and Energy, we began to put our ideas into effect and were able to resolve a wide range of issues between the energy sector and industrialists.

Figure 3.3 The Energy Strategy of Russia for the Period to 2020

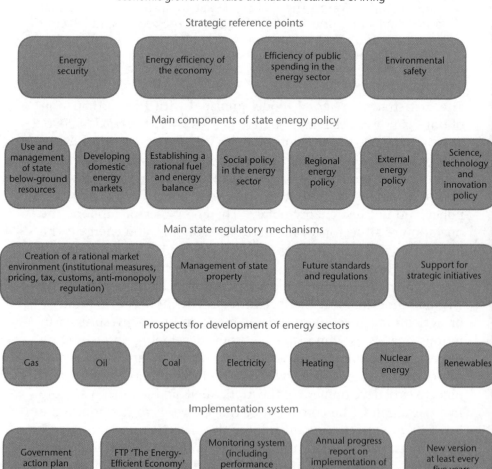

The key objective is to use the resource and production potential of the energy sector as effectively as possible in order to achieve economic growth and raise the national standard of living

Strategic reference points

| Energy security | Energy efficiency of the economy | Efficiency of public spending in the energy sector | Environmental safety |

Main components of state energy policy

| Use and management of state below-ground resources | Developing domestic energy markets | Establishing a rational fuel and energy balance | Social policy in the energy sector | Regional energy policy | External energy policy | Science, technology and innovation policy |

Main state regulatory mechanisms

| Creation of a rational market environment (institutional measures, pricing, tax, customs, anti-monopoly regulation) | Management of state property | Future standards and regulations | Support for strategic initiatives |

Prospects for development of energy sectors

| Gas | Oil | Coal | Electricity | Heating | Nuclear energy | Renewables |

Implementation system

| Government action plan | FTP 'The Energy-Efficient Economy' | Monitoring system (including performance indicators) | Annual progress report on implementation of the Energy Strategy | New version at least every five years |

Creating a system for balanced development of industry and energy in Russia, 2004–08

This section discusses the core elements of Russian energy policy. Based on balanced strategic development of the energy sector, and taking into account the potential for development of related sectors, we have been able to position Russia as a global energy player and participate in creating an international agenda for global energy security.

Achieving this required bringing together a whole range of factors, creating a unique management situation. The unique aspect of the situation at the Ministry of Industry and Energy consisted precisely in this combination of competences and powers to manage the development of industry and energy within the framework of a single ministry. To give a complete picture, I need to clarify the context.

Prior to 2004 when the Ministry of Industry and Energy was set up, taking decisions on the development of industry and energy directly involved several ministers and at least two sectoral vice premiers – one in charge of industry and one in charge of infrastructure.

The creation of the new ministry coincided with an administrative reform which left the prime minister of Russia with only one deputy in the government structure. This meant that all substantive discussions on the development of industry and energy were delegated to the Ministry of Industry and Energy.

It would appear (if only it were that simple) that it was only necessary to combine several related, but nevertheless different, economic sectors under the direction of a single ministry, and it would all start working immediately, some kind of breakthrough would occur and extra incentives for development would emerge. So why not take it to the extreme, go down the same route and create a Ministry of the Economy, Industry, Energy and Finance?

The answer lies in the extent to which the systems are connected. Industrial policy is never completely divorced from macroeconomic or financial policy, of course, but it is perhaps precisely in the interlocking of industry and energy, in addition to the managerial and logical connections, that one most clearly observes the physical connection.

Figure 3.4 Schedule map of the Russian energy sector

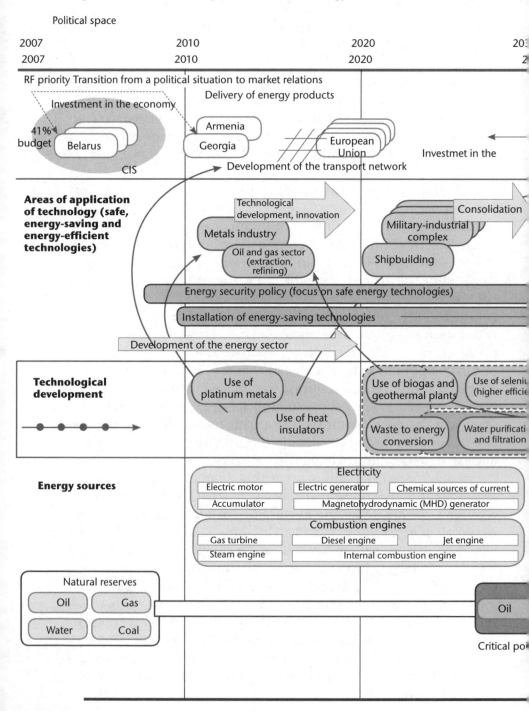

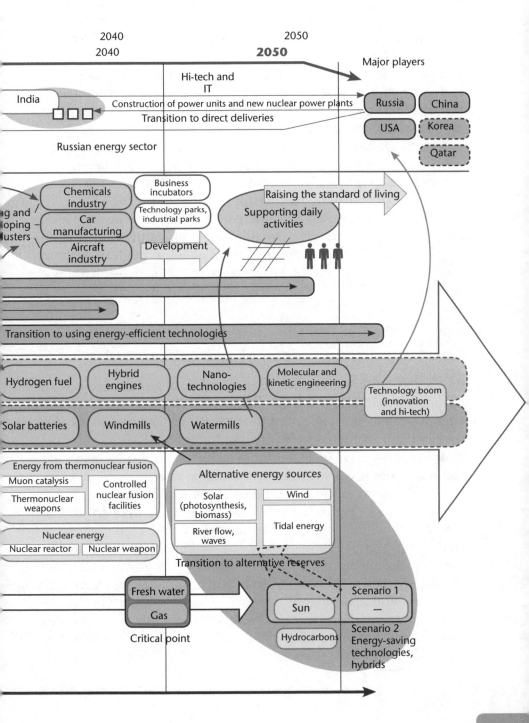

This interdependence between the industrial and energy sectors is the most striking example of a complex interaction of systems. Working with these systems contained within a single managerial team enabled us to radically improve the efficacy of decision making.

First, we were able to get away from unintelligent, one-sided sectoral lobbyism, where even after a given decision has been taken, it usually remains an area of conflict, because such decisions often favour only one of the parties.

Second, we were able to form an integrated vision of the strategic development of industrial sectors and the energy sector, taking into account the specifics of each, and harmonise different interests on the basis of private–state partnerships.

Finally, it was precisely this interdependence at the working level that enabled us to resolve the inevitable difficulties and friction between different interest groups operationally, so to speak, without taking them to the political level, and to build dialogue on a single working platform.

The oil and gas sector

Thankfully, market conditions are good, or the woes of oil[1]

Russia has the natural advantage of oil and gas resources – an advantage that must be used effectively. State regulation of the energy sector has two objectives: first, to ensure sustainable development of the sector at all stages from analysis of potential hydrocarbon resources to refining, transportation and sales; and second, to use the energy sector's potential effectively to diversify the development of the Russian economy and society.

The primary task facing us in the oil and gas industry was to develop a modern and effective regulatory and legal framework facilitating sectoral development and stimulating an influx of investments, including foreign investments. This was extremely demanding, and required many rounds of negotiations as we endeavoured to harmonise diverse interests. When a law was enacted on foreign investments in strategic sectors, for example, we proceeded on the basis that an investor's nationality is irrelevant and drafted

---

1 Translator's note: a pun on the title of Griboedov's play *The Woes of Wit* (1823).

the statute accordingly, taking the route already approved by a number of countries. This gave a clear signal to foreign investors that investment projects would be secure.

An equally important objective was to stimulate the development of the raw materials resource base for industry, as well as adequately expanding the transportation infrastructure, for both domestic and foreign markets, to meet growth in demand and production. This involved implementing major and unique infrastructure projects, such as the Eastern Siberia–Pacific Ocean oil pipeline, which in many respects had no analogues anywhere in the world. As we developed our infrastructure, we simultaneously addressed the issues of Russia's entry into the Asia-Pacific energy market and the regional development of Siberia and the Russian Far East.

Finally, a major element of our work in this strategic area was to create conditions for completing the final link in the chain: adding value to Russian territory by developing refineries. This involved a range of decisions, both strategic and tactical, from adopting a strategy for developing Russia's chemical and petrochemical industry to decisions on the utilisation of associated gas.

Thankfully, market conditions are good

From an interview with Gazeta, *15 June 2004*:

Viktor Borisovich, so the main objective of the new Ministry of Industry and Energy is to double our GDP, because everything that could double the GDP is under the jurisdiction of your ministry.

No, why? Other sectors also make a major contribution to the GDP, so other ministries have work to do too. You must understand that material production is not the key issue right now. We follow trends in developed countries and we see that the services sector – ranging from finance, transport and construction to consumer services – holds a dominant position. These changes are already happening in Russia. Half of our GDP already comes from this sector, and it will play a more and more important role in the Russian economy. Although the services market in Russia cannot exist and develop effectively without the material sector.

But all the same, if we're talking about the material sector, what sources of growth do you see in industry, not including the energy sector?

It's not right to separate some sectors from others, I think, because it's all interrelated. The energy sector is clearly well positioned for development: there's something to produce, someone to sell it to, and thankfully, market conditions are good. All the factors are there, and they're all positive.

A developing energy sector is a major boost to the development of all other sectors, whether that's production of pipes, steel structures for construction, conglomerate, pellets or coke. This boost from the energy sector involves mechanical engineering to a large extent too, of course. Not to mention demand for more complex equipment such as oil pump stations and gas compressor stations, and the process also involves aircraft manufacturers. This booster effect is clear, it's real. And there's an observable benefit in kind, a physical cross-flow of orders. Demand for energy products generates demand for the products of other sectors. It would be good if there was a similar movement of capital at the same time, not only these benefits in kind. This is the diversification of sources of development that's talked about so much. We need capital to start flowing into those sectors that can form a basis for future development of the Russian economy, and also occupy a more significant position in the overall structure of our GDP. This is not happening yet for the most part.

Why?

For various reasons. First, this is a long and slow process, and second, such movement of capital doesn't appear very attractive at present. Apart from the energy sector, if you look at the traditional Russian sectors, the metals industry – both ferrous and non-ferrous – is developing very rapidly; it has good dynamics, good demand and good market conditions.

Of the other more developed sectors, it seems to me that vehicle engineering has interesting market positions – mainly railways and cars. There's good demand for investment in this sector now and the situation for expansion of the domestic market is clearly very good. This has come about through our railway reforms, and the announcement of its plans by the railway company RZhD OJSC. The sector's focus on its own enterprises has already created a quite sharply rising dynamic. This sector is progressing the most rapidly now and demonstrating its potential. The same is true of freight vehicle engineering. Our freight vehicle manufacturers have quite good positions in both the domestic market and some foreign markets, but they can't supply enough to meet the growing demand. This is related to another source of growth, construction, which is starting to grow quite rapidly. There are other interesting sectors too, such as aircraft manufacturing. This is easier to say with regard to military technology, less so with civil technology. These very advanced high-tech sectors are the most interesting.

The President said in his address to the Federal Assembly that the government is delaying a decision on construction of the new export oil pipelines, and this is long overdue. What will you do to speed up this decision?

All the decisions on export pipelines are known and the priorities are known: east, north and north-west. In the north-west, the Baltic, it's all going exactly to plan. The Baltic Pipeline System (BPS) already has a capacity of 42 million tonnes per year, which we'll increase to 62 million tonnes. The east will carry up to 80 million tonnes of oil. There are two factors here. The first is to update the estimate of resources, which the Ministry of Natural Resources is working on actively now; that is, which fields can be put into production in the short, medium and long term, subject to developing the infrastructure. The second issue, regarding the eastern line, is the route itself. This was changed after the environmental report, and we're now talking about routing it from Taishet to Nakhodka with a branch to Datsin, instead of the specified route from Angarsk to Nakhodka with a branch to Datsin. The scheme is already being developed now for a feasibility study. This is a major and very costly process. The whole route has to be assessed, and not just on the map; you need to know the topography and do the necessary surveys, estimate costs, and say how much it will cost not just in total, but including the pumping tariff. The project has to be cost-effective for the petroleum companies, you understand. The feasibility study should be completed in July. Then we have to make the final investment decision, and subject to that, the wheels will then start turning to implement the scheme.

There's still work do on the plans for the northern line, looking at various routes. They're very different, both in price and even the end point. We're already considering the coast of the Barents Sea now, rather than Murmansk, because even the choice of the end point has a major impact on the costs. This is a vast permafrost area where the pipes are laid on piles, which isn't cheap. So there has to be a very clear appraisal of the routes, including a cost–benefit analysis. But I'm absolutely confident that the northern pipeline will be brought into operation, there's no doubt about that.

Not one comparison would favour private pipelines

You say 'investment decision', so will you have to decide the ratio of private and state investments?

That's a simplistic interpretation. Who's for which international company? For the second or the third? When all's said and done, this means only one thing: if a project is ready, you need to take an investment decision on it. To take this decision you need to arrange and combine all the required financial resources. You can't take a decision if it's not clear where and how you'll get the money. There are several ways of sourcing it. The first would be, as before, that we either use funds sourced from the market by Transneft, or loans, or bonds. We also have proposals from our foreign partners that we're working with directly on the eastern project. If the conditions are good and clear, we will gladly use them. There's also the option of involving private businesses with an interest in this route. But this doesn't mean that we'll split the finance 50:50 or something. There are plenty of other ways. For example, you can offer an option to pump at fixed terms, let's say, where the company financing the construction gets a guaranteed volume of traffic. You can discuss all kinds of other models. But all this relates to this project and this route, not to the whole Russian trunk pipeline network.

So state property is protected?

This is just a question of financial calculations, not a political issue of whether the pipelines can be private or not. This was never the issue for me. We must have a state-owned trunk pipeline network for now. What is there to complain about? That it's not cost-effective? Let's do a comparison. We have far more private than state pipelines, there are quite extensive privately owned large-diameter pipelines, so we do have something to compare. Let's see how cost-effective they are: what are their tariffs and conditions, and what are the tariffs on the trunk network? We have big joint projects such as the Caspian Pipeline Consortium, so let's compare that in terms of cost-effectiveness. Not one comparison would favour private pipelines. I don't want to go into the reasons, but for now, unfortunately, none of the facts support the revolutionary thesis that we need to decide whether or not they can be private. This is not the issue. The only issue is whether or not I have enough money to implement such a project, and whether the project is interesting enough to attract partners. So I need to think of a model that will keep them interested. Period. That's it. So we can never cede control of this system in principle, never.

The emphasis on equal access to the 'pipe' is still of central importance

Turning to the regulation of oil exports. Previously, as deputy prime minister, you headed the commission on this, and now a new regulatory scheme is being devised. What will it look like?

Since it was decided to reduce the number of government commissions, which most probably was the right thing to do, two forms of decision making remain: either directly in the ministry or, when required, at an interdepartmental commission. I personally believe that an interdepartmental commission on the use and development of the trunk oil and gas pipelines is essential. I therefore produced a proposal on this, a draft regulation for this commission, and I sent it to the seven or eight departments that I proposed be included in the commission. If we implement everything in the very near future, we will revive the same commission, just in a different format. Regardless, this commission is needed, as there are many issues that require confirmation by other departments.

Such as?

For example, under Russian law, only oil-producing companies have the right to access the Transneft system. To ascertain whether or not a company is an oil producer, you need to know whether they have a licence. And it is the Ministry of Natural Resources that can answer this question. This ministry can revoke or suspend a licence at any time, so it should be on the commission. It should tell us every time, 'Now this one has jumped the gun, he doesn't have a licence, he doesn't have anything yet, he isn't allowed to do anything.' Or take the Tax Service, now subordinate to the Finance Ministry. It is meant to track interactions with the budget. If there is a problem, the Tax Service should record it and say that measures should be taken to remedy it, in accordance with the law. The standard operating procedures that we had before should be retained. Moreover, the emphasis on equal access to the pipe remains of central importance. Incidentally, the setting up of the commission is good grounds for discussion of export prospects: it records export opportunities every quarter, and so can also identify current constraints on exports.

Independence in decision making is essential

Your new department was set up in March. As early as May, the number of services and agencies under its jurisdiction was halved. What was this related to?

To the latest step in implementing administrative reform. In terms of the supervisory functions that come under the remit of executive bodies, the decision was absolutely justified. I think that supervisory bodies should gradually be removed from the jurisdiction of the ministries, so that decisions relating to oversight are taken solely by supervisory bodies and can be overturned only by a court of law. End of story. All supervisory bodies should have a simple structure: the standards, and the measures they can take if the standards are not complied with (shutting operations down, levying fines, suspending activities). Independence in decision making is essential. This is why I believe that the process of removing the main services from the jurisdiction of the ministries is the correct course. This should apply to all the supervisory services. Moreover, in the future they could be consolidated.

From a speech given at the opening of the Fourth Russian Oil and Gas Week in Moscow on 26 October 2004:

Russia is a unique oil and gas power. We have among the largest potential fuel and energy resources in the world. Judge for yourself: Russia occupies 13 per cent of the Earth's territory and accounts for less than 3 per cent of the world's population, yet it has about 13 per cent of the world's proven oil reserves and 34 per cent of its natural gas reserves. Russia's annual production of primary energy resources is more than 12 per cent of global production.

Today, the energy sector is one of the most important, stable and rapidly growing production sectors of the Russian economy. It accounts for about one quarter of GDP and one third of industrial output, and approximately half of Russia's federal budget revenues, exports and foreign currency receipts.

A number of Russian and foreign experts sometimes use these figures as grounds for criticism. They claim that the figures show the Russian economy to be highly dependent on oil and gas production, and that our country is becoming the natural resource appendage of the global economy.

The availability of extensive oil and gas resources is a natural advantage, not a shortcoming. The main thing is to know how to manage them rationally. As an example, it will suffice to refer to the United States, the United Kingdom and Norway. The experience of these countries shows that when resources are used rationally, the oil and gas sector stimulates economic development and contributes to increased national well-being. I therefore view the Russian energy sector as a 'driver' of the national economy, not an 'addiction'.

State regulation of the energy sector can be divided into two sets of tasks: first, to ensure the stable development of the sector at all stages, from analysis of potential hydrocarbon resources to refining and transportation; and second, to use the potential of the energy sector effectively to diversify the development of the Russian economy and society.

1 The global oil market

Next year will be the end of the first five years of the twenty-first century. The global oil market has changed markedly over these years, and this has affected the whole global economy. Demand for oil has increased year on year and prices have risen. 2004 saw record growth in oil consumption, and this was the main reason for the record increase in oil prices this year.

In the five years since 2000, global oil consumption has increased by 7.5 per cent. The highest increase has been in the Asia-Pacific region. In terms of the rate of growth, the European and CIS oil market lags behind the Asia-Pacific and North American markets. Europe is our main oil export market, and we must carry out a realistic assessment of prospects for increasing sales of Russian oil to this market.

At present, developing countries account for more than 70 per cent of the increase in global oil consumption. China tops the list: over the last five years, its oil consumption has increased by 94 million tonnes a year, accounting for 32 per cent of the total increase in global oil consumption.

In this five-year period, industrially developed countries have accounted for 29 per cent of the increase in oil consumption. The United States has seen the biggest increase, while Japan, Germany and Italy have reduced their consumption. In Europe, it is Spain, Austria, Poland and the Netherlands that have accounted for the increase in oil consumption.

From 2000 to 2004, global oil production increased by 7.1 per cent. Consequently, the increase in oil production was lower than the increase in oil consumption. In 2001 and 2002 the increase in oil consumption was modest, and OPEC reduced oil production so as to maintain the price situation on the market.

Since 2003 oil-producing countries have effectively lifted restrictions on the production and export of oil, in order to meet rapidly growing demand. The increase in oil production in Russia, Saudi Arabia and a number of other countries has been partly offset by a fall in production in the North Sea, the United States, Venezuela, Iraq and Indonesia, caused by political and technological factors.

The stabilisation of the political situation in a number of OPEC countries will mean that production can be increased by 73 million tonnes a year. This will compensate for the fall in production in the United States and other countries resulting from technological factors. However, to meet growing global demand for oil, other countries must also increase their oil exports, including Russia.

From 2000 to 2004, Russia provided the largest increase in oil production in the world. Russia's increase in oil output was three times that of OPEC. Today, Russia is one of the main stabilisation factors in the global oil market.

2 Forecast for Russia's oil production and oil supplies to the global market

In 1987, Russia (excluding the other republics of the USSR) produced 571 million tonnes of oil. This was the highest oil output of any single country in the history of the oil industry. It was followed by a period during which oil production fell sharply, but this trend ended a few years ago. Since 2000, oil production in Russia has been growing rapidly.

Thanks to high oil prices on the global market, growth in production has exceeded the forecasts in the *Energy Strategy of Russia*. The forecasts for growth in Russia's oil production can now be revised for the new conditions.

With average prices for Russian oil on the global market of $25 to $35 per barrel, oil production in Russia could reach 550 million to 590 million tonnes a year by 2020, primarily by developing new oilfields.

To date, Russia has discovered and explored more than 3,000 hydrocarbon fields. Only half of these are being developed. These resources are mainly onshore. More than half of Russian oil production and more than 90 per cent of its gas production is concentrated in the Urals and Western Siberia. Most of the fields in this region have been well worked. Therefore, while retaining this region as the main source of hydrocarbon resources, alternative producing regions should be developed.

In the long term, the priority regions for oil and gas production are Eastern Siberia and the Far East. The development of these regions will be especially important both in socio-economic terms and also for Russia's strategic interests in the Asia-Pacific region.

It is also very important to develop other oil and gas hubs, including the Sakhalin Islands shelf, the Barents Sea, the Baltic Sea and the Caspian Sea.

Russian oil exports depend on both oil production and domestic consumption. It is forecast that until 2010 the growth rate of oil production in Russia will exceed the growth rates in oil refining for the domestic market. Consequently, until 2010 Russian oil exports will increase. After that, they will stabilise.

3 Developing the system for transportation of oil from Russia

The prospects for development of Russia's energy sector are to a large extent determined by Russia's size and geographical location. Geographically, Russia is linked to three main oil export markets: Europe, the United States and the Asia-Pacific region.

The Energy Strategy of Russia envisages the development of a system of trunk oil pipelines and sea terminals to supply oil to these markets. The main projects are:

1 To expand supplies to Europe: the Baltic Pipeline System and the Port of Primorsk, with an annual capacity of up to 62 million tonnes.
2 To access the Asia-Pacific market: the Taishet–Pacific Ocean Oil Pipeline System and terminals for loading tankers with a dead-weight of 300,000 tonnes in one of Russia's Pacific ports, for example, the Port of Nakhodka. Total annual capacity of up to 80 million tonnes.
3 To access the United States market: the long-term plan is to construct a pipeline system linking Western Siberia and the Barents Sea coast. By 2020 this pipeline system could also have an annual capacity of up to 80 million tonnes.

In addition, it is anticipated that oil transit from Kazakhstan via the Caspian Pipeline Consortium (CPC) will increase to 67 million tonnes a year (1.3 million barrels a day).

Implementation of all the projects, both large and small, should increase the transmission capacity of Russia's export trunk oil pipelines and sea terminals to 303 million tonnes a year by 2010 (6.1 million barrels a year).

Russia's oil companies are implementing their own projects to increase oil exports. For example, Lukoil is delivering oil to Iran across the Caspian Sea via a terminal in Astrakhan. Rosneft is organising oil supplies to Murmansk in tankers along the Northern Sea Route, and oil exports from the Sakhalin Islands are increasing.

Gradual implementation of all the projects to develop Russia's transport infrastructure will provide for stable growth in oil supplies to the global market.

4 Markets for Russian oil and oil products

Europe remains the main market for Russian oil. Currently, 93 per cent of all oil exports from Russia are to Europe. This includes the markets of North-Western Europe, the Mediterranean and the CIS.

Oil supplies to the Asia-Pacific region are increasing gradually. Supplies to China dominate this market, accounting for the bulk of the increase. In the American market, the main consumer of Russian oil is the United States, but these supplies do not play a prominent role.

In the future, Europe will continue to be Russia's main oil market, and Russia will provide the required increase in oil supplies to Europe. By increasing oil production, it is also planned to strengthen Russia's positions in the markets of the Asia-Pacific region and the United States.

5 Domestic requirements: Rising petrol prices

As well as supplying foreign markets, the Russian energy sector meets the needs of the Russian economy and population in full. Domestic requirements currently account for about one-third of total hydrocarbon production.

However, although there is not a shortage of energy raw materials and derived products, prices on the domestic market are increasing, following global prices. Since the beginning of the year, the price of petrol has gone up by about 40 per cent, which naturally is very concerning for consumers.

The problem of rising petrol prices is a complex one. When attempting to address this issue, a question arises: Should Russian domestic prices follow global prices, gradually approaching their level, or should domestic pricing be based on its own logic?

It would be wrong to think that monopolistic collusion on the domestic market is entirely to blame for the increased prices of oil products. Oil companies do have to follow the global market situation and consider their profitability in the domestic market. In the current situation, measures such as domestic intervention, stock exchange instruments and stricter anti-monopoly laws can have only a limited effect. The main balance is determined by two instruments for state regulation of taxes: royalty payments and fiscal measures relating to external markets (export duties). Currently, domestic royalty payments are linked by law to prices on the global market. Royalty payments affect domestic prices, while also minimising the regulatory impact of export duties. It is true that the current system originated in principally different price conditions. Today, when the price band on the oil market has been broken, it might be appropriate to return to this question again.

6 Minerals Extraction Tax (MET)

The question of changing the principles used to determine the MET has been raised repeatedly, and, it should be said, not very successfully. The latest round of work is under way on diversifying MET rates based on thorough analysis of the effects of royalties-related factors. Moreover, it is more important than ever to prevent royalties for natural resources becoming 'administrative' rent.

7 The law on mining

Revising the legislation on mining below-ground materials is just as important. One of the problems facing Russia's energy sector is the replacement of mineral and raw material reserves. Present investment in replacing reserves is clearly insufficient, as the increase in production is outpacing the increase in reserves. Unless appropriate decisions are taken in this sphere, reserves will continue to dwindle. A new version of the law on below-ground resources is currently being prepared. The main aims of this law will be to ensure the rational use of the entire domestic mineral and raw material base and to create the conditions for its replacement through the following: establishing stable, mutually beneficial relationships between the government and resource users; increasing resource users' liability for performance of their obligations; and stimulating investment in the replacement of mineral and raw material reserves and oil field development. It should be noted that the drafters of the revised underground resources law are drawing heavily on foreign experience of regulating resource use. Of particular interest is the shift in other countries from bureaucratic relationships to relationships governed by civil law. Indeed, it is harder for an official to defend their interests in a court of law than in an imposing office.

All of this work is aimed at making the relationships between the government and business more transparent and attracting domestic and foreign investment in the Russian oil and gas sector and related sectors.

The woes of oil

From an interview with Itogi, *21 December 2004:*

Viktor Borisovich, under the current government you have been given almost all of the real economy. Explain to me, what is the real economy today? There is a view that besides oil and gas, nothing is real …

Given that we do at least have a lot of oil and gas, it's a good start. Still, the share of the oil and gas sector is contracting: in 2000 it was about 17.5 per cent, and in 2003 it was just 15 per cent. That leaves another 85 per cent of the economy: the metals industry (ferrous and non-ferrous), mechanical engineering, car manufacturing …

Let's leave car manufacturing out of this: you won't find a car owner in Russia who wouldn't like to get their hands on an imported car.

You know, foreign makes can also be assembled in Russia, and therefore become domestic vehicles. I think that such companies put useful competitive pressure on our traditional manufacturers, although they too are increasingly willing to co-operate. And it is better than testing the resilience of Russian car manufacturing by liberalising external factors, by abolishing duties. In this case, only Korean suppliers would remain in the market. We need to give ourselves a chance.

But let's return to the structure of the real economy. The idea that it is contracting to the level of the oil and gas sector is hugely distorted by stereotypes. The oil and gas sector remains the driver of the economy. If it contracts, the remaining 85 per cent also contracts. This is the path to economic hara-kiri. We need to know how to use this economic buttress, and not get neurotic about it, as Russians are prone to, saying, 'Woes come not only from wit but also from oil.' Otherwise, however highbrow a conversation starts, it will always end up being about oil and gas pipelines.

And if you were the Minister for Culture?

We would still be talking about pipelines, because the search for sources of finance for culture would still come down to oil. 'If we find the money to develop culture, can't we have just a bit of pipe?'

The priorities of the Energy Strategy

From a report given at the meeting of the Government Commission on the Energy Sector on 31 March 2006, 'On the state of the

Figure 3.5 Degree of concentration of capacity for hydrocarbon production and refining

Oil production in 2005	Capacity of Russia's oil refineries for primary oil refining in 2005
Total – 470 million tonnes including: OJSC Lukoil – 76.5 million tonnes (16%) OJSC Rosneft – 67.1 million tonnes (14.2%) TNK BP Holding – 65.7 million tonnes (14%) Surgutneftegaz – 67.1 million tonnes (11.7%)	Total – 470 million tonnes including: OJSC Yukos – 47.1 million tonnes (18.6%) OJSC NK Lukoil – 41.35 million tonnes (16.3%) TNK BP Holding – 31.7 million tonnes (12.5%) OJSC Bashneftekhim – 29.3 million tonnes (11.6%) OJSC Sibneft – 19.5 million tonnes (7.7%)

For primary oil refining, Russia's refineries operate at 80% of capacity on average.

At more than 50% of the companies in the sector the refinery yield is 50–70%. At only five companies is the refinery yield more than 80%.

It is intended to increase petroleum feedstock refining capacity by 20 million tonnes by 2010.

domestic market for hydrocarbons and oil products and prospects for development of this market':

As a whole, in its current state the oil-refining industry is meeting current demand. In recent years, or to be more precise, until last year, the oil sector demonstrated good rates of sustainable economic growth. However, this growth is based to a considerable extent on assets and facilities inherited from the past. The oil-refining industry as it currently stands will be unable to satisfy forecast demand. The growth potential, which was put in place back in the Soviet era, has almost been exhausted. The sector could find itself in crisis in the near future.

The Russian oil-refining sector comprises 27 oil refineries, of which 19 belong to vertically integrated oil companies.

Most of the oil delivered to refineries is processed by vertically integrated oil companies.

Many of the companies (almost 50 per cent) are concentrated in the Volga region and the West Urals. Siberia (19 per cent) and the central Russian regions (16 per cent) are in second and third place respectively for the number of oil refineries. The most 'deprived' areas are the Southern, North-Western and Far Eastern Federal Districts, which are attractive today in terms of export flows. The location of the refineries does correspond to the structure of current domestic demand. However, this demand will change, and we must therefore develop a system of measures to manage long-term risks. One of the ways to address the problem could be the construction of new oil refineries to be linked to new trunk pipelines.

The majority of Russian oil refineries (with the exception of the Kirishinefteorgsintez and Tuapse refineries) are situated in the heart of the country, far from port infrastructure. Russia is practically the only country that extracts oil from the continent and has to pump its oil for export a distance of 2,500–3,000 km. For the other main oil-producing countries, overland transportation does not exceed 200–300 km. In fact, the transportation leg is the main factor hindering the expansion of oil product exports from Russia. (There is also the problem of fuel quality, but this is more a tactical issue than a strategic one.) The additional cost of exporting oil products from refineries in European Russia is $20 to $30 per tonne, and from the Omsk, Achinsk and Angarsk refineries it is as much as $80.

Because of the high transportation costs resulting from the geographical location of the majority of Russian oil refineries and

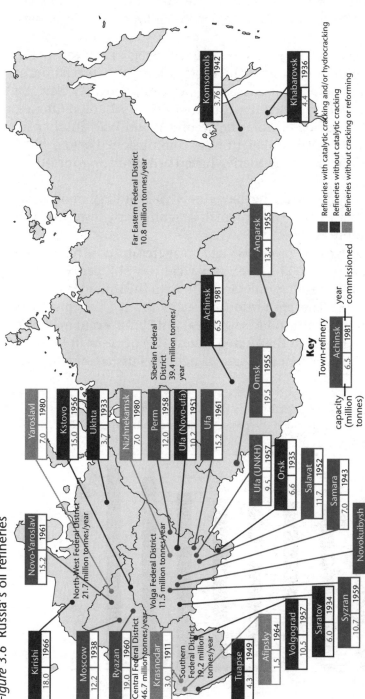

Figure 3.6 Russia's oil refineries

Oil refining capacity in Russia is distributed unevenly, creating:

- the prerequisites for the emergence of regions with 'surplus' production and regions with oil product 'deficits', both overall, and also for individual types of fuel;
- an increased burden on transport for the transportation of oil products.

Almost all Russian oil refineries are situated in the heart of the country, far from its borders and sea export terminals. The increased transportation costs reduce the cost-efficiency of oil product exports.

Most Russian oil refineries were built in the 1960s and are characterised by:

- a high level of depreciation of fixed assets (up to 80%);
- the use of obsolete, energy intensive equipment that is environmentally less than ideal;
- a low proportion of destructive refining processes (catalytic cracking, hydrocracking, coking);
- a low level of conversion of petroleum feedstock into more valuable oil products.

the low quality of the output, on the European market Russian oil products are sold mainly as raw material for further secondary refining.

A high level of depreciation of fixed assets is typical in the Russian oil-refining industry. The average level of depreciation of equipment at the oil refineries is 80 per cent, and they have by far exceeded their expected lifespans. (Of Russia's 27 oil refineries, six were commissioned before the Second World War, another six were built before 1950, and eight were commissioned before 1960. Therefore, 20 of the 27 refineries have been operating for 40–50 years.)

Despite a slight increase in the refinery yield at Russian oil refineries in the last three years, it remains significantly lower than in developed countries.

The average light oil products yield, in aggregate, does not exceed 55 per cent, and in 2005 the refinery yield was 71.3 per cent. This indicator is on average 1.3 times lower than in the United States and Western Europe. The proportion of secondary refining processes increasing the light oil products yield was just 20.3 per cent in Russia, against 73.3 per cent in the United States, 42.9 per cent in Western Europe and 32.6 per cent in Japan. As a result, Russian oil refineries

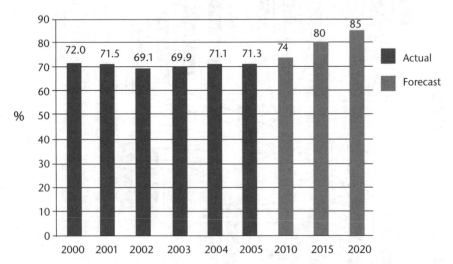

Figure 3.7 Refinery yield at Russia's oil refineries, 2000 to 2020 (per cent). Actual figures to 2005; projected figures from 2010.

Despite a slight increase in the refinery yield at Russian oil refineries in the last three years, it remains significantly lower than in developed countries.

Figure 3.8 Breakdown of production of the main types of oil products at Russia's refineries in 2005

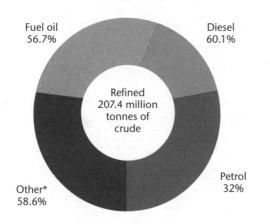

Fuel oil 56.7%

Diesel 60.1%

* jet engine fuel, petroleum bitumen, tar, lubricating oil, liquefied gas, aromatic hydrocarbons, etc.

Refined 207.4 million tonnes of crude

Other* 58.6%

Petrol 32%

Quality of the motor fuels produced:

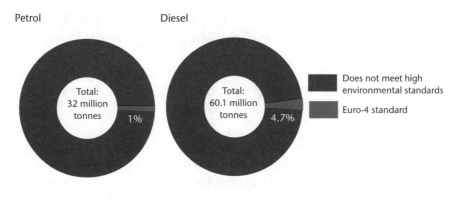

Petrol

Diesel

Total: 32 million tonnes

1%

Total: 60.1 million tonnes

4.7%

Does not meet high environmental standards

Euro-4 standard

obtain about 140 litres of petrol per tonne of crude oil. In the United States, it is more than 450 litres. Therefore, products with low added value dominate the commodity structure of the Russian oil-refining industry. This is primarily because Russian refineries lag behind in technology and the level of fixed asset depreciation is high.

Oil refining is currently focused on low-quality products, and the structure of output corresponds to the structure of demand that existed when these refineries were built in the 1960s.

Fuel oil and diesel account for a fairly high percentage of the output of the oil refining industry. However, there is insufficient demand for these products on the domestic market. Domestic consumption of the main oil products in 2005 was as follows:

◆ petrol – 83.4 per cent;
◆ diesel – 44.6 per cent;
◆ furnace fuel oil – 45.5 per cent.

Despite an increase in the number of vehicles on the roads, in 2000–2005 petrol consumption per unit of transport fell. The following factors contributed to this:

◆ replacement of obsolete vehicles with modern vehicles with more efficient engines;
◆ increase in consumer fuel prices;
◆ increase in the number of vehicles with diesel engines and gradual shift in motor fuel consumption towards diesel.

The main risk factor for the fuel market in the next ten years is a sharp change after 2010 in the structure of petrol consumption:

◆ increased demand for high-octane, high-quality petrol, meeting the Euro-4 standard as a minimum;
◆ reduced demand for low-octane petrol.

It can therefore be said that production is characterised by an archaic structure, with risks of an imbalance between the structure of supply (production) and the structure of demand (consumption) for oil products.

The industry has been given a signal, and in theory the market should have been able to cope with this situation by itself, bringing supply and demand more or less into balance. Companies have recognised this signal, but investment processes need to be triggered.

Hence, we need measures to supplement market mechanisms and to modify the market.

By adopting a technical regulation on environmental requirements for automobile engines, the Russian government has taken action to reduce demand for poor-quality fuel.

Experts forecast that between now and 2015 the number of motor vehicles in Russia will increase by 40.4 per cent, reaching 44.3 million. By vehicle category, the increases will be:

Figure 3.9 Forecast growth in the number of motor vehicles in Russia

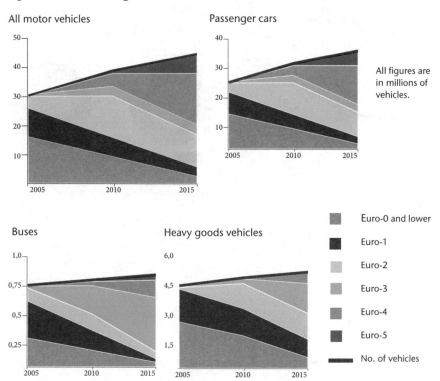

◆ passenger cars by 46 per cent;
◆ heavy goods vehicles by 14.6 per cent;
◆ buses by 7.7 per cent.

After 2010, the structure of consumption of motor fuels will show increased demand for high-quality grades of fuel that meet the Euro-4 and Euro-5 standards. The following factors will restrain growth in fuel consumption:

◆ an increase in the number of new motor vehicles with modern, more efficient engines;
◆ withdrawal of old, inefficient models, running on Euro-1 fuel, or lower grades, which account for more than 80 per cent of demand.

Figure 3.10 Forecast demand for motor fuel

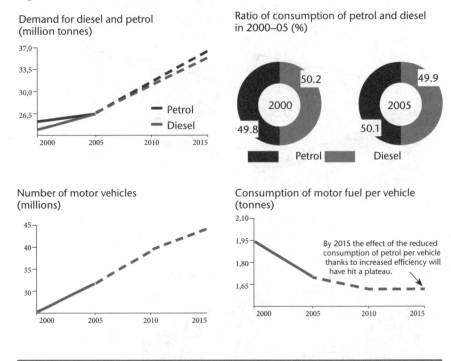

To stimulate the supply of high-quality products, it was decided to make equipment to modernise oil refining exempt from customs duties. Reducing export duty on oil products is another measure. These are just the first steps. New steps are planned for the following stage.

The following actions are aimed at managing demand:

◆ adoption of a technical regulation on fuel;
◆ differentiation of fuel duties;
◆ introducing stock exchange trade in oil products.

and to stimulate investment:

◆ adoption of amendments to the Law on Mining;
◆ differentiation of taxes on mineral extraction (MET);
◆ ensuring a stable customs tariff policy;
◆ support for infrastructure projects.

We believe that this package of measures will take the oil products industry to a new level in terms of quality.

Current and forecast (to 2015) growth in petrol production at Russia's oil refineries will outstrip demand on the domestic market. The task of the oil-refining industry in the near term is to change the structure of production of motor fuels in line with the forecast quantitative and qualitative changes in domestic demand.

The petrochemical industry

As for Russia's petrochemical industry, this subsector accounts for about 1.55 per cent of the country's total industrial output. This might not seem much, but the industry has 150 large and medium-sized enterprises, and 210,000 workers. Of the main local employers in towns and cities, 45 per cent are petrochemical companies.

For the last five years, the industry's economic and financial performance has been stable.

The level of consolidation in the industry is fairly high, with five financial-industrial groups producing more than 80 per cent of the products for sale. We are seeing a positive trend whereby petrochemical companies are becoming extensions of oil and gas producers, such as Sibur, Tatneft and Lukoil. The hydrocarbon resources used by Russia's petrochemical companies are extracted in Russia. At present, there are sufficient raw materials for the industry.

Based on Russia's potential hydrocarbon resources and the efficiency of hydrocarbon processing by the chemicals industry, future development of the sector will centre on production of synthetic resins, plastics, rubber, artificial fibres and thread, and paints and lacquers.

It should be noted that in terms of actual and potential hydrocarbon resources, Russia is in a better position than most industrially developed countries. The growing demand within Russia for petrochemicals is to a large extent met by domestic companies. At the same time, the export potential of Russian petrochemical companies is also constantly increasing.

The Ministry of Industry and Energy has held a number of discussions with petrochemical companies. There is a clear need to stimulate investment, which could be achieved by:

Figure 3.11 Forecast production and market for the main types of petrochemicals

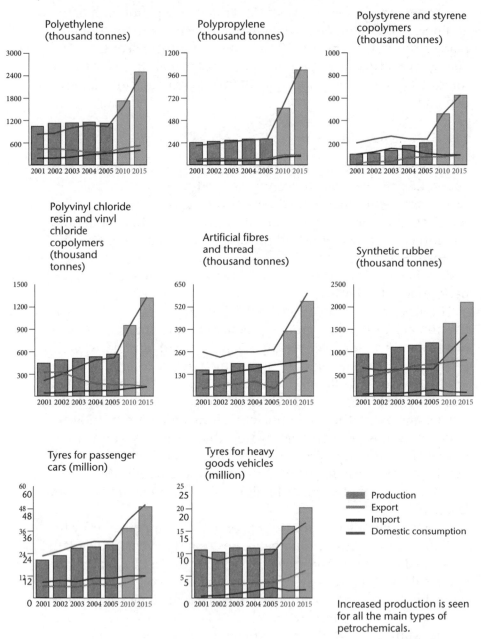

Increased production is seen for all the main types of petrochemicals.

- scrapping customs duties on imported high-tech equipment that is not manufactured in Russia;
- using the Investment Fund to provide loan finance for companies' technical modernisation programmes, and also direct investment in the infrastructure components of such projects;
- amending the tariff policy with respect to rail freight transport.

Government implementation of these measures to support the petrochemicals sector could significantly increase investment.

Technical regulation is particularly important at the current time. Companies in this industry face global competition both in domestic and global markets and this competition is to a large extent between states rather than companies. We are currently working on a programme to develop technical regulations. The aim is to create a system of standards and compliance evaluations to improve the quality and competitiveness of Russian petrochemicals, and also to create barriers to keep low quality products out of the Russian market.

2006 will be decisive for oil and gas fields

From an interview with Biznes, *21 February 2006:*

In its forecast for the development of Russia's oil and gas sector in 2006, the ratings agency Fitch notes that our country may have to decide whether it would prefer to export to the West or to the East. At present, neither the amount of resources being extracted nor infrastructure capacity are sufficient to develop both areas. So, which will be given preference, exports to the United States and Europe, or exports to the Asia-Pacific region?

Until 2005 the country was using almost 100 per cent of its pipeline capacity that was allocated for exports. Without a reserve, repairs cannot be carried out and unexpected situations cannot be overcome. The safety margin should be 10–12 per cent. Russia is still a very long way from this level. Last year, a small capacity reserve appeared in the pipeline system, of about one hundredth.

To ensure oil exports to the West we will complete the Baltic Pipeline System this spring. It will have a capacity of 60 million tonnes of oil per year. It is not intended to increase the capacity of the Druzhba system, as there are no new extraction projects planned for this pipeline system. At the same time, we anticipate increased supplies of Caspian oil towards the Black Sea, and also through the Caspian Pipeline Consortium, with respect to which fairly complex negotiations are ongoing. In addition, work is underway on plans for the transportation of crude via Bulgaria and Greece.

The main increase in production will come from the Eastern Siberian, Far East and Timan–Pechora oil and gas provinces. Resources from Eastern Siberia will be transported along the Eastern Siberian–Pacific Ocean pipeline (ESPO) to the coast of the Pacific Ocean, for export to the Asia-Pacific region, and we intend to take the Timan–Pechora northwards. In this respect, there is no competition between export areas. However, there are possible risks associated with the timescales for developing oilfields. It is planned that when we 'connect' new oil and gas provinces to export pipelines, they will be reinforced with output from the traditional Western Siberian oilfields.

And we should not forget about our Central Asian partners, in particular Kazakhstan, which supplies 18 million tonnes of its oil via Russia. By 2015, this figure could double.

But the start date for construction of the ESPO has been postponed again, this time because of another state environmental expert review. Isn't there a danger that the first stage of construction will end up behind schedule, given that completion is planned for 2008? Incidentally, the Ministry of Industry and Energy in its forecast for the development of pipeline capacity anticipates zero growth in transmission capacity in 2008.

There are no grounds for me to say that the first stage of construction will not be completed on time, in 2008. I remind you that the Baltic Pipeline System, for example, was built three times faster than would be expected, and moreover, without causing any harm to the environment or other aspects of the project. Furthermore, the pipeline was laid amid intense external pressure from environmentalists. Essentially, the whole of Europe was discussing the threat posed to the region by the pipeline and terminal facility. I can say in all good conscience: no other terminal in the Baltic has the same level of environmental and process safety as the Primorsk facility. It is time we required those states to bring their facilities into line with our terminal.

The ESPO is of just as much interest to environmentalists and environment agencies. However, reducing the environmental risks is a technical matter. The ESPO is a unique project: special grades and types of steel have been developed for a pipe with a reinforced wall thickness. In many places it will be an 'intelligent pipe', handling an amazing amount of telemetric data, and self-regulating. We must remember how important this complex project is. It is of enormous geopolitical significance for Russia, a 'window to Asia' in effect.

According to its own figures, Gazprom intends to increase production by 0.5 per cent a year until 2030. Experts say that such an increase is low in relation to the increase in demand. Moreover, the new large fields, which the company intends to augment in the next few years, are already tied up under the monopoly's long-term contracts. Can the state-owned company meet the growing needs of the domestic market as well as projects to supply gas to the United States and the Asia-Pacific region?

Without a doubt, Gazprom is balancing supply for the domestic market and foreign markets. When talking about production volumes, we cannot discount our Asian partners, Kazakhstan, Uzbekistan and Turkmenistan, with whom Russia is cooperating in the gas sector. The gas resources of these republics make a significant contribution to ensuring that the needs of both the domestic market and foreign markets are met.

Moreover, we must use opportunities to make huge savings in gas. Within Russia we already use 390 billion cubic metres of gas, and this at a time when, because our country is so large, the level of gas infrastructure development is not all that high. The average efficiency of gas usage at Russian power plants is 1.6 times lower than in countries that only just make it into the list of developed nations. The Ministry is currently working on the *General Scheme for the Development of the Electricity Sector to 2030*. Under this scheme, the capacity of each power plant will be calculated based on highly efficient gas use. Accordingly, domestic requirements for gas will definitely be covered.

As for new production, the Yuzhno-Russkoye field (and not only it) will be used as a resource for the North European Pipeline. Offshore fields, in particular Shtokman, are committed to the American LNG market. But in the east of the country there is also the Sakhalin oil and gas province, where the world's largest liquefied gas plant is being built. Construction is being completed here of a pipeline to transport dry gas to Khabarovsk Krai. With this capacity in mind,

Russia's first long-term contract has been signed for supplies of up to 3 billion cubic metres of gas by 2010 at market prices.

Because of the lack of agreement between TNK-BP and Gazprom about the Kovykta field, it is proving impossible to start developing it. Does the Ministry of Industry and Energy plan to somehow influence Gazprom's position with regard to connecting Kovykta to the pipe?

A special programme is being produced to develop the oil and gas sector of Eastern Siberia and the Far East, in line with the general assessments of the foreign and domestic gas markets, taking into account gas from our Central Asian partners. The programme will answer the questions, when and how should the Kovykta and Chayanda fields be 'uncapped'? Of course, the process here has been a little drawn out. But I hope that 2006 will provide breakthroughs on decisions, including with respect to the Kovykta project.

Three potential projects to construct gas pipelines in the Asia-Pacific Region are under consideration. Has it been decided yet which of the routes will be prioritised?

A gas market cannot work without properly defined, long-term relationships concerning supplies of dry gas. Active discussions are underway with our Chinese partners, and once the outcome is known it will be possible to decide the order of precedence for the transport routes: Altai, Kovykta–Irkutsk, the Far East, or all three. The choice of route should also be linked to the creation of a gas supply system in the east of the country.

Prospects for the development and use of systems to transport hydrocarbons and oil products

From a report to the Government Commission on the Energy Sector, 9 October 2006:

The system for transporting hydrocarbons and oil products includes the subsystems of pipeline, railway and sea transport, and the necessary port terminals. It is understood that rail and sea transport are general-use types of transport, in contrast to pipeline transport, which is a special type of transport providing the basis for the whole system for the transportation of hydrocarbon resources. My report will focus on pipeline transport.

The Energy Strategy of Russia for the Period to 2020 envisages:

◆ Development of the oil and gas sector's transport infrastructure: first, for the timely creation of transport systems in the new oil and gas producing regions; second, to diversify supplies to the domestic and foreign markets by area, means and route; and third, to increase the efficiency of gas, oil and oil product exports.

◆ Regulation of access by energy producers to the pipeline systems.

◆ Support for projects to create energy transport infrastructure, based on public private partnerships: coordination of objectives, pooling of efforts, and apportioning of responsibilities and risks.

It is with these aims in mind that the system for transportation of hydrocarbons and oil products is being developed. I just want to emphasise that, with regard to strategy, developing energy transport infrastructure requires everyone involved in the process (business, regional and federal bodies) to co-operate and take a long-term view.

Current forecasts (regularly produced by the Ministry to monitor the energy strategy in the light of changes in the economic growth rate and the situation on the external market) predict that by 2015 oil production will increase to 509–542 million tonnes (depending on the version of the forecast for the socio-economic development of the Russian Federation) as against 472 million tonnes in 2005.

It is forecast that volumes of crude oil exports in 2015 could be 272–300 million tonnes, as against 252 million tonnes in 2005.

It is anticipated that exports will increase as a result of increased oil supplies to the Far Abroad (a term for non-CIS countries). At the same time, there will be no significant change in oil exports to the CIS.

It is anticipated that primary oil refining will increase to 225–230 million tonnes by 2015, compared with 207 million tonnes in 2005. Petrol production will increase 1.2–1.3 times, and diesel production by 17–23 per cent.

The light oil products yield will increase from 57.2 per cent in 2005 to 62–64 per cent by 2015, with a considerable improvement in its quality, which corresponds to companies' plans for the rehabilitation and technical re-equipment of oil refineries. These were discussed in detail at the last meeting of the Government Commission. Oil product exports will remain stable.

It is clear that the foregoing (expanding production and exports of oil and oil products) will require commensurate development of the infrastructure for pipeline transport of oil and oil products.

Today, the pipeline transport system includes approximately 350,000 km of process-oriented pipelines (oil-gathering pipelines, pipelines for the supply of water to maintain formation pressure and for transporting treated oil), approximately 2,500 km of trunk pipelines owned by oil companies, including foreign companies (the Usa–Ukhta, Sakhalin–De-Kastri, and CPC pipelines) and also 50,000 km of pipelines belonging to OJSC AK Transneft.

At the end of 2005, OJSC AK Transneft had capacity of 221 million tonnes for the supply of oil to the Far Abroad, including north-westward, 72.1 million tonnes, westward, 66.5 million tonnes, and towards the Black Sea, 66.2 million tonnes. New lines will appear in the near future: to the east, 30–80 million tonnes, and to the north, 12 million tonnes.

The shortage of trunk pipeline capacity has been overcome in the last few years. OJSC AK Transneft now has surplus capacity of about 7 million tonnes a year, and the average utilisation rate for oil products is 92 per cent. However, for certain more cost-effective oil transportation routes there is still a shortage of capacity.

It should be noted that implementation of the ESPO project will increase pipeline transportation of oil towards the east from zero to 11.6–26 per cent, and, once the North project is completed (Kharyaga–Indiga), 95 per cent of oil exports will bypass the ports of neighbouring states.

These projects will increase the capacity of oil pipeline transport 1.4 times. Potential surplus capacity is estimated at 34–60 million tonnes (13–19 per cent), which would make it possible to diversify export routes and consequently make them more efficient.

Let me talk briefly about the progress of ongoing investment projects:

First, there is the Eastern Siberian–Pacific Ocean pipeline system (ESPO) to transport oil from Western and Eastern Siberia to a terminal on the Pacific coast.

The pipeline is 4,670 km in length (2,764 km in the first stage). Its design capacity is 30 million tonnes in the first stage and 80 million tonnes when completed. On 28 April 2006, construction began of the ESPO system's first start-up complex. In accordance with decisions taken at a meeting in Tomsk on 24 April 2006, chaired by the Russian President, Vladimir Putin, OJSC AK Transneft started

Figure 3.12 Structure of Russian oil exports by world regions

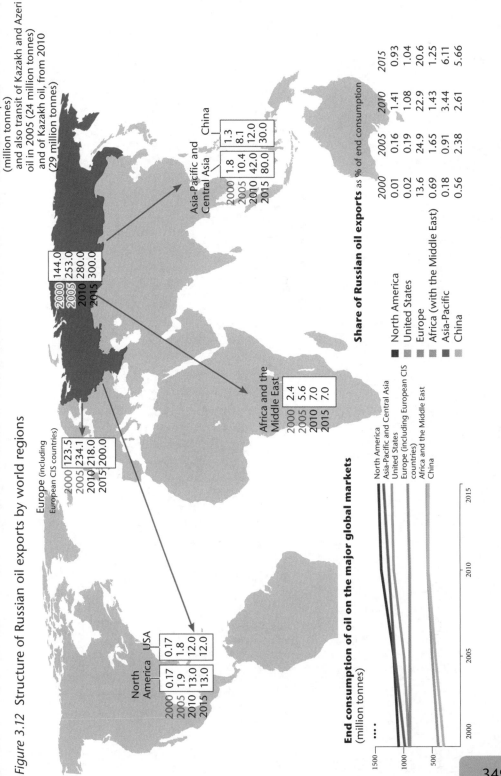

(million tonnes)
and also transit of Kazakh and Azeri
oil in 2005 (24 million tonnes)
and of Kazakh oil, from 2010
(29 million tonnes)

Europe (including
European CIS countries)

2000	123.5
2005	234.1
2010	218.0
2015	200.0

China

2000	1.3
2005	8.1
2010	12.0
2015	30.0

Asia-Pacific and
Central Asia

2000	1.8
2005	10.4
2010	42.0
2015	80.0

2000	144.0
2005	253.0
2010	280.0
2015	300.0

Africa and the
Middle East

2000	2.4
2005	5.6
2010	7.0
2015	7.0

North
America

2000	0.17
2005	1.9
2010	13.0
2015	13.0

USA

2000	0.17
2005	1.8
2010	12.0
2015	12.0

Share of Russian oil exports as % of end consumption

	2000	2005	2010	2015
North America	0.01	0.16	1.41	0.93
United States	0.02	0.19	1.08	1.04
Europe	13.6	24.9	22.9	20.6
Africa (with the Middle East)	0.69	1.65	1.43	1.25
Asia-Pacific	0.18	0.91	3.44	6.11
China	0.56	2.38	2.61	5.66

End consumption of oil on the major global markets
(million tonnes)

North America
Asia-Pacific and Central Asia
United States
Europe (including European CIS
countries)
Africa and the Middle East
China

2000   2005   2010   2015

1500
1000
500

Figure 3.13 Main pipelines in the Russian Federation

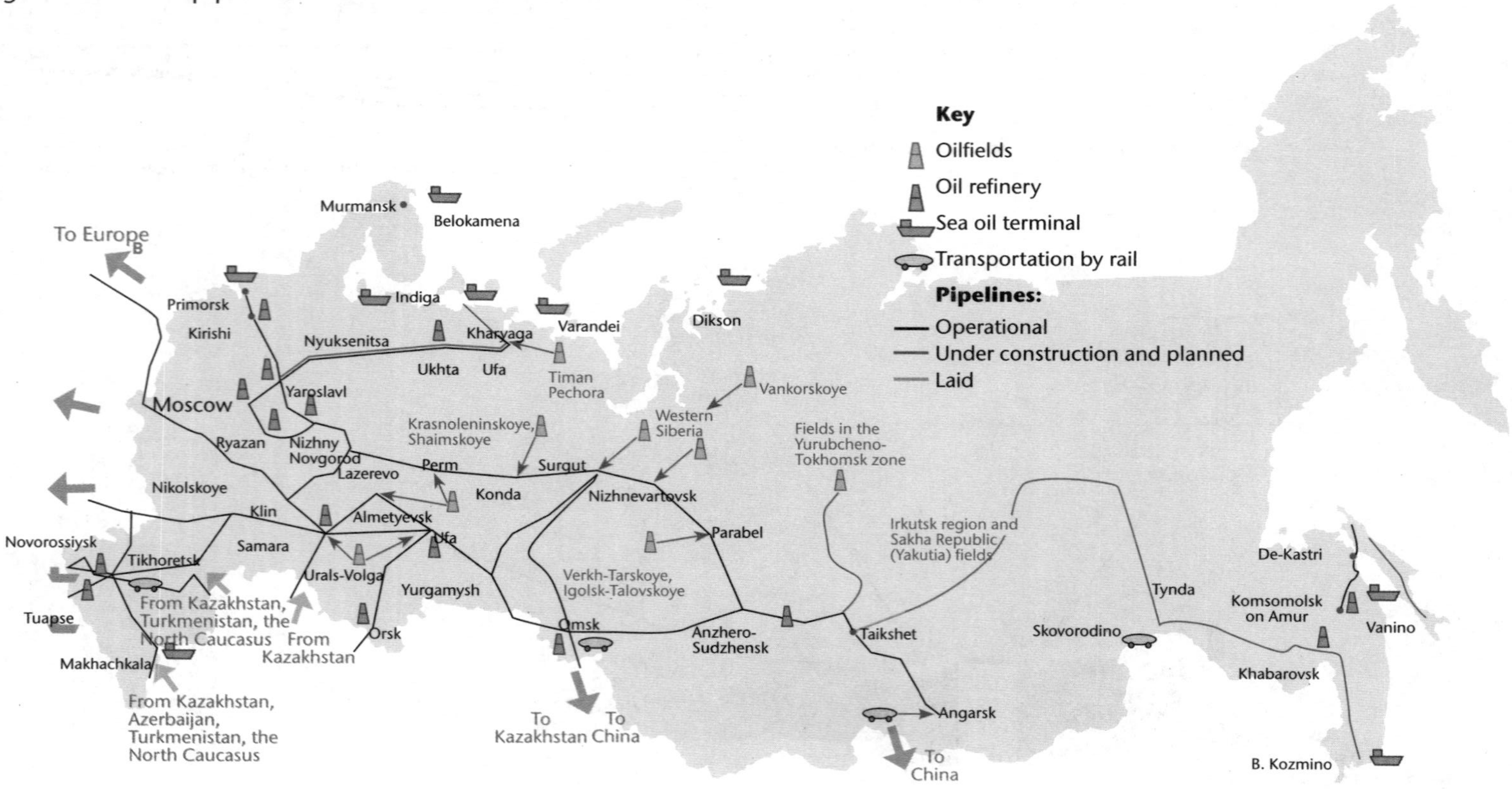

Key

- ▲ Oilfields
- ⬛ Oil refinery
- ⬛ Sea oil terminal
- ➤ Transportation by rail

Pipelines:
- —— Operational
- ═══ Under construction and planned
- ─── Laid

Table 3.1 Main pipelines in the Russian Federation

Operational

	Diameter (mm)	Length (km)	Design capacity*
Nizhnevartovsk–Kurgan–Samara	1,220	2,265	90
Ust-Balyk–Kurgan–Ufa–Almetevsk	1,220	1,844	84
Ust-Balyk–Omsk	1,020	964	46
Surgut–Polotsk	1,220/1,020	3,167	90
Kholmogory–Klin	1,220	2,431	42
Almetevsk–Nizhny Novgorod	1,020 + 820	580	58
Samara–Tikhoretsk	1,020/820	1,248	24
Samara–Lisichansk	1,220	980	82
Samara–Unecha–Mozyr	1,020+1,220	1,324	101
Michurinsk–Kremenchug	720	723	17
Ukhta–Yaroslavl	820	1,138	20
Aleksandrovskoye–Anzhero-Sudzhensk	1,120	848	60
Anzhero-Sudzhensk–Irkutsk	1,020+720	1,438	42
Perm –Almetevsk	1,020	445	50
Baku–Tikhoretsk	720/1,000	1,426	6
Baltic Pipeline System (Yaroslavl–Primorsk)	720+1,020	709	65
Caspian Pipeline Consortium (CPC)	1,016/1,067	1,580	28

Under construction and planned

	Diameter (mm)	Length (km)	Design capacity*
CPC	1,016/1,067	1,580	67
ESPO	1,067/1,220		30
Kharyaga –Indiga	1,220	467	12

* million tonnes per year.

design and exploration work for the route of the ESPO system beyond the water catchment area of Lake Baikal. With the aim of ensuring that the start-up complex is completed within the timescale set by the Russian Ministry of Industry and Energy, the extended route of the ESPO pipeline, covering a distance of 2,050 km, has been divided into three sections: Ust-Kut–Talakan field, Aldan–Tynda, and Talakan field–Aldan.

The next project is the Kharyaga–Indiga oil pipeline, which will transport oil produced in Timan-Pechora to an oil terminal near Indiga. The design capacity of the pipeline is 12 million tonnes and it will be 460 km in length.

In addition, the proposed expansion of the transmission capacity of the Caspian Pipeline Consortium, from 28 million tonnes to 67 million tonnes a year, is being discussed.

Expanding the capacity of the CPC would increase the supply of oil towards the Black Sea, which, given existing supplies to this market, would make Russian resources in the region less competitive. To avoid this, it is planned to build a pipeline from the Bulgarian port of Burgas to the Greek port of Alexandroupolis to transport oil bypassing the Bosporus and Dardanelles straits. This is the most economical of the

Figure 3.14 Oil resources and capacity of pipeline transport for supplies to the Far Abroad

Key

	2005	2006
Actual	XX	XX
Forecast	2010	XX
	XX	

Estimate

million tonnes

Northward

2000	2005	2006
—	—	—
2010	2015	
12	12	

Eastward (ESPO)

2000	2005	2006
—	—	—
2010	2015	
30	30	80

Export capacity surplus (including for transit supplies)

2000	2005	2006
	7.0	6.0
2010	2015	
11.0	38.0	27.0	34.0	60.0

Russian oil resources for supplies to the Far Abroad

2000	2005	2006
131.2	214.0	220.0
2010	2015	
220	231	224	248

Capacity of OJSC AK Transneft for oil supplies to the Far Abroad

2000	2005	2006
142	221	226
2010	2015	
246	258	308

CPC

2000	2005	2006
14.8	30.5	30.5
2010	2015	
67	67	

Towards the Black Sea

2000	2005	2006
53.8	66.2	67.0
2010	2015	
72	72	

North-Westward

2000	2005	2006
20.9	72.1	78.0
2010	2015	
78	78	

Westward (Druzhba)

2000	2005	2006
53.9	66.1	65.0
2010	2015	
66	66	

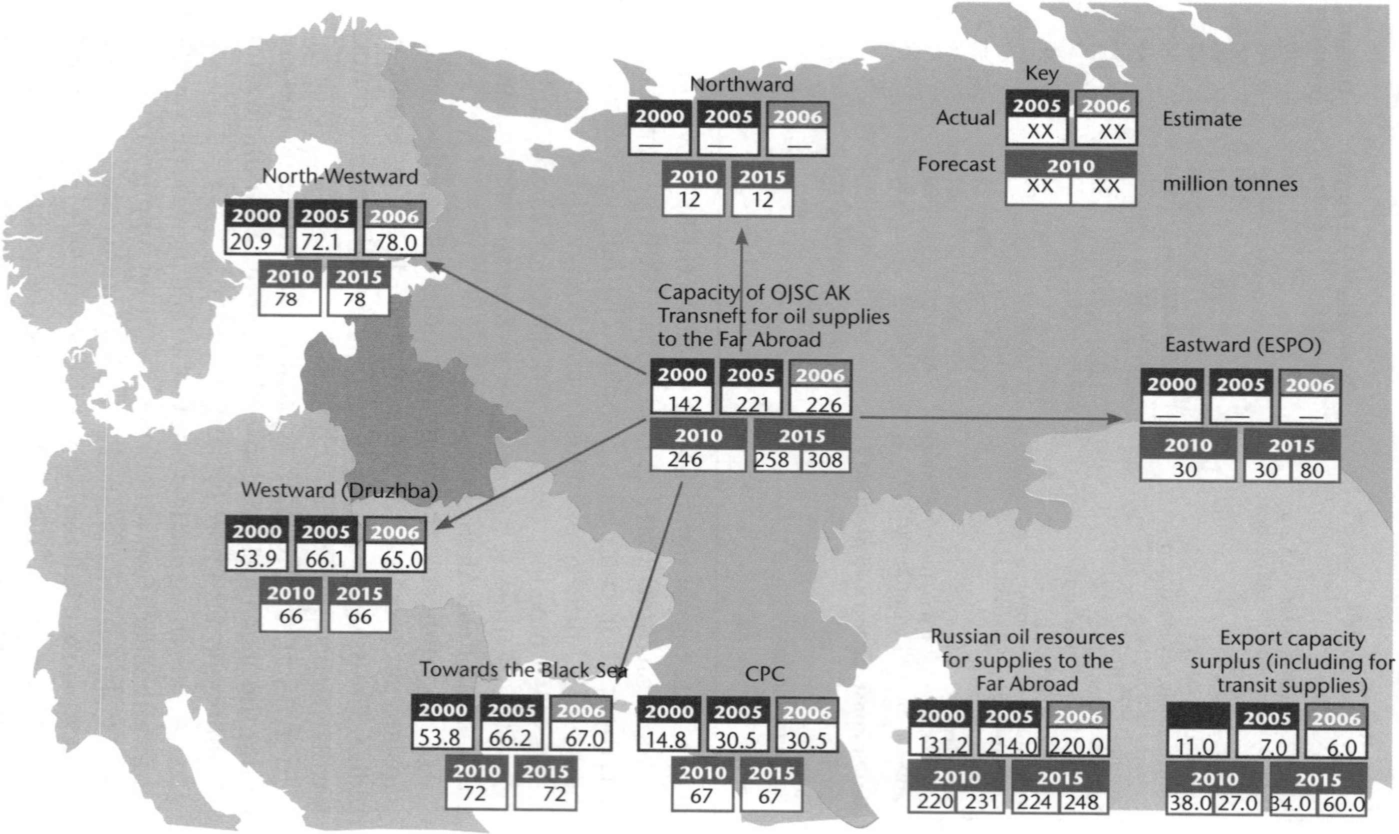

projects to bypass the straits. The design capacity of the pipeline is 35 million tonnes, with the option to expand it to 50 million tonnes. Its length is 287 km and the maximum deadweight of tankers in the port of Alexandroupolis is 300,000 tonnes.

Turning now to pipeline transport of oil products, the network for trunk pipeline transport of oil products runs in a latitudinal direction from the Kemerovo Region to the western borders of the Republic of Ukraine with Hungary and the Latvian port of Ventspils. The network is 19,100 km long: 15,200 km of trunk pipeline and 3,900 km of branch lines. The pipeline network transports light oil products (motor fuels) from 14 oil refineries in the European part of Russia. Two Belarussian refineries are also connected to the network (Mozyr and Novopolotsk).

From 2000–05, the volume of oil products pumped along the trunk pipelines of OJSC AK Transnefteprodukt's system increased by 20.3 per cent (from 23.1 million tonnes to 27.8 million tonnes). This was due to transportation of higher volumes of oil products both for the Russian domestic market (up 1.6 million tonnes) and for export (up 3.1 million tonnes, including 2.3 million tonnes to the Far Abroad).

The company's main objective for the next few years is to take the trunk pipelines to the Baltic Sea and Black Sea coasts. This would minimise the dependence of Russian exports on adjacent countries, help to develop Russia's economic infrastructure, and strengthen its defence capabilities. To this end, construction is under way of the Kstovo–Yaroslavl–Kirishi–Primorsk trunk oil products pipeline (the North project). The pipeline will reach the Baltic Sea coast near the seaport of Primorsk in the Leningrad region, where a terminal for shipment of light oil products is to be built. The length of the pipeline is 1,529 km (Vtorovo–Primorsk: 1,056 km; Subkhankulovo–Almetyevsk: 167 km; Kirishi–Primorsk: 306 km). Its design capacity is 17 million tonnes for the first stage (including 8.4 million tonnes for the first start-up complex) and 24.6 million tonnes when completed. It is planned that construction of the first start-up complex for the North project will be completed in June 2007.

Another promising project for the company is to take oil product pipelines up to the Black Sea coast. This project is being considered together with other issues relating to transport infrastructure for hydrocarbons and oil products in the Black Sea basin.

Other less capital-intensive projects are also being considered, including the construction of a branch line from Primorsk towards the port of Vysotsk, and completion of the Andreyevka–Almetyevsk oil products pipeline. The implementation of these projects could increase the capacity of the pipeline network of OJSC AK Transnefteprodukt from 50 million to 74 million tonnes a year in the period 2006–2012.

A key priority of the *Energy Strategy* is to preserve the Unified Gas Supply System and to expand it by constructing and connecting new facilities, ownership of which could take any form (including an equity interest).

It is anticipated that by 2015 gas production will increase to 742–754 billion cubic metres (compared to 638 billion cubic metres in 2005). The main increase in production is expected in the North-West region: 38 billion cubic metres (by developing the Shtokman field) and also in Eastern Siberia: 33 billion cubic metres (factoring in the development of fields in the Irkutsk region, including the unique Kovykta field). In the Far East it is planned that the Sakhalin-I and Sakhalin-II projects will reach design capacity and that work will start on the Sakhalin-III project, increasing gas production in this region by 42 billion cubic metres.

It is envisaged that the gas needs of the Russian economy and population will be met in full, with consumption forecast to increase from 442 billion cubic metres in 2005 to 470 billion cubic metres in 2010 and 490 billion cubic metres in 2015.

It is forecast that gas exports in 2015 could reach 274–281 billion cubic metres (compared with 207 billion cubic metres in 2005). Given trends in the global gas market and Russia's potential place in this market, and also the strategic decision to diversify exports, there will be a fundamental change in the structure of Russian gas exports:

◆ Due to the development of resources in the east of Russia (Sakhalin I and Sakhalin II) and also the Shtokman field, the share of liquefied natural gas delivered to Asia-Pacific markets and the east coast of the United States will reach 61 billion cubic metres (22 per cent of total exports).

◆ 30 billion cubic metres of gas (11 per cent) will be transported along the western route to China (the Altai project).

◆ Gas supplies to Europe will continue to increase, from 154 to 173 billion cubic metres (but the share of total exports will fall by 12 per cent, to 62 per cent), while gas supply routes will be

Figure 3.15 Structure of Russian gas exports by world regions

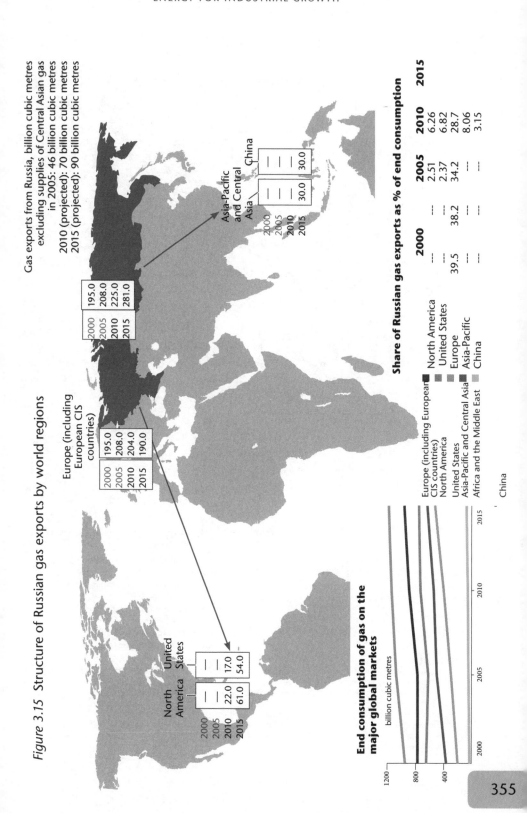

Gas exports from Russia, billion cubic metres
excluding supplies of Central Asian gas
in 2005: 46 billion cubic metres
2010 (projected): 70 billion cubic metres
2015 (projected): 90 billion cubic metres

Europe (including
European CIS
countries)

2000	195.0
2005	208.0
2010	204.0
2015	190.0

2000	195.0
2005	208.0
2010	225.0
2015	281.0

Asia-Pacific
and Central
Asia   China

2000	—	—
2005	—	—
2010	30.0	30.0
2015	30.0	30.0

North   United
America States

2000	—	—
2005	—	—
2010	22.0	17.0
2015	61.0	54.0

Share of Russian gas exports as % of end consumption

	2000	2005	2010	2015
North America	—	—	6.26	
United States	—	2.37	6.82	
Europe	39.5	38.2	28.7	
Asia-Pacific	—	—	8.06	
China	—	—	3.15	

Europe (including European
CIS countries)
North America
United States
Asia-Pacific and Central Asia
Africa and the Middle East

China

**End consumption of gas on the
major global markets**

billion cubic metres

1200
800
400

2000   2005   2010   2015

Figure 3.16 The unified gas supply system of Russia

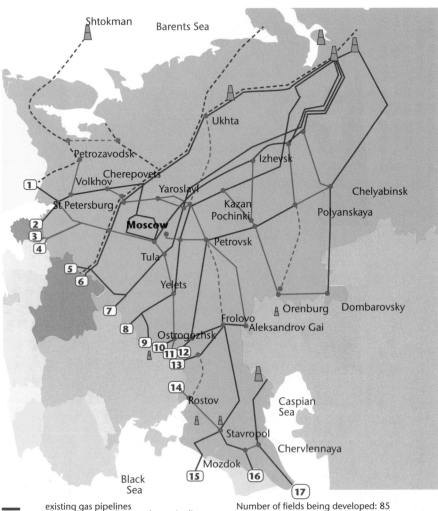

existing gas pipelines
planned gas pipelines and gas pipelines under construction
existing connecting gas pipelines
planned connecting gas pipelines and connecting gas pipelines under construction
fields
number of trunk gas pipelines for exports

Number of fields being developed: 85
Daily production in 2005:1.76 billion cu.m
Total length of trunk gas pipelines and branches: 152,800 km
Number of compressor stations/ sections:263/689
Installed capacity:44.2 million kW
Underground gas storage facilities:23

Name of gas pipeline

1 North Imantra (Finland)	9 Belgorod–Shebelinka (Ukraine)	13 Sokhranovka–Novopskov (Ukraine)
2 Kingisepp–Narva (Estonia)	10 Baluiki–Shebelinka (Ukraine)	14 Lugansk–Rostov-on-Don (transit through Ukraine)
3. Izborsk–Tartu (Estonia)	11 Ostrogozhsk–Novopskov (Ukraine)	15 Blue Stream
4 Izborsk–Riga (Latvia)		16 Mozdok–Tbilisi (Georgia)
5 Smolensk–Orsha (Belarus)	12 Pisarevka–Novopskov (Ukraine)	17 Izerbash–Shirvanovka (Azerbaijan)
6 Smolensk–Gomel (Belarus)		
7 Bryansk–Kiev (Ukraine)		
8 Kursk–Romny (Ukraine)		

diversified along the North European Gas Pipeline, and the Blue Stream will be extended to Central European countries and southern regions of Italy.

◆ Supplies of Russian gas to countries of the former USSR will be balanced (gradually replaced) by supplies of Central Asian gas. As a result, Russian gas exports to this region will decrease by 37 billion cubic metres, and its share in total exports by 20 per cent (to 6 per cent).

OJSC Gazprom's investment programme envisages a wide range of measures to eliminate bottlenecks in the Unified Gas Supply System.

One of the most significant investment projects in the sector is the construction of the North European Gas Pipeline (length: 1,200 km, diameter: 1,220 mm, operating pressure: 210 atm, design capacity: 27.5 billion cubic metres in the first stage and 55 billion cubic metres when completed). To connect the North European Pipeline and the Unified Gas Supply System, construction has begun of a new gas pipeline (Gryazovets–Vyborg), which will also meet the gas needs of St Petersburg and the Leningrad region. In implementing this project, particular attention must be paid to the environmental aspects of routing a gas pipeline along the bottom of the Baltic Sea.

A programme is being finalised to set up a unified system in Eastern Siberia and the Far East for gas production, transportation and supply, allowing for possible gas exports to the markets of China and other Asia-Pacific countries. Depending on the particular scenario, preliminary estimates put total capital investment in geological exploration, extraction, refining, helium storage and transportation of gas across Russia at $27–$59 billion.

As is clear from the foregoing, a fairly extensive package of measures is being implemented to develop the transport infrastructure for hydrocarbons and oil products.

Systemic implementation of these plans will require all the national energy policy mechanisms envisaged by the *Energy Strategy* to be used. The priority measures include:

◆ This year, the following documents will be ready: the *General Scheme for the Development and Location of the Gas Industry to 2020*, and the *General Scheme for the Development of Oil Pipeline and Oil Products Pipeline Transport for the Period to 2020*. These documents will be submitted to the Russian Government in December of this year. The General Schemes (once adopted), expanding on and clarifying the key provisions of the *Energy Strategy of Russia*, will provide a long-term foundation for the development of Russia's oil and gas industry.

◆ The Russian Government will continue to provide support for pipeline projects that are aimed primarily at diversifying exports and overcoming bottlenecks in the Unified Gas Supply System and OJSC Transneft's trunk pipeline network.

◆ Further work is required on the arrangements for access by oil companies to the trunk oil pipeline network and terminals. Specifically, the following should be introduced:

  ◆ the 'pump or pay' principle for using the trunk oil pipeline network (increasing the financial liability of oil producers for unused capacity)

  ◆ the principle of proportional allocation of the amount of oil for export that can be transported, by direction of transportation, with subsequent allocation among oil companies;

  ◆ a network tariff for the transportation of oil, based on distance and possibly direction also. This is of particular relevance in light of the ESPO project.

If these matters are settled, the functions of producing and implementing oil transportation schedules can be transferred to Transneft.

◆ Further work is also required on the arrangements for access to the Unified Gas Supply System by gas producers and consumers on the internal market. Access by independent gas producers to the Unified Gas Supply System for the purpose of exporting was addressed this year with the adoption of the law on gas exports.

◆ In accordance with the Government Programme, special technical regulations are being developed, in particular, a regulation on the safety of trunk pipeline transport by field and local distribution pipelines.

◆ A solution must be found to the illegal tapping of pipelines. In just the last five years, there were more than 3,200 cases of illegal tapping. The costs to OJSC Transneft alone were several hundred million roubles.

◆ In 2004–05 more than 20 acts of sabotage and terrorism were committed against pipelines. Special attention must therefore be given to increasing the protection of pipeline transport against terrorism. A draft law providing for increased protection has

Figure 3.17 Schematic diagram of a unified system for gas production and transportation in Eastern Siberia and the Far East of Russia

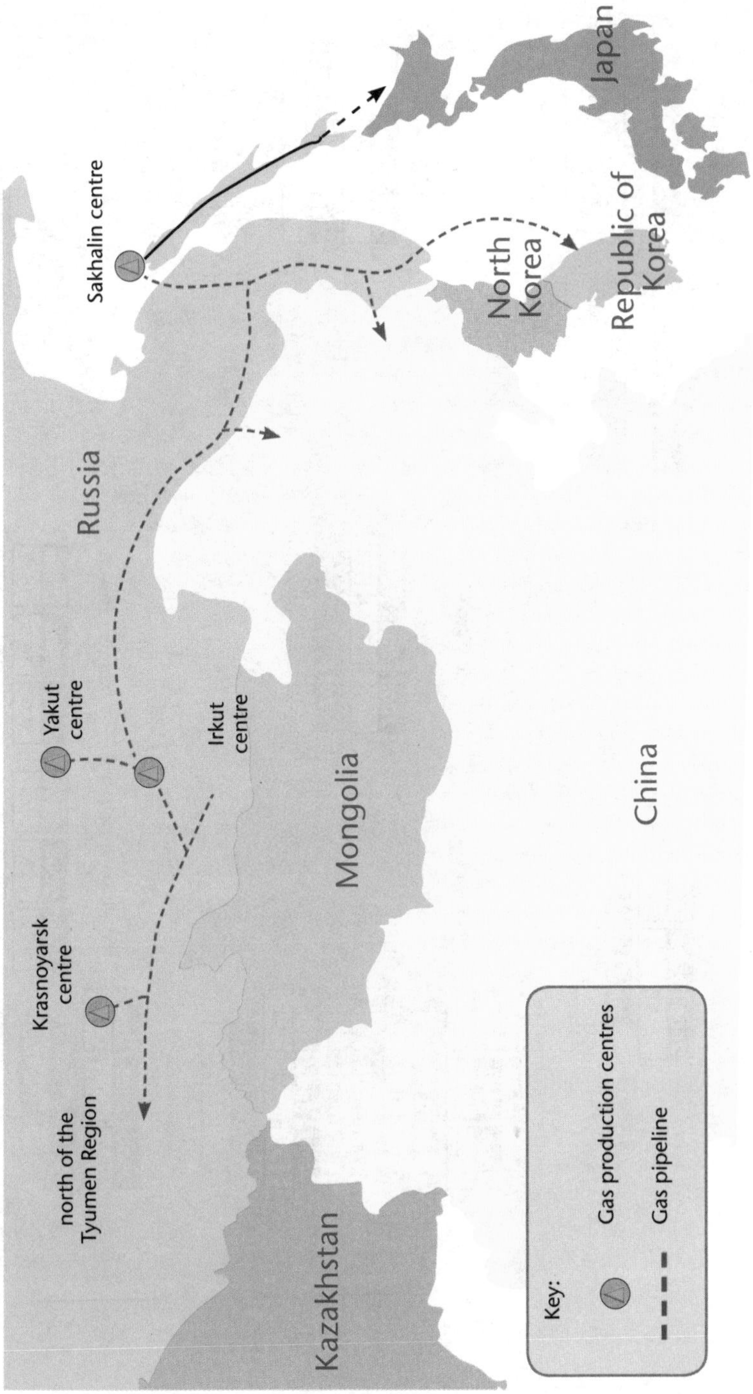

Figure 3.18 Gas resources and gas pipeline transport capacity for supplies to the Far Abroad

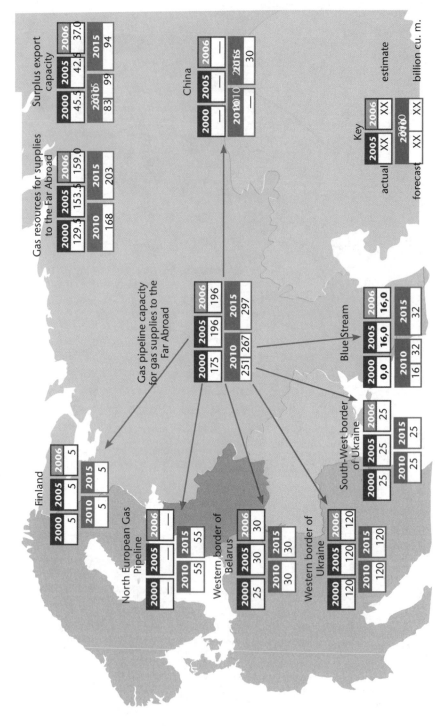

been produced by the Russian Ministry of Internal Affairs and is awaiting approval by federal executive bodies.

The electricity sector

The 'virtual incorporation' of the energy sector and industry

The reform of the Russian electricity sector began from with the sector itself, as RAO UES could be seen as akin to a Ministry for Electricity and the Electrification of the Whole Country (the electrification of the 'whole country' was one of Lenin's key objectives). The Ministry of Industry and Energy had the chance to link together or systematically organise the co-participants in the process, since ultimately fuel suppliers, large consumers and power plant engineering were all concentrated under the aegis of our department. Therefore, management arrangements and discussions about future management arose fairly organically within this structure. And, whether we wanted to or not, by virtue of our position, we were obliged to co-ordinate everyone.

The situation would have been quite different had I come to the Ministry of Industry and Energy from off the street, and not from a deputy prime ministerial position. However, coming from deputy prime ministerial position, which in 1999–2004 was about restoring infrastructure, I had vast experience of a holistic vision. I had worked on all the major infrastructure projects that are being implemented today, and thanks to my experience of working with industry in the Urals region, I could understand the fundamental nature of the processes taking place in this sphere also.

What was special for me, indeed for everyone, about this attempt to link the unlinkable was that it gave us the opportunity to set out new, intelligible, organisational and management schemes. Our task was to devise co-operative value chains in the oil–gas–electricity–mechanical engineering–metals cycle, and a kind of 'virtual corporation' arose, in which gas was the driving force.

The formation of 'virtual corporations' allowed us to organise work to bring together elements that at some point had been dispersed. Core infrastructure had been retained, and its future development depended on the future evolution of demand for electricity. This was a question for industrial development programmes. The virtual corporatisation did, however, mean that not only had we to find a common objective for the whole of the incorporated chain, we also had to ensure it was accepted by all the participants in the process. This meant there had to be a measurable economic benefit for all the participants, so that this format created a real synergy and the chance for everyone to profit.

What problems did we have to address? Russia had seen a stable upward growth trend in electricity consumption since the mid-1990s. Growth in demand for electricity was uneven, with regional and sectoral variations. At the same time, the capacity reserves that had appeared in the 1990s because of a fall in consumption were being gradually depleted.

A continuing trend for increased consumption, with continuing low levels of investment in electricity, inevitably led to an increase in the number of regions with capacity shortages and also to an increase in the size of the deficits. There was an increase in the proportion of requests by potential consumers for new connections to the power networks that went unmet, and restrictions on connections were much more typical for the rapidly developing regions of Russia.

The problems caused by rapid growth in electricity consumption were compounded by deterioration in the condition of the equipment in the sector. While the level of depreciation of fixed assets was falling for Russian industry as a whole, in the electricity sector it had increased. All of this meant that the sector was gradually becoming a hindrance to the country's economic growth and development. To remedy this, it was decided to embark on a programme to commission new generating capacity. Unprecedented in scale, GOELRO plan 2 would in effect be a second State Plan for the Electrification of Russia (the first GOELRO plan was the plan of the State Commission for the Electrification of Russia which was set up in 1920).

The government's policy for the development of the electricity sector comprised the implementation of a package of institutional measures to stimulate investment in the sector, public investment in systemically important companies, and attraction of private investment in thermal generating companies.

The new holistic model for the functioning of the electricity sector and the new legal and regulatory framework laid the ground-work for the publication of a strategic document, the *General Scheme for the Location of Electricity Generating Facilities to 2020*.

The purpose of the *General Scheme* was to provide a list of sites for the location of electricity-generating facilities of federal importance, and to ensure the supply of electricity for the Russian economy

Figure 3.19 Restructuring the electricity sector: interactions between the state and business

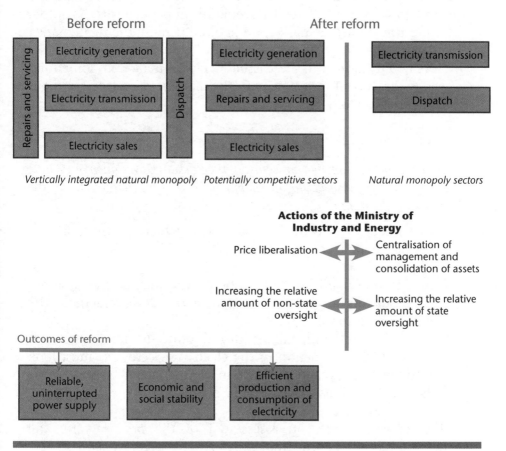

and population. As well as increasing nuclear and coal generating capacity, one of the core principles of the *General Scheme* was the 'hydropower renaissance'.

Growth in demand and increased generating capacity required a proportionate increase in fuel supplies. This necessitated instillation of the mechanism of long-term agreements between electricity providers and gas providers, synchronisation of their medium-term investment programmes, initiation of processes to ensure that gas prices on the internal and foreign markets were equally profitable, and amendments to the tariff policy.

The programme to develop grid assets was to be synchronised with the investment programme to develop generation.

To ensure the long-term reliability of electricity supply, it was also necessary to start up markets for capacity and system services and to introduce a new model for the electricity wholesale market based on long-term bilateral agreements. In parallel with liberalisation of the wholesale market, we had to liberalise the retail market and gradually eliminate cross-subsidies.

We had to address all these issues in close interaction, sometimes even in direct confrontation, with the main market players and our colleagues from different departments.

Prospects for developing the electricity sector

From a report presented to a meeting of the Russian Government on 7 June 2006, 'On the prospects for development of the electricity sector of the Russian Federation':

As we work on the *General Scheme to 2020*, which we will submit to the government at the end of the year,

◆ On the one hand, we must look a little further ahead, as we are producing a long-term vision for the development of the electricity sector to 2030.
◆ On the other hand, taking into account the long timescales involved in construction in the electricity sector, we must look at the next five years (2006–10) in as much detail as possible, as these are decisions that cannot be postponed.

This report provides an assessment of the prospects for the medium-term development of the electricity sector in 2006–10.

For the last eight years, Russia has seen a stable upward growth trend in electricity consumption. Prior to this, from 1990 to 1997, electricity consumption fell by almost 25 per cent, UES Russia found that it had significant capacity reserves, and the load on power plants fell noticeably. This period of falling demand ended in 1997, and a period of growth began, with demand gradually increasing and reaching a record level in 1990. The general trend for increased demand for electricity is seen throughout the whole country. An important feature of this growth is that it is uneven, varying both by region and by sector. In a number of cases, growth in demand has already resulted in capacity shortages during peak consumption periods in winter (the Moscow, Leningrad and Tyumen power networks). If the current trends of increased consumption and low levels of investment in electricity continue, there will inevitably be an increase in the number of regions with a shortage of capacity and also an increase in the size of the deficits. It is anticipated that this year the power networks in the following areas will see consumption reaching the 1990 level: Kaliningrad, Belgorod, Tomsk, Chitinsk, Dagestan, Ingushetia and Khakassia.

The problems caused by rapid growth in electricity consumption are being compounded by the condition of the equipment in the sector. While the level of depreciation of fixed assets is falling for industry as a whole, in the electricity sector assets are continuing

Figure 3.20 The electricity industry structure

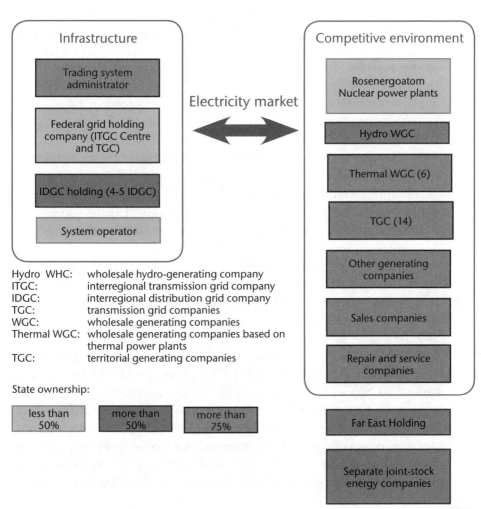

to age. If we allow this trend to continue, equipment will become much less reliable, resulting in higher risks of blackouts.

One of the issues of most concern is the extent to which requests for connection to the grid are going unmet. Unmet requests today amount to at least 10 gigawatts. This is equivalent to one and a half times the maximum load of St Petersburg, or more than 660,000 new flats, or producing about 5 million tonnes of aluminium a year. The percentage of requests for connection to the grid that are met is constantly falling. It is entirely possible that in 2007 less than 10 per cent of potential connections will be supplied. Analysis of the largest applications for connection reveals that it is mainly industrial enterprises that are not being connected; this category accounts for about 75 per cent of unmet requests.

It is forecast that if current trends continue, by 2010 a number of regional power networks could have a capacity shortage that cannot be covered: more than 16 gigawatts in total, from 1 gigawatt in the North Unified Power Network to 4.4 gigawatts in the Urals Unified Power Network. An increase in the restrictions placed on consumption by existing consumers is another problem.

The reasons include:

◆ An anticipated high level of consumption without sufficient capacity reserves (the classic case being the restriction on consumption during the especially cold winter of 2005–2006).
◆ Generating or grid equipment being removed from service for repairs and it not being possible to provide a substitute.

If the unmet demand for connection is estimated to be at least 10,000 megawatts, we can predict that if current trends continue (and consequently the demand continues to be unmet) in the medium term the annual shortfall in consumption will be about 50 billion kilowatt hours of electricity.

According to the forecast for 2006, 1 rouble of electricity consumption accounts for about 30 roubles of GDP. Therefore, the loss of 50 billion kilowatt hours of electricity consumption means an annual loss of about 1.5 trillion roubles of GDP, approximately 5 per cent of total GDP. Moreover, this is just the direct losses: that is, the products or services that businesses would have been willing to provide. In addition, because of the absence of an investment process in the electricity sector, the country also loses the increase in GDP that would have resulted from investment demand for the output of design, construction, installation and mechanical engineering companies.

Prompt decisions must be taken to correct the situation in the energy sector. The medium-term development programme for the sector is for a five to seven-year period. The programme is aimed at developing generating capacity and infrastructure to eliminate bottlenecks and to ensure the minimum investment reserve for the future, in line with the forthcoming *General Scheme to 2020*.

As a result, instead of constraining Russian economic growth, the electricity sector should provide a reliable energy base for sustainable economic growth.

When writing the medium-term programme, we factored in only those facilities for which there are designs and a construction site, and which can be brought into service by 2010. Preliminary assessments of investment for the necessary reserves to 2015 were also taken into account.

For the purposes of the programme, estimated demand is based on macro-economic forecasts for the Russian economy, the changes in demand in different areas forecast by energy companies (reflecting the uneven nature of regional development) and the development plans of large companies, stemming from the annual surveys conducted by energy companies on the basis of requests for connection.

The programme envisages the integrated development of generation and grid infrastructure. New generating facilities and grid assets will be based exclusively on modern technologies.

One of the key challenges facing the electricity sector is the provision of gas for the new power plants that are being built. The first steps towards addressing the problem have already been taken: RAO UES Russia and OJSC Gazprom have signed a memorandum on co-operation. The main objective of this agreement is to create the conditions for the supply of gas to the facilities envisaged by the medium-term programme. It still remains to develop and approve a procedure for annual co-ordination of investment programmes for the development of unified gas transport and energy systems, and also the arrangements for the supply of gas and the signing of long-term agreements for gas supply for the new facilities, including a future reserve. Long-term agreements are also required for the supply of gas to existing power plants.

The programme for grid infrastructure development takes the following criteria into account:

- increasing the reliability of the electricity supply for the Moscow, Leningrad and Tyumen regions;
- ensuring that the new generating facilities will be properly connected to the grid;
- removing the most significant grid restrictions and increasing the reliability of electricity supply for consumers;
- technological re-equipping and renovation of grid infrastructure.

The grid infrastructure development programme for 2007–10 provides for construction of new electricity transmission lines and substations to handle the power output of the nuclear, thermal and hydro generating facilities that are being built.

The medium-term programme for the development of the distribution network is designed to address two key problems: the high level of depreciation of fixed assets, which increases the fault rate and reduces the reliability of electricity transmission to the end consumer, and the inability to connect new consumers because substations are overloaded.

Investment in the energy sector will involve the full spectrum of sources of finance. Company profits will depend on the implementation of a long-term tariff policy in the sector as well as on performance in the liberalised sector of the wholesale electricity market. Connection fees should be one of the main investment resources for distribution networks. It is intended to give a significant role to public investment, long-term loans and private investment.

The main feature of the intended balance between sources of finance is that investment risks will be distributed between the state and private investors. The state will concentrate its efforts on systemically important companies (the Federal Grid Company, hydro system operator, nuclear), while private investment will be the main source of finance for thermal power plants.

As generating companies differ by territorial and geographical conditions, available fuel, readiness to attract investment, and stakeholder structure, each facility requires an individual, 'customised' solution.

When deciding the sources of finance for hydro generation the following factors must be taken into account.

The most important condition of setting up HydroWGC OJSC is that the state retains a controlling share in the company (50 per cent plus one share) after the restructuring of RAO UES Russia OJSC.

Figure 3.21 The Russian electricity industry's medium-term development programme

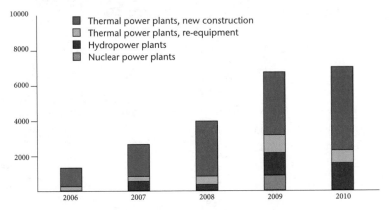

New capacity by type of generation until 2010 (MW)

Legend:
- Thermal power plants, new construction
- Thermal power plants, re-equipment
- Hydropower plants
- Nuclear power plants

New capacity (MW)	2006	2007	2008	2009	2010	2006–10
Nuclear power plants	0	0	0	1,000	0	1,000
Hydropower plants	49	69	368	1,348	1,931	4,375
Thermal power plants, re-equipment	165	264	419	1,006	637	2,491
Thermal power plants, new construction	1,359	1,516	3,160	3,221	4,649	13,905
Total	1,573	2,459	3,947	6,575	7,217	21,771

In this regard, one of the sources of finance should be the federal budget, and specifically a contribution from the federal budget to the charter capital of OJSC HydroWGC. Another specific feature of the hydro-generation development programme is that it is intended to include in its investment section extensive reserves for new construction.

It is intended that private investment be used only within the framework of a joint project to complete construction of the Boguchansk Electrometallurgical Complex.

The programme to develop grid assets is synchronised with the generation investment programme. The Federal Grid Company's investment programme will have a central role. It must be noted that the main sources of investment for transmission grid companies, as for hydro generation, are companies' own funds, public funds and loans.

Figure 3.22 Programme of measures to attract investment

A package of institutional measures will provide:

Trust:	Lower cost:	Efficient use
Investors	Loan funds	of investment
Creditors	Private investment	

All figures below in billion roubles.

Area of investment	Own funds	Private investment Debt	Equity	Federal budget	Regional sources	Total, 2006–10
Thermal generation	260	100	327			687
Hydro generation	140	50	21	39		250
Transmission networks	162	61		160		383
Distribution networks	433	158			41	632
Total	995	369	348		41	1,952

Proposed programme for nuclear power plants : RUB 337 billion. A more precise figure will be provided when finalising the Federal Target Programme.

A Russian Government stake in the charter capital of the Federal Grid Company will mean that the investment programme can be implemented without creating additional tariff pressure for the Russian economy. As for the distribution grid assets, specific programmes will vary greatly by region. The programme will be fleshed out for specific facilities by the end of the year, in the process of regulating tariffs.

To implement this large-scale investment programme, a package of institutional measures is essential, as set out in the report of the Russian Ministry of Industry and Energy submitted to the government. The proposed package of measures will provide for a transition to raising private investment in the early stages of market liberalisation by establishing a system of long-term agreements. In the initial stage, at the same time as moving to a system of long-term agreements, we must deploy the mechanism of investment guarantees. As a result, we will be able to achieve the policy of gradual expansion of private capital as the process of steered liberalisation proceeds.

Proposals are required for a programme to develop the regulatory bodies (in terms of their personnel and institutional development) and also to alter regulatory instruments. It has been recognised that we must create an effective system of state regulation of the electricity sector in line with the new conditions. This system should be based on measures to enhance the influence of state regulatory bodies. This will entail regulation of the quality of services, rules on the operation of companies in the electricity sector, indirect regulatory instruments, and development of anti-monopoly oversight, while also reducing direct price regulation.

'Recollections for the Future':[2] the relevance of the General Scheme for the Location of Electricity Generating Facilities

From a speech given to the Board of the Russian Union of Industrialists and Entrepreneurs, 2 October 2007:

Four years ago we adopted the *Energy Strategy*. And this *Energy Strategy* was essentially the first of its type. It was the first to use such a planning horizon and to be based on the logic of a strategy, specifying the core objectives, principles and mechanisms for this vital sector of the Russian economy. Since then, the *Strategy* has quite often come in for criticism, with people saying that the figures are out of date. This criticism is probably justified in part, especially if we recall that the key figures in the *Energy Strategy* were the parameters of the macro-economic forecast, insofar as it was possible to see 25 years ahead at that time. To remind you of the figures in the final version of the *Strategy*: average GDP growth was to be 4.5 per cent; according to exchange rate forecasts, the current rate should be about 36 roubles; and the assessment of the situation on external markets put the oil price at about $34 a barrel. Looking at these same figures from the macro-economic forecast today, it is clear that some of them do not just deviate slightly from the parameters set at that time; they have fundamentally altered the trend.

Of course this requires updating, as do certain parameters in the *Energy Strategy*. But the main thing is that the objectives, principles and mechanisms for development set out in this document continue

---

2 Translator's note: in the Russian this is 'Vospominaniya o bydyshchem', the Russian translation of the title of a German film, *Erinnerungen an die Zukunft*. The English translation is *Chariots of the Gods*. 'Vospominaniya' means a memory, a recollection. The author uses the word '*vospominanie*' twice in the body of his speech, referencing the title of the film, and translated here as recollection.

Figure 3.23 Steered liberalisation: the basis for attracting investment

2006: adoption of the medium-term development programme for 2006–10
2007: long-term vision for the development of the electricity sector to 2030 and the
General Scheme for the Location of Electricity Generating Facilities to 2020

2006: launch of the investment guarantee mechanism
2006: transition to a system of bilateral agreements between suppliers and
consumers, long-term agreements from 2007
2007: managed increase of 5-15% a year in the volumes of electricity traded at market
prices (while retaining regulated tariffs for households)
2007: launch of the capacity market
2008: transition to long-term grid tariffs allowing for a rate of return

◆ The creation of a regulatory system for the sector in the new setting, based on an
enhanced role for state regulatory and oversight bodies.
◆ Long-term agreements for electricity require long-term agreements for gas.

to be wholly relevant. They provided the basis for the development of a whole range of sectoral subprogrammes, including subprogrammes for the development of the electricity sector. All of the principles for reform of the sector were set out in the *Energy Strategy*. The *General Scheme*, which will be presented today in its final form, is the logical continuation of *The Energy Strategy of Russia for the Period to 2020.*

Apart from the *Scheme for the Location of Electricity Generating Facilities,* the *Energy Strategy* has also given rise to the *General Scheme for Development of the Gas Sector*, the *General Scheme for Development of Pipeline Transport* and so on. This is the 'first recollection'.

And now to the second recollection. The Ministry of Industry and Energy was set up three and a half years ago. This was the starting point for a difficult discussion, a difficult conversation about industrial policy. In the early phase, it was essentially a discussion – forgive me for the tautology – about whether we could actually discuss industrial policy. In the subsequent phases, once the first question had been answered in the affirmative, a whole range of sectoral strategies emerged for the major sectors of the Russian economy. I will not name them here; you know what they are. Many of us were involved in developing them, and it became standard working practice to hold joint meetings of the Board of the Ministry of Industry and Energy and the Bureau of the Union of Industrialists and Entrepreneurs to consider sectoral strategies.

Of course these two processes should have converged naturally, and they have converged, to a large extent in this document, which we intend to discuss today. A process of interlinkage began, a difficult process, and not always without scholasticism, but nonetheless during this period we acquitted ourselves well, overcoming quandaries like 'Which came first, a gas molecule or an individual electron?' All of this work is encapsulated in the document that will be presented to you today. We are in the decision-making home stretch.

Adoption of the *General Scheme* will not only answer the question 'How will the electricity sector develop?' It will also give a signal for the development of a large number of sectors related to the electricity sector, from power plant engineering to the metals industry and the extractive industries. Therefore it is very important that we complete this process as quickly as possible. There is also a view that we must consider all possible inputs more carefully, looking at how the *General Scheme* ties in with not only gas, coal or alternative energy, but also with transport, the development of transport mechanical engineering, the metals industry and so on. With this approach, you could take it as far as ore, and then come back round again in a loop. The proposition that 'everything depends on everything else' is valid, and I think it is useful for thinkers and philosophers, as it allows an uninterrupted process of reasoning. However, from my point of view, it is lethal for the manager: it simply paralyses their will and makes it possible to achieve nothing at all. When considering this document, it is essential that we remain sensitive to feedback in order to understand the risks and mistakes that could arise in the implementation of the *Scheme*, and to rectify them in time. In this regard, I urge you to help ensure that the decision is taken as soon as possible.

The Press attacks

The Russian energy industry in the global dimension, 2004–08

Economic growth that started at the beginning of the 'noughties' has led to a significant increase in demand for energy resources within the country. This has required a solution to the inherited economic problems that accumulated during years of reform under conditions of globalisation and intensified worldwide competition, escalation of the struggle for energy resources and the markets.

Differences between suppliers, deliverers and consumers of energy resources at a global level in the mid-2000s reached a very high level of tension. Indeed, Russia, being a full-fledged participant in each of these groups, has attempted to develop a system for the global sharing of energy risks. The issue of global energy security appeared on the agenda Russia proposed for discussion at the G8 Summit in St Petersburg in 2006. This subject became the lead 'frame' for the *Energy Strategy of Russia for the Period to 2020*.

Fundamental world energy problems today are the continuous confrontation between key players, fragmentation of the energy markets and consequently completely unfounded scaremongering. Two camps have developed historically and currently exist, holding opposing positions – the consumers and the producers of energy resources. Producers want to establish price control and generate the highest possible profits; consumers are demanding deregulation of the markets and as a result, a reduction in the price of the end product. Ensuring global energy security and countering threats in relation to other market players assumes the creation of a complex systemic organisation. This section of Part III of this book considers the concept of 'security' as a systemic-organisational activity for the prevention, removal and elimination of external and internal threats in relation to all users of energy resources.

Defining the problem of global energy security

From an address, 'Stability, security and sustainability of the Asian hydrocarbon economy', delivered at the conference of energy ministers of Azerbaijan, India, Kazakhstan, China, Republic of Korea, Russian, Turkmenistan and Japan, held in New Delhi, India, 25 November 2005:

Figure 3.24 A model for consideration, discussion and regulation: 'Global energy security or free and equal access to energy resources'

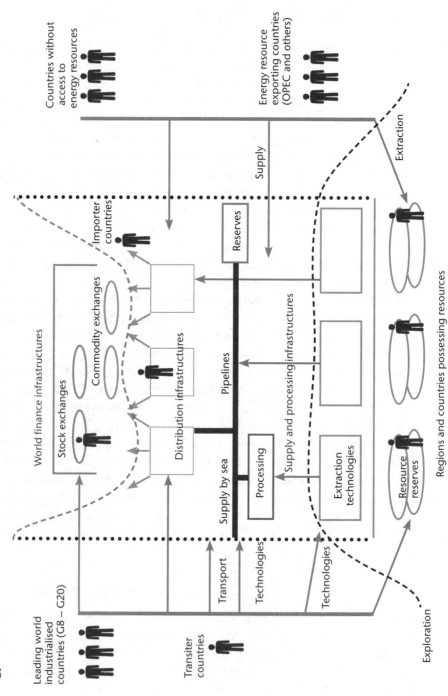

1 The Asia-Pacific region – a new centre of world economic development

The markets of the Asia region, and more broadly the Asia-Pacific region, including also the energy market, are the fastest growing markets today. According to an estimate by the International Energy Agency, demand for energy resources in the countries of Asia is growing faster than in all other countries of the world: demand for oil by 3–4 per cent a year, and gas consumption by 4–6 per cent.

At the same time, I would like to look at the situation more comprehensively. The Asia market is part of the global market, and its problems must be considered, among other things, through the prism of the processes occurring on the world energy market.

Russia's president, Vladimir Putin, very recently made a tour of countries of Asia – Turkey, Korea and Japan – during which the matter of energy was widely discussed, along with general economic and political issues. These included programmes such as development of Eastern Siberia and the Far East (a new oil and gas province emerging in Russia), a project for the Eastern Oil Pipeline connecting Siberia with the Pacific coast, the Sakhalin projects (development of the shelf will allow the creation of a new centre for the production of oil and gas: in fact production has already started, and the future appears to be more than optimistic), and the Blue Stream gas pipeline connecting Russia and Turkey through the Black Sea. Furthermore, we view Turkey not only as a consumer country and the transit termination point, but also as a prospective transport hub for new large-scale gas infrastructure projects.

All of these visits, meetings and discussions have once again provided us with an opportunity to participate in the complex nonlinear co-operation that exists today between domestic, regional and global problems and processes. I am deeply convinced that it is impossible to resolve the issues of the Asia energy resources market without clearly understanding and taking into account the global energy situation.

2 Global energy problems

According to available prognoses, world energy consumption could grow by one third over the next 15 years, and by approximately 45 per cent in the next 20 years. According to the same assessments, world demand for oil could grow by 35 million barrels per day (a

42 per cent increase) by 2025, and demand for gas by 1.7 trillion cubic metres per annum (a 60 per cent increase).

Today, the situation on the world market is characterised by the following four important conditions:

◆ a sharp increase in demand for energy resources by the countries of Asia (up to 45 per cent prospective growth in world oil demand);
◆ an increase in the separation between oil and gas consumption and production volumes in economically developed countries (for example, 60–70 per cent of Europe's gas supply will be imported by 2020, and today this value has already been surpassed by the majority of large Asian countries);
◆ a lack of oil refineries and transportation, and scarcity of additional oil production capacity;
◆ a lack of transparency in world oil trading.

In our opinion, all these conditions place a priority on the problem of energy security. Taking into account its positioning on the global market, Russia understands the problem of energy security not only as its own domestic security, but also primarily as a shared problem of reliable supply of energy resources to countries and the population of the planet, and as a problem of the world community.

We are aware that Russia holds a special position among energy suppliers from the perspective of reserve volumes, geography (a special role in the transit of energy resources) and reliability (stability) of supply.

While in Russia, Mr Aiyar, India's Minister for Petroleum and Natural Gas, said, 'The Soviet Union played an important role in securing India's territorial integrity over the past 50 years. I am sure that Russia will play the same role in ensuring our energy security over the coming 50 years.' I think that this involves more than just India.

In fact, Russia possesses some of the greatest potential fuel and energy reserves in the world. More than 34 per cent of natural gas, approximately 13 per cent of world proven oil reserves, approximately 20 per cent of proven hard coal reserves and 32 per cent of proven brown coal reserves are concentrated on our territory. Today, a world energy market without Russia is inconceivable. Russia occupies first place in the world for international trade in natural gas, and second place for natural gas and petroleum product exports.

Currently, more than 90 per cent of exported Russian energy products are supplied to the countries of Europe. However, we intend to focus more attention on the countries of the Asia-Pacific region. Overall, the share of countries of Asia in Russian oil exports is forecast to increase from today's 3 per cent to 30 per cent in 2020 (volume growth to 100 million tonnes) and natural gas export from 5 per cent to 25 per cent (volume growth to 65 billion cubic metres).

Proceeding from the understanding of its role in the world energy system, Russia put forward the problems of energy security and energy efficiency as the main issues for the G8 in 2006.

3 Global energy security agenda

Allow me briefly to present the format in which the Global Energy Security agenda is proposed for discussion within the framework of the Russian Government. We are proposing consideration of the following principal areas:

◆ sound underpinning of the world economy by traditional hydrocarbon resources at reasonable prices;
◆ diversification of energy supply by means of new energy sources;
◆ increasing efficiency and security of energy production;
◆ creation of conditions for the future transition to fundamentally new and ecologically clean energy production.

Common approaches to the following complex issues will have to be developed.

1 Stabilisation of the energy product markets, which, in turn, includes:
  ◆ development of global and new regional energy markets;
  ◆ ensuring predictability of the markets by widening the practice of long-term contracts, and developing dialogue between energy producers and consumers;
  ◆ ensuring greater accessibility and transparency of data on reserves, demand, stocks and production capacity.
2 Expanding investment in energy:
  ◆ improving the investment climate;
  ◆ implementing an insurance scheme and financial risk distribution.

3 Effective development of energy production and energy infrastructure:
- ◆ increasing efficiency of exploration, production, advanced refining and use of hydrocarbon resources, including their traditional forms;
- ◆ diversification of transportation of energy resources;
- ◆ development of gas energy production, including liquefied natural gas;
- ◆ ensuring the physical security of energy facilities and infrastructure.
4 Energy production and the environment:
- ◆ measures to improve energy efficiency and energy conservation;
- ◆ development of safe nuclear energy production, including with a closed fuel cycle;
- ◆ intensification of scientific research and implementation of new energy production (hydrogen, nuclear fusion, renewables, low-carbon, etc.);
- ◆ implementation of effective ecologically clean transport systems.

Essentially, the aggregate of the aforementioned areas comprises our vision of the main G8 agenda items within the framework of global energy security, and not only in the coming year. Of course, any of the listed themes could justifiably demand a broadened context of discussion. I bring this to your attention with a view to receiving feedback and a valuable response, which will allow for all the discussions that follow to be brought together.

The series of measures for developing energy themes that are already being developed within the G8, and a continuity of this, must be supported. In our hands we are holding a relay baton of sorts. The subject of ecological security, which has become the leading subject for the government of the United Kingdom this year, is closely connected with the matter of energy security. Incidentally, soon after our meeting with you, a conference will be held on 29 November in Montreal that is dedicated to climate problems. I would mention that this theme, relating to reducing emissions of harmful substances into the atmosphere by two-thirds, is also connected to the functioning of the energy industry. We must not rush to extremes in this regard. It is essential to strive to find compromises between ecological problems and the real conditions of economic development that take into consideration the special features of all market participants: both suppliers of raw hydrocarbons and their consumers. And this, in any case, is the formula of dependence of ecology on energy (two Es). This formula is easily and logically complemented by another 'E' – energy efficiency. In essence, the global response to the challenges of ecology and energy security is a growth model based on energy efficiency.

It should be highlighted that questions of long-term energy security require systemic actions by all participants in the global energy market. The possibility appears viable of discussion, preparation and consistent realisation of measures to improve energy security in an expanded format with the participation of countries that are the largest world suppliers of energy resources, and likewise countries with the fastest growing level of energy consumption.

In this regard, we believe it expedient to propose the creation under the auspices of the G8 of specific permanently operating groups in the principal areas of energy security, which would include, in addition to the representatives of G8 member countries, also the representatives of countries supplying and consuming energy resources – first and foremost, representatives of states attending here – to discuss matters of regional energy security and energy efficiency related to the G8 global agenda.

The most important results for us from realisation of initiatives ensuring global energy security should be:

◆ balanced markets for energy resources: first and foremost the oil market;
◆ formation of a new global liquefied natural gas market;
◆ attracting investments in the development of the energy sector and its transport infrastructure;
◆ broad exchange of technologies between countries;
◆ harmonisation of national energy policies, both among G8 member countries and among a number of leading industrialised nations, and likewise countries whose intensive economic development and growing energy consumption are significantly influencing both the world energy markets and sustained development of the entire world community.

Undoubtedly this is an important area. The world energy field cannot be conceived more simply than as the aggregate of businesses governed by corporate logic of survival and capable of covering all risks of current and future periods of economic development. A range of existing risks, particularly medium-term and long-term risks, cannot be brought to this level. These are not only domestic or regional risks, but also currently they are world-wide risks.

The world community has reached this understanding. Shared efforts must be systematised and attempts made to put them on an appropriate course. In this, Russia is proceeding on the basis that transparent and clear game rules should be maintained on the world energy market. We have published our *Energy Strategy* and are supporting it. We are not concealing information on plans for development of the Russian fuel and energy sector, production volumes and regions, plans for the construction of pipelines and our other actions that could impact on the world and regional energy situation. We do not resort to intrigue or play cunningly with partners and await the same response from them.

4 Energy security: Russia's position

It is our deep conviction that the stability, security and sustainability of the Asian hydrocarbon economy are impossible outside of the context of resolving the problems of global energy security. Only by taking into consideration the ratio of global, regional and domestic levels is it possible correctly to identify, diversify and cover risks emerging in the course of economic development.

In our opinion, effective management of non-political risks directly in the hydrocarbon sector of the economy is only possible with the comprehensive resolution of the following objectives:

◆ ensuring greater accessibility and transparency of data on reserves, demand and stocks;
◆ ensuring predictability of the market by widening the practice of long-term contracts, and developing dialogue between energy producers and consumers;
◆ effective development of the energy infrastructure, meeting market demands.

For its part, Russia is prepared to facilitate the solution to the objective of ensuring energy security, and consequently a reduction in risks, by the following means:

◆ Increasing export volumes, including in the area of Asia. (Over the past five years Russia has increased oil supplies to Asian countries fourfold, and export of natural gas has grown from zero to 5 billion cubic metres.)

◆ Diversification of the commodity structure, and increased supply volumes of more highly refined product. (Russia will increase the refinery yield of hydrocarbons, increasing the proportion of high-quality petroleum products and petrochemical products, and products from the chemical utilisation of gas, in its exports.)

◆ Expansion of the geography of external supplies on the condition that this is economically viable, with a primary view to the Asia-Pacific region. (Russia is making an infrastructural connection of the new oil and gas production centres in Siberia and the Far East with the countries of this region. Creation of port infrastructure for the Sakhalin-I and Sakhalin-II projects and construction of the Eastern Siberia–Pacific Ocean oil transportation system will make Russia's hydrocarbon resources accessible to the majority of countries of the Asia-Pacific region.)

◆ Promotion of foreign capital investment into Russia. A clear example is the successful realisation of the Sakhalin-I project, in the launch of which we were fortunate to have the participation of Mr Aiyar in October of this year, and in which large overseas partners from Russia, India, the United States and Japan are participating. It seems to me that this example of co-operation should be expanded and continued.

◆ In the development of new forms of international cooperation and the creation of mechanisms for co-ordinating state policy in the area of foreign trade in the energy sector.

Translation of the problem to the plane of the objectives

Organisation of world energy production should be founded on the following principles: open competition, sustainable development and integrated global infrastructure connecting isolated markets.

Infrastructure is a form of organisation, and not a transport network. The existence of infrastructure is founded on unified standards that unite all the components into an integrated whole. In the energy sector, the components are the extraction of resources, their processing, power generation, and the transportation of resources and energy. Infrastructure does not have a single master, it has a multitude of them: each user, is the master of their own component.

Figure 3.25 Principles of the arrangement of global energy infrastructure

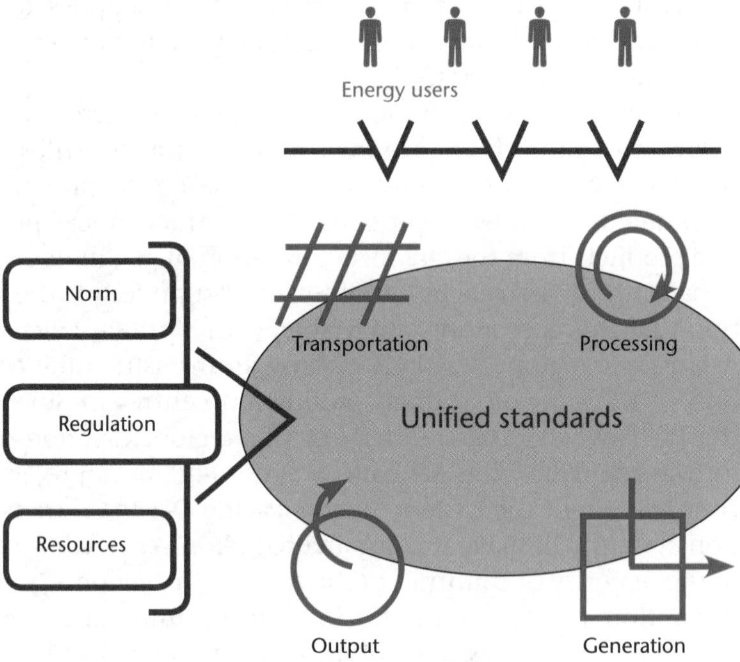

Those who use the infrastructure work with it as an integrated whole via terminals providing access to services rendered by the infrastructure. In order to support functioning of the infrastructure, a body of norms is essential, regulating integrated operation, ensuring access to infrastructure for new users, and ensuring access to essential resources for all users included in the infrastructure.

For realisation of the stated principles and stipulation of the corresponding objectives, a supervisory institute must be created for global energy infrastructure, which should consider the interests of all market players, the norms and principles of its activity, and conditions of access to infrastructure. Likewise, norms for the distribution of resources within the infrastructure must be created on this basis.

We do not need an institute that strengthens the positions of the producers, or an institute that protects the positions of consumers. This will lead to even greater detachment of interests and reinforcement of confrontation. A supervisory institute should support the representatives of producers and consumers who by joint efforts can form shared principles of operation in production,

Figure 3.26 Principles of the organisation of global sustainable energy development (GSED)

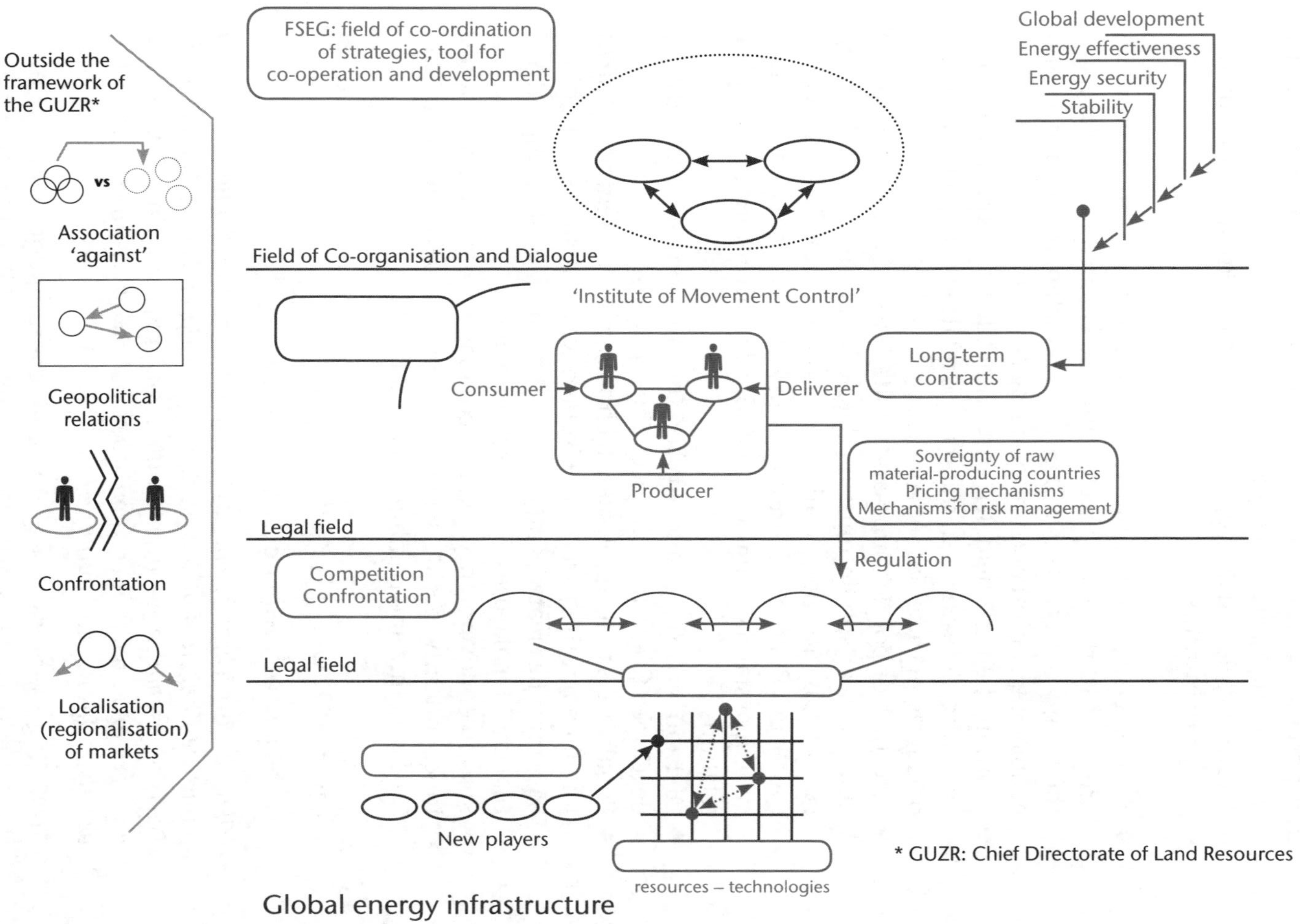

FSEG: field of co-ordination of strategies, tool for co-operation and development

Global development
Energy effectiveness
Energy security
Stability

Long-term contracts

Sovereignty of raw material-producing countries
Pricing mechanisms
Mechanisms for risk management

'Institute of Movement Control'

Field of Co-organisation and Dialogue

Consumer

Producer

Deliverer

Regulation

Legal field

Competition
Confrontation

Legal field

New players

resources – technologies

Global energy infrastructure

Outside the framework of the GUZR*

Association 'against'

vs

Geopolitical relations

Confrontation

Localisation (regionalisation) of markets

* GUZR: Chief Directorate of Land Resources

385

transportation and economic relations, and create the corresponding legal framework.

The principles that should be laid down in the work of the supervisory institute are:

◆ Transparency, predictability. Transparency of information on processes in the energy sector must be ensured for all players in the energy market. This will ensure predictability of changes and enable preparation of corresponding actions.
◆ Work in the legal field. Creation is needed of a system of rights and obligations that can standardise relations between all players operating in the global energy sector.
◆ Rejection of politicisation and militarisation. The energy sphere and political sphere must be defined and operate while being governed by accepted regulations and standards. Standardisation (of documentation, technologies and so on) is necessary. A shared system of standards must be developed to streamline and simplify relations.
◆ Division of risks. Standards for the division of risks must be developed to ensure resilience of the markets.
◆ Equal access to technologies. Technologies are essential resources for all composite parts of the infrastructure. A single technology base must be created, and access to it assured for all 'components' that could make use of such technologies.
◆ Resource sovereignty. Each company or country should independently decide whether or not to be included in the infrastructure and combine its resources with others.

Golden ratio of the pipe

From an interview with Itogi, *20 March 2006:*

Viktor Borisovich, in recent days leading Western media have published an article from the Russian president, 'The Upcoming G8 Summit in St Petersburg: challenges, opportunities, and responsibility'. This article expresses an idea for the creation of a global energy security system. What exactly is this Russian initiative?

According to forecasts, world energy consumption will grow by a third over the next 15 years. We are already seeing a sharp increase in consumption of energy resources by developing Asian countries, and likewise an increase in the disparity between consumption volumes and production volumes in developed countries. In addition we are facing a lack of oil refining and transportation capacity. All these conditions have thrust the problem of energy security into the spotlight. Taking into consideration its own positioning on the global market, Russia understands this problem primarily to be the reliable supply of energy resources to other countries.

And what needs to be done to accomplish this?

Work is being carried out in four main areas: reliable supply to the world economy of traditional hydrocarbon resources at reasonable prices, diversification of energy supply by means of new energy sources, increasing energy efficiency and security, and the creation of conditions for the future transition to fundamentally new and ecologically clean energy. Within the scope of its presidency of the G8, Russia proposes focusing on resolving these most urgent global problems. The energy dialogue is being conducted along the lines of Russia and the European Union, and Russia and the United States. The consequences of such dialogue are already clear; these are specific projects such as, for example, the North European Gas Pipeline (NEGP). You know, the experience of Blue Stream, which at one time someone called 'Blue Dream', shows that even under exceptionally complex technological conditions, at depths of greater than 2 km in the aggressive hydrosulphuric environment of the Black Sea, effectively operating infrastructure can be laid. The NEGP is also one of the real areas of diversification of Russian gas supply. Just such arrangements of reliable transit territories or extraterritorial zones must be developed for the long term.

The aforementioned article from Vladimr Putin contains the argument that the modern world suffers from 'energy egoism' – a dead-end track. Meanwhile, following the Russian–Ukrainian gas crisis, many in Europe are blaming Moscow for demonstrating just such 'egoism' and have become more cautious in their approach to the problem of energy dependency on Russia.

How can we speak of 'egoism' if Russia is taking active steps that are translating into joint investment projects with overseas partners (both governments and business)? We must differentiate lines of supply of hydrocarbons; we must not use exclusive routes, through which 80 per cent of supplies are currently being delivered, as is the situation with Ukraine, which is in essence a monopolist in the transit of gas into Europe. Rather we must have a selection of routes. Securing uninterrupted supply of energy resources at appropriate and economically substantiated prices, that supports market stability and ecological sustainability, is the cornerstone of development both for member states of the G8, and for the entire world community. The prosperity and quality of life of an enormous number of people directly depends on access to energy, the reliability of which is threatened by multiple challenges, both short-term and long-term in nature. The main challenge is to create such a global energy system that would fully preclude the possibility of destructive conflicts over sources and transit of energy resources, and would provide an effective and secure basis for the development of civilisation over the long term.

Is it possible to find common ground with our Western partners regarding energy security?

Opinions of the experts who worked ahead of the meeting of G8 energy ministers often coincided in an understanding of weak points with the scope of global energy security, but to say that the positions of experts from each of the parties were identical would be misplaced. Alongside this, specifically the dialogue that has already been initiated by experts and continues at the international conference and meeting of G8 energy ministers will determine the main factors of global energy security, since open discussion of them with the involvement of business and third-party countries is the only possible format for developing a common position.

Some of our partners say that Russia is aiming the use 'the pipe' as an element of political influence. Is this true?

The economic and political significance of energy resources are often inseparable. Most unpleasant of all is that we are now clearly seeing an attempt by many energy market players to politicise the process of resolving energy problems. Solutions should be reached completely pragmatically, within the framework of existing agreements and normal economic relations. Political posturing in this matter must be nipped in the bud. We have good relations with countries that are consumers of energy resources, and political actions must not undermine the foundation of our co-operation.

Why should Russia in particular play a leading role in maintaining world energy security?

In this context a country that is exclusively an exporter of raw material, which is categorically tied to the world pricing conditions for energy products, cannot be the leading power of the world. Nor, conversely, can a highly developed state setting the rate for technologies and striving to 'rid itself' of those possessing the deposits. A leader should take into consideration the interests both of suppliers and consumers of raw materials. I believe that Russia possesses both an accurate understanding of the situation and the mechanisms to reduce risks. We are a country with a market economy, and the Russian market is a composite part of the global market. On one hand, this reality brings Russia a series of challenges and problems, yet on the other hand, valuable opportunities in justifiably taking a rightful place in a new dynamic world, in a world where the relationship between politics and the economy has significantly changed. Whereas formerly the economy has often reaped the consequences of political ambitions, today politics are placed in the service of the economy. Therefore, in the energy dialogue we can and should take into consideration transport-related risks, infrastructural risks, risks of demand, risks connected with reserves, and political risks, to which the energy product market reacts quite sharply. Russia recognises its role as a large player – a seller of energy resources, as one of their largest consumers, as one of the most substantial transit territories, and as a member of the G8, where such problems can be discussed.

Is the G8 format sufficient for resolving the problems of securing energy resources that involve all countries of the world?

The G8 meeting is a convenient platform for demonstrating our position to leading countries and outlining the solutions to any particular challenges. But quite clearly the G8 format is not enough when taking into consideration the situation in the rapidly growing economies of China, India and Brazil. These are very large consumers of energy resources, and, in my opinion, it is inconceivable to discuss long-term energy prospects without them. Strictly speaking, this issue today is not limited to the G8. Furthermore, you could say that the very format of the G8, let's say in the medium term, could change significantly.

Global energy security

From an address at the meeting of the G8 energy ministers, 'Global energy security', 16 March 2006:

Our agenda today includes a matter that on the one hand has been quite widely discussed, yet on the other hand has a mass of unexplored facets. This is the issue of global energy security.

Reliability of access to energy, which at the current stage is subject to threats and challenges of both a short-term and long-term nature, directly impacts on the quality of life of the entire global community. Therefore it is essential to develop a joint approach to ensuring global energy security. Central issues in resolving the stated objective are sufficiency of resources, economic and infrastructure accessibility, and ecological tolerability.

We believe the St Petersburg meeting should become a significant milestone on the road to building a world-wide system of energy security. In the course of this meeting an authoritative, impartial and progressive document must be formulated that could achieve essential international recognition and the crucially important support of countries outside the G8.

Significant growth in world energy consumption is unavoidable in the twenty-first century, primarily because of dynamically developing economies. This will require additional development of the resource base of the global energy sector. Today more than 80 per cent of world energy resources are comprised of fossil fuels (coal, oil, gas). In spite of active inclusion of new energy sources in the energy mix, traditional resources will remain the foundation of the global energy sector for at least the entire first half of the twenty-first century.

The effect of advancing demand for energy from the natural or technological potential of the current hydrocarbon energy sector is demonstrably exacerbated by the lack of uniformity in the distribution of production and consumption of raw hydrocarbon material across the planet, inadequate sophistication of the infrastructure for its transportation and distribution, and the emergence of new dynamically developing consumer countries.

In this regard, collective efforts are needed to expand and invest in exploration and prospecting for new deposits of raw hydrocarbon materials on dry land and the continental shelf, increasing the efficiency of producing and refining oil and gas using new technologies, and the means of delivering energy resources to consumers.

Creation of an efficient and robust global energy supply system requires large investment resources, in aggregate comprising, according to IEA estimates, $17 trillion in the period to 2030, a significant part of which should be allocated to the areas of production, transportation and refining of energy resources. Conditions must be created by joint efforts for the effective mobilisation of these gigantic sums and for their optimum use.

Furthermore, special attention must be given to increasing the economic and financial viability of projects supporting reduction of risks of disruption in energy supply, using for this, among other things, mechanisms and arrangements for insurance and division of financial risks.

Mobilisation of investments essential for development of the world energy sector is only possible if a favourable investment climate and predictable political situation exist, both in countries producing and countries consuming energy resources, and in transit states. This assumes developed stable legislation, coherent and consistently applied tax regimes, the absence of unwarranted administrative barriers, categorical performance of contractual obligations and access to effective dispute resolution procedures.

In recent years consistent growth has been seen in the price of oil, which allows us to talk about a sustained trend in the change of scale of global prices for oil. The mechanism of this growth is being analysed by the global community. However there is not yet full clarity on this issue.

At the current time, the pricing environment is not particularly favourable because of the high level of the cost of oil on world markets, which is 'pulling up' the cost of other energy resources, and likewise a range of other types of products and services. The instability of the level of oil prices and its sensitivity to a number of non-economic factors are having a negative impact. All of this is impairing the world economic environment, in general and a particularly heavy burden is being borne by the economies of poor countries which are not particularly resilient.

It appears desirable, while maintaining the market nature of the relationship between exporters and importers, to look for adequate measures to impact collectively on the environment of the world oil market in order to maintain the level of prices and their fluctuation within tolerable limits.

It is essential to facilitate the creation of a highly reliable system of supply of energy resources to the world market. One of the most important conditions for achieving this objective is finding viable mechanisms to promote further development of pipeline systems, tanker transportation of liquid and gaseous hydrocarbons, and likewise intergovernmental systems of electricity transmission, having in mind the future creation of a global worldwide energy system providing technical capabilities for the diversification of sources and centres of energy consumption in all regions of the world.

The issue of international co-operation aimed at properly ensuring their physical security becomes critically significant when we consider the growth in the risk of subversive action at key sites of the energy infrastructure (nuclear power stations, pipelines, port installations, transmission system hubs, hydroelectric structures), their susceptibility to natural disasters, and likewise in connection with the widespread practice of unsanctioned extraction of hydrocarbons.

We must highlight the importance of further development and improvement of the effectiveness of energy dialogue between producers and consumers of energy resources, regular exchange between them of information on the energy situation in their countries, and on plans and programmes for the development of the energy sector in the medium and long term.

Issues of energy efficiency and energy conservation have been further developed pursuant to the G8 plans of action drawn up in Evian (2003) and Gleneagles (2005). Acting with the framework of this area of focus, we are expressing our aspiration to harmonise energy efficiency standards and improve the effectiveness of exploration, production and transportation of hydrocarbon resources, including their non-traditional forms. Energy efficiency is one of the viable mechanisms of managing demand for energy resources, which in turn facilitates stabilisation of global markets, including hydrocarbon markets.

We must not overlook such an important instrument as diversification of the energy resource portfolio according to types of fuel, suppliers and consumers, and likewise according to their means of supply, which reduces risks connected with ensuring energy security, not only for individual countries, but for the entire international community.

A significant contribution in resolving these strategic objectives can be made by the joint efforts of the G8 countries and of other states in relation to the more widespread use of renewable energy sources, development and application of innovative technologies in the area of energy, and development of low-carbon energy.

Figure 3.27 The evolving system of world energy policy and diplomacy

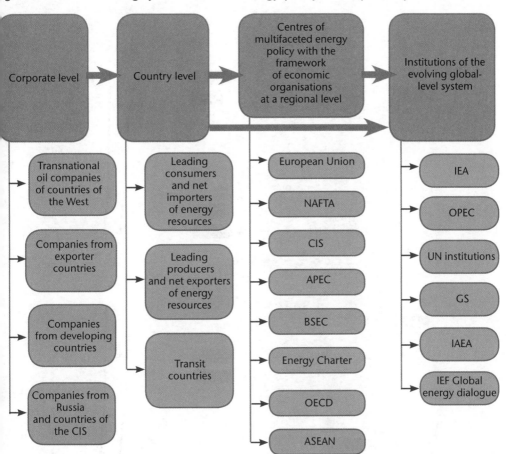

The development of safe nuclear energy and extensive application of hydro power are of special significance for the long-term and ecologically acceptable diversification of energy supply.

Being profoundly aware that the problem of supporting 2 billion of the world's population, who today do not have access to suitable and economically available energy services, is a most important component of global energy security and an imperative for the eradication of poverty and ensuring sustainable development across the globe, countries of the G8 shall further strengthen their work in eradicating energy poverty in third-world countries, including by means of transferring to them advanced technologies for the production of accessible and suitable energy, modern energy-efficient technology and equipment, provision of financial

Figure 3.28 The problems of energy poverty in the world

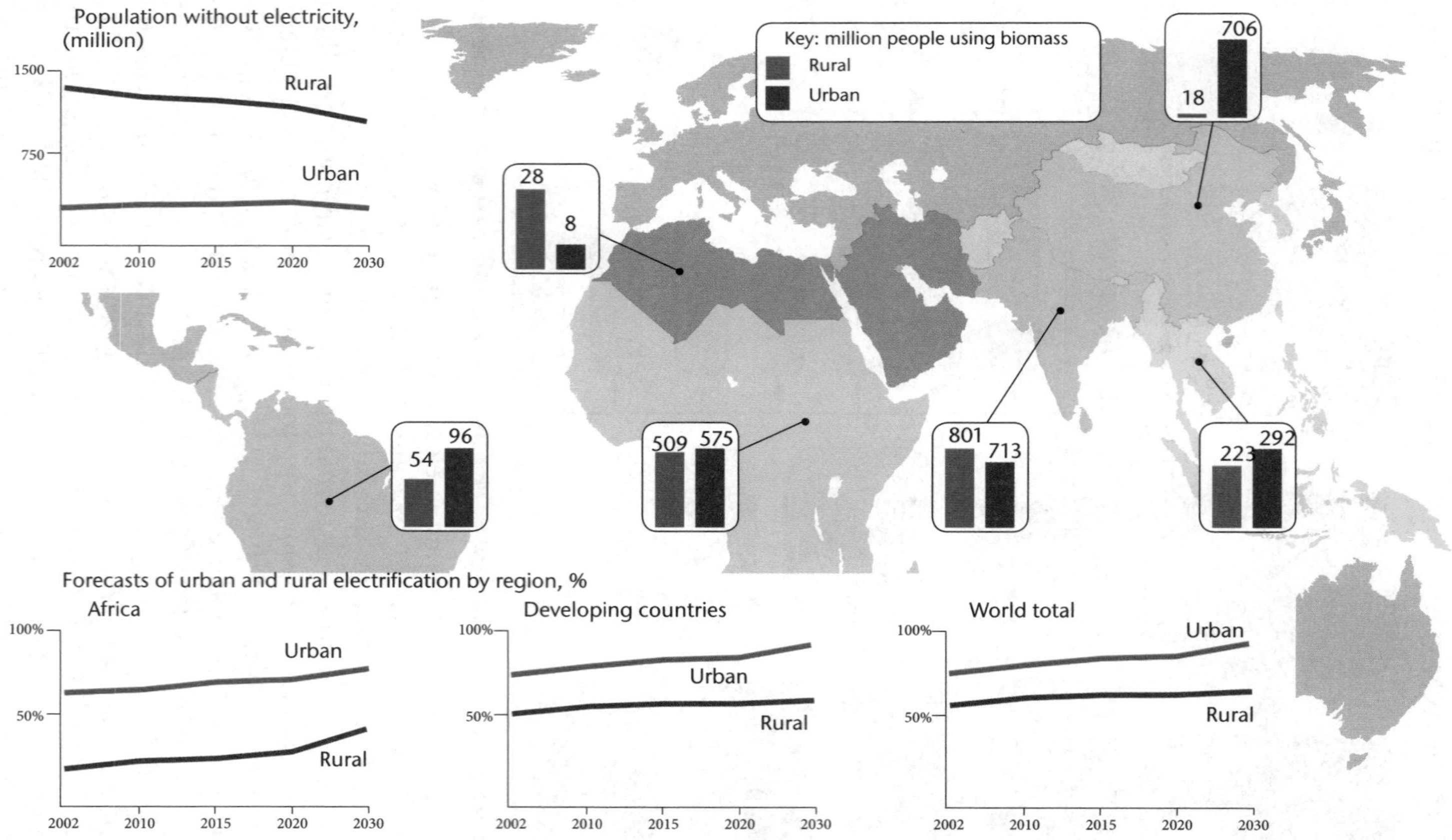

assistance, including from international donors and attracting private capital, and also by other available means and actions.

In conclusion we must say that the matter of energy security is not new. Russia is certainly not breaking new ground on this issue. However, in view of the objective imperatives of time, this subject affects the entire world community to some extent. Our objective in this regard appears to be the cataloguing of all significant previous initiatives in this area, with the subsequent organisation of a system of work across the entire spectrum of key issues of global energy security. We would like to express our hope that the solutions developed in the course of Russia's presidency of the G8 will be furthered in future joint measures.

It must be emphasised that the route to ensuring global energy security will require a lot of time and effort, namely internationally co-ordinated joint efforts both of producer countries and consumer countries that are capable of producing a positive result in the long term.

We must develop effective instruments and mechanisms to overcome the main energy challenges and threats of our time, such as persistent and at times economically unjustified growth in prices for energy resources, disruptions of any nature in energy supply, 'energy poverty', adverse environmental impact and a number of other challenges. Ultimately, our aim is to build a sustainable global market that precludes the destructive shocks of rivalry for energy resources.

In search of a security formula

From an interview with Moscow News, *20 March 2006:*

Does mutual understanding exist with G8 colleagues in relation to what energy poverty means?

In this regard, I recall a book by the distinguished Russian philosopher Losev, where a lay person poses the question, what is the meaning of life? The philosopher's reply is that the meaning of life is to live and act, and constantly return to the question of what is the meaning of life. If you substitute here the phrase 'meaning of life' with 'energy security', you will have an answer to your question. If we talk more specifically, then each of the G8 countries has its own strategy in the area of energy. These strategies rest upon a specific situation in one or other country in the energy sphere:

METHODOLOGICAL SCHOOL OF MANAGEMENT

there are producer countries and consumer countries of traditional energy sources, there are advanced countries and not such advanced countries in the development and use of new alternative energy sources. This being the case, states have different evaluations of their capabilities and risks, and this also finds expression in their national energy strategies. Discussion of the question of whether we coincide in our understanding of global energy security will rest on this. After all, the energy market became a global market a long time ago. So, the meeting of ministers is a platform for presenting national positions and interests, an idea of how far these interests are connected, and what routes exists to reduce risks.

In this case, what national energy priorities will you defend in the course of the meeting?

Our position includes an objective evaluation of the condition of traditional – hydrocarbon – energy markets and proposals to improve the predictability of these markets. Furthermore, in themselves natural resources are limited, which gives rise to the serious issue of new alternative energy sources, and their diversification according to fuel component and technology component. A third set of questions is connected to energy efficiency throughout the economic cycle: from obtaining energy to using it. And finally, a fourth set of questions concern ecological limits in energy development. In each of these platforms for discussion Russia is not an abstract observer of the situation, but an interested party capable of exerting significant influence on the development of events.

In connection with this, are you succeeding in establishing a dialogue with your colleague ministers while taking into account that our country is, after all, an energy producer and supplier, whereas their countries are mainly consumers?

I do not think we are interested in such opposing positions. I am absolutely certain that for a country to attempt to retreat within itself, even for the elite club of the G8, would be a mistake from the viewpoint of the prospects of global energy security. Therefore, we are proposing dialogue between the largest consumer countries with growing economies – China, India, Brazil, Mexico – and the largest OPEC producers. Only with such a structure can we adopt real means of strengthening global energy security. In addition, from the perspective of possessing energy-efficient technologies, unfortunately I can hardly list Russia among the world leaders.

In this context other representatives of the G8 have a far greater head start. In fact, we are interested in organising the transfer of energy-saving technologies. Ultimately our actions in relation to moving toward the synchronous operation of the electricity systems of Russia and the European Union are an attempt at realising such a principle of co-operation, so that we can absolutely equally feel we are partners on both sides of the border. In this, the boundary between the concepts of energy 'supplier' and 'consumer' simply disappear.

It is no secret that we occasionally hear talk from Europe of the need to reduce their dependency on our hydrocarbons. Does this create a field of dispute in relations with G8 partners?

There are different kinds of dependency: historically determined and geographically defined, and economically effective, and it is not easy to reject all dependencies. But, we also absolutely clearly understand that diversification is a course of risk reduction on the part of our partners. It is important both for the consumer of energy resources, and for the supplier. In this case, the consumer selects various sources, whereas the supplier selects various markets and routes. Russia's energy strategy is absolutely clearly targeted on this, because we consider the risks of transit territories to be substantial. Equally, we consider the opportunities of new growing markets to be substantial. So our strategy involves developing the new oil-producing provinces of the Far East and Eastern Siberia, which are primarily oriented towards the rapidly growing market of China and other countries of the Asia-Pacific region. Another province – Timan-Pechora – is oriented to the North American market, which is a new market for Russia. Transition from our own territory to sea terminals is a further key element of the strategy of reducing risks of transit territories. For this reason in the coming couple of months we will complete work on the final configuration of the Baltic Pipeline System and will reach capacity of 60 million tonnes per annum, which would have been difficult to believe just five years ago. Yet today it is no sensation, it is even difficult to say it is news.

Following the recent unforgettable gas conflict with Ukraine, rebukes of 'energy extortion' were voiced about our country. What do you think: has this problem now passed?

I don't want to play the role of Cassandra, foretelling what awaits us tomorrow. The arrangement of regulation that was found at the beginning of the year was probably far from ideal, if for no other reason than it encompasses the immediate period. The contract for delivery of Russian gas for RosUkrEnergo is calculated for just five years and not for 30 years as with the majority of European partners. On the other hand, progress on a series of bilateral areas that were stated as being strategically important has now simply stalled. This is partly connected with an agreement for the creation of an international consortium for the management and development of a gas transportation system for the Ukraine, which explains to some extent the recent situation with unsanctioned extraction of gas on the territory of Ukraine. So when such harsh terms as 'energy extortion' are used, I would really like to understand who here is the extortionist and who is being extorted. Because the only way in which the current situation differs from the situation, let's say of ten years ago, is that our Ukrainian colleagues have publicly announced: yes, we are taking more than the contractual gas quota, because it's cold here.

There is one other difference from the situation of the recent past: the price at which we are selling gas to Ukraine is five times higher ...

True, but when the price for gas has grown, it would seem that the sanctity of contractual obligations should only be deemed to be greater, at the very least, because this extra-contractual volume must be paid for at the new prices. Yet this did not stop our Ukrainian partners, while at the same time all other countries – our partners – were fully performing their obligations in relation to the transit of gas and took the exact volume of gas that they were due under contracts. So, when talk about the North European Gas Pipeline, this certainly does not replace the Ukrainian route, it is simply one of the areas of diversification of supplies of natural gas to European consumers. We are interested in there being more routes and more possibilities for storing gas. Another matter is that this all costs money; what's more, a lot of money, estimated in the billions of dollars.

Are you not concerned that our economy is too strongly dependent on the global pricing environment for energy products, and that sooner or later the environment could change for the worse for us?

Yes, that's true. The Russian economy is substantially dependent on the energy sector, or more accurately on the hydrocarbon sector – on oil and gas, the sale of which provides half of all our foreign currency receipts and more than one third of the entire state budget. But, it would be absurd to beat ourselves up over the fact that we have so much oil and gas, and say, 'If only we didn't have it, we would be more energy efficient, disciplined and technologically advanced.' Personally, I have no regrets that Russia possesses such colossal resources. Their availability creates opportunities for the country to develop non-extraction sectors, and likewise to perform its national obligations of a social and defence nature, and in all other areas. At the same time, the market environment is an inconsistent thing and can fluctuate in either direction. So it is most important not to try to inflate your desires and immediately use the fruits of a favourable situation. Otherwise, the injection of such large sums of money could stoke inflation and, most importantly, it produces permanent obligations, whose performance depends on the market environment. What if the price of an energy product falls tomorrow? Will we stop paying pensions or treating the sick? In this sense, the obligations that are included in the budget today should be protected unconditionally from the impact of the market environment. For this reason a harsh discussion accompanies the matter of the so-called cut-off prices for the Stabilisation Fund. We must remember that we are talking about volumes of real obligations of the state that it assumes in relation to its citizens.

From the viewpoint of ordinary citizens, energy security is needed so that the lights stay on and the heating is uninterrupted, and so that the price for these services is not too high. How are we doing in this regard?

The power failure that occurred on 25 May last year in Moscow allowed us to evaluate adequately the risks that exist in our power system, and just six months prior to the peak period of cold winter weather, to implement a whole series of measures that enabled us to get through the winter without serious failures or disconnections, only with partial localised limits on power usage. (Incidentally, not a single country falling within the cold zone on the European Continent was able to avoid these limits.) This is when we, in fact, have prices on monopoly energy products – gas and electricity – that are fixed for the year. We can recall the United Kingdom, where the cold of this winter led to the price of gas on certain days reaching $1,000 per cubic metre. I would mention that our price is approximately $40. With gas at such a price, no domestic motives exist to limit consumption, so we apply administrative decisions – so-called schedules. I must mention that it has been very difficult for us to introduce these schedules and somehow convince consumers to limit their consumption. Whatever the case may be, we honourably endured a very difficult period when the country encountered a season of anomalous temperatures, which was a record in both its duration and the territory affected.

What should be done with petrol prices, which also regularly increased even though this sector is not considered to be a monopoly?

Only a couple of years have passed since a shift occurred in social consciousness, and oil ceased to be viewed as a resource of corporations, which generated profits for them, and was instead seen as a resource of the state, which has been temporarily granted for use by these very same corporations. Therefore, the state should receive a proportional royalty from the pricing environment. In other words there should be a sort of floating tax that transforms a favourable market environment into revenue for the state, whereas an unfavourable environment does not lead to the sector suffering financial ruin.

Now, our tax legislation – tax on the extraction of mineral resources, export duties, excise duties on oil products on the domestic market – has reached the point where royalty components of the tax have become the dominant part. In general, we unwaveringly follow the world pricing environment, which is correspondingly increasing tax rates and budget revenues. But we must also remember that there are no such things as miracles, and any tax is always paid by the consumer. All these taxes are reflected in the price of petrol. However, this certainly does not mean that we must suddenly change our taxation policy. From my perspective, the sphere of tax regulation is closely connected with the conduct of investors, and should have some stability, at least in the medium term, if not in the long term. There is one further point: during 2005 we have had just 2 per cent growth in oil production, compared with 10–11 per cent growth in previous years. Clearly, there is a substantial fall in production rates, and with such a favourable environment! And this is not the opportunistic behaviour of Russian companies who have decided to hide something away somewhere. We are talking about real opportunities to develop new deposits, which are far greater than simply producing from the existing deposits of Western Siberia. So today we are deliberately moving in the direction of creating trade preferences, including tax preference, in relation to the development of the difficult-to-access provinces of Eastern Siberia, the Far East and Timan-Pechora, in order to create conditions for oil production that are economically acceptable to investors. Otherwise, we risk stagnation and even the failure of the Russian oil sector. Do we need to say that this would be bad news, and not only for the oil producers?

Ensuring energy stability and security

From an address at the Tenth International Energy Forum, Doha, Qatar, 24 April 2006:

Our session is dedicated to the issue of access to energy. Undoubtedly, access to energy resources is only an element, one of the conditions for ensuring stability and security on global energy markets. This condition is absolutely essential, but at the same time it is absolutely not enough.

What does access to energy mean? This is access to reserves deposited in different regions of the world, at different depths, in regions with climates from +50 °C to –50 °C, in countries with different political systems, faiths and so on. However, this is also access to the energy resources of countries that differ in their role on the world market. What countries do I mean?

◆ Countries where there are sufficient energy resources for domestic consumption, and even an excess. This also means access to energy sources.
◆ Countries where meeting domestic needs depends to a significant degree on resources produced thousands of kilometres or miles from its territory. And this is connected to access to energy sales markets.
◆ Countries where a significant part of the economy depends on the quantity of energy resources passing through the national territory to other countries. In this case, we are talking about access to the transit of energy resources.
◆ Finally, there are simply energy-poor countries that do not possess energy resources and stand apart from the main energy flows (be they on dry land or by sea). The issue here is energy accessibility.

In connection with access to energy, we can also talk about the technological aspect of this issue. From the perspective of energy consumption, while I am giving this address someone in the world will be using up enough fuel to heat an entire house just to fry an egg, while someone else will be using the very same amount of energy to build two houses. The issue here is access to energy technologies.

Can these issues of access, either exclusively to energy sources, or on the broader subject of energy security, be resolved while ignoring any of the listed aspects or any of the players on the world market? Probably, and possibly to the benefit of individual players, but not for long.

Today the significance is growing of such a factor as co-ordination of approaches and actions along the entire chain of production, supply and sale of energy resources. I am not talking about an exchange of market mechanisms but only about improving their effectiveness, including in relation to rules for accessing markets, infrastructure and ultimately resources.

If diversification of supply of resources according to source is relevant for the consumer market, then this unavoidably leads to diversification according to lines of supply on the part of the supplier. We are dealing with an objective process of correcting an imbalance in the distribution of risks. We should be aware that the concentration of all risks on the part of the supplier will ultimately not facilitate security of supply.

The question of diversification is also closely related to the issue of promoting development of energy infrastructure. One of the most important conditions for achieving the stated aim is finding effective mechanisms for promoting further development of pipeline systems, tanker transportation of liquid and gaseous hydrocarbons, and likewise intergovernmental systems of electricity transmission.

The same is also true for contractual relations between market participants throughout the entire energy chain. If long-term contracts for final delivery are not supported by reliable contracts for transportation then reliability of supply will simply become unattainable. There are very recent examples of this.

Access to energy also means access to capital. Creation of an effective and robust global energy supply system requires substantial investment resources, a significant part of which should be aimed at the areas of production, transportation and refining of energy resources.

Mobilisation of investments essential for development of the world energy sector is only possible if a favourable investment climate and predictable political situation exist, both in countries producing and countries consuming energy resources and, in addition, in transit states. This assumes developed stable legislation, coherent and consistently applied tax regimes, the absence of unwarranted administrative barriers, categorical performance of contractual obligations and access to effective dispute resolution procedures.

In this regard, Russia is probably not a benchmark, but it is conducting a whole range of measures to improve legislation and to form a transparent and effective domestic energy market. In the near future we shall be considering some very important draft legislation on taxation of mineral resource extraction, and new regulations on underground resource use, including conditions for the participation of foreign capital. These draft laws are aimed at making conditions for conducting energy business in Russia more convenient, transparent and predictable.

Access to energy also means access to assets. Reciprocal participation in assets between energy companies will play an important role in the division of risks. This is one of the instruments for improving the sustainability of global energy supply. Russia is already taking steps in this direction. In particular, we are working with our German and American partners and are open in this regard to the energy companies of other countries.

Access to energy also means access to energy technologies. In the first quarter of the twenty-first century, humankind will have to make a scientific and technological breakthrough onto the route to effective development of 'clean' nontraditional and renewable energy sources, including such areas of energy as hydrogen, nuclear, solar, biofuel and clean coal technologies. We believe that new energy, including advanced areas of nuclear energy, will in the very near future become an ecologically safe and economically effective source for supporting growing demand for electricity in many countries of the world.

Among other things, today's forum provides an opportunity to present national positions and interests, an idea of how far these interests are connected and what routes exist to reduce risks. This is an opportunity to replace incomprehensible variable values in our energy security equation with permanent ones, and to take decisions other than by guesswork. Today's audience is extremely important by virtue of the breadth of its membership. And value must be increased. I think that it is possible to consider providing additional impulse to this process, which has been formulated under the auspices of the International Energy Forum, and move our sessions with this group to an annual format. In Russia in recent years, within the scope of our presidency of the G8, our certainty of this has only grown stronger.

In this regard I shall consider separately nuclear energy. The majority of leading countries have stated – and what's more, done so very recently – their ambitious plans in the area of nuclear energy. Our country is among them. We intend to increase the proportion of electricity produced at nuclear power stations from 16 per cent to 22–24 per cent over the next 15 years. Furthermore, we are certain that the global nuclear energy alternative should also be accessible to other countries under nonproliferation conditions.

Our country has formed a comprehensive approach to the problem of energy security, which is determined by the specific nature of the geographical, economic and political position of Russia. We are both a large exporter and a large consumer of energy resources, at the same time as Russia is a significant transit nation. Therefore we are in a position to understand the viewpoints of many players in the global energy market.

It has been mentioned a number of times yesterday and today that two years have passed since the last forum was held. This is quite a long period of time for the current condition of the world market, allowing much to be accomplished.

According to the *Energy Strategy of Russia*, adopted in 2003, a series of measures are being realised that will have a positive impact not only on the energy sector of Russia itself, but also on global energy security. In realising our strategy, we have announced commencement of work for the production of hydrocarbons in new regions. These are Eastern Siberia, northern regions of Russia, and the continental shelf of the north seas and the Far East. These processes are accompanied by significant changes in legislation, including tax legislation.

A separate, already implemented element of the energy strategy is an offer to the world market of products that are new for Russia. Here I mean liquefied natural gas.

A huge amount of work is being undertaken in expanding the existing energy infrastructure, including in areas of export. One of the largest infrastructure projects is the construction of the Eastern Siberia–Pacific Ocean oil pipeline system. This is approximately 4,300 km of pipeline and more than 1.5 million barrels of oil per day, of which more than a third will be supplied to China. Construction of the first stage is planned for completion by the end of 2008.

Following this, we will progress to the creation of a gas transport system in the east of the country. Along with development of the Sakhalin continental shelf, this will ensure the delivery of oil and gas from new Russian provinces in the east to markets of the Asia-Pacific region. In 2020, the share of countries of the Asia-Pacific region in Russian oil exports could have grown from 3 per cent today to 30 per cent, and natural gas from 5 per cent to 25 per cent.

In order to ensure oil export flows from Russia in a westerly direction, construction of the Baltic Pipeline System (BPS) is finally completed and in April of this year it reached operating status with a capacity of 65 million tonnes of oil per annum.

Preparation is under way of a northern route for the transportation of resources to North America from the continental shelf of the Barents Sea. The deepest underwater gas pipeline –Blue Stream – has been laid across the Black Sea and has prospects of being extended to the southern regions of Europe.

Realisation of the North European Gas Pipeline project will help solve the problem of diversification of gas export flows, and the possibility of making good use of them will facilitate the expansion of gas supply to the countries of Western Europe and the performance of obligations under contracts for the supply of gas, including both those already concluded and future long-term contracts. In essence, this will afford direct connection of the Russian gas transportation system to the common European gas network.

Russia has been engaged in active energy dialogue for a number of years with individual countries of Europe, the EU bloc, the United States, OPEC and countries of the Asia-Pacific region. We are gaining concrete understanding of our own economic interests and the interests of our partners connected with development of the market, and of the problems that need to be discussed and resolved. The significance of any energy dialogue lies in the interface between any processes of realising national energy strategies.

States evaluate differently their capabilities and risks, and this evaluation also finds expression in their national energy strategies. Specifically, if we are sincerely striving to attain global energy security, we should be talking about ensuring the absence of conflict or inconsistencies of these aims and the means to achieve them.

Among other things, today's forum provides an opportunity to present national positions and interests, an idea of how far these interests are connected, and what routes exist to reduce risks. This is an opportunity to replace incomprehensible variable values in our energy security equation with permanent ones and to take decisions other than by guesswork. To repeat, today's audience is extremely important because of the breadth of its membership. And that value must be increased. I think that it is possible to consider providing additional impulse to this process, which has been formulated under the auspices of the IEF, and move our sessions with these partners to an annual format. In Russia in recent years, within the scope of our presidency of the G8, our certainty of this has only grown stronger.

Trust in Russia

Article from Allgemeine Zeitung, *11 July 2006:*

Trust – the foundation of good international cooperation. At the G8 summit that is to take place at the end of the week, the focus should be co-operation in the energy sector. In recent times, the production, transportation and consumption of energy have been considered primarily from the perspective of the reliability of suppliers. Reliability can be evaluated from the viewpoint of payment discipline, but first and foremost it is a matter of trust. Trust can only be achieved as a result of equitable dialogue between potential partners. For this reason, a few years ago we opened an energy dialogue with the European Union. Secretly, all the participants want this energy dialogue to result in an active economic union.

Any disagreements regarding Russia's reliability as a supplier of energy products should be based on fact. We have been a reliable supplier of energy products to European consumers for more than 40 years now. Russia has never disrupted the supply of its energy products to Europe, not even during the period of the cold war or the financial crisis of 1998, because historically we perceive ourselves as being part of Europe. This shows that irrespective of domestic problems or strained relations with the rest of the world, including countries with which we could end up in confrontation, Russia will never conceive of energy being a weapon, bargaining chip or some sort of pretext.

A recent discussion on the regulations for transit of Russian gas through the territories of neighbouring states proved to be brief, because it was possible to arrive quickly at a solution that was beneficial to all parties. An agreement signed in January between Gazprom and the Ukraine provides an opportunity, particularly in the still insufficiently developed Ukrainian economy, to adapt gradually to the realities of the global economy. Currently, Gazprom pays the young Ukrainian state significantly more for transit than previously. A satisfactory decision at a European level was found for all parties as a result of negotiation.

Nevertheless, certain journalists call into question Russia's reliability as a supplier of energy products. The sole comfort can be found in the fact that the vision of these sceptics, who out of old habits view Russia as the Soviet Union, is not appropriate for discussion with modern Russia. Over a year ago the Ukrainian president, Viktor Yushenko, understood that with the realities of a globalised world Ukraine is better off operating within the framework of pricing mechanisms of the world economy. The global community quite justifiably expects that the head of the young Ukrainian democratic state will also inculcate this vision in the heads of the members of his government.

Negotiations with our closest (at least, geographically speaking) partners are categorically based on economic principles. In addition, we should take into consideration the regular increase in prices on the part of our own gas suppliers (for example, Turkmenistan). Also, the World Trade Organization is continually reminding us that 15 years after the dissolution of the Soviet Union, Russia should not be providing any gifts to the businesses of neighbouring states – goods should be offered at prices that reflect the situation on the world market. For comparison: last year Ukraine received Russian gas at a price of just $50 per cubic metre, while European countries had to pay approximately $200 per cubic metre. In other words, in the case of Ukraine Gazprom has simply been applying free market economy rules since the New Year.

By means of new large joint projects we are trying to establish trust and ensure reliability and transparency. Among other things, we are building new pipelines in close co-operation with well-known European partners. These will, in practice and not simply hypothetically, lead to further diversification of supply routes, and consequently improve the reliability of supply to Europe.

Co-operation with foreign partners is very important to us, because Russia, as a European country, wants to achieve Europe's technological level of development quickly and with the support of foreign investment. In one interview my colleague, the European Commissioner for Energy Mr Piebalgs, spoke about investment in Russian infrastructure at a level of 'several hundred billion euros'. We welcome such a relationship and foreign participation in Russian businesses, but both at the current time and in the future we anticipate the same openness also from our European partner. Moreover, this does not only apply to in the energy sector. However, energy is an extremely important subject not only for the leading industrialised nations: about 2 billion people in the world do not have access to electricity. This circumstance does not support international economic development and is not merely a decisive factor for the survival of developing countries in the south. A lack of access to energy resources threatens modern civilisation with various consequences.

Russia's presidency of the G8 is a good opportunity to talk about Russia. Those who are prepared not to limit themselves to once more taking dusty 30-year-old tomes about the Soviet Union off the bookshelf can reflect with us on how to ensure equal, reliable and unhindered energy supply. At negotiations in St Petersburg we will sometimes utter words that differ from one another, yet we will all be speaking the same language – and this dialogue will create trust.

Practical development of a 'global sustainable energy development' concept: demand for gas should be transparent

From an interview in RBC Daily, *23 January 2007:*

Rosneft and Stroitransgaz are investing $1.3 billion in oil production in Algeria, Gazprom is proposing four assets in Russia to oil and gas company Sonatrach in exchange for access to gas fields in Central Africa, and Russian power personnel will be able to participate in a number of Algerian projects. These are the results of a visit to Algeria by the minister of industry and energy of Russia, Viktor Khristenko, which concluded last Sunday. The minister explained the details of the results of the visit in an interview with *RBC Daily* correspondent, Igor Naumov.

Viktor Borisovich, what is your assessment of the status and prospects of co-operation between Russia and Algeria in the energy sector?

This co-operation makes absolute sense. First, we are large players on the market. Second, we have similar production resources in relation to both gas and oil. Third, we operate essentially on the same market platforms. Each of the parties is interested to the same extent in exchanging both technologies and information on the situation that is emerging on the market, with the aim of stabilisation.

During a visit to Moscow in August 2006 by my colleague the Minister for Energy and Mines of Algeria, Chakib Khelil, memoranda were signed at company level between our Gazprom and the Algerian company Sonatrach, and also between Lukoil and Sonatrach. Within a short period of time Gazprom has been able to complete a fairly large range of joint actions with Algerian colleagues. As a result, in discussing prospects of co-operation with Algeria in the gas sector, we are talking about applying the most advanced practice in linking interests – asset exchange. What is proposed is participating in the production and exploration segment, and in refining and marketing: in other words, in all links of the process chain. Gazprom has offered eight sites on the territory of Russia, four of which the Algerians have deemed of interest to them. Further work is under way in relation to them. On their part, they are preparing proposals for Gazprom to participate in production assets on the territory of Algeria.

It has been stated that the interests of these companies are not limited to the territories of their own countries ...

Indeed, the intention has been confirmed to develop business in third-party countries where Algerian gas personnel are actively working – Mali, Morocco, and a whole range of other African states – or in places where Russian gas personnel are represented. This involves the use of substitution mechanisms in trade so that Gazprom and Sonatrach can expand the geography of their market presence, for example, by providing opportunities to our Algerian colleagues to enter the market of the Asia-Pacific region, and for the Russians to enter the Atlantic market. I am certain that these proposals are sure to be realised. Opportunities are also being discussed to conduct exchange operations with foreign energy companies working in Algeria: let's say, Gaz de France. But of course, processing is an extremely important issue for us – entering production of liquefied natural gas (LNG). Algeria has actually been a groundbreaker in this area. We proposed that our partners participate in the creation of a Baltic plant for the production of LNG.

How is co-operation developing in the oil sector?

There are also good prospects in oil production. Rosneft and Stroitransgaz have been working together with Sonatrach in the exploration of large oil fields in Algeria – the 245 South block. Two fields are already prepared for commercial opening. All materials based on the results of a five-year programme of works have been submitted to the Algerians, and agreement has been reached that in the near future the companies will obtain permits and licences for the production and operation of these fields. In addition, a third oil field has also been opened there and work on this is at the concluding stage.

Is the concern of certain European countries justified regarding the Russian–Algerian gas alliance?

Our co-operation with Algeria cannot be equated to a friendship that legislates against someone else. That is an absolutely ridiculous idea. It is essential specifically so that all participants in the energy chain, including consumers, can to a greater extent have a common understanding and awareness of the value of energy security and those factors impacting on it, and also for the development of appropriate instruments. This is co-operation for the sake of a stable energy market, for predictability and transparency of rules of conduct within this market by all its participants.

In this context Russia and Algeria are actively positioned in multilateral international organisations. We are initiating a process for the exchange of information and viewpoints, and for co-ordination within such organisations as the International Energy Forum and the Gas Exporting Countries Forum. An awful lot in the area of energy security depends on our countries, not only as large suppliers of energy resources, but also as system players on the global market. And this applies not only in the supply link, but also in following through on the correct viewpoint and balancing the risks of suppliers, consumers and those involved in transportation.

While in Algeria you confirmed that Russia is participating in a scheduled meeting of the Gas Exporting Countries Forum, which is to take place in Qatar in April. How relevant to Russia is a dialogue in such a format?

This allows gas-producing countries to develop a common opinion, a shared viewpoint on significant issues about the functioning and

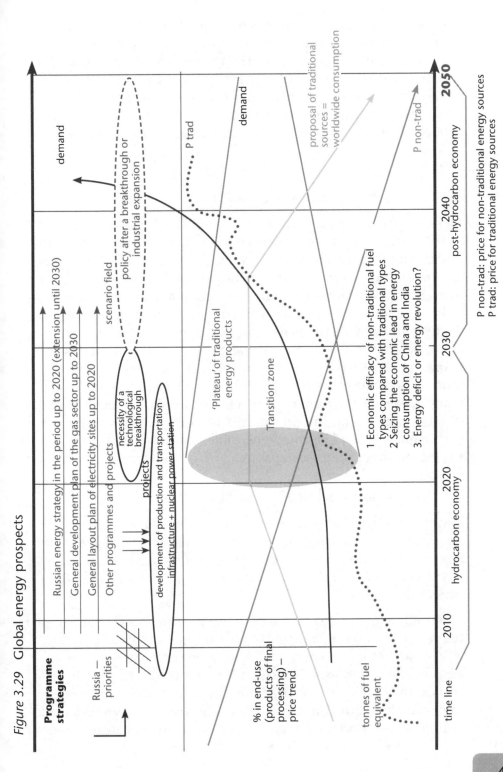

Figure 3.29 Global energy prospects

Programme strategies

Russian energy strategy in the period up to 2020 (extension until 2030)

General development plan of the gas sector up to 2030

General layout plan of electricity sites up to 2020

Other programmes and projects

Russia – priorities

development of production and transportation infrastructure + nuclear power station

projects

necessity of a technological breakthrough

scenario field

policy after a breakthrough or industrial expansion

demand

demand

P trad

proposal of traditional sources = worldwide consumption

P non-trad

'Plateau' of traditional energy products

Transition zone

% in end-use (products of final processing) – price trend

tonnes of fuel equivalent

time line

2010

2020

2030

2040

2050

hydrocarbon economy

post-hydrocarbon economy

1 Economic efficacy of non-traditional fuel types compared with traditional types
2 Seizing the economic lead in energy consumption of China and India
3. Energy deficit or energy revolution?

P non-trad: price for non-traditional energy sources
P trad: price for traditional energy sources

development of the gas market, which thanks to LNG is beginning to become global in nature, but along with this, taking into consideration the great significance of the gas pipeline, it also preserves specific regional characteristics – European, Asian and American. In this sense, a format of this kind – the exchange of opinions and the development of a shared position – is a factor for stability. We should not try to present this as rallying to fight with someone.

Priorities

How relevant is the creation of a 'Gas OPEC'?

I am not one of its supporters and do not believe that we should move along the route of a cartel agreement. But it is important to understand that a number of objective processes exist. Companies are becoming larger and transnational on the strength of an increase in risks connected with production at new fields that are more complex and costly. This is also occurring due to an expansion of the geography of the market and supplies. In essence, it is not a fad, but rather a response to challenges and risks of the global market. Companies will complement one another by virtue of mutual exchange of assets and distribution of risk. There will not be many players in the form of suppliers, but we should move in this direction, relying on the consumer, who must recognise primarily that demand should be comprehensible and transparent, and also the intentions of the gas companies.

Energy policy and energy security

The role and significance of energy policy of the Russian Federation in the general context of energy security in the region of the United Nations Economic Commission for Europe: from an address at the 62nd session of the United Nations Economic Commission for Europe (UNECE) in Geneva, 27 April 2007:

Cooperation in the area of energy has occupied a primary place over the course of the 60-year period of the existence of the UNECE. So it is no accident that the energy problem, as one of the most important areas of the Commission's sectorial operations, is reflected in the agenda for today's session. The Commission's activity and membership of its Committee on Sustainable Energy have always been aimed at unifying the efforts of all the Commission's member states to ensure a sustainable and reliable energy supply to their countries. Russia has taken and will continue to take an active part in this activity.

During this period the Committee on Sustainable Energy and structures operating under its auspices have become a platform for the exchange of opinions on the most varied energy problems. These include energy efficiency, gas supply, fossil fuels, coal, coalbed methane and electricity. One of these areas is energy security, which in our opinion is the key subject for today's energy sector, or even for the current stage of humanity's development. For this reason Russia raised this problem within the scope of our country's presidency of the G8.

In 2003 Russia supported the creation of an UNECE energy security forum. The research it has carried out into new risks to energy security and paths to their reduction was used in preparing the *Plan of Action for Global Energy Security* adopted at the G8 Summit in St Petersburg.

This *Plan* was the result of work conducted on Russia's initiative, generally in a multilateral format. 2006 demonstrated the efficacy of just such a multilateral dialogue in the energy sphere.

In spite of the fact that the increase in the number of communication platforms on which energy problems are discussed is sometimes ambiguously evaluated according to geographical or industry-sector principles, we believe that the emergence of new platforms for discussion is a positive phenomenon. Such a situation allows us to structure a set of problems contained in the G8 Declaration and Plan of Action, and to reach concrete solutions taking into consideration the specific nature of each segment of the global energy sector.

We must remember that opening any multilateral dialogue places certain demands on its participants. Dialogue is the ability not simply to talk (or dictate), but also to listen, and more importantly to understand another point of view, with the latter being the most important aspect. Pinning labels on them is an attempt to disparage sovereign states, discredit initiatives and disorientate public opinion, in particular, on the right to dialogue and joint resolution of industry sector and regional problems.

Therefore, I am to some extent bewildered by the initiative of the US Senate Committee on the Judiciary, which 'unanimously voted for draft legislation prohibiting foreign states from creating oil and gas "cartel" organisations such as OPEC'.

In a modern democratic society, any person is entitled to an opinion or suggestion. The objective of an effective state administration of a modern democracy is to sift through ideas that are ineffective, contravene international law and domestic legislation, or are unrealisable in practice. It seems to me that the second and third of these filters would sift out the idea voiced above.

Within the scope of the G8 presidency, last year Russia set out its position regarding development of the global energy sector and its place in it. Basic principles were developed to ensure global energy security – co-ordination of national energy policies, diversification both of supply and sales markets and of energy sources, improving market transparency, energy efficiency and access to energy.

In developing the principles set down in the G8 Summit documents, we started a process of discussion and co-ordination of our *Energy Strategy* with the long-term documents of other key players in the world energy market. We are actively working with the European Union in the course of this energy dialogue. In October last year we held a conference on aligning the energy strategies of Russia and the EU *Green Book* on energy. This year similar conferences will be held in the United States and countries of the Organization of the Black Sea Economic Cooperation.

Large countries, primarily consumer countries, have started presenting their updated energy strategies (the United States, the European Union, Japan, China, Italy and others). Is this not fundamentally proclamatory, a sort of tribute to a political trend? I am not convinced. Leading world consumers of energy resources, while making formidable corrections to their energy policy, are already today reinforcing them financially and legally.

Currently, Russia is working on elaborating its energy strategy. Without altering the basic prerequisites, we are building on it for the period up to 2030, taking into consideration, among other things, the new conditions and challenges that exist in the world today. This process is absolutely transparent and we are determined in the work to take into consideration the results of consultations with our partners, including the UNECE.

The basic principles of development of the Russian energy sector are:

◆ supporting the domestic energy market and meeting international obligations;

◆ deregulating the domestic energy market;
◆ improving investment opportunities in the Russian energy sector and its transparency;
◆ developing transport infrastructure with the aim of developing new oil and gas provinces and diversifying supply routes;
◆ establishing transparent long-term rules for interacting with consumers and transporters of Russian energy resources;
◆ improving energy efficiency of the economy and developing renewable energy sources.

Let me say a few words about how these principles will be realised in practice.

In November last year the Russian Government reached a general consensus on the need to be oriented towards an equal return on sales of gas within the country and for export. In other words, domestic prices should be brought into line with prices at which European consumers are buying gas, net of transportation costs and customs duties. It is suggested that parity of returns in the industrial consumer sector will already be achieved in 2011. Furthermore, we are successfully conducting an experiment in the exchange trade of gas.

Reform of the electricity sector is running in parallel to reform of the gas market. Here we are planning to deregulate the electricity market by 2011.

These decisions have enabled us to embark on implementing the programme for development of the electricity sector. While altering the priorities in forming the country's energy mix, we are paying ever greater attention to the construction of coal and nuclear power generating capacity, and likewise the use of renewable energy sources, in particular hydropower. In the period up to 2020 this will require the involvement of investments of up to $450 billion. The investors are eager to start. Large energy companies of Europe are already participating in this process. Incidentally, in the first quarter of this year total growth of investment in the Russian economy was 21 per cent.

Russia is moving to the same rules on the domestic market as on the external market.

Russia has proposed to its neighbours that they move to the principles of gas supply and transmission that are commonly accepted on the European market.

The UNECE is a 'Big' Europe, whose boarders are determined by economic and trade links and infrastructure systems. This growing level of integration is most clearly seen in the energy sector. So, when we talk about development of Russian energy infrastructure, we are in effect talking about developing the infrastructure connecting UNECE countries.

I would point out that our actions demonstrate that Russia does not imagine that the problem of energy security can be solved outside of a global and regional context. Therefore, participation in UNECE bodies and its sectorial committees is important for us, and we will not simply attend, but work.

Humanitarian principles of sustainable energy development

From an address at the Energy in a Changing World Conference, UNESCO, Paris, 31 March 2007:

There are a number of important and pressing issues requiring our consideration. Energy is the source of life on earth. Energy security is becoming a decisive factor in the future of the planet. Development of new energy technologies is a condition for economic growth and sustainable development, and also an implicit component of global energy strategy.

Today, the issues of energy security and energy efficiency have become some of the most relevant and critical questions. For this reason Russia consistently puts them forward for discussion at such respected international forums as the meeting of leaders of the G8 nations. We are convinced that energy development is a global process. We are also certain that states participating in this process should not limit themselves exclusively to economic pragmatism. Humanitarian values must also be taken into consideration – the values defended and promoted by UNESCO. Among them, the value of dialogue – of both governments and cultures – is fully shared by all of us.

Here, dialogue is of fundamental importance. At the current time all countries are presenting increased requirements in the energy sphere, while forgetting about the principles on which partnership should be built. First and foremost, we must discuss and approve principles and act on the basis of them, not fearing one another. For example, within the framework of the Gas Exporting Countries

Forum in Doha this year we used just such an approach – we started with a discussion of the principles of operating on the world gas market, and we are using this approach in realising Russian energy policy. The Russian energy sector is developing according to the principles set out in our country's *Energy Strategy of Russia for the Period to 2020*. This document has been published, and the principles contained therein conform to world-wide practice. They are congruent with the provisions set out in the G8 Declaration on Energy Security last year. These are security, demand and supply, diversification both of supply and the sales markets, division of risks, market transparency, rejection of politicisation and militarisation of the global energy sector, the priority of market principles, and so on.

We are facing challenges more far-reaching than simply Russian or European challenges – they are world-wide challenges. For this reason and specifically because of the people here today in this hall, we shall open a discussion of the most critical issues of sustainable energy development.

Please allow me to identify the three main problems that we must resolve together. The first problem is *energy poverty*. A huge gulf exists today between those who have energy, and those who do not. Luxembourg, with a population of approximately 1.5 million people, consumes the same amount of electricity as Ghana, with a population of 22 million people, or Kenya, with 35 million people. The United States consumes approximately a quarter of the total world volume of supplied electricity and oil, and it is closely followed by China.

Africa's economy is lagging behind in development because of a shortage of energy resources, which:

◆ restrains industrial and trade development;
◆ prevents people making use of the advantages of information technologies;
◆ arrests the promotion of ideas and culture;
◆ hinders dissemination of knowledge and technologies.

These are vitally important issues on which UNESCO has been working actively for a long time. Please allow me to share a few examples.

Across the world 1.6 billion people have no access to power grids. Of these, 535 million live in Africa.

In rural areas of sub-Saharan Africa, nine out of ten people have no access to electricity.

Africa is rich in natural energy resources – oil, coal, gas, and likewise water and sun – yet in rural areas up to 95 per cent of energy consumption is based on ineffective and harmful combustion of wood and so-called elementary biofuel.

More than 1.6 million people across the world, primarily women and children, die each year from respiratory diseases connected with the combustion of wood for preparing food and heating.

Africa's problems were stated by Germany to be one of the priorities of its G8 presidency. Yet the continent's development is impossible without resolving the problems of energy poverty. For many Africans the issue of access to energy is, with no exaggeration, a matter of life and death.

The second problem is the *development of new and ecologically clean energy technologies*. Access to energy presumes access to energy technologies. Over the course of the next 20 years, humankind must make scientific and technological breakthroughs with the aim of ensuring clean, safe and renewable energy sources, such as hydrogen energy, nuclear power, solar power, biofuel and clean coal technologies.

A central role in this process belongs to fundamental science, so we welcome the programmes being carried out with the support of UNESCO. In particular, Russia considers projects connected with study of the world's oceans to be extremely important. These studies are relevant for our country because comprehensive and large-scale development of the potential of the sea shelf is one of the priorities of the Russian *Energy Strategy*. Naturally, realisation of plans for the continental shelf requires that we pay greater attention to protecting the unique biospheres of the Arctic and Far Eastern seas.

Russia possesses phenomenal energy resources. We occupy first place in the world for oil and gas production. However, the ecological and energy efficiency of the infrastructure we inherited from the Soviet Union – let us be honest about this – is unsatisfactory. We repeatedly lag behind countries of the European Union, the United States and Japan according to these indicators, but we are pursuing a consistent policy to improve energy efficiency, and have the objective of halving energy consumption by 2020 compared with 2000.

Modern Russia is developing an efficient energy sector within the framework of international ecological standards and the strictest

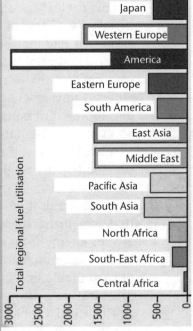

Figure 3.30 Schedule map
of fuel utilisation in 2007

environmental protection requirements. For example, 36 energy efficiency and energy generation projects will be implemented in the candidate city for the 2014 Winter Olympic Games. In total, almost $2 billion is earmarked for investment in the creation of new energy infrastructure for the region.

A range of initiatives are already operating today in the area of environmental protection. These include projects such as 'Zero Balance Waste Accumulation' and 'Zero Balance Greenhouse Gas Emissions'. Let me add that this programme proposes using renewable energy sources and plans to change the fuel used by Sochi Public Aviation to environmentally friendly hydrogen in the near future.

This is clear testament to the fact that Russia is developing not merely by virtue of development of underground resources and export of raw materials. Because of its educational, scientific and creative potential, our country possesses advantages for the creation of a competitive economy founded on intellect and knowledge, an economy where the primary engines are not only the pace of development of natural resources, but ideas and inventions and the ability to use them to good effect in daily life.

All the desired breakthroughs in the area of energy cannot be provided by any single country, so we cannot allow energy to become the cause of wars. It must become a source of co-operation. UNESCO is playing a unique role in ensuring such progress. The organisation can bring together scientists, engineers and experts in the area of energy from around the world, uniting our knowledge and know-how. I am certain the UNESCO's attention to the problems of sustainable energy development is a huge confirmation of the organisation's competence as a world-wide intellectual centre.

The third problem is the *worldwide dissemination of knowledge about energy*. It is important not only to develop new energy technologies, but also to distribute and realise them in practice across the world. New technologies must be used universally across the entire world: in homes and offices, cities and towns, and especially in developing countries.

In the interests of future generations, we must work on developing alternative and renewable energy sources. We should nurture a careful approach to energy, implement the relevant education programmes and standards, and formulate a new and responsible approach to energy at a micro level: that is, at the level of individual users of energy resources. Energy projects should take into account the imperative of preserving natural wealth and diversity, ensure respect for the culture of native and indigenous peoples, and be oriented towards the fair distribution of global energy resources with the aim of reducing energy poverty.

What are we proposing? Russia proposes that UNESCO member countries together create the architecture of a global energy system, in this way realising the UNESCO ideal as a global laboratory of ideas. In particular, we are proposing discussion of such projects as the creation of an international fund of energy technologies of the future to facilitate access to advanced energy technologies, to improve global energy efficiency and consequently the stability of the global energy sector.

We propose conducting long-term global scientific and technological forecasting, which will enable us to predict and mitigate risks to global energy security and energy development, including, very importantly, ecological risks.

We propose development of a system of standards in the sphere of energy education. In the long term this will create conditions for the development of technologies in the energy sphere (in order to create a global energy infrastructure), which will lessen the lag in energy development of a number of countries. In the short term this will establish an energy dialogue not only at a 'high' diplomatic level but, very importantly, on a professional and technological level.

We propose the development of classifications and standards of the quality of energy security (similar to systems evaluating public quality of life). In the long term, development will 'work' both in energy-developed countries and in energy-poor countries. The first group will obtain an additional instrument for developing energy efficiency, and the second group will obtain legal mechanisms for evaluating and combating energy poverty.

We propose that the G8 countries assume specific obligations in combating energy poverty. This will help us take the next step in jointly combating energy poverty on the planet, and will make a valuable contribution to global energy security.

Sharing energy

An article by the Minister of Industry and Energy of the Russian Federation, Viktor Khristenko, and the Director-General of UNESCO, Kotiro Matsuura, in the Guardian, *1 June 2007:*

The leaders of the world's richest countries, the G8, will meet for their annual summit, in Heiligendamm, Germany. Every year, these summits generate high hopes, and expectations too. Two years ago at Gleneagles, poverty in Africa was the major focus; last year in St Petersburg, energy security topped the agenda.

This year marks an opportunity for the G8 to advance on both issues, and to keep their promises – to those who need guarantees of stable energy supplies, and to those so poor that they have no electricity supplies at all.

At the end of this week, on the eve of the summit, energy ministers and specialists from around the world will be meeting at the Conference 'Energy in a Changing World' organised at UNESCO headquarters in Paris. We will debate all the interlocking problems of energy security, 'clean energy', new technologies, and the ultimate goal – sometimes seen as an impossible dream – of providing energy to the whole of humankind while mitigating climate change.

Our conference will address this conundrum. We will send a message to the G8 that sustainable energy is not a dream, and is not just for the rich. We will call on the world's richest nations to come up with new creative solutions, to share the technologies and know-how that will both reduce emissions of carbon and pollutants and bring power to those who lack it.

Germany, chairing this year's G8 Summit, has declared Africa to be one of its prime concerns. For many in that continent, the 'energy question' is literally a question of life or death. The lack of energy holds back Africa's progress in every way – it bars the development of industry, and it cuts off its people from the benefits of the IT revolution, on which much of the world has come to depend.

A cavernous gap exists between the 'energy haves' and the 'energy have-nots'. It is a long way from the bright lights of big cities in industrialised countries to the rural villages of sub-Saharan Africa. Globally, 1.6 billion people have no access to networked electricity. Of these, 535 million live in Africa. Nights in sub-Saharan Africa are dark, with almost 92 per cent of the rural population and 48 per cent of the urban population having no access to modern energy provisions.

Whilst Africa is rich in natural power sources (oil, coal, gas, but also water and sunshine), in rural areas, up to 95 per cent of energy consumption is based on the harmful and inefficient burning of biomass (wood, animal dung, crop waste). Unless drastic steps are taken, the International Energy Agency expects the number of people who rely on biomass to increase steadily.

According to estimates of non-governmental organisations, many women in rural sub-Saharan Africa carry 20 kilograms of fuel wood an average of 5 km a day. Researchers at the University of California, Berkeley and Harvard University have found that more than 1.6 million people world-wide, primarily women and children, die prematurely each year from respiratory diseases caused by the pollution from wood fires used for cooking and heating. By 2050, wood fires will release about 7 billion tons of carbon into the atmosphere – 6 per cent of Africa's total expected greenhouse gases. The transition from biomass fuels to kerosene and liquid propane gas alone could prevent 1.3 to 3.7 million premature deaths. The use of wind, solar and micro-hydropower would have further social benefits while reducing greenhouse gas emissions.

UNESCO is uniquely placed to make a valuable contribution to sustainable global energy development, taking into account the humanitarian dimension of this world-wide challenge.

The world's great energy producers cannot rest on their laurels. It is essential for new technologies and know-how to be disseminated around the world. We propose that the G8 create a system for the exchange of advanced sustainable and renewable energy technologies with the aim of enhancing energy efficiency and management and ensuring the stability of the world's energy system.

Access to energy presupposes access to energy technologies. In the next 20 years humankind must make scientific and technological breakthroughs to improve access to modern energy services for all through a wider use of environmentally sound, sustainable and renewable energy.

None of this can be achieved by any single country alone. We call upon the world's industrial champions, represented by the G8, to work together in sharing the energy for the benefit of the developing world and all humankind.

Who's left on the pipeline

From an interview with Itogi, *1 November 2007:*

International Energy Week (IEW) has taken place in Moscow, bringing together the elite of global oil and gas and energy companies, and also representatives of the authorities. The problem of energy security was at the centre of the discussion, or more specifically, the differences between suppliers and consumers of energy resources, resulting in a threat from the European Union to restrict access by outsider – primarily Russian – energy companies to its market.

Viktor Borisovich, what is the main objective of International Energy Week?

This event has acquired a special status after the G8 summit in St Petersburg, where the main focus was on energy security, and energy dialogue emerged as one of the main instruments to achieve this. Representativeness of the forum is testament to the significance our partners and the heads of corporations place on this event. For example, participation of the EU Commissioner for Energy, Andris Piebalgs, helps us to appreciate how the problem of energy security is viewed in the European Union – our main partner (three-quarters of Russian energy exports are sent to the EU – *Itogi*). Among other things we have also discussed the latest EU energy initiatives which will significantly change the shape of the market. The fact that only a month after announcing the initiative we are already in a dialogue with Brussels over this issue is evidence of our mutual understanding.

In your view, how much time does the European Union need to reach a decision? When can the new developments come into effect?

To some extent, a comparison with the procedure for adopting a new European constitution is appropriate here: the EU is ready to adopt an amended version, but in an 'easier' format. This is the fruit of compromise. I think that the energy initiatives are also complicated for discussion, because the greater part of the powers in this sphere are held by national governments, and each EU country has its own ideas on energy. For Germany, for example, which depends on the partnership with Russia, the current situation is familiar and understandable, but for others the opposite is true: they do not have long-standing connections with Moscow and are jealous of their neighbours. There are countries where large energy corporations are operating, and others that do not have such companies, so all of this leads to a complicated discussion. Within the European Union itself they estimate that a solution will be found in the second half of 2008 during the French presidency, but my experience indicates that this is an optimistic schedule. For us, the most important thing is to participate in the process of finding a solution; it is important for us to know what the consequences will be, although so far the discussion has shown that there are more questions than answers.

Will the new order have retroactive force? In other words, will our energy projects with Europe end up being reviewed?

One of the most important elements of the EU energy package is the division of assets. Furthermore, we are not talking about businesses (separating production from transport within a single company), but rather about right of ownership: assets for production and for transit should be owned by independent companies. From the legal perspective, this is a change in approach to current conditions. Another question arises, to which there is not yet an answer: if an intergovernmental agreement (duly ratified) existed, then according to the Venice Declaration it has a higher status than national or common European law. Another question is how to proceed if it is proposed to split up a company that is owned by the state. It isn't important which state – France or Russia. After all, it might not be Gazprom that is the partner in a deal, it might be, let's say, Eurogas, whose controlling stake might also be state-owned. What should we do in such a situation? This is not specific to Russia. France, Italy, Qatar have the very same problems .... According to new initiatives, states wishing to work in the EU supply network business should not only break up their companies, but also privatise them! What will Norway do in this situation? It is difficult to find EU members whose energy assets do not have state participation.

Will you put these questions to Piebalgs?

Yes, he's made a note of them. Any answers are important for us, not just good ones that we are happy with. After all, any answer provides clarity, and, conversely, the lack of an answer poses a colossal risk that we must avoid. To this end we, together with Brussels, are posing these questions and seeking answers to them peacefully, without hysterics, in spite of the fact that some commentators are perpetually trying to find an unearthed war axe in our actions.

What can Russian companies do in the absence of answers – block joint projects with the European Union?

On the contrary, they should be actively pursued. The more successfully they proceed, the easier it will be for us to take the dispute to

Brussels. There's no need to block anything! We'll operate within the framework of existing standards, while at the same time asking the European Union: what happens next? At IEW-2007 Piebalgs himself named all the important projects: Nord Stream, Burgas–Alexandroupolis, Baltic Pipeline System, South Stream. Realisation of these projects will allow us to resolve an important challenge for the European Union – diversification of supply routes for raw energy materials – and for Russia, the diversification of sales routes. In this our interests coincide. So new standards will be examined by the European Commission for these very projects.

Is this not too expensive a proving ground? Nord Stream alone costs tens of billions of dollars. And what if in a couple of years at the height of construction Brussels demands the breakup of the operating company?

This project has no analogies, and Brussels understands this fact. It is being actively realised: the first tender has been completed for the supply of pipes to the cost of €2 billion, which was won by Europipe (75 per cent) and our factories (25 per cent). In other words, Nord Stream already has obligations to suppliers. I do not believe that Brussels is full of masochists. In any case I have not seen them among our negotiating partners – there are no people there who are prepared to make an incomprehensible sacrifice of such a project as Nord Stream. In fact, it would be difficult to argue for such a decision because economic grounds do not exist for it, and ideology in Europe is out of favour in such a situation.

So the project will be carried out, come what may, which means that a decision has been made on its route. And what will the route be, taking into account that Estonia has refused to approve study of the seabed?

The Estonians have refused to discuss the route passing through their economic zone, which in my opinion is a violation of the Convention on the Law of the Sea. I am not a lawyer, but it would appear that a single country does not have the right to refuse to consider an issue. After all, there is freedom of transit under specific conditions. There is no point in politicising Nord Stream; the ecological and other risks should be discussed, along with conditions to mitigate them. Will the route be altered because of Estonia's decisions? Such an option is being developed. Incidentally, this involves ecology: at the request of the European Commission, Nord Stream is preparing a special address that will be presented at the end of the year. This is just a request, not a requirement: the European Union does not have an economic zone in the Baltic – it is shared between the countries. If there is the desire then any problem can be resolved, even a very complicated one. For example: Blue Stream has been laid at a depth of 2,300 m in the Black Sea where there is an aggressive environment – almost pure hydrogen sulphide – whereas Nord Stream is being laid at a depth of just 210 m in a far less aggressive environment. They say that the Baltic is full of unexploded ordinance. Really, so much? Why is shipping allowed then? These are technical issues, albeit complex ones, but they should not be elevated to the level of irresolvable problems. They could lead to the project being more expensive, but they can be resolved. At one time we were presented with a list of threats to construction of the oil loading terminal in Primorsk – a big fat tome – so we agreed with a lot and created the best port in the Baltic.

US Secretary of State Condoleezza Rice advised Russia not to turn its energy policy into an instrument of political extortion.

If I was an observing bystander, then I could feel indifferent about such statements. From a historical perspective, everything is clear: in a world where everything is shared, someone appears who claims their slice of the cake and intends to eat it. Of course, you'll hear the response: 'There's no point in you being here!' Incidentally, criticism directed at Russia can easily be redirected at the West. What happened in Iraq? We could talk about a victory for democracy, or we could talk about oil, and that would be the truth. So, political rhetoric and attempts to defend the interests of your investors are the normal reaction of politicians and diplomats, and are called upon the distract attention from the issue at hand.

We are getting the impression that oil companies are acting less as an independent force, and that their problems are ever more frequently being resolved at a political level.

Not a single large deal in the world passes unnoticed by the state's highest leadership. Everyone is interested in promoting their own companies, but a lot also depends on the status of bilateral relations: an international agreement needs to be signed with some partners, whereas elsewhere a verbal agreement is enough. Incidentally, the most universal formula for reducing risks is joint projects, involving the division of risks.

A joint project will probably not help where we are talking about global confrontation between sellers and buyers of energy resources.

We must not split everything into two camps – black and white. Although this is just what often happens: suppliers are completely ignored, and they advocate arranging everything so that it is good only for the consumer, but then the consumer ultimately ends up carrying all the risks. Energy is a harsh chain. If you ask a bank for credit to develop a deposit, then you must submit a plan for realising the entire project. In the gas sphere long-term contracts were always a guarantee that all the risks had been calculated. If we were to add gas because 'someone will buy it', this would inflate market prices. Here the gas and electricity markets significantly differ. Risks are of a different order in the electricity sector. It is both a consumer of raw material and at the same time a seller of energy. While you can locate a power station closer to consumers, you cannot produce gas wherever you chose.

In this regard, is draft legislation on strategic industry sectors an attempt to 'thin out' those who are allowed to develop Russian below-ground resources?

But has this stopped those who wanted to invest funds in Russian electricity? Foreigners have invested $20 billion in just the last year and will invest the same amount again over the coming nine months. I cannot see anything to suggest that they are concerned – if anything, they are fighting with each other at auctions. So the investors are supporting our case with money. In developing the draft legislation, we have been guided by international experience and common sense, and we have created the best possible document from those already existing. It is transparent. We do not have a formula, as in the United States, for rejection motivated 'in the interests of national security'. You can put an end to that phrase. And the barrier in the United States does not arise on purchasing a controlling stake, but a shareholding of just 5 per cent. Who determines the interests of national security? Correct – the president does. We do not have any prohibition at all; there is a licensing procedure for a limited list of investment areas. If there was at least one deposit in Europe that could be compared to the largest Russian deposits, then with such reserves they would declare it as pan-European wealth and would not let anyone hold it at gunpoint. Incidentally, our decisions are not taken by a single person, but by a commission. We drew up this draft legislation together with foreign investors – our colleagues on the Consultation Committee on Foreign Investments – and they involved their lawyers. What is important to investors is not a proclamatory level of deregulation, but the intelligibility of the procedure, and this is what they have received.

But you will not disagree that there are fewer foreigners in the Russian gas market? Kovykta, for example ...

I don't disagree, but there are various reasons for this. Russia has a single gas supply system, control of which the state will not hand over to anyone, ever. This is a monopoly by definition. No economy could support a multitude of such systems, and in this regard we cannot control the production process. Not a single deposit can be 'opened' without a prior long-term supply contract. Regarding Kovykta, this field will be developed pursuant to the East Gas Programme: the first stage in 2011, and the second stage in 2017.

Will Russia at some point be able to make money only on the transmission of energy resources?

Never; in fact there is no such objective. Our system should ensure diversification of routes. When we open the Eastern Siberia–Pacific Ocean oil pipeline system, we will gain the first oil transportation network to the west and east of the country, and then all that will be left to do is build on this.

Bilateral agreements and asset exchanges – are we moving towards a 'gas cartel'? A permanent secretariat of the Gas Exporting Countries Forum has been operating since April 2008.

This decision should be taken at the conference of forum ministers, which will take place in Moscow. In my view, such a proposal makes some sense, but there is a lot yet to do, for example, carrying out studies of price formation. By the way, it is already clear that the forum needs institutional development.

What should be done with agreements already in existence, such as with the Energy Charter?

The Charter was signed by 52 countries, but with the expansion of the European Union, the European Union has a majority of the signatories, so all discussions now revolve around the Russia–EU axis. A few years ago at negotiations in Brussels, the leadership of the Charter's secretariat proposed, 'Let's sign up to a protocol with any transit conditions that Russia will agree with the EU!' Clearly, the Charter was signed at the beginning of the 1990s and corresponded to the perceptions of Russia and the European Union that were current at that time. Both Russia and the European Union have since changed. We are prepared to ratify the Charter, but in a revised version that meets current realities,

Global energy issues

From an address at the Eleventh International Energy Forum, Rome, 21 April 2008:

Two years ago, at the Tenth Forum in Doha, I made an address at a session dedicated to the problems of access to energy resources. At that time I spoke about the fact that in the modern world access to energy resources should be considered from various positions, and that different focuses should be taken into consideration. We have moved away from treating this problem as simply a problem of raw materials, and now talk about the necessity of accessing technologies, capital markets, services, infrastructures and so on. Just such a multi-focus understanding of access to energy resources enables us to move to actions to reinforce global energy security and ensure sustainable economic development. This understanding, in and of itself, is already a significant addition to the results of our work.

From the presentations of colleagues from OPEC and the IEA, and studies from other respected organisations and companies (CERA [Center for Environmental Risk Assessment], the US Energy Agency, Shell and others), it is very clear that greatly differing evaluations exist today of the situation and development trends of the global energy sector. We see distinctly different evaluations of the role of renewable energy sources and nuclear energy in the global energy mix, different approaches to deregulation of energy markets, and often differing forecasts of the pricing environment. This list of differences could be expanded.

Nevertheless, almost all expert evaluations, including those presented today, contain a list of consultants whom nobody challenges.

First, the world energy sector has entered an epoch of change characterised by processes of globalisation, growth in demand for energy resources by developing economies, growing preoccupation with the problems of climate change, and problems of transition to an energy sector of the future – so the long-standing scenario of business as usual is unacceptable.

Second, it is clear today that the energy sector of the next two decades will be a combination of a stable high share of traditional energy (primarily hydrocarbons) and a constantly growing share of renewable energy sources, although these will not lay claim to the leading position for the foreseeable future. Correspondingly, the problems of the world energy sector can only be resolved by targeted systemic actions providing for improvement in the efficiency of each of these areas. It is a sort of yin and yang of the future energy sector.

Third, the world community has developed a mechanism for resolving global problems – the global energy dialogue. Its principles were formed as far as possible in the St Petersburg G8 Declaration on Energy Security, in the work on which not only G8 countries participated, but also colleagues from China, India, Brazil, Mexico as well as OPEC, the International Energy Agency (IEA) and IEF. These principles include the diversification of energy sources and transport routes, improving energy efficiency, market transparency, development of new energy sources, and the attention of the world community to problems of energy poverty and ecology.

These constants depend on changes in the global energy market, which could either accelerate or restrain events that are in essence unavoidable. However, we must take into consideration both the main risks and the special characteristics and stages of development of various energy markets and different countries. Without claiming to have the opportunity to throw light on all these aspects, at this point I would highlight the following in particular.

First, it is important not to overestimate the potential for development of renewable energy and new fuel types in the near term. Today, in many regions and countries of the world quite high aims have been set for increasing the share of renewables and new fuel types in the energy mix. Furthermore, some of the countries are putting forth the corresponding efforts, providing state financial support not only to studies aimed at creating this field of new technologies, which is fully justified, but also at the allocation of investment support to the use of these technologies (including the production of other sectors of the economy, for example agriculture in the production of biofuel). In this way the real economic environment is being distorted and the market is getting biased signals.

In essence, an attempt is being made to solve a market problem by non-market instruments, which results in an increase in the cost of energy, and problems in associated sectors.

In addition, the fact is often ignored that renewables have a complex structure. This applies to all of solar energy, biofuel and hydro resources. Therefore, different countries have a fundamentally different potential for developing renewables. So, in Russia we put an emphasis on developing both large-scale and small-scale hydropower. Along with a range of 'traditional hydropower' we are developing a new area, which includes the planned construction of powerful tidal power stations.

Second, a serious risk is posed by the resource-related uncertainty of traditional (primarily hydrocarbon) energy.

Russia believes the transparency of world energy markets to be a highly important condition for the stable development of the world economy. Furthermore, the extent of deregulation of regimes of below-ground resource use and the level of transparency of geological information in any particular country depends both on the level of their socio-economic development and on the level of protectionism of their energy companies.

We consider it to be simply ineffective, and consequently irrational, to create political barriers to the route to investments and to apply duplicitous standards in this sphere. We are trying to make our legislation as transparent, understandable, and naturally in keeping with national interests, as possible. For this reason the new Russian law on foreign investments in strategic sectors is substantially less regulated and more transparent than many of its Western counterparts.

Transnational companies are operating in Russia and also hold significant shareholdings in Russian companies. In addition, foreign companies together with Russian ones are realising a whole series of joint projects; an exchange of assets between Russian and foreign oil and gas companies and the creation of joint ventures are becoming effective instruments for development.

In our opinion, the reciprocal inclusion of capital allows risks to be divided, including resource-related uncertainty, increases the responsibility of corporations for efficient resource use, and creates a solid basis for long-term mutually advantageous cooperation.

Third, and perhaps the most discussed, is the application of integration and disintegration structural instruments in the energy sector. Every time we follow a route of splitting energy companies. or on the contrary merging them into unified ones, we face the risk of adopting an ineffective decision. In our country we have come to the following understanding in the area of electricity; separating electricity generation from the grid component allows us to increase the efficiency of generating electricity and attract significant volumes of investment funds.

At the same time, gas companies operating on the basis of long-term contracts that provide stability to the gas market in the event of their disintegration, will not be able to realise highly capital-intensive projects which are accompanied by enormous risks. Particularly hazardous is the adoption of insufficiently thought-through structural decisions under conditions of growth of the share of natural gas in the fuel mix in many regions of the world over the coming decades. We believe the most effective route for development of the gas market is development of the LNG segment, whose share in the future will grow to up to 30 per cent. This sector will provide price signals for the traditional pipeline gas market.

Fourth, the most serious risk zone is price fluctuations on energy product markets. Prices are pushed up by very different factors, from the fundamental ratio of global demand and supply, to military and political factors and conditions on the world currency market.

Without delving into a multifaceted analysis of the causes of price volatility and the methodology of price formation, I would like simply to turn our attention to the important role played by cost-push inflation in the oil and gas sector. Prices are rising for metal, engineering services, freight and so on, and the upward cost trend underlies and often surpasses the oil trend. Unfortunately, in this area we do not yet see the development of a free and competitive market that could facilitate a reduction in associated expenditure and ultimately in oil prices. In this way the risk of price instability is to a great extent derived from excessive monopolisation of the service sector, and this, in our opinion, is a serious cause for concern and taking appropriate measures.

Fifth, in many of the areas identified at the St Petersburg Summit significant projects are already being realised, including in Russia or with Russia's participation. Principles of diversification, division of risks and exchange of assets lie at the foundation of such projects as Nord Stream and South Stream, Burgas–Alexandroupolis and the Caspian Coastal Pipeline. Deregulation reform in our country is almost complete and a transition is under way to world gas prices. Energy dialogue mechanisms are functioning successfully: for example, the energy dialogue between Russia and the European Union. Work under the auspices of the Gas Exporting Countries Forum (GECF) is moving to a new level. One of the most striking examples of a global energy project embodying the principles of the St Petersburg Declaration is the ITER project for construction of a thermonuclear reactor in France with a perspective to 2050.

Nevertheless, current practice has shown that co-operation mechanisms developed over the last two to three years have proved to be insufficiently effective. We have all learned to talk the language of global energy security; however, each of us often continues to scatter its principles through the prism of 'national parlance' to acquire new or protect old advantages. New understanding and new knowledge are generally used as arguments in a fight, and not in co-operation, and the newspaper headlines on many of our meetings are reminiscent of briefings from the field of war.

The results of energy dialogues are interpreted in terms of new challenges and threats, even though there is an abundance of willingness for conflict in such a complex and resource-intensive sector as the energy sector, which is riddled with excessive costs. So it is not worth being surprised at what is occurring on the energy markets – price fluctuations, the increasing gulf between energy-poor and energy-rich countries, gradual 'erosion' of a number of very important global projects, such as Kyoto.

In our opinion, energy wars are futile and they have no victors. It is time to take a decisive step in the direction of 'energy peace' and start to turn the understanding that has been achieved into real sustainable structures of future world energy. Therefore, we are participating in an exchange of energy assets in the oil and gas sector and in the creation of new routes for supplying resources to the markets. Today in the energy sector, we are actively developing certain types of renewable energy, in particular, tidal power stations, and tomorrow in the energy sector we will be participating in the realisation of high-tech thermonuclear projects. This is the future of energy.

If the energy sector faces entering 'turbulence', as we often hear, then we must overcome it and not deviate from the primary course to improve global energy security.

Epilogue

I am writing this epilogue in the summer of 2012, about four years after the issues and events described in this Part of the book. In retrospect, I can see the consequences and lessons of the period of activity and the subjects raised in the book. Let me highlight some of the more significant themes that have already been and, in my opinion, should be refined. I shall separate them arbitrarily, in the same manner as the text, into two parts: domestic and foreign policy in the energy sphere. I shall start with domestic policy.

I was able to work at that time in the role of the energy minister, but the government of Russia did not include a Ministry for Energy,

V. B. Khristenko with his associates A. G. Reus and A. Dementyev

and the Ministry of Industry and Energy 'stewed in a single pot' state regulation in the spheres of energy and industry, and indeed many others, at the same time as ensuring normal current functioning of the sectors and maintaining oversight of the realisation of large 'breakthrough' development projects. This is in our country, where we have a nine-month heating season, three months of maintenance of networks and equipment, and a perpetual *force majeure* situation in the utilities sphere. Furthermore, large-scale energy development projects were being prepared and implemented, and in the new situation of the Ministry of Industry and Energy we were forced to discuss and co-ordinate these with all interested federal subjects and take into consideration their substantially differing positions.

If I compare the work of the Ministry of Industry and Energy with the work of restoring infrastructure which I performed in the position of deputy prime minister, it leads me to view infrastructure projects from a different perspective. It is always more effective to trade in a deficit commodity. However, when sellers of a deficit commodity turn out to be its consumers, then their interest in trading in the deficit commodity soon disappears. In my new position, I had to resolve the challenge of making the infrastructure accessible and convenient, and not scarce and expensive. Transneft is an example. As a result there was more transportation capacity than oil supplied to the system. This is what my team achieved. Therefore, the challenge of achieving fair access to pipelines, which during the previous stage was important, had now, in the grand scheme of things, become meaningless: anyone could come and get it. Whereas previously this had to be dealt with at a government level, in the new situation everything started to move to a corporate level, as it should.

Generally speaking, current functioning in the energy sector should have now rested on an effective corporate level, while the Ministry of Industry and Energy performed the function of overseer of the processes of energy development. We needed oversight as a means of retaining everything that we had obtained 'in the single pot', so the system wasn't torn up, but, during this period it was necessary to develop and start realising the toughest projects aimed at energy development. In the scale of things, this was all clearly no less significant than the Government Plan for the Electrification of Russia.

An overseer should understand what is happening in the processes subject to them and have an accurate picture of their arrangement. They need a continuously functioning communication platform in order to achieve this. While retaining strategic aims, they manage deviations, monitor undesirables, and seek out instruments of non-invasive influence on them. What exactly do I mean? There were many projects in the oil scene: the Baltic Pipeline System, ESPO oil pipeline system and others. In the gas sector there were Nord Stream and South Stream. I remember how I spent months in an aircraft. The gas market model was also developed during this period. A full-fledged oil transportation system was created, which became not simply a natural monopoly, but firmly connected the entire country. These were systemic projects that will determine the face of the energy sphere for hundreds of years. Our position was that we were not the developers of these individual projects, but were in a place where we could see the whole picture and where it was possible to monitor and oversee the spheres of the energy sector as a single whole.

We did not allow opportunities for misalignments to arise, and will did not allow the developers to deviate from course. The first phase of construction had to be the first phase and it absolutely had to end with something, and the second phase had to be the second phase. When working with these projects we tried to incorporate in them the interests not only of the oil and gas personnel, but also of the transporters, and then the pipeline workers and metallurgists. Then we tried to unify the capabilities of these projects with the objectives of the domestic positioning: both to have access to the ocean and to reach China, and at the same time to develop further manufacturing operations – to place a small factory at the end of the pipeline for it to deliver chemical products. In addition to resolving problems arising between business enterprises, we had to resolve conflicts that arose between administration units.

One situation was unique in its level of stress, when we were engaged in synchronising and harmonising relations between suppliers of hydrocarbons, electricity producers and the consumers of gas and electricity. It became an acute problem when energy industry personnel undertook reform. The metallurgists were the first in this, particularly the non-ferrous metallurgists, who realised that they did not only need to demand some sort of tariff, but they had to be active participants in the reform. And the gas personnel, seeing the situation with the reform of Russian Joint Stock Power Engineering and Electrification Company, said, 'Well, well, well, they are implementing reform there, and considering deregulation, setting themselves up, and we are paying for it all. Let's do our own deregulation!' And then the gas exchange market emerged, and spot and futures contracts appeared. On this basis the gas personnel started knocking the wind out of the electricity producers. What are you planning on building there? Where will you get the gas from? We haven't got any gas for you. And why would we provide you with gas at domestic prices at a loss, when we can sell it into Europe through Nord Stream?

I cannot boast that we at the Ministry of Industry and Energy were able to contain all of these situations, but we managed to create a platform on which we could build communication between all the participants, understanding on which site we wanted to build (to create a sort of pseudo board of directors) and that if we didn't all get stuck into building on this site, then we would not achieve anything at all. The participants had to realise that by being included in this virtual corporation, they would gain 2 or 5 per cent influence. If they were not included, then there would be a rupture of minus 2 per cent. The most interesting things occurred when this concept started to acquire its own legal anchor in the form of standards and regulations. Then the biggest fight started, and it is at its hottest today. The fight for regulations is still being waged.

A recent situation at the St Petersburg Economic Forum (June 2012) reminded me of a situation in the area of foreign policy. I was participating in a discussion that had evolved at a business round table meeting of Russia and the European Union which was moderated by the former prime minister of Finland, Esko Aho. While summing up, he posed a question to each of the participants in the discussion: what would they have done if today they had been in the place of their counterpart on the other side? In my case, that counterpart was José Manuel Barroso. This question took me back many years. Relations between Russia and the European Union at the beginning of the current century presented a full and convoluted story. Over the course of a few years I was responsible in government for these relations, in which regard I was even given the nickname 'Minister of Europe'. Regular meetings of partners from both sides sometimes resembled a reading to everyone of well-known texts containing reciprocal demands from one to other: from big to small, and even tiny suppliers of Finnish eggs and lynx pelts. I once even told Chris Patten, the 'Minister for Russia' (in his role as European Commissioner for External Relations; earlier he was the last British governor of Hong Kong), let's exchange files, after all we are well aware of what arguments they contain. It was obvious that it was impossible to try seriously to build relations on such a basis. We could not repeatedly discuss these petty dead-end issues without trying to construct a project plan of co-operation of the parties with a strategic perspective. A long-term megaproject was needed. If no such project exists, then it's impossible to know in which direction you are moving, and why you are doing all of this. Are you being carried along on the wave of the situation? If you try to manage the situation, then you should set out a project and find consensus for its realisation among all the interested parties. Then you will have a different approach to the small issues: either you resolve them, or you pass them by as being insignificant and don't waste your energy on them.

The project of the Four Common Spaces started to emerge: the Common Economic Space; the Common Space of Freedom, Security and Justice; the Common Space of External Security; and the Common Space of Research, Education and Culture. Permanently active dialogues started to be built within them. The scope of building the Common Economic Space included trade, investment, energy, industrial, regulatory and other dialogues – more than a dozen in total. They were conducted by ministers, and I, as a deputy prime minister, supervised these discussions and also conducted the energy dialogue, a limited part of which became a megaproject in the area of energy – a single energy space. It must be emphasised that the energy dialogue had special significance in relations between Russian and the European Union, and was particularly sensitive. The lion's share of our trade relations are composed of energy. We have a current situation in which we both hold a kind of controlling stake – the European Union for consumers, and Russia for the suppliers.

Energy is the area in which the level of propensity for conflict is extremely high, yet on the other hand mutual dependency is very deep, with 'mutual' being the key concept, and this is what represents the relationship between Russia and Europe. Both they and we are absolutely linked in this issue, which is why this space should be more progressive than the Common Economic Space, and we should be moving towards a single energy space.

Here, I must clearly define what I mean by 'common' and what is 'single'. What I am talking about is not a 'common space' so much as a 'single space'. 'Single' means a single set of standards for participants, not just a common set, meaning they are applied uniformly, in one place for all and directly effective for all participants. A single set of institutions are needed to regulate and maintain these standards, and so that all elements of democracy are observed. Romano Prodi (president of the European Commission) even proposed creating a European-Russian energy parliament that would organisationally and institutionally maintain these processes. This has been discussed in a very narrow format, but at the level of key people. We were fortunate: at a European level during that period our partners were some of the best specialists in their field, François Lamoureux (head of the Directorate-General for Transport and Energy) and of course a leader such as Romano Prodi (a creative man with philosophical thinking). For me this project was a dream. Even if it had been only halfway realised, then that would have had a colossal effect.

The political landscape changed noticeably after 2004. A change of priorities occurred in Europe and in the leadership team, and everything gradually ground to a halt. In the European Commission, the main objective was now expanding the European Union, and that is chalk and cheese. More than 20 new countries appeared on the 'field' who all had big demands of the Soviet Union, and now of Russia, and they started pursuing them on all fronts: from what happened in the 1940s to 'why was I short changed on gas yesterday?' Big projects for the long term were replaced with ad hoc behaviour, which was determined by the reaction of new EU members to Russia's actions. As a result, everyone lost out. Russia continued to develop relations with the grandees – Germany, France and Italy – which provoked yet further bitterness on the part of the neophytes. Now, in relation to Russia, Europe thinks more often in categories of 30 minutes, not 30 years. Basically, petty thinking cannot help to progress a big project. If when you have the power and hold the position of a high-level manager, you are not able to develop and realise a development plan, or to think in terms of long-term strategic projects, then you cannot hold such a position.

Let me return to my reply to Esko Aho's question at the St Petersburg Economic Forum of 2012. First and foremost, today I would secure a mandate for the European Commission to conduct negotiations with Russia on the basis of a new framework agreement, which would include one project from the past, namely the one that was included in the Russian–European agenda at the beginning of the 2000s. It is not merely the conclusion of formation of the Common Economic Space, but the formation of a single set of rules in the most important sectors of the economy, and in particular in the energy sector. That was the ambition ten years ago. Returning to it would allow us to create a mode of strategic co-operation not for 30 minutes, but for 30 years in advance.

The world is becoming more complex, and today another serious partner of the European Commission has appeared in negotiations, in which it can view itself not merely as the small entity it was in 1957, but as a great bloc in 2030. Therefore, this European mandate should take into account the new realities – the functioning of a Eurasian economic commission and plans for the creation of a Eurasian Union.

Part IV
Airplanes Come First

Principles and Plans for the
Implementation of Industrial Policies
and Development Strategies at the
Russian Ministry of Industry and
Energy and the Russian Ministry
of Industry and Trade, 2004–12

V. B. Khristenko

In the cockpit of the Sukhoi Superjet 100

In lieu of an epigraph: 'from the sewers to space'

... To establish the Ministry of Industry and Energy of the Russian Federation, which shall assume all functions related to adopting regulatory and legal acts in the designated spheres of activity of the abolished Ministry of Industry, Science and Technology of the Russian Federation (except functions related to the field of science); the Ministry of Energy of the Russian Federation; the Ministry of Atomic Energy of the Russian Federation; the Russian Munitions Agency; the Russian Conventional Arms Agency; the Russian Agency for Management Systems; the Russian Shipbuilding Agency; the Russian Federal Supervisory Authority for Mining and Industry, which is to be reorganised; the Russian Federal Supervisory Authority for Nuclear and Radiation Safety; and the State Committee of the Russian Federation for Standardisation and Metrology, the State Committee of the Russian Federation for Construction and the Housing and Utilities Complex, and the Russian Aviation and Space Agency, which are also to be reorganised.

From the RF Presidential Decree of 9 March 2004, 'On the System and Structure of Federal Executive Authorities'

...To transform the Ministry of Industry and Energy of the Russian Federation into the Ministry of Industry and Trade of the Russian Federation and the Ministry of Energy of the Russian Federation, with the appropriate delineation of functions between these ministries.

The Ministry of Industry and Trade of the Russian Federation shall assume all functions of the reorganised Ministry of Economic Development and Trade of the Russian Federation related to developing state policy and the regulatory and legal framework for trade.

Technical regulation and metrology shall fall under the authority of the Ministry of Industry and Trade of the Russian Federation...

From the RF Presidential Decree of 12 May 2008, 'On the System and Structure of Federal Executive Authorities'

Introduction

This book traces my many years of experience in public service, including positions in the Russian Government, particularly as head of the Ministry of Industry and Energy (2004–08) and head of the Ministry of Trade and Industry (2008–12). Within the federal executive branch, these agencies were responsible for developing and implementing industrial policy.

The most important management principle that my teachers taught me to rely on – sorting, extracting and accumulating the experience of personal victories and defeats – requires that we regularly and continuously process, interpret and apply this experience to subsequent actions. Therefore, this book is a compilation of materials taken from what metallurgists would call the 'first processing stage', effectively providing an outline of the work that was done over that eight-year period.

'Learn by doing'

I think an essential feature of my experience is that it was gained using a method held up to scorn by the great German Chancellor Bismarck: 'learning from your own mistakes'. This was because I was mostly dealing with things that no one had done before, and thus there was no way for me to learn from other people's mistakes.

This is by no means a matter of petty vanity or coquettishness about my own courage in the class struggle. This is simply a statement of fact regarding the situation in which we and the country found ourselves.

Every situation and every task that I received from the president and the prime minister was unique and unparalleled in the history of governance in Russia or abroad. Each demanded unique treatment and comprehensive analysis, as well as discussion and agreement with a large number of interested parties, including the political, financial and economic forces that backed them. On top of all this, there was the problem of relations with the various people representing these forces.

Yet it is these very complexities, and the very high risks associated with them, that were and remain for me the most attractive aspect of public administration. You are likely to get as much adrenaline from this kind of activity as if you were hunting or diving into the sea during a storm.

The most important feature of the economic management system of the Russian Federation in 2004 was a movement away from sectoral fragmentation (in Soviet times, dozens of different ministries, under the guidance of the State Planning Committee, had been responsible for controlling budget allocations), as well as a need to take a systemic approach using appropriate management tools. The energy, industry and finance sectors needed to work together harmoniously, regardless of which persons or forces claimed managerial authority. In order to enter growth and development mode, however, it was essential for the state to promote large projects and radical reforms without harming the efficient operation of the country's basic financial and economic infrastructure.

Our management team had considerable experience in solving similar problems, but we faced a difficult task: to convey our view of the situation to a majority of ministry employees, to the higher authorities, and to our partners and opponents. We had to change the mindsets, forms of communication and mutual organisation of numerous executives, professionals and experts, and thus change their ability to solve the tasks at hand.

We had to do this difficult job not just in a single instant, once and for all, but constantly, returning to it again and again in every decision-making situation and every discussion about new strategies and projects. This brings to mind an ancient Chinese curse: 'May your children live in interesting times.'

The impact of our core principles consistently shows through in the interviews, report abstracts and other documents presented here.

Industrial policy

During the Soviet era, industrial policy, which consisted of an assortment of strategic and operational methods, as well as means of direct management of industrial enterprises by the authorities, formed an integral part of the system of state management of the country's economy.

As soon as Russia embarked on market reforms, however, this industrial policy was rejected – intellectually, theoretically and in practice. For more than 10 years, industrial policy in the form of goal-oriented regulation of the industrial sector of the economy was effectively absent from the activity of the Russian state. In the early twenty-first century, industrial policy was partially rehabilitated – you could once again speak of it in positive terms, and this was not met with an immediate rebuff. Then, around the middle of the last decade, industrial policy became an officially recognised, basic type of government activity.

In the USSR, the state directly managed all energy-related and industrial assets through the authorities of the executive branch. Given the high level of centralisation of political power and financial and material resources, industrial policy mostly consisted in monitoring the implementation of decisions made at the very top. In those days too, however, there was intense competition among industries and sectors to be the state's primary focus, as this would ensure prioritised allocation of resources. This competition mostly occurred behind the scenes, hidden from public view, so it came across not so much as politics, which by its very nature is the result of competing interests, but rather as an assortment of ready-made solutions and prescriptions given to businesses from the top down.

Industrial policy in the full and precise sense of the term arises and becomes necessary when there are multiple authorities claiming to exercise management functions. No one can make decisions unilaterally, and it is necessary to begin the process of negotiations, approvals and the development of co-ordinated decisions that take into account the positions of all interested parties.

Reflecting on why industrial policy was forced to pass through a double helix, I eventually came to the conclusion that this was probably the result of interaction between differently directed factors.

The first factor was subjective: the radicalism of a substantial number of the people who had laid the intellectual and theoretical foundations of Russia's reforms, translated them into the language of regulatory acts and management decisions, and converted them into practical actions by the authorities. This involved a sincere, deep reassessment of former views, an intellectual epiphany, accompanied by a thirst for quick solutions and immediate trans-formations. As a result, the baby was often thrown out with the bathwater, and approaches, methods and management tools that practice later showed to be viable and fruitful were declared obsolete and basically wrong.

One such baby that got thrown out was industrial policy in the sense of the state's active and centralised influence on processes taking place in spheres of industry and energy. The removal of indus-trial policy from the state's management arsenal happened largely for ideological reasons. From the very beginning of the reforms, the prevailing opinion, not only within the expert community but also among a significant number of businesspeople, industrialists and officials, including those at a high level and a very high level, was that any attempts by the state to influence the development of industry were superfluous and even harmful. It was considered almost an axiom that properly implemented institutional reforms and the creation of a healthy business climate were all that was needed in order to ensure that domestic industry achieved rapid and steady development and a new, innovation-based quality of growth, and that it would become competitive in both the domestic and international markets.

The development of a negative attitude towards industrial policy was also exacerbated by the fact that the state's activity in the sphere of industrial management in the 1990s was basically reduced to granting subsidies and preferences to certain enterprises that had managed to 'extract' the relevant government decision. This was done in isolation from, and sometimes even contrary to, the long-term interests of domestic industry, divorced from the realities of the Russian and global economies.

The second factor was objective. By the middle of the first decade of the new century, the term 'industrial policy' had gradually ceased to be a bugbear. The attitude towards industrial policy had changed for the better, both within business circles and among the regulatory and administrative authorities.

To be honest, however, the legitimacy and effectiveness of industrial policy as a government tool for managing the development of the country's industry and energy sector – as a form of active state influence on the economy – is not accepted by everyone even today. Industrial policy has its opponents, some of whom are convinced and intractable. They can be found among academics and specialists, as well as within business circles, including some senior executives at major companies. It also has opponents within the government. Nevertheless, a fundamental shift did occur in people's minds, in the policy arena and in the state's management activity.

This was facilitated by the following objective processes:

◆ Success in achieving macro-economic stabilisation (the main goal of the state's economic policy, consistently pursued by the Russian Government). The public coffers now had resources that the state could afford to use not only for meeting the country's immediate needs, but also for implementing strategic programmes and long-term projects.
◆ The state's implementation of a number of measures aimed at regulating the fuel and energy complex, which, on the one hand convincingly demonstrated the effectiveness of state regulation of specific sectors and industries, and on the other, created an opportunity to redistribute investment resources to other sectors, including the processing industry.

◆ Positive changes in Russian industry (strong players emerged in many industries, creating innovation, using modern management techniques and producing competitive goods).

Experience has shown that institutional reforms and the creation of a favourable macro-economic climate alone are not enough to effect the structural changes and technological modernisation needed by domestic industry. These factors must be supplemented by real and effective state involvement in solving structural, innovation and investment-related challenges. In other words, they must be supplemented by industrial policy measures.

This conclusion is supported by the experience of many other nations that have dealt with, or are currently dealing with, challenges comparable to the one that Russia now faces. In countries with emerging markets, where the authorities prefer not to intervene in the economy, national companies are losing the competitive struggle to large companies from leading nations and transnational corporations, since the latter have far greater human, technological, industrial and financial resources. Meanwhile, countries that have pursued a policy of regulating industry (such as Japan, South Korea, Taiwan and China) have achieved considerable success in developing their industries, especially the high-tech sectors.

Thus, by 2004 it was clear that Russia had reached the point where its existing potential for dynamic growth had basically been exhausted. In order to move forward with confidence, achieve the high targets we have set, and approach the level of economic and social development of leading nations within a historically acceptable timeframe, we need to diversify the economy and make industry – especially the processing sectors – the main engine of economic growth. This means transitioning industry to an innovation-based type of development and effecting the structural changes that will make industry a dynamically developing and competitive sector of the Russian economy. This is the essence, purpose and substance of the Russian state's industrial policy.

A systemic approach

What prompted me to take up the pen? I suppose I had two main motives. First of all, the realisation that industrial policy is too important an issue for the country and for society to allow any lingering confusion in terms of approaches, principles and methods, or any insufficiency or inconsistency of information concerning the decisions that were taken. Industrial policy ultimately affects every family, even if only indirectly. This is, so to speak, the social orientation of this book. One might say that it performs the function of an information bridge between the state and society, without which the citizenry cannot really control the authorities. But there is also a second impetus, no less significant and powerful for me. I have worked in the executive branch at various levels and in various posts for over 20 years. Before becoming head of the Ministry of Industry and Energy, I was in charge of finance, economics and infrastructure as deputy prime minister of the Russian Federation. Because of the way events transpired, I was very often forced to create and refine plans, models and instruments of state administration under new conditions.

It cannot be said that my colleagues and I started completely from scratch. We carefully studied foreign best practices. We had at our disposal the know-how of Russian academics and specialists. I would especially like to point out the theory of organisation, production and management developed from the 1960s to the 1980s by G. P. Shchedrovitsky and his students. This Russian school was ahead of its time. Its theories came in very handy during the era of reforms. They became a reliable support for us in developing the tools we needed to solve problems posed by the practice of management.

But neither our team nor the country as a whole had any ready-made formulas for solving specific problems. The search for solutions, the complexity of the problems that arise, the need to remain highly creative, and finally the very realisation that all of these efforts will materialise and become concrete, tangible, positive changes in the management system and in the economy as a whole, remain for me the most attractive aspect of government activity. As a result, we accumulated a wealth of experience in designing tools to manage complex economic systems and applying these tools to managerial work at a high, national level.

Today we can see quite clearly that it was this systemic approach, which essentially consisted of improving the state's managerial role in the economy, that made it possible first to curb and then to overcome the problems associated with blind faith in the creative power of the market's 'invisible hand'. I do not think this faith is completely unfounded. It is just that markets differ. The Russian

Figure 4.1 Stages of implementation of Russian industrial policy

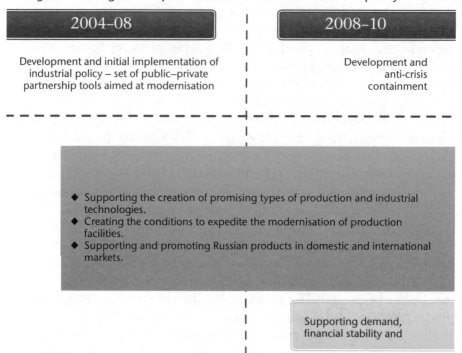

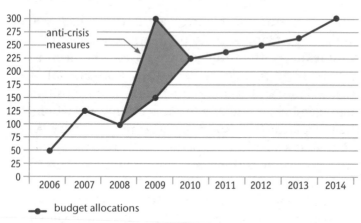

Expenditure of the Russian Ministry of Trade and Industry and the Russian Ministry of Industry and Trade (civilian industries) (in RUB billion)

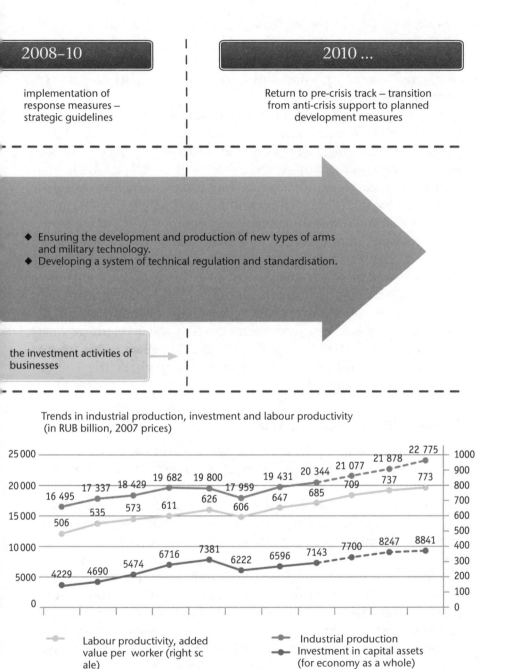

2008–10

implementation of
response measures –
strategic guidelines

2010 …

Return to pre-crisis track – transition
from anti-crisis support to planned
development measures

◆ Ensuring the development and production of new types of arms
and military technology.
◆ Developing a system of technical regulation and standardisation.

the investment activities of
businesses

Trends in industrial production, investment and labour productivity
(in RUB billion, 2007 prices)

Labour productivity, added
value per worker (right sc
ale)

Industrial production
Investment in capital assets
(for economy as a whole)

market, especially in the 1990s, was a nascent market, and therefore to a large extent a wild one. Only the state could stem the tide of market elements, which like any elemental force carried an inherent destructive charge, and turn this into a civilised market capable of constructive activity.

In addressing the issues of industrial development and growth, we could not overlook reforming the energy sector. In solving problems and promoting projects related to reorganising the aircraft industry, we could not have got by without developments in the area of technical regulation. Laying long-distance pipelines required extremely complex financial planning, along with estimates of the reserves that might fill these pipelines. In order to achieve growth and development, we needed to ensure that a variety of projects were moved forward under the auspices of the state. In some cases, this meant maintaining the growth of existing major companies (such as Gazprom and Rosneft); in others, it meant reforming the natural monopolies based on a wide variety of models (such as reforms of the electric power sector accompanied by the gradual disintegration of RAO UES of Russia); and in others still it meant creating major industry-specific companies (such as the United Aircraft Corporation, UAC).

Organising collective work

The main problem lay in agreeing on the delineation of activity between the Ministry of Industry and Energy and the Ministry of Industry and Trade, developing a common understanding of the situation, goals and operating methods among all their employees, and conveying our assessments and approaches to the higher authorities, our allies and partners, but also to our opponents.

When I say 'conveying', I mean not only informing them of our position, but also ensuring that they understand it. They do not have to agree with it, but they definitely need to understand it. This is extremely important, since many problems arise out of misconceptions and are therefore very difficult to solve. At the same time, we should realise that work on establishing intradepartmental, interdepartmental and extradepartmental communication must be done gradually. It is necessary to come back to it almost constantly, since realities change, and consequently so do our positions, along with the positions of our partners and opponents.

Thus, in order to fulfil the task of reorganising the activities of approximately 12 former industry-specific departments (in Soviet times there were 19 Union ministries), it was necessary:

◆ **to create a unifying 'platform'** in the form of a specific system of values, principles, and mechanisms for industrial policy and managing its implementation;
◆ **to convey a well-developed vision of the scope of activity** not only to Ministry employees but also to everyone with whom we would have to collaborate and interact;
◆ **to prepare a package of documents and plans** that anyone involved in our joint work would be able to use for their **self-organisation** and subsequent managerial actions.

What does it mean to organise a major joint undertaking? It means the totality of negotiations, discussions, meetings, seminars and specially designed game scenarios, in the course of which something objectified emerges: **programmes, projects, plans for collaboration, and mechanisms for adopting the appropriate decisions**.

This is all the work consists of; it may seem mundane at first glance, but it is actually creative, innovative, inspiring and at the same time exhausting.

How this part of the book is arranged

The materials collected in this part of the book are illustrations of the solutions we came up with from 2004 to 2012. I decided to present only the main documents and organisational and operational diagrams. The texts of the speeches, reports and interviews outline the framework of our activity, which consists of persistent and steadfast adherence to adopted and declared principles.

For each area of our activity I have selected materials in such a way as to show how we planned to fulfil our objectives – what we inherited, which actions we planned and implemented, and where we stand today. The main goal here is to demonstrate the productivity of our 'bureaucratic work' and show how we made the transition from theoretical strategising and planning to actually implementing the ideas that were outlined in our strategies and plans – how we worked with these ideas and moved things forward.

Figure 4.2 Long-term priorities of the Russian Federation's industrial policy

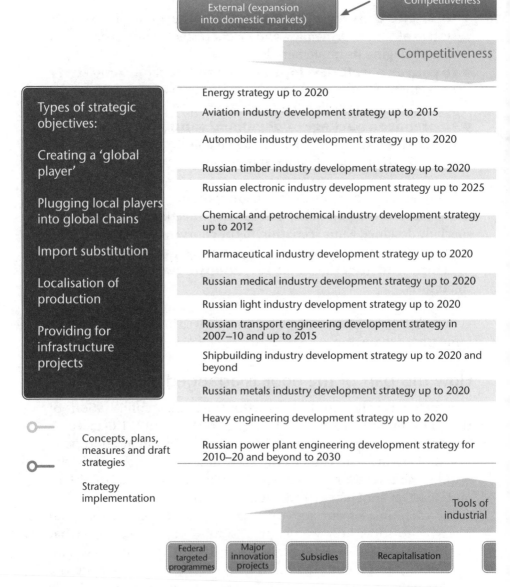

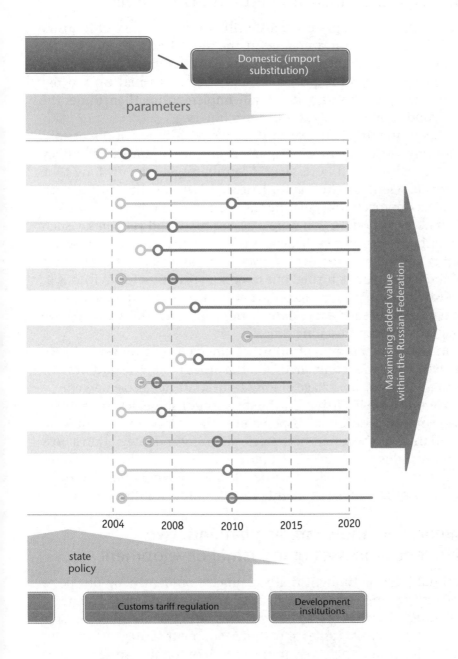

Strategy as an instrument of industrial policy

My change of workplace – transferring to the Ministry of Industry and Energy – meant a change in the areas I was responsible for managing and in the general scope of my activity. I had to make a transition from the principles and strategies I had worked out during the previous stage to actually implementing them under the real conditions of state executive machinery.

I spent my first half-year in this new post in urgent discussions with my government colleagues about 'what industrial policy means and why is it necessary?' I cannot forget how my long-time comrade, German Gref, an ardent supporter of the institutional, indirect approach to regulating the economy, said in the heat of an argument, 'I thought you were a decent man, and yet you say such rubbish... I do not even believe it is you saying it.' Now this seems rather amusing. At the time, however, it was a real battle. The heat of these discussions turned out to be somewhat useful. Without it, we would not have managed in that relatively short period of time to put together such a toolkit for action, and everything would have dragged on for quite a long time.

In the end a ranking of priorities emerged, and we were able to see why 'airplanes come first'.[1] On the other hand, the outlines of a plan for creating a package of long-term strategies also emerged.

We must dwell further on the question of strategies, since there are people in positions of responsibility these days who get the idea, when they see the results of strategic planning and integration across certain industries, that developing a strategy inevitably requires corporate integration, and they decide that applying similar arrangements to other industries might produce similar results there as well.

Integration and strategic planning: two different processes of industrial development

It should not be thought that the process of identifying prospects and setting long-term goals – in other words, the process of strategic planning – inevitably leads to the integration of an industry. This is not the case. We came up with development strategies for many industries where there was no need for corporate restructuring at

---

1   Translator's note: An allusion to the popular song 'Migratory birds' by Soviet composer Vasily Soloviev-Sedoy.

all: non-ferrous metals, for example. We did not seek to consolidate the aluminium industry. The same is true of iron and steel, pharmaceuticals and the timber industry.

Our task was not to bring about corporate integration at any cost. Our task was to outline prospects and prepare a development strategy. For each industry there were generally two effective players: the actual authorities that set about strategic planning, and the private sector, which was either present in the industry or virtually absent. Consequently where there was a private sector, we needed to manage the industry, not run it, since there were already players on the field who did their own goal setting. Of all their existing goals, we needed to select the ones that did not contradict or compete with each other but created a mutual synergy and were consistent with a national goal. After all, a unified goal, with shared risks and pooled opportunities, is the essence of strategy, and most importantly, the implementation thereof. We might provisionally call this the 'integration of goals', but it does not mean the physical integration of corporate bodies. In the latter case we would have had to undertake the integration of not only goals but also everything else as well: risks, responsibility, and resources.

Only a few of those 14 industries for which we developed strategies required corporate integration. These included three subsectors of the aircraft industry: airplanes, helicopters and engines, which simply cannot survive on the Russian domestic market. They need a global market and major sales volumes in order to succeed as high-tech industries. The Chinese are fortunate in this sense. Their domestic market can support at least a monopoly structure, if not a competitive one, in the aircraft industry.

For a number of industries the subject of corporate integration was completely irrelevant, since as it turned out, the subsequent fate of these industries was connected not so much with mergers and acquisitions within the country as with their development as transnational industries from the outset. They had already started making acquisitions outside the country, in the global market. That, after all, is how the market works. This is the trend in the aluminium business, as well as among producers of other non-ferrous metals: gold, copper and so on. The situation is slightly different but quite similar among iron and steel producers. They now need to be connected to the markets and hold on to the finishing processing stages in these markets.

Integration of finisher and assembly industries at the global level

The need for integration and structural reforms when formulating development strategies generally arose in relation to those assets that were considered strategic – that is, the ones that were off limits to privatisation, were under state management, and had reached the end of the road in terms of their development and financial position. No one had got around to reforming them, yet they were on the brink of collapse. Structural reforms in this case relied on state-owned assets, although there were also some private minority shareholders. In every story of integration, however, private shareholders accounted for only a minimal percentage.

We needed to reconfigure the state-owned assets that the bureaucrats would not exempt from strategic status but at the same time did not know what to do with, and that had long been part of globalised business areas. For these industries, strategic planning had to be accompanied by processes of corporate reform. That is how United Shipbuilding Corporation (USC), the United Aircraft Corporation (UAC), the United Engine Corporation (UEC) and Russian Helicopters came into being, with elements of private participation. In other words, integrated structures emerged as a result of the development of strategies when it became clear that a strategy could not be implemented without structural reforms and integration.

When the elaborated strategies enabled us to see the situation clearly, it turned out that structural reforms were also be needed for the purpose of dismantling certain already established structures. They had mostly been built according to the principles of vertical integration, where a corporation tried to keep a grip on everything, from mining ore to the finished product – all types of technology and know-how, as well as all types of processing. Consequently, any airplane or engine within such a structure will always be precious, since you have to keep everything at your disposal in order to make it. Obviously this airplane will not be in the least bit competitive, particularly given the scale of the Russian market. When the aircraft industry was being formed, entities of various types started to emerge, which were necessary for the normal functioning of the industry. The same thing was happening in the shipbuilding industry and the production of armoured vehicles.

Finished product corporations (UAC, UEC, Russian Helicopters) were formed, whose main goal was to preserve the function and expertise of system integrators. Such corporations needed to be capable of conceiving, designing and manufacturing products that would succeed in tomorrow's market. A product can only be kept and mastered if you possess the relevant design and engineering solutions. However, it was necessary not only to come up with a design, but to create it using a technology that would enable the corporation tomorrow, after coming down a bit from the concept level, to fully utilise every engineering tool, and then every tool of competition, to help make the product the best it could be. Sometimes this means assembling the product using components supplied by entities not affiliated with the corporation.

It is possible for an organisation to assemble an airplane because it holds the design, it understands all the risks, and it knows where to get a wing, where to get an engine, where to get avionics, where to get a chassis, and so on. The ability to integrate is the most important one for a finished good corporation. As for welding the metal or rolling the aluminium, someone else can do that. The same goes for making the avionics or the composite parts.

Therefore, entities of a different sort started to emerge, which were supposed to retain manufacturing competency. They were usually horizontally integrated. The integrator was the airplane, while the carbon-fibre composite materials were the horizontal manufacturing competency, which could work for airplanes, for helicopters, for rockets, for steamships and so on. The same applies to the manufacturing of avionics, which are used not only in airplanes and helicopters, but also in other areas of application.

There are many such assets strewn about the field. Russian Technologies was specially conceived, and a decision was taken to create it, so that it could work with manufacturing competencies and maintain this level of capability. This corporation emerged for the purpose of launching the process of forming entities to ensure the development of manufacturing competencies. Of course, the state also could have done this work, but the state has a very complicated mechanism for taking and approving decisions, and whenever property-related decisions have to go through various decrees, orders, directives, resolutions and God knows what else, all of the assets can get lost along the way.

We believed that the corporate model of consolidating all these assets would be easier and simpler, and we transferred all these enterprises from the level of the Ministry of Industry and Energy to the corporate level in the expectation that this would help solve tasks more efficiently and quickly, since management at the corporate or business level gives the ability to act not as a psychotherapist, like the state, but as a surgeon who saves lives. Therefore, Russian Technologies became the designer, to which the projects of 19 integrated entities and over 400 associated enterprises were transferred, from which these integrated entities were to be formed purely on a manufacturing basis. They did not seek to act as finished goods producers. They were, and were to remain, second- and third-tier suppliers and assemblers. They were also to understand in advance that the state would support the manufacturer of the airplane or the helicopter – the system integrator – in its own market or in the external market, because it was the face of the state. But it was up to the system integrator to decide what this face should have for its right eye, since otherwise it would not make an efficient machine capable of being sold on the world market.

In all truthfulness, it must be said that other assets also ended up being part of Russian Technologies by sheer chance, such as Oboronprom UIC OJSC, on the basis of which helicopter and gas-turbine engine manufacturing assets (Russian Helicopters and UEC) were consolidated within the framework of the development strategy for the aircraft industry.

Public–private partnership

When we first started talking about what a strategy consisted of, the first question was about goal-setting. In setting goals, we needed to specify clearly what the medium would be, and for which interests. Since the driving forces and players in this matter are different types of entity (public and private), a simple construct was established: strategy is a product of public–private partnership, in which a non-contradictory trinity must be achieved:

◆ the formulation of a unified goal acceptable to both the state and the private sector;
◆ a system for sharing risks;
◆ a system for consolidating and concentrating resources.

This construct lies at the heart of each strategy that was developed and adopted over the next eight years.

The next stage in developing a strategy is to assess the industry's position in the markets, both domestic and global. How is the national market plugged into the global one? Is the national market sufficient to ensure development? Which competitive advantages do the Russian players have, and what else do they need in order to strengthen their positions? After that, specific instruments of state influence were developed.

A diagram of the method

We chose several of the most important and interesting areas of the ministry's activity (aircraft, automobile manufacturing, pharmaceuticals, iron and steel, shipbuilding and technical regulation) to illustrate our strategic planning method. (A total of around 15 strategies and strategic documents have been prepared in recent years.) The essence of this method is presented in the flowchart that we used for developing strategies (Figure 4.3, overleaf).

In each specific instance, we delineated:

◆ the situation in 2004, in which we received our Terms of Reference and began our analysis and planning;
◆ the goals and horizons that were approved and outlined;
◆ the areas of our activities;
◆ the organisation of our work and the set of tools (organisational, financial and legislative) that were used;
◆ the shifts that occurred in the areas of activity that were subject to strategic development;
◆ the new situation (2011), which requires that we refine the focus of our efforts and develop new tools

Figure 4.3 Programme for transition to target status

Programme for transition
to target status

Legislative

Financial

Organisational

Goals

State of affairs
in 2011

2008

What would
have been if
nothing had
been done

Management
system

What we
received in
2004

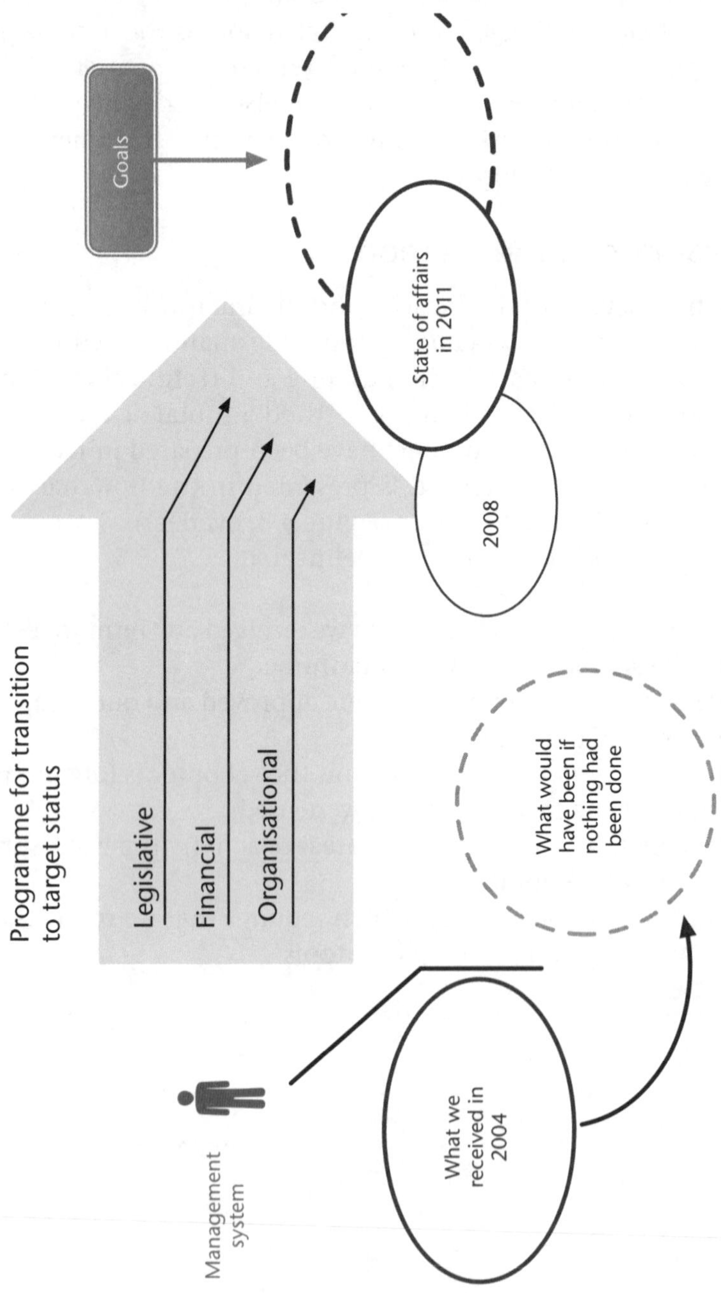

The aircraft industry

Why is the topic of developing the aircraft industry a priority for us? Why do 'airplanes come first'? The model for this strategy differs considerably from the model for the development of iron and steel or pharmaceuticals.

If we look at it from a product point of view, there are no products more intellectually rich than airplanes and gas-turbine engines. The major assets that existed in this area were nearly 100 per cent state-owned. At the same time, no one in the world, and we are no exception, could have taken new strides in engineering or developed new products in this area using business revenue alone. Therefore, in terms of the state's level of responsibility, the development strategy for the aircraft industry bears the strongest resemblance to infrastructure development. If the state had not supported this industry, it would have been destroyed. Subsequently, however, the state began to ask the industry: are you going to continue to do everything at the state's expense? We say: no. We need to create a structure capable of designing and manufacturing competitive products, the efficiency of which (both of the structure and of the products) is valued by the market – the same market that votes not with its hands, but with its money. We therefore wanted to remove the windbreak so that that public offerings of our companies on the market would prompt investors to vote with their money for the success or failure of our actions.

The uniqueness of the structure we ended up with is obvious. We currently have three major entities: UAC, Russian Helicopters and UEC. Each of them is responsible for the final products in its product line, performing the role of a system integrator. At the same time, no matter how much we huffed and puffed, insisting that all of this was economically interesting and intellectually rich, the Russian market is too small to enable aircraft manufacturers to prove their commercial efficiency and ensure a return on all their investment. It is easier for the Chinese, as was noted above. Even in an industry like aircraft engineering, the Chinese can rely on their own domestic market. Therefore, faced with this global market challenge, we need to meet more ambitious objectives and do so more aggressively.

The interest shown in the Russian companies by Boeing, India and China is a sign that we are meeting those objectives. They are taking the risk of a shared partnership with us in major projects.

Sukhoi Superjet 100 and Sukhoi JetFighter

Sometimes we are criticised for the fact that 2,000 of our engineers in Moscow are working for Boeing, which is exploiting their brain power. We reply that they are developing their brains by being involved with creating world-class products on a new technological level. The engineers will gladly work for us when we find a need for these brains and are able to pay them the same as Boeing. In fact this is already happening, as many of them are already working on our products, and this is a recipe for the effective transfer of technology, harmonisation of standards and best practices.

We are also criticised for the fact that there are too many foreign components in the new products manufactured by the Russian aircraft industry. Half of the parts used in the Sukhoi Superjet are supplied by the world's leading manufacturers of assemblies and avionics. This is indeed the case, but I see more advantages in this than disadvantages. We have shown that we are capable of acting as a system integrator and arranging the work of a huge number of designers, engineers and specialists using a single engineering language, a common digital environment and unified standards.

For the first time, we have begun to create not only a product but also a system for promoting it on the global market and supporting it throughout its service life. For the first time we have obtained certification in Europe with a minimum time lag from ARMAK (the Russian airworthiness authority). For the first time we have learned, together with our foreign partners, to unite our efforts and capabilities and share risks while moving towards a common goal.

I say we should continue this systematic trend, and further localisation will not be long in coming.

Woe from oil

From an interview with Itogi, *21 December 2004:*

You initiated the creation of a unified aircraft manufacturing company ...

This reform was long overdue. We merely suggested creating a unified aircraft engineering corporation that would absorb both the civil and military sectors and be able to consolidate industrial and design capabilities. With an entity like this, we can position ourselves effectively in the global market. After all, there are just four and a half major aircraft manufacturers left in the world today: Boeing, Airbus, Bombardier and Embraer, with Russia being the 'half' (our military aircraft are listed in the global market, but our civil aircraft are not). This consolidation of capabilities is demanded by the times. Not a single corporation in the world today is capable of developing the aircraft industry with domestic sources alone. The same applies to Russia. International integration is needed.

I doubt that foreign investors find the civil component of Russian aircraft manufacturing attractive ...

That is true not only of Western investors, but also of domestic air carriers, who prefer foreign aircraft even if they are heavily used. Russian banks are also in no position to finance aircraft purchases. So our air carriers buy second-hand planes from the West – this is far more profitable. A couple of years ago the government came up with an instrument for supporting domestic aircraft manufacturers: leasing. It worked to some extent. Now we want to expand this experience to support Russian aircraft exports. But it is still a bit early to speak of the rebirth of the Russian aircraft industry: we have

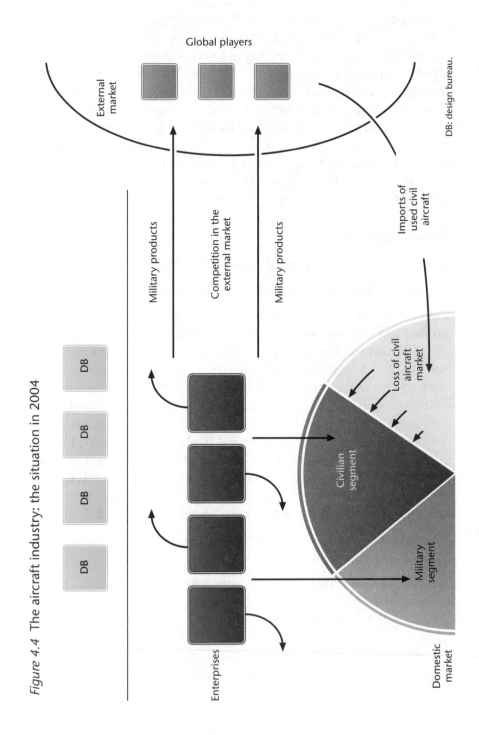

Figure 4.4 The aircraft industry: the situation in 2004

prepared a general document concerning its creation, but there will be a lot of problems getting it passed. As for the unfortunate plight of the civil aircraft sector, here, too, there are promising developments, such as a joint project with European companies and Boeing to create a regional airplane. But in order to make this project a reality, we need to structure the aircraft industry itself and create something that could be offered on the world market. And then, within a year or two, we will have stable partners in this business.

From a report on the Strategy for the Development of the Aircraft Industry up to 2015, delivered at a Russian Government meeting, Moscow, 22 September 2005:

There are currently 293 main enterprises and entities operating in the aircraft manufacturing industry, employing nearly half a million people. Despite a drop in production since the early 1990s, the number of such entities has fallen only slightly. A majority of them, however, are equipped with obsolete technology and machinery, which prevents them from competing in the open market. While the total annual volume of marketable goods produced by these aircraft enterprises stands at RUB 160.2 billion per annum, the volume of finished products sold in the civil aircraft industry was less than RUB 10 billion in 2005. At the same time, more than 50 per cent of the industry's enterprises are either owned by the state, or the state holds more than 25 per cent of shares in their equity capital.

The Russian aircraft industry's share of the domestic market for civil aircraft has been falling steadily, from 27.5 per cent in 1992 to 17.4 per cent in 2004. This is exacerbated by active marketing of foreign-made second-hand aircraft to Russia, while Russian enterprises are competing amongst themselves primarily for public funding. The pace of sales of Russian aircraft that were built in recent years but have already become technologically obsolete remains low, comprising around 1 per cent of total sales of civil aircraft in the global market.

In 2004, the domestic aircraft industry sold 12 civilian planes. While each of the leading companies (Boeing and Airbus) produces and sells approximately one airplane a day, the Russian aircraft industry produces and sells one a month.

Until recently, Russia's military aircraft exports accounted for around 25 per cent of global exports of military aviation technology. After a relatively successful period from 2000–03, when aircraft comprised more than half of exports of arms and military equipment, the volume of military exports started to fall. This was because contracts previously entered into, primarily with India and China, had entered the final stage of implementation. At the same time, new contracts and an increase in the state defence order cannot fully compensate for the decline in sales. Therefore, the current situation also requires serious efforts to develop the military component of the aircraft industry in order to hold onto ground that was won in global MTC (military-technical co-operation) markets.

In the area of helicopter manufacturing, we are holding our segment of the global market. In recent years, from 2000–04, the sales growth has been small but steady. We consider this sector quite promising.

Aircraft manufacturing is a capital-intensive business, where the return on investment can be spread out over 10 years or more. The industry is large in scale and technologically complex; the risks are high and accompanied by large-scale investments in new projects and significant competition in the global market.

The Russian Ministry of Industry and Energy, working in close collaboration with other interested authorities of the executive branch, came up with a development strategy for the Russian aircraft industry. The goals of the *Development Strategy for the Aircraft Industry* are: to retain the competencies of a system integrator; to ensure the engineering independence and global competitiveness of the new generation of military and civil products; and to return Russia to the global aviation market as a player among the top five manufacturers.

Solving the problems of aircraft industry involves defining the basic principles of the industry's development.

Our *Development Strategy* is oriented towards the global market through a transition to an open industry model, accompanied by collaboration with partners from the high-tech sector of industry. The *Strategy* also provides for collaboration with emerging aircraft manufacturing facilities in countries that import Russian aircraft, particularly India and China.

A reasonable combination of state and private capital, along with dynamic, co-ordinated efforts by the state and private sector, could produce the desired result: turning Russian aircraft engineering into an industry capable of competing in the global market.

Finally, the *Strategy* calls for consolidating assets: that is, integrating the industry's enterprises into large, stable research and production complexes.

The *Strategy* consists of three main blocks:

- ◆ completing structural reforms in the aircraft industry;
- ◆ selecting financial mechanisms and tools;
- ◆ adapting the legal framework to the tasks that are to be met within the framework of the *Strategy*.

Implementing the proposed *Strategy* will enable us to conquer at least 5 per cent of the world's civil aircraft market and ensure the production of military aircraft to equip the Russian armed forces.

In 2015 we plan to fundamentally change the share of civil aircraft, which will comprise 33 per cent of total industry sales, compared with just 6 per cent today, while total sales volume will increase 3.4 times over the course of the programme.

The problem of structural reforms in the industry occupies an important place in the *Strategy*. The Russian aircraft industry is currently characterised by a high level of insularity, low production volumes and financial instability, as well as isolation from external sales and distribution markets.

We need to realise that the Russian aircraft industry today is mostly a collection of small (by international standards), disconnected companies incapable of competing with global market players in either the long term or the short term. The industry is long overdue for the sort of consolidation that has already occurred in other countries.

In Russia, the state was, is and should remain a major owner of the industry's capital. It is in this capacity that the state should initiate the necessary changes at the organisational level. The central idea here is the creation of UAC.

The need to consolidate the aircraft industry under UAC stems from the following factors:

- ◆ The extremely high level of concentration of the aircraft industry in the world today. The minimum level of sales needed in order to become one of the five top players is currently estimated at US$5–6 billion a year. At the same time, the total annual revenue of Russia's entire aircraft manufacturing sector is currently estimated at just US$2–2.5 billion.

◆ The accumulated critical level of technological backwardness, which could lead to a loss of competiveness by 2010 if the appropriate steps are not taken.

◆ The industry's capital-intensity and project timeframes are such that no domestic manufacturer is in a position to take on all the existing risks.

◆ No project involving the creation of a new, competitive civil aircraft can be implemented outside the framework of international co-operation, especially at the stage of initial entry of unfamiliar products onto the market.

The process of forming UAC consists of three stages. In the first stage, draft regulatory documents on the formation of UAC were developed and co-ordinated at the interdepartmental level by the Ministry of Industry and Energy pursuant to the List of Instructions of the President of the Russian Federation, based on the results of a meeting of the presidium of the State Council of the Russian Federation on 22 February 2005. Aircraft manufacturers formed a nonprofit partnership, which is currently coming up with a unified development policy and preparing assets for the merger.

In the second stage, the state will contribute its assets to the corporation's equity capital. When acquiring stakes in the corporation, private shareholders will swap their assets for shares in UAC at an agreed price.

In the third stage, steps will be taken to increase the corporation's investment attractiveness and turn it into a public company with substantially increased capitalisation.

The strategy also provides for the creation of a united helicopter corporation of Oboronprom OJSC. The relevant decree of the president of the Russian Federation has already been issued. The corporation is being formed on the basis of a public–private partnership.

In addition, the strategy provides for the development of key elements of second-tier aircraft construction companies. Our fundamental position is that engine manufacturing, the creation of avionics and unit engineering should be developed with a focus on the global market.

Manufacturers of final products work with Russian second-tier corporations on a market basis: that is, they purchase only those products that are competitive with global manufacturers in terms of quality and price.

The strategy provides for a major restructuring of the afore-mentioned subindustries and changes to the principles of their operation. At the same time, I would like to emphasise that these process are already actively under way, and more than 50 per cent of the integrated entities have already been formed.

The second block of the strategy in question is dedicated to selecting financial mechanisms and instruments. The state's involvement in supporting the aircraft industry takes a variety of forms in different countries, but in every case the state plays the vital role of a stabiliser and offsetter of risks when creating new technology.

The state should engage in risk-taking at the stages of research, testing and design, the creation of critical industrial technologies and new materials, and when a new product is being introduced to the market.

In addition, for the purposes of creating financial leverage, the state should participate in the most important projects so as to create the conditions for attracting significant amounts of private capital to the projects.

The Russian aircraft industry is seen as a classic case of an industry to which the principles of public–private partnership can be applied. This development model is based on the principles of close collaboration between the state and private sector, and it allows us to effectively combine the ability of the state to concentrate resources in the necessary areas and the motivation of private owners to achieve positive business results. We believe that these approaches should also be taken as part of the development strategy for the shipbuilding and conventional arms industries.

The main financial mechanisms for state's implementation of the *Strategy* are the Federal Targeted Programme (FTP) for the Development of Civil Aviation, the State Armaments Programme, and a number of other measures that are not part of any programme (increasing the equity capital of leasing companies, interest rate subsidies on loans to air carriers, state guarantees for the promotion of Russian aircraft exports, and so on). Budget funds are also to be allocated for work on building the fifth-generation Prospective Airborne Complex of Frontline Aviation (PAK FA).

The favourable investment climate in the industry is enhanced by amendments to applicable laws, such as those concerning restrictions on the holding of equity interests in aircraft manufacturing

473

companies by private shareholders, including foreign ones, and updates to the laws on military-technical co-operation and the state defence order.

From a report on the steps being taken by the Russian Federation Government to reform and develop the domestic aircraft industry, delivered during 'Government Hour' at the State Duma of the Russian Federation, Moscow, 24 October 2006:

The country's aircraft industry is the largest among all the branches of the military-industrial complex (MIC). It provides for the interests of defence and security, air transportation and other areas of the country's economy. It accounts for more than one-third of the MIC's total production volume, around 40 per cent of production of military-purpose goods, and around 50 per cent of military exports. More than 450,000 people are employed in the industry. This is a quarter of the total number of people working in the MIC.

The aviation industry, like other branches of the country's MIC, has not completely recovered from the severe crisis of the 1990s. This can be seen in the fact that the positive growth trends of 1998–2003, when the aircraft industry's total production volume tripled, thereby outpacing the machine engineering sector and industry as a whole, started to reverse direction in 2004–05.

What can be said about the causes of this instability in the industry's performance indicators? For the most part, it is because of the flawed structure of industry's manufacturing output, and its dangerous reliance on the status of military-technical co-operation. The recent growth of production in the domestic aircraft industry is mostly attributable to exports of aircraft and aviation components. Exports of military aircraft are several times higher than procurement for the domestic armed forces, while exports of civil aircraft in some cases equalled or exceeded (in the case of helicopters) deliveries to Russian air carriers. The share of products used in civil aviation has once again dropped to pre-reform levels (less than 20 per cent). Deliveries of civil aircraft to the domestic market remain isolated events.

Over the past 15 years, the demand for the construction of new aircraft from both state aviation and the numerous but small private Russian air carriers has been extremely limited. Between 2003 and 2005, for instance, Russian manufacturers supplied only 29 aircraft (including light planes) to Russian air carriers, while 85 airplanes were produced. It should be added that the process of purchasing foreign-made aircraft, especially used ones, has recently intensified. As at August 2006, Russian air carriers were operating 116 foreign passenger planes (long-distance and regional).

As for helicopter manufacturing, of the 95 helicopters produced by the Russian aircraft industry in 2004, only three were supplied to Russia's domestic market, while the rest were exported.

The year 2004 saw a decline in the industry's economic performance (to about 89 per cent of the 2003 figures). This was primarily because of a noticeable drop in exports of military products, as well as the still dangerously low level of aircraft production for the Russian armed forces (a manufacturing rate of 77 per cent for military products). In 2005 this negative production growth continued, and sales of civil products also fell. The aircraft industry's total production volume in 2005 was 97.9 per cent of the corresponding level in 2004.

As for documents recently adopted by the Government of the Russian Federation, these include:

◆ *The Strategy for the Development of the Aircraft Industry up to 2015.*
◆ *The State Armaments Programme for 2007–15.*
◆ The new version of the Federal Targeted Programme for the Development of Russian Civil Aviation for 2002–10 and up to 2015, and a number of others.

They are all aimed at fundamentally solving problems in the development of aircraft manufacturing and aviation in the Russian Federation, including the creation of new models of military aviation technology, as well as the retention and development of new external markets for high-tech airplane and helicopter engineering products.

An analysis of the potential supply and demand for Russian aircraft has shown that Russian industry is capable of replacing the retiring fleet of domestic air carriers, particularly in the medium-range air transportation sector (the replacement of Tu-154 and Il-86 aircraft), as well as the local airline sector, which has been in deep crisis since 1992.

An integrated product strategy has been developed for the industry. It is consistent with the current realities and stringent requirements of Russian and international civil aviation markets.

A transitional project needs to be implemented on a new organisational basis to create a Russian regional airplane orientated towards the global market.

Work must begin on selecting and implementing a 'breakthrough' product – that is, a marketable product of the next generation – a short to medium-range airplane.

Simultaneously, in order to expand technological and organisational competencies, steps will be taken to promote integration into international co-operation programmes, such as the A-350 and B-787. Of course, co-operation with the leading Western aircraft companies, Boeing and Airbus, is important for implementing our product strategy in the area of civil aviation, but the main key to developing the domestic civil aircraft industry is to ensure that the industry retains its competency as a system integrator. In order for this to happen, work on the creation of scientific and engineering capacity and the development of the actual designs for the short to medium-range aircraft must be in place by 2006.

In the military aviation sector, efforts will be focused on a limited number of promising projects designed to meet the needs of the Russian Air Force and to develop the system of military-technical co-operation. It is also important to ensure the integrity of deliveries and high-quality after-sales service for mass-produced models.

In order to ensure the implementation of the decisions taken at the suggestion of the Russian Ministry of Industry and Energy, the Russian Government has provided for a number of measures starting in 2005. These include:

◆ Increasing the funds allocated for research and development (R&D) within the framework of the Federal Targeted Programme for the Development of Russian Civil Aviation for 2002–10 and up to 2015.
◆ The state's further involvement in increasing the capitalisation of Russian aviation leasing companies.
◆ Using federal budget funds to compensate air carriers for part of their lease payments and interest on loans obtained from Russian lending institutions for the purchase of new aircraft.
◆ Providing state guarantees to support exports of Russian-made aircraft, as well as domestic borrowing for the purpose of developing a new-generation Russian regional plane.

The set of measures provided for in the *Strategy for the Development of the Aviation Industry up to 2015,* and the concrete steps currently being taken to implement it, will help ensure the dynamic development of the Russian aircraft industry. The development of the industry will be achieved through public–private partnership, the introduction of modern mechanisms of corporate management, improvement of the legal framework and new methods of state support.

Ultimately, this will help fundamentally change the strategic competitive position of the Russian aircraft industry in the global aviation market. Russia will effectively return to this market as a global centre of aviation engineering, promoting new, competitive aircraft.

From a report on the development of aviation in the Russian Federation, delivered at a meeting of the Security Council, Moscow, 31 March 2011:

Aircraft engineering is one of the most high-tech sectors of industry. The industry's products are a key component of the country's defence and security system.

In 2006 we adopted a *Strategy for the Development of the Aircraft Industry up to 2015*. The goal of that *Strategy* is to create a globally competitive industry.

During this time we managed to stabilise the position of key enterprises, consolidate assets and competencies, and concentrate resources in breakthrough areas.

The creation of the main entities we planned to develop has for the most part been completed. UAC has been created, as have engine manufacturing, helicopter construction and rocket engineering holdings (UEC, Russian Helicopters and the Tactical Missile Corporation). Two key component companies (Aircraft Instruments Concern and Aviation Equipment Concern) are in the formative stage. This integration has made it possible to start to raise the economic efficiency of enterprises and to boost revenue.

During the five years of the *Strategy*'s implementation, growth in sales volume exceeded expectations, reaching 212.7 per cent in 2010 (compared with a projected increase of 196.1 per cent in the *Strategy*). Production grew from RUB 210 billion to RUB 504 billion. The share of products supplied to the domestic market increased from 42.2 per cent to 68.8 per cent (the share of exports fell from 57.8 per cent to 31.2 per cent accordingly). Annual output per person nearly tripled (from RUB 0.4 million to RUB 1.1 million).

At the same time, according to these indicators we still lag significantly behind the global leaders. By way of comparison, in the United States, sales volume was US$173.6 billion in 2005 and US$214.4 billion in 2010, while output per employee was US$0.531 million in 2005 and US$0.596 million in 2010.

However, the positive trend is obvious. In 2010 we posted revenue growth in all subsectors of the aircraft industry compared with 2009.

In the aircraft industry as a whole, production rose by 11.3 per cent last year [2010]. The best performers included military products, helicopter engineering and engine manufacturing.

The situation in the civil sector is still the most sensitive. We cannot yet boast of any large-scale manufacturing of civil aircraft, with just seven planes produced in 2010.

If we include military products, last year we produced 73 airplanes, 214 helicopters (half of them for export), 482 aviation engines and 95 land-based gas-turbine engines (we rank second in the world in sales of military airplanes and third in sales of helicopters). We expect further manufacturing growth in 2011, with deliveries of 267 helicopters, 27 regional planes, five mainline planes and six cargo and special planes expected.

To this end, the industry's enterprises are actively upgrading and optimising their production facilities. The implementation of these programmes will help reduce labour intensity by two-thirds, increase productivity two to three times over (given the appropriate workload), and increase production volume 1.3 times. Another important effect will be a substantial increase in energy efficiency.

All of this requires significant state support for the industry.

The main goal is to take the industry to a new technological level. This applies to the entire production chain: in the case of design, it means switching to digital; in the case of manufacturing, it means introducing the most modern technologies and utilising new, specially developed materials; in the case of sales, it means building a system of after-sales service based on international best practices.

The total amount of support we gave to the industry in 2005–10 increased by an average of 150 per cent a year, since during this period we needed to bridge the technological gap that had accumulated over the course of 15 years. As a result, new technologies, new projects and new production lines emerged.

Table 4.1 Sales volume in companies in the Russian aircraft industry (in RUB billion)

	2009	2010
UAC	114.9	164.7
Russian Helicopters	57.7	87.1
UEC MC	72.8	73.6
Tactical Missile Corporation	31.4	34.2
Aircraft Instruments Concern	31.3	36.2
Aviation Equipment Concern	9.3	9.9

The economic crisis posed a serious challenge. There was a risk that the resources set aside as part of the *Strategy* for achieving a breakthrough would by necessity be reallocated to cover more immediate problems.

However, funding for the development of the industry was not cut. Furthermore, additional funds helped prevent enterprises from going bankrupt, cover accumulated financial holes and continue taking the aircraft industry to a new technological level.

This year, state support has been maintained, including more than RUB 70 billion through the Ministry of Industry. These funds are specifically being applied to breakthrough projects, and in all our new projects we are raising enterprises' competencies and product specifications to the level of global players.

We see our ultimate goal as forming competitive entities capable of being offered in the free market.

The main challenge for the Russian aviation industry, and especially for its civil segment, is to gain access to the global market. Only this will generate enough demand to enable the intensive development of the industry.

Let me emphasise that as far as civil engineering is concerned, we are entering the world market for the first time. Russia has never been a global player in this segment. Domination within the COMECON (Council for Mutual Economic Assistance) does not constitute a market in the classical sense.

As we move towards the global market, we must accept all of its standards and trends. One of these is co-operation among major players and mutual cultivation of new competencies.

On a number of projects we already have successful examples of this. One is the Superjet-100, in both its airframe and its engine.

This machine is the first to be designed entirely digitally and is, technologically speaking, quite comparable to its Western counterparts, even in terms of promotion (it is a Russian-Italian joint venture). In the case of the Sam-146 engine, we have full-fledged co-operation with the French. Its mass production is under way.

A number of new projects are being actively implemented with extensive international collaboration. These include the medium-range MS-31, which involves developing new technology and using new materials ('black wing'), as well as the promising MTA military transport plane, which we are building together with our Indian partners, and the T-50 fighter plane, also based on digital technology.

In helicopter engineering, we are already at the stage of promoting the Ka-226 T on the market. This is also a collaborative project – the helicopter's engines are being supplied by the French company Turbomeca. Active work is being done on the Ka-62 and Mi-38 helicopters, for which we have also enlisted the help of French engine-manufacturing partners.

As for engine manufacturing, in addition to our successful experience with the Sam-146, for the first time in 25 years we have created a PD-14 gas generator for a new family of engines, and we have done this in just 1.5 years, as compared with the standard seven years for the development of such technology.

There is a whole cohort of new products created using fundamentally new technology.

First, in order to facilitate the development of the industry, in both the civil and military sectors, it is especially important to create advanced scientific and engineering potential. A pool of breakthrough technologies is being built around promising projects. The initial exploratory stage of work on the 'Airplane-2020' project is scheduled to begin this year. We are already looking at this area from the perspective of new opportunities for collaboration with global players, both established and emerging (India and China).

Second, the draft of the new *State Armaments Programme – 2020* calls for expediting the development and supply of new models of equipment to the armed forces. This requires striking a balance between the requirements of the Ministry of Defence in terms of product quality and cost, and proper regard for the market realities of enterprises' operations (the state defence order must be cost-effective). At the same time, we see modernising production capacity as one of our most important objectives. The structure of this capacity remains less than ideal.

In light of the start of work on breakthrough projects, the industry's enterprises will have to bring the technological capabilities of their production facilities in line with market requirements. This means a quantitatively and qualitatively new level. Modernisation will not be possible without state support. That is why we made sure the Federal Targeted Programme for the Development of the Military-Industrial Complex includes funding for R&D and capital investment in specific equipment models that are to be purchased within the framework of the *State Armaments Programme.*

Third, a key factor in the industry's global competitiveness is the ability of its enterprises to transition towards selling the lifecycle of their products. After-sales service accounts for up to 50 per cent of total revenue in any segment, whether it is airplanes, helicopters or engines.

Fourth, another important condition for the industry's development is to develop human potential. To this end, new professional standards are being created, and enterprises are participating in the accreditation of educational programmes.

Fifth, the prospect of Russia's accession to the World Trade Organization (WTO) raises the question whether measures of state support will need to be adjusted. This includes funding for the aircraft sales system. We are now actively working on this in collaboration with companies in the industry.

At the same time, it is equally important for us to provide systematic support to our air carriers. For the aircraft industry, this means stable demand, including from such niches as regional transportation.

Sixth, in order to meet the objectives formulated in the *Strategy*, as well as any new challenges that arise, we have developed a draft *State Programme for the Development of the Aviation Industry*. This programme document draws on previously developed and widely used instruments, as well as new ones that take into account key risks and opportunities for the development of the aviation industry at the current stage.

Figure 4.5 The aircraft industry: the situation in 2011

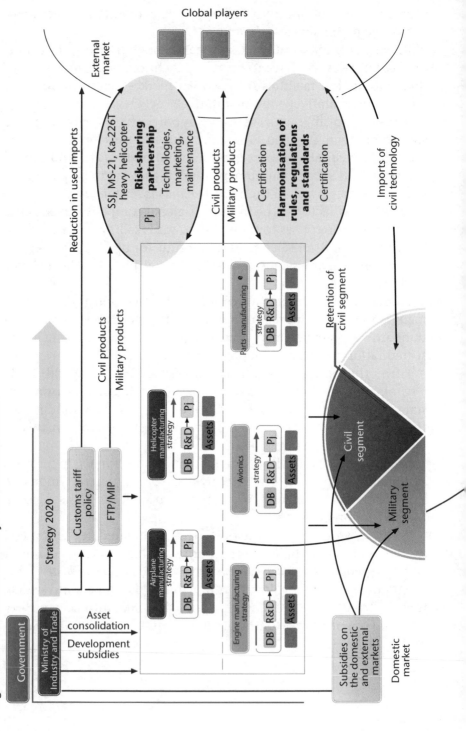

Development strategy for the automotive industry

This strategy has its own special history. Whereas the metals industry has enough resources to ensure its own development, and only in difficult times, such as an economic crisis, has it needed to find risk-reduction tools to support the projects incorporated in its strategy, the automotive industry must be treated differently.

This industry has never had its own internal innovations: platforms, engines and other critical automobile systems. To a significant extent these have always been products and technologies borrowed from abroad. Russia's automotive industry, unlike aviation, has never had a complete cycle for the creation of new products. We all remember the popularity of the Soviet version of *Za Rulem* (*At the Wheel*) magazine as proof of the creativity of our people, where half of its pages were devoted to the tricks mechanics and 'tinkerers' used to fine-tune and repair domestic mass-produced vehicles. It is impossible to explain to Germans how, after buying a new car, people must immediately put the finishing touches on it. They would immediately ask, 'But how would you be able to use your insurance tomorrow if something happened? How would you pass your roadworthiness tests, and so on?' We made millions of these cars, and they are all different. It has been 40 years since we invested in this industry, which needs to be completely upgraded every ten years. Otherwise it gets pushed out of the market. We have tried to break this vicious circle.

We launched a new cycle in the development of the industry, to which the fate of over 2 million people is tied. Otherwise it would be impossible to figure out what to do with this army of people. There is also a huge market, driven by pent-up demand from Soviet times. Our industrial policy dates back to 2004, when the first industrial assembly model was formed.

We spent a year debating, but in the end industrial assembly became the main model for the development of the automotive industry. Despite all the criticism directed at us, the work was soon in full swing.

Quite logically, we arrived at the second stage. 'Industrial Assembly 2' involves not just a package of operations aimed at localising components and technologies in Russia, but also mandatory requirements with respect to setting up R&D units and linking

intellectual property assets to created alliances. We already have projects that are implementing our strategic plan – a strategic partnership involving Renault, Nissan, AvtoVAZ, Ford and Sollers. From our perspective, these are projects with the potential not only to integrate our people into the production chains, but also to integrate them into global chains for the creation of new products.

All of this is more than just a beautiful story. Over the course of implementation of this industrial policy, the automotive industry signed about 20 'industrial assembly' agreements. Industrial assemblers invested about US$6 billion in the industry. The total amount of production capacity created under existing projects is over 1.5 million vehicles a year. In this sense, the point of no return to the old model of the automotive industry has been passed.

Even if we look at the four largest alliances, more than

US$7 billion still needs to be invested. If we add to this the nearly 300 memoranda with companies that supply auto parts, the amount of investment doubles, and all this by 2016–17.

We have become experienced at successfully using previously unimaginable tools to support the industry. During the economic crisis, 600,000 cars were sold under the programme for recycling old vehicles. While the preferential lending programme was up and running, 500,000 loans were extended for the purchase of new cars made in Russia.

Last year the automotive market in Russia was valued at US$100 billion, and it is still growing: 2.6 million new cars were sold in 2011, and in 2013–14 Russia will become the largest market in Europe. Throughout 2011, nine of the 10 best-selling passenger cars were produced in Russia, and in the first quarter of 2012 all 10 of them were. Car production in Russia reached 1.7 million units in 2011. This is a historic record.

Of course, much more needs to be done. The development of the industry within the framework of Russia's national strategy needs to be harmonised with the development of CIS integration formats and the emergence of a new reality – the Common Economic Space. We need to develop the practice of levelling risks, taking into account Russia's accession to the WTO. The fact that industrial assembly and the automotive industry have become the latest stumbling block in negotiations on Russia's accession to the WTO is an indicator of just how high the stakes are.

Nevertheless, the creation of a new image for the Russian automotive industry is in full swing. This will be a different industry and a completely different story.

From an interview with Itogi, *21 December 2004:*

Viktor Borisovich, in the current government you have been put in charge of virtually the entire real [products rather than services] sector of the economy. Please explain what this real economy consists of today, as we get the impression that we do not have anything real except oil and gas ...

If at least they think there is a lot of oil and gas in the country, that is already a good start. However, the share of the oil and gas sector is declining: it accounted for around 17.5 per cent in 2000 but just 15 per cent in 2003. It stands to reason that there is another 85 per cent of the economy: metals (ferrous and nonferrous), engineering, the automotive industry...

Perhaps it is best not to speak of the automotive industry: there is scarcely a car owner in Russia who would not prefer to ride an imported 'iron horse'...

But foreign brands can also be assembled in Russia, making them domestic cars. I think such enterprises put healthy competitive pressure on our traditional manufacturers, though they are increasingly keen on collaboration. And this is better than testing the strength of the Russian automotive industry by liberalising its external outlines: that is, lifting import duties. If we did that, only Korean manufacturers would survive in the market. We need to give ourselves a chance.

But let's return to the structure of the real sector of the economy. Ideas that shrink it down to the size of the oil and gas industry are badly distorted stereotypes. After all, the oil and gas industry remains the engine of the economy. A contraction here means a contraction of the other 85 per cent. This is the path of economic suicide. We have to be able to take advantage of the fact that our economy has such a support, and try not to fret, as is our cultural tradition, that woe comes not only from wit,[2] but also from oil. Otherwise it seems that whatever conversation you start in Russia about elevated matters, you always end up talking about oil and gas pipelines.

From a report on the medium-term implementation (2005–08) of the priority tasks set forth in the Plan for the Development of the Russian Automotive Industry, *delivered at a meeting of the Government of the Russian Federation, Moscow, 19 May 2005:*

The level of development of the automotive complex largely shapes the appearance of the country's industrial sector. The development of the automotive industry is also directly linked to meeting the strategic objectives for the development of the economy: doubling GDP and creating jobs.

The creation of new high-paying jobs, including jobs in the automotive sector and related industries, is an effective way to solve the large-scale problems of poverty, which cannot be overcome by redistributing income through budget transfers.

The state's ability to fulfil its social obligations and secure welfare gains depends on maintaining high rates of economic growth. Growth based on the raw materials sector will ultimately fall to

---

2   A reference to *Woe from Wit*, a play by the nineteenth-century Russian playwright Aleksandr Griboyedov.

Figure 4.6 The automotive industry: the situation in 2004

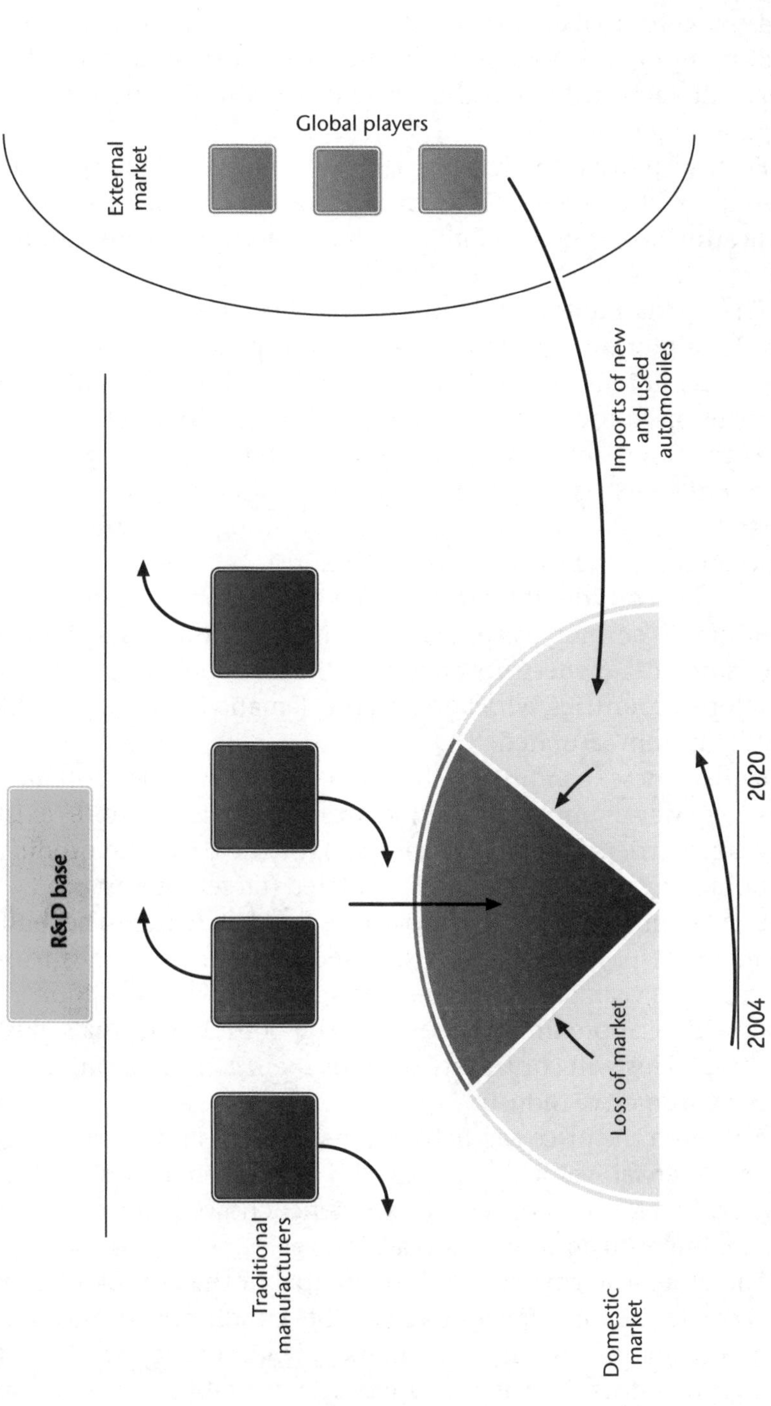

External market

Global players

R&D base

Traditional manufacturers

Imports of new and used automobiles

Loss of market

2004

2020

Domestic market

3–4 per cent a year, and trends beyond this level will depend on the pace of development of industries oriented towards the domestic market, such as the automotive industry and mechanical engineering in general.

Finally, refusal to develop the automotive industry and the absence of other comparable strategic initiatives is a negative signal, indicating the state's inability to implement a targeted industrial policy.

The Russian automobile market has become one of the fastest-developing ones in recent years. Sales of passenger cars increased from 1.2 million units in 2000 to more than 1.6 million in 2004. In value terms, it increased from US$7 billion to US$18 billion.

At the same time, given the stabilisation of domestic production in recent years, as well as a certain restriction of used car imports, most of the sales growth was achieved through an influx of cheap new foreign cars, mostly from South Korea.

We can confidently say that Russia's automobile market will continue to develop dynamically in the near future as real incomes rise, since car ownership rates are still low compared with other developed countries, which means the demand for personal vehicles is still far from saturated.

Under these conditions, the situation could develop in two possible ways: imports could continue to rise despite existing customs barriers (the inertia forecast), or the domestic production of promising models could be stimulated (target forecast).

It is estimated that if the inertia forecast, where the bulk of demand for passenger cars is satisfied by imports, comes to pass, then by the year 2010 imports, having reached 1–1.1 million cars a year, will be approximately equal to the output of Russia's existing factories. This will contribute towards maintaining negative trends in the automotive industry.

Although the price gap between new foreign and Russian models of commercial vehicles, lorries and buses remains significantly higher than for passenger cars, experience shows that this reserve of price competitiveness will not last forever.

Therefore, the government's main goal in the automobile sector is to create the most favourable possible conditions for positioning domestic manufacturers in the market, whether they are Russian or foreign investors. This is because of the capital-intensive nature of the industry and the relatively long period of time it takes to launch production. Special conditions will be created for potential investors through the framework of the industrial assembly of vehicles and vehicle components.

We believe the widespread use of industrial assembly, which domestic auto makers have mixed feelings about, is an inevitable stage in the development of the modern Russian automotive industry. It is important for the industry not to be held back at this stage in its development.

Regarding the potential adverse effects of industrial assembly, we should bear in mind not only the obvious benefits to the industry and the economy as a whole, but also the risks associated with government inaction.

If the inertia scenario comes to pass, we will end up with a complete 'bouquet' in the form of imports of ready-made automobiles in all price ranges, the need for a gradual reduction of current customs tariffs under the agreements on WTO accession, and a lack of desire among investors to invest in Russia's automotive industry.

At the same time, the Russian Ministry of Industry and Energy supports the auto makers' position on the conditions for organising automobile assembly and stimulating domestic production of auto parts, as well as the localisation requirements that must be clearly established within the framework of a specific investment project.

The new procedures for importing auto parts will increase the investment attractiveness and competitiveness of the Russian automotive industry, help establish a natural barrier to imports of ready-made vehicles, and ensure stable investment in the automotive industry, as well as the creation of new production facilities.

The urgency of the situation in the Russian automotive market stems from the fact that all competing manufacturers are forced to operate in a fairly low price segment, where the mass demand of Russian consumers is concentrated. This currently means a price range of US\$6,000–10,000 per vehicle.

I shall not hide the fact that we are heartened by the examples of Toyota, General Motors, Renault and Ford – investors who have announced their model range plans, since they will occupy the price niches at which the bulk of imports are currently aimed. Renault Logan and Ford Motors are positioned in the \$8,000–15,000 price niche, while Toyota Camry occupies the niche of the most expensive cars priced at over $20,000, which reduces the likelihood of price competition with domestic models.

Speaking of Toyota's recently announced project, it is worth noting a number of positive aspects. The volume of planned capacity allows not only for supplying our domestic market, but also exporting a substantial number of cars from Russia. Toyota requires a much bigger space for production needs than it would require for mere assembly – there is an assumption from the outset that auto part production will be located next to the assembly plant. These are all positive signals. We hope that this auspicious start will be continued by such auto giants as DaimlerChrysler and Volkswagen, and that existing assembly plants will not lag behind.

It is worth noting that all serious investors are planning to use Russian-made auto parts, and this is not the result of state coercion, but a natural business decision, dictated by the logic of private entrepreneurs. This will inevitably boost demand among auto assemblers for the products of related industries – metals, chemicals and so on.

Rapid growth and changes in market structure will most likely lead to substantial changes in the organisational and production structure of the automotive industry. In other countries, the structure of the automotive industry includes the main assembly companies, which own the trademarks, as well as a large sector of auto part manufacturers. The Russian automotive industry is more vertically integrated and less specialised, consisting primarily of large full-cycle plants.

The production of auto parts, especially complex ones, is a knowledge-intensive process requiring a high degree of specialisation in certain areas on the part of manufacturers. Another incentive to specialise is the significant proportion of industry products that consist of mass-produced, standardised components used by a majority of manufacturers. As a result, the production of auto parts is an important part of the global automotive industry; in the United States, for example, this sector generates about 50 per cent of the industry's added value.

Thus, the need to achieve a reasonable level of specialisation in large-scale automobile production shapes the momentum towards a new structure of the domestic automotive industry. The task of the government is to ensure that the emerging structure of the automotive industry is filled with the widest range of businesses, so that we do not replace the existing, somewhat suboptimal, vertically integrated structure of the industry with 'bare' industrial assembly. Assembly alone does not make the same contribution to the value-added chain as integrated production. In order to increase this contribution, it is necessary to develop the production of auto parts. One of the positive consequences of the automotive industry's new structure should be the active involvement of small and medium-sized businesses in the production of auto parts, which would make the production structure more flexible.

It should be recognised that the only way we can overcome the uncertainty in the development of the Russian automotive industry is by improving the quality of government regulation and with the help of public–private partnerships. Since the *Plan for the Development of the Russian Automotive Industry* was adopted, the government has taken a number of important steps. These can roughly be divided into four areas:

◆ Customs tariff block: barriers have been set up against imports of cars older than seven years; import duties have been reduced for certain types of foreign equipment without Russian-made analogues (welding, painting and conveyor lines); and as I mentioned earlier, duties on auto parts used for automobile assembly have also been reduced.

◆ New environmental standards: imports of lories and buses with diesel engines that do not meet EURO-1 environmental requirements have been halted; Russian auto plants have started to make vehicles with EURO-2 and EURO-3 environmental characteristics.

◆ The initial implementation of a programme for the development of diesel engine manufacturing: some preliminary work has already been done at the Zavolzhsky Motor Plant, and there are additional prospects within the framework of relevant diesel manufacturing programmes of the Union State.

◆ Pursuant to the Federal Law on Technical Regulation a programme has been adopted for the development of technical regulations for 2004–06, which provides for the development of two out of the six specific technical regulations envisaged by the *Plan*.

At the same time, the problems of quality, the development of a components base, and car import substitution have not been fully resolved. The proposed draft action plan offers steps to achieve this.

These are consistent with international practices in stimulating the development of the automotive industry, and involve regulating supply and demand in this market. These measures are also consistent with the priority objectives of the current *Plan for the Development of the Russian Automotive Industry*, and include:

- tax incentives for R&D in the automotive industry;
- the continuation of work on technical regulation, including a strengthening of safety and environmental requirements;
- customs-tariff regulation of imports of used automobiles;
- implementation of existing decisions concerning industrial assembly;
- use of the infrastructure of special economic zones;
- measures of state support for exports;
- finally, the critical issue of training personnel for the industry.

From a report on the development of the automotive industry of the Russian Federation delivered at a meeting with Prime Minister Vladimir Putin, Nizhny Novgorod, 23 December 2010:

The government is constantly focused on developing the automotive industry. This inevitably had an impact on performance results in 2010. Since April 2010, the market has posted double-digit growth month on month. In November 2010 alone, auto sales grew by 68 per cent compared with the same period the year before.

The market is now recovering from the economic crisis. We are seeing growth in all segments. One stable trend in 2010 was that nine out of ten market-leading models were made in Russia. This became possible thanks to an effective system of measures to support all auto makers in Russia. If we include used cars imported to Russia for the first time, the market may be approaching the mark of 1.9 million vehicles. One indication that the crisis has ended is the fact that consumers are returning to the auto dealerships; sometimes there are even queues.

A similar situation can be observed in the light commercial vehicles market. Qualitative shifts in the structure of the market are becoming increasing apparent. Business owners, who have become more frugal with their money, largely shape the demand for reliable foreign cars that are inexpensive to operate, including foreign cars that are manufactured domestically.

Among the key groups of companies and alliances, AvtoVAZ

remains far ahead of its competitors. However, large foreign manufacturers are steadily increasing their market shares. Production
volumes, when placed next to sales statistics, clearly illustrate the
differences in policies among foreign players on the Russian market.

Volkswagen and Toyota remain the most illustrative examples.
The share of their vehicles produced in Russia compared with their
total sales volume in 2010 was 80 per cent and 20 per cent respectively. At the same time, the increased localisation of production by
a number of manufacturers, such as Sollers, Peugeot and Renault-
Nissan, has been a key factor in the growth of sales in the country.

On the other hand, we have a special situation with Avtotor. It
operates in a special economic zone pursuant to Federal Law no.
16-FZ, acting as an assembly site for five foreign brands. Today, it
mostly assembles foreign cars in Russia. This is more than 200,000
cars a year (as at the end of 2011). At the same time, more than
90 per cent of these cars are produced either by the notorious
method of semi-knocked down assembly (SKD) (for instance, KIA
cars), which is the subject of heated debate, or simple assembly
operations using painted bodies (as for BMW cars). Only one car is
assembled through a full cycle, the Chevrolet Lacetti. This cannot
but cause concern. I am convinced that we will not be able to create
a level playing field in the automotive industry as long as such
loopholes exist. I think we need to support Kaliningrad as a production site, but only on conditions that are as consistent as possible
with the new stage of industrial assembly we have agreed with the
Ministry of Economic Development!

Within the structure of imports we can see a clear stratification of
the supply chain. Legal entities import new cars, while private individuals mostly import used cars. The growing volume of imports
once again demonstrates that, in terms of consumer preferences,
the Russian market has long been a developed one. One of the key
challenges for foreign companies seeking to maintain their market
share is to offer the fullest possible line-up. High duties on used cars
have led to a reduction in the share of imported used cars sold in the
secondary market, from 18 per cent before the crisis to 3 per cent
today. This measure has proved completely worthwhile.

This year the sale of lorries increased significantly, partly due to
government procurement programmes. At the same time, domestic
manufacturers of lorries were able to retain a dominant position
in the market. The growth of imports was mainly the result of

heightened demand for articulated lorries used in international transportation, as well as medium-duty lorries. We have also seen a substantial increase in imports of used coaches, which have nearly doubled (or tripled if we include imports of new coaches). It is time to think seriously about the safety of passenger transportation and to take the necessary measures to restrict the use of such used vehicles.

I have already mentioned that the state played a key role in all segments in 2010. For instance, state support for passenger cars amounted to 25–30 per cent of annual sales. The most effective measures included recycling and soft auto lending programmes. Incidentally, we completed the second stage of the latter programme and started issuing an additional 100,000 certificates to citizens towards the adjusted limits for 2011. The popularity of soft auto loans made the programme, which was extended in 2011, another driver of demand. Banks extended 160,000 loans and received over 340,000 applications.

State procurement turned out to be most effective for commercial vehicles. It accounted for 20–25 per cent of sales in these segments. However, we must focus on gradually phasing out state programmes aimed at stimulating the demand for light vehicles and on growing commercial sales. According to our estimates, this trend will be noticeable in the spring of 2011. At the same time, the state will continue to significantly shape the demand for lorries and coaches. This is dictated by the need to upgrade the fleet. One example: according to the Ministry of Transport, more than 50 per cent of coaches need to be replaced because they are technologically obsolete or excessively worn.

As we emerge from the crisis, we are beginning to address the main objective of the *Strategy* – to form and develop a full-fledged domestic automotive industry. What does a full-fledged automotive industry mean for us? It means having manufacturers in the country that either control or indirectly influence the entire chain of creation of added value.

The Russian market has gone through several stages in its development. The initial stage was a period of haphazard trade policies on the part of companies in the Russian market. Sales were largely made through 'grey schemes'. The qualitative and quantitative growth of demand then led to the centralisation of sales and the formation of dealer networks (Rolf, Musa Motors and so on).

Figure 4.7 Stage one, 2004

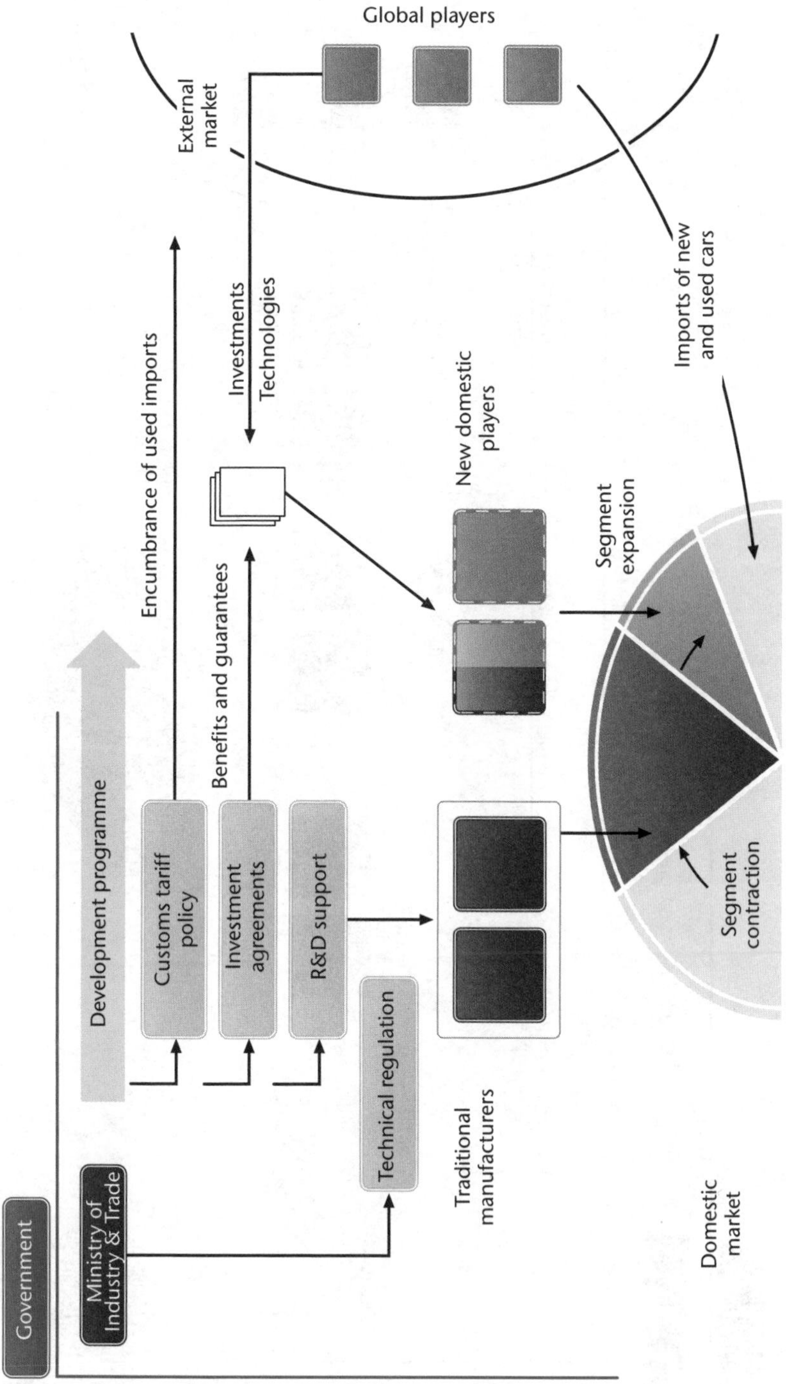

Figure 4.8 Stage two, 2020

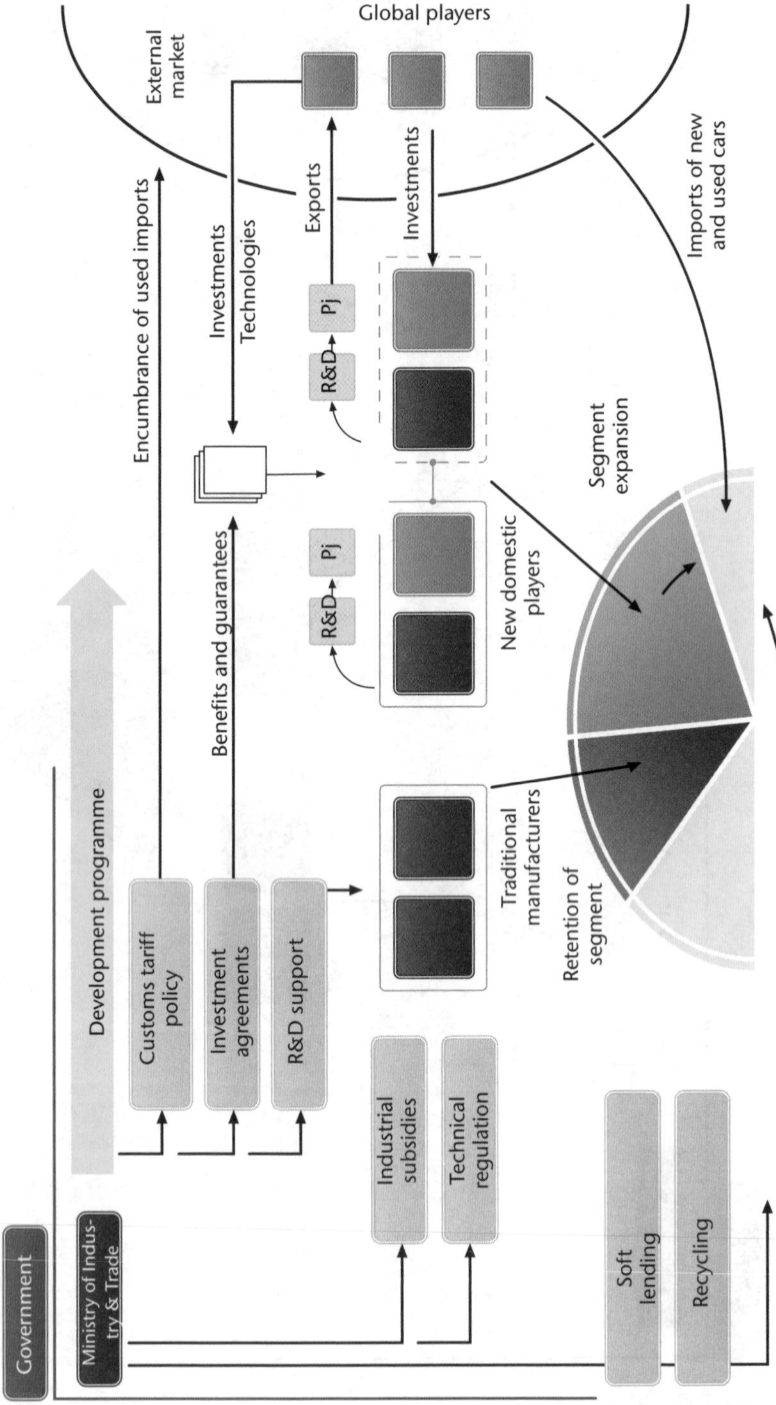

During the next stage, the state made its first attempts to attract foreign companies to set up production in Russia, since efforts by Russian businesspeople to establish joint ventures had been isolated events and had ended in failure.

The situation was changed by Resolutions nos 135 and 413 of 1998. These allowed for duty-free imports of components (through the mechanism of free customs warehouses) in exchange for investment in the construction of assembly plants. Only three auto makers – TagAZ, Renault and Ford – planned to take advantage of this regime. In the end, only Ford started operating under this regime in 2001.

Another mechanism for supporting the automotive industry was the federal law on the free economic zone in Kaliningrad. However, the latter has always been intended for just one player, Avtotor. All of these actions have had an impact on the market, despite the crisis of 1998.

The greatest impact on the creation of assembly sites was generated by Government Resolution no. 166 and the introduction of the mechanism of industrial assembly in 2004. This new tool gave a real impetus to the creation of production facilities in Russia by global players, resulting in the creation of 18 auto assembly complexes. However, their capacity exceeds current market demand and remains under-utilised. This is partly the result of market maturity and openness.

More than 370 models are already being sold in Russia today, of which only 130 are for mass use (sales of more than 1,000 units per year), while market volume does not exceed 2 million units. As a result, the localisation of production is going much slower than expected.

The proposed new regime will help solve these problems and support the large manufacturers that have not merely declared Russia to be a strategic market but actually treat it as such in practice. At the same time, we have always advocated equal operating conditions in the industry for all players. However, it is obvious that only companies with rights to the product and core development competencies will be able to create the backbone of the industry. I am convinced that support for assembly projects outside the perimeter of global auto makers will only be effective while customs benefits remain in place. As soon as these are phased out, interest in the projects might be lost. From the perspective of the *Strategy*, this makes no sense.

The current industrial assembly regime has served its purpose. The next step is to create effective tools for implementing the strategic scenario of 'partnership'. This will make it possible to 'close' the value-added chain by absorbing aggregate plants and engineering units – that is, to meet the objective of creating and developing a full-fledged automotive industry in Russia.

In figures, it looks like this:

◆ Up to 80 per cent of all automobiles sold in the Russian Federation should be manufactured domestically.
◆ The share of value added that is created domestically – in other words the localisation of production – should be at least 50 per cent.

By 2020, the value added that is created in Russia, in absolute terms, will increase 4.5 times to RUB 2.250 trillion. According to the *Strategy*, the passenger car and light commercial vehicle segments will develop in partnership with foreign companies through the creation of joint ventures or alliances. Foreign companies will produce up to half of the vehicles in the passenger car segment at their Russian plants. In the lorry and coach segment, a major exporter (national champion) will be developed.

The key condition for bringing about these scenarios is to preserve existing customs duty rates until 2014. Assuming that a compromise will be found regarding Russia's entry into the WTO, I think it is necessary to outline the basic parameters of a new industrial assembly regime. The main objectives of 'Industrial Assembly 2' are to reduce the number of platforms while increasing production per platform, assimilate partner technology, create a modern component industry, and integrate into global R&D.

Based on this analysis, we have drawn up and co-ordinated with the Ministry of Economic Development a joint decree that calls for:

◆ Granting additional benefits to importers of components 'for industrial assembly' for a period of eight years (but not later than the end of 2020) in exchange for a commitment to create new and/or upgraded facilities for the production of at least 300,000–350,000 new vehicles per year, as well as engines and/or gearboxes, at least 30 per cent of which must be installed in the manufactured cars.

◆ Calculating the level of localisation for value added, as well as establishing reporting requirements that will make it possible to determine conclusively whether a particular component is actually made in Russia.

◆ Undertaking to achieve an average level of value added (localisation) of at least 60 per cent for the declared line-up no later than five years after the date of signing of the supplemental agreement. This will enable the manufacturer to decide for itself which models should be localised, and to what extent.

At the same time, we are limiting the scope and timeframe of SKD assembly. It will still be up to the manufacturer to select the technology for specific models. Companies that do not wish to participate in Industrial Assembly 2 will be able to finish implementing their agreements under previously agreed requirements and deadlines.

An approved Action Plan for implementing the second stage of the *Strategy* was recently presented to the Government. I shall briefly outline what has been done and what remains to be done in certain areas.

Updating the vehicle fleet

Here there are two main objectives. The first is to create tax or economic incentives for purchasing new, environmentally friendly and energy-efficient vehicles. The second is to upgrade the lorry and coach fleet. We have done some serious work with market participants. This has shown that blind imitation of car recycling experience in these segments does not produce the desired effect. We should continue to focus on programmes aimed at upgrading specific types of equipment, such as public transport, along the same lines as the programme implemented by the Ministry of Regional Development in 2009–10. The Ministry of Industry and Trade and the Ministry of Regional Development agree that such a programme, coupled with a ban on the operation of coaches more than 15 years old, might not only support manufacturers but also greatly improve transportation safety. This initiative could then be developed for other types of transport. This concept is generally supported by manufacturers. That is why I suggest returning to a discussion about funding for this area in the coming year.

Figure 4.9 The automotive industry: the situation in 2011

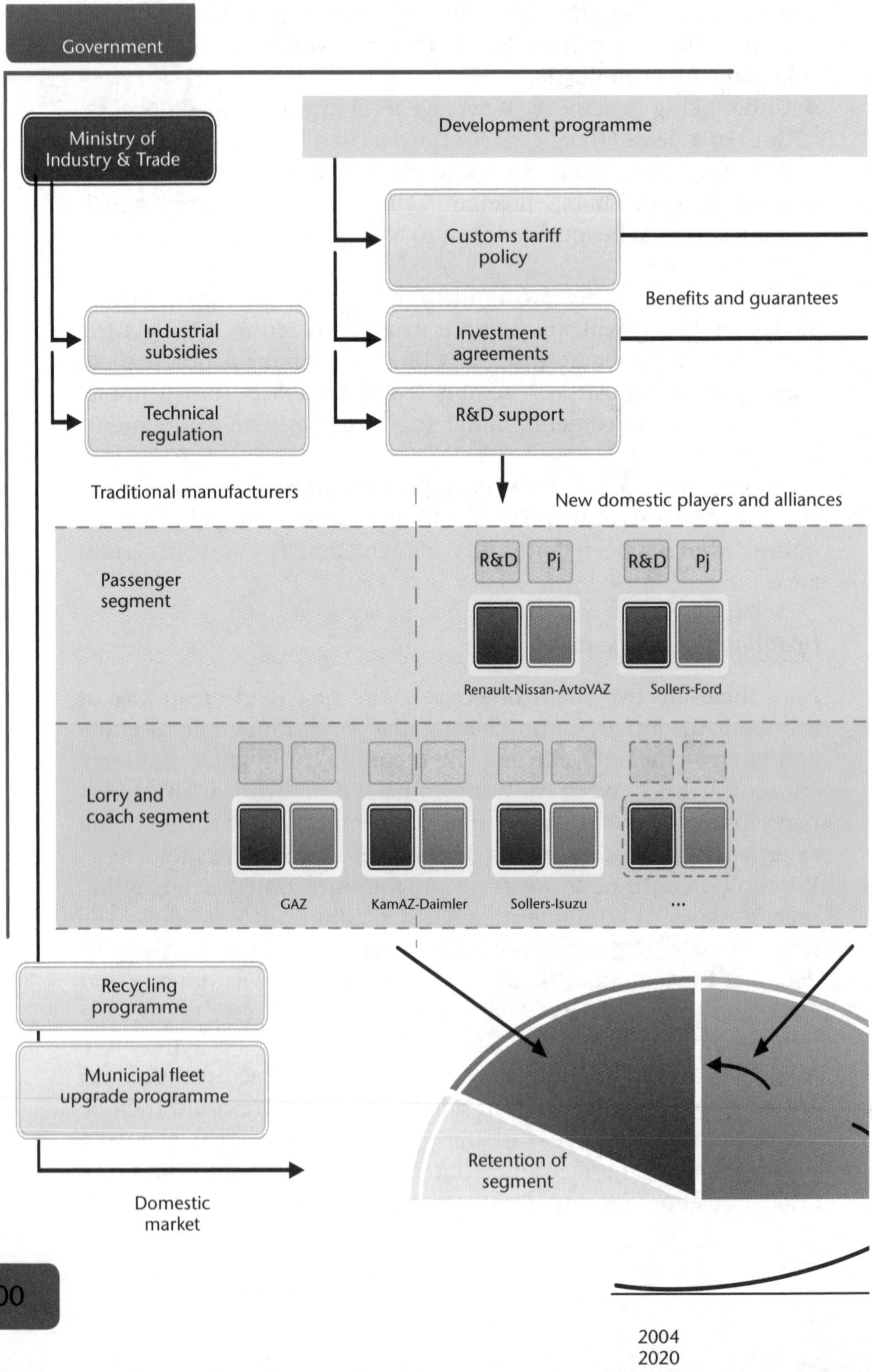

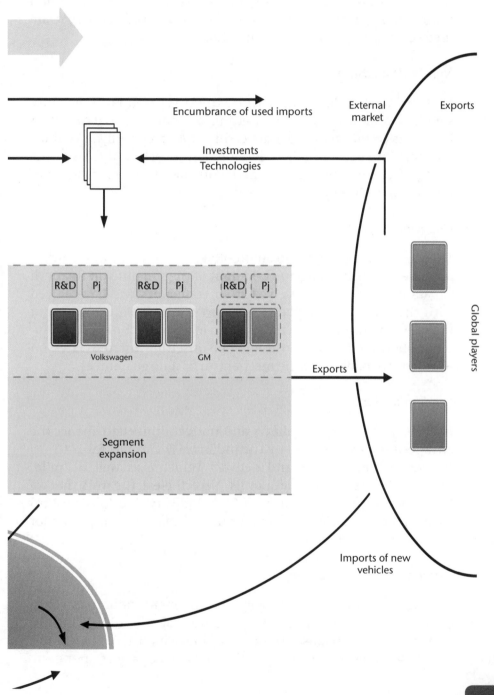

The expansion of exports

This occupies an important place in the *Strategy*. Special attention should be paid to the work of the Export Insurance Agency and the opening of export credit lines. These are the tools that are used successfully by all WTO countries.

Non-tariff measures

In the context of Russia's entry into the WTO, non-tariff measures should become a key tool for offsetting low duties on used cars. (Our European counterparts have used this tool successfully.) We must take this into account when developing the technical rules of the Customs Union, and tighten the requirements for certification of individual vehicle models.

Financial support

This is generally provided to automotive companies using resources set aside under the Budget Act. In light of the still difficult financial situation and requests received from companies, we have agreed with the Ministry of Finance to approve a possible expansion of the rules on offsetting interest rates on loans for technical re-equipping, allowing for the possibility of offsetting interest rates on restructured loans using the mechanism of state guarantees.

Funding for R&D

In 2010, the Ministry of Industry and Trade continued to finance the advanced research needed by the industry. The results for 2009–10 include hybrid coaches and delivery vehicles, as well as 'mild' hybrids with starter-generator units. Nevertheless, the work that we fund does not cover the needs of the industry. We look forward to further discussions regarding forms and sources of financing for research and development work.

Staffing

In conclusion, I would like to speak for a moment about the staffing of the industry. Despite the large number of educational institutions that train specialists for the automotive industry (17 institutes and universities producing up to 1,500 graduates a year), not more than 10 per cent of them go on to work in the industry. Here we can see a clear need to work with institutions of higher learning and the Ministry of Education and Science to develop a programme reflecting the combined interests of the institutions and the industry. Only then will graduates not only be in demand but also be employed in their specialty area. The implementation of *Strategy Auto-2020* gives young specialists clear prospects. A new milestone in training was the development of professional standards for automotive companies. The Ministry of Industry and Trade will fund this work in 2011. We are also counting on the support of businesses. Operating under alliances with foreign manufacturers, they are not only well aware of future needs, but have gone far in implementing advanced methods of training.

Only the implementation of this whole package of measures will enable us to create a full-fledged competitive automotive industry in Russia.

Figure 4.10 The shipbuilding industry: the situation in 2004

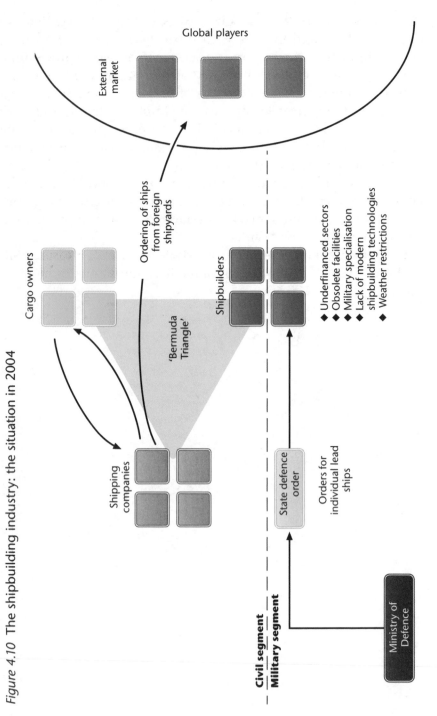

Shipbuilding

This is one of the few industries where the Russian market is big enough to support the highest level of competitiveness. There have been some extremely interesting developments in the industry in terms of both material science and unique products. However, an entire technological system was missed out, and the demand for equipment and the transportation of goods, as well as offshore development, disappeared from our country. Even a partial return of demand will create a solid base for developing the shipbuilding industry, particularly in the civil sector, since military shipbuilding has managed to survive one way or another.

Interview with Rossiyskaya Gazeta, *18 October 2006:*

Viktor Borisovich, what does the Russian shipbuilding industry basically consist of today?

First of all, we must differentiate between civil and military ship-building. Whereas military shipbuilding has survived over the past 15 years due to the state defence order and overseas orders within the framework of military-technical co-operation agreements, and has retained some potential, the situation in civil shipbuilding is quite complicated.

Today, domestic civil shipbuilding exists in a fragmented form. Enterprises have fallen behind technologically (with rare exceptions), and their production capacities are not in demand even among domestic ship owners. In addition, many types of vessels that are needed by Russian shippers (such as gas carriers with a deadweight of more than 90,000 tonnes) are still well beyond the capabilities of existing Russian shipyards. Thus, today we are basically talking about changing the face of the industry.

Is the industry's fragmentation largely responsible for its problems?

Definitely. There are essentially three groups of problems today. First, there are the structural imbalances of the shipbuilding industry: a mismatch between the scale and structure of production and the actual demand for civil products

Second, the industry today is characterised by an extremely low level of technology and organisational management. Building vessels in domestic shipyards takes two to three times longer, and involves higher costs, than in foreign ones.

A third but equally important problem is the flawed nature of domestic legislation and financial infrastructure compared with foreign conditions. The shipbuilding industry is very complex and unique, requiring large amounts of capital investment for relatively long periods of time. In other countries, for example, loans are extended in the amount of 80 per cent of the price of the vessel at 6–8 per cent APR for a period of 10 years or more. In addition, shipbuilding is directly subsidised to the tune of up to 6 per cent of the vessel's cost. In Russia, loans are short-term and expensive, and foreign lenders often make loans contingent on ordering associated hardware from the West and registering the vessels built with these loans under a foreign flag.

Is there any demand at all for products made by Russian shipbuilders? Surely there is no point in developing the industry if there are no orders?

The Russian economy has been growing in recent years. Ship owners are transporting more and more cargo. What kind of cargo? Oil, gas, metals, timber, grain, and products from the processing industries. The water transportation market is showing steady growth, and hence there is a need for new vessels. Therefore, when assessing the situation in the shipbuilding industry, we tried to look at it from the point of view of all market participants, and identified those priority niches in which our shipbuilders would be able to compete.

We must focus on developing several priority market segments, such as offshore development and the development of the fishing and river fleets, while continuing to focus on the concentration of efforts aimed at creating complex high-tech ships, including those that are designed to work in extreme climatic conditions. In other words, we must select those niches where we can and should be competitive. In each niche that is selected on the basis of analysis, the state must create the economic conditions for the emergence of a sort of magic triangle of equal interest, consisting of cargo owners, ship owners and shipbuilders. Let me also emphasise that this should be a market-based alliance, not an administrative one.

What does the Ministry of Industry and Energy propose for the development of the industry?

We have prepared a *Strategy for the Development and Reform of the Shipbuilding Industry*, in which we propose a range of modern regulatory tools, selected in light of the specific problems facing

the Russian shipbuilding industry. This document defines the optimal choice of potential market niches and mechanisms of state support for the industry. We start from the assumption that the resources used to create and maintain a modern military fleet – production capacities, technology, human resources, and R&D – can and should be used to develop civil shipbuilding. Conversely, civil shipbuilding should 'feed' its military counterpart with new approaches to management, new technologies and so on.

The strategy proposes solutions to the industry's problems in three areas. First of all, it is necessary to make timely and significant changes to the law. In the context of budget law, we propose that starting in 2008 the federal budget should reimburse the cost of interest on loans used to purchase or build ships. We also propose allocating budget resources to increase the equity capital of leasing companies and to reimburse Russian shipping companies for part of their leasing costs. Components that are not yet produced in Russia should be exempt from import VAT and import duties. We also think it is necessary to reduce VAT to 0 per cent for vessels manufactured in the Russian Federation for Russian companies, and to exempt shipyards from property tax and land tax.

The second area involves facilitating technological modernisation in the industry. We propose using the federal budget to finance Russian companies' acquisition of licences to advanced marine shipbuilding technologies, which are currently lacking in our country. The Federal Targeted Programme for the Development of the MIC, as well as the new targeted programme to promote shipyard products on the market in 2008–15, should play a decisive role in this. The bulk of resources should be channelled into the development of pilot projects, the development of the scientific and technological base, and the diversification and technical re-equipping of shipyards.

Finally, the third area involves optimising the structure of the shipbuilding industry. What is more important: integration or disintegration, diversification or specialisation? Decisions must be taken based on the effectiveness of particular methods of implementing priority programmes, as well as specific aspects of doing business.

So what do you expect from the implementation of the proposals made by the Ministry of Industry and Energy?

First, a qualitative change in the state of affairs in the industry. We estimate that by 2015 the utilisation of shipbuilding capacity will increase by a factor of at least three to four, to 70–75 per cent (it currently stands at about 20 per cent). Improving the financial and economic situation of enterprises will ensure a permanent rise in salaries of at least 15 per cent a year, which will noticeably reduce the problem of retaining qualified personnel. In general, we expect that Russia will take its rightful place among the leading maritime nations.

From a report on the status and development prospects of the Russian shipbuilding industry, delivered at a meeting with Prime Minister Putin, St Petersburg, 13 May 2008:

Over the past two years, special attention has been paid to the development of the shipbuilding industry. The main tasks have been defined as follows:

◆ maintaining Russia's status as a leading maritime power;
◆ winning and securing a niche for Russia in the world's civil and
  military shipbuilding market.

Specific steps have been taken to develop and maintain the
competitiveness of domestic shipbuilding.

A decree on the establishment of USC was signed in March 2007,
and the company was incorporated in November last year. Three
subholdings have been formed according to the territorial structure
within the framework of USC. These are to become regional integrators of the industrial and innovative capacity of the industry's
enterprises.

Given the potential of St Petersburg as a research and design
centre of the shipbuilding industry, this city was chosen as the
headquarters of USC. Work is now under way on the main area of
the USC development and production programme.

In September 2007, a development strategy for the shipbuilding
industry up to 2020 and beyond was approved by order of the
Ministry of Industry and Energy.

In February 2008, the Federal Targeted Programme for the
Development of Civil Marine Engineering for 2009–16 was adopted
in pursuance of the strategy.

The industry's enterprises produce over RUB 132 billion worth
of marketable products a year. That said, about 50 per cent of this
volume is accounted for by enterprises belonging to USC. Every
third shipbuilder works for one of these enterprises.

At the same time, the formation of seven shipbuilding industry
companies in the areas of instrument making, underwater weapons,
and an industrial design and shipbuilding technology centre is
nearing completion. Krylovskiy State Research Centre has been
given the task of developing fundamental applied science in the
field of shipbuilding.

An analysis of the structure of the industry's marketable production shows that military shipbuilding predominates. In 2007, ships
manufactured for the Russian Ministry of Defence as part of military-
technical co-operation accounted for 74 per cent of production.
Accordingly, civil shipbuilding accounted for only 26 per cent.

To ensure the stability of the industry and bring down the cost
of its products, including in the context of the state defence order,
we must actively develop the civil component of the industry. An

analysis of the product line of civil vessels shows that the industry has extensive capacity to satisfy first and foremost the needs of Russian customers, including in the context of Russian offshore development projects. That said, the bulk of demand for domestic shipbuilding products will be concentrated in the sector of high-tech vessels and offshore structures.

At the same time, there are a number of problems hampering the development of the domestic shipbuilding industry. First of all, there is a high degree of deterioration of production capacity. In addition, not all types of vessels and marine equipment needed by the civil sector can be manufactured at existing Russian shipyards because of their technical features and engineering capabilities.

Only 28 per cent of the total demand from domestic ship owners can be met by Russian shipyards for technical and economic reasons. However, only 8 per cent of the total demand will be satisfied by Russian shipbuilders in 2008. The remaining 20 per cent that could have been met will be built by foreign shipyards. The way to change this situation is through the ongoing restructuring of the industry, as well as its modernisation.

Another constraint is the fact that in both civil and naval shipbuilding, most of the models produced (70 per cent) are lead ships. In other words, virtually three out of four vessels produced in our shipyards are made according to individual designs. Thus, the advanced technologies and organisational methods that are used in mass production cannot be applied in this situation. This in turn pushes up labour and operating costs.

If we look at Russia's demand for ships and floating structures during the period 2008–15, the bulk of it consists of technical equipment for offshore development and vessels serving oil and gas production (about US$15 billion in total) and transport vessels (US$3.2 billion). Total demand comprises more than 500 vessels with a total combined cost of US$22.8 billion. In order to implement the presented plans at Russian shipyards, the problems that have accumulated will have to be overcome, and a wide range of new challenges will have to be met.

The *Development Strategy for the Domestic Shipbuilding Industry up to 2020 and Beyond* includes not only a set of specific measures, but also indicators that show the level of performance in achieving the goals and meeting the objectives of the strategy throughout the entire implementation period. One of these indicators is the increase in labour productivity in the industry. Naturally, in order to raise productivity at our shipyards we need to restructure the industry, change its technological appearance, change the mentality of workers and managers, and create new capacity.

If the planned measures are implemented, we can more than double the output of the shipbuilding industry by 2015 through the modernisation of existing facilities and the construction of new shipyards. In 2007, a number of such projects were submitted in a call for tenders by the Ministry of Industry and Energy. These will allow us not only to boost productivity through the use of modern production techniques and modern technology, but also to overcome factors currently hindering the construction of vessels with deadweights of more than 70,000 tonnes. The timeframe for implementing each of these projects is five to six years.

The *Development Strategy for the Domestic Shipbuilding Industry up to 2020 and Beyond* calls for using a number of tools to encourage the leasing and purchase of domestically produced ships by Russian ship owners. The state budget for 2008–10 provides for the allocation of RUB 9.3 billion for this purpose.

If the planned product range covers the basic needs of Russian ship owners, including the demand generated by ambitious plans for Russian offshore development, then consolidating the strengths of various enterprises, including the investment potential and initiative of private entrepreneurs, may enable us to achieve higher rates of development in the industry.

An analysis of the situation in the western region suggests that combining the efforts of USC and the United Industrial Corporation, for example, could bring down costs when fulfilling the state defence order. This can be achieved using fibreglass manufacturing technologies and other technologies for the construction of corvettes, support vessels and ice-class vessels. Private shareholders are ready to provide not only their unique technological capabilities, such as the Baltic Shipyard, but also investments and marketing experience.

Another project involves the idea of building a new shipyard in the Leningrad region. Private investors can contribute to this project by providing the bulk of investment, creating modern auxiliary production, and facilitating a transition to technologies for the construction of large ice-class vessels based on modern methods of construction in large blocks.

In addition, we expect to acquire the most important modern

technologies from other countries. These capabilities will be combined with the shipbuilding experience, existing technologies and brand recognition of Admiralty Shipyards.

This interaction will allow us to ensure the implementation of projects involving the construction of liquid gas carriers and tankers with a deadweight of more than 100,000–150,000 tonnes, as well as projects involving the construction of complex offshore structures for shelf development.

In the Northern shipbuilding centre, we plan to focus on improving the efficiency of the management system and restructuring the state assets that are present there. This applies first of all to Sevmash and the Zvezdochka Shipyard. A great deal of work has been already done, as a result of which six shipyards of the Ministry of Defence have been merged with the Zvezdochka Shipyard. The purpose of Zvezdochka's new branches, which are located at naval bases, is to ensure that ship repair and maintenance targets are met. In addition, these branches are expected to be involved in vessel repair work. It should be emphasised that Zvezdochka focuses on implementing priority tasks for the Navy.

In the Russian Far East, we plan to build a new shipyard in collaboration with our South Korean partners. Their expertise, technology and resources should enable us to meet the needs of the commercial fleet in the Far East, including the production of marine equipment for the Sakhalin and Kamchatka shelf.

We attach special importance to implementing the Programme for the Development of Civil Marine Engineering. Under this programme, 74 per cent of funding is channelled into R&D, while 21 per cent of funds will be allocated to maintain the laboratories and offshore infrastructure for the aforementioned research. In addition, more than 5 per cent will be spent on market research, quality standardisation, certification of production and so on. The main areas of R&D fully correlate with the objectives of the domestic shipbuilding industry and marine programmes.

From a report on the development of civilian marine technology, delivered at a meeting of the Government of the Russian Federation, Moscow, 6 March 2009:

About 160,000 people are employed by 168 shipbuilding enterprises. The main facilities are concentrated in the north-west of Russia. The industry works with more than 2,000 assembly plants.

In recent years, the industry has posted steady sales growth – RUB 148 billion in 2008, projected sales of about RUB 180 billion before the economic crisis in 2009, and around RUB 170 billion under current conditions. Military products are the dominant component of these sales, comprising around 70 per cent.

The share of civil shipbuilding products and services for the domestic market has grown over the past year, making up one third of total output including exports.

However, despite the positive indicators of recent years, the industry's systemic problems have yet to be resolved. These problems include:

◆ the low competitiveness of civil shipbuilding as a result of extensive deterioration of production assets and a critical situation with human resources;
◆ structural imbalances in the industry;
◆ a lack of long-term and cheap credit resources in the country's financial system (I should point out that this last problem increases the cost of domestic production by 20–25 per cent).

Unfortunately, the global financial crisis has only exacerbated this difficult situation.

In order to improve the competitiveness of domestic shipbuilding, we have prepared and approved a *Strategy for the Development and Reform of the Shipbuilding Industry for the Period up to 2020 and Beyond*. The main objective of the *Strategy* is to give the industry a new competitive character.

In order to solve the tasks outlined by the *Strategy,* the following three programme periods have been established:

◆ short term – up to 2010;
◆ medium term – up to 2015;
◆ long term – up to 2020 and beyond.

Each period has its own specifics, objectives, criteria and resource support. A step-by-step approach to solving these resource-intensive and time-consuming tasks, based on the principle of 'simple to complex', allows us first of all to concentrate our efforts on the most immediate goals, as well as ensuring that we maintain a long-range vision and strategic direction for the industry.

The objective of stage one (2007–10), which is currently under consideration, is to preserve the most valuable part of the industry's potential and to consolidate the positions reached earlier. In addition, at this stage we should form a list of promising projects that can be implemented by the end of 2010.

Civil production should be clearly oriented towards filling market segments in which such products may be popular and competitive. The core of the product range capable of ensuring the efficient operation of the Russian shipbuilding industry in particular consists of high-tech vessels. The main market niches are defined by the strategies for developing industries that consume shipbuilding products, as well as the corresponding federal targeted programmes (FTPs). Many of them will start to be implemented in 2009. So far, there has not been any significant growth in purchases, but we hope that despite the economic crisis all the plans we have outlined for the acquisition of the shipbuilding products will be implemented.

In addition, we are guided by the indicators of non-programme budget-funded measures taken by the Federal Service for Hydrometeorology and Environmental Monitoring (Roshydromet) and the Federal Atomic Energy Agency (Rosatom), the plans of energy companies, and USC OJSC's preliminary plans for co-operation with Cuba, Venezuela, Argentina and other countries.

Taking into account the strategic goals of a maximum number of market players will allow us to balance the interests of shipbuilders and buyers of these products. This approach becomes particularly relevant in crisis conditions, which increase the potential antagonism between different market participants.

At the beginning of the fourth quarter of last year [2008], the combined demand from domestic and foreign customers was consistent with the earlier estimates of the *Strategy*, and even slightly exceeded them.

Compared with the basic range of civil marine technology that has been under construction since 2007, the domestic shipbuilding industry is currently fulfilling non-recurrent but large orders. At the same time their total tonnage, compared with the combined orders of Russian ship owners, is insignificant. We believe that there is significant potential for import substitution.

Current measures of state support for shipbuilding include the following:

◆ In order to implement projects involving the leasing of domestically manufactured ships, funds have been allocated for the capitalisation of USC.

◆ Subsidies have been set aside for Russian ship owners to offset some of their leasing costs when acquiring vessels built at Russian shipyards.

◆ Interest payments on loans for the purchase of ships built at Russian shipyards have also been subsidised.

At the same time, it is obvious that some of these means should be considered to support orders of river vessels and fleets for small fishing and companies.

All measures of state support for the development of shipbuilding that are provided for in the budget up to 2011, including measures implemented by existing FTPs, amount to more than RUB 30 billion in total. In addition to the industry-specific FTP for the Development of Civil Marine Engineering for 2009–16, there are a number of other programmes that fund measures aimed at developing the shipbuilding industry.

With the help of the relevant federal executive authorities, the Ministry of Industry and Trade has developed and approved a *Comprehensive Action Plan to Implement the Strategy for the Development of the Shipbuilding Industry up to 2020 and Beyond.* The main sections of the *Comprehensive Action Plan* include:

◆ innovation projects and the creation of scientific and engineering capacity for the future;
◆ organisational and structural changes and the optimisation of industry potential;
◆ maintaining and strengthening human resources;
◆ legislative and regulatory support for shipbuilding development.

The comprehensive solution of problems facing the domestic civil shipbuilding industry will be effected primarily within the framework of the FTP for the Development of Civil Marine Engineering for 2009–16.

In developing this programme, we considered more than 1,500 recommendations from 80 entities in various branches of industry and science and educational institutions with an interest in the programme's implementation. In its final form, the programme

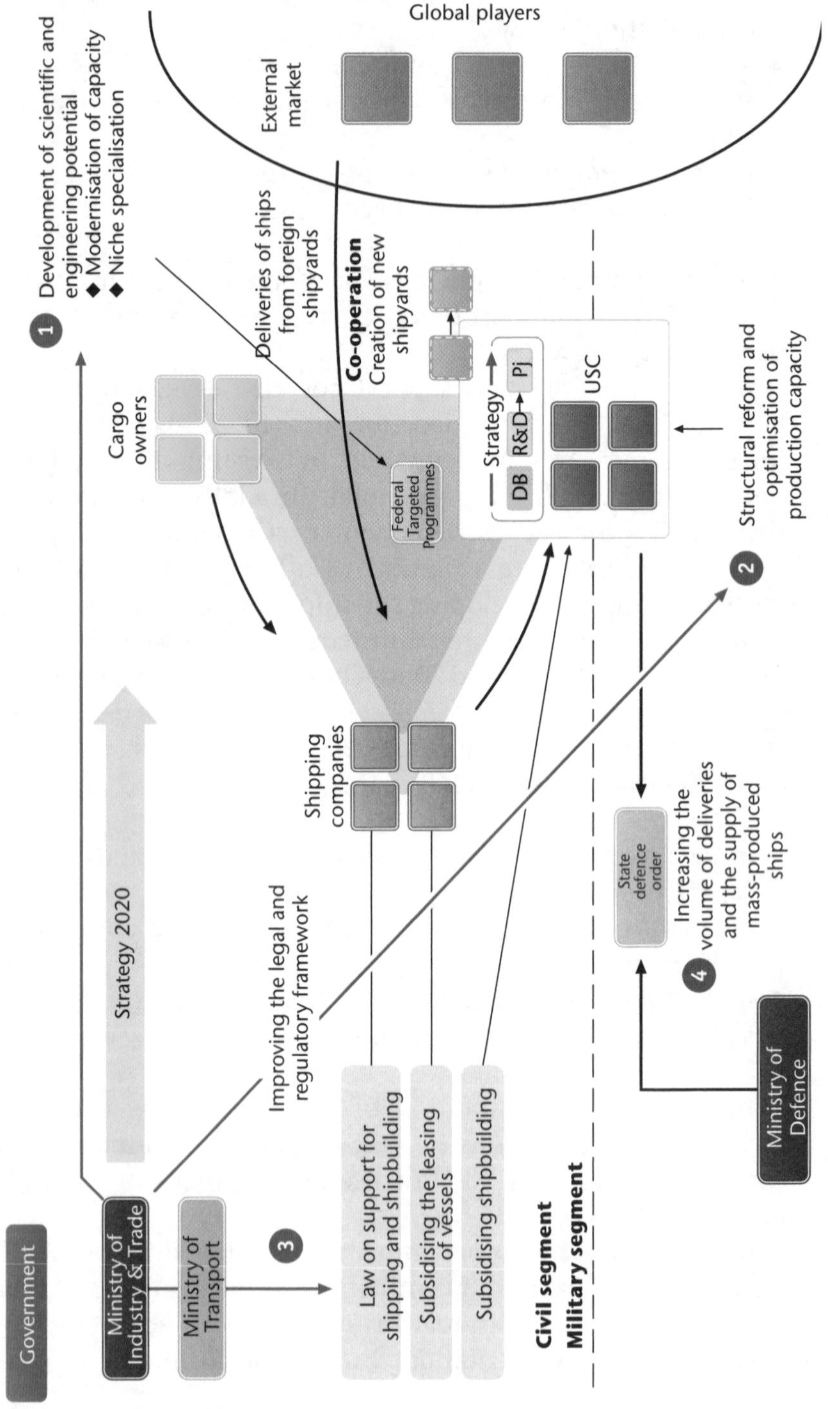

Figure 4.11 The shipbuilding industry: the situation in 2011

provides for the implementation of 138 R&D projects and 75 projects for the capital construction of scientific infrastructure. The total amount expected to be allocated to the programme for the period 2009–16 is RUB 136.4 billion.

In the coming decade, the most significant market for civil ship-building will be linked with the production and transportation of liquid hydrocarbons in the Arctic. Therefore, the programme's two main technological areas ('Offshore development' and 'New look') address urgent tasks associated with the shipbuilding industry's full-fledged participation in this sector. Within the framework of the programme, we expect to achieve the necessary level of scientific and engineering capacity for the creation of complex offshore structures – offshore platforms, facilities for the development of field infrastructure, and vessels for the transportation of hydrocarbons (with a special emphasis on designing and building ice-class liquefied natural gas (LNG) carriers).

Currently, the share of domestic shipboard equipment installed on ships under construction is extremely small, with this niche largely occupied by imported equipment. Therefore, one of the programme's technical areas ('Shipboard engineering and energy') is fully devoted to creating competitive prototypes and subsequently launching production of them.

Full implementation of the programme will have a high social impact by maintaining and creating highly skilled jobs in ship-building and related industries. The projected tax revenues payable to the federal budget for the period of 2009–16 from civil shipbuilding production will exceed RUB 130 billion as against RUB 90 billion in budget expenditures on implementation of the programme.

According to our estimates, a real breakthrough in the development of the domestic shipbuilding industry and an increase in its competitiveness can only be achieved if new high-tech shipyards are introduced. Since 2007, work has been under way in the industry to review designs for the creation of modern shipbuilding capacity in the Western, Northern and Far Eastern regions. We are studying the possibility of implementing these projects through the mechanisms of a public–private partnership (Vyborg Shipyard, Primorsk, and the modernisation of plants: Sevmash Production Association OJSC, Severnaya Verf Shipyard OJSC, Admiralty Shipyards OJSC and so on).

In the eastern section of the Gulf of Finland we are considering several locations for a multipurpose shipyard suitable for large-capacity shipbuilding. We believe the establishment of three to four new shipyards similar to the Primorsk Shipyard will be sufficient to meet the demand for new vessels.

The main products of the new shipyards will be floating facilities and transport vessels for the offshore production, processing and transportation of hydrocarbons.

Unfortunately, the implementation of the first stage of the strategy has coincided with the global financial and economic crisis, and negative events can affect our plans in terms of the scale and speed of deployment of new facilities and the creation of products. To put it more simply, the implementation of designated projects might be pushed back.

One of the anti-crisis measures being taken by the Ministry of Industry and Trade is constant economic and financial monitoring of strategic enterprises in the shipbuilding industry. A key factor in supporting the industry amidst the instability of global financial markets is to maintain appropriate lending conditions at Russian banks. After all, shipbuilding has perhaps the longest production cycle among all branches of industry, as well as the corresponding costs and risks. In addition, it is necessary to support the implementation of priority investment projects involving the modernisation of existing shipyards and the creation of new, high-performance ones. Therefore, the most common form of state support requested by enterprises in the industry today is subsidies on loan interest.

Despite this, the key objectives, targets and performance indicators of the Development Strategy for the shipbuilding industry remain valid and unchanged:

◆ providing for state needs in naval and civil shipbuilding;
◆ maintaining positions in the global military shipbuilding market at the level of 15–20 per cent;
◆ exports of civil products – 2 per cent of world sales.

The iron and steel industry

One of the key factors in developing a strategy for the development of the iron and steel industry is the fact that the industry is almost entirely in the private sector. It has stood firmly on its own feet, at least until the economic crisis, and was developing with funding from private resources. Tools for building the strategy were to a greater extent based on corporate development programmes, rather than on the formulation of a large package of 'external' objectives on behalf of the state. The only thing that needed to be done was co-ordination or harmonisation with the requirements of other industries, as well as national and global marketing in collaboration with the metals industry – for example, when the development strategy for the automotive industry made it clear to the metal producers that they, and consequently their projects and investments, needed to be involved.

Synergy across separate branches is another key principle of our strategic planning. Metallurgy does not only involve the automotive industry; it also includes construction and the infrastructure monopolies. It also means a change in the principles of technical regulation, which in the field of oil and gas production, for example, can produce major shifts in pipeline manufacturers' projects.

From a report delivered at a meeting with Prime Minister Putin in the city of Vyksa, 24 July 2008:

Over the past 15 years, the global market for steel and iron products has shown steady development. Since 1991, steel production has doubled. At the same time, the geographical distribution of the main production facilities and major markets has changed greatly over the years, and Russia has played a major role in this process.

In order to understand the past, and therefore the prospects, of the domestic iron and steel industry, it is important to note the qualitative changes. Earlier (in the 1980s) domestic metallurgists focused primarily on domestic demand, as in fact did their foreign counterparts. In the 1990s, in the context of a general industrial decline, there was also a sharp decline in domestic consumption of metal in Russia. In this situation, the only way to maintain and even increase the volume of production was by skilfully taking advantage of the global market situation. The sole scenario for preserving the industry was to boost exports.

Figure 4.12 The iron and steel industry: the situation in 2004

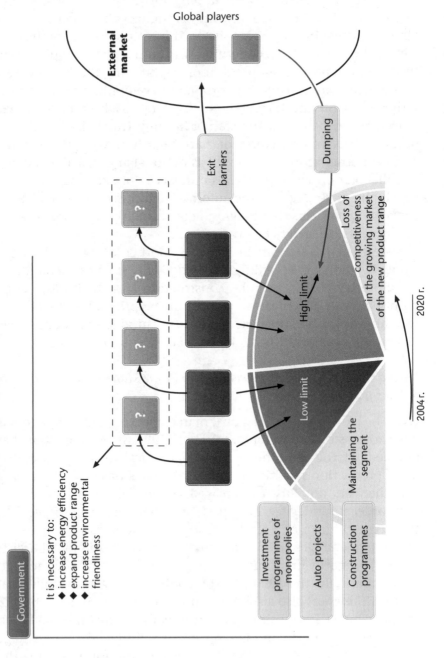

The favourable state of affairs for Russian steelmakers was largely due to rising demand for metal from the emerging markets of Asia and South America, as well as certain aspects of the metal industries' development in the advanced market economies (heightened environmental requirements imposed on enterprises, high labour costs and so on). As a result, the iron and steel industry (along with the oil and gas industry) became one of the first basic export-oriented sectors of the Russian economy.

Since the beginning of the new century, the situation has changed considerably. The most noticeable changes were caused by a large increase in the individual potential of those same developing countries, especially China, which has seen its production capacity triple since 1991. Even at this rate, however, China, India, Brazil could not meet their domestic demand at that time. The traditionally largest producers (the United States, the European Union and Russia) continued to see their share of world production decline.

In this situation, more and more countries started to resort to various measures to protect their domestic markets, and accordingly their manufacturers. Pressure from rapidly developing China contributed to this as well. In some countries, such as the United States and Canada, import duties on Chinese pipes reached 700 per cent. Russia, however, does not use this approach.

The growth of barriers in markets that were traditional for Russian companies in many ways predetermined the changes in their foreign economic strategies. An effective response to the emerging risks in the distribution of finished products was a shift away from exporting products in favour of exporting capital – the purchase of foreign assets by Russian companies. This was the only way for them to get around the barriers and gain access to foreign markets with their own highly processed products (foreign assets are usually the final link in the production chain of Russian companies). Thus, the capacity of Russian companies' foreign assets in 2007 totalled 25 million tonnes. In 2009, this figure will rise to 30.8 million tonnes.

All of this allowed Russian metal producers to maintain a prominent position in the global market. Four of the top 30 metal producers today are Russian enterprises, the largest of which ranks 15th.

At the same time, we cannot help noticing that most of these top 30 are Chinese companies. Moreover, their next actions are aimed at further integrating the industry's enterprises and capturing an even greater share of the global market.

As a result, in 2007 China became a net exporter of metal products. Today, China is able to satisfy virtually any consumer's demand for steel. At the same time, China has become the largest consumer of iron ore and coking coal.

Radical changes in the structure of the global metal market have been accompanied by ever-increasing prices. In spite of this, Russian producers on the domestic market continue to supply their products at a negative premium in comparison with the world level.

Only the stable influx of funds to the industry from outside allows Russian companies to build a consistent and active investment policy.

According to the results for last year, investment in fixed assets amounted to RUB 128 billion. This year the figure could already reach as high as RUB 160 billion. Tax withholdings are growing equally fast. In 2007, they amounted to RUB 135 billion. Metal workers' incomes are also growing.

At the same time, while the value of exports tripled from 2000 to 2007, the cost of imports to Russia increased by six times during the same period. Imports comprise such a noticeable share of certain types of commodity because demand is growing faster than new capacity can be brought on line. This is in part because of the economic impact of decisions taken by the government to develop certain branches of industry. For its part, the *Strategy for the Development of the Metallurgical Industry up to 2015* includes a set of import-substitution measures for the development of metallurgical industry, as a kind of point of common interest between the state and large companies.

The year that has passed since the *Strategy* was adopted has proved that the assessments made at the time, as well as the target indicators specified in the *Strategy*, were correct. The industry is developing slightly faster than the projected parameters. Domestic demand is growing actively, and the supply of previously exported products is increasingly reoriented to the Russian market. The year 2007 was a turning point in this regard: for the first time since the decline of the 1990s, the volume of exports was smaller than the domestic market. At the same time, a substantial part of exports goes to meet the demand of foreign assets acquired by our companies. In other words, they are actually an integral part of the domestic economy and help diversify risks related to demand.

The clear future of market development enables us to say even

The new workshop of the Chelyabinsk tube rolling plant

today that the domestic market will continue to grow at a fast pace, which in its turn stems from the strategic decisions recently adopted by the government.

Thus, the current *Energy Strategy up to 2020* gave a clear picture of the demand for metallurgical products for a variety of infrastructure projects. The plan for the development of the automotive industry identified the long-term demand for high-quality rolled metal. The targets specified for the production of rolling stock and elements of transport infrastructure in the *Strategy for the Development of Transport Engineering* and the *Strategy for the Development of Rail Transport* enabled metal producers to take a long-term view of the market for their products and rationally invest in the development of modern manufacturing capacity.

Most industry enterprises have already adopted long-term

investment-based development programmes. These programmes provide for significant amounts of investment, even during the period up to 2008, in upgrading and modernising production facilities, as well as developing the capacity to produce competitive products with high added value. Specific projects form the general shape of the industry.

The total amount of investment in fixed assets at all iron and steel plants increased seven-fold in the period 2000–08. During this same period, the depreciation of fixed assets decreased from 53.5 per cent to 43 per cent. In the period 2008–11, total investment will amount to RUB 700 billion, which will lead to a depreciation level of less than 40 per cent.

The metals business has already voted with its money for the solutions needed to develop these industries, as set forth in the strategies.

Obviously the momentum of the industry's development must be based on an adequate raw materials base. Russia currently has the highest level of proven iron ore reserves in the world (about 26 billion tonnes) and is fully self-sufficient when it comes to feedstock. Currently existing iron ore imports (which account for no more than 10 per cent of domestic consumption) are mainly attributable to the convenient logistics of importing from neighbouring countries to certain major steel plants (such as from Kazakhstan to the Magnitogorsk Iron and Steel Plant).

Recently, the trend among holdings to acquire their own iron ore assets has clearly been gaining in popularity, which could eventually lead to overproduction of basic products and an increase in their share among Russian exports – that is, a reduction of raw material risks.

The situation is similar in the coking coal sector. To a great extent, the shift in favour of self-sufficiency resulted from the absence of long-term contracts. Production of coking coal in Russia exceeds consumption, but for some grades, particularly high-quality 'fat' grades, there is a clear shortage, and many companies are forced to buy them in the open market. Here the situation is similar to the iron ore market, where companies are building long-term relationships with suppliers based on contracts with a price formula. Metal producers are already accustomed to this mechanism due to their integration into the global trade in iron ore and metal products. This practice should be expanded as part of multilateral co-operation among metal producers, raw material suppliers and consumers of metal production.

Over the medium term, metal producers will put into operation about 18 million tonnes of electric arc-furnace capacity. This will generate an 8–10 per cent annual increase in the consumption of scrap metal. Based on these figures, the share of electric steel in total production volume will rise to 35–37 per cent of total output, or 90 million tonnes a year.

Maintaining an adequate supply of scrap metal for Russian metallurgical companies for the foreseeable future will require special attention from the state and the adoption of the necessary legal, regulatory and economic measures. Due to the significant rise in prices for iron and steel scrap metal, the current rate of export customs duty is ineffective. Therefore, we must consider raising the specific component of the export customs duty in order to bring it into line with the *ad valorem* component.

The availability of the necessary amounts of alloying materials is an important aspect of ensuring the supply of raw materials for the Russian metals industry. The production of metal products for industries such as defence, aviation, shipbuilding, nuclear engineering, and the manufacturing of arms and military equipment largely depends on this factor.

Thus, one of the priority areas in developing the raw materials base should be to effectively solve the problem of ensuring the supply of scarce mineral feedstock. Therefore, taking into account the needs of the metals industry, it is necessary to analyse the existing mineral resource base and formulate a clear plan for the possible acquisition of rights to the development of such fields. This is important for the very specific subsector of special steels, where the situation differs markedly from 'big' metallurgy. During the period of sharp decline in domestic demand, special metals producers were effectively unable to find alternative markets. Such is the specific nature of this subsector: the main demand for its products is ultimately shaped by state procurement. As a result, over the past 15 years special metals producers have seen the profitability of their production remain at around 5–10 per cent, which prevents them from modernising and upgrading their production facilities. The degree of equipment depreciation in this subsector averaged more than 60 per cent, whereas in the 'big' metals industry the figure was closer to 40 per cent. The subsector's negative trends can be seen in the production of stainless steel. The condition of the special metals enterprises prevented them from responding to growth in domestic demand, as a result of which this niche was occupied by imports. Meanwhile, this subsector has strategic significance.

In contrast with the large-scale metals industry, here it is most reasonable and effective to use the mechanisms of direct state support. In particular, we propose to consider expanding the practices of long-term contracting and planning, R&D funding, subsidising interest rates on loans for the modernisation of production facilities and so on.

Implementing the proposed measures for the development of Russia's metallurgical industry will help increase the competitiveness of the industry, fully meet the needs of the domestic market (particularly related industries), and create conditions for strengthening the position of Russian companies in the global market.

From a report delivered at a meeting with Prime Minister Putin in Chelyabinsk, 27 July 2010:

The iron and steel industry often ends up being the focus of attention at various levels of government. Indeed, large annual meetings on the industry are now traditionally timed to coincide with Metallurgists' Day.

In my opinion, this attention is absolutely justified. After all, the industry accounts for about 4 per cent of the country's economy (GDP), 6.7 per cent of its exports, and 1.2 per cent of its jobs. Russia has steadily maintained a 5 per cent share of the global steel market, ranking fourth among all producing countries. In the foreseeable future, steel will retain its role as the main building material.

During the period of gradual pre-crisis development from 2000–08, the industry advanced a long way. Accumulated investments amounted to nearly a trillion roubles; annual tax revenues at the federal, regional and local levels increased from RUB 22 billion to RUB 152 billion (or more than seven times), while the average monthly salary increased from RUB 3,500 to RUB 17,000.

The amount of investment in Russian iron and steel enterprises per tonne of manufactured steel from 2004–08 was around $45–48, which is almost 1.5 times higher than the level of developed countries. As a result, metallurgy is perhaps the most heavily invested-in branch of industry today. Our leading companies are competitive on a global scale.

Despite hard times, Russian metal companies continue to bring the most important and unique facilities on line according to plan. Today's launch at Vysota-239 (Altitude-239) serves as the latest confirmation of this.

Of course, the economic crisis has had a significant impact on the development of the industry. All businesspeople sitting in this hall have felt it fully. The level of production of finished rolled metal in the industry decreased by 47 per cent in November 2008, which was the most critical month, compared with the average monthly indicators during the pre-crisis period (January–August 2008). Receivables and payables among the industry's companies grew by 50 per cent. Based on the results for 2009, metallurgical plants have almost regained the pre-crisis level of production, with a lag of only 7 per cent.

In the first half of 2010, the average monthly volume of finished steel production was still 4–16 per cent lower than the pre-crisis level, at about 3.7 million tonnes per month. The debt load of the most important companies has been completely restructured with the help of the state, but its size is only beginning to decline.

As a result, one year ago, when we talked about updating the previous *Strategy* (up to 2015), we basically faced a choice: to go for a deep correction of strategic objectives and investment ambitions, and thus abandon projects in associated industries, or to refine our priorities in light of the economic crisis and provide targeted support to the most important projects. In the updated version of the *Strategy for the Metals Industry,* just as in the strategic documents for the industries that consume steel products, the choice was made in favour of the second scenario. This decision was not accidental. It was made in light not only of the risks, but also of the opportunities generated by the economic crisis.

The document consolidated the corporate strategies of the major players in the industry and consumer sectors. It allowed us to formulate long-term goals and objectives for the development of the metals industry. By 2020, we expect to reach a production of level of 90 million tonnes of steel, 38 million tonnes of flat products and 37 million tonnes of rolled section.

These figures are not an end in and of themselves. It is important that the *Strategy* has enabled us to structure government policy in the industry so as to achieve a maximum multiplicative effect throughout the economy. Thus, the development of the iron and steel industry is a key factor in the development of the machine engineering and infrastructure industries. It is important to remember that the modern iron and steel industry itself is also a consumer of innovation-based products.

The set of anti-crisis measures is in turn reflected in the *Priority Action Plan* formulated at last year's meeting under your chairmanship. The main objective of this *Plan* is to keep the industry on the development trend set out in the *Strategy*. Based on the outcomes of 2009 and the anti-crisis measures laid out in the *Plan*, we can say that the goals and objectives specified in the *Strategy* we updated in March of last year [2009] were correct.

By adopting measures in a timely manner, we were able to get through the acute stage of the crisis without losing key investment and innovation projects, to save jobs at the enterprises, and to continue the programme of introducing new technologies developed through public–private partnerships.

A system of state support for the industry was developed in several key areas, above all for managing demand, supporting priority projects, protecting the market from unfair competition, promoting exports and supporting industrial innovation.

Effective support for the metals industry has come from preserving investment programmes to the greatest extent possible and creating a transparent, long-term demand pattern in the infrastructure sectors. I would like to highlight the efforts by key infrastructure companies Gazprom and Transneft to increase the share of Russian pipes in their procurement and their willingness to work with long-term contracts. Thanks to their use by end consumers, the practice of long-term contracts filters down the chain to raw materials producers, thereby stabilising the whole system.

Efforts by the government to support the major metal-consuming sectors – auto manufacturing, construction, shipbuilding, and so on – were an important factor in first stabilising and then revitalising the domestic market for metal products.

The task of supporting strategic investment projects has effectively been solved. This can be seen, for example, in the projects you saw today, which were launched without any delays. The crisis has changed the requirements imposed by financial institutions for the purpose of securing credit facilities that have already been extended or are to be extended in the future for key projects. The government has begun to provide state guarantees for such projects. Around RUB 53 billion in guarantees have been provided.

I would like to emphasise that these are repayable funds aimed at supporting key growth points in the industry. As a result, as I said earlier, virtually all the problem debts of strategic enterprises have been restructured.

As part of our efforts to support projects at the international level, we have made active use of the institutions of intergovernmental co-operation, as well as working out a mechanism for interaction with foreign financial and insurance companies.

In addition, reducing VAT to nil for processing equipment with no Russian-made analogues enabled metal companies not to withdraw about RUB 2.3 billion from circulation. Duties on processing equipment with no Russian-made analogues were also reduced to nil (the resolution applies to 91 types of equipment, including five for the mining industry and seven for the metals industry).

In supporting specific projects, we clearly understand which tasks their implementation is aimed at solving and which needs of the Russian economy they are aimed at fulfilling. The major investment projects reflected in the *Development Strategy for the Metals Industry* are aimed at meeting the demand generated by long-term strategies for the development of priority sectors of the economy (the *Transport Strategy, Energy Strategy, Strategy for the Development of the Automotive Industry, Strategy for the Development of the Shipbuilding Industry,* and so on), as well as the corporate strategies of the largest infrastructure companies.

It is now possible to say that the implementation of Nord Stream, South Stream and other international pipelines projects involving Russian companies can be entirely provided for by Russian pipe manufacturers and metal companies.

In 2011, the companies Mechel and Evraz plan to complete projects involving the creation of rail and structural steel mills to produce 100 metre rails that will allow Russian Railways LLC to start large-scale work on the development of high-speed railway networks in the country.

Thanks to the completion of investment projects involving the production of cold-rolled automotive sheet by the companies MMK and Severstal, it will now be possible to implement the 'Industrial Assembly' project in the automotive industry with the planned level of localisation.

Figure 4.13 The iron and steel industry: the situation in 2011

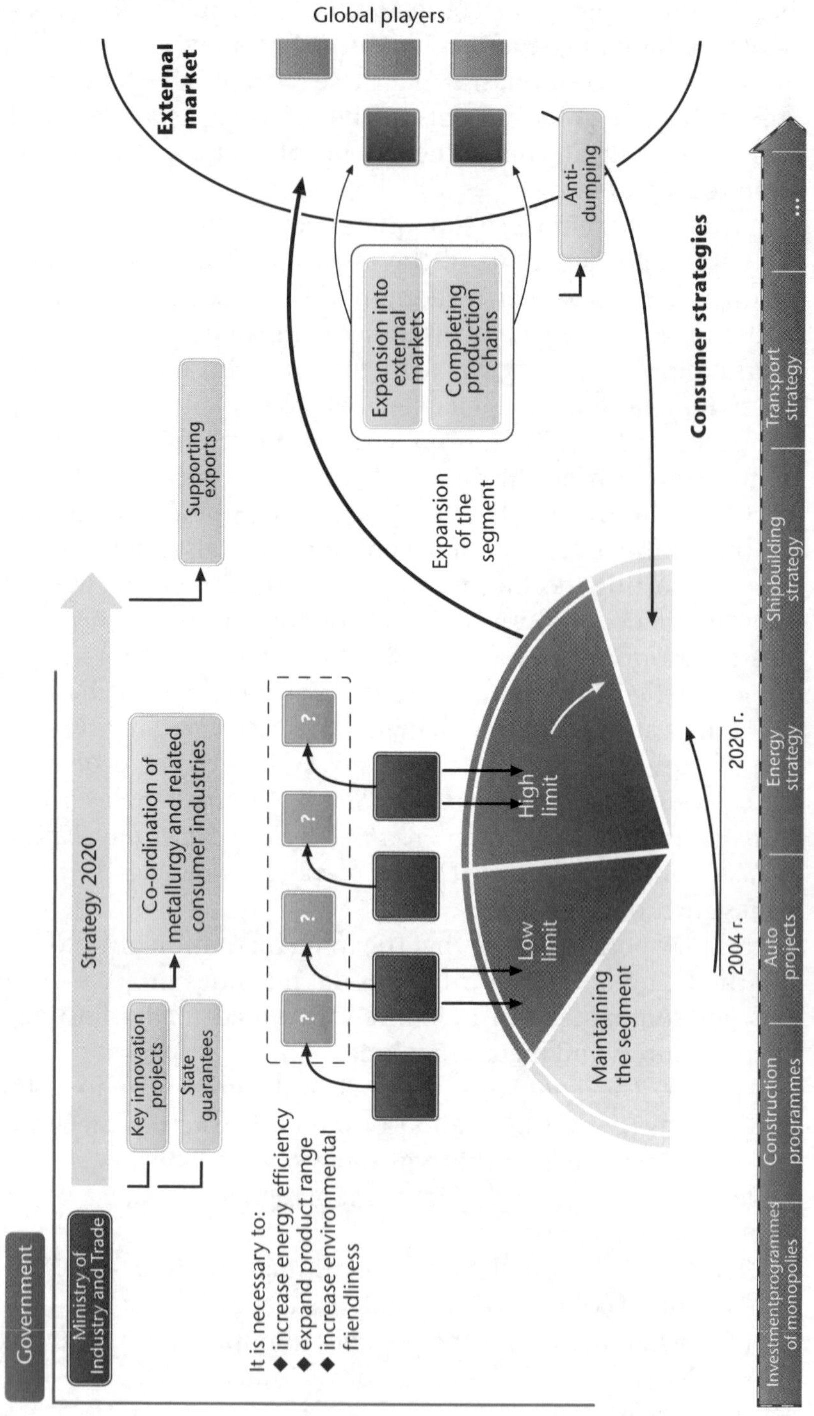

Global players

External market

Anti-dumping

Expansion into external markets

Completing production chains

Expansion of the segment

Supporting exports

Strategy 2020

Key innovation projects

State guarantees

Co-ordination of metallurgy and related consumer industries

It is necessary to:
◆ increase energy efficiency
◆ expand product range
◆ increase environmental friendliness

?   ?   ?   ?

High limit

Low limit

Maintaining the segment

2004 г.   2020 г.

Consumer strategies

Government

Ministry of Industry and Trade

Investment programmes of monopolies

Construction programmes

Auto projects

Energy strategy

Shipbuilding strategy

Transport strategy

...

We have a specific plan regarding the items that are to be introduced up to 2013. Timely decisions were taken to protect the domestic market. Import customs duties on certain types of rolled steel and steel pipes (more than 100 products) have been increased by 5–10 per cent. An arsenal of special protective, anti-dumping and offsetting measures has been implemented effectively. It is worth noting that our foreign partners do not hesitate to use similar measures against Russian companies. In many respects, this is an indication of how competitive our metal producers have become.

Further work is aimed at putting the industry back on its pre-crisis development trajectory, as defined in the *Strategy*. The *Action Plan for the Development of the Industry in 2011–13 s*hould be a logical extension of the solutions adopted over the past year, most of which have already been implemented. The new *Plan* includes mostly tried and tested tools to support the industry.

One of the key priorities within this construct is to encourage the development and implementation of innovations (with respect to both products and applied technologies) at metallurgical enterprises.

Since we started implementing the *Strategy*, more than 20 world-class technologies have been developed using the mechanisms of public–private partnership and are now being put into production. Despite the economic crisis, work in promising areas has not been curtailed.

The Ministry of Industry and Trade has drafted a sub-programme entitled 'Technologies for the Production of New Types of Metal Products, Steel and Alloys to Meet the Future Needs of the Mechanical Engineering, Automotive, Fuel and Energy, Aircraft and Shipbuilding Industries' within the framework of the National Technological Base for 2012–16 Federal Targeted Programme.

This subprogramme incorporates key areas of future developments for the next five years, co-ordinated with projected demand from key sectors of the consumer industries. At the same time, mechanisms have been created to co-ordinate the efforts of federal and regional authorities and metal companies, including the Government Commission on the Development of the Metallurgical Complex and the Coordinating Council for Industrial Policy in the Metallurgical Complex under the Russian Ministry of Industry and Trade, which will enable us move forward efficiently on implementing the long-term *Development Strategy* for the industry.

The biotechnology company Generium

The pharmaceutical and medical products industries

The pharmaceuticals industry and the medical product and device industry ended up being part of our sphere of responsibility quite unexpectedly. In late 2007, the government decided to transfer these areas to the Ministry of Industry and Energy (in 2008 they remained with the Ministry of Industry and Trade). Our team found itself in an ambiguous position. On the one hand, this was a brand new, undeveloped area of activity, which, in the public mind, is more closely associated with healthcare than with industry. Discussions at all levels were viewed through this prism. On the other hand, the fact that we were starting from a low baseline in the context of a rapidly growing market gave us an opportunity to try to create conditions for the creation of a new high-tech industry in Russia.

Indeed, the structure of the pharmaceuticals market evolved over the first 15 years of modern Russia's history. In Soviet times, there was virtually no serious pharmaceuticals industry in our country. The Russian Soviet Federative Socialist Republic specialised in bulk chemicals. Ready-made pharmaceuticals remained in the former countries of the COMECON. After 1991, the country needed pharmaceutical products, and Western companies were given fairly liberal access to our market. They, along with several leading Russian distributors, effectively shaped the structure of the market and rules that suited them. It was not until the mid-2000s that they made the first attempts to invest in assets within our country. At the same time, the first major Russian industrial players started to get on their own feet, Further, the overlap between the arrival of investment and the formation of companies capable of accepting this investment is no coincidence. The same applies, with certain exceptions, to the medical product and device industry.

The Russian pharmaceuticals market and the market for medical products are very similar: in recent years both have grown rapidly, placing new demands on suppliers, and the key customer in both markets is the state. However, whereas Russian pharmaceuticals companies have managed to keep their market share at around 20 per cent, their counterparts in the medical products industry have gradually lost ground.

As part of the *Pharma-2020 Strategy*, which we have been implementing since 2007, we attempted to identify the main barrier to

Figure 4.14 The pharmaceuticals and medical products industry: the situation in 2007

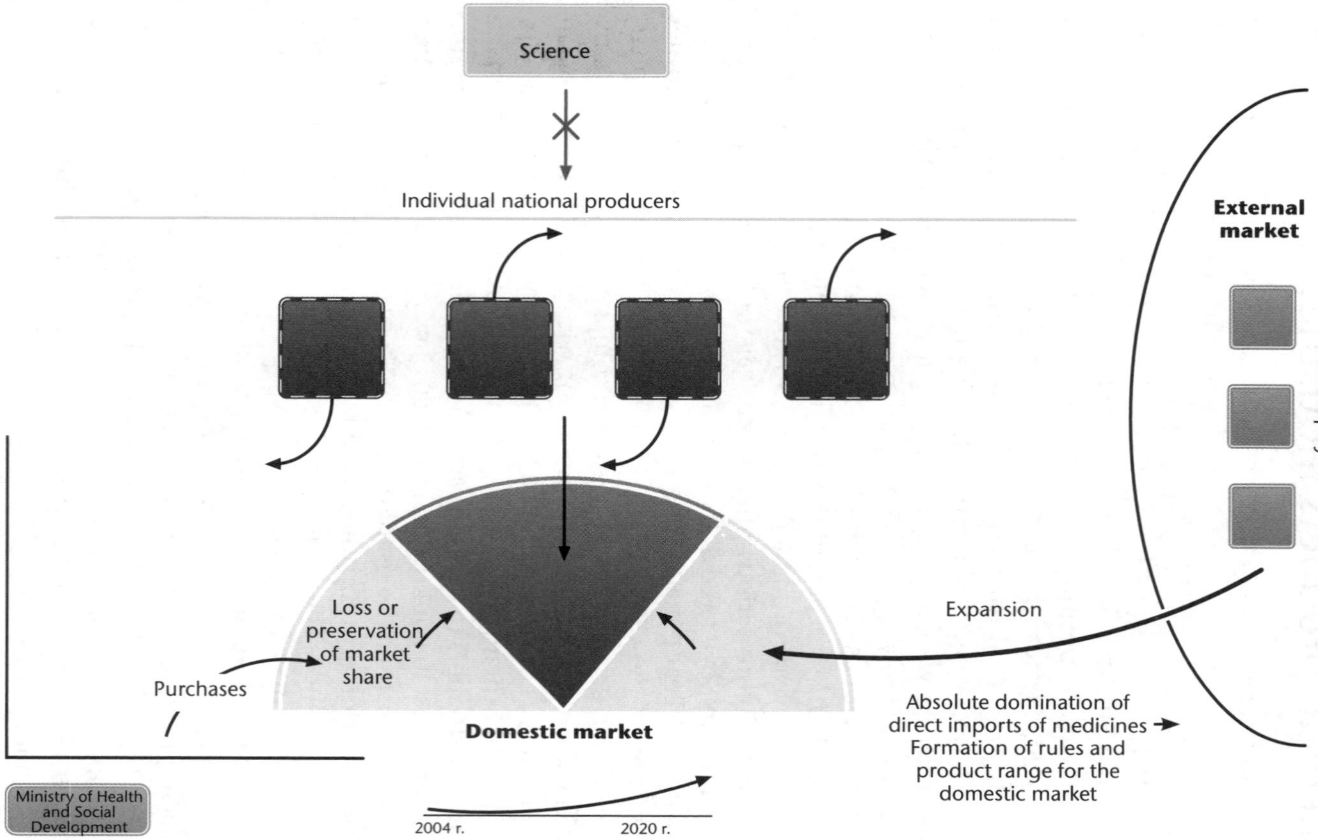

Science

Individual national producers

Global players

External market

Expansion

Absolute domination of direct imports of medicines
Formation of rules and product range for the domestic market

Domestic market

Loss or preservation of market share

Purchases

2004 г.

2020 г.

Ministry of Health and Social Development

the development of the pharmaceuticals industry. This we found to be the failure to fund applied research and bring new products to the market, which resulted from the fact that industry had transitioned to a market economy while science remained under a planned system of funding by the Russian Academy of Sciences and the Russian Academy of Medical Sciences, as well as small foundations and grants.

The situation began to change rapidly after 2007, when the government sharply increased its investment in the healthcare system. In 2009, the industry was identified as one of the president's modernisation priorities, and the *Pharma-2020 Strategy* was approved. Moreover, the *Strategy* became the first 'post-crisis' document of its kind in the implementation of industrial policy. In pursuance of the *Strategy*, the legal and regulatory framework underwent substantial changes. A new law on the distribution of medicines and a number of concomitant changes (such as the mandatory transition to GMP (Good Manufacturing Practice) standards starting in 2014), along with preferences given to Russian manufacturers, helped eliminate the situation where it was harder for Russian manufacturers to gain access to their own Russian market than for foreign distributors (especially large ones). Most importantly, they also provided a powerful impetus to the industry. These changes became statistically tangible in 2010, when the share of Russian companies on the market started to increase.

In 2009, President Dmitry Medvedev issued an order to draw up and approve an FTP for the industry based on *Pharma-2020*. In addition, a kind of sieve was formed within the framework of the Presidential Commission for Modernisation, through which more than 300 projects passed, many of which influenced the selection of priorities and the FTP that we developed. Work on the programme was completed in early 2011.

Implementing the FTP will provide a financial basis for the priorities of the development strategy. For the pharmaceuticals industry, this means achieving parity (50/50) between Russian and foreign drugs in our market by 2020. By 2015, this figure will be 37 per cent. At the same time, Russian pharmaceuticals will account for 90 per cent of the medications on both the SIM List (List of Strategically Important Medicines) and the VED List (List of Vital and Essential Medicines). In 2020, at least 50 per cent of the products sold in the domestic pharmaceuticals market will be produced in Russia.

The situation in the medical products industry is more complicated. We have included in the draft *Medical Industry 2020 Strategy* the target of achieving a 40 per cent share for Russian manufacturers by 2020. It is important to note that the Russian share of the pharmaceutical and medical product markets is growing against the backdrop of steady development of the domestic market and the simultaneous, albeit less ambitious, cultivation of export positions.

Discussing and approving the *Pharma-2020 Strategy* and the corresponding FTP, as well as updating the regulatory framework, has allowed us to start the process of localising some previously imported products. Further, both Russian players and foreign investors have begun actively building and upgrading their assets. Fruitful talks were held with the senior executives of all major international pharmaceutical companies. The volume of investment in ongoing and announced projects in 2009–11 was RUB 38 billion in the pharmaceuticals industry and RUB 12 billion in the medical products industry, for a total of more than RUB 50 billion. The most important thing is that some of these investments involve projects aimed at promoting Russian designs in foreign markets. We have begun the transition from 'pharmaceuticals assembly' to global strategic partnerships.

At first glance, the model for collaboration with global players in the pharmaceuticals industry resembles the model used in the automotive industry. In the automotive industry, we followed the logic dictated by the production chain – from final assembly to gradual localisation in the rapidly growing market. Industrial assembly mode was the instrument for this.

The subject of pharmaceuticals has enabled us take a completely new look at collaboration models within the framework of a global partnership strategy. The Russian market is too small to recoup investment in innovation or to grow full-fledged competencies independently, relying on the domestic market alone – especially if we recall that foreign players occupy a dominant position in this market. Meanwhile, the creation of new pharmaceutical products is a long, difficult, capital-intensive, rigidly structured process, regulated throughout the entire chain. The path from the exploratory stage through pre-clinical and clinical trials to commercialisation takes about seven to ten years and costs tens or even hundreds of millions of dollars. In addition, if a company does not already have a presence in the global market, it cannot break into it unless it partners with a global player.

Proceeding step by step, according to the standard industrial logic, from the final product to the molecule, it is virtually impossible in the pharmaceuticals industry to reach the desired extent of competency localisation or to create innovative products within a reasonable period of time. The latter fact has spurred us to incorporate various forms of interaction into the strategy and to apply them in practice, such as making use of contract manufacturing, where the manufacturing of previously imported products is placed at Russian sites; bringing the new products of 'big pharmaceuticals' to pre-clinical and clinical trials and subsequently dividing up the sales markets (for example, the Russian partner operates in Russia and the CIS, while the foreign partner operates in the global market); acquiring biotechs with innovation know-how in the Western market; using global partners to bring new Russian products to the global market, and so on.

This process has another important focus. The economic crisis has forced a number of major companies in the world market to partially reconsider their long-term portfolios. Russian players, through their partnerships, now have an opportunity to pick up the development of new drugs. In practice, the multi-format nature of global partnership allows us to share the risks associated with developing innovative drugs most effectively among the state, Russian companies and global players.

From a speech delivered at a meeting of the Commission for Modernisation and Technological Development of the Russian Economy under the President of the Russian Federation, Pokrov, 31 August 2009:

Biotechnologies have long been growth areas in advanced economies around the world. The global market for pharmaceutical and medical products exceeded US$1 trillion in 2008. At the same time, the top 15 pharmaceutical companies account for around 50 per cent of the market, while the top 30 manufacturers of medical equipment account for 80 per cent of the market. The Russian pharmaceuticals market, though relatively small compared with the developed countries (11th place in the world), is one of the leaders in terms of annual growth rate at more than 12 per cent per year. In total volume, our pharmaceuticals market has already surpassed that of India ($9 billion) and is comparable to that of China

($22 billion). The financial and economic crisis and current world trends are having a new impact on the development of the industry around the world, which in its turn opens up new possibilities for the development of the domestic industry. The dominant economic trends at the moment are as follows:

◆ contraction of the largest pharmaceuticals markets (the United States, the European Union and so on), which is leading to an increase in corporate mergers and acquisitions;
◆ migration of production and research facilities to China and India;
◆ evolution of products towards generics and bio-generics.

In formulating a development strategy for the industry, it is necessary to rely on projected indicators regarding the development of healthcare systems, science and the structure of morbidity. Changes in the demand for medical products are 'superimposed' on the structural and economic development trends of the global markets. That said, the two main trends are the rapid ageing of the population in the developed countries and a steadily growing standard of living in the developing countries. At present, there are about 450 million people older than 65 in the world (about 7 per cent of the world's population). By 2020 this figure will double, and by 2050 it will more than triple. As a consequence, health-care systems in the developed countries will come under increasing pressure, and the structure of causes of death will change.

The evolution of the morbidity structure is leading to a change of priorities in the development of new medical products. Recent advances in biotechnology will help fundamentally change approaches in medicine in the nearest future. There will be a shift in emphasis from mass treatment to the development of preventive drugs and personalised medicine. However, given the current economic situation, these trends are unlikely to become dominant in our country over the next two decades.

The structure of the Russian market differs considerably from the developed markets in that it is dominated by branded generics, mostly foreign-made. At the same time, the bulk of the product portfolios of domestic manufacturers are made up of low-profit generic drugs. This limits the amount of money spent by Russian companies on research and development to 1–2 per cent of revenue compared with about 20 per cent among the global leaders. Imports currently account for 80 per cent of the Russian pharmaceuticals market, while the share of state procurement is 35 per cent. In the medical device market, the share of imports is 70 per cent, and state procurement accounts for 90 per cent. Thus, the main determining factors in the Russian market are imports, and demand from the state.

After beginning preparations for the implementation of the *Pharmaceuticals Industry Strategy*, the Ministry of Industry and Trade conducted an analysis of state procurement of medicines in 2008. Our country has considerable potential for the localisation of generic drugs, as well as drugs whose patent protection will be expiring in the coming years. In this regard, it is necessary to pay special attention to the process of state procurement of drugs. First of all, this means making sure terms and requirements that discriminate against domestic manufacturers are not included in tender documents. At the same time, modern quality and safety requirements for supplied products should be established at the state level. As for drugs that are not manufactured in Russia, the creation of a special targeted programme will make it possible to start developing them and putting them into production.

The *Pharma-2020 Strategy* was developed with due regard for the current structure of the market and identified problems. It provides for several stages of implementation. In the first stage, it is necessary to make structural adjustments to the legal and regulatory framework, to focus state procurement and to expedite the processes of localising production and developing new drugs. After that, in the second stage, the localisation of generic drug production must reach the level of 50 per cent, while the goal of the third stage is to achieve 50 per cent import substitution for innovative drugs. It is important to note that the innovation cycle has to be launched now, so that the necessary quantity of implemented designs will be available by 2020.

Work on creating a system of strategic documents and regulations for the medical and pharmaceutical industries, taking into account current trends in the development of these sectors, has now entered its final stage. This preliminary work covers the period up to 2025, and provides for a gradual transition to an innovative track, and co-ordination between demand from the healthcare system and the capabilities of Russian industry.

The scope of strategic development described above shapes the areas of activity of the Working Group on Medical Equipment and Pharmaceuticals. These are:

◆ development and production of new types of medical equipment and medical products for treatment and diagnosis;
◆ development and production of medicines for the prevention, diagnosis and treatment of socially significant and rare disease;
◆ development of innovative nanotechnology, biotechnology, cellular and nuclear technology in medicine.

As part of the group's work, a list of strategic objectives has been formulated. These are directly derived from the programme documents that have been developed and approved in the field of pharmaceuticals and medical equipment. On the one hand, each of the projects that passes through the Working Group and the Commission can help solve certain problems. On the other hand, in order to implement each administrative task, it is necessary to amass a sufficient number of projects – a certain critical mass which will accompany their implementation, shatter existing barriers and give impetus to a breakthrough.

The large number of projects in the healthcare system, as well as their varied scale, require the Working Group to be fundamentally open and sensitive to new projects and initiatives. To this end, the Working Group established a register of projects, which will be expanded after thorough discussion and approval of suitable proposals.

The first systematic product of the Working Group's activity was the List of Priority Medicines for the Russian Healthcare System. Of the more than 3,000 pharmaceutical products circulating in the Russian market, 650 are included in the list of vital and essential medicines, and 248 of these are not manufactured in our country.

Relying on mortality statistics, the Ministry of Health and Social Development made up a list of the 15 most important drugs necessary for the healthcare system. We believe that from the point of view of national security and budgetary savings, the production of these drugs should be located in Russia.

The projects submitted for consideration at today's meeting of the Commission already cover six of the 15 designated items, and will save the state up to RUB 6.5 billion a year once they are successfully completed.

The first project is the creation of the Generium Scientific Research Centre. The centre consists of industrial and scientific sections. The production part of the project involves expanding the existing production capacities for the three already registered drugs and starting the production of five more drugs that are in late stages of development. The company has already invested RUB 600 million in the project, and plans to invest another RUB 2 billion of its own funds. The production volume of drugs currently in development will meet all the country's needs, and the total budget savings from all these products, once production reaches full capacity, could be as high as RUB 4.8 billion a year.

The project will involve the creation of production facilities providing 140 high-tech jobs, as well as a research centre that will employ up to 150 specialists, including some recruited from abroad and returning Russian specialists. The research centre will help solve any problems in the fields of biotechnology, cellular technologies, chemistry and pharmacology. Once construction is completed, as many as 8–10 new genetically engineered drugs will be developed and put on the market. Generium does not require additional funding from the state budget, as this is a pure business project.

The second project is entitled 'Plasmapheresis'. The goal of the project is to create domestic high-tech production of medical equipment for cascade filtration of blood plasma and related technologies for the treatment of a wide range of diseases through the purification of blood from pathogenic (harmful) substances.

Until now, blood filtration methods have been based on very expensive technology. This has made them unaffordable for most people, even in the most developed countries. Implementing the Plasmapheresis project will help solve this problem by making this service more accessible.

As a result of implementation of this project, high-tech medical equipment will be manufactured in Russia. According to the network plan:

◆ Design work will be carried out in 2009–10, product certification will be launched in early 2010, and construction of the Beta Scientific-Industrial Complex will begin in mid-2010.
◆ Equipment will be brought online as production facilities are created and expanded (2010–13).

◆ Production will be launched in 2012. By the end of 2012, utilisation should reach 60 per cent of planned capacity.
◆ The project should reach full capacity by the end of 2013.

The third project is the ChemRar Centre. The main goal of the project is import substitution. As much as RUB 1.5 billion in state budget funds could be saved each year. These figures will be achieved due to the lower cost of manufactured products than of the original imported supplies.

The average age of the centre's employees is 37; most are young graduates from Russia's top universities (Moscow State University, Moscow Institute of Physics and Technology, Moscow State Academy of Fine Chemical Technology and so on) whom we managed to sign up for domestic applied research. Many of the laboratories are run by Russians who have returned from abroad after gaining experience in Western industrial science.

The fourth project is represented by the Biokad company. This project will lead to the creation of a full production cycle in Russia for pharmaceutical products based on monoclonal antibodies, which are the most modern and expensive class of drugs. Russia currently lacks the technology to produce such drugs. These medicines are highly effective in treating the most common cancers. The annual cost for state procurement for this group of medicines is more than RUB 4.5 billion.

The impact of the import substitution that will be achieved by implementing this project will generate annual savings of at least RUB 1.5 billion, since the newly developed analogues will be cheaper than the original imported drugs. In addition, the new research and production complex will have the capacity to quickly develop and launch production of other drugs obtained through biotechnology and genetic engineering, including new innovative drugs.

Biokad has already created the necessary research infrastructure to carry out work in the field of genetic engineering and cell biology. Plans call for setting up pilot production and an entire package of work on developing and studying announced products.

The fifth project was announced by Medradiopreparat Federal State Unitary Enterprise of the Federal Medico-Biological Agency (FMBA) of Russia. It is designed to provide radiopharmaceutical products for diagnostic and therapeutic procedures performed in Russian cancer centres.

The project is characterised by specific working conditions, geographical dispersion of medical centres throughout Russia, and the short shelf-life of its pharmaceutical products. As a result, complex logistics systems will have to be built. The implementation of this programme will require co-ordinated efforts by institutions of the FMBA of Russia and the Rosatom Group of Companies.

From a report on the Federal Targeted Programme for the Development of the Pharmaceutical and Medical Industries of the Russian Federation up to 2020 and beyond, delivered at a meeting with Prime Minister Putin, Khimki, 8 December 2010:

Mr Prime Minister, the problems of the Russian pharmaceutical and medical product market have been discussed at various levels, including at meetings held under your leadership. A number of decisions were taken at these meetings, including a decision to approve the *Strategy for the Development of the Pharmaceuticals Industry up to 2020* and to order the drafting of an FTP for the industry. In addition, the Ministry took the initiative to draft a *Strategy for the Development of the Medical Industry up to 2020*.

The somewhat more favourable situation with the manufacturing of pharmaceuticals is partly due to the consistent state policy implemented in this sector over the past three years, and the fact that Russian enterprises started from a stronger position. We expect to turn the tide in favour of Russian manufacturers by 2015.

The FTP under consideration today is principally aimed at overcoming the major barriers that prevent pharmaceuticals and the medical industry from developing at a faster pace than the market. It is based on a strategic vision of the industries' development, co-ordinated with our colleagues in government and the private sector.

State procurement accounts for a large share of the market in monetary terms, comprising around 38 per cent of pharmaceuticals and around 85 per cent of medical products. Thus, the state has a powerful lever for changing the situation in favour of Russian manufacturers. By 'Russian manufacturers' we mean not only native domestic companies, but also foreign players that are prepared to localise substantial elements of added-value creation within Russia.

The priority strategy in both the pharmaceuticals market and the medical industry is to form global partnerships with major global companies. On the one hand, implementation of this strategy has been facilitated by market growth combined with the transparent long-term priorities of state policy. On the other hand, implementation has been hindered by number of negative factors that have their roots in the early 1990s.

It is safe to say that that discussing and adopting the *Pharma-2020 Strategy* and substantially updating the legal and regulatory framework enabled us to start the process of localising some previously imported products. Moreover, both Russian players and foreign investors began active work on the construction and upgrading of their assets.

We have started doing the same work in the medical equipment segment. In the coming months, we look forward to receiving specific proposals from major manufacturers regarding the localisation of key products and components.

The localisation of foreign competencies with respect to developing innovative products, and the integration of Russian companies into global chains for the creation of innovative products, require a more active stance from the state. In this area too, however, we have already achieved positive results.

Approving the FTP is an important condition for the continuation of this process. The main goal of the FTP is to transition the Russian pharmaceutical and medical industries to an innovation-based development model – that is, steering it away from conventional 'screwdriver assembly' to a full-fledged cycle, from development to production, with obligatory integration into international markets.

The FTP mostly focuses on filling the gap in funding for applied science. This gap has formed as a result of the fact that industry has transitioned to a market economy while science has remained under a planned system of funding by the Russian Academy of Sciences and the Russian Academy of Medical Sciences, as well as small foundations and grants. This is why the programme is mostly 'technological' in nature.

The FTP is made up of two stages, consistent with the *Pharma-2020 Strategy* and the draft *Medical Industry-2020 Strategy*.

During the first stage – up to 2015 – the pharmaceutical and medical products industries will be modernised with the help of R&D on the design and organisation of import-substitute production. As part of this work, extra-budgetary funds will be used to upgrade enterprises' fixed assets, while budget funds will be used to develop technology and carry out installation and start-up work with a view to launching production. Simultaneously, starting as early as 2011, innovation projects will need to be launched in the pharmaceuticals sector. This will include transferring designs for the purpose of putting innovation-based products on the market starting in 2015.

In addition, the first stage calls for starting to build an innovation infrastructure, including investment in state enterprises and institutions of higher education. It will also include retraining staff to master new technologies, taking into account such factors as the transition to international manufacturing standards (GMP).

In the second stage – from 2015 to 2020 – the innovation and export potential of the pharmaceutical and medical industries will be developed by implementing R&D programmes to develop innovative pharmaceuticals and medical products. By that time we expect enterprises in the pharmaceutical and medical industries to have limited development potential based on import substitution, and the only way for them to compete effectively in the global market will be to have innovative, patent-protected products.

The total budget for the programme is more than RUB 185 billion (RUB 185.348 billion), including about RUB 123 billion (RUB 122.95 billion) from the federal budget and more than RUB 62 billion (RUB 62.398 billion) from extra-budgetary sources.

The rollout of the FTP is significantly affected by the lengthy duration of the development cycle: the starting dates of projects are contingent upon the need to achieve systemic changes by 2020. This is a difficult task in itself, since R&D projects in the pharmaceutical and medical industries often take 8–10 years. That is why it is so important to finance development in the early years of the programme.

The FTP we have developed is an R&D programme, and in addition to managing the product portfolio (that is, launching the production of pharmaceuticals and medical products) it aims to create a sustainable system of development and commercialisation of innovative products. Therefore, the bulk of funding for the programme – 77 per cent of its public funding – will go towards R&D. Capital investments will account for 21 per cent of the programme's public funding, and 2 per cent will go towards miscellaneous expenses.

The programme measures are divided into seven groups. The first two groups consist of measures to modernise and develop the pharmaceuticals industry. Groups 3 and 4 consist of measures to modernise and develop the medical products industry. Group 5 involves developing the human resources and information infra-structure of the pharmaceutical and medical products industries. Group 6 consists of capital investments, and Group 7 consists of organisational, technical and information support for the programme.

The thematic content of the Group 1 measures is based on the priority lists developed by the Russian Ministry of Health and Social Development and approved by the Government of the Russian Federation: the SIM List and the VED List. By implementing projects within the framework of Group 1 measures, we plan to develop and organise the manufacturing of approximately 155 pharmaceutical products from the SIM and VED lists that are not currently manufactured in Russia.

All measures in this group are structured according to two criteria:

◆ the method of obtaining the drug – by chemical synthesis or using biotechnology;
◆ the degree of patent protection in Russia.

In selecting areas for the development of innovative pharmaceuticals (Group 2 measures) within the limits of available funding, our main reference points will be:

◆ the main causes of mortality and morbidity, taking into account forecasts up to 2030;
◆ the sizes and growth trends of the relevant markets;
◆ the portfolios of international pharmaceutical companies;
◆ the availability of promising domestic product designs.

Priority will be given to monitoring promising areas in the development of innovative drugs throughout the world. Therefore, Group 2 measures largely focus on creating an effective model for technology transfer in Russia.

Thus, areas for the development of innovation-based pharmaceutical products have been formulated. The measures in this group are aimed at developing the innovative capacity of the pharmaceuticals industry through the forced development of domestic innovation-based pharmaceuticals. I should point out that for Group 2 measures, budget co-financing will constitute from 50 per cent to 75 per cent of the total project costs. This structuring is predicated by one of the programme's key objectives – to cover the high-risk gap in the processing chain for the creation of new pharmaceutical products.

Groups 3 and 4 are devoted to developing the medical industry. In formulating these measures, we have taken into account both market priorities and the types of medical product that will be most needed by the healthcare system over the short term (2011–15).

A key factor in the growth of Russia's medical product market in the coming years will be the implementation of a number of large-scale public health programmes. These include:

◆ regional programmes for the modernisation of medical institutions (including reforms of the compulsory medical insurance system);
◆ the 'Health' Priority National Project;
◆ the development of nuclear medicine in the Russian Federation.

Thus, in the coming years Russia's medical products market will receive a substantial financial infusion.

Russia's share of global consumption of medical products is insignificant today – about 1 per cent, or US$3 billion annually in monetary terms. At the same time, the amount of pent-up demand suggests that the domestic market has far greater potential. According to the most pessimistic estimates, the volume of purchases by 2020 will increase five to six times at 2010 prices. The model for the future structure of healthcare has become the basis for formulating areas and measures within the context of the development of medical equipment.

The FTP highlights areas of innovative breakthrough into global markets. Foremost among these are technologies in the fields of nuclear medicine and biomedicine. The types of projects provided for by these modernisation measures will help meet the primary needs of the Russian Ministry of Health and Social Development in terms of the provision of quality services.

One of the key objectives in developing the industrial base is to implement projects in the early stages of the programme (2011–13) aimed at organising and developing the manufacturing of components for medical equipment and special materials for medical products within the Russian Federation. This will enable us to master the technologies incorporated into modern equipment and

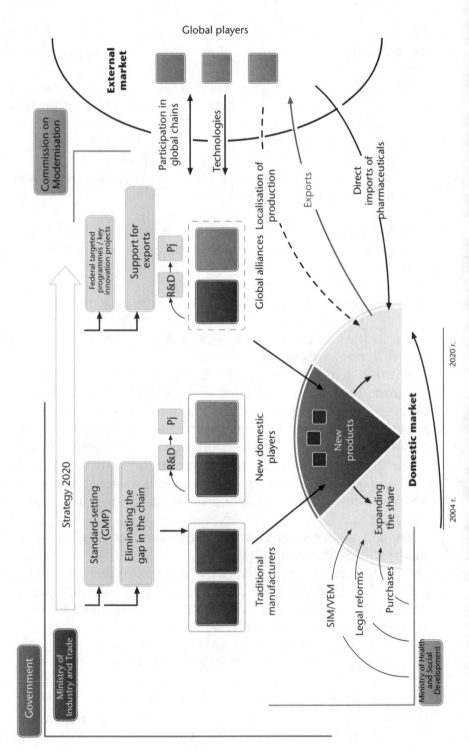

Figure 4.15 The pharmaceuticals and medical products industry: the situation in 2011

prepare the industry for the development of innovative products in years to come.

Given the variety of designs for most types of modern medical equipment, the FTP calls for establishing functional and operational requirements for new products during its implementation stage. This will help synchronise demand on the part of the healthcare system with measures implemented within the framework of the programme, and reduce the risk of manufacturing products that are unwanted by end users.

Group 4 comprises areas that have the greatest potential for innovative development. These include various diagnostic imaging devices and the field of biomedicine – the development and production of special (including biological) materials.

Thus, the adoption and implementation of the FTP for the Development of the Pharmaceutical and Medical Industries of the Russian Federation up to 2020 and Beyond will provide a financial basis for implementing the priorities set forth in the industry-specific development strategies. Once again, the priority in the *Pharma-2020 Strategy* is to achieve parity between Russian and foreign pharmaceutical products in our market by 2020. In the draft *Medical Industry 2020 Strategy*, we have made it a priority to achieve a 40 per cent share for Russian manufacturers.

Figure 4.16 Technical regulation: the situation in 2004

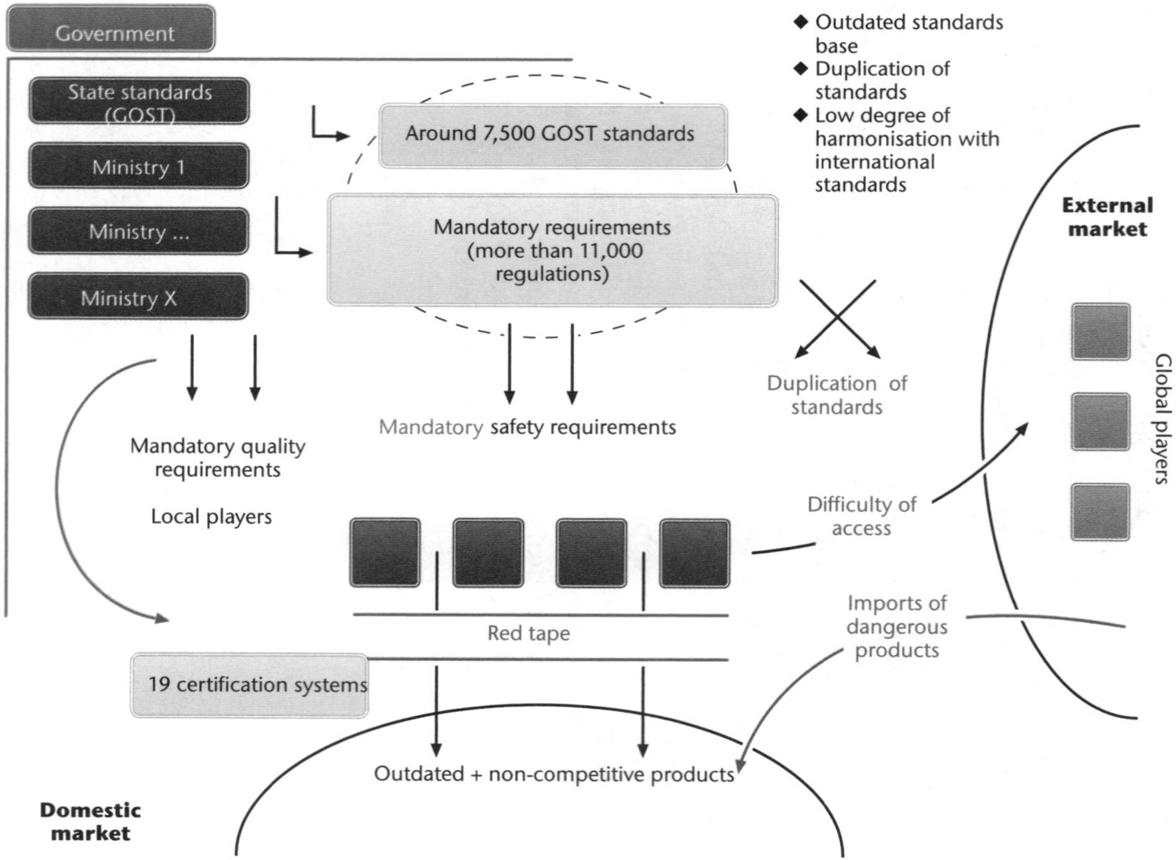

- ◆ Outdated standards base
- ◆ Duplication of standards
- ◆ Low degree of harmonisation with international standards

External market

Global players

Duplication of standards

Difficulty of access

Imports of dangerous products

Government

State standards (GOST)

Ministry 1

Ministry ...

Ministry X

Around 7,500 GOST standards

Mandatory requirements (more than 11,000 regulations)

Mandatory safety requirements

Mandatory quality requirements

Local players

Red tape

19 certification systems

Outdated + non-competitive products

Domestic market

Technical regulation

The Law on Technical Regulation entered into force in 2003. The adoption and implementation of this law was supposed to be a revolution for the Russian economy and lead to a change in the old system. The outdated standards did not meet modern requirements and were extremely confusing: GOST, SNiP, SanPiN[3] and other documents containing mandatory requirements all operated in the country simultaneously. Pre-market control was exercised within the framework of 19 certification systems created by federal departments and agencies on the basis of the Law on Certification. In addition, there were a number of other laws in effect (72 in all) that established the rules for state control (supervision), and additional requirements regarding certain aspects of technical regulation. As a result, the mandatory certification of all products largely became a formality, a kind of superfluous red tape. Companies had no incentive to modernise their production, and product safety was not really controlled.

Implementing the Law on Technical Regulation was the task of my team from 2004 onwards, first at the Ministry of Industry and Energy and the Federal Agency for Technical Regulation and Metrology, and then at the Ministry of Industry and Trade. We found ourselves in a situation where the revolution, with its righteous slogans, had already been accomplished; its logic, goals, objectives and instruments had been formulated before we came along; and there was just one little thing left to do – essentially, to completely update the system of technical regulation, come up with all the necessary technical regulations from scratch, and create a system for effectively updating standards. What had been written on paper had to be converted into a working administrative machine. In light of the administrative reforms that were in full swing at the time, this was no easy task.

The role of the Ministry of Industry and Trade as a federal authority for technical regulation was primarily to provide legal, organisational and methodological support to the process of reforming technical regulation, and to co-ordinate and provide informational support for the actions of all participants in the reform process.

Work in the field of technical regulation involves two stratagems:

---

3   These are acronyms for Russian standards.

◆ Maintain the balance between safety (including from 'dangerous' imports) and excess barriers.
◆ Define the desired technological level of economic development. At the same time, it was understood that regulations would be imposed by directly applicable laws, which would eliminate the ability of departments to create additional administrative barriers.

This work was extremely hard. Because of the imperfection of the law and the cumbersome procedures for adopting regulation, technical regulation turned into an arena for lobbying wars. Typically, the warring parties lacked a full understanding of the boundaries between the actual technical regulations (that is, mandatory product safety requirements) and industrial safety, fire safety, health and safety and so on. After all, technical regulations only account for about 5–10 per cent of the total framework of rules and regulations that a business has to take into account. The search for compromises in the process of adopting regulations led not only to long delays, but also to a loss of substantive conceptual aspects. As a result, we ended up with camels. What is a camel? A camel is an Arabian horse that passed through the approvals process.

Prior to December 2009, technical regulations were a piecemeal affair. I had to take fairly tough management, personnel, organisational and political decisions. In 2008, the ministry added the position of deputy minister, who dealt exclusively with technical regulation, and every industry department added a technical regulation department. Simultaneously the law was substantially amended. Important changes to the Law on Technical Regulation were made in 2007, which led to the adoption of six technical regulations in 2008 and eight in 2009. Nor were we idle in the years following the enactment of the Federal Law on Technical Regulation. A significant number of specialists in various fields were recruited to work on technical regulation – not only standardisers and certifiers, but also economists, lawyers and workers in the technical sphere. The scientific and technical community actively joined in this work.

Nevertheless, the years 2009–10 finally allowed us to turn the situation around. As we started to develop our own technical regulations, we simultaneously began to the process of preparing international agreements on the harmonisation of technical laws within the framework of the CIS, Single Economic Space, the

V. B. Khristenko with President Dmitry Medvedev

Eurasian Economic Community, and the European Union. In 2009, this work came to intermediate completion with the creation of the Customs Union of Belarus, Kazakhstan and Russia.

On the one hand, the creation of this supranational structure, to which the three countries have transferred their powers in the sphere of technical regulation, has meant relinquishing some of Russia's national authority over technical regulation; on the other hand, it was a way out of the vicious circle of national procedures capable of stopping and freezing everything. All of this has largely helped resolve the inconsistencies that had accumulated.

Below I would like to share a speech that is extremely important to me, which I delivered at a meeting of the Presidential Commission for Modernisation. It happened at the very peak of the turning point in early 2010, and reflects the transition from a purely national

Figure 4.17 Technical regulation: the situation in 2009

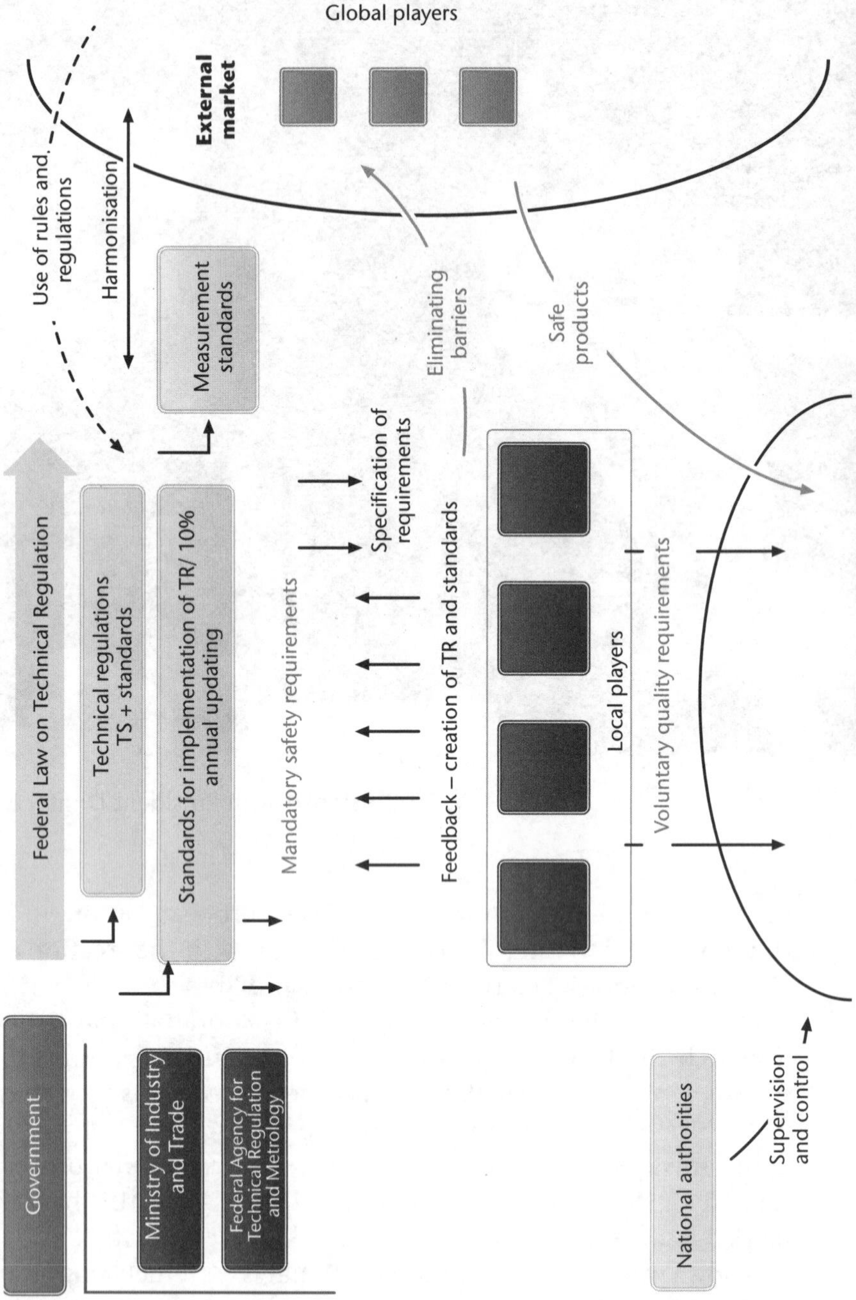

perspective to the format of supranational technical regulation, which was completely new for Russia.

From a speech delivered at a Meeting of the Russian Presidential Commission for Modernisation and Technological Development of the Economy, Lipetsk, 20 January 2010:

Technical regulation is an internationally recognised tool for adapting a country's economy to modern safety and quality requirements, and creating clear and transparent rules of the game, thereby generally promoting the modernisation of the economy. This system includes a large number of mutually linked components, each of which helps solve specific problems.

Technical regulations establish requirements for product safety. Standards help ensure quality and competitiveness. A system for assessing conformity and providing metrological support makes it possible to assess whether products conform to the established requirements.

The tools of technical regulation are traditionally varied and complex in design. This is normal. In our country, however, much of this system became outdated during the post-Soviet period and stopped helping the economy move forward.

About 7,500 state standards and more than 11,000 regulations issued by various departments contained mandatory product requirements, creating excessive red tape for business. We therefore began reforming our system of technical regulations in 2003. This involved optimising the structure and content of mandatory product requirements, ensuring the necessary level of safety, as well as making quality requirements voluntary within the framework of the standardisation system. This should help achieve the overall objective of the reform: to reduce technical barriers to business, including obstacles to bringing innovative products onto the market.

Creating a system for developing and adopting technical regulations took a considerable amount of time. It was not until 2005 that the first technical regulation, limiting the content of harmful substances in car emissions, was adopted. This gave impetus to and set the course for the modernisation of the automotive and oil industries. The imperfection of laws governing technical regulation impeded the natural continuation of this process.

In 2007, with your direct involvement, President Medvedev,

significant changes were made to the law on technical regulation, which led to the adoption of six technical regulations in 2008 and eight in 2009, including one in the area of construction. The need for change in this area was outlined in the Presidential Address to the Federal Assembly last year.

In 2009, work on improving the law continued. Amendments to the law dated 30 December simplified the procedures, making it possible as early as this year to provide technical regulations for all products subject to mandatory conformity assessment, and to create a foundation for further integration within the framework of the Eurasian Economic Community.

In addition, under a provision of the law introduced in December of last year, the requirements of 19 technical regulations adopted in Kazakhstan pursuant to European directives will be temporarily applied to those product groups for which Russian technical regulations have not yet been adopted.

In 85 per cent of cases, the standards used in these regulations are standards developed in the Russian Federation, which will facilitate their integration into the Russian system. Thus, we are not only taking a step towards forming the Common Economic Space, but also towards harmonising our standards with the European Union.

National standards that include quality and competitiveness requirements and reflect the technical level of the national economy form the basis for modernising the economy. The extent of their harmonisation with international standards is about 40 per cent, and they are being updated at the rate of 5 per cent a year. In leading industrialised countries, national standards are updated at the rate of up to 10 per cent a year. We made this our objective for 2010. This would enable us to reach the target level of harmonisation with international standards – about 63 per cent – by 2013.

The December legislative amendments provide for updating the standards used to verify compliance with regulatory requirements at least once every five years.

In a number of industries, the level of harmonisation is quite low. Often, however, there are a variety of objective reasons for this. On the one hand, not so many Russian industries are export-oriented and consequently interested in harmonising the relevant standards. On the other hand there is the example of the Russian metals industry, which because of its export orientation has effectively switched to Western standards by its own initiative.

In order to reach the intended rate of updating of standards, the amendments to the law of 30 December 2009 establish a mechanism whereby companies can apply advanced foreign standards for the purposes of conformity assessment.

Any interested market player can prepare a translation of a foreign standard and contact the national standardisation authority. The authority will send this document for an expert assessment by the Technical Standardisation Committee. The Committee consists of representatives of the authorities, businesses, non-governmental organisations and trade unions. The Committee's decision will determine whether the standard can be used as evidence of compliance with the requirements of technical regulations. The Committee has a maximum of 50 days to decide whether to register the standard.

This mechanism will allow enterprises to use modern foreign standards and technologies to prove the conformity of their products, including those that are the result of innovation and modernisation activity, with Russian regulatory requirements. All of this will make it possible to expedite the harmonisation of Russian standards with advanced foreign and international standards.

The second crucial area of harmonisation is improving the instruments of technical regulation within the framework of regional integration. The objectives for technical regulation within the framework of forming the Common Economic Space were defined by decisions of the presidents of Belarus, Kazakhstan and Russia, The relevant action plan provides for preparing an agreement on common principles and rules in this area, and adopting uniform or harmonised technical regulations of the Eurasian Economic Community. The Russian Federation is responsible for the development of most of these documents.

For integration purposes, it will also be necessary to apply the so-called 'new' and 'modular' European approaches to technical regulation. These approaches provide for the use of only general safety requirements in technical regulations, and allow for the possibility of simplifying the choice of conformity assessment procedures.

I would like to emphasise that the use of these approaches will require amendments to existing laws. The current law allows the use of 'new approaches', but at the same time it requires that only standards with direct force be applied. The resulting legal conflicts make it extremely difficult to work with the new instruments. As a result, one such regulation – and a relatively small one at that – regarding the safety of low-voltage equipment took five years to adopt.

Returning to international issues, I would like to point out that in the future we will create a common information system – a kind of 'early warning mechanism' – about dangerous products, and by 1 January 2012 we will switch over to a single conformity mark for products in the market of the Common Economic Space, along the same lines as the European CE mark and the Russian STR mark.

An important step for integration was the decision taken by the heads of governments of the Eurasian Economic Community member states in St Petersburg this December regarding the formation of an Association in the area of accreditation and its subsequent accession to the International Laboratory Accreditation Co-operation (ILAC) and International Accreditation Forum (IAF).

The task before the Association is to form an accreditation system in each state according to a single international principle 'One certificate, one test – recognised everywhere'.

In this regard, the Russian system of product certification needs serious updating, as it hinders the access of domestic products to European and other markets. Once again, the December amendments to the Law on Technical Regulation helped get this process under way. They provide for a transition to international principles of accreditation. Not only will this move us forward in the process of integration, more importantly it will enable us to erect an additional barrier to the entry of dangerous products to the domestic market. Therefore, the task of forming a new, more liberal system for admitting products to the market is a priority.

At the same time, the transition from a rigid model of certification to the declaration of regulatory compliance must necessarily be accompanied by heightened liability for participants in processes within the framework of technical regulation. The two lists that were approved in December – the unified list of products subject to mandatory certification and the unified list of products for which conformity assessment may take the form of a declaration of conformity – include 2,340 items. Of these, 1,500 (or 64 per cent) are subject to mandatory certification, while 860 (36 per cent) are subject to declaration of conformity.

The fines provided for today in the amount of RUB 500 to

RUB 50,000 for improper certification and testing and for the circulation of substandard products are completely incommensurate with the level of risk and potential consequences. We deem it necessary to amend the Code of Administrative Offences to increase the liability of manufacturers, certifying authorities, testing laboratories and other market participants for violations in the sphere of technical regulation and, most importantly, to establish clear liability for fraudulent declarations. All these amendments must be differentiated according to the nature of the products in question.

We cannot effectively adjust the system of technical regulation without the understanding that the law operates within a whole system of Russian laws containing safety requirements. This area is regulated by more than 50 separate laws.

The process of developing technical regulations has led to a clear understanding that without a simultaneous adjustment of related legislation, products will be subject to a multiplicity of requirements. Legal contradictions occur as a result of imposing standards on the regulated item as well as rules concerning the procedures for allowing a product onto the market. The existence of this situation requires that we amend existing related laws as soon as possible in order to eliminate the duplication of product requirements and avoid creating excess procedures for admission to the market.

We already have a very relevant example of such a contradiction. Last year, the Technical Regulation on Pharmaceutical Products and the Law on the Circulation of Pharmaceutical Products were developed simultaneously. In this situation, a decision was taken in favour of the law. In the food industry, meanwhile, we believe it makes sense to develop the technical regulations and to eliminate the duplicative provisions of the Law on the Quality and Safety of Food Products. The specific decision in each situation depends on the particular nature of the regulated products.

In light of the foregoing, the Russian Government's plan for top-priority actions in the sphere of technical regulation consists of five main tasks:

◆ adopting a programme for the development of technical regulations to be completed in 2011;
◆ supporting new technical regulations with updated, harmonised national standards;
◆ implementing the action plan on harmonising technical

Figure 4.18 Technical regulation: the situation in 2011

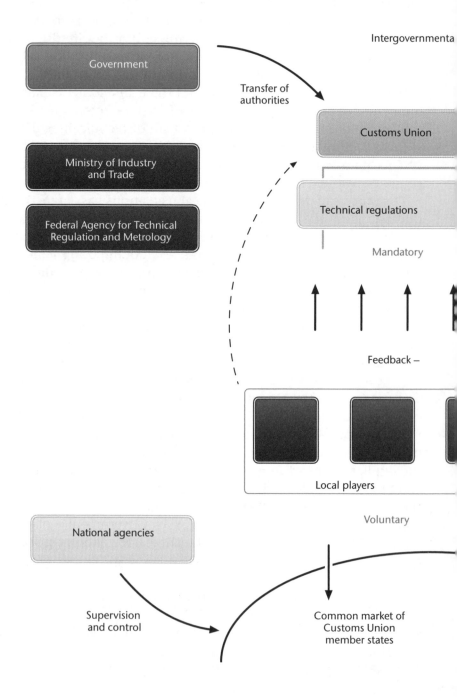

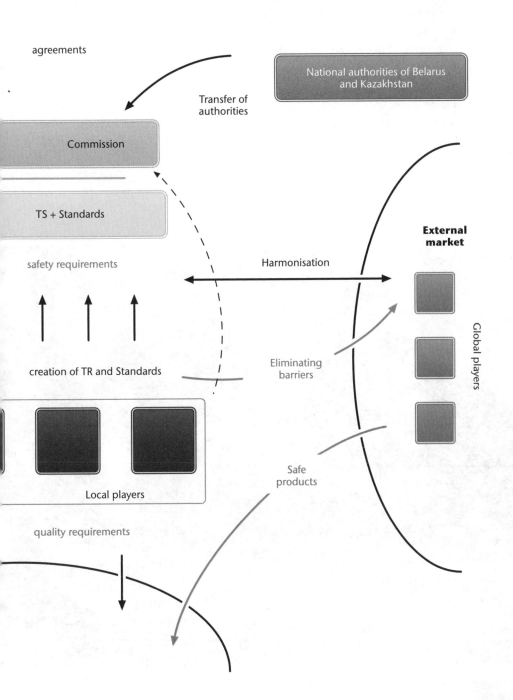

regulation within the framework of the Common Economic Space which will enable us to switch to a single conformity mark for products in the CES market by 1 January 2012;

◆ amending the Code of Administrative Offences, the tax code, related federal laws, and the Law on Technical Regulation;

◆ developing the Law on Standardisation.

These actions will result in a streamlined, understandable system of unified rules and regulations in accordance with best international practices, which will actually enable us to modernise our economy.

Together with the team in the State Duma

Overview of work completed so far: management, administration and politics in the sphere of industry and energy

The texts collected in Parts II, III and IV of this volume were already in the public domain. These are fragments of articles, reports and interviews, and they were assembled into a unified whole according to a certain logic – the logic of demonstrating the methods of our work. But there are also some general sketches that lie at a higher level of abstraction. They emerge after and on top of the completed work and the highlighted logic of its description. These are the conceptual distinctions that enable us to highlight the key points, qualify situations and events, and draw fundamental conclusions for the future. The experience in contemplation that I have gained over the past several years has forced me to see the path I have travelled in a new light. The essence of the matter becomes clearer as you become wiser. You acquire the ability to make generalisations and formulate thoughts that you simply could not have formulated before. Some of these thoughts and distinctions, which seem important to me today and which I would like to pass on the next generations of managers, I will present in this section.

In particular, these include the vital distinctions between management, administration and politics. My monographs do not claim to be methodological studies. Besides, the arrangements in place today are no longer the same – not the ones that were developed by the methodologists who specialised in organisation, management and administration in the 1970s and 1980s. But there are three conceptual focuses that we needed to retain, and I must tell you: it is very important, my friends, at a certain stage, in reflecting, understanding and so on, not to lose sight of, or fail to appreciate, what has happened in the various types of activity – management, administration and politics – taking into account the full depth and complexity of the situation: the collapse of industry, new forms of integration, public–private partnership and so on. When you work in the future, you will need foresight to understand: in this case we are dealing with politics, but here we need actual administration and practical management.

Guided by the precepts of teachers and methodologists of history,

I understand that history is always written in hindsight. The seeds of what we are dealing with today were planted many years ago.

> It is important to know what happened as a result of the historical process so that we can grasp the essence of this process, for this essence actually consists in the result.
>
> (A. Zinoviev, *The Factor of Understanding*)

Not a single management decision or executive order could be prepared or issued without conflicts and struggles among the widest variety of positions, interests and people representing them – and, naturally, real political forces whose will was expressed through these positions, interests and people. For me it is very important that these distinctions were not developed in an abstract, theoretical way, but, to put it mildly, paid for with my own sweat.

How things turned out for us

Our involvement in real politics became apparent when we were refining the concept of public–private partnership. We planned to start formulating a unified goal within this policy framework with all the parties to the partnership, but it turned out that each had its own interests. Corporate goals had to give way to this unified goal. This was followed by an attempt to do two things: unite efforts and share risks. Long-term risks were supposed to be assumed by the state, and the private sector could thus create development projects with real profitability. Such attempts were made, and the instruments were put together.

During the economic crisis (2008–10), this concept and the 14 development strategies based on it in various branches of industry underwent an 'integrity test'. A lot of people told us: you have to reconsider the strategies, because this is a crisis! We replied: But why? What does this have to do with the strategy? They told us: Let's see how resistant these strategies have been to the crisis. You promised 134.5 by 2012, for example, and you ended up with 128.4. We replied: So what? And when people started looking closer, it turned out that all the strategies had weathered the crisis just fine. Not a single goal, not a single objective was changed or lost its priority status or its precedence. Some estimates were changed in terms of re-evaluating risks. Here and there we had to regroup our forces.

Now we can calmly point out that the reason it was easy for us to formulate anti-crisis measures and get a substantial amount of funding for these measures during the crisis was because it was clear where these funds would go in order to keep moving forward with the given strategy. With the strategies at our disposal, we clearly understood that we needed to invest in a particular area of the automotive industry, and then the process would continue. Or that one particular thing, and nothing else, needed to be done in the metals industry, such as helping the main investors with credit histories for a short while without pushing anyone towards nationalisation or assuming full responsibility for any assets. At the same time, there never was, nor is there still, any shortage of dimwits – those 'executives' with their understanding of industrial policy as a set of instructions on how to manage industry. And they do not stop huffing and puffing: They still need to be helped; we'll take their assets away, and they'll recover! We'll tell them what they need to do, and everything will start working out for them!

Historical reconstruction leading to a definition

There are general definitions that we rely on, but there are also applied definitions dictated by the specific nature and circumstances of our activity. I use the general definition of politics that I borrowed from G. P. Shchedrovitsky:

> Politics is a clash between two or more systems, where they try to control each other and where they try to usurp each other and claim control but are ultimately unable to do so. Conflict and struggle erupt between them. And when they arrive at the mutual understanding that each wants to be in control and that each is unable, they switch to political activity, and then another type of work begins, more complex than leadership and control.

Managing industrial development processes

The starting point in the structure of a field of activity is the 'cell', or object, which lies at the heart of the system of our activity. For us, such objects consisted of groups of industries, an industry or a sphere of activity, the remnants or parts of which needed to be analysed and which needed to be given a precisely measured and accurately aimed 'kick' towards development. In order to explain the reasons for the decisions that were taken, I must highlight at least four types of objects that we had to deal with:

Figure 4.19 Managing industrial development processes

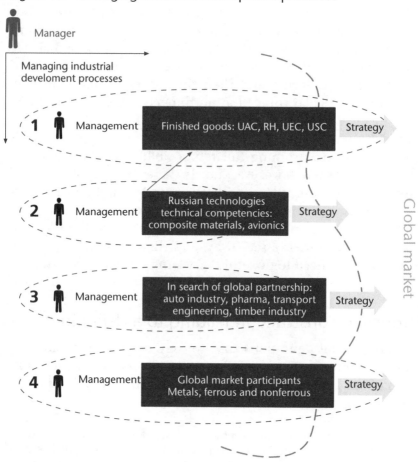

◆ Strategic industries, where we retain the competencies of system integrators and finishers – we offer competitive products on the world market and remain among the world leaders. These primarily include the aircraft industry, helicopter engineering, aviation engine manufacturing and shipbuilding .

◆ Industries that act as second and third-tier suppliers for the finished products industries. Their function is to support existing manufacturing technologies and develop modern ones: composite materials, special alloys, avionics components and so on. They work not only for our leading finished products industries, but also for a wide range of others, where products based on the relevant technologies are in wide demand.

◆ Industries that also have to compete at the global level but do not have the necessary traditions, new products and competencies for this. They need to become full-fledged participants in global production chains with the help of the state, attracting to our country and assimilating modern research, engineering and technological competencies. Obvious examples of this are the automotive industry, pharmaceuticals, transport engineering and the timber complex.

◆ Industries that are fortunate enough to manufacture products that enjoyed demand in the global market from the outset. These include the iron and steel industry and non-ferrous metals.

The first type includes the aircraft industry, engine manufacturing and shipbuilding. The principal assets of these industries are concentrated in four corporations: Russian Helicopters, UAC (United Aircraft Corporation), UEC (United Engine Corporation) and USC (United Shipbuilding Corporation). They require the firm hand of a tough manager. USC needs to act in accordance with a plan that defines clear product goals ('breakthrough' projects) as well as financial goals (changing the industry from an extractor of budget funds into an efficient – profitable – business). On this type of objects and at this stage in their development, we should use primarily management tools: orders, personnel appointments, direct infusions of public funds and so on.

At the interim finish (late 2011) we had more than 10 such entities with well-developed strategies. I shall not list them all here or enumerate their characteristics. What matters to me here is something else: identifying yet another set of tools, administrative ones. In order to form and co-ordinate the development of such a large number of businesses of a type that was new for us, we needed to:

◆ put the drafting of a development strategy on the conveyor belt;
◆ identify methods for approving and co-ordinating public funding for the upgrading of what remained, as well as the necessary innovations;
◆ develop appropriate legal provisions, financial arrangements and organisational tools;
◆ dive headlong into developing programmes to recruit and train specialists for the new integrated entities;
◆ constantly track ongoing changes and adjust the proposed plans.

In order to retain this idea and illustrate the distinctions, I shall use a graph. In the first edition of my first monograph (Khristenko, 2004), I provided a flow chart that showed the gist of our activity at that time. Politics could be seen 'between the lines' or in transmuted forms. However, in order to understand the essence of the conflicts and clashes in the decision-making arena at the state and industry levels, we need completely different charts showing specific items – the vehicles for certain interest and programmes.

Figure 4.20 gives a very rough sketch of the object of our administrative position, where the multiplicity of 'cells' – types of industry – are shown in their autonomous flow within the general scope of activity.

All of our strategies need to be differentiated by type of interaction with the world. There is the aircraft industry, where Russia is turning itself into a global player. We think of ourselves as finalists (unlike our football players). In the aircraft industry, engine manufacturing and shipbuilding we are always in the finals.

There are also other industries though, such as the automotive industry, where we have never been in the highest league, and we cannot afford this today. That is why I say that the principle of strategic partnership with global players needs to operate here. This means creating such entities and types of connections as would install our representatives in every chain of product creation, from design to marketing, so that these competencies will find a place within our automotive industry. That is why I include engineering centres here. Throughout the world today there are about 10 centres where new platforms and new models of automobiles are developed. I want Russia to become one of these centres and to be included in the global chains for the creation of new products.

The process in the pharmaceuticals industry is moving along the same lines but with greater difficulty, because the development of this industry also requires access to a global market with a limited number not only of global players, but also of innovative products – so-called blockbusters. That is why at the research stage of creating such products the state assumes 75 per cent of the risks in our *Strategy for the Development of the Pharmaceuticals Industry*.

Metal companies are a special breed. They do not need state resource support, and there are no top-down structural reforms required in the industry. The companies have a common understanding regarding the existing risks. For instance, it is very

Figure 4.20 Overview of processes managed

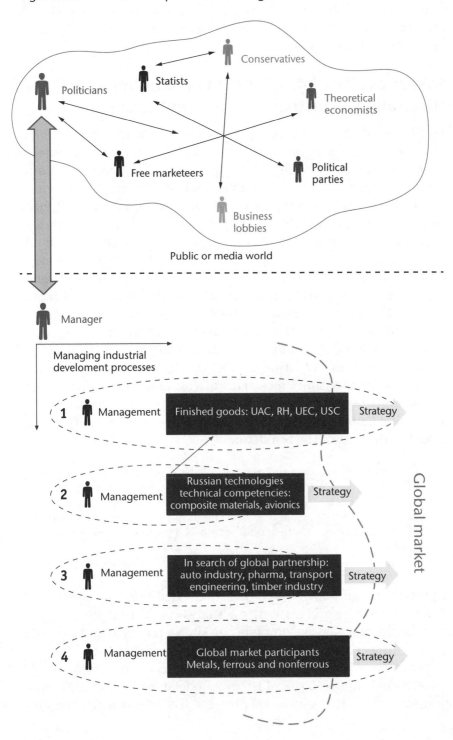

important for them to get policies across to management that will work in the industries that consume their products, and they expect the state to protect them from 'miscreants' – competitors that want to break into their market.

Politics as a battlefield and an environment for elaborating industrial development strategies

No matter what I do, being in charge of the Ministry of Industry, it will in fact be industrial policy – such was the assertion made by my colleagues when my team had just started figuring out our scope of activity and developing our tools for action. The political arena, though built on top of the field of administrative activity, shapes many aspects of that activity – if not directly then indirectly, through the interaction and communication of active players in this area. The tools we need in this area are quite specific: an understanding of other positions, ways of expressing our interests and goals, and the will and ability to win others over to our own position.

From the outside, however, the political arena looks like a communicative mess. The fact is that statements by responsible players – politicians involved in administrative activity – or, as people sometimes say, 'real politics', stand side by side with the absolutely irresponsible 'messages' of the numerous people who take advantage of the modern capabilities of the mass media.

Nothing better describes the general nature of this mess than the model of the 'Age of the Feuilleton':

> ... the empty chatter, the inflation of words, where a famous chemist or pianist is asked, for example, what he things about certain political events; popular actors, ballerinas, athletes and pilots are asked about the causes of financial crises, and so on. The only thing that was thought to be important here was the combination of a prominent name with a current topic.
>
> (Herman Hesse, *The Glass Bead Game*, 1943)

The scope of our activity was roughly divided into two layers. The lower layer was for administrative activity and the practice of taking decisions. Strategies were developed in such a way as to give working assets – infrastructures, enterprises, cities – real prospects.

In the upper layer were the outlines of the virtual world, or the media world. All the work of the theoreticians of economic reductionism was carried out at this level. Crises are constructed and organised precisely in this area, since this is where risky financial schemes are created and macro-economic indicators are calculated. But for those who organise production or work in the factories, little changes. They have no idea about any crisis.

My positions in the public arena have been noted, but evaluating the actions of colleagues who are still active is a risky business. I am not going to start any intrigues with anyone. These are special times, and this could be interpreted as opportunistic speculation – something I have never been known to do. Besides, politics is not a means of settling scores, but an instrument for filtering out questions (petty, secondary ones) that the government should not be dealing with.

Politics, strictly according to the definition, consisted in the fact that we had to assemble and focus in the right direction the activities of numerous important persons – the heads of federal structures, powerful regional figures, owners of major business entities and financial institutions – who were responsible for their particular area and ultimately for the overall success in implementing the decisions that were taken in the area of administrative activity. For this purpose it was necessary to organise the substantive communication and understanding of all these completely different people. We held a lot of working meetings and planning and analysis sessions on the most important and incomprehensible topics. This was painstaking and onerous work, which generally speaking always goes unnoticed.

The experience we gained here came in handy when working on designing the infrastructure for global energy security. This was politics in its more refined manifestation. We had to work with the leadership of the European Commission, the leaders of gas-exporting countries, the leaders of oil-exporting countries (OPEC) and the leadership of international organisations – UNESCO and the International Energy Agency.

Today we can speak of three approaches to industrial policy. The first is that there cannot be any kind of industrial policy, only economic policy. Everything else is a partial derivative – and you should not meddle in this business.

The second approach: you will not get anywhere. Industry is a hands-on affair. You have to take it by the hand and lead it – run it. And when you ask how, people say: nationalise it; let everything belong to us. And we will sit at the top and hand down goals and objectives. This is a normal, clear army system, where no one has the right to set their own goals. And you also have to act according to the Charter. They told you 'what', they told you 'how'; to ask 'why' is forbidden.

And there is a third approach, which we quietly tried to implement, since public relations was never the most important thing in life for us, although people around me were always trying to convince me that it is not what you do, but how people talk about it that matters. But we made a meaningful effort to follow a certain third path, creating new tools or fleshing out our activity with tools that merited inclusion.

You can examine these tools in more detail by returning to the texts of my monographs. How it all turned out in the end is not for me to judge.

Afterword: transitioning to a plan for further action

In eight years of work on designing and implementing Russia's industrial policy, I and my team managed to achieve quite a bit. I am referring not only to tangible things: new manufacturing complexes, new products, and new models for the operation of Russian companies in a globalised, highly competitive environment, which are described in detail in the pages of my monograph.

No less important is another aspect. As Bulgakov's Professor Preobrazhensky (in *Heart of a Dog*, 1925) wisely observed, 'Dereliction is not in water closets; it is in people's heads.' It is from this starting point that the transformation of reality must begin. Of course this is the hardest and most time-consuming task, which does not fit neatly within the rigid project framework of a particular ministry. However, it is our ability to solve this problem, no less than tax policy or the cost of credit, that will determine our success in managing the development of complex systems, whether they be infrastructure or branches of industry.

My team does not claim the distinction of having created a new mentality in Russian industry. However, I sincerely believe that significant positive changes in this area were the product of our collaboration with colleagues, partners and opponents of this work.

Removing restrictions on systematic thought has led to the realisation that industrial policy should be an area of constant attention on the part of the state, and it should be systematically organised. It is possible to have consistent, pragmatic interaction between the government and the private sector based on developing common goals, uniting efforts and sharing risks. For me, this has a high value.

The list of subjects and themes presented in the pages of my three monographs is a kind of map of the current industrial policy of Russia, which it is now impossible to imagine in isolation from the global context.

Russia has now been admitted to the WTO. Over the years of the negotiating process, both the WTO and Russia itself changed. Today, it is a changed Russia that has joined an organisation currently undergoing its own changes. This is a serious challenge for the Russian Government, for legislators, and above all for businesses. I am convinced that along with risks, it brings new opportunities.

Simultaneously, the process of economic integration within the

CIS is under way. Over the past four years there has been a qualitative shift: the Customs Union of Russia, Belarus and Kazakhstan has emerged. The three countries apply the provisions of a unified Customs Code, unified customs tariffs, a unified system of foreign trade and customs regulations, and a common legal framework in the field of technical regulation.

On 1 January 2012 we began the next stage: forming the Common Economic Space. This work has only just begun. In the next few years we want to create a qualitatively new integrated economic association, the Eurasian Union.

I am confident that the development of the Customs Union and Single Economic Space will be associated with many new, interesting and ambitious projects.

As we work on their implementation, we will continue to adhere to the principle of consistency and, in the manner typical of our team, avoid switching from pragmatic to emotional logic in our decision making.

Part V

Knowledge in Management and the Management of Knowledge

An Experience of Integrating High-Technology Industries

A. G. Reus

A. G. Reus

Foreword

The material in this section was initially intended more for internal company use than for a wider readership. It contains a broad summary of working principles, models and case studies taken from my own personal practice. It should not be regarded as a complete and in-depth analysis of my work, but outlines the important stages of a flexible and versatile system of managerial work that has been subject to political pressures and economic risks. These are most definitely not my memoirs, but rather the developments of an as yet unfinished lifetime of work. For the time being, there is not a huge amount to show or tell – it is still very much a work in progress.

However, I believe that the time has come to share my experiences and knowledge with a new generation of managers, and this is the aim and objective of this section. Knowledge increases when it is shared. This is probably precisely why I have such a great respect for education, and like to study in my spare time whenever I am free from the responsibility of having to make managerial decisions.

There is also a very specific group of people to whom this book is aimed: the current and future participants in the many events going on at the OAO UIC Oboronprom Corporate University. It is largely to them that the majority of my conclusions are addressed.

The experience of the Soviet and Russian managers who established and developed our industries is known to only a very few people. For a number of different reasons none of these managers made a special analysis of the methods and managerial ideas employed during their work. It was believed that everything they had done was only made possible as a result of the watchful and faithful guidance of the Communist Party and its leaders. And those elements that had been sensible and placed on record were glossed over and forgotten. Today students in business and management schools study the managerial achievements of Henry Ford, Jack Welch and Bill Gates, the theoretical constructs of Peter Drucker, Russell Ackoff and Philip Kotler, because the art of management has always been greatly esteemed and valued by the business community in the United States.

Through this rather complex collection of ideas, principles, and excerpts from articles and interviews I should like to share with my readers my personal experience and methodological reflections on management.

In particular, I believe it is vital for anybody aspiring to become a manager to get to know the concept of a system, which is a vital tool for all organisers, leaders and managers. I happened to initiate and organise the publication of two anthologies on this subject: *A Guide to the Methodology of Organisation, Leadership and Management* (Shchedrovitsky, 2003) and *A Guide to the Basic Concepts and Systems of the Methodology of Organisation, Leadership and Management* (Shchedrovitsky, 2004). These anthologies collected the published works of my late teacher G. P. Shchedrovitsky (for more details see www.fondgp.ru). To my knowledge, his texts are the easiest and most accessible of their type for any reader. Unfortunately this great teacher is no longer with us, but we have to move on without him. I shall attempt to demonstrate how systematic tools can be used to restore Russia's economic, military and political might.

In addition, regular methodological reflection is needed not only to deliberate over the problems faced in our own practical activity while using the requisite tools, but also to analyse which types of thinking have worked and which have failed. Naturally, during the course of business the team that I have had the good fortune to work with faced various tasks, and new problems arose which the existing tools were unable solve. Thus new constructs, models and concepts emerged. We recorded them not so much in order to have them published but to use them for future solutions and to share them with our colleagues.

My experience of working for the Russian Government for ten years, my aspirations to work using a methodology, to use systematic tools, to put in the groundwork before making decisions and to analyse decisions that have been taken, and my attempts to think about them in a methodological way, have led me to the simple conclusion that very few of the people I address actually understand what I have been doing. As the saying goes, it's 'a very narrow and restricted circle of people'. They are the sort of people who aspire to get to the very top of their area of business, the sort of people who believe that the most important task facing them is to know their business better than anyone else in order to have the right to lead people and determine their future. The only thing is that these are the sort of people who also need to think systematically. This is not an ability that is a vital prerequisite for poets, scientists, inventors, experts and cultural aficionados (the list could go on forever). Therefore, only those who by dint of their circumstances, position and calling in life are required to create management systems and regularly make managerial decisions will find it worth their while to analyse this text any further.

The principal task

It was not all that long ago when I discovered for myself just how difficult it is for managers to make decisions even when they have heard and read a lot about the subject. Thanks to the feedback I have received from my colleagues I realise that this is a skill that I have managed to master, and continue to perform quite well.

The position that I currently hold requires me to make the following sorts of decisions every day:

- ◆ immediate decisions (who to meet in the next few days, how to organise my trips over the next week and so on);
- ◆ medium-term decisions (how to best place people in the businesses' management systems, in the investment programme teams, in the breakthrough projects, how to set up crisis management groups and new product developers);
- ◆ long-term decisions (how to implement strategic plans, how to beat our most powerful competitors);
- ◆ personal decisions (how to keep myself in good physical shape, socialising with family and friends);
- ◆ other miscellaneous decisions.

It is clear that the orders, instructions and directives that are the manifestation of the decisions we take have a direct impact on the lives and activities of many people, be they top managers, engineers, workers or family members. They have the right to know why and how we plan our work; how we analyse, deliberate and work out the plans that organise the activities of large teams of people.

The meaning of the title of this book

I have already had to live through several different meaningful incarnations in my life. I have the right to say this because at a certain stage in my life I acquired the ability to reflect (to constantly analyse what I have been through and done) and learned to respect culture deeply. In other words, I accept the need to view what is past and done from a position of declared and accepted principles.

Initially, this involved preparing myself for possible future scenarios, in particular by taking part in organisational activity games, better known as 'life games'. The next step was to take part in decision-making processes as part of a strong managerial team, and to carry out and master various different functions in extremely responsible positions. And, finally, it is necessary to discover how to work as a decision maker when there is no one to back you up and the responsibility for your each and every word and deed lies with you and you alone. Figure 5.1 is an illustration chronologically representing some of the most important milestones of my life over the past 20 years. (I refer briefly to this later in the section.)

I think that by the age of 50 I have occupied practically every post and experienced every trial that a manager can face in government service and in private business. And now I fully realise that an efficient system of management should encompass a multitude of other systems, organisations, people and the results of their thinking processes, and co-ordinate them in order to reach the goal set by the manager and to attain the appropriate products and results. Depending on the type of management system, this can be done in any of three ways: direct management intervention, the setting of standards, or developing integrated ideas and skills oriented towards the same goal for all the systems, organisations and people, and the results of their mental activities. In this day and age, the third scenario is the only possible option for a hi-tech corporation competing in the world market. The best known umbrella definition for these kinds of operations is 'knowledge management'.

I received my training in how to act using this third scenario at the Russian Methodical School, working together with the school's leading light, G. P. Shchedrovitsky, along with a team of his students. What savvy consultants today call 'knowledge management' had various different names 20 years ago, such as 'organisational activity schemes' for example. The crux of the matter is not in the name but in the substance. For me, knowledge management is a synonym for the art of management and the fundamental production processes of any large hi-tech corporation, and this is what I hope to draw to your attention with this collection of principles, schemes, case histories and ideas.

Figure 5.1 A. G. Reus: developmental milestones over the last 20 years

MMC   Moscow Methodological Circle
OAG   Organisational activity games
NML   Network of Methodological Laboratories
TAM   Togliatti Academy of Management

The principles of management

Over the past 15 years I have been through many tricky situations in my work as a manager. I gradually accumulated experience and refined the processes and tools. I decided to summarise and formulate the essence of what I had understood in a few principles without which, in my opinion, it would be impossible to make sensible and long-term decisions in any field of activity.

But first of all, I would like to say a few words about the nature of these principles, who might need them and what they might need them for. The concept behind these principles has been borrowed from my teacher and mentor:

> Life differs from the existence in nature of natural bodies in that it relies on principles that are being proposed by people themselves, and they make up the foundation of life itself. Moreover, real life is in fact the pursuit of a certain ideal principle.
>
> G. P. Shchedrovitsky

If things go well, a management system can rest on standardised schemes and documents such as those for planning, budgeting and verification. But if the situation is uncertain (for example there is a world or country-wide crisis), the field of operations gets into a

581

complete mess and the decision-making process has to be based on the most general principles.

The principles of organisation in a management system can only be defined by a group of like-minded top-level associates. General and subsequently French President Charles de Gaulle famously and aptly said that 'The ten commandments are brief, clear and lucid because they were written without the aid of consultants and experts.' Today, when it is often the done thing to be engaged in a game of 'democratically discussing issues with specialists, experts and the public at large', a fallacious illusion emerges that a collective decision can be smoothly worked out from these varied and separate little jigsaw pieces, which have their roots in the separate personal experiences of the process's many participants. In actual fact this is merely a cover for management systems, which are always designed to convey a veneer of objectivity.

About 15 years ago I happened to read a thin booklet by Henri Fayol called 'General and industrial management', which was written in 1916 and which I believe is still by far the best manual for top-level managers (see Appendix 5.3). Fayol set out six basic facets of activity, five functions and 14 principles that should be implemented in the work of top-level managers. In the decades following him, many deep-thinking managers have tried to refine and add to this list. The most famous of these are the 14 principles postulated by W. Deming and the 14 principles of the Toyota production system (see Appendices 5.2 and 5.1 respectively).

I have included summaries of these principles in the appendices for your comparison and use. Try to use them, if you can. I certainly still use them. That said, I still remain true to the Russian school of management, and keenly follow the works of A. A. Bogdanov, A. K. Gastev, G. P. Shchedrovitsky and many other great managers who have left us their body of work but did not have sufficient time to provide a 'debriefing' of their findings and a formulation of their techniques and instructions for later generations.

The five principles that I rely on in management

The first principle is to understand who you are working for. Understand the set-up of the organisation you are working in, observe its power hierarchy, and understand the mission, strategy, purpose and function of your organisation.

The second principle is to work specifically in the place that you have been assigned in the organisation and carry out your functions to the letter. Very often employees in big organisations do not understand what they are responsible for, while high-ranking managers often try to be responsible for everything. This can break an organisation, seriously disrupting efficient operations and impeding any sensible co-operation between the people working in it.

The third principle is to work as a team. I hope this does not require any explanation.

The fourth principle is to think and act in accordance with the tools provided by a project and programme-oriented approach. This means to think according to the rules of the systems concept, to use techniques for structuring your thoughts and actions in order to pass them on to colleagues who are working with you on a common task. It vital to understand that you can only manage the process of moving from the past to the future, and this process is manifested in terms of management in such forms (documents) as projects, programmes, scenarios and plans.

The fifth principle is to work in accordance with the models of knowledge management. I shall dwell on this principle later on because I believe that in a modern hi-tech corporation, knowledge management is in fact the principal production process.

Junior manager at the
Chelyabinsk Tractor Plant

Training

In 1988, at the age of 28, I was working as a junior manager at the Chelyabinsk Tractor Plant when I happened to attend an organisational activity game (OAG) in the city of Rostov-on-Don. The game was entitled 'The development of a region within the framework of the development of a town'. It was there that I first met G. P. Shchedrovitsky.

This was an occasion that was to change my life completely. I went to seminars on methodology, read articles and books, and took part in OAGs as a player, game technician and organiser. This was during the difficult *perestroika* period, or *catastroika* as it was so aptly called by the writer A. A. Zinoviev. Industrial, economic and social infrastructures that had been built up over the course of many decades were breaking down. The opportunity emerged to take part in the radical changes that were taking place, and I did not want to miss out. And back then I had an abundance of energy.

As evidence of this I would like to quote some excerpts from an important document from my private portfolio.

To the General Director of the Chelyabinsk Tractor Plant, Comrade N. R. Lozhchenko

On the organisation of a concept for the development of the Chelyabinsk Tractor Plant

With each passing year, it is becoming less and less prestigious to work in large plants (and this goes for the Chelyabinsk Tractor Plant as well). This is particularly the case amongst energetic, forward-thinking young people, and is the cause of a good deal of ill feeling. Our plant, like many others of its type, is facing the onset of a crisis that is linked deeply with a lack of any *perestroika* restructuring processes aimed at accelerating the production, economic and social development of the plant and its subsidiaries. Practically all our problems are decided using methods that were developed decades ago when the plant was first commissioned, and which are simply not good enough today. The old-school method of fighting to keep to the schedule means that 12-hour shifts by factory section heads are the norm, along with constant shouting at staff, the organisation of extra work shifts during days off and so on.

Consequently we find ourselves faced with the same situation time and time again: the times, technology and people have changed but working patterns have not, and this is currently leading us into a dead end. Our actions are based on old methods and traditions, which means that we are not developing but reproducing the conditions that have led to stagnation. This might have kept us afloat ten years ago, but it is leading us into crisis today.

In our opinion, the main trend that is leading us into crisis today is the haemorrhaging of qualified and promising personnel (primarily young people) who are endowed with business sense or the potential for it.

Moreover, this inability to attract highly qualified experts into the plant is depriving us of our future, because our intellectual potential is our primary asset, and everything else, including our economic mechanisms, is just a byproduct of our intellectual labour. However, the sad reality is that we are currently paying money for nothing more than a nameplate : head of factory section, accountant, designer category I, II, III and so on.

Today, the restrictions on entrepreneurial activities have been lifted; the processes have been launched in our country that are aimed at liberating people, restoring their rights, and the respect for the individual, the restoration of the institution of property and the rebirth of intellect, democratisation, economic efficiency and decentralisation.

In view of this, we would like to suggest a number of ideas and proposals for discussion:

1 The plant requires independence, with the right of ownership of the means of production and the products that it manufactures. What's more, it needs the selection of a form of economic management that will be entirely up to us.

2 We need to set up our own bank for internal accounting purposes, with our structural subunits as well as external organisations (following the example set by the VAZ car assembly plant). Moreover, shareholding forms of ownership will become a possibility, simplifying the creation of co-operative, leasing and state co-operative organisations.

3 It will become possible to organise ourselves along the following lines: as a production association, a corporation, a concern or a consortium. Thus, it might be possible to solve the issue of the Kolyushchenko plant by making it a co-operative attached to our concern, to make the Chelyabinsk branch of the Tractor Research and Development Institute a part of the plant, and to develop co-operative and leasing arrangements throughout the region.

4 Considerable changes should be made to the organisational structure of the plant. The time has come to eliminate the head plant as such with its specialised production facilities, and create three to four smaller plants on its foundations: for example a tractor assembly facility, a foundry and forging plant, and an experimental and pilot modifications facility. All our subsidiary plants should be affiliated as newly formed legal entities, together with the creation of administrative subunits with their own headquarters and strategic functions. It should be noted that the granting of legal entity status to the plant's structural subunits is the prerogative of the plant's management.

At a later stage, the plants could switch over to rental and co-operative forms of property ownership. A scientific research institute needs to be established on the foundations of the plant's design and technology departments, and this should also have legal-entity status, with all the rights and responsibilities that come with this.

Cost accounting should be introduced in the procurement, sales and servicing departments and elsewhere.

In order to discuss the first steps that need to be taken to improve our in-house economic mechanisms, we should like to propose the following measures:

i Speed up the development of our in-house, planned, pre-calculated and accounting pricing. Pricing should become an important tool affecting production efficiency, which will make it possible to:
   • plan profit (income) at all the subunits and thus evaluate the actual contribution that each subunit is making to the profit being generated by the plant;

- use subcontracting, leasing and co-operative types of organisation for labour and for payments;
- use the positive experience of employing team and personal cost accounting as measures of economy.

ii Make radical changes to the current systems of operational and accounts reporting:

- Change the in-process accounting report from an unfinished to a semi-finished type of accounting report.
- Immediately introduce in parallel with the current reporting system an account for material costs, earnings and income (applicable to a form of economic calculation based on a standardised distribution of income).

In addition work needs to be carried out on the implementation of previously adopted measures to improve the operational accounting, such as:

- the universal introduction of the documented transfer of finished products between the subunits;
- providing the subunits with the tools to verify, measure and account for all types of fuel and energy resources.

iii Start work to set up all kinds of technologies in the plant, including technologies for education, information support, and management of the economics and production. A research subunit will need to be set up to achieve this. While there is a Chief Technologist's Office tasked with the creation of production technologies, there is no one who deals with any other technologies. Consequently, there are no records of the activities of management at the subunits, with each subunit being a law unto itself. This is one of the reasons that it is practically impossible to automate a lot of the management work at the plant.

iv Facilitate operations to define the assortment of products manufactured, or the strategic zones of economic management – to use Ansoff's term.

Serious research is needed to look into the requirements of the country's economy, but not by using our current method of extrapolation, which leaves us absolutely confident that the demands for our technology are boundless.

We have to listen to various statements being made that tractors are being overproduced in our country. In order for a rational system of economic management to take root, the possibility that foreign-made machines might appear in our markets needs to be taken into account, along with the need to freeze big construction projects.

I believe that it is vital to diversify our production. Bulldozers are one type of diversification. Other possibilities are computers, electronics, management systems, horticultural equipment, and so on and so forth. It should be noted that the production of consumer goods in their current form will not fit into future diversification plans. The issue of conversion should be resolved within the framework of the diversification process.

5 We must move away from the idea of 'production for the sake of production' to an idea that we need to meet the demands created by a marketing system.

These and many other entrepreneurial issues can be explained by the following:

- We are incapable of envisaging a future for our consortium without the tractor-servicing company, when we are fully aware that this company already has some small auxiliary service centres in various locations but only one serious centre. This line of business is one of the most strategically important for us in order to determine the demand for our technology, its quality, how our sales should be organised and how we are to become profitable.

  Obviously, we are talking about the creation of a company, with centres and bases, which will be able to operate using co-operative, leased and other forms of property. Should this be organised properly it would be possible to raise funds, involve people and other organisations interested in these new types of centre, and to establish shareholding companies and other types of work set-up.

- I believe that without this kind of organisational work it will be extremely difficult to break into foreign markets.

  'Wherever our products are, we should be influential and popular' – this is the main idea that should be imbued into the philosophy of the association, corporation and consortium of the Chelyabinsk Tractor Plant.

6 We must quickly make use of the opportunities that a foreign trade company has to offer. Going forward, this should be an independent member organisation of the consortium. If we are looking ahead to the next 10 to 15 years, the initial emphasis should primarily be on studying foreign markets, their laws and standards; on instilling entrepreneurial ideology into our business by enlisting specialists to work with foreign partners; on expanding trade, setting up centres abroad, and examining the issues involving the creation of joint ventures with foreign partner.

7 Review the structure of the labour collective councils and give them a new professional (and specialised) form of organisation. For example, we could set up economic, technical, personnel and social commissions each with a transparent structure, and consolidate precisely the rights of the labour collective councils in each of these areas. The role of these commissions should significantly increase in the event of leasing other types of property (so there would be a leaseholder's council).

   Professionals should be enlisted into these commissions. Workers need to study how to set up a knowledge data base in order to make decisions. The labour collective councils could become a means of studying management during the very process of making decisions. Leaving these labour collective councils in their current form undermines the very idea of democratising our business.

8 Put into practice the widespread use of temporary creative teams set up to deal with specific problems.

   We would thus end up with an incredible situation. Our business would be able to order in solutions from an outside organisation. Having its own accounts this organisation would be able find employees from our business to do this job, and profit as a result of their enterprise. Our business is routinely unable to carry out operations of this sort and is consequently losing its qualified specialists and wasting funds. This issue needs to be settled immediately, by raising salaries for the most highly qualified specialists and terminating inefficient working relationships.

Such a policy would allow us to identify and designate highly qualified teams. The business's philosophy would become more oriented towards being an organisation that has its own intellectual potential and high profitability as result of its use.

9 We need to create a system of ongoing personnel training, to sign contracts with colleges and universities, to take on second and third-year students to look at specific problems facing our business (for example to look at development concepts), and to provide training on special programmes with internships, like they do at the Massachusetts Institute of Technology or the ZIL Truck Plant.

We have to realise that investing in people is the most effective kind of investment. The Chelyabinsk Tractor Plant's philosophy should be 'Spare no funds in the training of personnel'.

The issue of personnel training that is oriented towards the development and implementation of the business's development will become one of the most important departure points for our progress. We have to set a course in accordance with a development strategy, which should be discussed along with any proposals that are produced through a system of personnel training. Role-playing games should be used in order to enlist teams of employees to create new economic mechanisms.

Measures are under way in the country to set its economic entities free. According to the forecasts only 60 to 70 per cent of our enterprises will survive, and we need to be in that number. In order to do this, our business must immediately set out on the road towards change and transform itself from being a victim of *perestroika* to an object of *perestroika*. By becoming a collective owner, we will build ourselves a launch pad for not only entrepreneurial activities, but also state activities, by extensively using the philosophy of experimentation and experimental launch pads.

This means experimental production – an experimental plant, experimental plant sections and workshops in other subunits, a co-operative workshop, plant leaseholding, commercial profit and loss management or state co-operative management, experimental workshops providing ongoing training and education systems, and many other things as well.

It is common knowledge that *perestroika* has made managers' work much more difficult. Therefore we now face the double task of working out a development concept while delivering it. There are the traditional ways such as:

a) ordering the work to be done by some institute or other;
b) assigning parts of a task to the subunits and appointing a coordinating centre;
c) a combination of a) and b).

But we need to bear in mind what managers the world over have been debating for decades, and this is the relationship between formal and informal structures in businesses. Strategic issues will not be resolved without using informal structures. When forming a business it is vital that club-like structures are created and that existing ones are utilised. These might be labour collective teams, various types of ongoing training and education (role-playing training for example), an economist's club, a board of directors or a board comprising the heads of the workshops. If a director's 'team' informally decides what needs to be developed and implemented while organising a concert or even better over a cup of tea, then this would also be an element of the informal structure mentioned earlier.

The first step will be to have a comprehensive and open discussion of the concept, which would then be followed by a meeting and further discussion with the general director.

The second step will be to analyse all our contracts with a view to possibly retargeting them to complement the implementation of the concept.

The third step will be to create a temporary creative team with a programme and a plan based on the available structural subunits.

N. A. Chudinov, deputy general director of the Chelyabinsk Tractor Plant

A. G. Reus, deputy head of the Department for the Improvement of the Chelyabinsk Tractor Factory's Economic Mechanisms

4 August 1988

Naturally, it was extremely difficult to implement all the ideas detailed in this document at that particular time and at that particular plant with the resources available. The important thing for me is that these ideas had been well thought out, well put together and well formulated. But if you have understood something and are unable to implement it, then you have to look doggedly for even the smallest opportunity to test your ideas. And OAGs provided me with exactly this opportunity. These games can be used as an experimental model for a new way of organising operations.

The possible outcomes of the game can be tested on a model before its subsequent application in reality in a working organisation. Having created 'experimental scenarios' and models as an organiser, player and deputy manager, I have devised and carried out several large and, as it subsequently turned out, extremely far-sighted OAGs. I shall mention only a few of them.

- 'Ways of developing and raising the efficiency of the servicing of Kamaz Trucks for the national economy' (11–18 November 1988, Naberezhnye Chelny, Kamaz);
- 'The prospects and strategy for the development of systems at AvtoVAZ Technical Servicing' (23 November–2 December 1988, Togliatti);
- 'An industrial enterprise for the 21st century' (7–16 April 1989, Chelyabinsk Tractor Plant, Chelyabinsk);
- 'The methods and contents for training cross-disciplined engineers' (22–30 April 1989, State Committee of the Soviet Communist Party, Ulyanovsk Technical Institute, Ulyanovsk);
- 'Prospects and programmes for the development of automobile manufacturing in the USSR' (16–24 December 1989, VAZ Research and Development Centre, branch office of the Minavtoprom Institute of Advanced Training, Togliatti);
- 'A programme for the regional development of the city of Chelyabinsk and the Chelyabinsk Region' (26 November–3 December 1990);
- 'Prospects and programmes for the development of education and culture in the city of Chelyabinsk and the Chelyabinsk region' (7–14 December 1991, Chelyabinsk, I-93).

In 1992 I joined a team of development engineers and played a part in implementing the Educational Programme at the Network of Teaching Laboratories. Later I became one of the heads of development, and in 1994 I became the financial director, of the Innovation Educational School (now the Togliatti Academy of Management). I recently enjoyed rereading the summaries of my report to the Congress of Methodology (1994, Moscow), where I formulated my own principles at the very beginning of my management career. I don't think that I would repudiate a single one of these principles even today.

The concepts and requirements of networks for the organisation of work

Unlike the prevailing concepts of networks as a form of organisation that acts like a parasite on infrastructure, we believe that the principles of network organisations are principles for the personal organisation of head office staff when solving specific issues and tasks as a part of a strategy that they are developing. Naturally, none of these networks exist in reality: no production facility, let alone a society can be organised as a network. However, the network principles for the self-organisation of head office staff place certain demands on the organisation of operations at the subunits subordinate to the head office.

First, all top-level managers should have a certain vision and understanding of the organisation as a whole, along with its horizons and main lines of development. The programme is presented to the public in the form of a number of diagrams.

Second, when line managers organise the operations of their subunits they are obliged to correlate their actions with the objectives of the organisation as a whole and adhere to the principle of consistency.

Third, a system of working with personnel should bring across the principles of intellectual work to all specialists, in particular regarding the technical organisation of reflection pertaining to their own actions.

Fourth, the principle of openness should also extend to analytical work, since this guarantees people's conscious self-determination both in existing places of work and in future jobs.

The model for the organisation of head office operations

The main peculiarity of managerial thinking activities is that they take place in relation to other acts and systems of organisation and thinking processes. Consequently, from the outset there is a higher level of thinking activity (an all-encompassing one) and a lower level of thinking activity (inclusive) which can be extremely complex. The specific feature of network organisation is the simultaneous existence of several managerial or organisational focal points, in relation to each of which all the remaining focal points act in an all-encompassing way. Network organisation does not presuppose the position of the person who is taking the decision (the decision maker). This is a separate, external position in relation to the head office of the network. The sole function of the head office in relation to the decision maker is to make this position more consistent with overall strategy. The chief function of the head office is to maintain its own operations and deliver a product that is consistent with strategy in the event of a change of situation or the imposition of external elaborations.

On strategy

Strategy is a function of a school of tradition, within the framework of which a team of developers work. This is the principle of the team's self-organisation, which determines its thinking processes. The head office is responsible for working out uniform patterns of actions and work for the executive machine, which are aimed at goals and objectives arising from the strategy.

Our team, which had set up an innovation university, followed the teaching of its teacher and understood perfectly well that the main thing when planning a modern learning institution is the content of the training and education programme (something that the present leaders of the Russian education system fail to understand completely in my opinion). The contents of a manager's training should of course include the history and culture of management, an activity of vital importance for both the country and society. But what is more important is to condense and pass on to new generations the principles of managerial thinking that are relevant and operating here and now. That is why I began actively to take part in developing relevant concepts, forms and methods of training. I analysed the works of the great managers and management theoreticians. But I also kept my own experiences in mind because they were the most interesting thing I had encountered in my life.

The chief measure of any activity is its productivity. My participation in the development of the content of a managerial training programme gave me the opportunity – which I used – to write a dissertation and thus gain my doctorate in economics. The subject was 'The mechanisms for transforming the current managerial systems of industrial enterprises' (1997).

This research provided me with the requisite training and a powerful impetus to take things onto the next level – working for the Government of the Russian Federation. And indeed, all my current work involves the use of the ideas and schemes that I have mastered during my training. I left the academic community in order to test my abilities in practice and to experience my own on-the-job training in the field of managing large technical and organisational systems. Twenty-two years have passed and over that time one or two things have become clear.

A. G. Reus with V. B. Khristenko

The Russian White House: designing and testing managerial principles

In 1998 I had the good fortune to become a member of Deputy Prime Minister Viktor Khristenko's management team.

Five years of working as the head of the Secretariat of the Deputy Prime Minister in the Russian Government is a long enough time to draw the following conclusion: in this environment you will have absolutely nothing to offer without solid disciplined thinking and efficient intellectual tools. Over the years, our team had to research many situation schedule maps, infrastructures and corporate conflicts, and disentangle them using a multitude of situations in the country's economy.

By a quirk of fate I ended up working alongside Viktor Khristenko in the upper echelons of the federal executive authorities during a very tricky period for Russia. In this environment my many years of training came to the fore and I was able to improve upon it out of sheer intellectual interest.

I realised that although advisers are not required to take decisions personally, it would be wrong to say that they do not bear any responsibility at all, because they 'live and die alongside their superiors', and in this way share responsibility with their bosses. Therefore, in this situation anyone constantly asks themselves which methods and techniques need to be applied.

What was used, where they were used and why?

I would like to dwell in a little more detail on the concept of a 'system', which I consider to be the mother of all intellectual battlefields. We needed it when researching the ways and means of managing new facilities (which had previously never existed in Russian economic management practice). We would begin by organising the head office operations and solving the main systematic problems. This would involve building new cohesive schemes and constructs on the ruins of an economy which had been systematically planned at one time but lacked a new generation of professional managers.

Interested readers will find a description of the operations and procedures for categorised systematic thinking activities in the appendices to this part of the book. Note that this text is fairly complex for new and untried managers. However, these guidelines have been worked out and applied in practice by my colleagues and me. The guidelines bear a strong personal imprint and therefore should only be used by others with the necessary adjustments to suit their personal experience, situation, time and place.

Participation in the overhaul of infrastructure

Without analysing each particular case I shall describe the most typical situations we faced and worked in, and consequently better explain the system of management for the Russian economy. The economic collapse of August 1998 was the result of the lack in Russia of a system for managing the country's economy, and testimony to the need for one. We could observe how sensibly planned and reasonably functioning systems were deliberately destroyed for the sake of the transition to market forms of regulation. Elements of the whole, ripped out of the structure of connections, were transformed into private (and essentially partial) enterprises. Anything that was not an interesting target of privatisation continued to function out of an inertia that had become embedded a long time ago. Back then it was far from clear how the particles and remnants of the whole were to function and manage themselves – in accordance with the magic flourish of the 'invisible hand of the market'.

After all a market is essentially war. It is a war between manufacturers, trademarks, corporations, states and intergovernmental alliances, which is waged using much more sophisticated armaments and technologies than are employed in a conventional war. This includes advertising, public relations, preferential treatment for close associates, dumping, financial manipulation and of course various forms of power politics, ranging from sabre rattling to simply stoving heads in with a baseball bat.

It is perfectly obvious today that without a clear and transparent picture of the object of its system of economic management, Russia with its energy and industries would simply not be able to survive as a prominent country on the world stage in the modern globalised world of financial and trade wars.

How to choose an object of management correctly

The choice of a model for an object of management determines the logic of a manager's actions. Here is an example. In my free time

I used to research the road-building industry, and I came to the conclusion that the object of management for this important area of the economy had been incorrectly chosen. The object of management for those who are employed in this system is the road itself and the properties associated with it. But what needs to be managed is the quality of the road surface, its carrying capacity, infrastructure support for transport and personnel, travel speed and so on. In other words managers should be looking at an entirely different construct, with all the relevant schemes that entails.

If the choice of the object is wrong, the economic interests of all those involved in the process are not being directed towards the efficient functioning of the transportation industry as a whole. To put this another way, construction workers build roads, road menders mend roads, road users use them and traffic police blow their whistles on them. And not a single one of these players in the overall process is working efficiently. This is not because those involved in the process are bad apples, but because the wrong object has been chosen. And this forces everyone to act in the wrong way and leads to the collapse of the transport system, as we can clearly see in Moscow, for example.

Another example is the helicopter-building industry. One of the themes that we have discussed is the choice of a business unit. What does this choice comprise? Until a certain time the business unit for helicopter manufacturers was the technology itself: that is, the production of helicopters. But a business unit such as the life-cycle of a helicopter from its production to its utilisation requires a totally different approach. In this instance, attention has to be paid to completely different aspects and the work needs to be done using a totally different logic.

The very same principle needs to be applied when determining the outlines of the object of a system of management for the economy of a country as a whole.

Just one glance at the basic diagram of the system of the 'unified factory' regulated by the Communist Party and Gosplan (the state planning agency) inherited by Russia from the USSR (see Figure 5.2) and the basic diagram of overall competitive equilibrium (the invisible hand, or the economic lifecycle, as Paul Samuelson put it) is sufficient to enable anyone to clearly understand the meaning and extent of the shock therapy to which the country was subjected.

I should like to quote some of principles of the 'unified factory' construct (the term was coined by Lenin, but the set-up itself was created several decades after his death):

◆ The economy is arranged as a network of production hubs inter-connected by ties of production co-operation (an industry-specific organisation of the economy).
◆ There is no free trade, and a system of distribution is built on the back of this production co-operation.
◆ The basic unit of social organisation in society is the workforce.
◆ Production is organised for the purpose of obtaining the necessary quantity of products with the appropriate characteristics.

In comparison here are some of the principles of the market economy:

◆ The economy is set up as a multitude of private enterprises competing in a free market.
◆ People's freedom and equality is the principle of social organisation.
◆ Individual free enterprise and economic rationalism organise production for the purpose of generating profit.

Figure 5.2 The 'unified factory' model

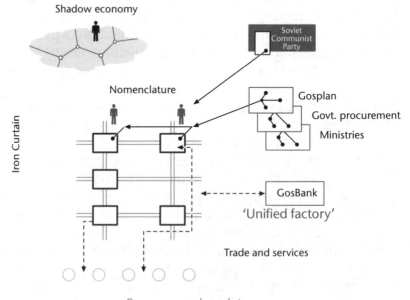

Figure 5.3 The economic lifecycle model

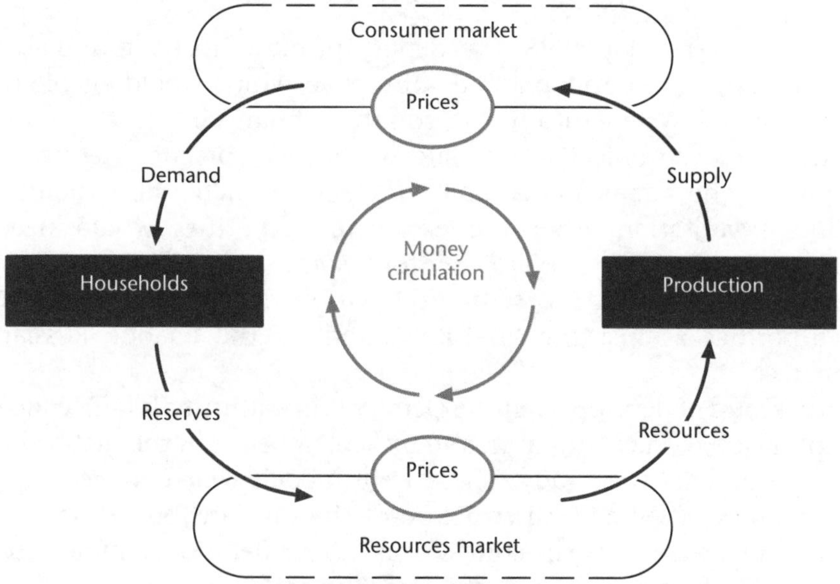

We realised that our task was to build a new, third model that would encompass all the necessary principles of the market economy with the effective managerial tools developed by a generation of the best Soviet managers: not the 'red directors', but the 'captains of industry'.

It was vital to find the sort of organisational principles on the basis of which the Russian economy would be able to become an inseparable part of the world economy while maintaining its historical advantages. It was clear what had to be done, but the road towards the end result and the amount of work to be done initially seemed insurmountable. But we worked doggedly, systematically and sequentially.

We began with a number of attempts at constructing the whole picture from scratch. We had to play our part in saving the country's energy, transportation, communications and industry infrastructure from the crisis. As the situation unfolded we were forced to act as crisis managers, developing the principles of immediate industrial policy from scratch. I would like to stress that this work did not involve theoretical and confrontational debates with supporters of free market liberalism, although we did take part in such debates whenever we could – after all we do live in a democratic society. Our actions were initiated by the awareness of how acute the situation

601

was, especially in the backbone infrastructure sections of the Russian economy.

As early as May 1998, the deputy prime minister formulated an objective: to develop a body of models which would enable us to visualise systematically the country's financial and economic structure. The objective was laid out in very practical terms: to outline the main operational processes, functional structures and organisations that the executive authorities would need to work with. We had to confront some very unsophisticated economic arguments by setting the 'visible hand' of the executive authorities against the 'invisible hand' of the chaotic Russian market.

A group of developers in the Deputy Prime Minister's Office took up the job with enthusiasm, and by September 1998 the first batch of documents was ready. These were models that embraced the principles of the federal structure of the Russian Federation, the idiosyncrasies of the structure of the various fields of activities, the public finance models and inter-budgetary relationships.

These became very useful when Khristenko's team worked on the system of inter-budgetary relationships within the Russian Federation. (I must mention the contribution made by A. Lavrov here.) We were able to solve the issue of the confrontation between the regional leaders with the federal centre by developing transparent and clear decision-making principles. (V. B. Khristenko later used these materials as the basis for his doctoraL dissertation.)

In a very short period we were able to turn a conflict situation into simple and easily comprehensible models. I can confidently say that these managerial actions carried out on the instructions of the country's leadership allowed us to radically change the whole system of regional financing in the country. In fact, what actually happened was a changeover from traditional old-school feudalism to a genuine form of federalism.

But more importantly, I would now like to speak in more detail about the purpose and structure of the third model, and how it differed from the Soviet unified factory model and the 'economic life-cycle' model. I outline one version of it below. We obtained this model as the result of numerous staff discussions and by testing it in various conflict situations. It represents the basic principles of public–private partnerships (see Figure 5.4).

In its most general form a public–private partnership is an

Figure 5.4 The system of the principles of public–private partnership

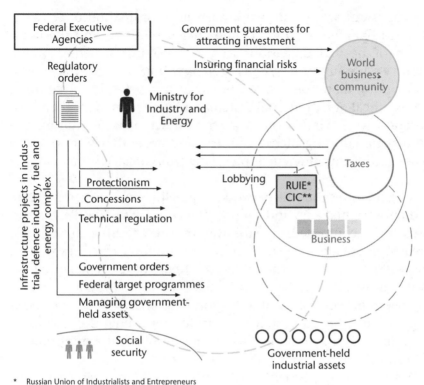

* Russian Union of Industrialists and Entrepreneurs
** Chamber of Industry and Commerce

approach where the government takes the responsibility for defining strategic priorities while at the same letting business know that the entrepreneurial risks in these areas may be minimised.

In each situation it was the job of the deputy minister or minister to resolve an atypical type of problem: when and how do you use principles, models and schedule maps if the landscape of the field of activity is constantly changing? Many failures in government policies are the result of the fact that they are based solely on systematic models, and entrepreneurial games are not sufficiently taken into account. When certain regulations and laws are adopted it is presumed that the government will work strictly in accordance with the principle declared and that business will act exclusively as an economic entity. In reality, both operate with an element of free choice and not always in accordance with the rules.

The infrastructure approach

An important area of our work was the co-ordination of activities between branches of the fuel and energy industry, and the restoration of normal operations in the main infrastructure of the country's life-support systems – energy, housing and transportation among many others. We began to understand the nature of big technical organisational systems and how to manage them. For instance, we separated out infrastructures that were vital for the normal functioning of the country, and areas that were open to business and entrepreneurship, serving as financial resources for the state.

It was obvious that the networks of pipelines, electric supply lines and railways make up and support the country's cohesiveness and need to be controlled in some way by the executive authorities. Created in Soviet times, the country's state infrastructures were in many respects ahead of their time and should have been maintained as much as possible. Before privatisation no urban construction, engineering, technological and economic analysis had ever been done to identify the state's priorities regarding the country's economic set-up, which to this day has resulted in a multitude of uncontrollable consequences.

We had to implement large anti-corruption operations. We worked out and implemented a number of objectives and well-founded ground rules which were then translated into simple rules when making decisions that were transparent, clear and acceptable to all the companies with an interest in gaining access to the pipelines and power networks.

Later on, this approach became the predominant one in our work. We tried not to be too hands-on when resolving conflicts, but rather to work out rules that were clear to everyone involved in the conflict situation.

Alan Greenspan's *The Age of Turbulence*, published in 2007,[1] starts with a description of the 11 September 2001 terrorist acts, in which he reminisces that at the time he was worried first about the security of his wife, followed closely by that of the US system of payments. He argued that if the payment infrastructure was upset there could have been a snowball effect for the US economy. He talked in detail about how this infrastructure operates and what he did in order

1   *The Age of Turbulence: Adventures in a new world.* London: Penguin, 2007.

to keep the system of payments functioning normally in such circumstances.

Russia's infrastructures were completed in 1917, but later, under the planned economy, they had to be created from scratch, then it was decided to dismantle them again. Today we are beginning to build them up all over again. This requires large expenditures by the government because infrastructure is a very expensive and can only be created with the help of the state. During privatisation in a mere two years we succeeded in destroying much of what had been built up over decades. And now we had to repair it, or to be more precise, to practically rebuild a reliably functioning infrastructure from scratch by assembling a totally new one piece by piece (there was simply nothing left of the old infrastructure to restore).

This means that the manager's attention needs to be focused not on manufacturing products but rather on creating a body of research, engineering and design solutions and certification tests. Without these, product lines cannot be updated and consequently new buyers and customers cannot be attracted. Also vital are high-class servicing and post-sales service, which is where the bulk of income is earned in today's world. In other words, this 'new cohesive whole' needs to correspond to the new competitive conditions of the world market and drive new processes for the development of the corresponding branches of industry. But here we get into the same hole that we dug for ourselves a little bit earlier. You need experienced personnel in order to ensure there is research into engineering solutions, design projects and marketing promotions. And all these people had either left the country, retired or died during the period when everything that had previously been accumulated was sold off.

We realised that we needed to kick-start the next era by quickly and efficiently training up new generations of a new type of expert who would be able to ensure the systematic design and reliable performance of our modern economic infrastructure.

In the aviation, space exploration, atomic and innovation industries we still enjoy a strong position. Injections of cash are not sufficient in themselves to ensure that our infrastructure reaches maximum performance; human and intellectual capital also has to be nurtured.

Organising team operations during the design and planning of the Ministry of Industry and Energy

For the sake of clarity, let me quote a couple of excerpts from Presidential Decree no. 314, 'On the system and structure of federal executive agencies', dated 9 March 2004:

> In order to form an efficient system and structure of federal agencies of executive power and in accordance with Article 112 of the Constitution of the Russian Federation and Federal Constitutional Law No. 2-FKZ on the 'Government of the Russian Federation' dated 17 December 1997, I hereby decree: ...
> 13. To form:
> The Ministry for Industry and Energy of the Russian Federation endowing it with functions to adopt regulatory legal acts in the established sphere of operations of the defunct Ministry for Industry, Science and Technology with the exception of functions in field science, of the Ministry of Energy of the Russian Federation, of the Ministry for Atomic Energy of the Russian Federation, of the Russian Munitions Agency, the Russian Agency for Conventional Armaments, the Russian Agency for Management Systems, the Russian Agency for Shipbuilding, the reorganised Federal Mining and Industrial Inspectorate, the Federal Nuclear and Radiation Safety Inspectorate, and also the reformed State Committee of the Russian Federation for Standards and Weights and Measures, the State Committee of the Russian Federation for Construction and Housing, the Russian Aviation and Aerospace Agency ...

Our team of managers had already accumulated a good deal of experience in solving complex problems, but now we were faced with the unique task of communicating our vision of the situation to the majority of the employees at the newly formed Ministry for Industry and Energy, to the higher authorities and to our partners and opponents. We had to change the ways in which many leaders, professionals and experts understood, communicated, interacted and organised things, and thus change their ability to deal with the tasks that they faced. And this complicated job needed to be done gradually rather than all at once and once and for all. It required people to constantly return to it at each stage where decisions were being taken and new projects discussed.

In order to reorganise the activities of around 12 industry-specific ministries that had been integrated into one new ministry, it was vital to:

◆ create common ground in the form of a defined system of values, principles, mechanisms of industrial policy and the management of its implementation;

◆ communicate the vision of the new activities that had been developed both by the employees at the Ministry and by everyone else they would need to work and co-operate with;

◆ prepare a body of models and documents that the employees could use for their personal organisation and subsequent management activities.

What does it mean to organise a large common undertaking? It involves a combination of conversations, discussions, meetings, seminars, specially designed game situations, which give rise to a certain objectifying function in the form of models for the adoption of responsible decisions, programmes, projects and plans for joint operations. By 2006 the conceptual model for the Ministry for Industry and Energy looked like Figure 5.5.

Figure 5.5 The conceptual model for the Ministry for Industry and Energy's scope of activities by 2006

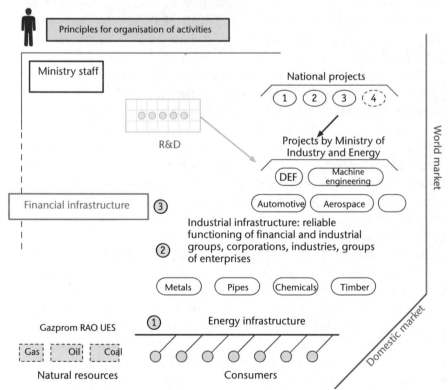

Industrial policy

Industrial policy is implemented by the state. In military language, the industrial policy that is implemented is referred to as the 'view of the battlefield'. The manager concerned must be able to survey the battlefield and understand it.

Up until the 1990s Russia had an industrial policy, but then it ceased to exist. In my opinion, in 2004 we once again acquired an industrial policy. By this time discussions about the necessity for an industrial policy as such were over. The end of the discussions was marked in quite a cut and dried manner when the president simply said that an industrial policy was a must.

Our opponents' main thesis was that the best industrial policy was to have no industrial policy at all. And that is exactly how they acted. The main mistake of the 'era of having no industrial policy at all' was that it basically equated economic policy with privatisation. The only ideology that could be cultivated in industry was privatisation. Success in industry was appraised in terms of the size of the privatised sector. In my opinion, the lack of an industrial policy prevents industry in our country from being competitive. A manager needs to understand industrial policy, to take active part in its creation, to fight for it and to be able to survey this battlefield.

Today, we realise that it was the systematic approach based on the idea of maintaining and improving the managing role of the state in the economy that had made it possible initially to diminish and then to overcome the difficulties linked with blind faith in the creative power of the 'invisible hand' of the market economy. Markets differ. The Russian market, especially in the 1990s, was only at its inception and was therefore chaotic. Only the state was capable of calming the chaos of the market, which like any form of chaos contained within itself an element of destruction, and only the state was capable of civilising the market and creating something new.

Being involved in the issues regarding the development and growth of the country's industry, we had to keep a constant eye on the reform of the energy sector. When solving problems and promoting plans to reorganise the aviation industry it is imperative to keep up with the latest developments in the field of technical regulation. Laying long-distance trunk pipelines requires extremely complex design and financial planning that accords with the calculations of the natural resources that will be travelling along these pipelines. In order to ensure that various projects enter the growth and development stage, the patronage and promotion of the state is vital. In some cases this will mean the maintenance and growth of existing large companies (such as Gazprom and Rosneft); in other cases it will mean reforming natural monopolies using fundamentally different models (such as the reform of the electricity sector with the gradual dismantling of RAO UES of Russia, and the reform of the highly integrated OAO RZhD, Russian Railways); in other cases it means setting up large industry-specific companies, such as United Aircraft Corporation (UAC).

Many problems in management are caused by a lack of general understanding and are therefore difficult to solve. It is worth noting that the job of setting up communications within agencies, between agencies and with outside agencies cannot be accomplished in one day and for all time. We have to return constantly to the issue of communications because day-to-day realities constantly change, and along with them our attitudes and the attitudes of our partners and opponents.

Head office analysis

In order to solve newly formulated systematic problems we held OAGs where needed, enlisting the support of leading managers and specialists from business and government.

A good example was the OAG held on 19 March 2005 at the Institute of Private Property and the Public–Private Partnership. One of the results of the work carried out during this game was a model that represented the principles of public–private partnerships (see above).

Another example was the OAG 'Russia 2050' (held on 19–24 March 2007), at which a large team of specialists, experts and businesspeople gathered in order to outline future trends in development for energy, industry, finance and education in Russia. A consequence of this was a schedule map for world energy development to 2050 (Figure 5.6). How did it emerge and what functions did this solution play? For several years I was a Russian observer at OPEC, and was also working on a project to set up an organisation for gas exporters. Under our plan the International Sustainable Energy Development Centre was set up under the auspices of UNESCO.

In order to understand the setting-up of any activity we need to look at its prospects (again, see Figure 5.6).

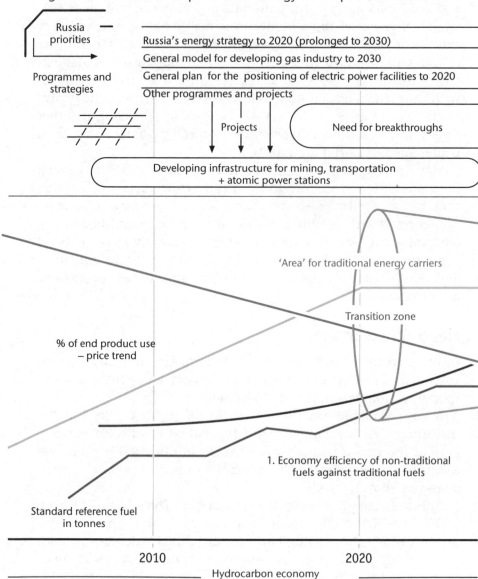

Figure 5.6 A schedule map for world energy development to 2050

Price non-trad.: price of non-traditional sources of energy
Price trad.: price of traditional sources of energy

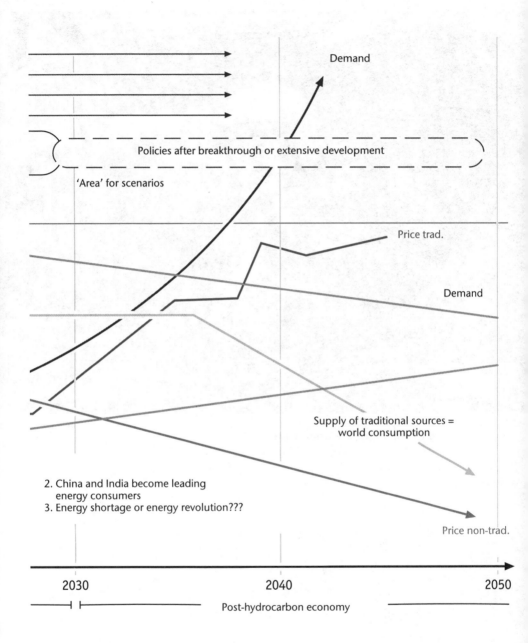

In the cockpit of the Kamov 52 helicopter

At the controls of OAO UEC Oboronprom

The situation

I had been working in government for ten years and was by then looking at the world through the eyes of a government official. It is now almost three years since I started working at Oboronprom. In my last four years at the Ministry for Industry and Energy I had been overseeing a full range of industries and developing strategy, and now I was in the process of implementing some of these strategies.

Oboronprom's management system carries out assignments from the government leadership, and ensures integration between the helicopter and aircraft engine construction industries. Development strategies are worked out and approved by the board of directors. A package of breakthrough programmes and projects of various types for helicopters and gas turbine engines has been developed and is being implemented.

In the course of implementing strategies, serious problems that need to be kept under constant surveillance by the management system are pinpointed and resources are assigned for their solution as a top priority. At the majority of our plants the primary problem is the poor organisation of the management, and extremely low productivity levels and discipline in the workforce in comparison with the rest of the world. The outlines have been approved of the programme for the reorganisation of production at the corporation's enterprises for the implementation of breakthrough projects.

In order to implement breakthrough projects, for which serious funds are being earmarked, the corporation will have to resolve the problem of achieving efficient co-operation between its teams of design engineers and staff at the multitude of enterprises that will need to be involved. Using its own engineering centres and those of other organisations in the aircraft engine business, the corporation will need to set up research, design and engineering solutions, production and after-sale services for its products in accordance with the 'stage gate process' project management models that are being used by the world's leading corporations. This means implementing a transition from an administrative type of organisation to a collective, networking and team organisation, and also the adoption of a rigorous technical set-up. The corporation needs to engage only with things that increase the value of its products, and cut out anything that is not essential.

In order to resolve specific issues as well as immediate difficulties and disruptions, we need the right kind of people in place: those with a mindset (and to be more precise a way of thinking) that is open to communication and the implementation of anything new and more efficient in the management systems for their programmes and projects.

Managing a modern industrial corporation

Achieving consolidation and programming for the development of a hi-tech industry requires an appropriate management system to be designed and applied. This needs to correspond with the complexity of the activities of the dozens of plants, design and engineering departments, institutes and other organisations involved, and the interests of those employed in them. If the management system is not conceived as a cohesive whole, the managers will be blind.

How should an advanced technology corporation perceive itself? First and foremost, it needs to make a break with its previous history, with the endless issues of everyday reality, and move into a totally different world – a world of concepts, models and onto-logical diagrams. It is vital to analyse what is going on in order to identify the existing state of affairs and understand what needs to be done. This requires the appropriate sort of thinking (the sort that works). As soon as it becomes clear how everything needs to be set up in theory, it will then be possible to think about what to do with the unsatisfactory state of everyday reality. This purely intellectual process takes quite a lot of work and time. A couple of days of working at this will produce no results, but a couple of years might. People who do not work this way are always finding quick and easy answers which pretty soon turn out to be ineffective solutions.

The mega-machine and the system

Today many people continue to perceive the corporation, its design and engineering department and its plants, as one big mega-machine. This concept was first introduced by Lewis Mumford, an American sociologist who researched the structure of human society and various types of organisations. He believed that the

Figure 5.7 The mega-machine as an object of management

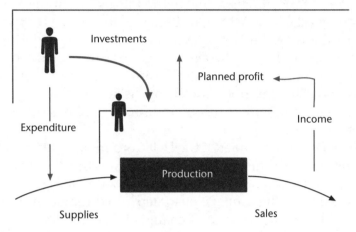

Mega-machine as an object of management

first and most basic form of organisation for human society was the mega-machine, or a machine consisting of people. This is the model for those who were engaged, for example, in the construction of the Egyptian pyramids.

The plants and design and engineering departments of the former Ministry for the Aviation Industry were also built in their time as mega-machines (see Figure 5.7). A plant was supposed to set up production, produce something and organise procurement. The plant's management system was located at Gosplan, which decided how much of the profit would be allocated to the plant and how much would be retained by the state. In addition, there was the Ministry for the Aviation Industry, which decided what would be produced, where it would be produced and in what quantities.

From machines to systems

Some time in the 1960s a number of thinkers realised that the age of the machine and mega-machine was over. The most advanced countries started to live and think about the activities that they were engaged in systematically. Russell Ackoff, the most famous of all the systems thinkers, wrote a book called *Creating the Corporate Future* in which he rather beautifully explained that we live in an age of transition from the age of machines to the age of systems. In Russia it was G. P. Shchedrovitsky, the organiser of the Moscow Methodological

Circle, who taught his pupils to think systematically. In his team we tested out principles of systematic thinking.

Ackoff and his colleagues, the methodologists from the Moscow Methodological Circle (MMC), realised that to regard a corporation as a machine is to think at a level that was prevalent during the industrial age. Today, in the age of large organisational technical systems, a corporation also needs to think systematically. It is vital to think about systems not statically but as involved in a process of change. Today new authorities are in fashion, and it is these that I shall refer to now.

Michael Dell, the founder of the Dell Corporation, said that 'The only constant in the modern world is that everything is changing.' Heraclitus understood this perfectly well 3,000 years ago when he famously said that 'It is impossible to step into the same river twice.' If we do not grasp the process of changes in a corporation, and do not perceive the change process in terms of systems, we are not even in the industrial age but still in the prehistoric era.

How does a machine differ from a system? A machine is a technical design that we can understand. It has a blueprint: an automobile, a gas turbine engine, a nuclear power station or a submarine. A system is something totally different. It is something that constantly eludes us, changes, and we can never get an accurate graphic representation of it. This is because a system is always in a state of transformation. Of course, an automobile also changes over its life span: it gets rusty, falls to pieces and finally ends up at the dump. But even when it is at the dump its design is unchanged. It looks pretty much like a new car, only rustier and a lot the worse for wear. A system is completely different. At the current time its design and make-up might be such and such, but it will become completely different in half an hour. These ongoing changes are impossible to stop.

That is why a management system needs to put a bridle on the change process and drive it towards the goals set by the manager. (It should be borne in mind that a system must have more than just one goal.) A modern corporation's management system is not like the one for the Ministry for the Aviation Industry, which understood the industry, had a budget at its disposal and could set up everything in the industry's factories in accordance with its model. A corporation's management system requires a different set-up.

The type of object of management: the project–programme approach

To summarise, we could say that while the ministry's industry-specific management system was completely clear-cut, with precisely designated limitations and a clear and comprehensible object of management, the modern corporation has no such clear object of management. There are no stable conditions, no clear-cut borders to corporate property rights, no unambiguously drafted models of activity arrangements, no single location where decisions are made (a top manager has to mentally adopt the positions of a multitude of stakeholders). From the point of view of a machine organisation, a modern corporation is utter chaos.

However, the experience of a huge number of global corporations testifies to the fact that they undoubtedly do have systems of management, and very often these are working very successfully. Moreover, what they apply is not so much an idea of an object, but more a project and programme approach.

The thinking and actions of modern managers at large hi-tech corporations are focused not on objects in the usual sense of the word (such as factories, design and engineering departments, products, markets and financial resources), but on such things as directing activities, managing solutions, implementing projects, rotating experienced personnel, maintaining the pace of movement towards set goals and designating milestones.

Unfortunately, it has to be stated that the majority of our current Russian senior executives understand absolutely nothing about these things. For them, the industry-specific models of the Ministry for the Aviation Industry era are still the benchmark. But this is a model that dates back to the age of machines. A modern corporation is managed using project and programme-approach models, and its management system must have analytical and project centres. What is needed in a manager in this context is a totally different sort of person who is flexible, imaginative and ready to assimilate the new.

In the West, where questions of management have always been a priority, this became obvious a century ago. Over there, corporate management systems are operated by young and bold people who are unsentimental about the fate of the material that gives the system its very existence. That is why they are capable of calmly coming up with new rules that, when applied, will mean that people who might have been greatly respected in the past but are now holding things back will have to be removed from their current posts. A different use has to be found for the experience and wisdom of the older generation.

The system of managing a corporation

Thus a management system is a constantly changing entity, and because of this it is vital to distinguish those parts that we can and should control.

We create this system in this way in order to control and influence changes in the following principal processes:

◆ ongoing functioning: the manufacture of the business's principal products (including breakthrough projects), and the replacement of personnel and technologies;
◆ development (in other words, determining what the organisation will capable of and will be manufacturing in 5, 10 and 15 years' time) (see Figure 5.8).

For this purpose, a corporation needs to have an analytical function in order to follow what is being done and how things change. Another must is for the function of project planning to be located outside the framework of the corporation's management system, in order for it to generate projects and visions of the future, which will have a bearing on the creation of future plans.

These days, in order to keep the management system up to date and in good shape, these functions are guaranteed by a transparent and stable structure of internal communications (meetings, conferences, seminars between managers and other specialists of all levels).

The corporation as a polysystem

The problems that have arisen during the process of resuscitating and sustaining the aviation industry and its management permit the assertion that in this particular case we are dealing with a polysystem, and are in need of the appropriate concepts and schemes. In other words, the principle that 'a system is that which is located within the reach of an outstretched arm' will not work in the case of the engine-building industry. The system is so big and complex, and it has such a multitude of multidirectional processes,

Figure 5.8 The management model according to the project and programme approach

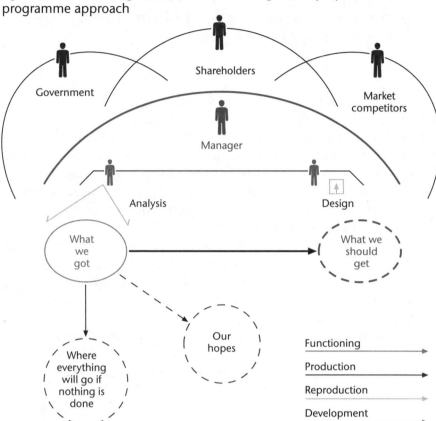

structures that are so branched out and diversified, that even the longest outstretched arm would often be unable to access the most hard-to-reach places.

What does the term 'polysystem' mean? What concepts and models are required in order to analyse its processes and understand the situations, and more importantly make balanced long-term decisions? In order to figure out these issues it is vital to construct a succession of logically and historically associated models. The models that I discuss here are still a long way from functioning as analytical models, and indeed they make no claim to do so.

These models should be detailed and refined during the course of analytical research. In their present form they are quite suitable for the designation and discussion of the types of management system that need to be taken into account when implementing Russian Helicopters and United Engine Corporation (UEC) strategies.

The principles behind the set-up of the organisational power verticals of the Soviet Ministry for the Aviation Industry

Features of this system are:

♦ rigid power verticals and a centralised budget;
♦ mega-machine-type organisation of activities;
♦ fast consolidation of resources for the resolution of new strategic objectives, and efficient managers for the resolution of these objectives (a pool of factory managers and chief designers);
♦ artificial competition created between design-engineering centres and production plants in isolation from the world's markets and the world's latest solutions;
♦ a management system with experienced professionals who had been through the Second World War and various occupations in various types of production plants and design-engineering departments (and a vision of the whole gained as the result of their experience);
♦ the accumulation of scientific and engineering projects (taking

Figure 5.9 The organisational structure of the power vertical for the Soviet Aviation Industry Ministry

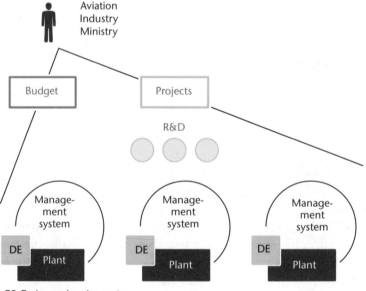

DE: Design-engineering centre

Figure 5.10 The absence of any system management in the aviation industry

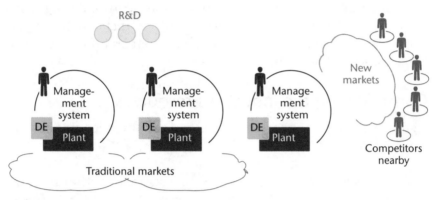

DE: Design-engineering centre

into account German contributions) during the arms race against potential opponents;

◆ the particular Soviet way of organising production processes (the Standardised Organisation of Labour);

◆ inexhaustible human resources: the prestige afforded to the professions in the USSR and a well-developed system of training.

The collapse of the Ministry for the Aviation Industry

Factors in the collapse were:

◆ There was an absence of any system of management in the industry for 20 years (see Figure 5.10).

◆ The main strategy was simply to survive.

◆ Production plants and design-engineering departments were forced to look for market niches for obsolete products.

◆ Some production plants and design-engineering departments succeeded in starting joint operations with world leaders and striking out on independent development programmes.

◆ There was competition in the markets between entities that were previously a part of a single industry.

◆ The lack of orders for research and development led to the degradation of the corresponding institutions and subunits. Production plants were still working on old projects.

♦ There were attempts by groups of enterprises to restore a comprehensive system of engineering operations.
♦ Meanwhile world market leaders were consolidating their assets, continuing to work in conditions dictated by market competition, and concentrating their resources in order to make technological breakthroughs.

Consolidating the industry's resources

Figure 5.11 shows how the industry resources could best be consolidated.

♦ This calls for the formation of a single centre of authority in the management company, taking into account at least three aspects: the interests of the state, business efficiency (profit made from the principal activity) and internal consolidation, with the corporation gradually moving towards working in accordance with modern models.
♦ The seizure of enterprises and their integration into a single corporation using the 'carrot and stick' approach. One basic everyday function of the management company is to support

Figure 5.11 Consolidation of aviation industry resources

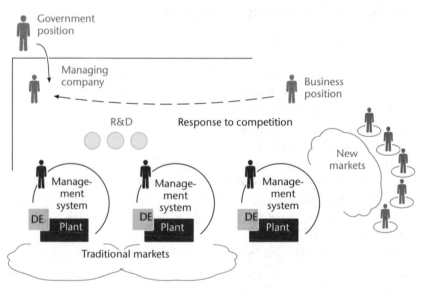

DE: Design-engineering centre

loss-making enterprises in order to maintain the industry's basic competencies that have been built up over the years.
◆ The industry needs to be reorganised from scratch in accordance with the development programmes (breakthrough projects), and to do so while continuing its normal day-to-day production work.

Programmes for production and innovation integration

In the new phase of its activities the management system needs to systematically solve the problem of integrating its principal activities, or ensuring the dovetailing of several managerial focal points, which are competing for resources, and in need of their own management systems. In order to achieve this the following steps are needed:

◆ elaboration of a development strategy;
◆ the management of programmes and projects that are aimed at development;
◆ the reorganisation of production processes based on modern economic models, in crisis conditions and amidst social upheavals;
◆ the organisation of research and development centres to ensure the success of the breakthrough projects and the restoration of operations to make in-house technological advances;
◆ a search for, and selection and training of, human resources to be placed in key areas of activity.

Programmes to concentrate industry resources in order to advance the breakthrough projects that will carve out and increase the corporation's share of the world market

See Figure 5.12. The core steps are to:

◆ designate priorities and determine the corporation's most promising product lines;
◆ set up teams that will implement programmes and projects using all available resources;

623

Figure 5.12 The concentration of aviation industry resources in order to advance breakthrough projects

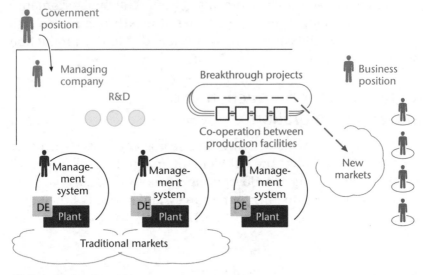

DE: Design-engineering centre

◆ manage co-operation problem number one – between enterprises as a part of the process of creating value for the client – involving the placement of orders for the manufacture of products;
◆ manage co-operation problem number two – within the framework of the 'technical refit' – setting the objectives for technical solutions, research and development centres.

As a part of managing the corporation's projects, senior managers should strive to achieve acceptable financial results in keeping with the basic laws of business.

Programme to enlist managers, design-engineering staff and plant engineers in operations to implement lean production tools and models

As part of the lean production implementation programme, the main objective of senior executives is the retraining of personnel and the transformation of the way senior managers and line managers think (see Figure 5.13).

Figure 5.13 The enlistment of managers, design-engineering staff and plant engineers in operations to implement lean production tools and models

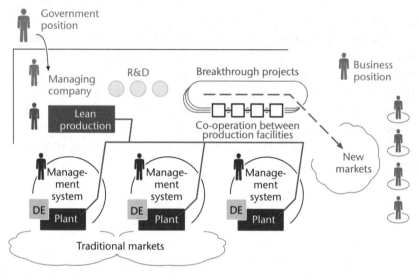

DE: Design-engineering centre

Programming the innovative growth of the corporation

This is a communications process co-ordinated for the purpose of programme and project co-operation, allowing for the discussion of various projects by development engineers at various levels of the corporation's polysystem, as well as a whole range of operations to promote breakthrough projects, research and the design of new materials and technologies.

Programming a comprehensive organisation to ensure the development of the corporation's programmes and projects

The difficulties and problems in managing the development of the corporation are caused primarily by a lack of sound ideas in the management system regarding the principles of the setting-up of organisation and communications between the research and development centres and the processes for the creation, production, sale and servicing of the new technologies.

At earlier stages in the development of aviation manufacturing this kind of organisation was guaranteed by the Communist Party and the Ministry for the Aviation Industry's administrative resources, as well as the personal abilities and resources of the specialists (the chief designers and directors of the trial production and production facilities), and not recorded in special models and rationalised knowledge sets or passed on to future generations. The little that was set down became hopelessly obsolete over the course of 30 years when there were no prospective projects in the industry at all. In the meantime, the world's leading companies were moving far ahead. We are now faced with having to create the necessary models and knowledge sets based on outside global experience, but primarily by acting by ourselves.

During the project analytical session

Knowledge management:
the corporate university

It is clear from what has been said that the integration of a hi-tech industry is a task that needs to be resolved by its leading specialists, using the tools that a systematic approach and organisational activity models have to offer. Special forms of organisation are needed to bring a team of specialists together, provide them with the necessary tools and organise them to carry out joint development research. And it is precisely for this purpose that the corporate university was conceived. I should like to stress that this is a way of organising the work of the corporation's specialists that is not a part of the production process, but in close proximity to it and conditioned by the problems that arise from it.

Many people mistakenly believe that the corporate university is a special type of educational establishment. For example they conceive it as a miniature university attached to a large corporation, created for the retraining and professional development of personnel through conventional lectures and seminars that are designed to serve the interests of the corporation as opposed to wider educational goals. The Soviet factory technical school is an analogy that often comes to mind. However, a corporate university is rather a way of selecting and training people, and a modern approach to developing large organisational and technical systems.

Corporate universities as a particular form of training first emerged in the 1980s. So what principles are they built on?

Over the course of the last two centuries the number of people that have gone through universities and business schools has grown exponentially. And over the last 50 years as a result of the efforts of the mass media, publishing houses and internet technologies, the world has become 'saturated with information and knowledge'. Resolute managers of the world's largest corporations have decided to use these resources economically and sensibly, in order to be sure that the corporation's specialists have all the skill sets that they need, and the thousands of people who work for the corporation know everything that the corporation needs them to know.

Once this is established, a simple and logical step follows: the necessity of organising the sharing of experience within the corporation, setting it down in convenient forms and transferring it to a place where it can and should be used. In essence this is what is known as the 'management of (available) knowledge'.

We need to move from people management to knowledge management. This assertion does not mean that we have to stop working with people, but is more about the fact that instructions to executives need to be delivered taking into account their knowledge, skills and abilities. At the same time it is imperative to organise the change taking place in this system and the set-up as a whole, in keeping with the tasks that a particular employee should be handling. The experience of business as well as government service has taught me that giving people a job that does not correspond with their skills and knowledge can lead to the most stressful outcomes.

A role in a functional structure requires a very clear cut set of skills, ideas and techniques in order for its holder to execute the necessary functions. Accordingly, there need to be a selection of models that make it possible to maintain and develop further structural ties. Otherwise the whole system would collapse, because the structure would cease to operate, functions would not be carried out, and malfunctions would occur and have to be identified and corrected. Even if an activity is described in detail, which unfortunately in our country is a very rare occurrence, an operation specially dedicated to knowledge management is still very much needed.

The most appropriate structure for this type of operation is the project team. Managing knowledge is pretty effective when project teams are used. One of the biggest problems in any structure is installing project teams in an existing structure.

It is a good thing if this operation is successfully embedded into the information system and experienced specialists are persuaded to share their knowledge. For example, after a project seminar appropriate information about it should appear on the company's portal. Then any corporate employee, regardless of their location, would be able to enter the system, ask a relevant question and find the answer.

Why do I, as chief executive of JSC UIC Oboronprom, feel that the corporation needs a corporate university? The objectives that our company has to meet require people of a new generation with the appropriate training. These people must have, among other qualities and skills:

◆ awareness of the state's needs;
◆ business talent;

- understanding;
- systematic thinking;
- perseverance in getting to the bottom of a designated problem;
- fluent command of modern technical tools of the trade (the English language, information technologies, an engineering approach, knowledge of anthropotechnology and social engineering).

I know of no single educational establishment that can provide all this. Most of what I have listed above is gained by people from the 'university of life': by working in a responsible position, solving a technical issue or during the creation of a new organisation. In other words they learn by solving problems in their own personal practice.

The ways of organising work practised in the corporate university anticipate special answers to the following questions:

- What is knowledge?
- What is knowledge as the object of management?
- How can and should we manage knowledge?

It is at this stage that we come to some important conclusions and answers. A concept such as knowledge should not be regarded as a thing that can be transferred, saved and bought, and so on. The knowledge that is used by specialists in their practice has to be examined from a pragmatic viewpoint and approach. Knowledge has a defined place and function in practical activity. Knowledge is what enables a specialist to act correctly.

Knowledge management is invoked in order to solve the problems of organisation and management in large organisational and technical systems. The principal and constant problem is a complicated issue: how to attain manageable networks of organisations consisting of thousands of different people located at different sites who are separated by huge distances and engaged in a multitude of different types of activities. Knowledge management is marshalled by such organisational forms as the corporate university.

A localised management system comes within reach of the manager's 'outstretched hand' when they are able to reach every member of the organisation and then apply an order, an instruction, an incentive along with other tools of direct intervention. The

629

traditional tools for localised systems are discipline, authority and incentive.

A network management system is required in organisations where the size and quantity of the tasks are too great for any one 'outstretched arm'. In this instance, managers need to have the tools of indirect intervention at their disposal, such as semiotic management, corporate culture, a 'learning corporation' and a network of communications. These take the place of an administrative hierarchy.

Knowledge management is the result of the systematic synthesis and constructive assembly of management tools in big organisational systems arranged in accordance with the principle of the network.

Ideas such as the exchange of knowledge and collective thinking, which are referred to today using the borrowed Western term 'knowledge management', were devised a long time ago in our country.

The corporate university enables us to work on knowledge management, the sharing of experience and collective thinking in a systematic and transparent way as opposed to a random and haphazard way. It is precisely for this reason that I created the corporate university, and why I shall be maintaining and using it in my own personal interest and the interests of the corporation as a whole.

A talent pool

The big projects and investment programmes that we are involved with these days are beyond the scope and capabilities of any one single human life in terms of the time scale and human resources required for their implementation, even if this person were a true giant among humans. Global experience and practice has shown us that the average senior manager only has the energy reserves to last about five years, and the toughest manager spends no more than 12 years in any one job. Therefore, a manager who takes on a big project needs to build a team and nurture a replacement.

Those who fail to do this (or are incapable of doing it) are either too careless or too incompetent to hold down the job they occupy. Today, we can look back and say that many of our industry's leading captains failed to leave us either a replacement or a productive description of their activities. In the situation that we currently find ourselves in, we have no right to repeat the mistakes of the past, and must always remember that the task of a senior manager is not only to maintain the normal functioning of their organisation but to encourage and clear the way for the next generation. Without this there can be no development, which is what we so desperately need today.

That is why the work of selecting, training and promoting the talent pool is so vital for our corporation. And it is the corporate university that provides those involved in this work with the tools that they need.

The principles behind working with a corporation's talent pool

In the situation faced by our corporation today we need to move on from corporate consolidation to the systematic integration of the industry, which means setting about forming a single management system for UEC and thus providing new and substantial impetus to the process of corporate consolidation.

When implementing our strategic plans we need to redevelop our technical expertise in the form of a new generation of engineers, designers, process engineers and production managers capable of creating world-class engineering products, and guaranteeing their sale and efficient servicing over the long term.

During the project analytical session

It is precisely for the implementation of this mission and the attainment of the goals associated with it that we are gathering together the combined managerial, engineering and production resources of the Russian helicopter and aircraft engine construction industry into one joint corporation. This concentration of resources of itself would be pointless if we did not organise them sensibly and use them properly.

In order to achieve these goals and to gradually make such serious changes a reality, we have to change the way that the majority of those involved in these upcoming operations think. Stalin famously said to the head of the writer's union, who complained to him about the calibre of his members, 'I'm afraid I don't have any other writers for you.' We need people who are competent professionals while at the same time being promising, young and dynamic. That is why we have undertaken a series of operations aimed at establishing a human resources policy in the corporation.

We need to concentrate the best specialists, resources and efforts into breakthrough projects. As a part of our helicopter and aircraft engine development strategy the main objective that we have set ourselves and are implementing is to develop hi-tech products and solutions that are on a par with the rest of the world and will occupy a respectable niche in the global marketplace. To this end we have put together a package of breakthrough projects and a prospective range of models, and are busy planning and implementing them. In order to meet this objective we will need to make several breakthroughs in terms of the way our business is organised and the way that the corporation's people work.

We need to increase labour productivity significantly and to transform all our plants to work in accordance with lean production models. This extremely complicated task requires a change in the mindset of thousands of experienced specialists. The experience and performance of Russian machine engineering enterprises, including ours, suggests that this is going to take quite a lot of time. It reminds me of the famous Russian comedian Arkady Raikin's much quoted joke, 'Forget everything that your university taught you.'

We need to set up design-engineering solutions, the production and post-production servicing of our products, as a part of a project management approach that is in keeping with the models (based on stage gate processes) adopted by the world's leading corporations. This means moving away from administrative to team-based organisational structures, and the adoption of a strict ideology that we will only spend time on things that add value to our products, and cut out anything that is not essential.

This breakthrough in labour productivity will require fewer but much better qualified workers. To an outsider it might appear that we are simply reducing our workforce. But in actual fact we are creating opportunities for those who are striving to become better and to move up their professional and career ladder.

I cannot do better than quote Jack Welch here. He managed General Electric from 1981 to 1996, and is a man that I respect greatly:

> I shall begin by changing the company. I want to raise productivity, radically improve quality, to halve the number of hierarchy levels and so on. These are the only conditions that the company can survive under; this is not my choice but the law of competition. I invite those who are

ready to build a new company to come and join my team. I won't be firing anyone, but those who can't keep up with the changes and the leaders who introduced them are just going to have to leave.

In the long run all this should lead to the integration of our enterprises under the guiding principle of a learning corporation. The corporations created by Oboronprom should guarantee that our country becomes a global leader in terms of its technology and the market share enjoyed by its products. Naturally, we need to set our sights on the latest ways of organising and working with our human resources, our intellectual capital. Our design-engineering centres, businesses and people should be imbued with the idea that they constantly need to be learning and the desire to be the best in the world.

Our best specialists should be given the opportunity to join the corporation's management pool and to be trained accordingly. If we do not train up the next generation of our industry leaders today, instead of development and growth we will just be left with the decay and collapse of those available resources that still remain. Setting up teams of managers for the areas of operations that have been earmarked is the most complex task that we need to resolve.

Programmes and actions: excerpts from open source articles and interviews

The principles behind the creation of a new system of training for personnel in the aircraft industry: an opinion

A speech at the 'Creating Systems for Personnel Training in the Aircraft Industry' conference, 24 August 2007:

I am speaking today not only as a part of my professional duties but also because this is a subject that concerns me personally.

Ever since 1988, I have been a member of a team headed by G. P. Shchedrovitsky that began working out a fundamentally new system of education in Russia. Since then a great number of theoretical, experimental and pilot solutions have been developed. Several innovative educational platforms have been set up. Experience has been accumulated and principles for the training of modern, up-to-date specialists have evolved, which should make a significant contribution to the realisation of the country's innovation development strategy. Since 2004 we have been trying to put the main results of this work into practice at the Ministry for Industry and Energy. We do it in our work with the Ministry's own staff, where a programme for managerial training has been under way for several years, and also when designing strategies for the development of some of our subdepartmental industries and areas of operations. In addition to this, my colleagues and I strive to keep abreast of all the innovations and breakthroughs being practised throughout the world in the training of engineers, researchers and managers. And it is on the basis of this that I would like to elaborate a number of fundamental assertions with regards to the subject of this conference.

'High-accuracy weapons as a substitute for carpet bombing and shelling'

This is a principle that is already well known to defence industry specialists, but I believe that it is also a key principle with regard to modern training systems for defence industry personnel. So what do I mean by this? When we were laying the foundations of our defence industry between the 1930s and 1950s we acted without counting the costs in terms of resources and human lives, which at that time seemed inexhaustible. A host of design-engineering centres, factories and testing grounds were commissioned. In order to provide the defence industry with personnel, dozens of identical higher education establishments were set up that churned out a surplus of freshly moulded young specialists. I would particularly like to stress this word 'moulded', because these graduates then had to undergo lengthy on-the-job training and retraining (I know this full well from my own personal experience). Sheer numbers and natural selection were sufficient to solve some very complex problems, but today we are faced with tasks that are a lot more complicated. Those who really strived for it became highly qualified professionals. However, the surplus of engineering graduates who were happy to accept the salary of a machine tool operator led to a devaluation of the engineering profession.

Everybody here knows that there is a huge void of professionals in the 20 to 60 year old age bracket. Unfortunately, there are practically no 40 year olds working in our production facilities. Having created the UAC to implement hi-tech projects and marketing operations, we also need to devise highly specific plans for training the industry's managers, designers, researchers, engineers and operators.

We have to move away from wasteful mass-produced training to clear-cut, goal- oriented training plans for specific groups of specialists. In our country we have a lot of experience and a deeply held tradition of practising this approach.

*'Let the dead bury the dead, but we have
to act and give life to others'*

Over the course of a mere ten years we have succeeded in effectively losing the intellectual and engineering stock that had been accumulated by the selfless work of many generations of Soviet people. The problem is, how are we going to regenerate and develop it? Everyone here is fully aware of the generation gap that exists in the industry. As the wise old folk saying puts it, 'If only youth had the knowledge and old age the energy.'

When growing a new generation of specialists we can no longer just rely on the knowledge and experience of veterans (despite our deeply held respect for them). In the modern world many traditional knowledge sets have lost their transferable value, and the education system has ceased to be the main bearer and source of knowledge.

Explaining something to V. Putin

We need to reject the Soviet system of training personnel, not just because it is not possible to bring it back in its previous guise, but because it is not capable of ensuring the attainment of the objectives set by the development strategy for the aviation industry, or indeed for the country's other industries for that matter. Today we need to support teams of working professionals who are capable of not only 'getting things done' but also understanding the importance of passing on this ability to their junior colleagues. In other words, we need good old-fashioned mentoring by a master of a novice, or 'knowledge management' as it is called in global practice these days. Of course, this approach is not a return to a medieval workshop model of organisation, but on the contrary enables us to apply the latest technology when working with knowledge. The technology of knowledge management is used in all the largest aviation

637

corporations, and UAC is up there with them. Knowledge born out of the daily practice of solving design, engineering and production tasks is becoming the main asset of a corporation as a whole. (Just take the examples of General Electric, Boeing, Toyota and British Petroleum.)

We should not go wasting our time and efforts resurrecting something that does not meet the new challenges facing us. Meanwhile the human, intellectual and engineering potential that we do have available should be painstakingly accessed, recorded and augmented, or to put it another way, capitalised.

A new personnel policy is not about providing new jobs but about defining specialists' development prospects (including their material prospects)

The Soviet system of assigning people to production facilities ceased to exist a long time ago, and the labour market has become much more mobile. The principle of identifying prospects needs to be distinguished from the principle of providing new jobs. By using such an approach an expert's capitalisation grows in proportion to their participation in important projects. Practical training needs to be acquired on the job while the requirements of a general level of education need to be passed on at the discretion of the specialists themselves.

So what is practical training? It is the suitability of a person to the requirements of a defined place of work, while general education should be acquired at the individual's discretion. For instance, the question of learning a foreign language or not has always been a matter of personal choice. If you want to get involved in operations connected with exports to South-East Asia or if you want to go to Iran, then you will need to learn Chinese or Persian, but if you don't, you will end up working in a place that doesn't require a foreign language.

UAC can and must become a leader in creating a corporate system of targeted training

New generations of personnel need to be nurtured in centres of competence, and for all intents and purposes UAC is one of them.

Over the last few years I have spent a fair amount of time with the Sukhoi Corporation's senior management, and I am well acquainted with the Sukhoi Corporate University's set-up and development projects, and also its finely tuned system for the selection and promotion of specialists within the company. It is quite possible to put the experience that Sukhoi have gained at the very heart of UAC's plans for a corporate university.

I believe that the system of training for personnel in the aviation industry should be as separate as possible from the general system of Russian higher education, while it still remains unclear in what direction the latter is likely to be reformed. Fifty years ago new fields of activity used to be generated within personnel training systems themselves. However, today the opposite is true: newly developing fields of activities create all types of 'custom designed' training systems for professionals.

A new format of technical assignments for training specialists should be formulated at special centres for the creation of intellectual capital. And this is precisely why I propose creating a centre of this sort as a part of UAC. It should create new systems and standards of training. The experience of creating a centre of this sort could then be transferred to other fields of activity and other industries.

Industrial policy: the infrastructural approach

From Vedomosti, *28 February 2008:*

Over the last 15 years we have seen several epochs come and go in terms of changes to the management systems in Russia's economy: from the removal of the 'red directors' right up to the infrastructural architecture of economic activity.

A short course in crisis

During the complete removal of the 'red directors', decisions were taken that generally favoured a new breed of owner. It was said (and with a good deal of justification) that most Soviet directors were not capable of thinking independently and taking responsible decisions. It was believed that during the course of privatisation a new, more efficient, Western type of owner and manager would emerge, who would be more entrepreneurial, independent and ready to compete in the tough conditions created by market competition. As soon as these leaders emerged, the economy would get back on track and the country would make a decisive leap forward in its development. Privatisation basically became equated with economic policy, and as a result for a time it became the ideology of the Russian state.

This equation was the main economic error of that period. New owners and managers arrived, but it quickly became clear that they were only successful in those businesses and areas of activity where their products already enjoyed a degree of demand on the world's markets. Foreign trading houses and swarms of intermediaries flew in wherever there was something worth selling. Fuel, energy, metals and chemicals, timber and fish products saw a brisk trade. Then the new managers learned how to trade themselves and do without the intermediaries. But at the same time it was the government's job to pursue the country's interests: to collect taxes, prevent monopolisation, ensure product safety and so on.

The enterprises that had been appropriated by the new breed of owners and managers were left without government investment: that is, without centralised injections of funds into depreciating assets and the development of technological capabilities. Gosplan and government supervision were a thing of the past.

As a result there was a deep-seated collapse in our technical and engineering capabilities, and a growing lag behind the leading world economies in terms of technology innovation. The dilapidation of our equipment in the energy engineering, machine building, transport and other key infrastructure industries grew to catastrophic proportions. Engineers became traders selling goods in the large cities and the markets of the world, teaching departments at the universities decayed without being set any specific practical tasks to solve, young people went into professions where there was money to be earned – as bankers, lawyers, economists and sales managers.

The situation was even worse in the defence industry. In the Soviet period it had enjoyed guaranteed sales in the countries of the Warsaw bloc and in other countries that were friendly to the USSR. After the collapse of the Soviet Union, our defence products were not in demand in the outside world, while inside Russia there were no government orders for them either (we have only just got into other markets in the last few years). As a result, the huge potential that had been accumulated in the industry – in its research institutes, its design-engineering centres, its testing grounds and experimental production – was now on the verge of total collapse. Moreover, the fundamental principle that the defence industry's finest brains are the country's capital and they will only stay in those places where they are being properly nourished with state funding was completely forgotten.

Crisis management

This was the situation that we found ourselves in at the Ministry for Industry and Energy (under the leadership of Viktor Khristenko) where we were forced act like a team of crisis managers while developing the foundations of a high-priority industrial policy that had been ordered by the president. I must stress here that our actions were not the result of furious theoretical debates with the supporters of market liberalism. Our actions were prompted by a recognition of the acute problems that were plaguing the Russian economy's most important industries.

It was vital that the attempts to carve up and privatise the country's network of Gazprom pipelines and RZhD railways be halted in its tracks. The issue at stake was no more and no less than the very disintegration of the country itself. We simply could not afford to lose control over the transport and machine engineering capabilities of the defence industry and other sectors of the economy that were vital to the country's economic safety. We prepared and launched a huge number of development strategies for the most important branches of the country's economy. What was the purpose and content of these development strategies that at first glance appear so chaotic?

The modern global economy is essentially infrastructure-based. In the twentieth century new rules in global trade and financial interaction were put in place. For instance, it is impossible to sell products in a region that lacks a well-developed network for their repair and servicing. From the standpoint of an infrastructural organisation, the issue of having access to a reliable supply of goods and services is much more important than their cost and volume. The best example is the Internet, but the same principle applies to trading in electricity, gas, oil, transportation services, machine tools, automobiles, airplanes and rockets.

Infrastructures have been growing in developed countries for over 400 years. Soviet managers were able to establish infrastructures over the course of several decades. During privatisation we managed to destroy much of what had been created over decades in the matter of a couple of years. And now we need to create everything from scratch piece by piece (there is simply nothing left that can be restored).

This means that the focus of our attention needs to be not only on manufacturing products, but rather on their after-sales servicing and the creation of a body of research, engineering and design solutions and certification tests without which product lines cannot be updated, and consequently new buyers and customers attracted.

Our technological backsliding is not just the result of a lack of financing of innovation in the defence industry's production assets and research and development activities, because backsliding was already evident in a number of areas by 1990 despite ample financing. The same could be said for domestic appliances, measuring instruments and machine tool production, to name but a few sectors. Our country's lack of a special technological infrastructure enabling the nurture and growth of new competitive technologies and products played a fundamental role here as well. In order to create this infrastructure it is vital to ensure that there is an efficient system linking the design engineers creating the various different hubs, parts, materials and processes with each other. Another important matter is the creation of a feedback system with the consumer, because in the final analysis it is the consumer who determines what technology is required, and which solution is competitive and will repay the investment that has been put into it.

Efforts to construct such an infrastructure are under way now. They include technology parks, special economic zones and innovation cities. However, here we find ourselves in the same Catch-22 situation that we found ourselves in earlier. In order to ensure the success of research and engineering solutions, design projects and marketing campaigns you need qualified and experienced personnel, but all these people left the country, retired or died in the period when everything that had previously been accumulated was all sold off.

The new era

Today, we need to kick-start a new era by quickly and effectively training up new generations of a new type of expert who will be able to enable the systematic design and the reliable performance of our modern economic infrastructure in machine engineering, in the defence industry and in the innovation industries where we still enjoy a strong position.

It would be rash of me to assert that with the arrival of Oboronprom all these problems will be solved immediately

From 'Russia's Aviation Industry', a supplement to Izvestia, *18 August 2009:*

UIC Oboronprom currently faces the difficult task of creating a modern, world-class machine engineering company capable of uniting such hi-tech industries as helicopter and aircraft engine construction (Russian Helicopters and UEC) and ensuring the smooth functioning of its enterprises and the production of competitive products. Andrei Reus, the general director of Oboronprom, talks to Izvestia about how UIC Oboronprom is progressing.

UEC's strategy has been worked out, you have talked about it on more than one occasion to the press and at public events. How would you best sum it up?

In our country we need to ensure the regeneration and support of a modern engineering philosophy in the field of gas turbine engine production. This can only be done only by setting objectives for the design and organisation of the serial production of modern engines that can be competitive on the global market. We need to build the best and most reliable engines for the military air force and civil and transport airliners, we need to produce a promising range of engines for Russian Helicopters, as well as industrial facilities involved in the production of oil and gas and energy. In other words, we need to raise a whole new generation of engineers, designers, technicians and production managers capable of creating world-class modern technology while ensuring long-term sales and efficient servicing. If you take the international aspect of this strategy for example, we are planning to be in the top five leading engine manufacturers in the world by 2020.

The plans are impressive. What is being done to implement them?

First of all, we have installed a new system of management based on a programme and project approach. We have determined the holding company's priority projects and placed senior managers in charge of them who will be responsible for their implementation. These senior managers have been given the necessary authority to use all the resources available to them at our businesses to make sure that these projects are implemented.

Second, work is currently under way to set up an integrated single model line, and we are also identifying specialised production plants. I have to say that this is a very tricky job. Over the last 15 years practically all these enterprises have been operating according to principles of self-sufficiency. In other words they have been trying to set up a complete infrastructure ranging from the solutions produced by their design-engineering departments to the manufacture of the final product. This had led to the duplication of many functions and destructive competition between these plants for government resources and clients. This is the mess that we are currently busy sorting out! UEC's engineering centre was set up specially on my orders for this particular task. After we complete the list of the range of engine models that will need to be manufactured at the corporation, we will approve it at a session of the corporation's council for strategy and investment.

I have to point out that the heads of all the corporation's companies play a part in the work of the council.

Yet another innovation is our transition to a lean production system of operations, or on other words low-cost production. Among the organisations pioneering this approach are the Ufa Engine Industrial Association, Saturn and the Perm Engine Company. Lean production will be embedded at all the holding company's enterprises. We estimate that as a result of this system alone we can reduce costs by 15 per cent. And that means an increase in labour productivity and incentives for our employees.

So moving on from theory to practice, have there been any specific practical results in the engine manufacturing industry arising from Oboronprom's activities?

It would be rash of me to assert that with the arrival of Oboronprom all these problems will be solved immediately.

The main very positive factor that I see is that we have analysed and taken into account all the problems in the industry, and we now have a clear and realistic action programme. It goes without saying that the plants that we have acquired are experiencing varying degrees of difficulty. For example, the Samara cluster requires the creation of a single integrated research and production facility on the foundations of the current structures at Motorostroitel, JSC Kuznetsov and the Samara Design and Machine Engineering Centre

(SKBM). We have already started the merger process and the sale of non-core assets and the optimisation of human resources. There are also plans to establish a scientific development and production centre to design and manufacture aviation and gas-pumping engines. In addition, we have succeeded in obtaining government support for these enterprises. Motorostroitel has been allocated RUB 1.46 billion for additional capitalisation. In addition to the credit line opened to the 'Saturn' scientific development and production centre from VTB Bank it will be getting RUB 5.2 billion in additional financing for work on the promising SaM146 engine as a part of Oboronprom's additional share issue.

The Chernyshev Moscow Machine-Building Enterprise is getting government funding to the tune of RUB 2.9 billion.

Likewise production programmes for the UAC (United Aircraft Corporation), the Defence Ministry, Gazprom and Roscosmos have been developed and are up and running.

On the whole, I can say that currently it is only state support that makes it possible for the industry to exist and develop. Our task is to use this assistance and not waste it, by creating an efficient business that produces competitive products and earns profits. We have the complete support of Sergei Viktorovich Chemezov, the head of Russian Technologies and the chairman of our corporation's board of directors.

Taking into account the tricky situation that engine building is in, can you really say that Russian Helicopters is developing successfully?

It is important to remember what the starting position was. Our two businesses – the engine-building and helicopter-building business – earned over RUB 100 billion in 2008; of these UEC earned almost RUB 60 billion and Russian Helicopters over RUB 40 billion. What's more, Russian Helicopters put on production and financial growth of 30–40 per cent, but at the same time the engine-building industry is making considerable losses amounting to several billion. Therefore compared with engine building, the helicopter industry looks in much better shape.

But if you look beyond the ongoing results such as earnings and profits and into the deeper processes at work, then you will see that Russian Helicopters requires just as much attention as UEC. Our own available industry resources are clearly insufficient for it to develop and compete effectively on the global markets. We have designed a range of models for Russian Helicopters that includes models that are capable of occupying certain niches in the market. The government is also helping us to implement these plans. For instance the Bank for Development is financing the serial production of the Ka-226T and there are Ministry of Defence orders for the Mi-28N and Ka-52 helicopters. We are counting on government support to produce a promising high-speed helicopter.

On the whole, I can say that despite the problems we have, given the systematic and painstaking work being carried out with the support of the state and the plentiful financing, Russia's helicopter and engine industries have every possibility of not only working efficiently but making a real breakthrough at the technological level.

The work of the Samara businesses is critically important for our strategic aviation

From Volzhskaya Kommuna *(Samara), 1 April 2009:*

In February of this year our famous Samara engine manufacturing aerospace industry enterprises came under the control of the United Industrial Corporation (Oboronprom). This state-owned holding company plans to create an integrated modern structure on the basis of these Samara businesses in order to launch the serial production of aviation engines. However these plants are currently in a difficult situation and practically on the verge of bankruptcy.

Oboronprom general director Andrei Reus talks to us about the programme for pulling Samara's plants out of the crisis situation and the prospects for their development.

How does Oboronprom plan to pull the plants out of their current crisis?

I would like to stress that Oboronprom only became the legal owner of OAO Motorostroitel, JSC Kuznetsov and the JSC Samara Design-Engineering Centre in mid February 2009 when we were given the state's shareholdings in these companies. At the current moment, consolidated enforcement proceedings have been brought against all these companies and their property and bank accounts have been frozen. Total debts for the Samara cluster are in excess of RUB 7 billion against annual sales of roughly RUB 3.5 billion. As a production site JSC Kuznetsov is barely functioning at all. The situation requires prompt crisis intervention measures. The specialists at Oboronprom and UEC have devised a reorganisation plan to take us to 2015. The key element is the restructuring of the management system of all three enterprises through a merger. The main site will be Motorostroitel. This will make it possible to reduce the plants' costs and create a streamlined and efficient production facility. The programme has been forwarded to the country's and region's governments.

Technically speaking, how will this process be carried out? Which structures and production facilities will have to be jettisoned and which are going to survive?

I would like to stress straight away that we are not going to close production! We are going to keep and develop the key competencies of all of the three businesses. The merger process itself will involve the elimination of all the services that are being duplicated at the three enterprises. For many years these businesses have been duplicating each other's work on a number of questions and effectively ending up in competition with each other. This can be demonstrated with the example of the Gazprom orders. On the one hand, Gazprom's requirements for NK engines could have been a financial lifeline for the plants and helped them to regenerate their operations. On the other hand, it was these contracts that became the reason for the controversy, and resulted in Gazprom orders for engines being divided between Motorostroitel as the serial production plant and JSC Kuznetsov, which only has a test production facility. Gazprom repeatedly filed claims against JSC Kuznetsov regarding the poor quality of its engines. The result of this conflict was deplorable, with both plants suffering serious economic and reputational damage. It will take a lot of effort to put the situation right.

We plan to set up an integrated structure based on Motorostroitel that will provide the design, production and repair of engines for the Strategic Air Force as well as the needs of the space programme. It will also manufacture equipment for Gazprom and other raw material companies. The brand name Kuznetsov will be kept. Moreover, JSC Kuznetsov's engineering team will focus on designing and updating units, while Motorostroitel will remain the only enterprise in the region mass producing gas turbine engines. JSC Kuznetsov has a modern testing facility and lift-off production methods that cannot be transferred to other sites. Therefore, these facilities will continue to function at JSC Kuznetsov while the remaining unused premises and space will be sold. An efficiently functioning enterprise will provide stable jobs, decent incomes, the uninterrupted payment of taxes, and create conditions for the further development of the enterprises. It is so much easier to survive as a part of an integrated structure. This has been demonstrated by the experience of Russian companies and the world as whole.

What other measures will the crisis programme entail?

We are counting on government support for the plants in the form of credit guarantees and an increase in the government's shareholding. These funds are needed to repay debts and restore the plants' operating capacity. The borrowed funds will be repaid between 2011 and 2015. Yet another stage in the plants' emergence from the crisis is to create and operate strict short-term three-year programmes for orders, commencing from 2009. We are talking here about a government order for the production of engines for Roscosmos space programmes as well as technical support and repair of the whole family of NK engines for the Strategic Air Force. The allocated funds and long-term government orders will lead to the immediate solvency of those enterprises that have key competencies and demonstrate efficient development. The programme is currently being considered by the Russian government. We are hoping that this programme will also be supported by the Samara regional government.

Are there any other possible ways to save the plants other than a merger?

Over the last year we have thoroughly analysed the situation at the plants and made decisions on how the Samara cluster will work as a whole. Oboronprom also took an active part in implementing measures to prevent the plants' bankruptcy throughout the whole of 2008. At the end of 2007 government subsidies were paid to JSC Kuznetsov amounting to RUB 676 million, and RUB 1.129 billion to Motorostroitel in December 2008. The funds were used to repay payroll debts and tax arrears.

Oboronprom loaned the Samara plants a total of RUB 615 million of its own funds and provided bank guarantees for RUB 2.126 billion. However, that failed to radically change the situation. As a result, we came to the conclusion that the only possible solution in the circumstances was to merge the enterprises. We need to restructure production. Right now our companies are seriously falling behind in comparison with their Western counterparts. The productivity of a single worker at the Samara plants is several times less than that at other motor construction businesses in our country and many times less than similar plants abroad.

In your opinion, what are the reasons for the current state of the plants?

The current situation is largely because since 1991 the government has not placed a single order for the mass production of engines for the Strategic Air Force. Over the whole of the last 18 years the plants have had to share the meagre market for the repair and maintenance of engines manufactured in Soviet times, and that inevitably led to a duplication of functions and unproductive competition. Experience has shown that the private owners did not turn out to be very efficient managers. The enterprises found it difficult to survive when faced with tough market competition. The defence production plants were effectively left without any government investment and without any cash injections to ameliorate the amortisation of their assets and develop their technology. This didn't just happen in Samara, it happened everywhere. As a result, the huge potential that had been built up in the industry over the years was on the verge of collapse.

Do you feel you have support from the regional authorities and the state?

It would be quite impossible to change the situation without the support of the government and the regional authorities. Oboronprom has already applied to the Ministry for Industry and Trade and the Ministry of Finance as well as the Samara Regional Administration for extra support. Essentially this would involve raising federal budget funds to assist the strategic enterprises within the framework of increasing Motorostroitel's authorised capital. This would enable us to settle the enforcement proceedings, and set up a property mortgaging fund, to implement the consolidation of production and to create the preconditions necessary to receive state guarantees in accordance with the rules approved by the government. In addition we have been offered state guarantees for bank credits for up to five years. This is all vital in order to refinance debts and to replenish our working capital financing.

With regards the assistance from the Samara regional government, we welcome the constructive relations that we have with the administration and are working on the best possible solutions, in particular to create favourable conditions to provide the plants with electric power, heating and gas. Yet another important issue is the provision of jobs for employees that have been laid off as a result of the streamlining of staff numbers.

Are staff redundancies going to be obligatory?

Yes. Enormous ongoing costs are making the operations of these huge enterprises unprofitable. These enterprises need to be downsized to a level where their operations will become profitable. It is not possible at the moment to say exactly at what point the plants will cease to be loss-making because of the complexity and the sheer size of their operations. But a 10 per cent reduction in the administrative and managerial staff would save us over RUB 100 million a year. In the current situation this sort of money would be vitally important to these businesses. But right now we are only talking about a 10 per cent reduction in the administrative and managerial staff. Moreover, first and foremost we will be getting rid of posts that have become vacant and administrative jobs. We are ready now to offer jobs to some 340 specialists from JSC Kuznetsov at Motorostroitel. This has become possible as a result of reductions in managerial staff. Production workers, especially qualified ones, are in acute demand, and we will be opening up new vacancies for blue-collar specialists. In other words, there is no question of thousands of people suddenly being made redundant. Redundancies will be carried out gradually, and everyone who is laid off will receive a redundancy package in line with legislation.

How large are the payroll arrears at present?

Last week we paid off JSC Kuznetsov's payroll debt for November and made an advance payment for December. At present, wage arrears stand at RUB 52 million. The Motorostroitel plant payroll debts for January and February are RUB 103 million, and advance payments for these months amounting to over RUB 0.8 million have been paid off. The issue of paying salaries is important for us because it is directly linked with the implementation of the production plan. We are handling this issue in real time and will fulfil our obligations to our employees.

What is the situation with the backlog of orders? How are things going with potential clients?

So far this year, contracts have only been signed with Roscosmos, but we are negotiating deals for three-year contracts with the Defence Ministry and Gazprom. The situation is complicated by the fact that the principal production assets are critically obsolete and the machine tools have not been upgraded for several years. In order to survive, the plants are in need of government support and defence orders.

Experts believe that without the orders from the Ministry of Defence there would no future for the Samara plants, and that the only possible product the plants would be able to produce will be natural gas pumping stations. Is this a possible scenario?

It is out of the question. Seamless and high-quality work operations at the Samara plants are extremely important to ensure the Strategic Air Force's combat readiness and the efficiency of the manned space programmes. That is why we are currently doing everything possible not only to support these operations but also to give them the impetus they need for their further development.

I believe that it's vital to keep all these processes under my own personal control

From RBK Daily *(Moscow), 2 April 2009:*

UIC Oboronprom was set up in 2002 as a multi-profile industrial corporation to concentrate on four areas of business.

However, over time it has become clear that the size of the tasks faced by the industry requires narrower specialisation. While helicopter production has been producing stable profits, aircraft engine production is facing a large number of unresolved issues. Our correspondent Sergei Starikov interviewed Andrei Reus, the general director of Oboronprom, about how these issues are going to be addressed.

Recently there have been rumours regarding the liquidation of Oboronprom and the transfer of its assets directly to Russian Technologies. Would you care to comment on this?

I regard these rumours as pure speculation which has no foundation whatsoever in reality. Oboronprom has been set the task of creating integrated and fully fledged facilities in the fields of helicopter and aircraft engine construction. This is not just a question of consolidating shareholdings but also setting up efficient management systems for production, sales and servicing. We are only at the start of this long journey, to say nothing of such issues as the corporate procedures to transfer these holdings into a single shareholding. In its turn, Russian Technologies is also faced with a huge range of work with the assets that it has acquired. In addition, the following well-known fact should not be forgotten: Sergei Viktorovich Chemezov is the chair of Oboronprom's board of directors. Besides, after the government's orders have been implemented, a block of Oboronprom shares that belongs to Rosimushchestvo will be transferred to Russian Technologies. Therefore, the relations between Russian Technologies and Oboronprom are completely transparent and have been determined for many years ahead.

Andrei Georgiyevich, tell us about what has already been done – the results of the work carried out at Russian Helicopters in 2008.

The helicopter construction industry is one of the few industries in Russian machine engineering that has been producing good production results over the last five years and even in the current climate. In 2008, we delivered 169 helicopters to our clients. This is a 3 per cent increase on the planned figures for 2008, and 40 per cent up on our results for 2007 (120 helicopters). The Kazan helicopter plant completed 55 helicopters, Rostverto 44 helicopters, the Ulan Ude Aviation Plant 59 helicopters, and the Kumertau Aviation Production Enterprise 11 helicopters. The bulk of the helicopters built have been the ever-popular Mi-8/17 (114 of them), but we have also carried on producing the Mi-24/35, the Mi-28N and the Ka-27/32. In 2009 we are planning to sell about 230 machines. According to our preliminary figures the helicopter holding's earnings were in excess of RUB 40 billion, which is 20 per cent up on the RUB 33.7 billion earned in 2007. The holding's profits have gone down slightly to RUB 1.56 billion (in 2007 they came to RUB 1.8 billion). This was because of an increase in prices for spare parts and materials, a rise in interest rates and the strengthening of the rouble throughout nearly all of last year. Nevertheless, this was a good year considering the overall situation in the Russian machine engineering sector and the global financial crisis.

How are things going with regards helicopter servicing? It is well known that this market is worth some US$200 million.

Helicopter servicing is the most important thing for us. We had 2009 marked down as 'helicopter servicing year' at Russian Helicopters. We have made after-sales service one of Russian Helicopters top priorities; without it there will be no sales. Marketing begins with after-sales service, logistics and a clear understanding of how quickly your technology can be repaired. There is no point confusing spare parts sales with after-sales service. Historically, it is a service that our domestic producers are not fond of providing. It has not been easy for us to overcome this old-fashioned mentality and to operate in line with the idea that we are selling services throughout the whole of the product's life-cycle, but we have started this process.

According to our estimates Russian Helicopters may soon count for half of the world's servicing market, which is worth some US$100 million a year. And then we shall see how things develop! In India we have set up a joint venture with a company called Vektra to service our products, and this venture is now becoming the main legitimate player in the Indian market for the delivery of spare parts and repairs. In China we have signed a framework agreement on organising after-sales services for Russian helicopters. We are on the approach route to setting up a centre in the Middle East. We realise that we need to build up our servicing infrastructure globally because Russian helicopters are being operated in some 80 countries throughout the world and are being actively sold in 40 countries.

How is the Ka-226T project, which was given a loan by the Bank for Development, progressing?

The bank issued a US$100 million investment loan for eight years. Despite the crisis the credit terms have not been reviewed and the interest rates remain as they were. A project team has now been set up and is currently working on the project. At Oboronprom we are analysing its implementation practically every week. We have settled the issue regarding the engines.

We have signed a contract with Turbomeca to build and certify a modified version of the Arrius 2G1 engine. At the same time, we are working on the sales of the Ka-226T to the Ministry of Emergencies, the FSB and Gazprom, and through the good offices of Rosoboronexport we are planning to take part in an Indian tender for light helicopters.

What is going on with the Mi-38 project? We have heard that there are some problems with the engine supplier for this helicopter?

This is a very good machine but work on this project is currently a bit slow.

Unfortunately we have not been able to raise financing for this project, therefore we are busy working on this issue despite the current tricky conditions. Pratt & Whitney Canada's refusal to supply engines for this helicopter despite a signed protocol of intent has also had a fairly important effect. Perhaps some negative experience of working with Russian enterprises in the 1990s played a role. Nevertheless, the work is under way to fit the Mi-38 with

653

the TV7-117 aircraft engine, which can be converted for helicopter use. It is proposed that the end producer of this engine will be the Chernyshev Moscow Machine-Building Enterprise.

Do you still have plans for an initial public offering (IPO)?

There is a government decree approved to create a single Russian Helicopters shareholding in the next two years, and that is the preliminary step before entering the capital markets. I would like to stress that an IPO for us is not an end in itself. It is a means of raising investment. That is why an IPO will be considered depending on how the situation develops in the holding company itself and the markets.

Is the partnership with AgustaWestland still under way?

Our distribution joint venture is up and running. The project to set up production of the AW139 helicopter under licence is progressing according to plan. We are on course to sign a licence agreement. In the near future the Italian side will appoint a general director and the Russian side will appoint a first deputy in charge of finances. We believe that the first serial production helicopter will be produced by the end of 2010 and delivered to our clients in 2011.

Will the scope of the targeted development programme for the helicopter industry be reviewed in the light of the crisis?

Despite the successes of the helicopter industry in terms of the production side we should not forget that we are using models that were developed decades ago. The industry urgently needs investment and new solutions that will enable it to maintain its potential. Therefore, the development programme for the helicopter industry as targeted remains unchanged.

Today we are just introducing some minor adjustments to the model range. In particular, this goes for our light helicopters, the 4 tonne payload helicopter that may be built on the basis of the Ansat. The most important task for us is to build a promising high-speed helicopter that would define the position of the Russian helicopter industry on the global market for the next few decades. Work has already been started on this, but it will need a great deal of support from the government.

Are you planning on increasing domestic helicopter orders?

I very much hope so. Russian Helicopters have definite plans to increase these orders.

Now a question about the other holding company, UEC. When will the first phase of the merger be over?

The phase involving UEC's extensive expansion is practically finished. Oboronprom has already received the government-held shareholdings of Saturn, Motorostroitel, JSC Kuznetsov plant, Metallist-Samara and the Perm cluster of plants. One of the latest vital acquisitions was the purchase of a block of Metallist-Samara shares from private shareholders. By the end of 2009 we should have completed all the legal procedures to set up UEC. Right now we are in the process of implementing the integrated management concept for all the enterprises through the auspices of the UEC managing company. We will eliminate redundant management systems, such as the Perm Engine Company management company. At present, from a management point of view the structure of UEC is at maximum efficiency and we do not want to overload it with new personnel. This is not only to keep costs down but also to keep the management system as transparent as possible. Practically all of Oboronprom's senior managers working in UEC hold more than one post.

Why did you take up the post of the UEC general director? Was there no better candidate?

Thank goodness, our industry is blessed with many experienced and professional managers. But at the initial stage of creating the UEC it was important to work out a unified action programme and to find a consensus among all the participants. That is why I believe it is important to keep all these processes under my personal control.

Has Yury Lastochkin already transferred his shareholding in Saturn to Oboronprom?

The deal has already been done and the payments for Saturn completed. We have also received a block of shares for the Ufa Engine Industrial Association. Oboronprom controls both these enterprises now.

Will MiG's engine manufacturers be transferred to Oboronprom? How are you going to solve the problem of replacing helicopter engine imports?

Decisions have already been made to provide state support to the Chernyshev Moscow Machine-Building Enterprise to the tune of RUB 7 billion, including an additional issue of the plant's stock worth RUB 2.9 billion. There were a number of speculative press reports concerning this process. All I can say is that we have had no disagreements with the Chernyshev management regarding Oboronprom's shareholding in the plant. There were some technical problems with filing the deal but they are settled now.

As for replacing imported engines, OAO Klimov is capable of building the TVZ-117 and VK-2500 helicopter engines using repair kit components. The Chernyshev plant will produce TV-117 engines for the Mi-38 as well as repair kit components.

When will UEC merge with the Salyut plant? Did the president's visit to the enterprise speed the process up or slow it down?

We have a number of serious objectives ahead regarding the restructuring of our assets. The Salyut plant is now resolving the issue of its conversion into an open joint stock company and the creation of its own holding company in accordance with the president's decree. Each party has to complete the reorganisation work that has been started in each of the holding companies. But currently we are co-operating with Salyut in a number of different areas. The enterprise has everything that UEC needs.

In your opinion which of the enterprises that have joined UEC are strong and which weaker? Will some plants be closed down, for instance in Samara?

I would like to underline here and now that we are not closing any of the Samara production facilities. We will keep and develop the key capacities at all three of the plants: Motorostroitel, JSC Kuznetsov and the Samara Design and Machine Engineering Centre (SKBM).

We plan to set up an integrated structure based on Motorostroitel that will guarantee the design, production and repairs of engines for the Strategic Air Force as well as the needs of the space programme. It will also build equipment for Gazprom and other raw material companies.

The brand name Kuznetsov will be kept. Moreover, JSC Kuznetsov's engineering team will focus on designing and updating units, while Motorostroitel will remain the only enterprise in the region mass producing gas turbine engines. The Kuznetsov facility has fairly modern testing facilities, which for technical reasons cannot be moved to another site. Therefore this production facility will continue to function at this plant, while its remaining idle premises will be disposed of. In total, the Samara plants are in debt to the tune of about RUB 7 billion, and the production facilities are in urgent need of modernisation. It's already too late apply standard approaches here, which is why we have started a series of urgent crisis measures. As a whole the Perm cluster is making stable progress, but now it needs to be consolidated. Despite the financial situation the Saturn plant is a strong enterprise with modern production and technology facilities, where for the first time an engine is being certified according to European standards. The Ufa enterprise has a promising future, and we are planning to use it as a specialised facility for all the plants in the holding company.

Maybe it would be easier to pull everything down and start from scratch?

No, we're not going to do it that way, although sometimes a green-field site is easier to build on than regenerating old ones. The Chernyshev plant has 10 hectares of idle land that requires constant funding to pay taxes, housing expenses and so on. Obviously, these sorts of costs make no sense. We also plan to get rid of some of the non-core assets in Samara. We are not in the property-developing and tourism business, and we cannot afford to maintain the hotels and resorts that are currently on the plants' balance sheet.

Our employees' social benefits need to be measured in monetary terms and not payments in kind. We will only keep those hostels and accommodation buildings that are needed to attract personnel.

Do you plan to reorganise the Perm cluster of enterprises? As a shareholder of the Perm Engine Company what is Pratt & Whitney's attitude towards these plans?

As I have already said, the Perm plants are fairly stable from both a financial and production point of view, but they also need serious restructuring. We have begun the procedure of transferring manage-ment operations from the Perm Engine Company to UEC, and the merger process is under way between the Perm Engine Company and other plants that are technologically allied with it. We are discussing all the procedures with the shareholders, including Pratt & Whitney, which we regard as an important strategic partner in the Perm Engine Company.

What goals have you set UEC?

We have determined that UEC's strategic goal is to support and regenerate a modern school of Russian engineering in the field of gas turbine engine production. Hence, the main task is to build engines that meet the requirements of the domestic and foreign markets. We have declared that by 2020 we plan to be among the top five producers of gas turbine engines in the world. Our work will be aimed at implementing these plans.

We have also determined UEC's most promising projects. These are the SaM146 project, a new engine for civil aviation (the MC-21 engine), a new engine for the Air Force (the advanced front-line aircraft system project) and a new engine for the high-speed helicopter. We will, of course, continue working on the engines that we already have: for instance, the certification of the PS-90A2 engine in collaboration with Pratt & Whitney. The strategy for the development of the industry will be completed by UEC in the very near future and will be presented to Oboronprom's board of directors. Then the strategy will be submitted to the government for consideration.

What sort of structure do you envisage for UEC, and what will be the principles of operations for the holding company?

Eight committees have been working on UEC's structure. The committees included all the plant directors, experts and scientists. The process was completed on 27 March. It is evident to me that the UEC managing company needs to focus on its international activities and financing. But this is co-ordination, and no substitute for the work that is being carried out at the enterprises. The fundamental principle behind UEC's work is the projects and programme approach. All human resources decision are considered from the standpoint of the expediency of applying the experience and skills of a specific manager to a specific position.

This is very important for me, since directors are the UEC's main 'combat unit'. The appointments to the holding's leading projects were made on the basis of this principle. The SaM146 project will be implemented by Saturn general director Yury Lastochkin, and the programme for producing helicopter engines will be headed by Alexander Artyukhov, the general director of the Ufa Engine Industrial Association. Aviadvigatel general director Alexandr Inozemtsev will be in charge of creating an engine with a 9 to 18 tonne thrust. The programme for industrial gas turbine plants has been entrusted to my deputy at the UEC managing company and Oboronprom, Dmitry Petrov. My other deputy at UEC, Ilya Fedorov, who headed the OAO Dubna Machine Engineering Plant, will be responsible for the advanced front-line aircraft system engine project. The foundry project that we are looking into as a possible common solution for our helicopter and engine holdings is headed by Gennady Zubarev, UEC's deputy chief designer. All the orders for the appointments have been signed by me. There are a number of other profiles such as composite materials and tool production which will be headed by directors who will be appointed in the very near future. All the projects will be examined at Oboronprom's council of experts, and their financial arrangements will have to be approved as well.

What were the financial results for UEC's enterprises in 2008?

This year for the first time we consolidated all the financial figures of UEC's enterprises. According to the preliminary figures our enterprises' earnings were in excess of RUB 57 billion in 2008. But the industry is generating a lot of losses as a result of wage and tax arrears and so on. This is testimony to systemic problems in the industry that we still have to resolve.

I have always been and remain a team player

From Natsionalnaya Oborona, *August 2009:*

Andrei Grigorievich, today Russia and indeed the rest of the world find themselves in a tricky economic situation; has the crisis affected the implementation of your corporation's plans?

You have to divide Oboronprom's activities into operations connected with the helicopter industry and engine construction. Oboronprom began dealing with these issues at different times, therefore each of these projects is at a different stage of development.

From the standpoint of design and flight performance, we are serious players in the global arena. Our helicopters are flying in 80 countries around the world and we supply them to 40 countries. But in order to compete on the global markets and to operate at the same level as our foreign partners, the country needs to have a powerful holding structure with a single brand name. I don't want to take anything away from such brand names as Mil and Kamov, which are already famous in their own right. When I use the word 'brand' I mean it first and foremost in the sense of a form of organisation. Everybody knows AgustaWestland, Eurocopter and Sikorsky. And Russian Helicopters also needs to become a key player in the world market just like the other companies that I just mentioned.

Russian Helicopters has only quite recently been set up as a single structure, therefore the advantages of co-operation, the restructuring of production, the increases in efficiency and proper redistribution of its managerial functions have not been fully felt yet. There is still lot of work ahead.

We have declared 2009 'helicopter servicing year' because it is my firmly held belief that servicing is what really tells when it comes to sales, image and gaining a competitive edge. We have to get our servicing to the highest global standards. But this is not going to be easy because unfortunately many of our senior management and production staff lack the mentality that is needed to provide good servicing. There are still a lot of people with old-fashioned mindsets and an oversimplified understanding of the issues based on the fallacious idea that servicing is just a question of selling spare parts. We have to break out of this sort of approach and build a new modern system. We have just started to take the first steps in this direction, but we need to deal with the issue of servicing logically and persistently. A servicing centre has been set up in India, and a similar centre is planned for China and a number of other regions.

Another real problem is operational efficiency. We are losing out to our competitors in terms of the way we organise production, productivity and a whole range of other areas. We have already embarked on a programme to significantly improve our performance figures in order to be at the same level as our competitors. What we need are lean production, a programme and project approach to organising our operations and so on. A particularly big issue is our suppliers of sets and stock. Our production programme sometimes depends on the capabilities of our suppliers. This particularly goes for transmissions and gearboxes. A key decision was taken to build a new plant to produce gearboxes, without which we simply wouldn't have a future.

The same goes for our limited foundry production capabilities. It is vital that we modernize the facilities that we already have and possibly build a new modern foundry, and thus launch a complete restructuring of our production as a whole. After all, our cost efficiency is also very much linked to our lack of a necessary level of specialisation. One of the maladies of the Soviet economy was its insistence on complete production cycles, which creates subsistence economics and kills all notion of efficiency.

How do things stand with investment in Russian Helicopters projects?

Before the onset of the global financial crisis we worked out our helicopter manufacturing strategy, approved it at board level and submitted it to the Ministry for Industry and Trade and the relevant documents to the federal government.

There is one piece of helicopter technology that feeds the rest of the industry, and that is the Mi-8/17 helicopter. This helicopter was designed quite a long time ago, and it is reliable, but despite its recent modernisation we will soon need new models. Our new strategy proposes creating new helicopters that are capable of winning us serious niches in the market. Naturally, these projects require big investments and primarily government investments.

We have received a loan from the Bank for Development for the serial production of the Ka-226T helicopter. We are expecting a great deal of interest in this helicopter from Gazprom and the Ministry for Emergencies. We are preparing this helicopter for the Indian tender (the Indian armed forces plan to buy 197 helicopters). We have some serious competitors, in particular the Eurocopter. Russian Helicopters has signed an agreement with the French company Turbomeca to supply engines for the Ka-226T that have been adapted for operations in the Indian highlands and in their hot and humid climate. So far work is going according to schedule.

Obviously in the conditions that we are facing today it's no easy task getting the necessary level of investment. Therefore, we are using every resource available to us in order to finance these priority projects. One plan is to improve production efficiency and investment by using Russian Helicopters earnings from the sales of its technology, and indeed sales are on the up. In 2007 we sold 120 helicopters, while in 2008 we delivered almost 170 machines. This represents an increase of 40 per cent. We anticipate that in the future, despite the general negative economic situation throughout the world, helicopter technology will remain in demand and that our helicopters will continue to be called for.

In 2009 we are planning on growth to be up by 20 per cent on 2008. Another source of investment will be budget financing. Helicopter construction has been included in a special targeted federal programme for the development of civil aviation from 2011–20, and this stipulates the provision of the necessary funds for the most promising design solutions, including a high-speed helicopter. Everyone understands full well that the team that launches their high-speed helicopter first will grab a significant segment of the market.

And of course, we want it to be our helicopter technology that provides for the needs of Gazprom, the Ministry for Emergencies, the Ministry for the Interior and the Federal Security Service (FSB). Russian Helicopters is capable of efficiently carrying out a whole range of operations over the territory of the Russian Federation. Just one example is the high rate of mortality on our roads because of a lack of prompt medical assistance for traffic accident victims. Because of the huge distances on our roads, the only way to solve this would be to use emergency helicopters.

In my view every single region of Russia should be equipped with reliable Russian-made helicopters. High-speed, time-efficient transport is an issue of vital important for the effective management of our huge territories. I have been talking with my colleagues from many different regions, and it turns out that in order to get from a regional centre to a smaller district centre it is often easier to fly via Moscow. That is simply absurd!

It would be logical if every governor in the country had a Russian-made field helicopter, which would allow them to control the everyday situation on the ground in even the most remote regions.

I believe that's absolutely right. Because a management system is only effective when it can be monitored at arm's length. Accordingly you have to be mobile and able to see what is going on with your own eyes.

What share of the global helicopter market are you planning to carve out and what are you expecting to get?

In our strategy we have identified a target objective of up to 15 per cent of global sales. This is a very ambitious plan considering that the Eurocopter is not wasting any time and is bustling ahead very fast. Another of our strategic goals is to change the correlation between the domestic and export market in favour of the domestic market, at a ratio of 50–60 per cent. We have a strong team and very able leaders at our production facilities, and I am confident that we will succeed in implementing our plans.

We will also use our international experience. Our strategic alliance with Agusta-Westland is one of the elements of this strategy. We are getting ready to start building a plant near Moscow to assemble the AW139 civil helicopter. This joint venture should become a kind of a training ground for a model organisation of our own production processes and servicing activities.

How important are government defence orders for you?

They are very important since they help us design new models of helicopter technology. This is true for the Ka-52 and the Mi-28N. The Ministry of Defence has been very receptive to the Ansat helicopter and it is expected to become the basic training model for the Air Force.

Who are you planning to collaborate with when designing and manufacturing helicopters?

It is impossible to talk about modern production without global co-operation. We need to be working with those countries and in those regions where our technology works best and is most in demand. We will be co-operating extensively with India and China. For instance, we are working on the idea of building a heavy helicopter with our Chinese partners. We are also planning to offer a number of projects to investors in some Arab countries who are interested in Russian helicopters. Strategic alliances in designing technology with other global producers are also a possibility. We are open for business.

Are you expecting an injection of new personnel in the industry?

Very much so! In fact, we need to nurture a whole new generation of engineers, designers, technicians and production managers in the country, capable of creating world-class modern technology while ensuring long-term sales and efficient servicing.

We haven't been idle and are doggedly determined to meet this objective. In order to do this we have set up close ties with universities to look into both helicopter and engine construction. Our target is to have students working at our enterprises from their very first year so that they can be inspired by the production process and become a part of it.

Another important element is our system of knowledge management. Oboronprom's corporate university has been up and running for some time now, where particular attention is being paid to training up management specialists, and also exchanging the experience and knowledge that already exists in our teams.

Now that Russian Helicopters has been established, is there the possibility of the Kazan and Ulan-Ude helicopter plants competing against each other?

No. That is out of the question. A certain element of competitiveness between them remains, and that is as it should be in my opinion, because this provides an extra incentive and impetus to work even more efficiently. But it's quite a different matter when it comes to helicopters that are already being produced. They need to be unified so that Russian Helicopters can offer its clients the basic Mi-8/17 model with a number of different extra options.

Are you planning to increase your shareholding in Rostvertol?

Yes we are, because in accordance with our strategy at Russian Helicopters these shares will be transferred into a common shareholding. Today there is good co-operation and collaboration between Russian Helicopters and Rostvertol. I am sure that the logical development of the business will lead to Rostvertol becoming a fully fledged member of the group, and that will be reflected in terms of its shareholdings as well. It's just a matter of time.

Are you planning to launch on the global financial markets?

Definitely. This primarily goes for our subsidiary companies, Russian Helicopters and UEC. Despite the fact that the very idea of an IPO elicits a wry smile from certain experts, you have to remember that crises come and go but the financial markets aren't going anywhere. The position of Russian industries in the global economy is the key issue here. Either we operate in the generally accepted system for co-ordinating business or we don't operate there at all.

Will the reprivatisation of whole branches of the economy get in the way of your plans?

The increase in the government's share in certain segments of economy, especially the backbone industries is still perfectly logical. Show me at least one private investor who would have been able to invest the billions necessary to develop an engine-building industry capable of manufacturing modern engines. No one would have taken that sort of chance!

When I was a deputy minister for industry and energy I used to explain that a public–private partnership is about the government acting to keep the risks taken by private entrepreneurs down to an acceptable level. In other words, to a level where they are ready and able to invest their money. The government underwrites their risks in those areas of the economy that are absolutely key, and thus provides private business with the opportunity to realise its entrepreneurial initiative and potential.

A comprehensible arrangement has now been created that clearly shows which functions should be performed by the government. The government cannot control the production of titanium, engines, aircraft, ships and a whole range of other operations. But the Russian state cannot allow itself to be in a position where it cannot guarantee its own national security. The rest, however, is up to the market.

It has come to light that over the past few months the engine-construction industry has been the subject of fairly lively debate and that the consolidation process has not all been plain sailing. Have the key issues now been resolved?

The accumulation of the engine construction assets is now practically over. The presidential decree and the government directives regarding the transfer of the government-held shareholdings to Oboronprom have been carried out. Saturn, the Ufa plant and the Perm and Samara plants are now part of Oboronprom, which controls 83 per cent of the industry's assets.

Now the key issue is to set up an appropriate management system to match. These enterprises have large credit obligations, the industry sector is fraught with serious systemic problems, and I make no secret of the fact that it generated a loss in 2008. We are already taking the steps needed to improve the efficiency of the industry's production and organisation, because our efficiency and productivity are way behind that of our competitors. We are competing with companies that are famous throughout the world and have excellent reputations. These steps include a programme and project approach, the approval of a new model range and a shift towards lean production systems, to name just a few of the tools we are using.

Russia hasn't made any new engines for the past 20 years with the exception of the SaM146 engine, which is being produced in collaboration with Safran. Our mission, as far as the project to create an engine-building corporation is concerned, is to regenerate the way we think about engineering to make it capable of creating innovative new engines, and the requisite organisational, financial and staffing conditions to launch large-scale production. That is the key issue.

We realise perfectly well that there are top priority, strategic projects such as the SaM146 engine for the Sukhoi Superjet 100 jetliner. The European certification of this engine is an entirely new challenge, as we have never done anything like this before, but it is a very important one if we are to launch ourselves onto the world market.

Among our other priorities are a new engine for the Air Force, a new engine for the civil aircraft industry and a new engine for a high-speed helicopter. The work on these projects is under way, the heads of these projects have been appointed and the co-operation and co-ordination needed have been determined.

What does the future hold for Russian engine manufacturers and Motor Sich?

Our attitude towards Motor Sich is exactly the same as it is for any of our other partners such as Safran, Pratt & Whitney and so on. The main thing for us is to have a guaranteed supply of engines for our helicopters. We are in daily contact with the Ukrainians within the framework of our contractual relations. The issue of a merger between Motor Sich and UEC is a long-running one, and it has been debated repeatedly. Right now we are not in negotiations to buy out Motor Sich. This would require fairly serious financing, which is a problem considering the conditions we are all facing today. Nevertheless, we are ready to examine various other ways of working together.

Can you provide us with any insight into who is going to produce the advanced front-line aircraft system engine?

This engine could only be produced as the result of a collaboration between all the enterprises in the industry. Among them will be Salyut, Saturn, the Ufa plant and a number of other plants. The technical details are currently being fine tuned.

What is the situation with the engine-building cluster in Samara?

For me the Samara plants are primarily about the manned space programme and the Strategic Air Force. We have a clear operations programme worked out with Roscosmos and the Defence Ministry. We have started with a decision to restore production of the NK-32 engine for the Tu-160 strategic bomber. We are definitely not giving up the production of power-generating units, since this is what keeps the plants afloat financially, but we will be concentrating on the production of strategic products.

We will set up one organisation on the basis of three plants: Motorostroitel, JSC Kuznetsov and the Samara Design and Machine Engineering Centre (SKBM), but we will be maintaining all their current capabilities, as well as the Kuznetsov brand name. We will dispose of any non-core assets and any premises that we don't need and we will also downsize the labour force.

As you probably know, the local trade unions and minority share-holders are not very happy about this. But economics has its own laws and it's just not possible to keep everyone happy. And I'm not going to try, because I have been set a number of objectives by my superiors to turn them into effective and efficient business units.

The government has repeatedly helped the Samara plants by providing them with subsidies running into many millions. This year, the government has once again allocated some RUB 5.2 billion for the Samara plants. This cannot go on indefinitely, which is why these funds are going towards restructuring the production facilities and refinancing and settling bad debts in order to make it possible to normalize the production and financial situation.

Will you be discussing the issue of restructuring production within the framework of the whole holding?

Our goal is to launch a process of specialised production. This will allow us to cut down production costs drastically and to optimise our expenses. Everyone involved is perfectly well aware of this. This is manifested in the discussions that go on in UEC's strategy and investment committee, of which all the heads of the holding's enterprises are members. Because right now most of the plants use a 'continuous cycle' production system running from the foundry to the final assembly. We are looking into creating specialised foundry operations facilities and a specialised blade production unit. In the mid-term we are looking for all our production clusters to become specialised operations but with a high degree of co-operation between all of the UEC member enterprises.

Are you confident that Russia will be able to remain a global centre for engine construction?

I am positive. This is one of the goals that we have set ourselves, it is a strategic priority. There are five key players in the world, and we need to remain among them.

Describe your normal working day.

I get into the office at 9.00 to 9.30, but my appointments start at 10 o'clock. Before that I have a look through my documents and handle any questions that require immediate attention. My working day can finish anywhere between 9.00 in the evening and midnight. Saturdays are usually devoted to the corporate university and knowledge management activities such as seminars, the head office and brainstorming.

What are your hobbies?

I like to play tennis. I train at least four times a week. If I didn't do it, I wouldn't survive. I believe that a sport of some sort is a must for a modern senior manager with the high level of stress that we face. It clears your mind, reduces your blood pressure and generally keeps you in good shape. I insist that all the senior managers at our company take up some sport or other.

It has been almost two years since you took charge of Oboronprom. Since your move from government service into business have you had to change your habits?

There is never enough time, because the volume of work is very high. There is one thing that I'm very glad about – I no longer have to spend three and a half hours a day wading through documents and orders. At Oboronprom I can focus on specific subjects, I am in charge of my working time and I make most of my decisions myself.

There is another important point. In my previous position I worked out industrial strategies, I worked on legislation and regulations, but now I am directly involved in implementing those strategies. I believe that this has been the right move, since I am now able to evaluate what I used to do previously. You can learn from your own mistakes.

Of course, my ministerial background helps me a huge amount. I can't imagine how I would be able to work in my present capacity if it had not been for my past. Because the objectives that I have to meet now require close interaction with some very serious government officials, and having a mutual understanding with them is half the battle.

What's your favourite tipple? When you're not playing sports of course that is!

I like red wine and a good Scotch. I couldn't claim to be a wine expert, that would be going too far. But I can tell a good one from a bad one. However, I believe that Russian vodka is second to none.

How do you relax?

I am a big fan of trekking; I have been on a lot of different trekking routes, including some in the Himalayas. I like downhill skiing and diving. I decided to try to master all the sports that my children go in for so that I can at least give them some competent advice.

What is your philosophy in life?

I was very fortunate to have Georgy Petrovich Shchedrovitsky as my teacher; you can see his photo on my desk here. He changed my view of the world, he provided me with the means of solving complex issues and helped me create the necessary theoretical tools to make this possible. Unfortunately he is no longer with us, but I consider myself indebted to this remarkable man and do everything in my power to be worthy of his memory.

I am used to working in situations when it is not clear what needs to be done with everything around you. If you manage to create something out of all the chaos that is well constructed and well organised, then that of course is a source of satisfaction. Engine building is precisely this kind of a challenge. Besides, I always have been and still remain a team player. Nearly all the solutions to problems come to me during team games.

On the other hand, I would like to see the country that my children live in become a better place. If it had not been for my desire to leave them with a reasonable and organised environment in which to live, I might well have taken up some other occupation.

The image of us as Oboronprom 'terminators' is just a figment of someone's sick imagination

From Vremya *(Samara), 7 September 2009:*

The process of consolidating the assets that will become a part of the United Engine Corporation has ground to a halt. The Samara cluster of enterprises – Motorostroitel, JSC Kuznetsov and the Samara Design and Machine Engineering Centre – have been picked for a very special role: producing solutions for the manned space programme and servicing the needs of the Strategic Air Force.

Andrei Reus, the general director of UIC Oboronprom, talks to us about the situation at UEC's Samara plants and the upcoming changes there.

Getting on with the competition

Under the presidential decree signed on 16 April 2008, Oboronprom needs to consolidate the controlling interests in the enterprises that are going to become a part of UEC. What will UEC look like in its final manifestation? At what stage is the holding company now?

Right now the process of consolidating the engine building enterprises is practically over. Oboronprom now controls 83 per cent of the assets for the whole of the industry; the remaining 17 per cent belong to the Salyut engine-building plant based in Moscow. The government held shares in the Saturn plant and its technologically allied enterprises, the Ufa Engine Industrial Association, and the Perm and Samara clusters have already been transferred to Oboronprom. In other words we have already implemented the main elements of the presidential decree and the government directives.

On the other hand, putting the presidential decree into practise is about not just merging all these assets together, but a whole range of corporate procedures aimed at putting these facilities back on their feet. The biggest headache is to set up a clear system of management at the plants. After all, any corporation only ever works as well as its management system. If the management system is smart, the corporation will be smart.

We want to create a management system that is capable of operating in modern conditions, and many of the enterprises that have joined UEC are currently not up to the job. We are taking the necessary decisions to increase the efficiency of our production: we are bedding in a lean production system, which is improving the quality of our operations, and we have started the process of specialising the production facilities. These are top-priority measures because our efficiency and productivity are a long way behind those of our competitors, and we shall need to compete with some of the worlds' best known companies.

What role will the Samara plants play in the corporation?

The Samara plants definitely have their own role to play, and what's more a fairly specific one. First and foremost they will be supporting the manned space programme and the Strategic Air Force. Everyone gets very worried when I start talking about Samara and fail to mention the Gazprom power unit projects. But this area, the so called civil production side, will definitely remain unchanged and is currently increasing in volume.

Are these strategic plans backed up by genuinely new plans or is this just a repeat of the template that was used in the 1990s, and the Samara plants are going to be left just repairing old engines?

This is a totally wrong way of looking at things. First, there is an objective that is currently being set to regenerate the production of the phase 1 NK-32 engine. We need to submit a feasibility study for this project to the Defence Ministry by 2013. Samara has not built a single new engine for the Strategic Air Force since the early 1990s. All work up until now has been restricted just to repairs, and we are rectifying this situation right now.

Second, there is another objective to restore production of the NK-33 engine. By next September we are planning to sign a contract with the Samara Progress Central Assembly and Design Engineering Centre to finance testing and design operations for the NK-33. We estimate that the total amount spent on testing and design operations will come to some RUB 700 million. There is the possibility that some credit lines will need to be raised, but this is not critical: the engine is popular and there is a clear demand for it. The project is expected to be profitable.

Oboronprom has put together a clear and precise crisis programme that sets real objectives and has analysed how these objectives are going to be realised. Before we came no one had ever done this.

What other measures are you planning to implement in order to save the Samara plants?

I am not a big fan of the word 'save'. I am not in the saving business, I don't work for the Emergencies Ministry. I am convinced that we need to consolidate these three enterprises in order to get them working more efficiently. This programme has been worked out and I believe that it is realistic. In order to meet the targeted objectives and goals that have been set for us, the configuration between the production and management processes at the Samara plants needs to be defined, and that is how we are organising things.

Why do you think that the Samara plants are incapable of existing as separate business units?

There will be one single structure; that issue has already been decided. For us the most important thing is to keep the skills and knowledge that we now have in Samara, rather than keep these bankrupt legal entities going.

After all, we are not creating anything new, but rather regenerating what was destroyed after 1991. In the Soviet times these enterprises were integrated in exactly the same way. JSC Kuznetsov did not have a serial production facility and Motorostroitel did not have a design-engineering department. I just don't understand this irrational fear of changing the organisational structure. By uniting the enterprises it will be much easier to bring back a normal level of operations to these plants. We need to preserve the engineering and design traditions that have grown up at JSC Kuznetsov and the Samara Design and Machine Engineering Centre, as well as the serial production traditions of Motorostroitel.

We are not going to destroy anything. Within the framework of the new single enterprise, designers will continue to design and production professionals will continue to produce. The image being put about of us as Oboronprom 'terminators' is just a figment of somebody's sick imagination.

Outsiders (in other words, Oboronprom) are being accused of creaming off the business's scientific component with the merger, and it is being claimed that without this scientific component serial production will not be possible.

I believe that the designer-engineering centres and the engineering schools are the most important components in the industry, and that is why we will be maintaining, developing, nourishing and cherishing them. This is the key issue. A glaring case in point is the NK-33 engine. The engine is so good that it is way ahead of its time. We are going to restore it and it will be used for another 40 to 50 years to come because the school of Nikolai Kuznetsov, which produced the engine, did a brilliant job.

Our corporation's stated mission is to maintain the skill and knowledge sets needed for the design, creation and launch of new products for large-scale production. This is not going to happen without a proper engineering school.

Have there ever been any other options on the table to solve the Samara plants' problems?

You have to understand that every solution is situation-specific and that every management situation is original. On the other hand, you find yourself using off-the-shelf solutions because of your experience and practice, and this is something that must always taken into account. But there are also real situations when you have to maintain design-engineering departments and pay people salaries and so on. Every strategy has a tactical component, and only time will tell whether the solutions used in various situations by managers have been the right ones or not.

There are also some objective appraisals that can be made. After all no one remembers now what state the plants were in when we took over their management. No one remembers what it was like when the staff at JSC Kuznetsov had not been paid for seven months, when the debts rocketed to over RUB 100 million and the electricity at the plant was switched off because the bills had not been paid. Now it turns out that before we came the businesses were rolling in money and everyone was happy until that nasty Oboronprom came and everything turned bad. Let me tell you what happened: we came, we paid the salaries, we turned on the electricity, (because I was personally able to do a deal with the energy grids, since I happened to know their bosses) and we provided the plants with work. We have already invested over RUB 5 billion if you count all the government injections and all the funds that Oboronprom has put in itself. I have never invested as much money as I have in the Samara plants.

Why then does Oboronprom have so many opponents?

I appointed outsiders to command positions at the plants. This has happened before in other places. Everywhere where you appoint an outsider, the local people feel very strongly about it because they naturally feel that they are no less competent. But the teams at the plants have been kept intact, and only a few of the managers have been appointed by me. It's possible that some may be feeling uncomfortable that they are no longer at the helm. I also don't rule out the possibility that we might have put a spanner in someone's illicit side-business, but that sort of thing goes on in every plant. And when side-earnings come to an end, there are always people who are going to be unhappy. I realise that the interests of some people in the region might have been ignored, but it's just not possible to take everybody's interests into account when there's a crisis and all hands are on deck. But economics is governed by its own laws and you can't keep everyone happy.

Operation 'Resuscitation'

What are your time scales for solving the problems at the Samara plants?

According to our calculations it will take another two years. We have started some measures now that require regular and systematic work. A technological overhaul is in order and we will allocating some RUB 150 million between 2009 and 2010 to this end. It is not a huge amount but you have to start somewhere. Taking into account the current state of the plant with equipment that dates back to before the 1970s, this is vital.

How do you currently rate the situation at the plants?

It's operational. At least it's clear what is going on. Everybody knows that there are definite problems. I realise that downsizing is always painful. But how can you be profitable if productivity in Samara is down by a factor of three on the holding's other plants in Rybinsk, Ufa and Perm? And I haven't even started talking about our overseas competitors! The situation in Samara is now improving somewhat: increased orders from Roscosmos and Gazprom and staff cuts have helped.

The crisis isn't the issue here. You have to understand that there is such a thing as an acceptable level of production profitability. If productivity is below this level then the work force has to be optimised. We cannot continue to generate losses and then go to the government and ask for yet another tranche of aid. There isn't anyone anywhere that has been allotted as much money as the Samara plants. Not that I'm saying that the funds going to the Samara plants are sufficient: they had, after all, been neglected for so long. I don't know where all these people who are so critical of us now were back then. It's very easy for them to say now that our crisis programme is no good, that the solutions are inadequate and that we need to do everything differently. But in order to do that, totally different decisions need to be taken and they just aren't an option. In addition, you have to remember that change costs time and money. And the Samara plants have neither. We have to follow one programme and see it through to the end.

What's more, this programme is already bearing dividends. We have a clear and achievable programme with Roscosmos and the Defence Ministry that is being implemented. We have begun repaying our debts to Gazprom, and the production process is ongoing, which is an achievement in itself. These businesses' bank accounts were only unfrozen last week. These bank accounts had been blocked for five years for repeated failures to pay taxes and other compulsory payments, although our opponents insist that everything was hunky dory.

Recently a government decree was signed to increase Motorostroitel's capitalisation by RUB 1.461 billion. When are you planning to carry out an additional issue?

I think we will have all the corporate issues settled by September so that we will have the funds by approximately early October.

What does the other big shareholder Kaskol think about the additional issue? Is it planning to buy out the issue in proportion to its share or is it ready to let its shareholding be diluted?

We are in negotiations with Kaskol now. It's not an easy decision for them: they either have to settle for a dilution of their shareholding, spend funds to buy up the shares, or block the decision on the additional share issue. But I think we will find a solution and settle the problem. We will carry out the additional share issue, and the plant will get the money, there is no doubt about that.

We are in a strong negotiating position: if you don't want to dilute your shareholding then stump up the money. It may sound tough, but this is a real-life situation. If I am the co-owner of the company and the plant is in severe trouble then I need to do something about it. The government subsidy is also real money. The government is investing its funds in its plant, and it wants the other shareholders to either make an adequate contribution themselves or reduce the size of their shareholding.

Last April, the Finance Ministry interdepartmental committee for the support of strategic enterprises and defence industry organisations approved the allocation of RUB 3.5 billion in government guarantees to Motorostroitel and JSC Kuznetsov for bank loans worth RUB 5 billion. What do you need the money for?

For a technical overhaul and for restructuring. To keep the financial situation under control and take steps to expand production in all areas.

The senior management at the plants are also planning to restructure the debts owed to the regional and city budgets. Do you know how the authorities have responded? Are there specific plans and proposals with regards the restructuring of the debts?

The authorities have responded positively and understand that we are doing everything possible to stabilise the situation. That is why I am confident that they will meet us halfway. After all, the restructuring is taking place in a situation where we are beginning to pay current regular taxes. We are ready to get rid of our non-core assets. If they are on the market now, they will need to be sold and the money used to plug up the financial holes. For instance I sold a sanatorium and several hectares of unused land and bought some equipment.

Are there currently any wages owed to the staff? And if so, how much?

There are no salary debts now.

New horizons

Gazprom has repeatedly complained about the poor quality of the products made at the Samara plants. In addition, over the past few years the Samara plants have accumulated big loan obligations to their clients. Can the Samara plants count on any new contracts from Gazprom in this situation? How do relations currently stand with Gazprom?

We are gradually repaying our debts and trying to rebuild our relations. And new contracts are expected. Most notably, a decision has been made to use the NK-36ST engine at the Vorkutinskaya compressor station on the Bovanenkovo-Ukhta gas pipeline. This is an order for nine engines plus one in reserve. The contract is expected soon. This will be the first order for new engines that the plant has had in several years. And also there are the five engines that are going to the Novogryazovetskaya station. Gazprom has already seen that the situation is changing at the Samara plants. One of Gazprom's conditions is that we fully repay our debts accrued between 2005 and 2006 by the first quarter of 2010.

Are there any plans to increase work for the space programmes?

Yes, from the beginning of next year. We will increase the number of engines being produced for the Samara Progress Central Assembly and Design Engineering Centre. I don't want to quote the precise figures.

The deal for 25 per cent of Metallist Samara was frozen. What were the reasons for this? How does Oboronprom plan to take this further? Will the deal be renewed? If so, when, and will there be any changes in the conditions or the price? Are there any claims against the current owners of Metallist-Samara?

I would rather not discuss issues of corporate purchases and sales. Metallist is a very attractive enterprise, we have worked with it in the past, are working with it now and will work with it in the future. We now have a block of shares and we are in a position to influence the decisions it makes. There is nothing unusual in our not increasing our stake to a controlling shareholding. The same goes for the rest of UEC's assets. When the financial situation in the country, and in particular in the industry, becomes more stable we will return to this issue.

We need to be predicting the market and not reacting to it

From AviaPort.ru, 28 January 2010:

Early in 2009 Oboronprom established the United Engine Corporation (UEC) and began to prepare the Russian Helicopters holding for an IPO. Andrei Reus, the director general, talked to AviaPort about which projects were a top priority for this engine and helicopter manufacturer, how relationships between the plants were structured inside UEC, and how Oboronprom was planning to work with its foreign partners.

What are the preliminary results for Oboronprom, Russian Helicopters and UEC for 2009?

The total earnings of Oboronprom's enterprises for 2009 were RUB 131.5–132 billion according to our preliminary figures. In 2008, this figure was RUB 101.5 billion. The group is demonstrating a steady increase in earnings. Russian Helicopters earnings came to around RUB 60 billion, nearly 40 per cent up on 2008. The profits of the company's enterprises almost doubled to RUB 4.5 billion. The results from UEC's plants were more modest in comparison with the helicopter manufacturers, although essentially the holding was only set up in 2009. Nevertheless, earnings have increased by 20 per cent to RUB 72 billion.

UEC had negative net profits in 2008. Will there be losses in 2009 as well?

677

Yes. But we have managed to cut our losses by about 60 per cent. More precise figures will be available some time in March, when the completion of the annual financial statements is due. A number of contracts were signed before the New Year, which will probably have an influence on the results for the year.

Current debts are inevitable as the production cycles are fairly long, and even the most generous advance payments do not exceed 25 per cent of the total. A particular problem is the toxic debt that the enterprises inherited in the period before they joined Oboronprom when they were carrying out their production programmes. Thanks to the financial assistance from the federal budget in 2009 we have eliminated these debts. By increasing Oboronprom's capital, the engine and helicopter manufacturing enterprises have gained RUB 16 billion. In addition to this Oboronprom is planning to place a bond issue.

When do you expect to place this bond issue and what amount will it be for?

The decision regarding the terms of the issue should be made during the first quarter of 2010. The loan will be some RUB 21 billion, and in all likelihood VTB-Capital Bank will be acting as the organiser. Normal working procedures are currently under way with the Finance Ministry. The main purpose of the loan is to refinance the corporation's debts to Russian banks that arose during the consolidation of the engine-building industry, and also to implement obligations to purchase the non-governmental stakes in our enterprises.

Are you planning an IPO in the future?

Access to the capital markets is a strategic goal for us in order to raise funds for development. We are now looking into an IPO for Russian Helicopters in 2012. I wouldn't want to risk naming a date for the engine-building holding, but we are working on it.

What could the capitalization of Russian Helicopters be by 2012?

It is hard to evaluate it right now. The main thing now is to maintain investment. The government has helped plug the holes financially speaking, but it is up to us to put modern efficient production facilities in place, which we can then offer as shares to private investors.

During a meeting devoted to the engine construction industry in St Petersburg in August 2007 the then President Putin ordered that four holdings be set up that would then be united into one company. UEC has already completed this phase. Is this a good or bad thing?

It is definitely a plus. We are forming new UEC production centres and we are using a common policy for our relations with our clients. As a result, all unnecessary competition has vanished. One project to build the MS-21 engine involves the Motor Research and Development Enterprise, the Aviadvigatel design-engineering centre, the Ufa Engine Industrial Association, the Perm Engine Company and the Samara plants. Before the merger NPO Saturn refused to work on the project, but now it is an active partner in the process.

Had we gone down the road of setting up an intermediate stage with the creation of several holding companies, we would have never agreed to produce one engine. Four holdings mean four ranges of models, which would never have resulted in a single common denominator. And I haven't even mentioned government support! Can you imagine what would have happened if they were all fighting for the same government funds?

How many helicopters are you planning to deliver in 2009?

Russian Helicopters has delivered around 180 helicopters, and of them 70 per cent have gone for export. Overall this is a little bit less than had been planned. The crisis has nothing to do with it. I keep telling senior managers at the plants, 'Start the production cycles, do not wait for firm orders! Get the plants up to full steam! You need to take chances!' The helicopter market is growing despite the financial crisis; we should be anticipating the market, rather than catching up with it.

As a result of the hard work put in over the last few months the helicopter holding company now has a backlog of orders for the next two years. On the one hand, this is an unmitigated success for our technology, but on the other, it is a huge responsibility, since we cannot afford to slow down the pace and we need to respond rapidly to the demands of the market.

Have your products gone up in price over the last year?

Yes, they have. This goes mostly for helicopters, which is natural, because the market has undervalued Russian technology in the past. The main factor in this price rise was our suppliers. We are going to work hard on them in 2010. We have developed a range of proposals on how best to work with our suppliers. We are setting up centralised organisations that should be able to drive the prices down due to long-term economies of scale and purchasing power. We are planning to sign a number of long-term agreements, one of which is a five-year contract with the Urals Optical Instrument Plant.

The situation with the foundry and gear box business is not ideal: the available production facilities can't cope with the orders, and production growth rates are quite high, so we run the risk of having to put the brakes on growth unless we solve the problem with the foundry and gearbox production. The Perm gearbox plant Reduktor-PM has been transferred to Russian Helicopters. On the one hand, transmission production is an integral part of helicopter production throughout the world, but on the other, this area requires very special attention. We are currently working on a project to establish a modern gearbox production facility at the Reduktor-PM plant. A new foundry plant is under construction at Arsenev to meet the needs of the whole holding. But we are not limiting ourselves to Russian suppliers, wherever possible we are looking at foreign suppliers as well.

I am always nagging my colleagues to learn English so they can communicate with any company in the world. I for one try to work without an interpreter, and I expect the same from my subordinates.

How much are you expecting earnings to increase in 2010?

There will be growth of around 30 per cent, although the difficult financial situation at some of our enterprises will offset that. Overborrowing and debt servicing are big problems in the engine-building industry. The government has provided serious assistance to the industry, and the most acute debt problems have been resolved, but they have not been sorted out completely.

The debt burden at NPO Saturn is very great. We are in the process of consolidating some of the most vital engine-production operations at the plant, but the financial model in operation there is very complicated. I am planning to work on this pretty well on a daily basis in the first quarter of 2010. The Chernyshev plant is also in a financial quandary, and we are currently working on the financial model there as well.

Regarding the tender for an engine for the advanced front-line aircraft system, when do you expect to know the date for its go-ahead to be determined by the military?

The delay was largely because there were two possible manufacturers, UEC and Salyut. I have now more or less come to an agreement with Yury Yeliseyev (the general director of the Salyut plant) regarding co-operation, and UEC will be responsible for the front-line aircraft engine. The Defence Ministry is supposed to be making a decision on the issue in 2010. Nevertheless, we have already started work on the project.

What part of the engine will the Salyut plant be responsible for?

I'd prefer not to discuss this before the contracts are signed.

Is there any discussion about the holding that is being set up at the Salyut plant being integrated into UEC?

There are no specific plans at present. Salyut is working to implement the presidential decree to set up a holding company of its own. It has a 17 per cent share of the assets in the industry compared with UEC's 83 per cent. Naturally, some competitive factors remain that I don't always find very productive. I think that the front-line aircraft engine project will get us working closer together, and could over time become a launch pad for our integration. My view is that in the future the engine-building business will have a single integrated structure. This would be logical from a production and financial point of view, as well as being a competitive force on the world's markets. But in any event it will be the government that makes this decision.

Currently, the helicopter and engine building industries make most of their earnings from overseas military orders. Is there a drive to increase your share in civil production?

The civil helicopter segment is on the up. Three or four years ago defence orders made up around 90 per cent of our total, whereas now civil production makes up over 30 per cent. Helicopter servicing is increasing dynamically, and the civil aviation market is keenly aware of this. As soon as Russian Helicopters' servicing infrastructure is put in place in a certain region, the local market immediately picks up. When we certified the Ka-32A11VS to EASA standards, interest in this helicopter grew considerably. The Ka-226T helicopter that is being readied for the Indian tender is in great demand on the civil market. We are now working on an improved version of the Mi-34 (the Mi-34S2 Sapsan with a gas-turbine Arrius-2F engine), and the Mi-38 and Ka-62 are also being readied for market.

A thorough update of the Mi8 is also planned. This model will be exactly the same for the plant in Kazan and the one in Ulan-Ude. This is a very important point. If we are offering our clients a standard product, then this needs to be a basic model with clear costs. I am sure that the Mi-8 will keep its share in the world market for a long time to come, because the technology functions almost perfectly.

As far as engine manufacturing goes, it will be the energy industry that will be the primary source of growth in the civil sector. UEC is working as a part of the government energy efficiency programme to modernise and improve the supply of thermal energy. Combined thermal energy production pilot projects will be launched in Yaroslavl, Bashkortostan and other regions in 2010. Orders from Gazprom and oil companies are on the up. By the end of December a project will be approved to produce 110 MW turbines. In one and a half to two years, UEC should be able to produce five turbines of this capacity a year. The production of aircraft engines for the civil segment still remains important, especially the SaM146 engine for the SSJ-100.

At the MAKS-2009 international exhibition, you gave a presentation on UEC's strategy where you noted that the share of civil aviation engines was 36 per cent in 2008, that it would go down to 18 per cent by 2015 and then recover to 30 per cent by 2020. Are you still sticking to this forecast?

Our plans for civil aviation engine production are tied to the United Aircraft Corporation (UAC). Things are changing rapidly in the aircraft and engine construction industries; we therefore have to take the time factor into account. In addition, during the same period engine production for helicopters and energy units is forecast to go up.

Some RUB 13 billion were allocated for the recapitalization of NPO Saturn, the Chernyshev plant, the Samara plants and JSC Klimov from the Russian Federation budget, and credit lines were opened with VTB Bank. Will you be asking the government for extra financing to support your enterprises?

The government is providing constant support to the industry through a mechanism of targeted programmes and targeted assistance. This assistance will be continued in 2010 but in a different way. It is now very important that the plants are supported by subsidising interest rates, because the 15 per cent annual interest rate for the machine engineering plants is just not affordable. At the same time we have quite rightly been set strict requirements to reduce our expenses. Oboronprom is implementing a centralised lean production programme that should reduce work in progress costs by half and significantly increase productivity. The Samara plants have fulfilled their production plan for 2009: the space programme and energy industry products are developing well.

In 2010 we will have completed the merger of the three plants into a single enterprise, and empty premises will be sold off. I believe that the crisis at the Samara plants is over now, and they are operating at a normal pace. Of course, productivity levels at these plants remains lower than in the industry as a whole, but positive shifts in production and financing are evident. We are expecting to break even in 2010.

Right now we are busy optimising the management structures at the Perm cluster of enterprises, and improving the quality of the PS-90A engine, which is currently the second most important engine at the Perm Engine Company in terms of earnings after the energy unit engines. At the end of December last year the Aviadvigatel plant certified the improved version of the PS-90A2 engine.

JSC Klimov and the Ufa Engine Industrial Association will be in the black in 2009. At the end of December the UEC project committee approved the Klimov project to build a new design-engineering facility, and vacate space in downtown St Petersburg. The project is realistic and financially sound, and the city authorities have been providing great support.

Apart from selling premises in the city centre, how is JSC Klimov planning to raise funds to build the new facility?

Through borrowing.

Some time ago JSC Klimov's strategy was based on producing helicopter engines, which currently provide most of its earnings. Now that helicopter engines are going to be assembled at the Ufa Engine Industrial Association, how is the Klimov plant going to fill the void?

To make it possible for JSC Klimov to earn more, we are building a modern centre and design subunit with test facilities. JSC Klimov is going to become the main design-engineering facility for continuous research and development, and design and testing, operations to maintain the latest technical standards of our existing helicopter engines and their serial production. JSC Klimov will also be responsible for creating breakthrough projects such as the new generation of helicopter engines.

Supporting the lifetime cycle of a product is always a stable and profitable source of income. In addition, the federal targeted programme is allocating considerable amounts of money for the implementation of our projects. That is why I am confident that JSC Klimov has a good future.

It is important to have serial helicopter engine production at the Ufa plant, because you can never feel completely safe without your own production facilities. In the meantime, we will continue to co-operate actively with foreign companies such as Turbomeca on the joint project for the Ka-226T helicopter engine and possibly for the Ka-62 engine. We are also examining the creation of a possible joint venture or managing company with our French partners to co-ordinate the work in these areas.

What do you make of the proposal by Vyacheslav Boguslayev, the head of Motor Sich, to set up a joint company to manage the Ufa project?

I don't understand what a joint managing company with Motor Sich would do. Jointly manage the UEC's assets? Why would our Ukrainian partners want to do this? In my view, a management company needs to have an object that it is going to manage. This might be some sort of common large-scale project. Yes, Motor Sich has made a number of proposals regarding the joint production of helicopter engines, but our analysis shows that these proposals would run counter to UEC's own plans. Therefore, for the time being we are perfectly happy with our current contractually based relations with Motor Sich.

What projects will be financed by the Development of Civil Aviation in 2011–2020 Federal Targeted Programme?

The Development of Civil Aviation Federal Targeted Programme will become one of our key programmes from the beginning of 2011. It details our priority products, such as the Mi-38 and the Ka-62 high-speed helicopter and the engine for it. Essentially, the federal budget will be ensuring that we maintain our capabilities and keep coming up with new solutions. However, this is not going to restrict our efforts to look for other sources of financing. We will be offering strategic partnerships on these projects to companies in India, China, and other countries.

How much will it cost to develop an engine for the MS-21?

We estimate the cost at RUB 35 billion.

UEC president Alexei Fedorov has said, regarding the MS-21 project, that a little over half of the programme will be financed by the federal budget (RUB 70 billion out of a total cost of RUB 150 billion for the programme according to the figures in July 2008), and that the rest would be borrowed. Will you be raising borrowed funds to develop the engine?

So far we are doing the work using the government money. Naturally, when we reach the serial production stage we will have to raise credits based on our contracts and market predictions. Fortunately, the industry has not created any solutions that are like this one. If we do not get the skills and capabilities to create new technology we will not be able to compete and simply degenerate. That is why one of the engines for the MS-21 will be developed by UEC.

For us a situation where the engine for the plane is developed by two companies (a tender for the first engine for the MS-21 was won by Pratt & Whitney) is the most welcome outcome. This is genuine competition that will provide us with an incentive to work hard but more importantly to the highest quality levels.

Is everything clear with the PD-14 engine? The aircraft makers are saying that the design has been shelved?

Everything is quite clear. There are a number of fundamentally new ideas in the so called risk areas regarding the application of new technologies and new materials that require some very intricate and precise work.

We attracting young people to work on this project – young able designers, engineers and technicians. One of the biggest problems is that it is impossible for someone to train a designer if they have not personally been involved in a project. This is one of the peculiarities of the profession. I am confident that thanks to projects like this we will regenerate our capabilities by independently designing and developing new engines in our country.

Has the senior management at Pratt & Whitney discussed with you what part of the work on its engine for the MS-21 could be carried out by the Aviadvigatel design-engineering centre?

Yes, we are discussing these issues. Our experts are already meeting regularly. Co-operating with Pratt & Whitney on this project will mean that, in the case of their engine UEC will be acting as the subcontractor for some units and systems, and in the case of our engine we will be turning to the Americans. This kind of co-operation suits me perfectly.

What date has been set for the engine's certification?

Obviously, the development and certification of the engine will be linked to the development of the plane itself. The first planes are expected to appear in 2015–16. So all the issues related to the engine should be resolved by the end of 2014. Engine certification is an extremely complicated job, and is something that we are not able to do in Russia yet. The certification process for the SaM146 engine used a lot of solutions that had already been worked out, but in this instance we will practically be starting the work from scratch.

Will you continue to consolidate the assets of the Perm cluster of engine plants?

At the moment a number of businesses that had been technologically allied to the Perm Engine Company but were then spun off, are once again being merged with the company. We have a schedule plan for creating a single structure with the participation of the Perm Engine Company and the Aviadvigatel design-engineering centre that has been agreed with our American partners from Pratt & Whitney, which will have a 25 per cent interest in the new vehicle. However, I see no need right now to speed up the merger process.

When does Oboronprom plan to sign a licence agreement with AgustaWestland to set up an assembly line of Italian helicopters in Russia?

We still have some issues that we will resolve in this current quarter. But I have no doubts that the production plant for the AW139 will be built.

Have you considered producing the AW109 model in Russia?

The AW109 has a growing market, but Russian Helicopters have the Ka-226T and the Ansat occupying this particular niche. We have a number of options worked out and agreements with operators, therefore the AW139 will get its share of the market.

Oboronprom has signed a cooperation agreement with Eurocopter, which stipulates the production of units for the Eurocopter, the development of the NTN heavy helicopter and a light helicopter of up to 2.5 tonnes. Is some sort of development being made on this agreement?

A number of memorandums of understanding were signed with Eurocopter, but there was no development beyond that. I don't see any particular desire on the part of the Eurocopter to share their competencies. They have decided to build a heavy helicopter on their own. There was an offer on their part to organise the assembly of the technology in Russia, but I don't see any need for this. Nevertheless, I don't rule out the possibility of a joint project. I can say that this would be something that would interest Russian Helicopters.

A. G. Reus with A. P. Zinchenko

Appendices

Appendix 5.1: The 14 principles of 'lean production' (Toyota Production System, 1980)

1 Base your management decisions on a long-term philosophy, even at the expense of short-term financial goals.
2 Create a continuous process flow to bring problems to the surface.
3 Use 'pull' systems to avoid overproduction. The organisation of production requires that the client gets what it wants at the right time and in the right quantity.
4 Level out the workload. In order to create proper lean production and improve the quality of servicing, it is vital to level out the production schedule by not always sticking strictly to the sequence in which orders arrive.
5 Build a culture of stopping to fix problems, to get quality right the first time.
6 Standardised tasks and processes are the foundation for continuous improvement and employee empowerment.
7 Use visual controls so no problems are hidden.
8 Use only reliable, thoroughly tested technology that serves your people and processes.
9 Grow leaders who thoroughly understand the work, live the philosophy, and teach it to others.
10 Develop exceptional people and teams who follow your company's philosophy.
11 Respect your extended network of partners and suppliers by challenging them and helping them improve.
12 Go and see for yourself to thoroughly understand the situation.
13 Make decisions slowly, thoroughly considering all options.
14 Become a learning organisation through relentless reflection and continuous improvement.

Appendix 5.2: 14 principles of quality management (W. Edwards Deming, 1950)

1. Create constancy of purpose for the improvement of products and service.
2. Adopt a new philosophy. We are in a new economic age. Managers must awaken to the challenge, must learn their responsibilities, and take on leadership for change.
3. Cease dependence on inspection to achieve quality. Eliminate the need for inspection on a mass basis by building quality into the product in the first place.
4. End the practice of awarding business on the basis of price tag. Instead, minimise total cost. Move toward a single supplier for any one item, on a long-term relationship of loyalty and trust.
5. Improve constantly and forever the system of production and service, to improve quality and productivity, and thus constantly decrease costs.
6. Institute training on the job.
7. Institute leadership The aim of supervision should be to help colleagues do a better job.
8. Drive out fear, so that everyone can work effectively for the company.
9. Break down barriers between departments. People in research, design, sales and production must work as a team, to foresee problems of production and in use that might be encountered with the product or service.
10. Eliminate slogans, exhortations and targets for the workforce, asking for zero defects and new levels of productivity. Such exhortations only create adversarial relationships, as the bulk of the causes of low quality and low productivity belong to the system and thus lie beyond the power of the workforce.
11. Eliminate work standards (quotas) on the factory floor.
12. Remove the barriers that rob hourly workers, and people in management, of their right to pride of workmanship.
13. Institute a vigorous programme of education, and encourage self-improvement for everyone.
14. Senior management should show a permanent commitment to ever-improving quality.

Appendix 5.3: 14 principles of administration by Henri Fayol (1916)

Henri Fayol (1841–1925) has more right than anybody else to be called the founding father of modern management. He began his career as a mining engineer in a French industrial company. As a director of the company he turned the company from being almost bankrupt into a highly profitable enterprise. In 1916, at the age of 75, Fayol wrote a book entitled *Administration Industrielle et Generale* (*General and Industrial Management*) which summed up his 50 long years of experience. Fayol singles out six basic facets of activity, five functions and 14 principles that should be implemented in the work of top-level managers.

The basic facets of activity

1   Technical: the production of a product.
2   Commercial: buying goods, the sale and exchange of ready-made products.
3   Financial: the acquisition and use of capital.
4   Providing safety at work and security of property.
5   Accounting.
6   Management, where Fayol singles out a manager's five functions or types of tasks:
   1   Planning. Setting goals, searching for ways to achieve them and determining the direction that an enterprise needs to move in.
   2   Organising. Designing and creating structures that are appropriate for the goals and the means targeted during the course of planning.
   3   Instructing. Operational control of planned steps by managers.
   4   Co-ordinating. Co-ordinating and streamlining the activities of subunits and representatives of the organisation that are aimed at reaching the greatest overall efficiency.
   5   Control. Evaluating efficiency in accordance with a developed system of rules.

He designed 14 principles to explain to managers how exactly to execute these functions.

1   Division of labour. The number of duties and tasks of every single worker should be kept to a minimum through the narrowest possible specialisation. Fayol believed that the division of labour always leads to higher labour productivity and a reduction in costs.

2   Authority. Authority and the right to make decisions, give orders and require their performance by other people are the key elements in any organisation. Authority may be obtained through a formal position or through nonformal status.

3   Discipline. To ensure orderliness and performance control is essential. The best way to maintain discipline is to select good managers, clear and simply expressed rules setting out the rights and mutual responsibilities of managers and subordinates, and to implement disciplinary action only on the basis of the established rules.

4   Unity of command. Every worker should receive instructions from only one manager. This principle determines the direction of communications inside the organisation.

5   Unity of direction. All the activities of the organisation in one direction are under the control of one manager and are determined by one plan.

6   Subordination. Personal interests should not take priority over the interests of the organization as a whole.

7   Remuneration. Wages should correspond to the services provided. Fayol realised that remuneration should be determined by many factors that are not dependent on the merits of the person being remunerated or the wishes of the person paying the remuneration, but he realised that managers should strive for a greater conformity between these two factors.

8   Centralisation/decentralisation. The idea of centralisation implies a state when all decisions are made at the highest levels of the organisation, while the role of the lowest levels boils down to the performance of these decisions. Decentralisation implies a state when the right to make important decisions is delegated to the lower levels. In big organisations decentralisation is vital.

9   The vertical line of authority. Relationships of subordination link the manager of the whole organisation with every worker through a chain of lower-level managers. However, a hierarchy that is too rigid reduces the flexibility of the organisation and its ability to respond to change. Therefore organisations acting

in an unstable environment permit violations in the vertical line of authority and the participation of subordinates in the decision-making process on an equal footing with their superiors.

10 Order. A sequence or arrangement of things, events and people that ensures each their own place. This principle demands that each organisation has a plan that reflects its own order.

11 Equity. The attitude of a superior to subordinates should be tactful, benevolent and fair. No one should be given preferment on the basis of personal motives.

12 Stability. Relationships with personnel should be based on stable principles that make the actions of managers predictable to their subordinates. This provides for security in the future and a feeling of security.

13 Initiative. Subordinates should be encouraged to submit new ideas and suggestions that could be used for the benefit of the organisation.

14 Corporate spirit (*esprit de corps*). The task of the managers is to cultivate a sense of harmony and unity in the organisation.

Appendix 5.4: The tools of systematic thinking and the organisation of work by head offices

The standard of our work inculcated by the Moscow Methodological Circle (MMC), known as methodological reflection, was realised during the course of research into models at which decisions were taken, supervision was exercised and the improvement of the systematic tools being used was carried out. We solved practical problems and tasks pertaining to the regeneration of the Russian economy. These problems involved for instance certain defined enterprises, infrastructures and spheres of activities.

We moved on from old models of managing industry that were outdated and obsolete in search of new ones that were suitable for the new historical conditions. We used models produced by head office analysts for our self-organisation in team, analytical and research work (see Figure 5.14).

Analytical and research work was conducted within the framework of a standard operational system:

1 The recording of disruptions, difficulties, problems (the inability to carry out a technical assignment).
2 Collective multi-positional reflection on the situation in the head office schedule maps.
3 Testing the tools and models of the systematic approach to understand and outline scenarios for decision making.

During the course of work we needed to master the rules for the structural assembly of models of hundreds of different objects, make a transition to the research of management systems (on models), the practical use of diagrams and schedule plans, and finally the standardisation of this work for future use.

What kind of standardisation are we talking about?

The essence of the systematic problem is that we have several different concepts of the object and, in theory, these concepts are not associated with each other, for each one of them exists in its own special 'subject space'.... But at the level of practical activity and engineering we are in reality dealing with the objects of this practical activity and engineering that are not divided and dispersed in accordance with various different departments.

Therefore, willingly or unwillingly, we have to join all these things together. And it is precisely in this situation when we have several

Figure 5.14 Head office analysis model

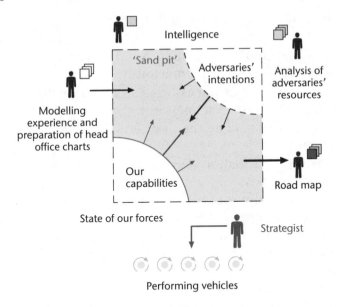

different concepts and we surmise that only one cohesive object corresponds to them, when we should be using all these concepts together, it is then that we start saying that our object is a system, meaning the banal and obvious fact that it is presented in several different representations, and that they should be regarded and examined as a whole thing, but their simple mechanical combination and amalgamation is impossible since these concepts go their different ways 'to different departments'. It is then that we also start to solve the task of how to assemble these concepts, amalgamate them and transform them in order to get a single systematic picture of the object.

G. P. Shchedrovitsky

It is possible to systematically conceive only the object that you are planning to manage. You end up with a tautology, which nevertheless contains a fully defined meaning. The foundation on which this assertion rests denies the possibility of the existence of 'natural systems', or systems that do not have a managing superstructure.

For instance, there are, and can be, no systems in nature (apart from those created by the will of a creator), just as there can be no 'invisible hand' of the market. Take a closer look and you will always see the iron hand of the manager lurking somewhere behind the scenes.

The concept of a 'system': a user guide

1 We need 'thinking' in our interpretation of this word only when we find ourselves in a situation. We are in a situation when we are unable to act any more in accordance with a certain tradition, model or stereotype; when our previously acquired skills and knowledge are useless; when our associates, partners, fellow workers and colleagues are just as helpless as we are. We have to move into search mode and assume the most efficient of positions in life, that of a student.

2 In order to perceive a situation detachedly from above, we have to assume a certain position, and for that we have to separate ourselves from our daily routine and the familiar and comprehensible ways of working that have led us into the situation. At first glance it might seem that the source of trouble lies close at hand, somewhere within the situation itself. But in order to see and discern it we have to move outside the system.

   We have to understand that a break in the work process, whatever the situation, does not depend on the readiness of people and their everyday working methods, but on the concepts, models and ways of thinking that those people use.

3 In order to think properly from the technical point of view (we can imagine how this expression might jar to the ear of a person who believes thinking to be the result of insight, enlightenment, inspiration and so forth), it is vital to:

   • maintain mental discipline and follow the model (we must be reminded again that those who create management systems will understand, and it is not necessary for everyone else to do so);
   • carry out a case study;
   • begin to analyse the situation with models;
   • set our goals in motion in accordance with the strata and places in the models of the situation, identifying priorities and building target trees.

   I would like to talk about the functions and purposes of models in our work (you will have come across them more than once), and explain them with the following clear and concise quote:

   Unlike words and texts, a model is a specific semiotic form that enables us to build and perform structural and systematic thinking and at the same time structural and systematic comprehension.
   — It is the emergence of complex, heterogeneous and multidimensional

models (all models are like this, which is why it is possible to talk about the emergence of models) that has made structural and systematic thinking possible.

— Models make it possible for us to depict what is being done. Methodologists were the first to depict what we do in our thoughts.

— Work with the semiotic form became interconnected with the semiotic form itself. In traditional thinking (the common as well as the scientific sort), work with semiotic forms is never interconnected with the semiotic form itself.

— This leads to a lot of surprising things, in particular to new opportunities for the development of our own thinking.

— The general conclusion: structural-systematic thinking is not possible using the language of words.

G. P. Shchedrovitsky

4 The analysis of a situation, as well as target setting, requires us to identify afresh the boundaries of the whole (our system). The boundaries should at first be drawn no further than the distance of an outstretched arm, in other words as far as we are able to look and reach.

At the same time as defining the boundaries we need to define the process (processes) that are already going on or which we want to launch into our system (or a system that we want to remove from our process). In general, a process is a flow of changes, but because we are initiating it artificially on the course and direction we need, we have to consider it as a process of development. Why should people bother with management systems at all? After all, destruction happens of its own accord when management is lacking.

Formulated assertions should be attached to the model of an organisational and technical system and the model of the processes that it organises. See the illustrations from the seminal works of G. P. Shchedrovitsky (Figures 5.15 and 5.16).

5 In any case it makes sense to identify the borders of a management system, if only to transform it into a new state – from a situation in the past to a situation in the future. The latter should be represented as a project – a selection of models of each of the most important parameters for us. We must try to understand the meaning of the organisation of design and engineering practice and the techniques of model building. But the assertion is a tough one: modern thinking should be recorded in the appropriate models.

6 The next step is the design of structural models that should

identify the most significant places to ensure the functioning and production of a system, and also in order to continue the business that we are preparing to develop, the processes necessary for reproduction and development. For this purpose, we need to take stock of what we have in any given situation for the business that is being proposed or for an activity we plan, and to create an inventory of defects, in other words the knowledge of what it is that we lack. In various different situations, depending on the field of activity, these may be structural models of the life-cycle of a product, of basic business processes, of organisational structures, of work structures within the framework of a project, and so on. With regard to any 'thing' from our environment, a systematic thinking approach requires the separation of the phases of its conception, the transition of the concept into a project design (into something material), the organisation of tests for its use, strength, beauty (according to Vitruvius) and its maintenance in working condition during the course of its use.

7 In models of the structures of connections there is a search going on for the best options: that is, the most successful connections in the construction of a new organisational form of a system. Here the dependence of places on each other and the contents of the activity connections between them are determined. These may be co-operative connections (logistics), communicative connections (transfer and development of skills), or communications (the understanding and reflexive depiction by some places of the goals of other places).

8 Later on, we have to determine the forms of organisation and decide what kind of material will be used for the various places in the structure that is being created by us. These forms of organisation might be borrowed from past work on the existing material. They will be transferred into the future with new functions that will require force (retraining, partial replacement) applied to the old material (the material that makes up the form of organisation: people, technologies, computer programs, technical gadgets).

9 Naturally, we always want to see the forms of organisation we need designed from new. But in this case the preparation of a material for them will be required, which will be able to ensure the functions that have been designated. But this takes a lot of time and effort.

It is specifically in the stratum of the form of organisation that

Figure 5.15 Models from G. P. Shchedrovitsky's work

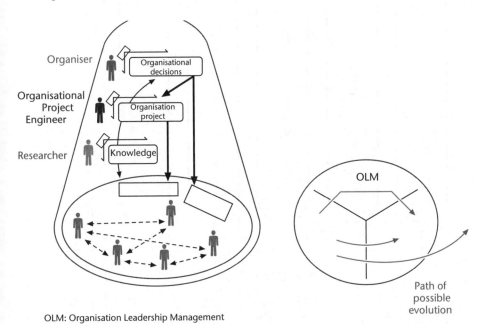

OLM: Organisation Leadership Management

our rational designs and projects meet with the substratum or material that is the bearer of the systems. And the bearers of the systems have a life that is governed by its own laws. These are the life-cycles of people, the regulations governing the lives of human communities (traditions, religion, rights), the laws governing the changing generations of technical devices.

That is how the principles of systematic thinking compiled into a model by G. P. Shchedrovitsky have been recorded in this user's guide (see Figure 5.16).

As a result of working on the picture of the whole gained during the analysis of a situation using five strata of systematic concepts we can arrive at the models of the object of the management system.

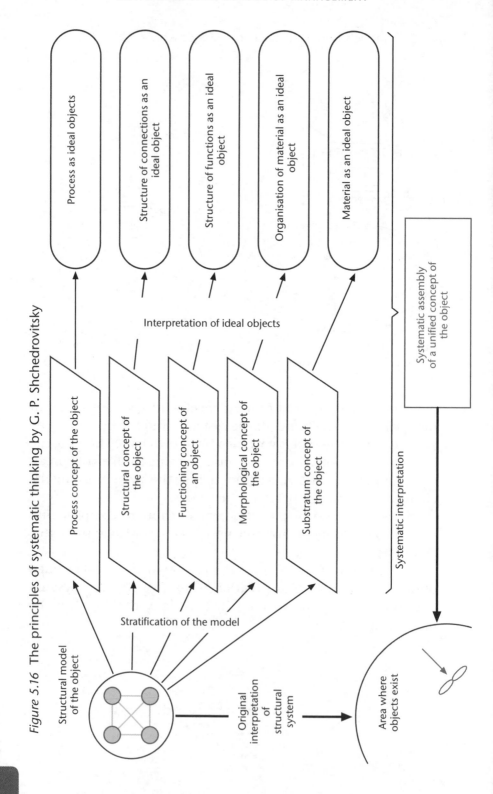

Figure 5.16 The principles of systematic thinking by G. P. Shchedrovitsky

Process as ideal objects

Structure of connections as an ideal object

Structure of functions as an ideal object

Organisation of material as an ideal object

Material as an ideal object

Interpretation of ideal objects

Process concept of the object

Structural concept of the object

Functioning concept of an object

Morphological concept of the object

Substratum concept of the object

Systematic assembly of a unified concept of the object

Systematic interpretation

Structural model of the object

Stratification of the model

Original interpretation of structural system

Area where objects exist

Part VI

On the Knowledge Management Method

Integration processes for a mechanical engineering corporation

A. G. Reus, A. P. Zinchenko,
S. B. Kraichinskaya and D. S. Talyanskiy

A. P. Zinchenko and D. S. Talyanskiy

Methodology: how we work

What do we mean by knowledge management?

The term 'knowledge management' (KM) is a highly abstract expression or metaphor. This phrase embodies a system of work that has developed historically and has the purpose of removing, as far as possible, the need for managers to command, order, compel and punish failure to comply with commands and orders. At the same time this system ensures compliance with manager's decisions by all members of the team, organisation or executive apparatus, with awareness and understanding of what needs to be done, how it should be done, and within what time frame it must been done. In essence, managing an organisation implies self-motivation of people within the organisation who ensure the performance of defined functions used in areas determined by the manager. They should move towards objectives set by the manager. How can this self-motivation be achieved?

Everyone can easily understand the straightforward army principle: 'If you can't do it, we'll teach you. If you don't want to, we'll make you!' It seems that many find it simpler to force others, but it is not always possible to achieve understanding and completion of a task, even when following army discipline. Failed attempts to 'force' others are followed by direct manipulation and physical coercion of people, and then chaos. This is all the more so when we are talking about business, design and engineering developments, effective organisation of manufacturing, and other business activities that demand participants' creativity, initiative, and personal interest in achieving the end result. People in these fields of activity will not tolerate blunt commands. They need to decide independently how to act according to processes set down for them by managers. Also, they must have conviction in the rationality, viability and attainability of the set objectives.

In recent times, public relations people and political and psychological specialists have seized a monopoly on the means and methods of persuasion. Their methods though are aimed at changing human behaviour with no regard for the work being done, and, primarily, they find success with social misfits, and 'orphans and charity cases'. The management system and its agents need schemes, concepts, evidence, analogies, experimental data and other constructs rooted in reality, collectively referred to as 'knowledge of activity'. And even the most effective applied psychology will be found wanting here. Managing knowledge as such is the same as managing hammers, saws and planes. These are the tools of the carpenter and are used by craftspeople to perform specific types of work. In the very same way, knowledge performs the function of tools in conducting specific types of intellectual work: in particular, managerial work. Using and by means of such tools as knowledge, people have learned to manage other people.

So 'knowledge management' is a reference to a particular approach and a fitting set of tools, methods and technological processes that ensure the development and transfer to the executive apparatus of such concepts, schemes for the organisation of activity, regulations and operating standards, which provide the 'self-motivation' of those performing the work that the manager needs. In other words, it is management by knowledge, which is such a shift in the processes and understandings that motivate people in an organisation that it changes the activity of the organisation as a whole, providing new management technologies and transforming it into a focused system, a system directed at achieving the manager's objectives.

How it works: the 'knowledge management' arrangement

A distinction must be drawn between such thinking instruments as topica and logic. Topica (from the Greek *topos*, or place) is a special technique for the spatial organisation of thought and under-standing, and likewise, the cognitive place organised on its basis. An illustrative example of topica is the PowerPoint 'slide sorter' option. This option allows you to display all slides on the screen at the same time on a small scale. We can then immediately (or, simultaneously) see all key points of the presented message. Thoughtful people in the course of long training courses have acquired the ability to view and collect fragments of the content, or different slides, into the structure they need to achieve the stated objective. In essence, this is the operation of thinking construction as such.

The name topica was received from Byzantine thinkers in one of the texts comprising Aristotle's *Organon*. Organon was the name given to the body of perceptions for the organisation of thinking, or the 'weapons of the knowledge of truth', as they would say at that time. The topica of Aristotle is the instrument for systemising the body of these weapons, and indeed also for the conceptions of the thinker. Topica must be mastered to be able to understand and to think. Logic is a different set of tools. This is a body of rules developed by humankind to express thoughts and to communicate them to other people in texts (or by discourse). The purpose of topica and logic is to serve in the structuring targeted actions aimed at achieving specific products and results.

The subject matter we are exploring is developed according to a specific topica. It can easily be reconstructed by selecting from the following text all the schemes we are using and placing them on a large table or pinning them to a board (and there are more than a dozen schemes). In order to unpack and describe these schemes in the text, we must follow the rules of logic and set out their descriptions sequentially in the following order:

◆ the 'business card' of the corporation where we apply and develop the technology process of KM;
◆ our position;
◆ fundamental methodologies of KM;
◆ description of basic schemes and technical devices we use in organising work with KM;
◆ technologies of large-scale application of KM;
◆ typical case of the application of KM technologies;
◆ principles of working with people under KM conditions.

Who needs to manage knowledge and why?

OJSC UIC Oboronprom. The company was created in 2002 as a diversified industrial group in the field of mechanical engineering and high technology (http://oboronprom.ru).

According to the RA Expert-400 Rating, in 2009 our corporation held 33rd place in the largest 400 companies in Russia and first place in terms of revenues among mechanical engineering companies (RUB 137 billion). In 2010 we strengthened our position, achieving revenues of RUB 192 billion. Pursuant to the company's development strategy, in 2015 we are planning to achieve revenues in excess of RUB 500 billion.

Here is a quote from an interview with the managing director of OJSC UIC Oboronprom, A. G. Reus, broadcast on the RBC television channel:

Our slogan is 'Knowledge management is the fundamental production process in the corporation.' This is no joke, or simply a wish, it is a reality. For us, both the Corporate University, and working with personnel, and competitive selection we conduct for managerial positions are an integrated chain, because education, personnel training and knowledge management are the key that should allow us to achieve ambitious aims.

Position and objectives

KM does not need to be applied left, right and centre. These technologies only function when solving tasks of a particular scale. To solve an engineering problem, it is enough to ask a competent engineer. However, to solve problems of integration in fields of mechanical engineering, which in Russia went 20 years without advanced specifications, and which were essentially ransacked and gradually degraded, it is impossible to do without KM.

Here, we need people who are capable of analysing the situation and working in multi-skill schemes. We need people who are able to foresee market prospects and determine a series of 'breakthrough' projects. We need competent developers of programmes.

People are needed who are capable of organising meaningful communication among professionals from different areas of activity, and constructing a structure from differing ideas that can be applied by all participants in a common endeavour. Such people are rare in the labour market, and they are greatly valued. Therefore, it is desirable to find them and train them up within the company. But further, we must rationally and systematically organise their interaction in moving towards the set objectives. The experience of world leaders in KM, such as General Electric, Motorola and British Petroleum, shows that such a form of organisation is effective and yields results.

When organising operations on the basis of KM, the management system of a large corporation can expect to solve two major problems:

- establishing uniformity across all enterprises for effective co-operation, standardisation and control of the operation of hierarchical management systems;
- raising all divisions and specialists to the highest levels.

Numerous other problems in any given situation will be resolved by a hands-on approach.

Again, we would emphasise that to ensure reliable performance,

Figure 6.1 Management system object scheme

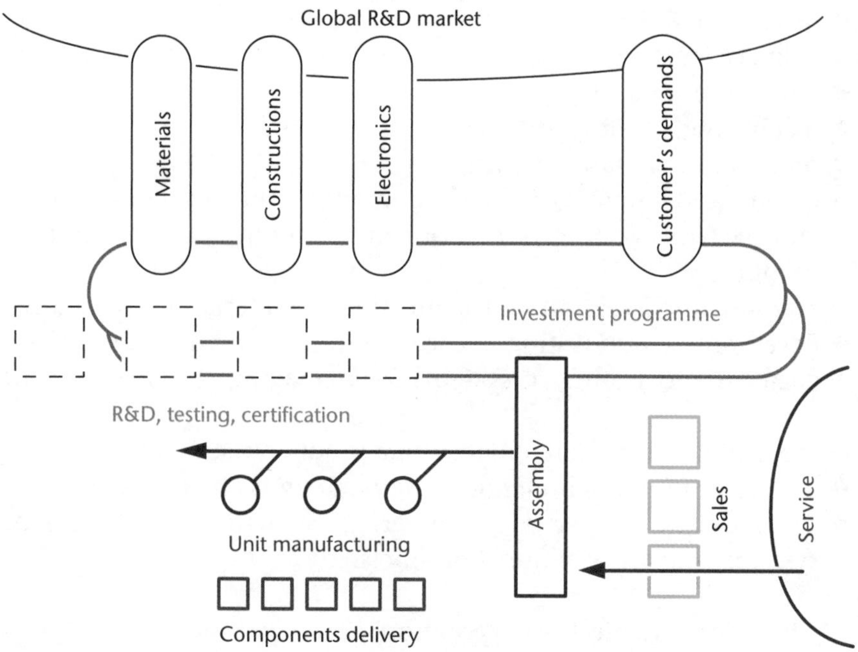

for example, of a small enterprise, KM is not required. According to Henri Fayol, when organising operations in a functional management system, KM is not needed if professionals can be deployed competently according to specific functions: technologists, salespeople, financiers, suppliers and others. Only in the case of big organisational and technical systems (BOTS – a term coined by Russell Ackoff) is it impossible to do without KM.

The knowledge manager's area of activity

Our corporation is just such an organisation. It includes design and engineering divisions, specialised factories, factories for final assembly, test centres and so on. This complex cannot function correctly or develop without an adequate management system incorporating the 'big picture'.

Processes arranged within the organisation are:

◆ lifecycle (process) of the corporation's products;
◆ product usage processes – service, technical support, repair, and extending the service life (lifecycle);

- sales (of flight time), handover of products to the client;
- assembly of products for the client;
- delivery of units for assembly;
- delivery logistics;
- fabrication of units;
- machining, reinforcement, surface coating;
- production of blanks, casting;
- design and engineering developments, fabrication of models and patterns, testing of demonstration models, certification of products;
- manufacture, creation and acquisition of materials for products;
- development and testing of the structural elements of products;
- creation and testing of systems for managing the operation of products;
- study of consumer preferences for a product (marketing);
- search for fundamentally new engine designs and aircraft;
- study of the properties of materials, structures, management systems, and areas of use of products.

KM functions within the corporation:

- top management needs a picture of the area of activity;
- market capture requires understanding of laws of the lifecycle of our products;
- project managers need to understand market prospects;
- improvement of manufacturing systems (Toyota Production System – TPS and others) requires active sharing of experience;
- scientific research and development work cannot be organised only to support manufacturing, because in this area innovative ideas and permanent upgrades are created;
- the talent pool must not learn from the mistakes of experienced personnel, but should develop when designing its own visions.

Methodology: historical forms

The earliest, yet the most reliable means of acquiring essential knowledge is to learn from a master teacher. Find a master teacher who possesses the secrets that interest you, win the right to become their student, live alongside them for seven years (that was the pattern of medieval apprenticeship) and perhaps you will become an equally accomplished master worker.

A training system with the sharing of experience arises by virtue of the fact that there are insufficient master teachers for everyone desiring to learn something. The master's work method needs to be described, transformed into regulatory prescription, an instruction, code of rules, and set out in readily comprehensible language in a textbook, and then the textbook must be accompanied by a teacher. The teacher cannot do or show, but must explain something from the experience contained in the textbook. Higher education institutions, which have today in Russia lost their dominant position on the market of developing specialist competencies, were established in this way.

Large technical systems develop new areas of activity, and create new products for new markets far faster than an education system that preserves previous experience is able to supply the relevant specialists. Consultancy groups have been created and were founded within this niche and are working for global companies (see Paul Dickson's *Think Tanks*, 1972[1]). The consultancy field has divided up on the basis of databases accumulated on the results of work with numerous and varied clients. Specifically, it is consultancy firms that are introducing the concept of KM in order to systemise and consolidate the accumulated experience of 'breakthrough' developments so that it can be explained and shared with clients.

We work according to what are called next-generation schemes – knowledge management within the framework of a corporate university. These have been developed by large corporations to overcome the dependency on traditional systems of training and service provided by consultancy firms. The best of the well-known corporate universities are those of General Electric (created and personally headed by the head of the corporation, Jack Welch) and British Petroleum (the experience is described in C. Collison and G. Parcell's *Learning to Fly*[2]).

The principal objective of a corporate university is not to train the corporation's employees, as many believe, but to search for experienced and knowledgeable people who are willing to share their experience, and people who are striving to gain this experience. We call them the 'talent pool'. Specialised organisational forms of collaborative work are needed for these people (see below), as well as

---

1   New York: Ballantine, 1972.
2   *Learning to Fly: Practical knowledge from leading and learning organizations*, 2nd edn. North Mankato, Minn.: Capstone, 2004.

specialist schematisation and sign engineering techniques, without which it is impossible to harvest experience, or package it, share it or use it in a new location.

Methodology: techniques of schematisation

'The thought spoken aloud is a lie!' (F. Tyutchev). First and foremost, the management of knowledge requires schemes and carriers of thought, rather than texts, which are more readily used to conceal thought. The person who does not master the technique of schematisation does not think.

The authors of this work are the students of G. P. Shchedrovitsky (see www.fondgp.ru). His Russian Methodological School paid special attention to matters of the schematisation of thought and action. As he put it, 'Schemes, in contrast to verbal texts, are a specific form that allows you to construct and implement structured and systemic thinking.'

We must make a distinction between different types of schemes:

◆ mnemonic schemes are useful to all: for example, the popular flash cards;
◆ schemes for visualising processes: charts, graphs and other graph-emes that are incorporated in Excel, Visio and numerous other programs.

In our work, two types of schemes perform the main functions:

◆ object-ontological (of which ideal-object schemes are a special case);
◆ organising-action (such as road signs).

We should present the arrangement of the 'objects' we manage (for example, a scientific and technical centre, management company, technology service centre, and market capture scheme) as object-ontological schemes. Clearly, such schematisation is only necessary when the management objects are not within arm's reach of the manager. They are needed where thousands of employees are in motion, and dozens of factories and design departments are working. A manager at a small enterprise always has the workforce in their field of view, so they can lead each of them by the hand.

However, this thesis must be qualified and moderated. Today, even a manager of a small enterprise must 'think globally and act locally' (this principle was formulated by one of the leading fraudsters among modern financiers, Michael Milken). This means that if you create a network for selling pastries, you must understand trends on the world grain markets, trends in switching to healthy eating, and so on.

So if a BOTS manager does not have an object-ontological view of their company (a concept of their area of activity or management object), then they are essentially incapable of taking responsible decisions.

The second type of scheme is the organising-action scheme. These are similar in function to road signs and signposts, since they prescribe in detail how we must think and in what sequence we must act so that we move directly to the set objectives.

Methodology: three concepts and three types of knowledge

In normalising knowledge management, we must accurately comprehend the arrangement of the mechanisms that need to be managed. This means having a working understanding and schemes of knowledge structure. Working in the tradition of the Moscow Methodological Circle (MMC) and the school of G. P. Shchedrovitsky (see www.fondgp.ru/gp/biblio), we distinguish between three types of knowledge, depending upon their purpose and the circumstances of use:

◆ knowledge in action;
◆ knowledge in thought and communication;
◆ knowledge providing understanding.

The first concept – knowledge in action – supports actions to transform source material into a product. This is generally a description of procedures and operations that must be performed. This description always draws on the past. In place of knowledge (see below), we can use an experienced coach, user instructions, reconstruction of textbook rules, a computer program, a test case: in other words, we can use anything that will help us achieve our goal. A pragmatic understanding of knowledge asserts that knowledge is everything that enables us to act without mistakes. The absence of

Figure 6.2 Knowledge in action

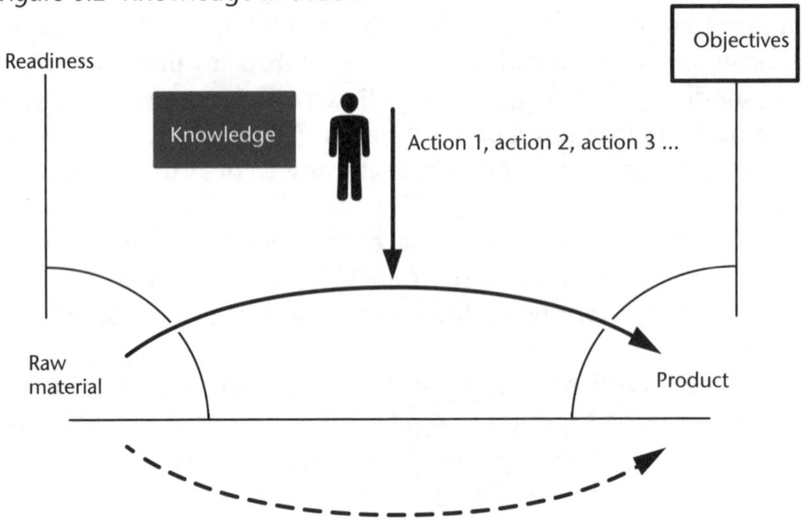

knowledge forces us to conduct business by trial and error, which is risky and slow.

The second concept is knowledge in thought and communication. This performs the function of ensuring understanding. For example, you need to ask someone with experience, 'How do you do this?' and then reconstruct the scheme of the action that interests you according to their response; once you have had a consultant's schemes presented to you and have considered them, you reformat them in a way that you can use in your work.

We exchange texts, and to highlight the content that we understand, we use metatexts – we ask questions for clarification and wait for an elucidatory answer. This is required in the majority of work situations.

For example, designers state that a new product will be ready for testing and certification within two years, but the financial specialists respond, 'If we do not launch this product to market within a year, then it is not worth developing, because our competitors will overtake us.' This exchange of metatexts should result in finding a constructive way out of the situation: for example, reducing the development period through co-operation or involving additional resources.

The third concept refers to knowledge that supports the

Figure 6.3 Knowledge in thought and communication

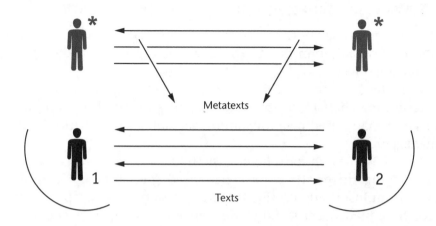

progression from understanding to constructive intellectual work aimed at changing the objects being operated on and managed, to create something new.

We pose questions on various aspects of the behaviour of the object we are handling ('How does this work?'), capture its various manifestations in signs and schemes, and attempt to construct such schemes that allow us to make comprehensible and transparent decisions for organising the actions of those executing the work. The third concept of knowledge is a shift in the schemes in an attempt to answer the questions 'How is it arranged?' and 'How does it work?'

Figure 6.4 Knowledge providing understanding

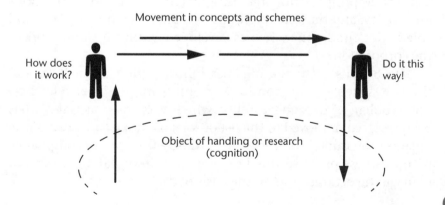

Phases and stages of the technological process of knowledge management in stage gate schemes

In the terminology of the stage gate process, Gate 0 is the creation of a new organisation or the arrival at the organisation of a new managing director.

Gate 1 is setting out the problem of managing the company; determining the lack of structural schemes, methods of communicating managerial decisions and loyal staff members in middle management.

Gate 2 is a search for schemes, methods, and managers capable of applying them; attracting experienced specialists and consultants from inside and outside the organisation to solve a problem; recording inadequacies and insufficiencies of available experience and managerial resources.

Gate 3 is organising the talent pool (seeking out employees) for search operations to resolve established problems in the manner of cross-corporate communications (participative planning) and project analytical sessions (PAS). The result of such organisation of work is project proposals, structures and ideas that allow the manager to make non-standard decisions, introduce new schemes into the organisation's operations and rely on new people to do this.

Gate 4 is the transition from schemes that clarify the structure of the organisation and the capabilities of its people, to schemes under which it is possible to work. These are known as organisational-activity (OA) schemes. They require work in specifying and developing schemes and regulatory instructions in specialised staff groups.

Gate 5 is the development of a set of regulatory documents establishing new principles for organising activity, regulatory instructions for activity, and training of groups of managers who are ready and able to work under the schemes developed within the framework of the corporation.

Gate 6 leads us to the organisation operating normally under the new schemes, and continually improving terms of reference. The problem of unmanageability, which was posed at Gate 1, has been resolved or moved to the list of solvable tasks. The head of the organisation can rely on the work of those who monitor compliance with business processes in the company's information flows and manage the organisation on the basis of deviations.

Figure 6.5 Stage gates in the process of knowledge management

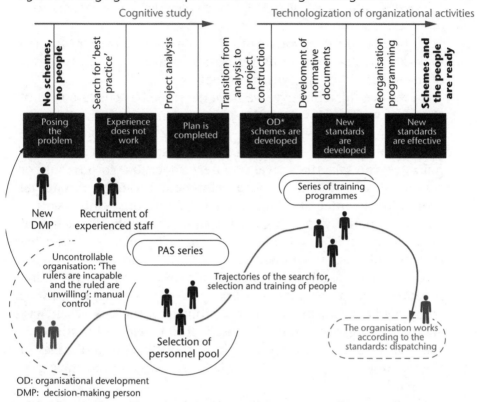

OD: organisational development
DMP: decision-making person

Knowledge engineering: general concept and typology of forms of working with knowledge in the corporation

Historically, there have been a number of fundamentally differing approaches to mastering essential means and tools for the organisation of intellectual work, and likewise to the content of training. For example:

Give people the opportunity to gain reliable information, and to undergo targeted training with experienced consultants, teachers and trainers.

You can only learn something from a master of their trade who wants and is able to become your coach.

We only need knowledge when we find ourselves in an abnormal (problematic, emergency) situation and are forced to comprehend and act quickly: in other words, to seek and develop knowledge as we go along.

To respond to the questions arising in each of the approaches and to look into the stated positions, we must have an appropriate typology of the forms of working with knowledge.

To resolve this objective, we have developed a schedule map of 'Types of work with knowledge in a corporation'. Different types of work are linked within the structure of the KM process. The schedule map is displayed as a sequence of schemes. As a reference point, we can take the arrival of a new leader to a corporation, or a more simple situation, the development of an organisational project for the integration of a number of enterprises into a corporation. Figuratively speaking, such a situation can be characterised as 'unmanageable' or it could be said that 'The rulers are incapable and the ruled are unwilling.' The new leadership has its own set pieces based on previous experience, but does not have any working schemes or people prepared to work by them. The situation must be considered as problematic, and the problem of the lack of schemes and work reorganisation plans must be formulated, as has the team that will perform the work (see the section 'Phases and stages in the technological process of knowledge management in stage gate schemes').

Figure 6.6 shows two hypothetical enterprises symbolising the multitude of enterprises in a corporation such as ours, each of which is represented in two states: the current state and the optimum state. The current state is that the corporation leadership, and indeed the leadership of the enterprise itself, is dissatisfied, whereas the optimum state is one they would like to achieve.

The talent pool, by definition, consists of people (a specially trained team), from whom the leadership expects effective actions in the transition from situation 1 to situation 2. In other words, the talent pool is only needed when and where we are unable to change the state of affairs by relying only on the existing management system and those working within it.

In management practice, a number of methods are known that can be used to resolve the problem without the creation of a talent pool group. These methods assume viewing the situation at the enterprise as a 'gap' (where solution options known to us are insufficient to achieve the required result, and we understand what we are lacking) or 'difficult' (when we do not have a means of solving the

Figure 6.6 Assignment of the talent pool

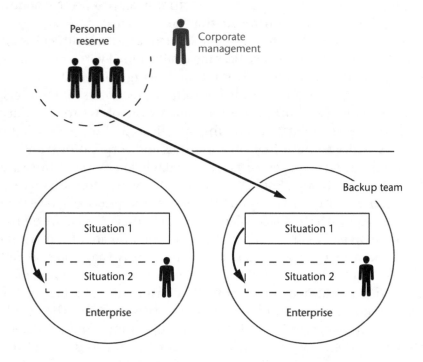

problem and cannot approach the situation, but we are aware that such means exist and they can be used). Here we should note, so that we can return to this subject later, that we only need a talent pool in a problematic situation: that is, when the means known to us to bridge the gap or overcome the difficulty are no longer effective. But for now we will focus only on these problematic situations.

The first method is authoritative and popular among those who still remember how the Ministry for the Aviation Industry worked. We shall call it command management. How does it work? If the management system contains certain inadequacies – it is not important whether they are difficulties, shortcomings or problems – we issue an order, appoint people to carry out the work and await reports of a change in the state of affairs. Sometimes this method is can be used successfully today, but rarely. The possibilities and limitations of command management are determined by the transparency of schemes for decision making and organising the activity of those carrying out the work, and also the willingness of those performing the work to undertake the appropriate action. Clearly, in our situation (where there are processes of change, obscurity of activity, and a lack of specialists with the required qualifications) the majority of orders are left hanging in thin air irrespective of how strong the systems of control are that we have created.

The second method to eliminate inadequacies and difficulties is used by managers who have become disillusioned with the efficacy of command management. This is called 'using world best practice'. In practice, this means inviting consultants, recruiters and trainers, who are willing at short notice and for a reasonable fee to introduce you to the consolidated working practices of hundreds of the world's leading enterprises, organisations and corporations, and 'to headhunt' their best specialists. They will tell you in straightforward language how Toyota, Boeing and General Electric achieved success, how many clients McKinsey and PricewaterhouseCoopers have, and provide you with the success-laden CVs of managers who are on the labour market. Possibly you will hear information about something that might serve as a model. The limitation is that you will not see the model, but will end up in an informational, psychological or even physical dependence on the consultants. The fact of the matter is that the situation in your enterprise is unique, the people have other values and a different mentality from those elsewhere, they have their own history, region, climate and so on. Beautiful schemes from outside will mostly be irrelevant to your organisation.

Peddlers of 'best practice' feed off our respect for knowledge and assert that they will provide us with the most up-to-date knowledge, which (pay attention here) will radically change our organisation if we are able to utilise and apply it. However, they do not say whether this will change it for the better.

The pragmatic approach to management that we operate is based on a simple principle: knowledge is only those concepts, schemes and models that you yourself have developed and which change your system pursuant to your goals. Incidentally, what the consultants trade in came about as a result of using just such an approach.

So let us say that the workforce initially opposes outside pressure, it is beaten, but some time later it 'recovers' and carries on work as before. The leadership becomes accustomed to dependence on outside advice. Everything is so wonderful for people in that faraway fairy-tale kingdom the consultants describe. The irresistible attraction leads to a management system that essentially prevents independent thought, in which the managers renounce their own will in subjection to others – in essence, to a beautiful picture!

Figure 6.7 Routine methods of transition to the future

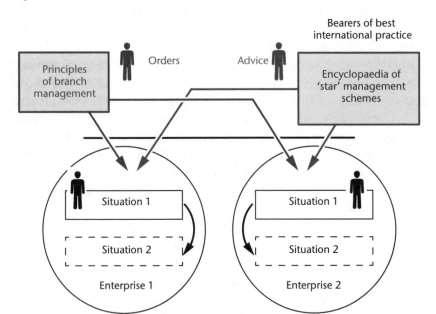

A third method relies on our own strengths, and its use requires setting the objective to develop our own talent pool. This is well known to all as sharing experience.

In Figure 6.7 we show situations that require changes, and a number of well-known means of making organisational changes. The situations are again at the bottom of the scheme's schedule map, whereas the management system views them from above (where you can 'see everything'). Each subsequent method that we discuss lies above the previous ones and is aimed at improving the activity of the corporation from within (in a way analogous with the French *centres de perfection* and Japanese *Kaizen*).

Experience sharing is a situation where we invite people from different enterprises, who are specialists in their field, have solved specific problems and can serve as an example for others, to engage in collaborative work. In the practice of leading companies who apply KM technologies (see for example, Collison and Parcell's *Learning to Fly*), this is the main manner of working. We need to find within a corporation those people who are most able to do what needs to be commonplace, convince these people to share their experience with others, to demonstrate their methods and techniques (at their own enterprise and in their own workplace) and even to become coaches for the inexperienced. The main difficulty in organising sharing experience is the lack of reciprocity. The best specialists in their field prefer to maintain professional secrecy or to sell their skills at a high price.

Literature on sharing experience and parallel criticism of consultants and business schools today have become one of the most popular subjects of so-called business novels (such as E. M. Goldratt and J. Cox's *The Goal*, 2004, and R. Immelman's *Great Boss, Dead Boss*, 2003). We should take into consideration that in the situations contained in literature, the industrial structure and material security of employees have almost reached perfection. Only one small thing remains – reasonable organisation of the activity of, and work, with the employees.

Orders should and can be performed, and consultation can and should be obtained, directly at the workplace. However, to organise experience sharing you must leave the workplace and have a detached view of your work from the position of a person who is improving. From this position, you can see how others operate in similar places and construct a scheme for sharing. In contrast to methods 1 and 2, we are not dealing here with an objective (for which there is a way to find a solution), but with a problem for which no one has a solution, so special work is required for its construction. In other words, to resolve it you will not be engaged in your business of manufacturing, but rather in some new and incomprehensible tasks, involving semiotics, epistemology and schematisation. How, where and when you do this, while neglecting your day-to-day duties, is an important question. Just such an opportunity is offered to experienced specialists, and requirements are made for them by a corporate university.

It is wonderful if the application of accumulated experience allows us to resolve the problems of managing and organisation. This works perfectly adequately in the vast majority of cases.

However, if the tools we are aware of do not work and we are unable to move to a desired condition, then we must proceed to the next level and engage in the organisation of communication aimed at establishing mutual understanding (this is not to be confused with the work of a moderator, and even less so that of a facilitator) or the development of new concepts allowing us effectively to organise activity. With each level, the forms of work become ever more abstract and refined, but they are precisely the forms that top

Figure 6.8 Workplace of the corporate university: sharing experience and normative description

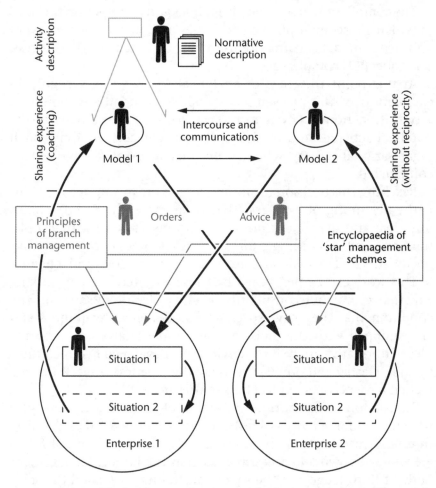

managers use. Their purpose is to provide their team (or talent pool, or backup team) with an understanding of strategy, objectives and business directions that will bring their people into a unified whole.

The problem is to organise a unified understanding of the aggregate of the tasks and functions of managers in the management system. Work in organising communication and understanding is not subject to standardisation and regulation, and will always be an expression of managerial skill.

We shall not dwell on the special work of constructing concepts, which is provided by the organiser of understanding. This work is methodological and philosophical, requiring special forms of organisation. At the Corporate University of OJSC UIC Oboronprom we use such formats as organisational-activity games (OAGs) and project workshops in the structural organisation of communication.

The compilation of schemes, principles and concepts, on the basis of which subsequent phases and stages are built in the process of knowledge management, leads us to Gate 3 in the stage gate process. The concept is completed.

At this point the stage of analytical (in this sense, cognitive) elaboration of the problems is completed, and there should be a transition from analysis to project design. On the basis of the obtained schemes and models, the manager decides from which organisational-activity schemes the management system will be constructed.

Reaching this decision means moving to organising activity. This is the beginning of a process that is far more protracted, labour-intensive and dependent on various forms of work with people, training and retraining, for the development of normative documents that regulate work based on new principles and schemes.

This work can be performed by those who have actual working experience (but not consultants or university professors), on the condition that they have special methodological techniques and are equipped with the tools for operational analysis. The principles of normative analysis of activity were developed in our country by A. K. Gastev and others, yet today the Japanese, Americans and French have become our teachers in this area.

Translation of a normative-methodological description into prescription for activity is a task requiring training and experience. In essence, we currently have no models, although cultural forms are widely known and accessible (such as the Project Management Body of Knowledge, the theory of constraints (TOC) and the stage gate process). Many foreign methodologies and standards are useful in our activity, but we have to adapt them, then define the problem and nevertheless develop our own approach. This is where we need common linguistic formats, concepts, schemes of descriptions and instructions. At the level of sharing experience, this is not necessary; friendly contact and meaningful communication are sufficient.

Work in the reorganisation of various divisions within the framework of new standardisation is developed in parallel.

◆ Gate 5 –new standards are developed. Schemes and people are available that allow the main processes in an organisation to be controlled using operational control instruments.

Figure 6.9 Concepts necessary to make activity meaningful

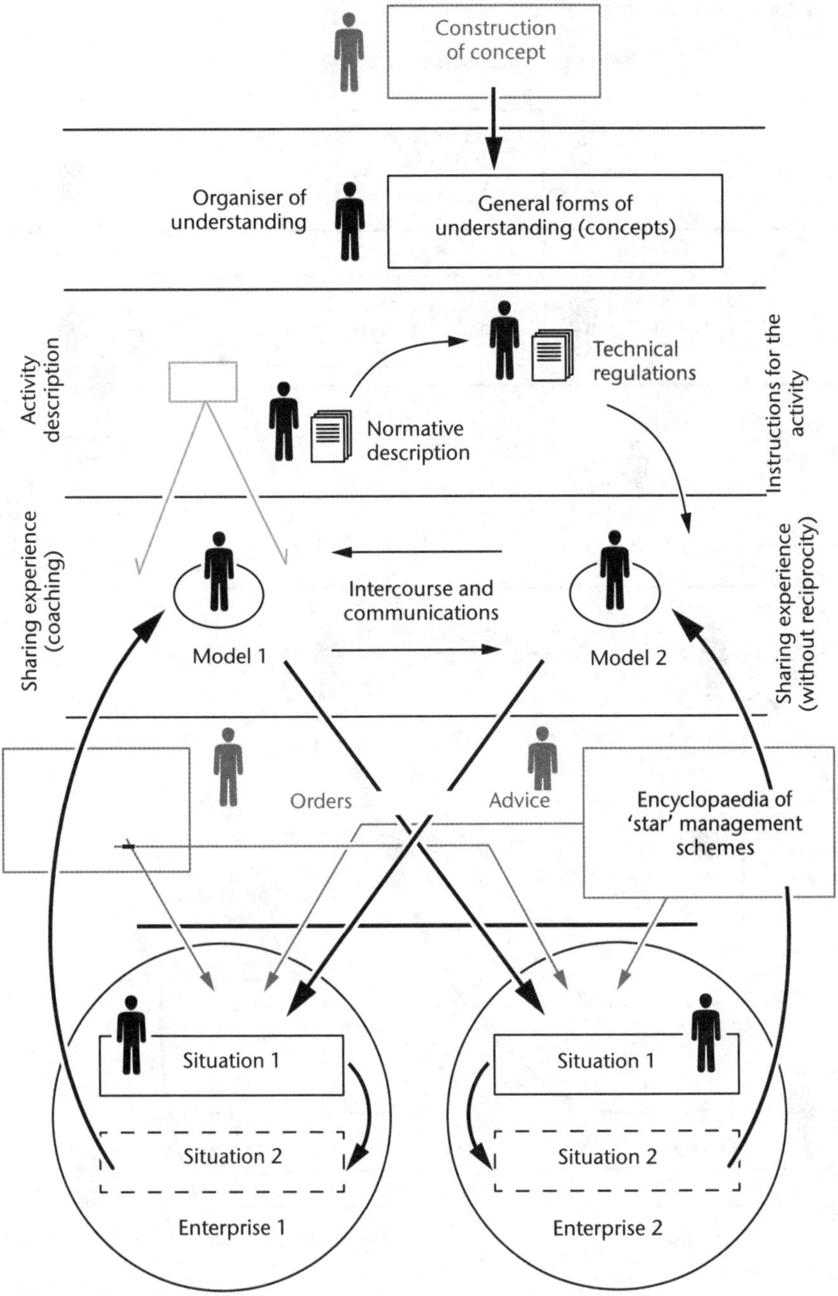

Figure 6.10 Changing the norms and rules of behaviour of corporate managers and personnel

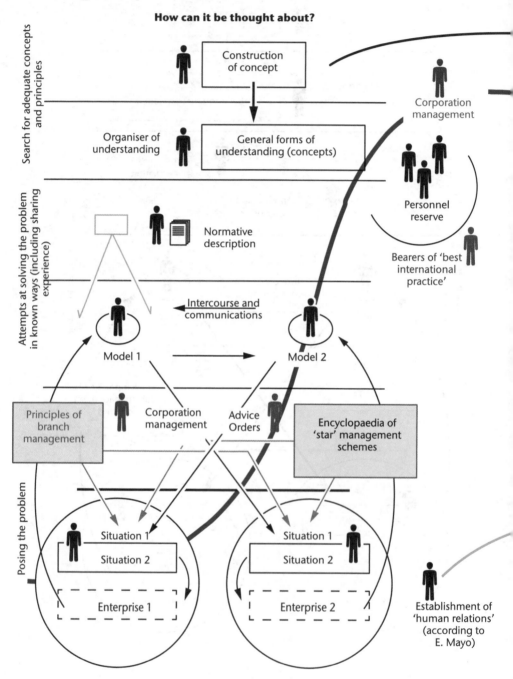

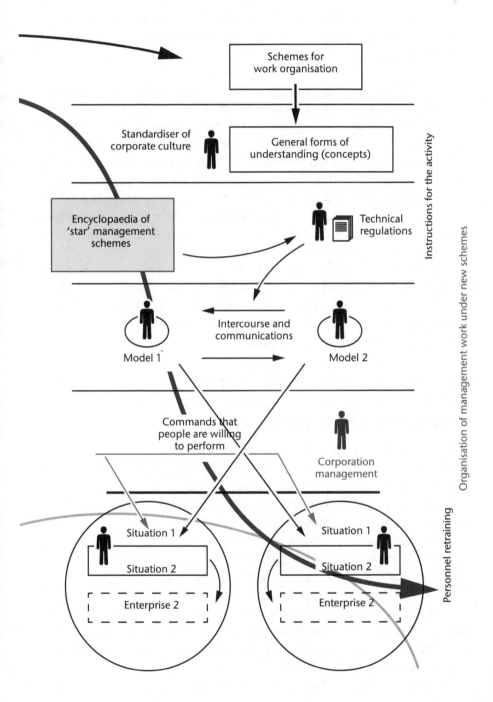

◆ Gate 6 – new standards are effective. This allows the manager to see working processes adequately reflected in information flows (indicative documents) and to trust the personnel monitoring these processes and preparing accompanying information documents.

In completing the structure, we must consider one further method, without which all the preceding methods will not work; we shall borrow its conventional name of tribalism from Ray Immelman. Specialists in lean manufacturing fully understand the purpose of this method. Irrespective of the correctness of the orders, instructions and schemes that are delivered from above to an enterprise, if its employees do not make a daily effort or strive 'from below' to improve their activity, the enterprise's operation will not change. Each wave of organisational innovation will die out even more quickly than its predecessor.

We could call this method motivation, corporate culture, education or prosthetics of mentality, or we could also call it tribalism, but the fact of the matter remains unchanged. For people at an enterprise to work effectively, we must work with them constantly and view them as people.

The way we organise the work on an industrial scale: the place of the corporate university in the management system

The corporation's activity is founded on the development and realisation of a body of investment programmes to advance in traditional markets and capture new markets for our future products. A model composition of types of work within the framework of the investment programme is given in Figure 6.11.

Work within the framework of the programme should not be monitored according to deadlines and costs, but on the basis of the achievement of specific financial and organisational stage gates. The structure of the investment programme, which should be developed over decades, cannot be determined by trial and error, and requires the organisation of work in systems of knowledge, and prototypes and demonstration models, in order to reduce as far as possible all potential (calculated) risks.

In support of this work it is essential to be diligent in collecting

Figure 6.11 The principle of the investment programme

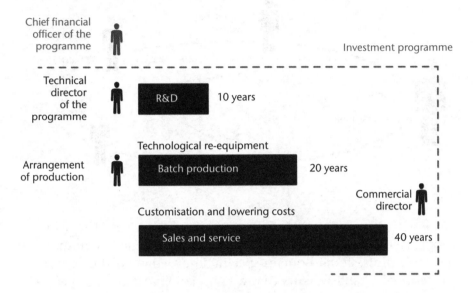

(in databanks and using other effective types of media, such as paper and white boards) details of:

◆ methods – regulatory instructions;
◆ domain-specific knowledge systems (on specific types of ideal object).

Figure 6.12 The stage gate process (according to Robert Cooper)

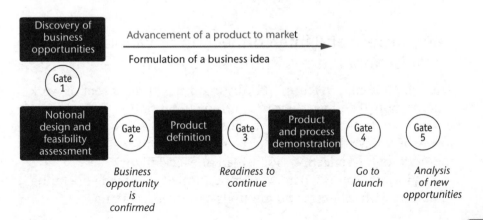

Figure 6.13 The core situation of knowledge management

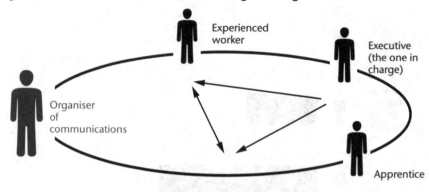

Work with people is organised separately, categorising them into people with knowledge, methods and experience; communities with professional domain-specific knowledge on the activity; educational establishments that accumulate and maintain people who have the methods, knowledge systems and experience; and the resources available through the labour market.

Special forms of communication and knowledge transfer should be applied in organising activity and linking knowledge and people. The elementary organisation of any activity is at the heart of these forms: the executive – the experienced (those with knowledge) – the trainee. This also ensures the development of new bearers of experience and knowledge. KM is possible in this framework by using a number of well-known forms of organisation: conversations, messages, discussions, lectures, methodological workshops, PAS and OAGs. But there are some forms that are preferable for resolving our objectives.

The purpose and interconnection of various organisational forms in the KM system

The schedule map (Figure 6.14) distinguishes three layers of work organisation. The lower layer is current functioning. This is what is done in the corporation, but is not specifically reflected in forms of knowledge. The subject of analysis and management in methodological reflection is specified one level higher.

The lowest layer is where work is performed to provide operating managers with schemes and methods of decision making.

Figure 6.14 Typology of work on knowledge management

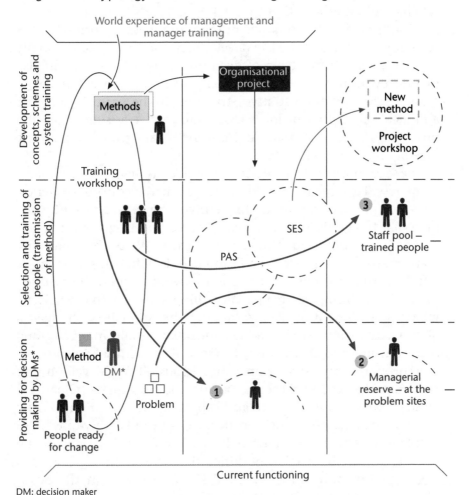

DM: decision maker

The middle layer is the selection and training of people who perform the decisions that have been taken.

The upper layer is the development of concepts, schemes, knowledge systems and methods that ensure people are trained and decisions are taken by managers.

Using the distinctions that have been set out, it is possible to distinguish three scenarios and three types of forms, according to which the work of the corporate university is organised.

The first scenario is the search for and development of intellectual prostheses for decision makers (DM). This work can be developed in traditional lecture and consultation formats, and based on concepts, schemes and methods that successful managers have developed in previous practice. The product and result of work performed in the scenario is assumed to be the development of a group of randomly selected people into a team of like-minded associates. We can also mention winning authority and real powers within the framework of the existing administrative structure. If the existing schemes and ideals are sufficient for managers to resolve arising issues and problems, then they can stop at this scenario (and the corresponding type of organisational work).

The second scenario is the selection and placement of the management pool. This scenario is used when the experience in our awareness does not provide the means for resolving problems faced by the manager. Integration of the mechanical engineering sector is a task that is invariably unique in its complexity. We do not have any methods that have proved viable and practical. In this situation, we must record problematic situations and work to build the required methods and bring together people willing to work with them. Here, we apply the tool of the PAS, gather together specialists who have a direct relationship with the problematic situation, and arrange a group brainstorming session according to a special problem-solving process. The corporate university assumes the responsibility of developing an organisational project of the session and leading team participants at all stages and phases of group and general communication. During the PAS, the people who demonstrate a desire and ability to work in problem areas can be extended such an opportunity. They will occupy those areas where the relevant difficulties have arisen.

Completing work in the second scenario results in the possibility of achieving a new method of resolving problems and finding people who can use it. Clearly, only set pieces are useful in the first scenario.

The third scenario is work targeted at the creation of a talent pool (not to be confused with a managerial pool). The organisational form is a session of experience sharing (SES). All participants analyse the experience of their work, try to convey it to others and record it in working concepts and juxtaposed schemes, and then on this basis determine possible areas and forms of using the selected experience at their own enterprise or organisation. The SES is not built around the problem, but around a particular growing point, where the participants share their knowledge of 'how to do it'.

Conducting an SES results in the formation of a talent pool; a group of people who have undergone shared events and who have become familiar with specific knowledge systems, but are not yet ready to take up new places.

The project workshop has a special place in this typology – it is work for the selection and formation of new concepts and schemes, on the basis of which PAS and SES can be conducted. This is special work, in which a small group of specialists is involved and which is conducted within the corporate university by the developers of PAS and SES organisational projects with the application of world experience.

The work of the communications organiser in designing concepts, schedule maps and organisational-activity schemes

The forms of work organisation adopted by the corporate university assume that such an object as knowledge cannot be considered simply as something that can be transferred, accumulated, purchased and so on. Knowledge that is used by specialists in an activity must be viewed from the perspective of an active approach. Knowledge occupies a defined position and function in practical activity. Knowledge is what enables the specialist to act without error.

The principal and constant difficult challenge we face is how to we achieve manageability of organisations that are comprised of tens of thousands of people scattered over immense distances and engaged in different types of activity

A local management system is within arm's reach of managers, where they can directly communicate with each member of the organisation and use compulsory orders, incentives and other tools that have a direct effect. Traditional tools for local systems are discipline, vertical authority and incentivisation.

A network management system is required for companies that because of their size and the number of task processes are beyond arm's reach. Managers need tools of indirect effect: semiotic management, corporate culture, a learning corporation, and a network of cross-corporate communication, which take the place of the administrative hierarchy. We apply the structure and mechanisms for organising communication that are relevant to the

Figure 6.15 Participative planning (according to R. Ackoff)

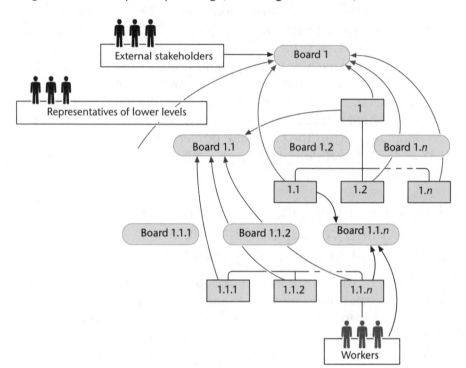

structure of the corporation. They pervade its management system and working body (management object), affording top managers the possibility of controlling and managing industrial processes without commanding, but rather by creating and transferring shared knowledge (an understanding) of what should be done, and how and when it should be done.

As a prototype we use the principles and schemes of so-called participative planning, which were developed and presented in *Creating the Corporate Future* (1975) by Russell Ackoff. Examples of the successful realisation of this scheme and its corresponding principles are provided by Jack Welch, the long-standing head of General Electric, who we judge to be among the top three leading managers of the twentieth century (he has written numerous books), and Carlos Ghosn, who orchestrated the corporate merger of Renault and Nissan (a detailed description is given in the book *Citizen of the World* [3]).

---

[3] This was published in French: Carlos Ghosn and Philippe Ries, *Citoyen du Monde*, Paris: Grasset, 2003.

Figure 6.16 Organisation of communication at a project analytical session (PAS)

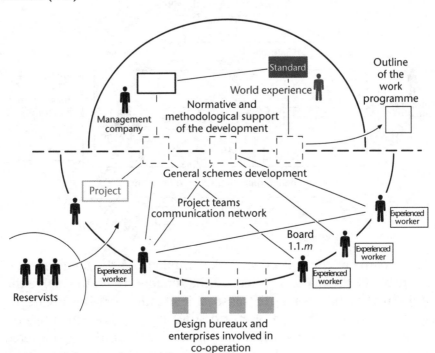

Principal schemes for organising communication on KM in PAS

For us, the principal and leading organisational form – PAS – has developed over the course of two decades of practice of this type of work.

The leading team (of those with relevant knowledge) presents its developmental work and performs the function of a breakthrough group. Representatives of other teams (from the corporation's enterprises) perform the function of technical auditor of the developmental work, and experts perform the function of comparing adopted decisions with best world practice. The teams work to develop and critique proposals according to their own objectives and capabilities.

The working process begins (see Figure 6.17) with a technical objective being posed by the leadership. The work develops according to standard operating procedures. This work is performed in the workplace, and in essence it represents sharpness or practical acumen.

Figure 6.17 Principal schedule map of the value creation stream at PAS

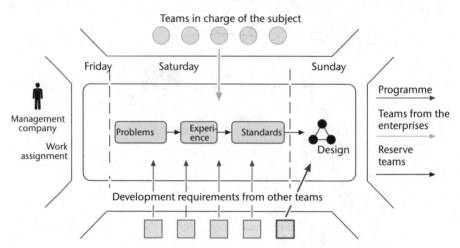

Participants in the collective work compile from the range of tools available to them a set or method that enables them to resolve the objective that has been set in this specific situation, or to formulate the problem, if the existing toolset and proven methods are insufficient.

Situations where acumen is required are constantly encountered by working specialists. Those with experience understand what they need to do and persistently repeat efforts to resolve the problem, to find and select the required tools and the method of using them. The inexperienced ask for assistance or retreat helplessly. Incidentally, one of the most popular uses of acumen by the experienced is to jump away from their previous course like a hare concealing its lair (to use the vocabulary of seasoned hunters), and remain at a distance from the inexperienced who are asking for help.

With this organisational form, other participants are afforded an opportunity to gain a reference point to clarify their own proposals and schemes, and to be included in the collaborative development work. Further group work is aimed at discussion of the identified difficulties, shortcomings and problems. This allows the participants to progress to the work with a project approach and to determine which solutions are needed to overcome the identified problems.

Delivery of performance results

In order to understand the principles of the organisation of work at the UEC Oboronprom Corporate University, we need to designate their place within the framework of the historical typology of the forms and methods of managerial training (see Figure 6.18).

At the bottom of the scheme there is a case that does not fit with the typology. This is individualised development or training (in the past, typically of royalty and aristocrats), which is called 'tutoring' today. The most well-known case is Alexander the Great and his tutor Aristotle.

Figure 6.18 is divided into two columns. The right column is designated for forms of organising manufacturing that have historically developed and become more complicated, whereas the left column is for forms of training organisation that have historically

Figure 6.18 Typology of forms of manager training

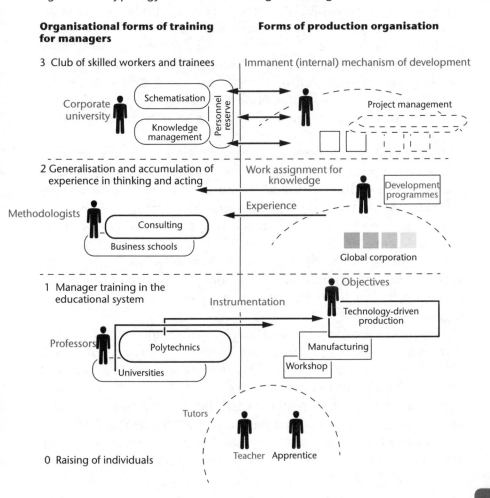

developed and become more complicated along their particular trajectory.

The first historical type of organisational form of training in the education system is instrumentation. This was provided by university professors and masters at polytechnic schools. Here, people were engaged in updating and passing on forms of thinking and organising activity accumulated by humankind (universities did not appear to meet the needs of nascent large industry, but they functioned as institutions for handing down culture). Students mastering them were progress-drivers in relation to the then current forms of organising production: the workshops of tradespeople, manufacturers and large technology-driven enterprises. The education and engineering training they received enabled them to understand the structure of manufacturing, to set goals and to organise the work of a large number of people. We can say that the foundation of manufacturing management systems and the corresponding knowledge are laid down according to this pattern in the education system. Clearly, this type of organisation of training remains the most widespread today, and will continue to exist for a long time to come, but it now performs the function of familiarising the flow of students with the history, elements and basic skills of various specialist fields.

The second type is the compilation and accumulation of experience of managerial thinking activity. It arose in the first half of the twentieth century, primarily at business schools – educational institutions that came to replace the universities and were intended to eliminate the managerial illiteracy of specialists in narrow fields. The emergence of these was dictated by a deepening division of labour and lack of co-operation in industry. Teachers at business schools and consultancy firms develop the content, focusing on and selling to managers effective schemes for making decisions and organising management.

Complex corporate schemes are developed within forms of manufacturing organisation, with a financial effect not directly connected with the manufacturing efficiency of the company (mergers and acquisitions). Transnational corporations are formed that organise their activity in different regions with the aim of minimising costs and capturing new markets (approach to market expectations).

A reversal takes place in the relationship between manufacturing and education. Business schools and consultancy firms do not nurture managerial candidates, but work on technical assignments from companies and corporations. After all, it is from here that they obtain their basic human resources (those with experience of management thinking and training content) or cases – examples of adopting managerial decisions that have had a noticeable impact on the development of manufacturing.

The focus of laying down development programmes shifts from the area of education to the area of corporate governance, whereas systems of managing corporations prove to be knowledge-dependent on the consultancy firms.

The third type of training involves KM within large corporations. This is formed as an inherent or integrated mechanism of the corporate management development system. It assumes that managers are equipped with systemic ways of thinking and schematisation techniques, and have the communication skills for passing on experience and training a talent pool who are on the heels of the decision makers and ready to replace them at any moment.

Work on KM schemes is not developed at special educational establishments, but within the corporation in forms of situational analysis, project workshops and PAS, to overcome specific shortcomings, difficulties and problems in current activity and in determining strategic plans.

The differences in content and organisation of work between training at the corporate university and other forms of training and education are:

- selection and choice of participants in events, rather than a determined group of students;
- pedagogy according to the principle 'teach everyone everything';
- solving challenges and problems relevant to the situation, rather than textbook solutions;
- identification and transfer of methods of operation;
- construction of concepts, schemes and knowledge systems;
- work within environments of thinking-action systemisation (TAS) and epistemological and technical methods.

Figure 6.19 History of work in supporting decision-making practice by knowledgeable and trained people at OJSC UIC Oboronprom

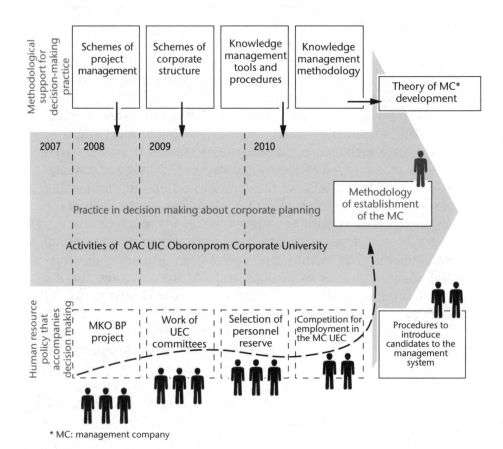

* MC: management company

Practice: two examples of our development work – OJSC Russian Helicopters and OJSC United Engine Corporation

OJSC UIC Oboronprom manages two of the largest mechanical engineering corporations in Russia. In organising work for the consolidation of helicopter construction and engine construction assets, we were compelled to press forward and simultaneously control two processes of change. Although such dichotomisation creates additional difficulties, it also provides unique advantages and opportunities for the manager whose managerial techniques are founded on the principles of KM. In order to make use of the advantages open to us, we conducted almost all the activities of the Corporate University on related subjects and in conjunction with managers and specialists from the helicopter and engine construction companies. In some areas the helicopter engineers took the lead, and in other areas the engine builders did, but the experience of discussions and the schemes that emerged for organising work in each situation were shared achievements and assisted both parties in their work.

In this section we present two examples of the development of work, by virtue of which new managerial tools emerged and became an asset to us, augmenting the decision-making process. We shall highlight major stages and milestones separately for each corporation.

Changing object patterns in managing the reorganisation of OJSC Russian Helicopters: the situation, the problem and the objectives

Historically, the Russian helicopter sector has developed cyclically according to programmes of expansion and modernisation of the country's helicopter fleet. After the breakup of the USSR, the sector fragmented into local enterprises and production decreased significantly. With the aim of developing domestic mechanical engineering pursuant to Presidential Decrees of the Russian Federation of 29 November 2004, no. 1481, and of 11 August 2007, no. 1038, and under the management of OJSC UIC Oboronprom, an integrated structure of enterprises developing and manufacturing helicopter machinery was created.

Today, the helicopter industry is effectively using its scientific and technical potential (drawn from world-class design-engineering schools) in the process of creating a future model line. The engineering schools of M.L. Mil and N.I. Kamov that arose during the Soviet period give the sector priority positions on the world market. Any disadvantage is not seen in the technical sector (here, the accumulated groundwork can and should ensure long-term superiority), but rather in the area of ineffective business decisions.

The main reason for creating the holding company OJSC Russian Helicopters was to ensure an effective business in helicopter construction based on existing accrued scientific and technical experience.

As of April 2011, we can isolate three stages of transformation of the integrated enterprises comprising the holding company, and accordingly, three types of schemes of the objects with which we worked in the process of managing reorganisation of the corporation.

◆ the stage of integration and anti-crisis measures;
◆ the stage of restructuring for the required model range and agreed production programmes;
◆ the stage of systemic reorganisation according to principles of managing the life-cycle of products, including the creation of technology competence centres (TCC) and a modern global after-sales service network.

Corporate integration and anti-crisis measures

The first project analysis session on 'Development of terms of reference for the project of integration of the Russian helicopter sector' (a project concerned with setting up OJSC Russian Helicopters) was held on 22–24 November 2007. The session was attended by the heads and leading specialists in the following areas:

◆ marketing policy;
◆ prospects for design and engineering research and development;
◆ reconstruction of the production platform;
◆ personnel policy;
◆ finance policy.

V. Putin and A. G. Reus

Constructive discussions resulted in determining a strategic development programme for the holding company:

◆ creation of a competitive, highly profitable and self-developing helicopter company;
◆ reorientation of the business from the sale of products to sale of the product lifecycle;
◆ modernisation of a diversified and competitive model range (creating a new product line in the helicopter sector);
◆ integration and co-operation with world leaders;
◆ upgrading of the after-sales service system and network.

On the basis of results of the session, a management team was formed for the holding company and the heads of the management company OJSC Russian Helicopters were appointed.

Figure 6.20 Scope of activity of OJSC Russian Helicopters in 2007

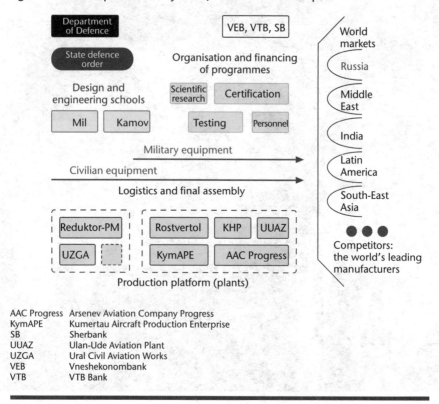

AAC Progress	Arsenev Aviation Company Progress
KymAPE	Kumertau Aircraft Production Enterprise
SB	Sherbank
UUAZ	Ulan-Ude Aviation Plant
UZGA	Ural Civil Aviation Works
VEB	Vneshekonombank
VTB	VTB Bank

Restructuring for the required model range and co-ordinated production programmes

Our competitors – European and American helicopter manufacturers – are operating successfully on world markets. We have studied the world experience of integration and transition to programme management.

From November to January 2008, on our instruction consultants from the Roland Berger company prepared an analysis of the condition of the helicopter market and the experience of world leaders in organising activity. In March 2008 they submitted to us a suggested sequence of steps for the transition to modern forms of activity and the corresponding administrative structure (see Figure 6.21).

In order to analyse the situation and resolve the problem of transition of the corporation to programme management, we organised

Figure 6.21 Evolution of the organisational structure of OJSC Russian Helicopters

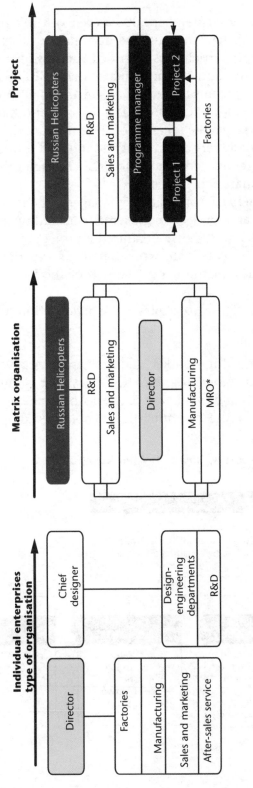

Individual enterprises type of organisation

- A clear, tried and true structure in which each company operates independently.
- The company board manages and co-ordinates all the elements.

Matrix organisation

- This implies double subordination: to the heads of departments or plants within the organisational structure and to the programme managers within projects.
- The main problems are contradictions in the criteria for performance evaluation and ensuring information symmetry.

MRO: Maintenance, repair and overhaul

Project

- This implies work according to the project principle:
  - The programme manager is responsible for the budget and the final result of the projects.
  - The factories delegate authorised representatives for different projects.
  - During the project implementation the direct management of the delegated staff shifts to the project manager.

743

and conducted in June to September 2008 a cycle of three project analysis sessions, which had the outward appearance of training activities. More than 50 participants attended the sessions: heads of the holding company and its individual enterprises, and also (this is most important) teams of developers for the main product programmes (Mi-28 NE, Mi-8M, Ka-62, Mi-38, Mi-34 and Ka-226). As a result, we received a detailed picture of the situation, the characteristics of leading designers and managers, and also introduced employees from remote divisions and enterprises to each other, so they could meet and share experience.

To convince experienced corporation managers of the advantages of programme and project management according to the KM scheme, on 14 March 2009 we organised a project workshop. The key speaker was M. Pogosyan, who shared his experience of developing programmes for the market launch of the SSJ (Sukhoi Superjet) aircraft.

The results of the first two stages of reorganisation of the corporation were:

◆ A model range meeting market requirements. Analysis of current programmes comprising the MCO (Master of Command Organisation) project and evaluation of the people realising these programmes enabled the creation of the holding company's

Figure 6.22 From the report by Roland Berger, March 2008

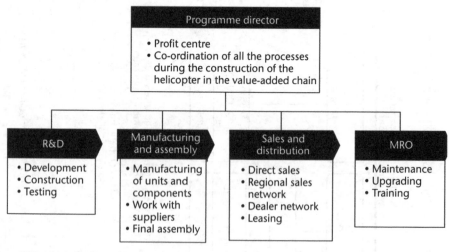

MRO: Maintenance, repair and overhaul

744

model range, and thus concentrated the resources of design and engineering departments on promising programmes and ensuring that they are financed.

◆ Transition to the programme and project method at enterprises of the holding company (the design engineering department and mass production factories).

◆ A talent pool group of people capable of holding key positions in corporation development projects. The MCO programme resulted in the corresponding personnel decisions.

On course for systemic reorganisation and an initial public offering

The first stage of the transformation is essentially complete. In 2010–11 schemes, projects and programmes of work of stage two were being discussed and realised.

On 19–20 February 2010 we held a PAS on the subject 'Realisation of the strategy of OJSC Russian Helicopters', and on 1–2 April 2010 a session was held in Kazan on the subject of 'Breakthrough projects of OJSC Russian Helicopters'. During these events a principal schedule map (Figure 6.23) was developed showing the main directions and bottlenecks in the corporation's activity.

The realisation of the programmes of OJSC Russian Helicopters and elimination of the bottlenecks in the corporation's activity require the creation of TCC. Each centre provides localisation of a special form of organisation (virtual, product-based, technology-based, in association with enterprises) and management systems. A competence centre has been created for non-ferrous casting (OJSC AAC Progress), and competence centres are currently being created for 'Rotor blade production' and 'Design and manufacture of gearboxes and transmissions'.

A typical example of developing the principles and schemes of management for programmes is a project analysis workshop on the subject of 'Restructuring of the management companies Russian Helicopters and United Engine Corporation in the course of corporation programme and project management' (10–12 December 2010). The workshop was conducted with the aim of training a talent pool for the corporations. During the event teams of developers on the Mi-171M and TCC Non-Ferrous Casting programmes, with the direct participation of heads of the management companies, prepared schemes for organising work on programmes for the Oboronprom

Figure 6.23 Main directions and bottlenecks in the corporation's activity

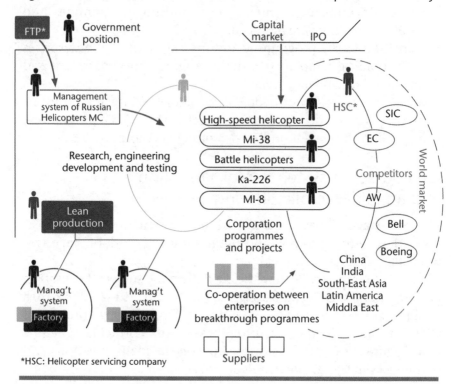

*HSC: Helicopter servicing company

project committee (see Figure 6.24). The aims and objectives of the PAS were:

- analysis of the situation, management of projects and programmes in terms of the projects of OJSC Russian Helicopters (Mi-171M) and OJSC UEC (TCC non-ferrous casting);
- development of terms of reference for organisation of the activity of management companies ensuring realisation of programmes and projects;
- testing of technological schemes for sharing experience and managing knowledge in the course of project analysis development on subjects that are relevant for the two holding companies;
- training of the corporation's talent pool in terms of non-standard managerial, financial and technical tasks.

The results of the workshop were:

- Changes to the management system of the Russian Helicopters

Figure 6.23 Cross-functional discussions of principles and schemes of programme management

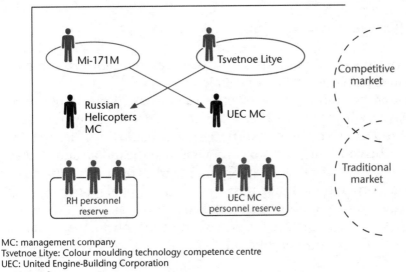

MC: management company
Tsvetnoe Litye: Colour moulding technology competence centre
UEC: United Engine-Building Corporation

holding company in relation to the management of key programmes (primarily the Mi-171M programme). This was brought to the level of the management company and the heads of these programmes were given the status of deputy directors-general of the holding company's management company.

◆ Designation of the primary principles of programme management and requirements applicable to their heads.

New organisational business schemes at the holding company require training of people with the required way of thinking.

The mission of the helicopter holding company, as it was envisaged in April 2011, is:

1 Gain a foothold in the world helicopter market as a recognised global market player (15 per cent market share by 2015).
2 Move from the sale of products to the sale of the product lifecycle.

Key components of the Russian helicopter industry are:

◆ systemic integration of the product lifecycle;
◆ research and development (R&D);

◆ load-bearing system (including the rotor blade);
◆ transmission;
◆ final assembly;
◆ after-sales service up to disposal.

A new organisational business scheme at the holding company requires a new generation of people.

We are entering a new round of development of the helicopter sector in Russia, which will grow because of the need to upgrade the existing fleet and launch new models. The need to re-equip the helicopter fleet of the Russian Army, and growing demand in the Indian and Chinese markets, will generate large government orders right up to 2020.

The corporation is preparing for an initial public offering (IPO) on the world's leading stock markets, and is actively examining proposals and scenarios for developing work on further systemic restructuring of the corporation.

Changing object patterns in managing the reorganisation of OJSC United Engine Corporation

The situation, the problem and the objectives

We shall identify the subsequent stages and, corresponding types of objects in the process of reorganising the corporation:

◆ corporate integration and anti-crisis measures;
◆ restructuring for the required model range and agreed production programmes;
◆ systemic reorganisation based on a divisional structure, management of the product life-cycle, management based on programmes and the creation of a TCC network.

The first stage is essentially completed. Currently, schemes, projects and programmes of work under the second and third stages are being discussed, with the aim of systemic reorganisation of the corporation.

Corporate integration and anti-crisis measures

United Engine Corporation OJSC is the leading Russian industrial group in the manufacture of engines for aviation, rocket launch vehicles, electricity generation and gas transmission. The corporation was created in fulfilment of Presidential Decree of the Russian Federation of 16 April 2008, no. 497, and Government Order of the Russian Federation of 4 October 2008, no. 1446-r. UEC OJSC was an integrator of the aviation engine-building sector in Russia, established in 2008 as a 100 per cent owned subsidiary company of OJSC UIC Oboronprom.

At the current time, the process of consolidating assets of the engine-building sector in Russia is essentially completed. As a result, a conglomerate of design and engineering departments, factories and other enterprises is under the management of UEC MC (the UEC management company). The corporation's management system is rapidly following a path taken by its competitors towards organising economically efficient activity, but naturally with its own special features.

On 6–8 February 2009 the objective of transforming the conglomerate into a modern global corporation was put to the top managers of the individual enterprises of UEC. A management system was created. The heads of leading enterprises and design and engineering departments headed eight working committees and determined areas of progress:

Figure 6.25 The UEC management system

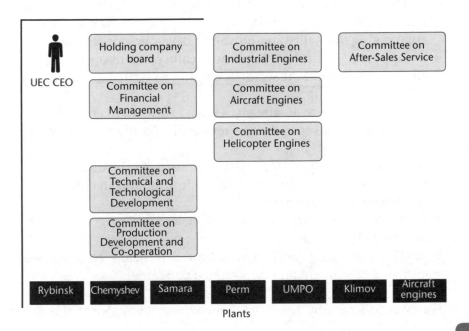

749

Figure 6.26 Where UEC is positioned among world manufacturers of gas-turbine engines

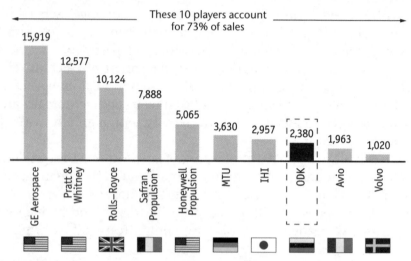

The civil and military aviation engines market is dominated by four major players

The top 10 main players in the world market, by turnover in 2009 (in US$ billions)

These 10 players account for 73% of sales

15,919	12,577	10,124	7,888	5,065	3,630	2,957	2,380	1,963	1,020
GE Aerospace	Pratt & Whitney	Rolls–Royce	Safran Propulsion *	Honeywell Propulsion	MTU	IHI	ODK	Avio	Volvo

* includes Snecma, Turbomeca, Snecma Propulsion Solid and Technospace Aero

◆ to integrate industry sector resources of the design and engineering departments and enterprises to reproduce a creative engineering mentality and move to a development regime;
◆ to support the transition to economically efficient operation of a strategically important sector according to principles of public–private partnership;
◆ to preserve (where it already exists) world market share and capture new market niches in regions favouring the use of our products;
◆ to organise co-operation with the world's leading companies within the framework of technical and technological re-equipment programmes;
◆ to support the search for, selection and training of modern managerial personnel;
◆ to eliminate excess facilities that have historically accumulated, outdated equipment and unoccupied personnel.

This was followed by the development and adoption of the first strategy option for UEC MC (February–April 2009). Three years passed. A lot had been done, but systemic shifts had not yet taken place. The management company is monitoring the situation, training the talent pool, and engaging in headhunting. Today (2009), the corporation has not yet managed to be among the five world leaders in gas turbine engine production.

At the end of 2010, the leadership of UEC MC set out an objective for the managing director, who had recently been selected by competition and appointed to the post, to review the strategy and provide a new structural model for the management company and corporation.

This work has been significantly arrested by a lack of adequate forms of thinking and methods of operation by the main participants in this work. As the experience of world leaders (Jack Welch, K. Krapek and others) shows, finding the solution to an objective begins with the systematic organisation of thinking and doing, first and foremost by the top managers, and then resolving the problems of the systematic organisation of work within the corporation by relying on the talent pool.

Three approaches to resolving the problem of system organisation

There are numerous approaches, scenarios and ideas of how this work can be accomplished. Specialists clash at the project committee and various operational meetings, where they state their positions. We shall consider three basic approaches.

The first approach involves reorganisation of UEC MC into a network of TCC. This is supported primarily by directors of factories. Each of them considers their factory as a nest of competencies represented throughout an entire autonomous closed production cycle. Naturally, the director wants to develop their factory by constructing new workshops and buying modern equipment in order to create what is known as a competence centre – including a foundry, rotor blade production, tool manufacturing and so on. Clearly, on this basis (a division of investments) there will be constant conflicts between the directors and the management company.

The second approach involves transition to a divisional structure, and has been voiced for a number of years now. This approach is built on the principle of expansion, with a transition from a dozen enterprises to five divisions, which should improve manageability and help dump ballast. However, here there are serious grounds for conflicts within the corporation. For example, each factory has its programme for the production of cash cows[4] and does not aspire to hand them over to the power division. Our factories, in essence, are autarchic economies, and if we diverted reliable revenue streams (which they had created over a number of years with much difficulty) from them it would place many of them in a difficult financial position.

The third approach is transition to managing the corporation on the basis of programmes and projects. It is not yet clear how to reorganise the system of management of the corporation according to this scheme, but it is clear that assigning programmes to factories, and correspondingly, appointing the factory director as head of the programme, will have a damaging effect on the programmes since funds will be redistributed in the interests of the factory. Our competitors have not worked in this way for a long time.

We have listed enough; what we are saying is clear. In order to understand this situation and find grounds to reach a decision, adequate means and methods are needed. In particular, to begin we must have a working understanding of TCCs in mechanical engineering (primarily, to differentiate between factories and TCCs), understand the principles of divisional structures (where and under which conditions they are effective), discuss problems of organising work within the framework of breakthrough and other UEC programmes, and understand what is known as the technology platform. Then on a foundation of mutual understanding, we can return to a discussion of approaches to building a new model system for management of UEC and a corresponding elucidation of corporate strategy.

Efforts at briefing to resolve identified problems which are in essence semiotic and epistemological – and we see them in great number – are fruitless, primarily because of a lack of time for deep discussion and reflective analysis of participants' forms of thinking, and second because of the absence of participants with the required technical means of intellectual work. The questions remain unanswered. This work could be handed over to overseas consultants. The corporation does do this. Our order for development of a strategy and road map to resolving problems was been fulfilled by Roland Berger. Experience shows that we can take certain

---

4   Translator's note: in Russian, GTI.

generalised schemes and methods of organising work from consultants and use them in our own work.

There is another way out – to use the work organisation schemes that the world of global co rporations calls the corporate university. This is by no means an invitation to listen to some wise professor – no one of that type has the means of resolving the tasks we face. It means rather that we ourselves must become cleverer. In other words, we need to take what we require from the entire world – bring together experienced managers, a talent pool, representatives from other advanced corporations – and, working according to standards of organising collective intellectual work, try to resolve the objectives.

Constructing a model of the corporation (the integral picture) for the future

How can we achieve the desired structure? How can we develop a map of competencies for gas turbine engine production? We can construct such a map for each of our products: shafts, rotor blades, disks and so on, but with such an approach we will unavoidably reach a special-isation matrix: one factory (or workshop) producing disks, another producing shafts, while the competencies remain in a cell within the matrix, and retrieving them from there is highly problematic.

The construction should be made on the basis of concepts – constructs or prototypes – of the structural schemes and models used by world leaders. Moreover, in doing so we must think systematically. In order to achieve a project structure in which the component parts will function as a new whole based on strategic principles and ideas, we need to do this work not in the office environment of 'Whoever knows something should speak up', but according to the princi-ples of participative planning (Russell Ackoff's concept), or in other words, with the participation of those who will be implementing the adopted decisions and creating the elaborated structures.

The construction should employ the experience of General Electric (1993–2003), Pratt & Whitney (1993–2000), Turbomeca and other world leaders, much of which has been accumulated over the course of more than 20 years when they started to move from conglomerates to systems. Today, we can take advantage of our cata-strophic time lag to avoid repeating the mistakes others have made, so as to move directly to the organisational and technological levels they have achieved.

753

Figure 6.27 A map of priority competencies and innovative programmes for UEC

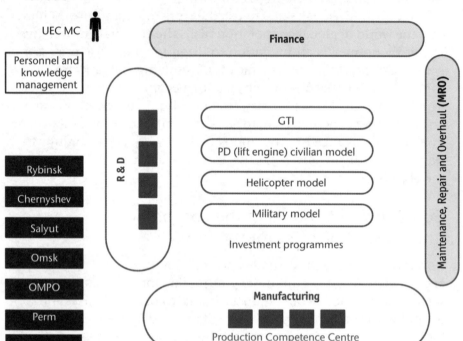

One approach is the transfer of experience: examining in detail specific successful decisions adopted at different times in relation to different aspects of activity of the leading companies (such as lean thinking, centres of technological excellence and an after-sales service system), and try to copy them. Consultants offer their services on many specific matters, but they will never provide us with an entire system since they cannot see it themselves, because it is in the domain of the head of the management system.

Another approach is design by prototypes: building a systemic (holistic) model of a high-tech mechanical engineering company, using the concepts of infrastructure and value chains that have developed among world leaders. Those parts of the system that we already have (design and engineering departments, factories) must be reorganised within the framework of functional support programmes. Those parts that we do not have, such as financial services infrastructure, a support system for technology consumers, a system of distributed engineering development, a network of centres of technical excellence, and a system of liaising with personnel and

Figure 6.28 Core competencies of gas-turbine engine building

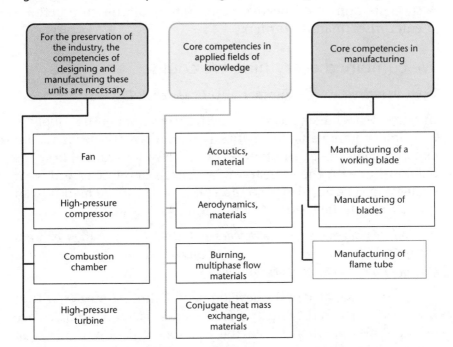

knowledge management, must be created from scratch on open territory within the framework of development programmes.

The advantage is the opportunity to preserve our priority competencies (primarily R&D) and achieve effective restructuring. The disadvantage is resistance from leaders of autarchic enterprises who think within the boundaries of schemes of industrial manufacturing. The problem is the lack of a body of managers to organise new directions of activity. The key strategic targets of UEC (based on project structures) are:

◆ providing strategic independence for the Russian aerospace sector;
◆ the process of organising a financial infrastructure for the creation of stable and long-term cash flow;
◆ conducting a range of work to retain traditional markets and capture new market niches (MRO system);
◆ organisation of design and engineering work (R&D), promotion of the corporation's breakthrough projects, and development of engineering expertise and a new generation of developers of gas turbine equipment;

- ◆ a move to working according to principles of lean thinking;
- ◆ specialisation and effective co-operation of the corporation's enterprises (manufacturing).

We combined everything we could

From an interview with Kommersant, *13 March 2012:*

In recent years Russia has started actively developing the supply of helicopter equipment and engines, both for domestic needs and for export. *Kommersant* correspondent Ivan Safronov learned how the relationship with the Ministry of Defence is developing and what strategy must be pursued to secure a place on the world market in an interview with the head of Oboronprom, Andrey Reus.

A trend has developed in the defence industry of co-operation between enterprises within the holding company, and this is what has happened in Oboronprom. Do you support this idea?

I directly participated in the development of those strategies, within the scope of which this integration was undertaken. This took place during 2004–07, when I held the position of deputy minister of energy and industry, and also had oversight of machine building and defence. Development and realisation of a strategy for such co-operation was our response to an instruction of the country's leadership to form industrial policy in principle. Until that time, the dominant notion was that the best industrial policy was an absent industrial policy.

Is this the right course for machine building?

I am certain that we have taken the right course. My work at Oboronprom over the last five years has convinced me that financial, organisational and political infrastructure have played a defining role in the regeneration of the engine building industry. For example, five recognised players operate in world-wide helicopter production: Sikorsky, AgustaWestland, Eurocopter, Bell and Boeing. Now, this club of sorts has been joined by Russian Helicopters. Indeed, at the beginning of the 2000s, Russian helicopter production did not exist as a world-wide business factor. True, there were a number of individual factories that were fighting for survival and producing extremely low volumes of equipment. The market share of Russian helicopters at this time was reckoned to be 3 per cent –

approximately 80 helicopters were being manufactured each year. People had stopped even noticing us.

The starting conditions of our competitive fight and those of our overseas partners were different from the outset. Challengers to Russian Helicopters were finally formed as holding companies in the post-war period, and by the time of the breakup of the USSR they were already serious world players. Incidentally, this also applies to engine building, where Unified Engine Corporation (UEC) will have to compete with grandees such as General Electric, Pratt & Whitney, Safran and Rolls-Royce. So if you want to reach the same level as the leaders, within a very tight time frame you must concentrate intellectual, manufacturing, financial and personnel potentials and create a structure that will be acceptable in this elite club. We have created such a company, which within eight years has taken third place by volumes of sales of helicopter equipment in monetary terms. Russian Helicopters now holds 14 per cent of the market in value terms and is recognised by leading world companies as a genuine player. It is my conviction that such a policy, at least in terms of helicopter production, has demonstrated its efficacy, and should continue its development.

Is competition possible in such an environment?

As our experience has shown, it is difficult, but possible. I believe that only in such a competitive environment is it possible to construct an effective structure capable of creating new products, carrying out modernisation, and developing a service system. It focuses enough intellectual potential and competencies that they enable the company to develop according to world trends.

Do you not agree that creating such holding companies reduces competition within the country and in this way arrests the pace of development?

That is certifiable stupidity! Only world-wide competition exists in modern machine building. All the leading players both in aircraft and helicopter production, and in engine construction, almost always represent one country or one company. It was suggested to us that we create a number of structures that would compete among themselves within our own country. And what would this have achieved? None of them would have been a player on the world market and they would have eventually been absorbed by world leaders. By virtue of just one consolidation, we immediately achieved a synergy of approximately 15 per cent efficiency increase.

Only by virtue of the consolidation?

In the helicopter sector we were, of course, very lucky: after all, we had very talented designers and excellent engineering schools. Thanks to their capabilities we were able to break into the market quite quickly. Now, we have the resources necessary to develop new products. We combined everything we could to achieve a specific goal. There simply was no other way of entering the world market. This was the only way, and we took advantage of it.

There is now controversy over whether industrial enterprises are oriented towards the domestic or foreign markets. What is the proportional split of Oboronprom products?

Currently this proportion is shifting towards domestic orders. A few years ago the ratio was 70 per cent to 30 per cent in favour of overseas deliveries. The ratio of export products to domestic products has levelled off and is now at parity.

An important role in internal market demand has been played by long-term contracts from the Ministry of Defence, with which we have signed large and strategically important contracts right through to 2020. The military order comprises up to 30 per cent of our product volumes. Moreover, we do not under any circumstances want to lose the external market: this is, after all, an indicator of the company's status. If people are buying your product on the world market, it means that the consumer trusts you. Overall, Russian Helicopters is growing year on year, and at quite a pace: in 2011 we produced 265 aircraft, whereas in 2012 we are planning to increase this number to up to 300 units.

Is that realistic?

It is a formidable leap, but the development strategy of Russian Helicopters defines both the necessary resources and the route to realising this goal. By 2015 the company should actually reach a level of 400 aircraft.

Some time back, the Ministry of Defence announced a tender for light heli-copters. The conditions of the tender show that the machine chosen will not be the Ansat or the Ka-226T, but some similar foreign aircraft. What is your opinion?

When a government department effectively brings into the country a direct competitor to a domestic manufacturer, it is unpleasant news. Russian Helicopters have the necessary technology in this sector: in particular the Ansat and the Ka-226T, which you have mentioned. We proposed them to the Ministry of Defence. We are continually monitoring the situation with their production and are ready to the greatest possible extent to assemble and after some time to deliver this technology not only to the Ministry of Defence, but also to the market. I would add that world practice of relationships between the military and industry shows the need to include R&D within defence procurement.

What is the current status of the Ka-226?

The Ka-226 is a working machine. It is being manufactured and sold. There is also the Ka-266T, mass production of which is to commence in the near future. We have attracted an investment loan from Vnesheconombank, focused design-engineering and manu-facturing resources on this project, and fitted the aircraft with the French Arrius engine. In this regard, an Indian tender for 197 light helicopters is extremely important to me. A direct competitor to the Ka-226T in this tender will actually be one of the aircraft from Eurocopter (AS-550 Fennec–Kommersant), which the Ministry of Defence is planning to buy.

In your opinion, what are Russia's chances in this tender?

Very high, I believe. This aircraft (Ka-266T–Kommersant) fully meets all the technical conditions of the tender.

Have you preserved plans for the creation of a joint venture with Eurocopter?

Various collaborative projects have been discussed with Eurocopter, but none of them have come to fruition because of differences in the development strategies of our companies. But we are focused on co-operating with the world leaders in those sectors that will make us stronger. By its nature, the creation of a joint venture is a complex issue. For example, we spent 2.5 years working on the creation of a joint venture with AgustaWestland, but only this year will we start production of the first aircraft, the AW 139, and then the AW 119. In comparison with our volumes, production of these aircraft is not so great, but the co-operation is very important to us. We are training personnel according to contemporary business standards, and we are learning to use a modern production arrangement and develop after-sales service. Of course, we will expand localisation of produc-tion but, taking into account that we are oriented on the world

759

market, for me localisation is what we are able to do for the whole world – we're competitive in this area.

Let's refresh our memories about what happened with State Defence Procurement in 2011. At that time you signed the first long-term large-scale contracts. How many Ka-52 aircraft did will the Ministry of Defence buy?

In the order of 140 units.

Did any problems arise when concluding the contracts?

Negotiations with clients are always quite rigorous, the issue is often centred around commercial viability. I believe that machine building is not the place to generate excessive profits. The target standard of commercial viability should be higher because this enables the sector to develop and invest in new products. But under the contract for Ka-52, I believe the conditions were acceptable. For us a long-term relationship was important, because a five- or seven-year contract affords the opportunity to conclude concurrent long-term contracts with suppliers and parts manufacturers. This is a completely different economic model because an understandable pricing formula is emerging. And if there is understanding of the price, then there is the possibility to maintain it.

What will you sign with the Ministry of Defence in 2012?

A series of documents is currently being prepared for signature, both in engine building and additionally in the area of helicopters. In engine building, as formerly in helicopter production, we are moving to long-term contracts. This year our collaborative work is proceeding much faster than in the past, and we are now discussing a supplementary agreement for the supply of the Mi-35. All together we are planning delivery to the military of in the order of 1,000 helicopters up to 2020.

Developmental work on the fifth generation of PAK FA jet fighter is currently actively under way. Who will be the chief developer of the engine for the fighter?

The UEC structure is built on a divisional principle: an energy division has already been created, and at the end of last year the helicopter engine and military aviation divisions were created. All management for creation of the PAK FA engine is concentrated in the latter. The base design engineering office for this project is the Lyulki research and development centre. But, in essence, this project became a collaborative one within the framework of UEC, and it includes factories in Ufa, Rybinsk and Moscow.

Have any challenges been made on the part of Sukhoi Civil Aircraft (SCA) regarding engines for the SSJ-100?

There is not an aircraft manufacturer that has not complained about the engine manufacturer. UEC is in close contact with SCA regarding the supply of engines. There have been problems, for example with time frames for certification of the SaM146, but these are problems that any new product encounters. A schedule has now been approved for delivery of engines literally for each aircraft.

However, for us the SaM146 programme is, to put it mildly, not effective in monetary terms. For this reason we will raise the issue of subsidisation of this project. That is standard world practice – when launching a new engine at a requisite production cost, some state support is needed. Of course the state is already providing such support, but we must remember that it takes a long time to launch a new aircraft on the market and to recover the costs.

How much time needs to pass to reach the break-even point?

From the initial order for the SaM146 that we have – approximately seven years.

And what is the current status of the NK-93 engine?

UEC is operating under current market conditions – where there is demand, there will be an offer. We have not encountered demand for the NK-93. UEC is not planning to use this engine on aircraft under development or in use. The NK-93 engine was developed as an alternative to the PS-90A base engine for the Il-96-T and Tu-330 aircraft, but the plans of aviation companies do not envisage production of these types of aircraft.

I can see the same case with the NK-93, where results obtained in the course of performing development work in relation to this engine will become the basis of technological development and can be used in the development of future medium- and high-thrust engines for passenger and cargo aviation, or military transportation. But I would stress that in this case UEC is acting in the role of parts supplier and will proceed on the basis of the needs of the aviation companies.

Is integration of enterprises in the engine-building sector appropriate?

The answer to this question is clear. We brought together the entire intellectual and manufacturing resource of the sector, and the enterprises ceased fighting among themselves and started working on the world markets. A single engineering centre is already operating at UEC and unifies the design-engineering personnel of all the holding company's enterprises. The corporation has already compiled a list of main projects that should ensure the competitiveness of domestic products on world markets over the coming 40–50 years. These projects comprise a family of PD-14 engines, an engine for the PAK FA and advanced high-speed helicopter, and a gas-turbine assembly for small-scale power generation. Industrial policy has just such an innovative characteristic, it is directed at supporting such projects, and to a great extent it is making this work easier for us. We are planning for UEC to secure a place among the five world leaders by 2020.

Is the government supporting your enterprises?

State support given to some enterprises has been, you could say, decisive: about a dozen factories were on the brink of bankruptcy, but the instruments of industrial policy – direct investments in authorised capital, subsidisation of interest rates, state credit guarantees and so on – enabled the situation to be stabilised and allowed us to start normal development, technical re-equipping, and upgrading of manufacturing. Almost all our breakthrough projects – the PD-14, advanced high-speed helicopter (AHH), and the engine for the PAK FA – are financed by funding from targeted state budget programmes. In particular, RUB 400 million were channelled into the AHH project, RUB 2.5 billion to the Mi-38 project, RUB 652 million to the Ka-62 project, and approximately RUB 14 billion to the PD-14 project.

What is the current status of the contract with the USA for supply of 21 Mi-17V5 helicopters to Afghanistan? How many aircraft have been delivered?

The contract is being fulfilled according to its conditions; nine units have already been delivered to the deployment site. This is a sign for the business community, a sort of certificate of recognition that our equipment is of a very high standard.

How have our helicopters proved themselves in India? Was the client happy?

When clients are unhappy, they do not buy. Sometimes you will hear the opinion that you can sell anything you want to India, China and other countries. That is not the case. Our Indian and Chinese partners, for example, are very thorough in their selection of equipment and in arms procurement. Overall I can say that India and China are our strategic partners. A contract for delivery to India of 80 Mi-17B5 helicopters, which has already been signed through the line of Rosoboronexport, is already being realised, we are participating in a tender for light helicopters with our Ka-226T, a joint venture is operating there for servicing helicopters, and so is a factory for the assembly of engines under licence.

Which countries, in your opinion, are the most important for Russia as partners, now and in the future?

India has been, and still is. Now, after something of a pause, we have started developing deliveries of helicopter equipment to China. Traditionally we have supplied a lot of engines; now, the volume of deliveries is continually growing. In 2012 we are planning to reach the objective of US$2 billion in deliveries to this country.

What equipment is being supplied?

The most recent deliveries have been a contract for 32 Mi-171E units, we are also supplying the Ka-32A11BC, which Indian customers are also buying from us.

What is the relationship like with Latin America?

This is a very important market for us, and we fought a long time for it. Deliveries of the Mi-35M are being made through the Rosoboronexport line. Of the civilian equipment, Russian Helicopters has started to supply the Mi 8/17 and Ka-32A11BC to that region. It plays into our hands that Brazil operates an open skies policy, including over large cities. This issue is currently being examined in China and India. The usage density of helicopter equipment will increase, which will significantly expand our opportunities.

And what about the markets of South-East Asia?

I would highlight Vietnam.

Is it possible to create a joint venture with China?

We are considering proposals from the Chinese regarding joint production of helicopters on the territory of China, and discussing collaborative design and production of heavy plant. In addition, the construction of a helicopter service centre in Qingdao Province is near completion. Regarding the creation of an international network of service centres, I would like to emphasise that we are moving to a new logic of running the business in our work with consumers. Demand for our equipment is determined not merely by the specifications of the product itself, but also by the availability of an accessible and effective working service system. Therefore, we are learning to build the business on the sale of the entire lifecycle of the product.

Have any negotiations taken place with Saudi Arabia?

Civilian equipment has not been supplied to this country. Rosoboronexport, as far as I am aware, has held negotiations with Saudi Arabia for the supply of military helicopters.

The government has now allocated support of approximately RUB 3 trillion to UEC. How much will you get?

Approximately RUB 10 billion will be allocated for projects and programmes of Oboronprom in 2012 through the route of the Federal Target Programme. In total, for the period from 2013–15, it is planned that approximately RUB 40 billion will be received.

Do you use loans?

We have to. The interest rate for rouble accounts in state banks comes to 7–10 per cent, and for foreign currency that is 8–12 per cent. Yet in the United States, the United Kingdom, Germany and France our competitors obtain long-term loans at rates of 2–4 per cent per annum. To be really competitive, we need financing conditions no worse than those of our competitors. When the price of money on the domestic and world financial markets differs, our machine building starts to lose in the competitive battle.

Will you change the structure of Oboronprom in the near future?

Fundamental changes were made at Russian Helicopters last year, and they were connected to preparation of the company for an IPO. Russian Helicopters moved over to IFRS [international financial reporting standards] and independent directors were brought onto the board of directors. And even in spite of the fact that the flotation did not take place, today Russian Helicopters is operating as a public, open company. The structural changes at UEC, as I have already mentioned, were connected to the shift to a divisional system of management. If we are talking about new types of business, then here I must mention the matter of unmanned aircraft, which we are developing using technologies from the Israeli company IAI. We see a future in this market.

What are the financial indicators of Oboronprom in 2011?

Oboronprom's revenue as a holding company structure comprised RUB 229 billion, with net profit of RUB 15 billion. Engine construction broke even for the first time in 2011.

What indicators are set out this year?

We say minimum growth of 15 per cent. We should be making products and providing services amounting to RUB 500 billion by 2015. That's what I promised Vladimir Putin during the MAKS-2011 exhibition.

What sort of relationship is there with the aerospace sector? Previously the head of Roscosmos, Vladimir Popovkin, announced that engine building is in crisis.

Work in the aerospace field remains one of the most stable areas of activity of UEC. Over the last two years Roscosmos has significantly increased orders at our Samara site. I believe that we are sufficiently focused to meet all the demands of Roscosmos.

Would you like to take control of other factories, for example, those manufacturing space rocket engines?

There is a certain logic in this, we have a team of anti-crisis managers, and ten years ago Oboronprom created a business incubator, which is forming out of isolated enterprises an effective business organisation capable of competing on world markets. The example of Russian Helicopters and UEC is confirmation of this. We are not banking on this work, but if we are instructed to manage these factories, we will cope.

Personnel reserve training

Work on the instruments: the concept of competence in mechanical engineering

A catastrophe of understanding

This metaphor was introduced 20 years ago by S. V. Popov (in *The Reforms are Going Through Russia*[5]) to define the phantoms, superstitions and other idols of consciousness that, with the systems of secondary and higher education, have essentially occupied the consciousness of the Soviet people. It is far from easy to throw off the yoke of this occupation, and for strong leaders it is almost impossible.

The following has been noted in the system of management of UEC over recent years in the course of numerous debates:

- the lack of working mutual understanding in resolving specified objectives (deficiency of working concepts);
- the lack of systemic vision of the corporation on the part of leading managers;
- the lack of methods of working with prototypes and their substitution with an attempt to transfer directly work experience to unprepared ground;
- the lack of means of productive collective thinking with the participation of competent (experienced) and knowledgeable (talent pool) people.

To make decisions on the reorganisation of UEC, in particular decisions on the creation of TCC, we need to understand clearly what this means and have an appropriate typology of working concepts.

Forms of thought and typology of working

What is a concept? In the European thinking tradition this is a form of thinking that enables us to construct an object of thought and make it an object of manipulation and transformation in the ideal reality of thought, and then to go out into the world and to organise work in the available (suitable) matter according to the new scheme

---

5   This was privately printed and is not available in English.

Figure 6.29 Words, concepts and the reality that they capture

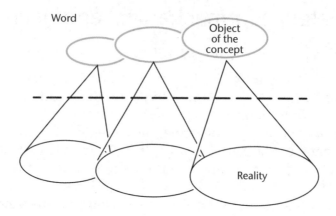

of the object. Initially, it is essential at least to discern the words, forms of thought and what we think with the use of these forms.

Let me digress slightly. What we should now consider is the desktop instrument of those who are engaged in intellectual work – management, design, engineering and analysis. The principles and rules of working with concepts have been discussed by many wise thinkers in the history of European thought. Let me mention a few works that can be considered a basis for literacy in this area.

According to Aristotle, every single thing is the unity of matter and form. Form is not something material, but it exists, for example, in the method of work of a craftsperson creating a copper sphere. The sphere is the unity of the substance (copper) and the form (spherical), which is given to the copper by the craftsperson. In the sphere that is actually in existence, the form comprises a whole with material or substance. A designer and constructor should understand all of this perfectly well, since they work in just this manner, with special concepts and structural elements.

A second important text is René Descartes's *Discourse on the Method*. Descartes made an attempt to collect and collate rules of intellectual construction so that not only philosophers could work with concepts and think constructively, but so could anyone who might need to do so.

A third key text is Karl Popper's 'Epistemology without the cognizing subject'.[6] How is science structured? The scientist has an

---

6   An article that can be found in Popper's *Collected Works*.

object of research, whereas the subject – the scientist – constructs knowledge about the laws of the object's existence. Popper, following Aristotle and Descartes, develops the understanding of the world of content (similar to Plato's world of ideas), which exists independently of reality – the objects of our research.

A fourth, transparent and understandable text is G. P. Shchedrovitsky's *On the Structure of Attributive Knowledge*, published in 1957, which distinguishes definitions, concepts and other subtle instruments of intellectual work.

Unfortunately, at one time a 'catastrophe of understanding' occurred in our country, so the majority of Russians think in so-called 'modified forms' (a concept introduced by G. W. F. Hegel) as a result of school and higher education training. In other words, they 'attribute' the form of thought to the material of the object. For example, they say 'competent person', although competence is a general concept and is not attributable to an individual. There are no competent people – this is a phantom created in pure thought (as they now say, 'virtual reality'), but people can possess competencies.

So to complete targeted collective intellectual developmental work we must differentiate the words, the form of thought or concepts, and the objects of contemplation that capture the reality of our activity and help us create the (virtual) constructs of what reality should be.

What is reality? Reality is what we hit against and cannot pass through, because it is material.

What are words? They are polysemantic and can imply a multitude of concepts and objects of thought. A well-known example is the word 'board'. What is a board? Is it a flat, wide piece of wood? Or a group of people making decisions? Or the food provided when you stay somewhere? It is a word that we use to mean many concepts, and there is a reality which we capture in these concepts (in German the word for 'concept' is *Begriff*).

One further example – a man is sitting in front of me and I am looking at him. Then I turn away and do not look, but I remember what he looks like. I learned to draw and I can even draw his portrait. So how and where does he exist – in reality or in my perception (my memory) or in the portrait I have drawn? After all, when I draw the portrait I will probably exaggerate his features or even grotesquely distort him. This is what working in concepts enables: we can imagine reality in the way we want to see it, and not as it truly is in substance (another conceptual object in German is *Vorstellung*).

The objectives of researching materials and resistances to them in our constructs are set by scientists, whereas designers create constructs of what they want to obtain. They should not depict how it is in reality, but rather express what does not yet exist, and search for suitable material for its fabrication.

There is one further important distinction: the rule for using individual concepts and general concepts. In the English language this is expressed by the articles 'the' and 'a'. *The* tree and *a* tree – a specific tree and any tree in general. The concept of competence is general, and requires appropriate use. Notably, in our country a number of objects are used in reference to the concept of competence. For example, people say 'competent authorities'. Here we are discussing competencies in mechanical engineering, where representatives of the competent authority – the Ministry of Industry and Trade – will decide whether we are correct in our thinking or not. Another example is from the education field. In Europe, for 20 years specialists have been attempting to move from the concept of the transfer of knowledge to that of the mastery of competencies. (And in our country a heated discussion has now started regarding the new FSES – the Federal State Educational Standard – which supposes a shift from the concept of the transfer to pupils of knowledge, skills and abilities (KSA), to that of their acquiring competencies). What does this mean? Hegel wrote, 'The student is like a gun that takes a long time to charge so that it can fire at the exam and be left empty.' That is why knowledge is needed: we should be teaching students a *modus operandi* and the readiness to apply it.

Competence is, in essence, the instruction for a method of activity that must be mastered. A person can work as a lathe turner, driver, scuba diver, parachutist or climber, but the competence exists separately from the person. They can master it and receive a certificate (and then confirm it). People stand separately from the competency. Some people have become excellent learners, yet have mastered nothing. Here is an example from the area of production. Twenty years ago the Americans and the French moved from the organisational form of manufacturing as the factory to that of the competence centre (centre of technological excellence). We also want to make this transition in order to work as effectively as they do, and therefore we must understand exactly what competence in mechanical engineering is.

The concept of competence in mechanical engineering

The competence centre (CC; technology competence centre – TCC) substitutes for the traditional enterprise (where all competencies are gathered under a single factory roof) and the communication infrastructure between the enterprise and suppliers (a network of mines, factories, design-engineering offices and scientific research institutes created by directives from the State Planning Committee and industry sector ministries of the USSR). The CC is a modern organisational form of commercial, manufacturing and design-engineering activity. Technology-driven manufacturing is aimed at the capture and long-term retention of customers. It 'compels demand', as it were, and so it should 'hook the consumer'. It uses a programme-and-project approach for the development of traditional factories (which must specialise and become technologically flexible modules, or disappear), and investment programmes (with the expectation of a return on funds invested in a calculated long-term outlook) into a targeted orientation on the product. This product is no longer a manufactured item, but a service that the item provides to the consumer (for example, the 'flight hours' of an aviation engine). For such a product-oriented investment programme it makes no difference who manufactured the product. It is important that the product works for the specified time and generates the specified money. To support the operation of such programmes, various competency centres arise (engineering, technological, financial), which can be rolled out in economically, geographically or socio-politically convenient regions of the world.

Organisational forms in manufacturing

Using the distinctions stated above, we can return to the concept of competence in mechanical engineering. In order to build a typology and map of competencies in gas-turbine engine building, we must reconstitute the historical series of types of manufacturing organisational forms. We will start with pre-forms. These are described in detail in Karl Marx's *Capital*. The simplest form is the workshop, where the master craftsperson fabricated certain items, keeping the method secret. In manufacturing production the process of fabrication was taken from the master craftsperson and divided into separate operations not requiring any particular craftsmanship or operational performance.

The industrial enterprise

An important form of organisation for us is the industrial enterprise, where the process is divided into operations performed by machines and assembled on a production line, which allows for productivity to be increased many times over. Theorists assert that this form of organisation is inherent to the market economy in its classical mode. Numerous enterprises producing products of the same type compete against each other for consumers on the open market. Only the strongest survive. This is an ideal model, which is not encountered in the world. Competition has always been dishonest. The strongest have striven to gain a monopoly or to conclude cartel agreements in order to impose their will on consumers. The state has constructed customs concessions and other preferences for 'its own' enterprises.

The Russian industrial enterprise consists of a design-engineering department, test divisions and mass-production factories, all working in seamless unity. Production rests on transformation of the source material into a product. Everything else – the system of management of production, sale and servicing manufactured items, fabricating plant and equipment for the production

Figure 6.30 On the concept of the 'industrial enterprise'

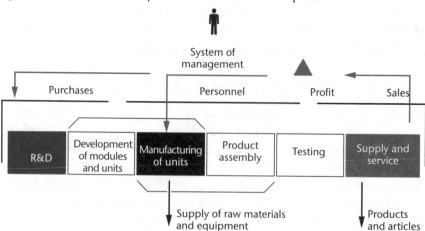

process – lies in the external sphere and does not have any direct relationship with the organisation of production. This type of organisation was characteristic of the industrial period (in Europe and the United States in the eighteenth and nineteenth centuries).

The organiser of such production should ensure that the manufacturing process (or as people now say, the process of value creation) runs smoothly so as to obtain the greatest quantity of products that meet specific standards (in their technical and tactile characteristics). These standards are defined in contracts with the client and by licensing authorities.

Industry was organised in the USSR in the form of sectors for identical types of products. The majority of sectors in the domestic economy of the USSR were organised as a project based on the concept of a single factory, and the principles of specialisation and co-operation were followed.

All of the competencies necessary for the manufacture of a product existed within such an organisation (including, obviously, supplementary ones specific to the type of product, such as making bricks, acetylene, rubber, screws and so on). This corresponds to a type of 'autarchic economic unit'. The real boss is the director. Today's directors of enterprises think according to the very same scheme, so for them the phrase 'technology competence centre' implies the creation of yet another new workshop, preferably at their own factory (with an accompanying request for financial support), without understanding or taking into account the scope of the corporation's activity as a whole or its leading competitors. Objectives are resolved for the coming five to ten years, but there is a lack of vision of strategic developmental horizons corresponding to the life-cycle of gas-turbine engines (20–40 years).

Technology-driven production

The second important form of organisation is technology-driven production. The technology-driven process supports growth in the productivity of enterprises and their aspiration to increase their share of the market. In other words, it does not involve a straightforward division of labour between those performing the work, but a substitution of people with machines, whose productivity is ten times greater than that of people. Karl Marx wrote, 'Complex technology-driven production cannot wait for favour from the consumer. Supply compels demand.' Today, this is the work of marketing analysts, advertising agents, after-sales service systems and so on, yet clearly all of this was already in existence 150 years ago.

Here we must remember Frederick Winslow Taylor, the father of the scientific organisation of labour. He was the one who analysed how workman Schmidt carried iron ingots at a factory of the Bethlehem Steel Company, rationalised his activity and then directed all of Schmidt's movements and pattern of rest. Schmidt's productivity carrying the iron increased threefold, and Taylor increased his wages for this by 15 per cent. Thus, normative descriptions of activity emerged that could be separated from the described activity and transferred in space and time to another type of activity at another enterprise. Lenin wrote that we need to make use of Taylor's developmental work (for what was then called 'sweatshop practice') to increase labour productivity in industry.

In our country this work was taken up by Alexei Kapitonovich Gastev, the great methodologist and organiser. He created the Central Institute of Labour (CIL). Gastev was executed in 1938, and the CIT was transformed into Orgaviaprom (and is now called NIAT, the National Institute of Aviation Technologies). This institute designed Russian aviation factories, whereas we bought the design of automobile and tractor factories from the Americans.

Unfortunately, the work on describing and standardising industrial processes in our country was stopped. We could spend a long time analysing the reasons for this. Probably the people who were engaged in methodological reflection became too clever. Apart from that, the proletarian ideology in the country (which has not yet disappeared) claimed that everything in existence was created by the hands of workers and peasants, so the idea that someone needed to think about how to create and organise that creative work was deemed to be less important. And now, when our great designers have passed on, we are forced to buy any know-how that we require from overseas. In almost every sector there is a lack of cohesion of the specialists who provide our competitive advantages.

The technological type of organisation of social production provides the opportunity to recreate the manufacturing process in another location and under different conditions on the basis of its description (through know-how). The complexity and specific nature of such manufacturing requires the emergence of a special community of professionals – methodologists who also need to be paid (one of the first of them was Frederick Winslow Taylor). This description, particularly for complex manufacturing processes (which in addition to manufacturing operations, involve requirements for raw materials, machine tools and plant) should include qualification requirements for workplaces (it might be that the required specialists are not available, in which case the technology transfer should incorporate a system of personnel training), the structure of production organisation and management, and much more. The criterion for evaluating production, in addition to the quantity of products (and profitability), was the criterion for its adaptability to manufacturing or being reproduced in a new location and with different people.

Large-scale technology-driven production changes the requirements for products. Let me say again, 'It cannot wait for favour from the market.' The organisation of sales, repairs and servicing products is incorporated in technological chains, and the technological description (and indeed the very design of the product) must also include methods of operation and convenient servicing of the manufactured product. The concept of product quality becomes most important. This not only includes the engineering specifications of the product (for example, power or speed), but also ease of service and repair, design, and the possibility of using the product as a symbol of social status. The requirements for the quality of products have started to change the manufacturing process: the most important criterion for evaluating production is not the quantity of manufactured product, but rather its quality. The ecological movement that developed in the 1970s and the energy crisis led to end-of life disposal requirements being applied to products, and stringent low-waste requirements to production.

Manufacturing in the USSR was generally organised along industrial lines, but looking to the West, we started to refer to machine tools arranged in a chain (ordinary production) as technology, and to quality as technical standards of the product (GOST compliance[7]). The substitution of stereotypes of industrial organisation with the word 'technology' resulted in an enormous number of mistakes when managers bought machine tools and equipment, yet forgot to buy systems to manage the technological process (it did not occur to anyone to buy the qualification).

---

7   Editor's note: GOST is a Russian certification system.

AvtoVAZ is the best example. The Italians described the manufacturing technology for the Fiat 124, which at the beginning of the 1970s was considered the best mass-produced car model in Europe, and 'wrote off' the obsolete machine tool stock to the USSR, thus freeing their project design and technology competencies for the creation of a new model range, and at the same time capturing a huge market. We struggled on with their old equipment, whereas they, now in possession of instruments to drive technology, continued to 'write off' their technologies to us and retain a body of engineers engaged in new developments.

Technological organisation of the manufacturing process provides:

◆ stable functioning of the main production process (reliable cash flow from the service and supply of spare parts);
◆ reproduction of technology in any location according to a description (know-how);
◆ production of products of a high quality (in the opinion of the consumer!);
◆ quick changeover to a different kind of product and replacement of obsolete equipment, easy recycling of products.

Figure 6.31 On the concept of technology-driven production

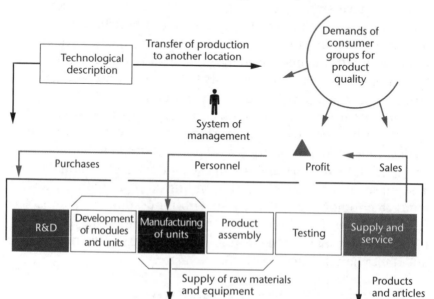

Implementation of this set of conditions enables us to define the concept of competence in mechanical engineering. It is present only in forms of modern technology-driven production, and implies the willingness of specialists to consider and combine the competitive advantages of a specific type of activity and thinking, and produce a description of the activity to that end, distinguishing it from the source material (the medium) and constructing on this basis a set of machinery and technical facilities that can replace the existing form of activity and simultaneously exceed its productivity. Those who are able to perform this work become cleverer and stronger and gain the opportunity to develop and move forward faster.

The CC is the focus point, for reproduction and dissemination of a given community of specialists, and likewise a cluster of opportunities for organising a specialist field and co-operation on the basis of transferring technologies in their entirety or fragments of them to locations with favourable economic, social and geographical conditions for a fundamental reduction in production costs.

The infrastructure form of organising manufacturing

Since the middle of the twentieth century, the infrastructural type of manufacturing organisation has developed. It takes advantage of networks that supply any manufacturing processes and technologies. Transport, power supply, water supply and utilities are arranged according to the principle of functional networks. With the development of communication systems and the Internet, this form of organisation started to proliferate at great speed.

This signified a new step in organising production: by separating specific production processes and their common requirements, it is possible to change production like changing a pair of socks or even to organise sales without manufacturing. To do this we must introduce a system of norms, standards and typology of products (using the instruments of certification to remove competitors from the market).

A well-known example is one of the world's largest computer manufacturers, Dell Computers. Michael Dell created and developed just two competencies – organisation of the sale of custom-configured computers (cash flow) and development of types and options of computers, anticipating and shaping consumer demand (research and development).

Dell founded his company in 1984 in Austin, Texas, and his thinking was based on the unprecedented idea of selling computer systems directly to each consumer. He created effective computing solutions that met the needs of consumers. Currently, more than 41,000 employees of service centres in approximately 90 countries, as well as 60 technical support centres and seven global operating centres, assist clients in achieving business goals using Dell computer technologies.

In the modern world, developed countries do not have manufacturing problems: they retain the science, and production development, marketing, sales and servicing, and likewise personnel training (reproducing qualifications and competencies) and specific production facilities (plants and factories) can be moved anywhere, transferred and sold to anyone. The technological organisation of manufacturing allows them to do this, and there are plenty of places in the world with cheap labour for the transfer of 'dirty' work and plants. In this way the Asian and other 'tigers' are emerging.

At the same time, production is not disappearing from the United States and Europe: the world infrastructure of transport, trade and finance provides connections between production and all consumers, irrespective of where they might be. The type of world domination has changed: neither the manufacturer of the end product nor even the creator of the technology holds everything, but rather the owner of world infrastructure of sales and after-sales servicing does.

The system category: principles of organisation

The main problem of systemic organisation of work in a corporation is a lack of adequate forms of thought and action by principal participants. Special training is needed to master thinking operations in the system category. The main operations are presented in Figure 6.32. The concept of infrastructure lies outside of the scope of systems analysis. Infrastructure is a materialised possibility for the existence of a number of heterogeneous systems of different quality in a single material. The problem of co-existence of a number of systems that cannot be represented as subsystems of a single system was discussed by V. A. Lefebvre (with the concept of systems drawn on systems) and G. P. Shchedrovitsky (in the category of a polysystem).

Principles of infrastructure organisation enable us to resolve

Figure 6.32 Operations of thought in the system category

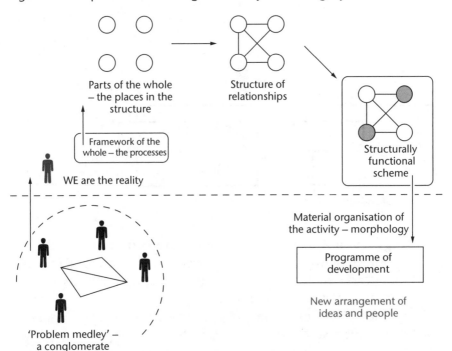

Parts of the whole
– the places in the
structure

Structure of
relationships

Framework of the
whole – the processes

WE are the reality

Structurally
functional
scheme

Material organisation of
the activity – morphology

Programme of
development

New arrangement of
ideas and people

'Problem medley' –
a conglomerate

conflicts between the processes of function and development. Redundant infrastructure networks simultaneously ensure the functioning of existing systems and create conditions for the development of others. Therefore, the formation of new regions of development starts with the creation of infrastructure networks that are redundant (in relation to actual needs).

Strategic horizons

One further problem is the conflict and compromise between two approaches to development and realisation of UEC strategy, and resolving current tactical tasks (moving back-to-front) and the designed construction of the system arrangement from strategic planning perspectives.

Approach 1 is the movement from opportunities and objectives of preserving parts of the conglomerate to building an integrated system of work within the framework of the corporation. The advantage of this is that it maintains current functioning and identifies growth points. The disadvantage of this is that it means

Figure 6.33 Two approaches to strategy

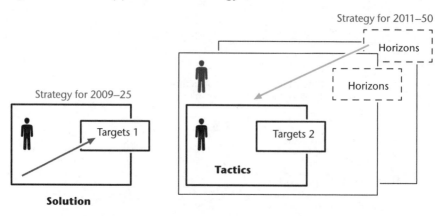

working according to a scheme of 'catch up and overtake', and back-to-front movement. The problem has become obvious to all over the past four years – each part is attempting to use the system as a whole in the interest of self-preservation.

Approach 2 is the movement from a detailed design of the systemic picture (in our case, of UEC) as a whole to a distant perspective over 40 years (up to 2050). (For nuclear engineers this period is 50 years, and for electricity generation engineers it is 30 years.)

Design according to prototypes versus the transfer of experience

To avoid being 'hooked' on overseas achievements, we must master the means of planning according to prototypes. Let me highlight a number of the most obvious prototypes of the structural elements for project development. Figure 6.34 is an example of how Roland Berger consultants depict the distributed structure of value creation. In the figure, constructed according to the basic points in the product value creation chain (segmentation can be further defined), we can isolate the prototype structure of the basic competency centres of a global mechanical engineering corporation:

◆ development of a concept of the technical device and the creation of demand for it;
◆ work of engineering thought (design of a new device – a machine, design study and supporting research and testing of materials and assemblies) – in short, R&D;

Figure 6.34 Distributed structure (for outsourcing) of the value creation process

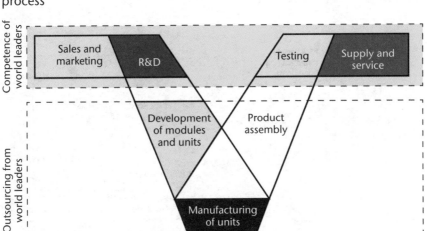

- ◆ technological preparation of production (development of modules and assemblies);
- ◆ mass production of various types of components and assembly units (CAU), for example, rotor blades, shafts, disks for engine manufacturing;
- ◆ final assembly of the machine according to the options of the specific customer;
- ◆ performance testing;
- ◆ delivery and after-sales service – MRO.

World leaders have their own financial infrastructure performing the function of budget management (cost reduction), sales management (leasing, credit), raising funds from the state budget (in Russia's case, Federal Target Programmes) and the stock market: primary (IPO) and secondary markets.

Each type of centre requires a special location, form of organisation (virtual, product-based, technology-based, linked to enterprises and so on), and a management system.

Two types of problem-solving programme

Programmes to support operating and development programmes should be drawn up relatively independently. Otherwise, under our conditions, as many years of experience have shown, operations inevitably consume and destroy resources allocated for

Figure 6.35 Distribution of competencies across countries of the world (the example of Pratt & Whitney)

development. Only the second approach allows us to start restructuring, not with what we already have, but with what we need to create. ('You need to search not where there is light, but where you lost something.')

Nevertheless, the results secured by world leaders are not based on design, technological or manufacturing achievements, but are primarily achieved as a consequence of the application of the following:

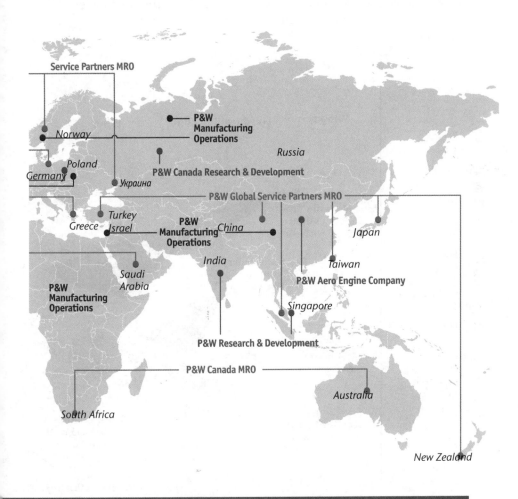

- adequate management technologies;
- diligent study, collation and adoption of all effective discoveries by competitors (the Japanese, Europeans, Russians, and Chinese);
- traditionally high standards of manufacturing and motivation of personnel to work. ('He who does not work three shifts a day, seven days a week, shall not eat').

Figure 6.36 Distribution of manufacturers of parts of the Dreamliner based on technological descriptions, standards and norms by managers of Boeing

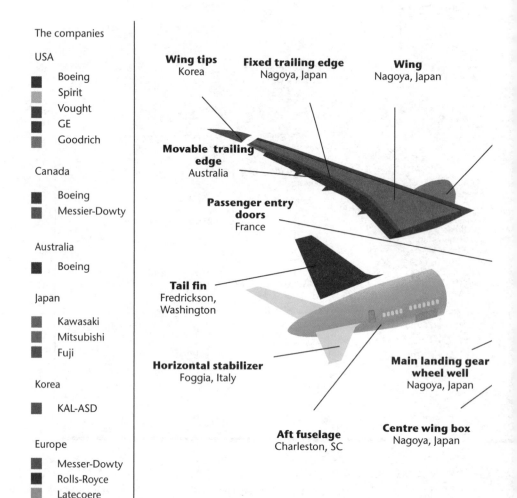

The companies

USA
- Boeing
- Spirit
- Vought
- GE
- Goodrich

Canada
- Boeing
- Messier-Dowty

Australia
- Boeing

Japan
- Kawasaki
- Mitsubishi
- Fuji

Korea
- KAL-ASD

Europe
- Messer-Dowty
- Rolls-Royce
- Latecoere
- Alenia
- Saab

Wing tips
Korea

Fixed trailing edge
Nagoya, Japan

Wing
Nagoya, Japan

Movable trailing edge
Australia

Passenger entry doors
France

Tail fin
Fredrickson, Washington

Horizontal stabilizer
Foggia, Italy

Main landing gear wheel well
Nagoya, Japan

Aft fuselage
Charleston, SC

Centre wing box
Nagoya, Japan

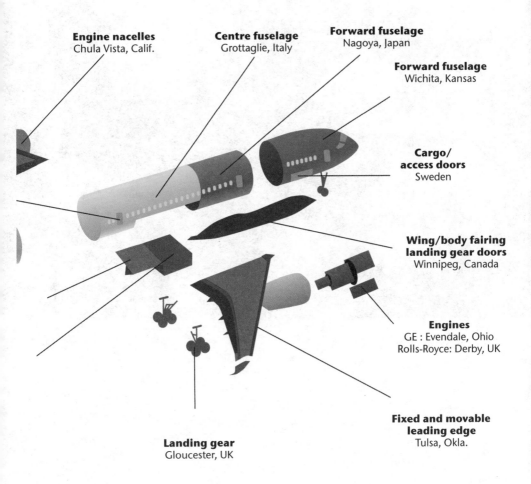

Engine nacelles
Chula Vista, Calif.

Centre fuselage
Grottaglie, Italy

Forward fuselage
Nagoya, Japan

Forward fuselage
Wichita, Kansas

**Cargo/
access doors**
Sweden

**Wing/body fairing
landing gear doors**
Winnipeg, Canada

Engines
GE : Evendale, Ohio
Rolls-Royce: Derby, UK

**Fixed and movable
leading edge**
Tulsa, Okla.

Landing gear
Gloucester, UK

During the project analytical session

Demonstration and mastery of knowledge management instruments: principles of personnel policy

Corporate personal development games

Everything set out above is impossible to achieve without the proper selection, training and placement of managers and overseers – people who can be trusted, people with a keen understanding and an ability for constructive thinking, and people who are willing and able to act in their assigned function, in a co-ordinated and accepted system of work.

First, no Russian corporation would start to say publicly on the strength of its activity that it is investing in people and is engaged in the development of its people. You can promote the creation of products, upgrade production and innovation, but personal development is not a corporation's core activity. Nevertheless, in any corporation the issue of people (personnel) is one of the priorities both for ongoing operations, and for development.

Second, historically the situation has come about that corporations and business structures believe that the education system is responsible for personal development, so if development of people is needed to resolve some problem, then they need to be immersed in the education system for a period of time, and then return to normal work, having been developed.

Third, to discuss the issue, a fundamental question must be answered: do people need to be developed at all? Who faces an issue of this type, and why?

What is the talent pool? We can highlight a number of currently employed understandings of this concept. The most widespread and commonly accepted understanding of the talent pool is that it is a reserve to fill positions in an organisation that is functioning normally. There are defined standards for different positions and posts, which determine the opportunity for progression to the next, higher position in the hierarchy. Games and game situations are not needed for the formation and development of a talent pool, because they interfere with normal work, during which the person becomes familiar with their workplace and function.

There is another situation connected with new positions and functions. Requirements applied to positions and the people

Figure 6.37 Structure of the system of working with personnel at OJSC UEC Oboronprom

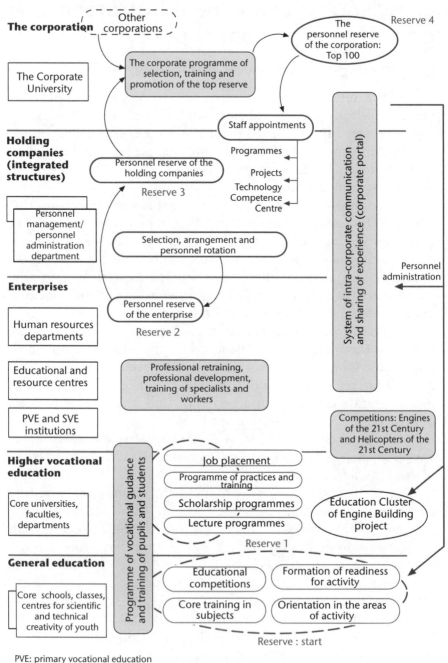

PVE: primary vocational education
SVE: primary vocational education

occupying them are formed and changed accordingly in the process of their creation. A game is unnecessary in this situation because work in the new position, and in the new structure of functions and positions, is in a certain sense of the word a game. A person occupying a newly created position can, on the strength of their understanding and competencies, do everything they deem necessary, reconciling their role with that of people in other, already functioning positions. They can 'play' in a relatively confined space, building contacts and relationships with other positions, and start to interact and reorganise the activity.

Then there is a third situation, which is used when working with the talent pool at Oboronprom. We have used examples from UEC, which at the current time represents a group of functioning enterprises that have not yet formed a single entity. At the same time, the aim of this structure is to become one of the five world leaders in its activity sector within a short period of time. Consequently, the systemic integration of all areas of activity needs to be completed, and in fact a corporation needs to be formed. In order to create a new organisation with defined and sufficiently ambitious goals, the existing organisation of activity needs to be replaced and a new one formed. Essentially, a new system of positions and functions needs to be created that will also establish the new corporation. When changing the corporation, the people need to change accordingly. It is not yet clear which positions and posts they will need to fill; however, if the forms of thought and modes of action of these people do not change, then what is currently called a corporation will also not change. This is the third type of talent pool – a personnel reserve for the future systemic integration and formation of a world-class corporation.

Currently, the corporation is a virtual organisation with a 'human dimension': that is, a circle of people who are included in discussions on the prospects, strategy, mission and development programmes of the corporation. This situation requires a game that also actually forms the corporation into a society of people comprising a common semantic and conceptual field that defines the future of the corporation.

The first and second types of talent pool are active in the corporation. A system of filling positions is operating, and all managerial posts of each enterprise have a succession candidate who is ready to take over the post at some point. When forming new areas of activity (for example, the corporation's production system based on lean manufacturing), a competitive assessment of candidates is conducted and a new system of posts, functions and work is formed.

Employees who are needed by the corporation can be:

◆ located on the labour market – both the domestic and international markets (or enticed away from leading companies possessing advanced technologies);
◆ developed within existing training systems (for example, at training courses using special methods and programmes);
◆ developed within the corporation using a specially constructed corporate system for the training and development of personnel.

The programme for forming three types of talent pool is a permanently operating corporate programme. However, the game form is only applied for the third type of talent pool as the main work instrument for people. At the same time, the principal position is that the education system cannot provide a solution to the task of developing people in the process of developing the corporation, specifically because their development should be integrated with, and not isolated from, the development of the corporation. When we take people off a job and place them in the education system, we must clearly understand the possibilities and limitations. The possibilities include training people for a standard position, mastering technology-driven skills, orientation in the structure of the area of activity, and so on (the list could be expanded and clarified). Limitations of the education system should include the claim to possession of knowledge, and likewise a monopoly on the technology of transferring this knowledge. In our corporation, the process of KM has been defined as the principal production process in contrast to the monopolism of the education system.

What do we do and how do people change in corporate games?

The first step is Selection no. 0, which is the selection of bearers of certain knowledge and their inclusion in the game. All people, by virtue of the fact that they have been employed in various jobs, are bearers of specific knowledge, competencies and qualifications. People who are potentially able to present their experience and knowledge in an abstract form should be selected for the game. At the same time, the game must include people who possess a different type of experience in the same field (for example, representatives of other corporations), and who speak a different cultural or professional language. Newcomers without experience in this field are also very important in the game. The game can commence with such an opening opposition.

Further, a space must be specially arranged where available knowledge can be presented and set out. This is Selection no. 1 according to the criterion of people's willingness to be engaged in further work, to participate in communication and reach understanding. At this stage, some people always stand out as being better than others at explaining what they can do.

At the next stage it is essential that people are included in the game situation. This means, in fact, inclusion in actual projects or programmes that are currently being developed and launched in the corporation. At this point the following limitation arises: how can participants use their knowledge in other work and transfer this knowledge to another situation, apply it to a different job? At each stage of the game the circle of people prepared to move further narrows. Generally, stratification occurs – separation of those who have some plans or aspirations from those who believe that they have already achieved everything.

At the next stage, it is necessary to move from fundamental organisation of work to a plan for the organisation of practical activity, and then to translate the plan into the organisation of work in daily activity. Here, the circle of participants in this type of work again narrows, because not everyone is prepared to realise in practice what has been discussed as an ideal construct. At this time a selection of developmental work should be made, and only what has been adopted by the management team for implementation should be put into practice. One of the most problematic issues in the game form of organising activity is how the rules and standards that were developed in the game should be implemented in order to change the activity that is already established.

Finally, the concluding step is when people, having worked in a different way and changed established standards and rules, are now able to explain it to others. If this does not take place, then the unique experience remains at the level of the individual people who were able to do something differently, and will not become the norm for the corporation. This game form has been practised at Oboronprom for three and a half years.

Let me give the following example of the game form of development of people at the corporation: 'Competition for filling the position of managing director of the United Engine Corporation management company'. In order to search for candidates for the position, an open competition was announced and a shortlist of candidates was drawn up. As an initial task, the candidates had to prepare a corporate strategy realisation programme, which is a typical part of the recruitment process in Russia.

The special feature of this game situation was to stimulate a situation of adoption of the programme by those working in the corporation management system and to organise their participation in the final development of the programme. To this end, the following groups were created in the game, representing different positions:

◆ current managers – the directors of enterprises within the corporation;
◆ future managers – the talent pool;
◆ representatives of other management systems – the heads of ministries and government departments with whom the head of the management company has to interact;
◆ experts – the top managers of other corporations.

Collaborative work situations and candidates' communication with each of these groups were organised in the game scenario. Candidates had to demonstrate their willingness to use the experience and knowledge of these groups of people in their programme, and build a relationship with the existing management system at different levels. In essence, the main criterion for evaluating the candidates was their ability to change within the special game situation, which imitated ('in vitro') the operation of the corporation management system, and to demonstrate their willingness to interact with all levels and positions in the management system.

In terms of the competition result (selection of a winner) the game had only just begun, since the selected candidate had to integrate the corporate strategy realisation programme that was constructed during the competition into current corporate activity.

The word 'game' is not generally used in the corporation; it is substituted by other more 'appropriate' words (see the first thesis), such as 'learning', 'workshop', 'session', and so on, although in the future it is quite likely that games will become just as much an integral part of the norms of corporate management as project management according to the gate model, lean manufacturing, and other terms which are already generally accepted current management practice. Games just need to be used exactly as intended – in problematic situations that do not have traditional solutions. Otherwise, the games could have an adverse effect on the functioning of the company.

I shall return to the answer to the original question: is it necessary, and why, to develop people (in particular, people in the corporation)? We can identify different approaches and perspectives on this question.

First, only children can be developed, and that has to be with parental consent, concluding a kind of contract for development with them.

Second, internal corporate standards can be changed and developed by changing the existing system. The purpose of such action is only comprehensible from the position of the first person who wants to demonstrate new standards and rules of the game to the staff, selecting the key issue for the organisation (as in the presented case – the issue of competitive appointment to a leadership position). In order to indicate the subject of change and development, it must be stated what is the system of norms currently in effect, what innovation is being introduced, and what old system is to be replaced by a new system. If the implementation process proceeds, then we can say that the standards have developed. If this does not happen – for example, the system rejects these standards – then it can be recorded that an artificial action for change occurred and the development did not take place.

Third, the question remains what extent the system of standards can be considered to be an autonomous object of development without anything else. It could be the case that if the techniques of activity do not change concurrently (for example, 6D-design is not implemented), then it will not be possible to find a new chief designer because the person taking this position is trained in old technologies. A minimum system of development must be outlined.

Fourth, experience in conducting competitions for candidates shows that people chosen through such a selection process and appointed to positions typically do not remain working long-term at the corporation. An analysis is needed of long-term prospects (not less than 15 years) of how these appointed people are included in and implement the corporation's activity. People can be developed and a talent pool can be created that occupies a position in the corporation management system (the task of which is to include all people in this activity), and not in some metasystem. With such an approach it is not important whether these people remain working in the corporation or not. Then, theoretically speaking, a contract with the corporation is required stating that the corporation agrees to provide its staff as a source for the development of people, and if people leave their job and start to criticise the corporation, or actions are taken outside of the system, then the corporation's leadership has given its agreement to it in principle. A good and wise head of the corporation should include the staff in the process of development.

Part VII

Knowledge Management in Working with Corporate Personnel (Corporate Anthropotechnics) at OAO UIC Oboronprom

A. G. Reus, A. P. Zinchenko and S. B. Kraychinskaya

Andrei G. Reus

Foreword

Part VII of the book is written with a specific group of people in mind. It is intended for expert professionals working in large mechanical engineering corporations, for those in charge of product programmes, divisions, technology competence centres, design engineering departments and enterprises, and for their employees. It is also intended for the managerial personnel reserve: professionals who wish to develop and implement programmes designed to create modern management systems and to train skilled employees in management and engineering.

It should be stressed that we are not talking about personnel officers and experts in the field of human resources (HR) management, although such people may also find this study useful. We refer, above all, to experienced practitioners and young, ambitious careerists who understand why it is so important to allow new generations to benefit from and assimilate the experience of others. These are the people who will be responsible for passing on experience effectively and reliably and for developing professional working practices. This, after all, is what employee training systems are normally designed to do – to prepare new generations to participate actively, meaningfully and successfully in the climate of global competition.

Our aim is to supply this group of professionals with the methodological foundations, concepts, methods and tools that will allow them to organise appropriate work in this area.

The present study is the logical continuation of a number of previous works by the authors. It continues to throw light on a series of methodical and methodological developments in the elaboration of concepts and schemes relating to the thinking action system (TAS) in organisation, leadership and management.

Our approach is systematic. We consistently single out and analyse certain aspects, projections within one general overarching theme: the management of the integration and development of mechanical engineering corporations.

Young engineers

Introduction: what is corporate anthropotechnics?

The term 'anthropotechnics' refers to the technical attitude of an adult individual towards their own individual realisation and development. This attitude is based on a particular approach and method. This can best be described by contrasting it with other approaches and methods.

Anthropotechnics is not a pedagogical programme

Pedagogy is the professional skill and area of activity concerned with the raising and education of children. Whereas the approach found in teaching is 'let others teach me', the basic principle of anthropotechnics (the professional skill of transforming adult individuals), is 'do it yourself'.

Anthropotechnics is not educational work, nor is it psychotechnics

It is rather a means of organising work which is designed to change ways of thinking and activity in collective organisations and in teams of professionals facing practical challenges in their sphere of work. As both domestic and international experience has shown, the best means of promoting ideological development, education and mental organisation in professional bodies is the indirect acquisition of practical experience through involvement and association.

Of central importance to anthropotechnics are people who are able to demonstrate models of thought and action, or methods, which others are then required to learn. Such people are known as masters. Masters are able to do and to show things. Masters should not deliver lectures or recite homilies, but should answer any questions concerning their working methods that might occur to interested students. By understanding questions about their work and answering them, masters, together with their students, move from the realm of work into that of learning and mastering working methods. The philosophers of ancient Greece had a succinct formula to describe this principle: 'You can only learn something by doing it.'

Anthropotechnics is not a school but a workshop

A school, unlike a workshop, requires the presence of teachers: academic authorities who are more intelligent than their listeners and know the answers to all of their pupil's questions. A teacher has the right to give moral lessons and take part in ideological instruction. The school model works in stable situations within a limited geographical area. A good example is a rural community. In such a situation, children accept what they are told by their parents and grandparents and by their school teacher as the truth, because it is all there is available to them. This is still possible in the modern world, but only in a limited set of situations. There is another and more powerful set of situations in which children see and hear not only their teacher, their grandparents or mother, but are also exposed to the opinions of many others, by reading books and by allowing the Internet, television and various other media into their lives. For people in such situations, the 'schoolroom' model of moral mentorship has become almost pointless. They have the opportunity to choose their own way of thinking and behaving, and they copy models of activity provided by masters, selecting whatever models appeal to them most in connection with whatever goals they have set themselves.

Anthropotechnics is not concerned with 'consciousness-changing', but with showing how to *think through* work

It is an opinion often expressed by HR professionals and many senior managers that any changes in work must start with changes in employee consciousness. On the other hand, many others claim that any attempt of this sort is bound to founder on the rock of the backward Russian mentality (that is to say, on the habits produced by that same consciousness). The notion of consciousness and how difficult it is to change has become a tempting catch-all excuse for a number of disastrous management decisions.

So what is consciousness and how sensible is it to set yourself the task of changing it? For those interested in a recent perspective on the problem, we would recommend looking into Joseph Nahem's work *Altered Consciousness: Narcotics, Meditation and Gurus.*[1] Those of

---

1 Published in Russian and not widely available in English.

the old school who studied Marxist–Leninist philosophy at college will be more familiar with the classic distinction between matter, existence and consciousness. Matter is primary – it is provided to us through sensations. Our consciousness, on the other hand, reflects objective reality, but can make mistakes, and sometimes needs to be slightly 'corrected' with the help of educational or propaganda work. Another matter debated by philosophers is the relationship between consciousness and existence. For materialists, being defines consciousness, but for idealists quite the opposite is true. Philosophers debate these questions, and as they do so, they train themselves in the techniques of debate. Our position in anthropotechnics, though, is that there is no need to work with consciousness and to try to alter it. Neither should we attempt to alter existence, hoping in this way to bring about changes in consciousness, even though legions of specialists are engaged in work of this sort.

We believe that in order to bring about changes in activity (in production/manufacturing, construction work and so on) people must be brought into goal-oriented production activity and shown effective *means* for organising their work, such as 'lean thinking'. If we can interest people in the activity itself and enable them to acquire the necessary methods, then the challenges facing us as organisers and managers can find a productive solution. Given that engineers, product engineers, organisers and managers are people who have a certain ability to think, acquired during specialist training and the solving of practical tasks, they can then use this ability to create new structures of activity: to plan activity. Thinking 'contains' activity. It allows us to describe our activity in the form of plans (made by analysts) and to proceed from this to planning directives, on the basis of which we can design future activity.

Thinking can describe and prescribe. It is always active, taking our own ideas out into the wider world. In this way, thinking does not reflect, but creates the world.

If people wish to concern themselves with their consciousness, they can do so in their free time, through hobbies, without any risk to their health.

Corporate anthropotechnics

Now we can explain what is meant by corporative anthropotechnics. It is a set of approaches and methods which aim to prepare a person to occupy a specific space within a given organisation and to management of organisations through the placing of personnel. Historically it has always sat alongside, offset and complemented pedagogy, psychotechnics and mind manipulation, all disciplines designed to raise individuals. Today corporate anthropotechnics is in competition with these disciplines and is increasingly gaining the upper hand over them. The present study is devoted to resolving a particular issue that has arisen out of the conflict, the mutual accusations and reproaches, and sometimes even the direct confrontation between Soviet management models and corporate integration models. This opposition is expressed diagrammatically in Figure 7.1.

In traditional personnel policy, the director gives orders to the personnel officer, who recruits people from the labour market or from special educational establishments which cater to preparing people to fill familiar and clear positions in an organisation that functions in the regular way. This type of conventional personnel officer may be quite unconcerned with the actual jobs people will fill and what they are needed for. Interviews make it possible to weed out unsuitable individuals. There is a probationary period. If an employee is not coping with the work they may be removed and replaced. As Stalin said, 'our human resources are inexhaustible'.

What is different about our situation today? Nowadays, we are engaged in integration, in transforming activity and developing organisations. There is an obvious shortage of educated specialists

Figure 7.1 The priorities of personnel management for a Soviet enterprise

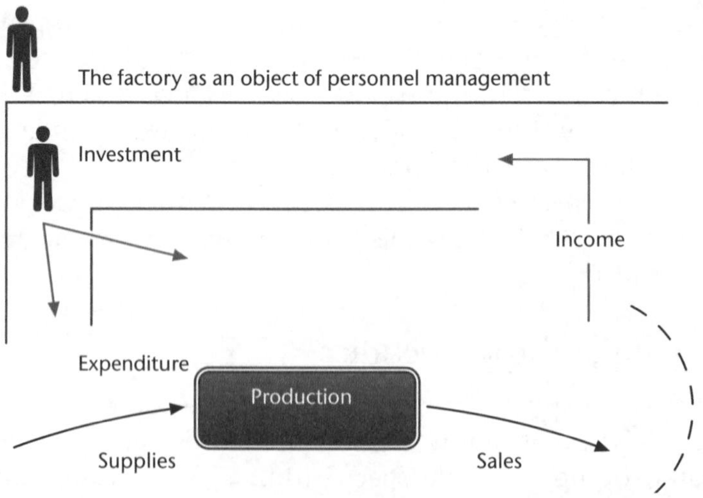

Figure 7.2 Priorities of personnel management in conditions of corporate integration and system reorganisation

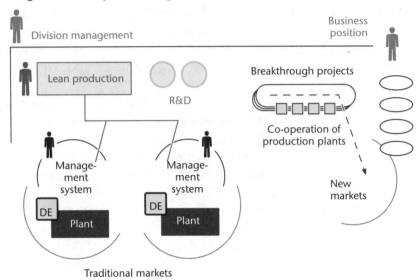

Traditional markets

DE: Design-engineering dept.

in this area of work. It is a sad fact of our lives. Without going into the details of why this is, it is clear that in order to find solutions to the challenges that face us, we need people who can be fitted into a precise position within a system of activity and who, at the same time, are able to transform that position in accordance with the challenges facing them. Currently, personnel services are not able to identify and train such people, because HR staff lack the necessary training themselves, because they do not have years of experience, and because of the general novelty of the situation. They have had not had the time or place to learn such skills. Here, then, is the problem which is solved by the drawing up of a new discipline of anthropotechnics, or personnel policy in conditions of rapid changes in work organisation.

In order to solve this problem we need:

◆ co-ordinated work between the planners and organisers of the new structures of activity;
◆ work in selecting a reserve workforce (consisting of already experienced but still ambitious professionals);
◆ work in training members of this reserve to occupy new places in the systems of activity organisation, and deployment.

All this must be done simultaneously and concurrently.

The right specialists are still to be developed, and this is why we need special modes of organising collective thought, so that appropriate tasks can be solved using the abilities of those people to hand, as well as through knowledge management (KM) schemes which are able to source the best international experience and expertise available at a distance.

Nowadays, attempts to shape people's professional and personal qualities are no longer the preserve of the realm of education. A professional and a personality in the contemporary sense is someone who is able to lead forward an organisation and all the people within it, to determine its future. Such a person is unlikely to be the immediate product of an educational establishment. They will have been shaped not only by the general social and cultural environment, but through their own struggles with an organisation and their attempts to get it to submit to their own aims. This is one of the most important features of the present era: the importance and the role played by education have gradually been eroded, and at the same time, a technique has been created for developing and training people within corporate and other organisational environments. As one famous piece of advice for anyone entering a corporation has it, 'Forget everything you ever learned' (A. Raykin).

The purpose and function of corporate anthropotechnics in management

There is no place for 'pure thought' and abstract theorizing in our work. We rely on our own experience for the corporate management of OAO UIC Oboronprom, JSC Russian Helicopters and the United Engine-Building Corporation (UEC). These organisations are currently implementing strategic goals designed to bring them into the ranks of world leaders in the field at some point in the foreseeable future. To achieve these goals we need to create new management systems and change the way in which work is currently organised. In transforming a corporation, above all we must transform people. It is not clear yet exactly in which capacity these people will need to be deployed. However, if people do not change the way they think and their modes of operation, the corporation will not change either.

From this it follows that the main purpose of a corporate personnel policy is to create a reserve of staff for the future reorganisation of the system, and to form a world-class corporation. The necessary staff for the corporation may be:

◆ located on the labour market – both domestic and global (or enticed away from leading companies that use advanced technologies);
◆ trained in-house using existing training systems (for example, using simulators, special techniques and software);
◆ developed within the corporation using a specially developed corporate system of training and staff development.

We work on all three fronts, with emphasis on the third one, as these are the only options available at present. 'Needs must', as the saying goes.

Discussion during a project analytical session

Experience in organising the training of a managerial reserve

Practice is the organisation of changes in activity in order to promote development in thinking.

(G. P. Shchedrovitsky)

Our principles (A. G. Reus)

What is a managerial reserve and why does a corporation need it?

A managerial reserve is the name given to a group of people selected during the process of various undertakings on the basis of a number of indicators. Through their project proposals and the actions they take in the course of their jobs, these people will determine the future of the corporation. Many people will still remember the Soviet concept of the managerial reserve. This was a formal entity, whereas we are dealing with an actual, working reserve. The Soviet managerial reserve was a group of people whose names had been entered into the appropriate documents for senior administrative bodies, but whom nobody had any actual intention of promoting to management positions. There were no places for these people to occupy. The managers actually in place were serious people who 'had no wish to die' and who therefore pushed themselves to work 'to the bitter end', as a result of which, they made the group of formal reserve managers redundant, to all intents and purposes.

In the Oboronprom Corporation the managerial reserve is prepared, and regularly, according to a plan, its members take up positions in management systems for product programmes, divisions, technology competence centres, businesses and design engineering departments.

The managerial reserve needs professional training

Perhaps the most harmful thesis ever formulated by a Soviet leader was Lenin's claim that 'any cook could take on the running of our country'. To this day, the results of attempts to make this thesis a reality are still evident.

Management is skilled work requiring no less effort and time spent in training and honing a set of skills than design engineering, research, or any sort of highly complex engineering work.

807

At the core of doctrines such as communism and fascism is the notion that complex issues can be solved using simple methods. But for senior managers such an idea is unacceptable: they have no right to adopt such a primitive attitude towards their work.

The corporate management system of a company in
the process of development must itself develop

The system of corporate management needs to establish:

◆ training processes for the managerial reserve, the design and engineering personnel;
◆ processes for acquiring and employing the best current models of thought, experience and practice the world has to offer;
◆ a process whereby senior managers, designers and engineers conduct a reflexive analysis of their own experience.

If the system of corporate management does not have people who are able to put this experience to use, modify it and develop it, the corporation is doomed to failure. It has no future. And any other organisation that wants to have prospects for 20, 30 or 40 years ahead must use in its activities all that experience which 'progressive humanity has accumulated', in the words of classics of the Soviet era.

Demands on members of the managerial reserve
arise logically from the purpose and function of
the managerial reserve in the corporation

In order to have an adequate understanding of development processes, you need be constantly growing and developing yourself. This is what lies at the core of managerial professionalism. The most important working process within the corporation is KM. Any professional who wishes to become a senior manager must master the techniques, basic operations and procedures of this working process. Apart from this, it is vital that future senior management staff master a minimal set of basic ideas which constitute senior managerial activity.

The work of senior managers is, above all, intellectual work. It demands a particular type of understanding, it demands reflective analysis of the situations in which senior managers find themselves, and mastering of the means of cogitative planning and patterning. The most important requirement for anyone wishing to become a leader and to move up through the career ladder in the management system is to master these intellectual techniques.

The next vital requirement for the modern senior manager is multilingual communication: the ability to understand and speak many languages. Those who know no other language than Russian should not become members of the managerial reserve. All members of this reserve must be ready and willing to work in any place in the world and to communicate freely with business partners and competitors, whoever these may be. If business negotiations are conducted in the language of the party contracted to carry out work, the process is speeded up and the negotiations are more likely to be successful. If work is done through an interpreter, much will depend on the interpreter. With a bad interpreter it is highly unlikely that any agreement can be reached.

A member of the managerial reserve should keep well informed about innovative business practices used by the world's leading companies. If a corporate management system does not possess knowledge of cutting-edge experience in its own sphere of activity, it cannot be sufficiently competitive. At the very least, a professional who joins the managerial reserve should have a good knowledge of the tools used in design and programming approaches such as the 'gate system' and 'lean thinking'.

A member of the managerial reserve must have mastered the patterns of systems thinking, as without a knowledge of this it is impossible to work with complex facilities. This idea can be illustrated with a simple diagram: see Figure 7.3.

There is a well-defined set of requirements for systems thinking, which, when performed, will lead managers to the facility they have to control. Managers always begin with these processes, as the logic of systems analysis and design requires. Figure 7.3 indicates three basic processes which should be emphasised from the first when working with any system.

The circle in the diagram represents the limits of a system as a definite whole, and the three arrows are the minimal set of processes that must be first set into action, and later maintained and controlled. These are the processes of development, operation and disposal. The way in which processes are initially conceived will affect all the actions that can be undertaken and realised by the manager.

Figure 7.3 Basic processes in systems thinking

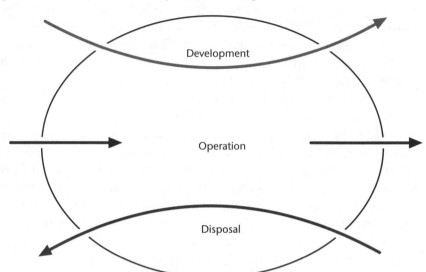

How do we approach the process of development? Here we need to go back to our third principle. As we have already mentioned, if an organisation wishes to continue to function in a healthy manner, it must have a development strategy, a training system which can put such a strategy into practice and the ability to analyse and employ the best practice the world has to offer both in training and in the main activities of the organisation.

Operational work is the fundamental process of any organisation. Any organisation must work, it must have a product or service to sell, and create this in accordance with certain standards. In addition, most management work should also be standardised, made to adhere to standard technological modes. These standard modes actually make up 90 per cent of a manager's activity. If a company's operational work were dependent on human agents only, then if an employee made a mistake, or, God forbid died, all activity would cease.

The third process is disposal. It is clear that managers need to be able to get rid of outmoded practices and superfluous people. The manager needs a clean desktop in order to start work.

The training of the managerial reserve should be efficient and productive. While acting managers are not relieved of their responsibilities – they remain in their positions – the managerial reserve must come up with a model of activity towards which the organisation should gear itself – and not only a model, but a course to follow and an action plan to make realisation a possibility.

Effective goals must be identified for the managerial reserve. Corporations need new business models and new ways to make these models a reality, but more importantly, they need people who understand this. Corporations need people who are willing themselves to change and who are able to achieve the productive goals that have been set.

The requirements listed here do not apply to everyone, but only to the intellectual elite of the corporation, which we call the reserve. It is this set of requirements that distinguishes the managerial reserve of a corporation from the cook of whom Lenin spoke.

Assessing the state of affairs and 'environmental' factors in conducting personnel policy

Since the late 1960s, the leaders of world industry have been reliant on:

◆ operations analysis and a systems approach;
◆ participative planning (end-to-end communication within the organisation);
◆ methodological reflection and analysis of real innovation;
◆ an awareness and an insistence that the manufacturing process should be shaped by the demands of the market, and be structured on the principle of market 'pull'.

In Russia, however, we are to this day reliant on the idea of 'sole command':

◆ total secrecy and corresponding discreteness of subdivisions and developments;
◆ a zealous ban on describing or conveying the experience of leaders;
◆ lack of innovation without orders from above (the centralised distribution of initiatives);
◆ execution within the period of the industrial and financial plan, resulting in the creation of process work and emergency situations;
◆ the expectation of an endless stream of funds from the state budget.

The main features of modern technologies of production management are:

◆ the integration of research and development with production;
◆ systems of digital automated design and planning;
◆ flexible manufacturing systems using computer numerically controlled (CNC) equipment;
◆ close collaboration with suppliers and buyers;
◆ horizontal co-operation;
◆ creation of joint ventures and strategic alliances;
◆ a radical shift in management systems towards working with investment (business) programmes that are geared towards supporting the lifecycle of the product.

The influence of these factors on personnel policy in mechanical engineering

The creation of multifunctional working groups bringing together various specialists – managers, engineers, designers, marketing consultants, economists and so on – comes to the fore. Staff training and attitude development moves to the workplace (so-called 'work mentoring'). Final assembly becomes the privilege of the most advanced or recently established plants. Others may compete for positions as multi-functional 'technological refinement centres'. The design and manufacturing of technologically simple modules and the parts-and-assembly units is transferred to enterprises and regions with low labour costs. We start to see global infrastructures of production units, technological competence centres, engineering centres, maintenance and repair centres and sales centres.

The most complex aspect of programme managing is not even the importance of establishing and effectively organising the co-operation of a multitude of different enterprises, drawing up transfer pricing and ensuring reliable logistics, because there are specialists who know how to do this. The problem is that financially successful ideas have to be found at different stages of the manufacturing process. Currently the design of a technologically sophisticated mass product is extremely expensive. In order to succeed, recoup costs and make a profit, only the most promising business ideas must be brought to the stage of batch production. This list could go on but what interests us is how personnel are selected, trained and deployed in a climate of frequent and extensive change. Figures 7.4

Figure 7.4 Essential characteristics and priorities of personnel management within a Soviet enterprise

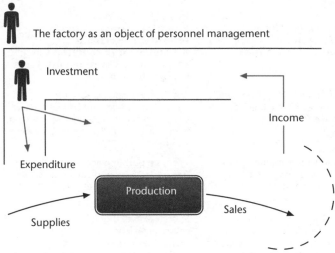

and 7.5 and Table 7.1 show the fundamental differences between traditional personnel management schemes and personnel management schemes in conditions of corporate integration and systems reorganisation.

Figure 7.5 Essential characteristics and priorities of personnel management in conditions of corporate integration and systems reorganisation

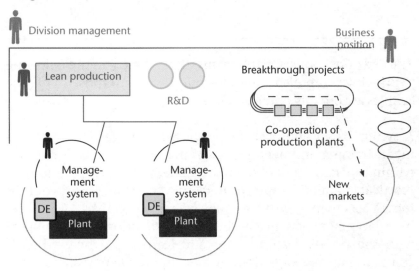

DE: Design-engineering dept.

Table 7.1 Essential characteristics and priorities of personnel management

Essential characteristics and priorities of personnel management within a Soviet enterprise	Essential characteristics and priorities of personnel management in conditions of corporate integration and systems reorganisation
The standards of the Labour Code and industrial ministries are adhered to, protecting workers' rights and state interests	The Labour Code is subject to discussion and debate. Employment may be through contract work, outsourcing, freelance work and 'grey' employment schemes.
A system of social consumption funds is in operation – nurseries and daycare centres, recreation centres, canteens, healthcare and labour protection	The state puts in place 'emergency' responses to social problems in specific regions, cities and enterprises
A system of distribution, placement and support of 'young professionals' is in operation. Industry-specific career enhancement schemes are also in place.	Specialists 'sell themselves' in a competitive labour market and must themselves seek to improve their qualifications and find means of earning enough to pay for accommodation, to support their families and to maintain a decent standard of living
The pensions system provides assurance for the future	The pensions scheme does not ensure a decent standard of living after retirement. Employees must themselves actively seek means of sustenance.
The company is the main social asset and the nucleus of society (one's 'own' factory). People act as material in executive machines.	The primary social values are family, home ownership and employment providing a decent standard of living. People change jobs, actively seeking better positions.

The personnel policy of an organisation is based on the following key principles (applied here to our own enterprise, but the principles are broadly applicable):

◆ A system-based approach to personnel management – recruitment, training and deployment of personnel are all carried out within the framework of the management of the corporation.
◆ Practical landmarks – we seek to recruit, train and place people in jobs in accordance with corporate strategy objectives.
◆ International experience and domestic traditions – we compete with the world's leading firms and learn from them when it comes to business organisation models, but we rely on our own people, on their talents, their potential and their initiative.

◆ A system of recruitment, training and deployment of personnel based on recovering, reorganising and supporting surviving and still operational remnants of the education and training system built up by the Soviet aircraft industry.

◆ A corporate culture that does not seek to manipulate the consciousness of employees but to communicate openly without lies – showing people the benefits which working to achieve the strategic aims of the corporation can bring.

The scope and organisation of human capital management work within the organisation

The practice of decision making

Since 2007 we have been describing decision-making activity in corporate structure HR management. Over the last five years a whole multitude of initiatives and activities have taken place. These can be divided into several key areas (not in order of priority).

*Change in leadership and management systems
in the enterprises within the organisation*

As a rule, the strategic objectives set for an enterprise by the management of a corporate grouping require the formation of a new management system. Therefore, the organisation has adopted the practice of replacing the heads of the enterprises wherever new tasks demand a leader with different competencies. This practice is supported by a system of rotation of managerial personnel. Experienced managers, released from the leadership of the company, move to new stations of work, where their experience and managerial skills can be used most effectively. Thus, a specific corporate culture of work with management personnel is formed, based on the principle of KM – every leader is effective in the place where their knowledge can be put to maximum use.

Example: The director of a batch plant may be replaced if production is being reorganised on the basis of 'lean thinking', as this would require a leader with practical experience in transforming production systems. Or, in another case, the director might be replaced in connection with a priority task to set up batch production, as this would require a leader who is a specialist in production, with knowledge of engine technology and experience in managing production.

The formation of a personnel reserve

As already noted, these people are intended to occupy managerial positions, and a series of organisational-activity games (OAGs) can be used for training the personnel reserve. The personnel reserve is a specially trained team of people from which the company's senior management expects effective action in order to change an entrenched situation. To put it another way, the personnel reserve is needed when the existing management system and those working within it are not able to change the state of affairs.

The personnel reserve programme includes the identification of potential candidates, and their selection in the course of specially organised activities (which simulate decision-making situations), the training of selected candidates in a team training regimen (which enables them to develop abilities in analysis and project work), deployment within the management system, evaluation of the effectiveness of their work, and subsequent rotation.

The programme is graded according to key categories of reserve personnel (in compliance with the strategy):

◆ programme leaders (business organisers);
◆ engineering and design personnel and directors of research and development (R&D);
◆ production organisers (experts in transforming production systems);
◆ functional managers/leaders (sales, finance, legal and corporate issues, personnel, quality control and so on).

Example: The creation of a list of 'golden heads' (a club of corporate engineers) with competences in design and engineering, from the pool of engineering and technical staff engaged in the development and maintenance of corporate production.

The selection and design of the content of management training according to knowledge management models

The KM system of a particular organisation should include only those concepts, patterns and models that have been worked out during the process of solving practical problems and which have led to changes in the system in accordance with the company's objectives. It is precisely this corporate knowledge that must constitute the content of management training, both of the acting body of directors and the reserve personnel. At the heart of the content of management training is the idea that 'What a corporation needs to know, it already knows.' Whatever a corporation does not yet know, it must find out from other sources: from foreign competitors and partners (world leaders in the field) and from the best domestic corporations. In addition to this, all knowledge 'lives' in people – people are the carriers of knowledge – and in order to identify, extract and accumulate the necessary knowledge, the appropriate people must be included in this work.

Example: Staff at the organisation studied programme and project management using the experience of the Sukhoi Company, the first organisation in domestic practice that mastered these techniques during the implementation of the Sukhoi SSJ (superjet) programme. Here, the speech addressed by the company's chief executive M. A. Pogosyan to the senior management of the company became the starting point for the transition of the organisation to a system of programme and project management.

The implementation of lean thinking within all the enterprises in the group, the organisation of efficient production systems and the raising of teams of production organisers

The idea of lean thinking (also described as lean production, the theory of constraint, a production system and so on) involves changing the patterns of thinking of employees in every place in the system of production organisation, from an employee at a specific work station right up to the director of the enterprise or the leader of a corporation. This is why this approach is seen as being within the sphere of HR management. By contrast with the scientific organisation of labour (SOL), in which emphasis is laid on the external normalisation and regulation of human operations, lean thinking presupposes that employees organise themselves to achieve, in the first stage, a properly organised production process, and in the second stage, continuous improvement of the process and a reduction in wasted resources. For this reason, it is essential to begin the gradual introduction of a new type of production organiser, someone who is able to ensure value for the client.

Example: The format of trainings for the teams of production organisers changed according to the stage of development the programme had reached – from open OAGs run by visiting experts (at the programme's launch) to workshops on the transformation of the production system (when the programme was being rolled out in all companies in the group).

Conducting an open tender for the position of managing director of UEC and the organisation of a new management system for the organisation

The organisation of the new management system included:

◆ involving all acting managers in the public discussion of problems and disadvantages in the current system;
◆ including reserve personnel in the collective planning of the new system;
◆ recruiting an external managerial reserve – managers from other branches of mechanical engineering with experience in transforming management systems.

The open tender was used in order to create open competition between different plans regarding the structuring of future management systems.

Example: The recruitment of senior managers through a process of competition has been a basic factor in appointments to key management positions since 2010. In addition, it has been also adopted by domestic corporations not only for selecting applicants for particular posts, but for planning strategic change.

The creation of divisions, modern business units on the basis of existing design bureaux and companies in the group, and the creation of systems of divisional management

During the finalisation of the strategy for UEC, it was decided to restructure the corporation – to move from individual enterprises (production facilities and design bureaux) to divisions organised according to products. The divisions are based on management systems for product programmes. These are designed with one particular product in mind (engines for civil aircraft, helicopter engines, land-based power plants and so on), and control the entire lifecycle of the product, from marketing and technical specifications for that product's development through to its employment and subsequent disposal. Divisional organisation must structure the business of the company and concentrate all its resources on creating competitive products. During this reorganisation process, it is essential to identify the current and prospective product range, design resources (a basic design bureau – DB), final assembly sites, and technological and industrial competence centres for every division.

Example: The creation of the Helicopter Engine Division as a compe-tence centre for the development, manufacturing and after-sales service for all types of domestic helicopter engines. The basic production facility and co-operating facilities for various programmes have been determined, and a product lifestyle management system is being created for the division.

Reorganisation of R&D management

In contemporary R&D organisation, an infrastructure approach and network-style working predominate. It is vital that we move on from the system of fully functional, autonomous DBs (which tend to be self-referential organisations), and use all available design and engineering resources in projects designed to create advanced technological models and modernise the current product range.

Example: The restructuring of the system of R&D management for the helicopter engineering industry is geared towards creating a single national centre of helicopter engineering on the basis of the integrated resources of two leading design bureaux, which will reap the benefit of the science and engineering knowledge of two different design schools. At the same time, engineering and design work will be organised on the basis of a single, integrated infrastructure of research, development and testing.

The transition from business management to programme and project management, and the selection and trying-out of potential programme leaders

The challenges relating to management change are the result of changes in the company's business philosophy – the move from the mere sale of technical products to the sale and maintenance of those products throughout their lifecycle. The service life of products is at least 30–40 years, and demand for them depends not only, or not so much, on the products' characteristics, but rather on whether or not a lifecycle management system is available for them. Programme and project management gives us an overview of the lifecycle of the product, allowing us to manage it.

There are no specialists being trained in programme manage-ment; in fact there is no such profession. It is, in point of fact, a

819

special administrative competence, which must be acquired during the process of solving practical problems presented by managing a particular programme. All programmes are divided into several types: programmes for advanced products (such as advanced helicopters or advanced engines), programmes for serial production products, and programmes for upgraded products.

Example: A special training programme for programme managers of the Russian Helicopters company was organised in 2008. In the course of the programme, teams for key projects were trained, and potential programme and project managers selected. Out of 50 participants in the programme, nine received a certificate of 'Expertise in Team Organisation Management' and six received a 'Managerial Reserve' certificate. Three and a half years after completing the training programme, seven participants have become programme managers, and the rest are either deputy programme managers, or managers of functional units.

The creation of an educational engine-building cluster based on specialist departments of national higher education institutes and technical colleges

The creation of a cluster provides a solution to the following challenges:

◆ It ensures co-operation between businesses and institutions, primarily vocational education institutions, in order to meet the challenges of staffing and the organisation of collaborative work in R&D, design and engineering, and education.
◆ It provides a communication platform for the employer (the organisation), the student (the higher education institution) and the specialist (the personnel reserve) in order to facilitate the attraction and recruitment of staff and to set goals for practice-oriented training.
◆ It sets the terms of reference for all members of the cluster for long-term training and the development of training programmes using new content and new formats.

Figure 7.6 shows the basic structure of the educational cluster.

Example: In April 2009, the following organisations became part of the educational engine-building cluster: the corporate university; 10 HR services, 15 basic specialist vocational educational institutions, 12 institutions of secondary vocational training (in areas where companies

Figure 7.6 The basic structure of the educational cluster

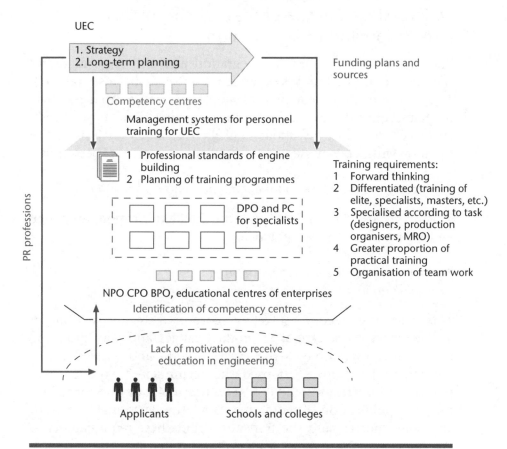

in the group are situated) and 7 educational, training and production and resource centres based in companies in the group. In the space of three years, the following communication platforms were organised: a course of lectures given by the managing director of the organisation for students and employees of specialist higher education institutions; public strategic seminars for the personnel reserve with participation by students (in Kazan, Perm and Samara); topical seminars at educational institutions, in particular on the lifecycle management of sophisticated technical systems; scientific and technical conferences held at enterprises, with the participation of students from specialist higher educational institutions; and corporate education programmes with the participation of senior executives as part of a number of industrial, engineering and innovation forums (Seliger, Skolkovo, and the Baikal Forum 'Engineers of the Future').

The personnel management system at various stages of the process of corporate integration and reorganisation

The first stage of corporate integration and anti-crisis measures was the recruitment and deployment of crisis managers (2008–11). This involved the deployment of employees into a rapid response programme for the existing situation, selecting from those already available and from the labour market. It included analysis of the situation within businesses, and immediate assessment of personnel.

The creation of an educational engine-building cluster

This involved a series of measures for the identification, exchange and accumulation of best practice.

A programme for the implementation of lean thinking in all enterprises

This was the second stage of corporate reconstruction in accordance with sought-after product ranges and corresponding industrial programmes (the recruitment and selection of development designers). It used the accumulated experience of reorganisation (from 2009–11). Activities included the formalisation and publication of requirements for the personnel reserve in corporate sources, and the transmission of these requirements to the enterprises through the leaders of integrated structures.

The personnel reserve was trained through initiatives run by the corporate university on KM models.

A planned transition to the creation of a new generation of management systems

For the corporation, this involved a move from managing a conglomerate of factories and design bureaux to managing programmes, divisions and technology competence centres, and the progression of the reserve to new management systems.

The third stage of systemic reorganisation according to the principles of programme management involved guaranteed management of the product lifecycle, management of value creation for customers, and the creation of a network of centres of technological competence (TCC) (2011–13).

Systemic staff rotation

This included the simultaneous replacement of company directors, appointment of programme managers and managers of TCCs and other key projects. Such packages are evidence of targeted personnel policy in management, a move away from the practice of 'plugging holes'.

The appointment of directors from among the personnel reserve

These appointments were announced publicly so that corporate teams understood they were systematic rather than random (emergency) actions.

New models of work organisation require a new generation of people with the appropriate forms of thought. For the long term, we are planning appropriate forms of work.

The instigation of competition among the management team

This will develop within the corporation over a period of 10 to 15 years, with the setting of policy objectives within the strategy implementation framework. (Opportunities for career advancement are intended as a primary motivator for staff.)

◆ *Contests* are a core element of training. There is competition not only between people but between programmes, energy, perspectives and so on.
◆ *Competitions are being organised* with global competitors in order to secure niches in the international markets and leadership in design and engineering developments.

Public demonstration of the principles of the personnel policy

This uses the examples of rotation within management systems for programmes, projects and TCCs with related technological content:

◆ Management teams are formed for divisions and problematic enterprises (with replacement of the director, followed by reorganisation of the management system, and so on).
◆ Management (and responsibility) are clearly designated for all divisions, product projects and UEC programmes. (Leaders should be people for whom this work is the main area of

Figure 7.7 The present system of corporate staff training

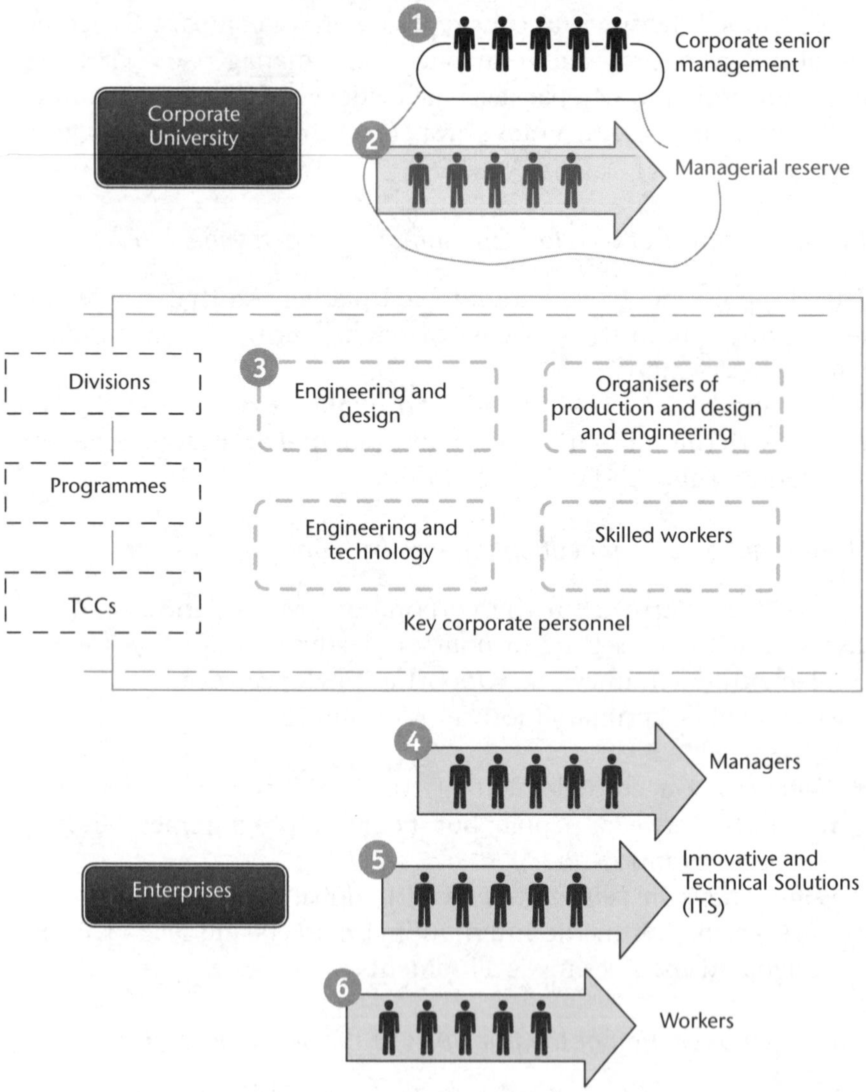

responsibility, and not directors of enterprises, as experience has shown.)

Long-range planning of solutions for corporate staffing issues

This involves prioritisation and identification of primary tasks and appointment issues (in accordance with the strategy), and later, persistent implementation of these appointments.

Traditionally, the training and professional development of

workers, engineers and managers within enterprises has been the work of personnel services. They keep personnel records, make plans for professional development and training, send staff for retraining and so on.

Work with the senior management of corporations and training of the personnel reserve is carried out by the Corporate University as part of strategic OAGs and targeted training programmes.

At the same time training is provided by both in-house resources (specialised training centres) and primarily external providers (mainly educational institutions and training companies). There is a gap between these strands of work (see the middle part of the scheme), since there are no targeted developments for the selection and training of key corporate personnel – those professionals who must ensure the implementation of 'breakthrough projects' within the organisation.

In order to implement strategy and meet strategic objectives, this gap needs to be filled, and, accordingly, substantial change needs to take place in personnel management. It is not possible to make the transition to a divisional structure (while maintaining a single system), to establish TCCs, organise programme and project-based product lifecycle management, to organise world-class maintenance, repair and operations (MRO), or to introduce lean thinking or continuous improvement of industrial systems if there are not people with the right level of expertise in the key positions in the newly formed structures.

Key categories of staff contributing to the development of the corporation and to the implementation of the corporate strategy are:

◆ engineering and design personnel;
◆ engineering and technological personnel;
◆ organisers of production and design engineering work;
◆ skilled workers;
◆ organisers of MRO systems (service people).

If the organisation does not have a uniform training policy, this means that there are no corporate standards for key strategic areas, it also means that practical training is organised locally and not systemically (there is no system of internships for the group and its partner enterprises, and no rotation of experts) and the resources of the federal and government programmes, which include relevant divisions for personnel training, are underused.

In long-term strategies for personnel training, it is important to define areas of responsibility in shaping human resources:

◆ *Initial conditions* are provided by schools, working according to educational standards, and (in the best-case scenario) directing students to specific areas of activity. The attention and influence of the corporation extend particularly to the specialised schools, which offer an in-depth education in physics and mathematics with a technical bias (modelling, design and so on) and which have close ties with the regions where the group has enterprises.

◆ *Basic training* (familiarising students with their future profession and its foundation, 'materiel', and eliminating gaps in schooling) should be provided by vocational institutions.

◆ *Special training* and the formation of specialists are the responsibility of enterprises (working in collaboration with higher education institutions). It is only possible to train a specialist within the system of their practical activity, through work experience and placements within the enterprise, and early involvement in solving practical problems during specific projects.

◆ A very important function in the staffing of any work is *rapid reconfiguration* – the possibility of rapidly retraining employees on a mass scale, allowing them to change specialism or develop new skills. This requires an infrastructure for continuing professional education, which can update the content of training programmes, develop 'express' training modules and implement practical training exercises in the workplace.

◆ *Key competencies* for a corporation can be formed only in the appropriate competency centres – for design and engineering, production and technology, service or management. The formation of competencies should take place through exchange of experience, rotation, training, and the continual inclusion of particular members of the personnel reserve in new types of work.

The Corporate University: its purpose and the results of its work

Since its inception, the Corporate University of OAO UIC Oboronprom has focused on the work of selecting and training the managerial reserve. Terms of reference for the creation of this structure were formulated at MAKS 2007[2] in a report given by A. G. Reus to the roundtable 'On the development of personnel training systems for the aviation industry' (24 August 2007). The initiator of the event was the United Aircraft Corporation (UAC). The event brought together managers and representatives from almost all educational institutions (universities, colleges) and other organisations that engage in training for the aviation industry.

The speaker declared that the most important task which would need to be addressed during the forthcoming integration of the industry was to change management systems and completely retrain or replace senior executives and managers at all levels. At the same time, the main problem identified was the fact that Russia lagged behind global competitors in the technology of work organisation. In the 1980s we were among the world leaders, according to production volume and performance characteristics of our products, but over 30 years, during which there was a lack of orders for production of high-tech aircraft, we started to lag behind seriously.

It was precisely in order to close this gap that a modern personnel reserve was needed, and a mechanism like the Corporate University was needed in order to train that reserve. In effect, the manager of the Corporate University and the commissioner of training services is the managing director of UIC Oboronprom.[3]

From 2007 to 2012 the Corporate University organised over 50 events. (Appendix 7.1, page 899, lists events organised by the Corporate University at different stages of the corporation's work.) All of them were organised in response to particular situations and had their own goals and outcomes. We will not enumerate all of these here or dwell on any particular details now that the situations have come and gone. Our task is to describe the essence of this work, the approach and method used.

As far as outcomes are concerned, by the beginning of 2012 38 people out of a changing contingent of 100 people from our personnel reserve had obtained appointments to new positions in management systems. On the whole, the Corporate University is consistently fulfilling the tasks that were set for it in 2007. As

---

2   The International Aviation and Space Salon, known as MAKS in both English and Russian.

3   More detailed information on the working methods of the Corporate University can be found in A. Reus, A. Zinchenko, S. Kraychinskaya and D. Talyansky, *On the Method of 'Knowledge Management' in the Integration Process of the Engineering Corporation*, Moscow: Delo, 2011.

Figure 7.8 Stages in the creation and development of UIC Oboronprom

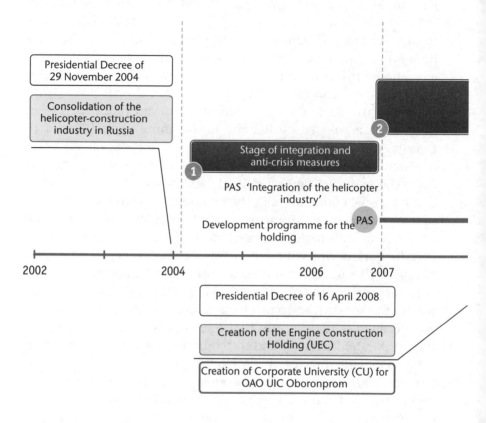

we train managers and build new management schemes, we must analyse the work that has been done, preserving good decisions in the form of standards and rejecting unsuccessful ones. In this key component of management technology we are still lagging behind our competitors and have to constantly redouble our efforts.

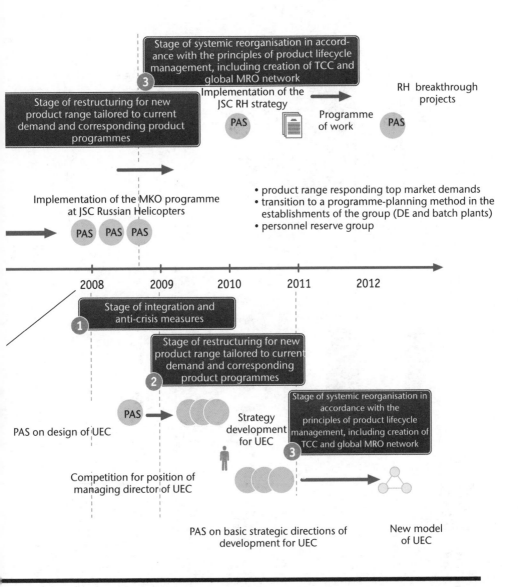

The programme of work carried out by the Corporate University

The various strands of our work can be categorised and considered with the help of a diagram: see Figure 7.9, which is made up of several layers. The bottom layer on the right represents the regions where our enterprises are located and the situations in those

Figure 7.9 The work of the Corporate University

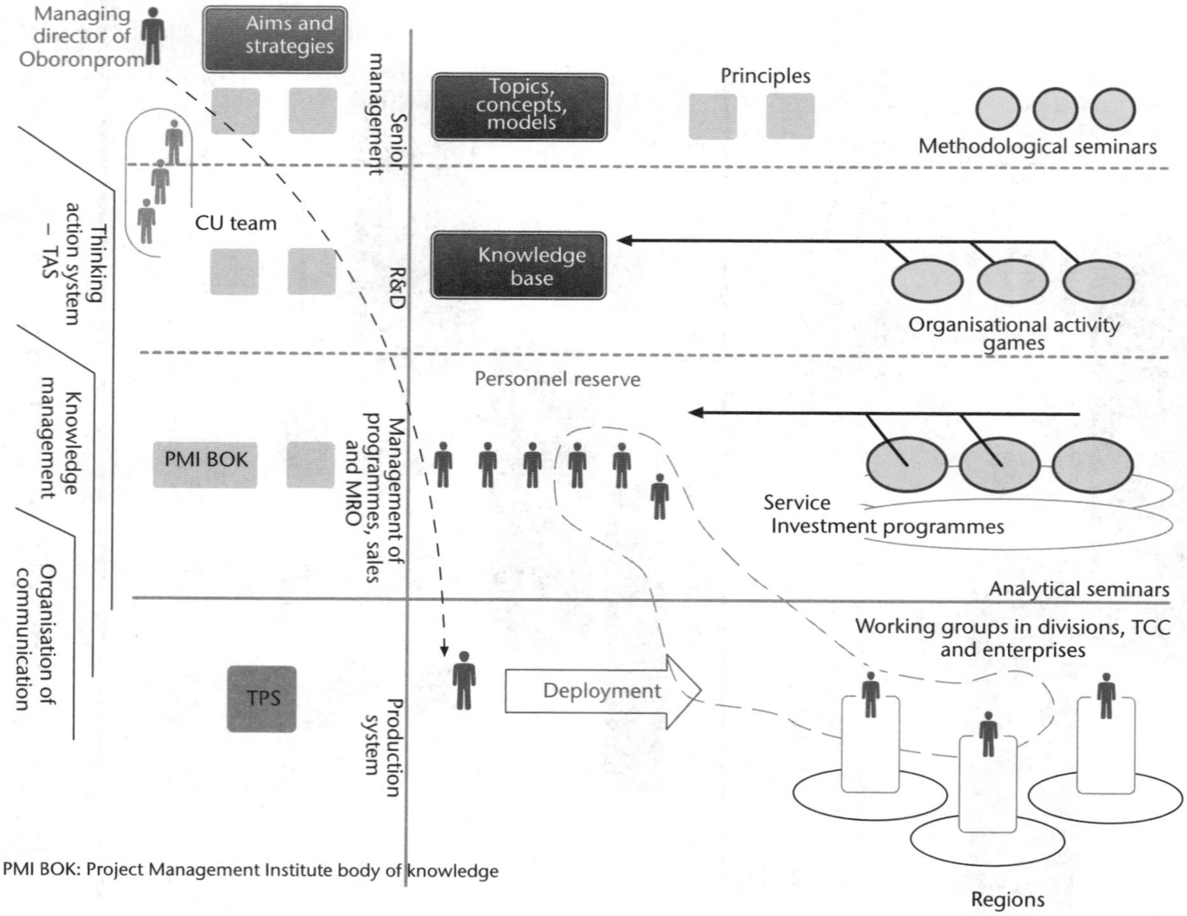

PMI BOK: Project Management Institute body of knowledge

enterprises which require a change of management system. These are situations of transition to new management schemes (the creation of divisions and TCC); situations of transition from the management of factories to management using programmes, as well as the standard 'tightening up' of management if it cannot cope with the appointed tasks.

The upper left corner of Figure 7.9 shows the position of senior managers of the corporation, who must have a group of possible candidates for deployment in appropriate posts. Selection and training of this group is provided by a team of employees at the Corporate University. Their work allows managers to chart and implement practical options and scenarios regarding personnel decision-making using various types of initiative depicted in the diagram.

These types of initiative are:

◆ Training sessions, analytical seminars and project sessions which enable the selection of the personnel reserve during their attempts to tackle pressing issues and challenges for the corporation.
◆ OAGs, arranged according to KM models, to encourage partici-pants to gain experience and knowledge, and to set problems and tasks in connection with the development of their projects.
◆ Methodological seminars with a small circle of senior managers, to work on principles, concepts and schemes (in particular, the important tool of systems thinking), on which management decisions should be based (examples are given below).

The people who take part in these initiatives and pass through the 'filter' of analytical discussions, project sessions, training sessions, and tests to determine aptitude for systems-based thought and so on, make up the group of the personnel reserve. So work is carried out on three different levels with the people who are sought out and selected for the personnel reserve. Decisions regarding the deployment of personnel in new positions are taken by the manage-ment, and since the managing director of the corporation, who is also the director of the Corporate University, is engaged in almost all of these activities at different levels and in connection with various thematic slants, he is well able to make informed decisions.

The main types of employment position for the management reserve

These types of positions are shown in Figure 7.10.

The most important area for the corporation today is the after-sales service system for our products. In this area we are lagging seriously behind our competitors. We know that up to 90 per cent of the income they receive comes not from the sale of goods, but from sales of the 'lifecycle', or flight hours. The second type of important position consists of directors of major investment programmes, technically competent organisers of co-operatives, traders and developers of financial models. The third type consists of organisers of R&D. The fourth type consists of project developers and organisers of TCCs. The fifth type consists of those specialists we were seeking when we started work three years ago: experts in the organisation of lean production.

Figure 7.10 Potential positions for members of the managerial reserve

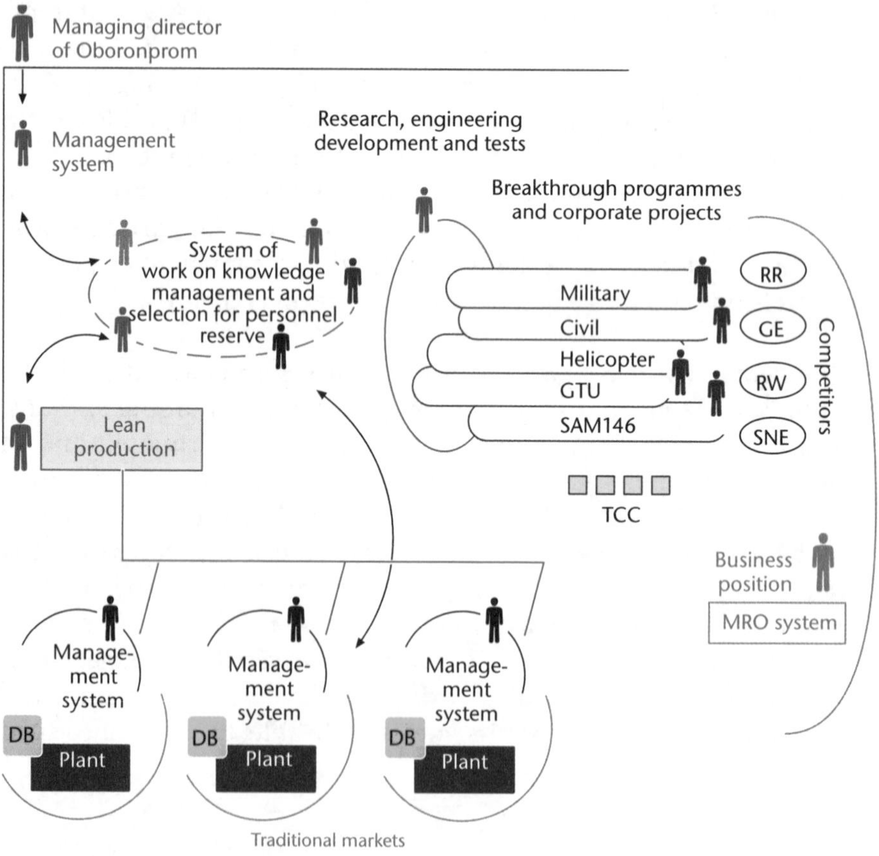

Targeted areas of training for the managerial reserve

◆ The transition to divisional organisation within the corporation – the network of enterprises and MRO centres as an organisational principle.
◆ The transition from separate DB to infrastructure organisation of R&D.
◆ The transition from the management of factories to programme management.
◆ The transition from 'natural economies' (full-cycle systems – from metal to finished product) to centres of technological competence.
◆ The formation of a network of compact industrial complexes based on the principles of lean production (involving transformation of the production system). Change of consciousness among industrial/production workers.

The scope of the Corporate University's work

In accordance with the areas of work outlined above, training is structured according to types of selection and training programme and requirements for specific positions.

Conclusions to be drawn from current results of work at the Corporate University

◆ At the moment, the Corporation is willing and able to define in figures its demand for different types of professionals required to implement our strategic plans for major restructuring and promoting breakthrough projects and programmes.
◆ The current system of education and training lacks the intellectual or material resources to enable a rapid roll-out of appropriate training programmes for candidates for the vast majority of positions needed, so the implication is that the corporation will have to 'take what it's given'. At the same time, educational institutions (with some rare exceptions) are using state money provided by educational reform programmes to strengthen their position in the educational services market, regardless of the requirements of industry.
◆ Over the last 30 years, although they have received virtually no orders from the national defence sector, the corporate plants

and design bureaux have managed to preserve fundamental and technological competences.

♦ Work on integrating design and production assets of the aviation industry into corporations has yielded initial encouraging results. There has been an increase in revenue and productivity, long-term development strategies have been drawn up, and designers and engineers are concentrating their efforts on long-term programmes and activities leading to the creation of modern TCCs. All this has allowed the corporation to break away from a situation of decline and degradation and outline clear, realistic plans. It is in order to put these plans into practice that we are now in urgent need of specialists, professionals and managers of a new type, which the existing system of education is not able to produce. We must regard it as an established fact that the necessary corporate competencies and appropriate personnel can either be trained using through internal corporate structures (the Corporate University, specialist training centres, regional higher education institutions with close relations with DBs and enterprises) or they must be head-hunted from other industries or from abroad.

♦ Corporations have become viable centres for the creation of intellectual capital. It is now possible to carry out labour market analysis and run local training projects (preparing managers, engineers, designers, technicians and machine operators for specific, highly specialised positions) within corporations themselves. Thus, corporations may actually become 'design bureaux' for creating new specialisations and new forms of training. The experience of creating such centres can be carried over to other areas of industrial production.

♦ High-precision weapons must take the place of carpet bombing. This principle is one that is now well understood, not only by experts in the defence industry. What do we mean? When the foundation of our aviation industry was laid in the 1930s to 1950s, when we acted without taking into account expenses, resources and the fates of individual people, all of which seemed to us inexhaustible at that time. We created a great number of design bureaux, factories, test sites and types of apparatus. In order to provide the industry with employees, dozens of higher educational institutions were created, which churned out vast quantities of experts. Domestic competition and natural selection permitted us to solve difficult problems, but today we are faced with more complex problems. To implement high-precision industrial programmes we need to develop forward-looking high-precision training programmes for professionals: designers, engineers, managers, planners, researchers and machinists. We need to pass from wasteful, large-scale operations to lean production – targeted training programmes for specific groups of specialists

◆ We can define the contours of the terms of reference for the design and creation of the Corporate Training Network (CTN), based on the existing capabilities and resources of the educational establishments in the group. The network should ensure co-ordination and co-operation among management systems for existing and future programmes in order to work out a cohesive personnel training mission. It should also work to realise this mission, using its own efforts where possible, and outsourcing when necessary.

The functions of the CTN are:

◆ Ensuring communication between the educational establishment, industrial plant, design bureau, test site and research centre.
◆ Practical training of students and professionals; education in the workplace.
◆ Organisation of a KM infrastructure, and mentoring and training in workshops that will provide that infrastructure.
◆ Training of a group of managers to allow the continual development of the enterprise by deploying staff in development projects.
◆ Specialised training of tutors, chosen from among the personnel of the enterprise and DBs. In the technical field, particularly as regards the design and manufacture of complex technical devices, staff must be trained according to a 'stepped' principle: no member of staff is able to proceed to the next level without having gone through the previous one. It is not possible to become a leader without having first acquired the basics of engineering (in specialised secondary college and university), then worked as a manual worker, then a technician, next a master and finally an engineer, just as in the field of medicine it is impossible

Figure 7.11 The scope of the Corporate University's work

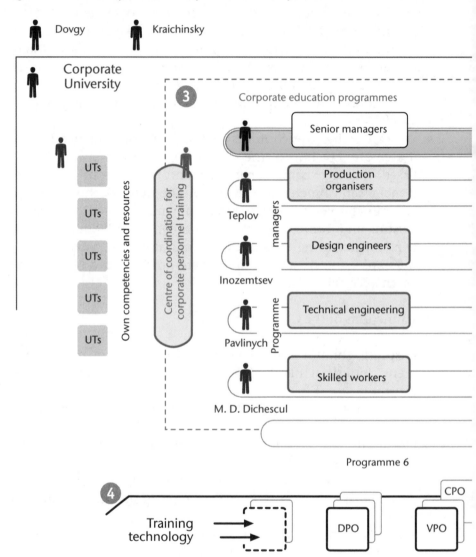

External (including international) providers of training programmes

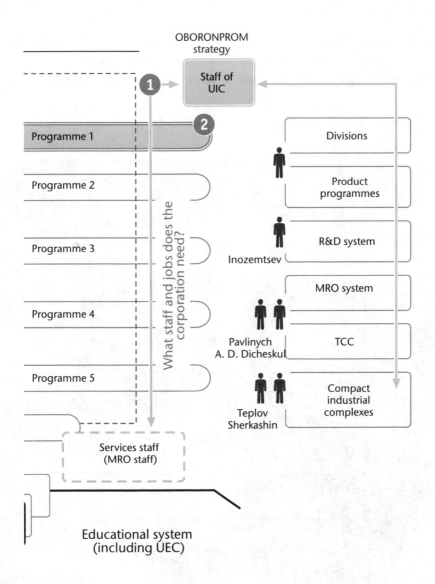

to become a consultant without first having practised dissecting frogs and afterwards gone through each successive stage of professional development.

◆ Training of teams consisting of specialists in various areas who are able to quickly integrate into an existing or emerging technology.

◆ High-level language training in the course of placements abroad.

Discussion during a project analytical session

The managerial reserve workshop

"We can't solve problems by using the same kind of thinking we used when we created them."

(Albert Einstein)

Schola – an ancient Greek school

Why a workshop and not a school?

The concept of the 'school' has its origins in the Greek *schole* ('leisure or activities undertaken in free time'). Children must go to school before they become engaged in serious work. The seventeenth-century scholar and educator Comenius formalised this idea when he wrote in 1658:

> "School is a place where young souls are brought up to be virtuous.
>   The teacher sits on a chair, the students on the benches. The teacher teaches and the students learn.
>   Things are written up for them in chalk on a blackboard. Some of the students sit at tables and write.
>   The teacher corrects their errors.
>   Some stand up and read aloud what they have learned by heart.
>   Some speak and behave like mischievous and inattentive students.
>   They are punished with a cane and a rod."
>
> (*The World of Sensible Things in Pictures*)

So school is a place where the teacher teaches, and the students listen and read. It is a place where young souls are brought up to be virtuous, where some of the students sit and write, and some speak and behave mischievously and inattentively. Around 400 years ago, in the time of Comenius, teachers could punish students with canes and rods. If there are no canes or rods in a modern school, it is not a school, according to this description. Children are kept there for many years, forced to get their Leaving Certificate and then released into the wide world.

The Corporate University does not deal with children, but with adults. There is no point at this stage in trying to bring them up to be virtuous, we must take them as we find them. There cannot be a teacher here, because what needs to be learned is not written down in any textbook. There are students here, but they learn from one another. They learn from one of their number who knows how to do something better than everybody else, and they must correct their own mistakes, at their own work stations. Here there are no mischievous and inattentive students, as they will immediately find themselves rejected from joint projects and will not be invited to take part in them again.

In conditions such as these we use a more rigid and robust form of education than a school. We use a workshop – a type of educational structure older than a school. In the workshop, people learn to work, whereas in the school they spend their free time profitably.

While the modern school assumes that students should be crammed with knowledge, the workshop is constructed around the idea of enabling students to acquire and develop the right tools, around the idea of changing people. In the 'workshop' students learn ways of doing things and master the appropriate tools by trial and error, under the supervision of a master who can show them 'how to work' and answer any questions about methods and tools. As they learn new ways of working, the students themselves become different people. The main figure in the workshop is the person who is able to show others how to do things, and on the basis of this, assumes the role of a master. Somebody must take on the role of student and begin working on a product under the supervision of the master. At the same time, the master should be interested not only in the finished product, but above all in how it is made, and with what tools. It is important for students learn to use the instruments properly and not to make a hash of the work. In this context, the preparation of the product or article itself lies within the sphere of practical activity, while learning to use the tools of a trade lies within the sphere of education.

In a workshop, students gain experience and become familiar with

Fig ure 7.12 The workshop

the tools of their trade. Sometimes it is possible to have a situation in which neither master nor student is able to achieve a result from the work. Then it is essential to identify the problem and to move on to design and analytical work in order to identify and develop appropriate tools and a new method of working.

The purpose and function of the workshop

The purpose of the managerial reserve workshop is to support and maintain the intellectual capital of the corporation and to organise, for this purpose, systematic anthropotechnic training for the personnel reserve intended for managerial positions. As far as the HR policy of the corporation is concerned, the workshop works in two directions:

◆ to ensure normal operations and increase the 'life span' of people and organisational mega-machines;
◆ to ensure the roll-out of programmes for the development of businesses and integrated structures, their organisation and personnel.

The most important components of the corporation's nucleus of activity are:

◆ intellectual capital (R&D);
◆ the brand (that is, important consumer attributes of the product);
◆ the employees who are 'carriers' of intellectual capital and brand principles (everything else can nowadays be divided up between global production sites and production modules).

The form taken by work in the workshop involves:

◆ the organisation of work within a strictly defined timeframe and thematic structure;
◆ self-monitoring by each participant of progress in mastering the content of the training programme;
◆ the organisation of collective tests and graded exercises for the sake of transparency and competitive ranking of participants;
◆ a change in place of work (and type of production activity) as the chief outcome of participants' efforts.

In the programme of works on KM organised by the Corporate University, the workshop acts as a way of accumulating methods and knowledge, and of passing these on to new generations of managers within the corporation.

Goals and objectives of workshop training

Employees in personnel reserve groups who go through workshop activities must master the following:

◆ the technique of rapidly grasping the specific characteristics of various administrative and organisational structures;
◆ the ability to join the group that draws up the rules of the organisation and the rules of the game within the management system;
◆ a willingness to clearly define their own position (by asking what must be done and what can be done by them);
◆ the ability to identify and schematise the field of activity for management seen from this perspective (developing maps for situational analysis and diagrams of facilities in order to analyse the situation);

- various approaches and methods for programme and project development;
- the principles of inventory building for large groups: the ability to identify partners. rivals and saboteurs in the field;
- practice exercises involving the deliberate creation of opposition to the organisation (in order to define managerial direction).

They must also, on the basis of periodic training and the accumulation of experience, acquire:

- the ability in a given situation to understand and to technically define (and thus manage) what is going on, what the situation involves, who is going where and who has ended up where, and so on;
- the ability to identify a strategy correctly: to ask, in the given situation, what needs to be done and what can be done by someone in their position;
- a set of models for possible transformative action (persuading, exerting force, outplaying, controlling the situation, managing the process of change);
- techniques for staging and predicting potential results: what outcome is desired and what outcomes are possible;
- methods of evaluating possible outcomes in accordance with strategic goals and intentions (long-term goals);
- the techniques of schematisation in order to translate meaning into knowledge (essential for the preparation and transfer of what has been understood to business partners, or for drawing up work plans for staff responsible for performing a given task).

The principles underpinning workshop training

The principle of practicality: an emphasis on the accumulation and transfer of experience

This principle is necessary in situations where people are being transformed gradually, step by step. It stands in opposition to the principle of 'cultural transfer', which, instead of altering people, involves filling them with 'theoretical' knowledge that has been accumulated by humankind. It is useless to accumulate an enormous mass of knowledge for future use – it goes in at one ear and out the other. In today's world, it is less important to replenish your stock of knowledge than be able to forget superfluous information you have accumulated.

The principle of the training of intellectual functions

Each cycle of work in the workshop is considered as training under the guidance of a master – a coach in the practice of accumulating experience. Just as sports training leads to an improvement in muscle strength, training in a workshop leads to a deepening of understanding, until reflection becomes automatic, and you are able to state your opinion accurately and to the point, make yourself understood correctly, and so on. It is possible to test how far you have progressed in your training by comparing yourself against and competing against others. Those who cannot stand the workload are weeded out.

The principle of team organisation

What we call learning is only possible in an appropriate work environment. Learning is a function of the rules of behaviour and communication of whatever group a person happens to be in – a family, company, team or crew. More often than not, a person ends up in such a group naturally, as it were. Targeted training should be structured as a specially organised communicative space. An effective model of just such a space was created during the Soviet era. It was made up of a series of organisations and corresponding groups which were embedded in one another – the 'October Children', the Young Pioneers, the Komsomol, party members, trade unions and so on. People were brought right up through this system. Organisers and managers grew up through this 'public work' and there was no need for any special management training.

The disciplinary approach and the position of a 'student'

This is the fostering of the ability to submit to standard thinking (or action) and to adhere strictly to it. Subordination to your seniors is a direct expression of the social hierarchy. The ability to consciously submit to standard thinking is not regarded as a tool of leadership and subordination, but is encouraged and developed during the course of some exciting and involving activity. Today, most educational institutions are structured as enterprises that basically pass on systems of subject-related knowledge to students, in which a local system of discipline (attendance, behaviour in class and performance during exams) is in operation. It is only possible to get practical discipline training – that is to say genuine discipline training – by independently adopting the most effective position, that of the 'student', as a rule outside the education system.

The contents of the practical workshop training programme for the managerial reserve

'Pressing issues'

Participants from the managerial reserve are invited to the workshop to discuss pressing issues in the system of corporate management. For instance, in 2011 the following issues were discussed:

- reorganising the corporation into a divisional structure;
- the move from managing factories to managing programmes;
- organising R&D and programme management for the product lifespan;
- lean thinking and organising final assembly according to plans that 'extend' the process of value creation.
- efficient organisation of supply chains;
- designing a modern MRO system;
- other issues, depending on the situation.

Willingness to change

During workshop activities, the members of the personnel reserve must demonstrate a high level of readiness to change. They must show, in the first instance, that they are willing to change themselves, and on this basis to take on the challenge of new tasks from adjacent and undeveloped areas of activity, undergoing experience in various areas of work and thematic groups in the course of training.

General management training (GMT)

GMT is a complex of disciplines which ensure that specialists master the modern techniques of self-organisation. An employee who wishes to become a senior manager – that is, to lead others and establish goals for them – must be able to:

845

◆ set meaningful and achievable goals;
◆ plan their own activity and organise the work of a small group, team, enterprise or organisation;
◆ acquire experience without the help of specialist educators (in other words, to learn);
◆ to this end, analyse their own thinking and activity (to think about activity methodologically);
◆ organise communication during complex work with the participation of numerous specialists and professionals (people from outside their own circle);
◆ quickly grasp the essence of a given task in a rapidly changing situation, understand precisely and keep their own position as well as the position of those with whom they are in communication, during any job and in any situation;
◆ most importantly, have the mental and physical preparedness or fitness to do this as long as it needs to be done, in order to achieve the intended result.

Schematisation and project design

Participants of the personnel reserve group should master the techniques of schematisation and project design. (This is discussed in greater detail below in the section 'Constructive thinking: what it is and how it works', page 872). The selection of the managerial reserve group is carried out in a competitive environment. A group of 80 people begin training and at each successive stage there is a weeding-out of those unable to meet the demands of the training. As a result, by the end of the training cycle we have a hierarchical grading of the entire group, plus a small group of people who can be deployed in corporate management.

The workshop curriculum

The package of projects organised in the workshop joins together three types of process:

◆ the formation of a working environment in which not textbook problems, but real, practical problems are presented, in which competitiveness is encouraged and management ambitions nurtured;
◆ the use of play simulations, which make it possible to gain

experience in taking complex management decisions without risk to your own career;

◆ the development of schematisation techniques and design of ad hoc knowledge systems as supporting rationale for management decisions.

It is clear that it is impossible to organise work of this sort in the form of standard classroom lessons. The fact is that these competences, techniques and aptitudes are essentially indivisible from the individual employee. They cannot be taken in, read and memorised; they must be acquired as a result of training, of competition, reflection on your own successes and failures, and through specially organised simulations and artificially created problem situations.

Organisational activity games (OAGs) are the basic structure on which the workshop curriculum rests. All other types of work and training are in some way or other dependent on the OAGs. They serve as a performance platform in which people can receive experience in management decision taking in the course of collective team confrontations. Solving genuine management problems gives participants training in the development of management techniques: self-organisation and the organisation of others, design, analytics and so on. The use of problematisation techniques, worked out during OAGs, enables participants to break out of stagnant patterns of thinking, and ensures a concentration of collective mental activity. This makes it possible for the participants to achieve the intended result, and they can then be asked to reflect methodologically on the events of the session.

The topic of an OAG cycle is worked out by the senior management of the corporation based on problems and challenges that are of immediate importance at any given time, or about to become important in the future. During the sessions, work is carried out according to a standard model: first: solution of analytical problems; second: familiarisation with the techniques of thinking; third: designing and planning of managerial work. If the participants in these sessions are to be able to carry out the analytical and design work and devise the required projects and programmes, they must master the methods needed to actually perform this work. Therefore, at each session, the organisers decide how to equip the participants with the essential tools and methods of constructive thinking: the basics of schematisation, methodological reflection, understanding and so on.

The design of a series of organisational activity games (OAGs)

The basic plan of the series configures a number of production, work and game processes. Every participant follows an individual trajectory during these sessions. Each session of OAGs is structured in such a way as to simulate a particular problematic situation in the work of the corporation. During the games, these situations are worked out through simulated confrontations between teams and specialists, and cast in forms that a modern manager might have to deal with. All the participants in a session can have a go at assuming the role of manager of a small group, project, programme, enterprise and so on.

At the same time, participants develop management techniques which will help them to lead their group or project. This is a specifically administrative (mega-machine) organisation of activity – by team, corporation, infrastructure and so on according to the situation. For each type of 'management object' different management tools can be tried out, leading to corresponding management result.

There is also room for homework in the workshop. Homework gives participants the opportunity to monitor how ready they are for the work in hand and to reflect individually on the topic of the sessions. But the most important thing is still the group work organised by game technicians, in which participants pass through the 'centrifuge' of the game.

Differences in the organisation of work in the managerial reserve workshop and in the 'class and lesson' system of education

Comprehensive schools and universities that prepare fully developed, balanced personalities, make use of the educational techniques known as the class and lesson system of education, which is about 400 years old. This system was developed in a particular historical period to solve the problems of a particular time.

The 'conveyor belt' of the class and lesson system is constructed as follows. The teacher conveys to each student during the appropriate lesson (or lecture) a particular fragment of a specific system

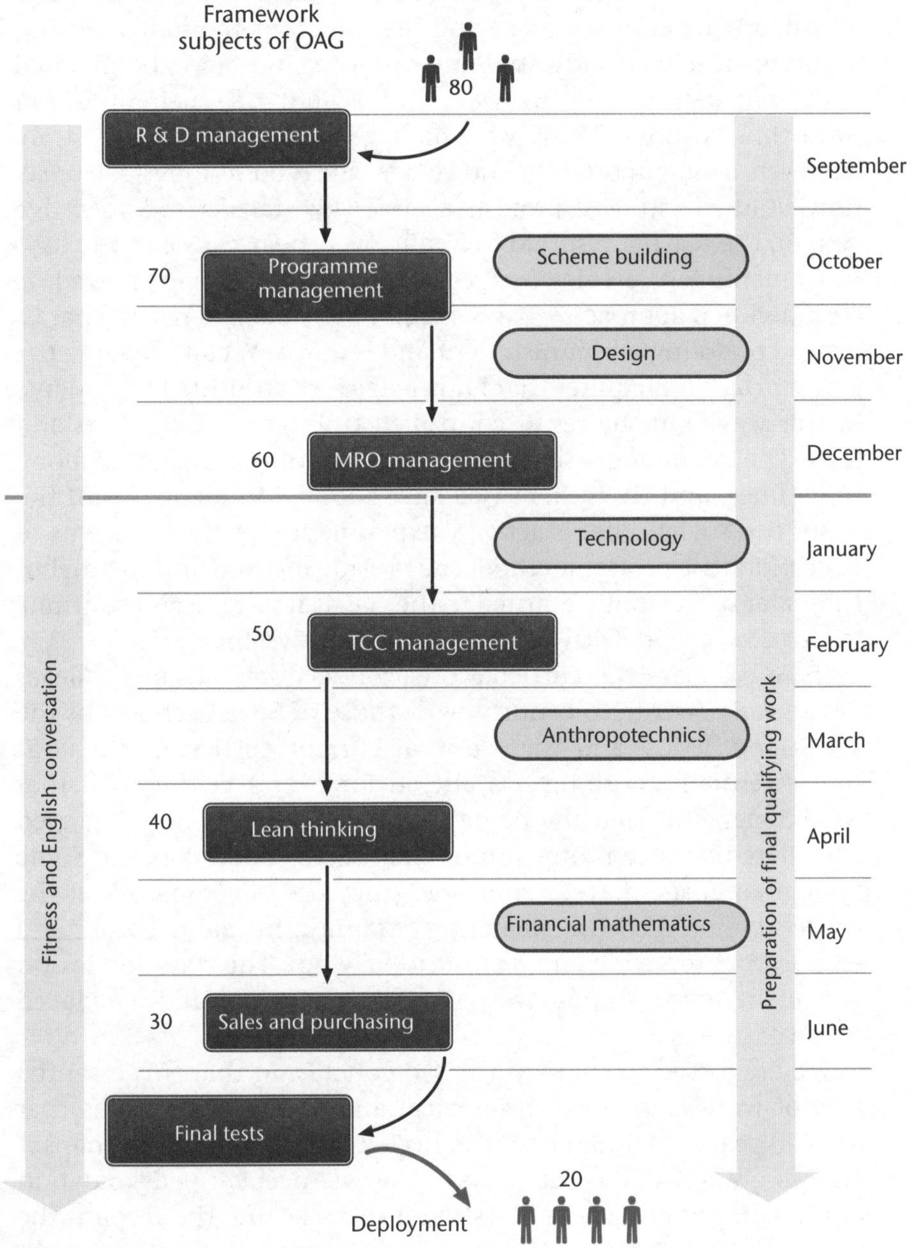

Figure 7.13 Construction of a series of organisational activity games

of knowledge. For the first lesson, an English teacher arrives; then there is a break; for the second lesson, a mathematician; for the third lesson, a teacher of language and literature; for the fourth lesson, a physics teacher. Many students cannot stand being bombarded with information in this way, and switch off their attention from time to time. Those who manage to withstand the test are left with a hotchpotch of knowledge. Everybody longs for break time. And if a student protests against this transfer of knowledge system, the teacher resorted to a cane over the backside in the days of Comenius, or a ruler over the knuckles, or perhaps nowadays an individual approach – pandering to the student's needs, that is, instead of doling out punishment and rewards. Yet all the same the core curriculum requires that knowledge be transmitted to students in this way, and the result controlled through examinations and tests. The German classical *gymnasium* school was organised along these lines, and the system was later adopted in Russia. Until the 1930s the Soviet schools actively experimented with new forms of education (the project method, the brigade method and so on), but they later successfully returned to the classical system, and continue to this day to work with the class and lesson system.

If we compare the curricula of secondary schools and colleges of the early twentieth century with those of Soviet schools of the 1930s and 1940s, and then look at current curricula, it is clear that essentially, nothing has altered for over a century. All that has happened is that the names of certain subjects have changed and there have been some minor changes to course content. Some foreign languages have disappeared (they used to study five at the *gymnasium*) and so has elementary training in manual work and engineering (drawing and technical drawing). The class and lesson system in school supports a classical curriculum and a reduced menu of subjects.

We are forced to come to the sad conclusion that this essential area of work employs technological and technical solutions that are 400 years old and, of course, hopelessly out of date. Perhaps it is precisely this that is the cause of the ever-deepening degradation of humankind as a whole. We should also take into the account the obvious fact that managers of any kind wish to avoid situations in which those they are supervising turn out to be more intelligent than they are themselves. Nothing solves this particular problem better than falling standards of education – although at the same

Table 7.2 The class and lesson system and the managerial reserve workshop compared

	Class and lesson system	**Managerial reserve workshop**
Organisation of content	A lesson (lecture) organised by a teacher with a group of students of approximately the same age (or a class consisting of up to 25 people) in order to pass on some information or working method familiar to the teacher.	Organisational activity games, run by organisers of team work for participants (in ten groups of from five to seven people), applying knowledge management to find solutions to problems posed by the client.
Aims and objectives	The transmission of accumulated human culture in the form of scholarly subjects. The principle of Comenius – 'teach everyone everything'.	Preparation for organisational projects which do not yet exist but which should be created, bringing in the necessary tools for this from outside.
Regulators of the learning process	Text books, methodology, use of example, timetables, educational law.	Simulated future scenarios, practice to enable the development of tools, learning by trial and error.
Maintenance of discipline among students	Leadership of teachers, system of punishments and rewards.	Self-organisation, assuming standards of team work.

time there is a risk that the quality of the managerial contingent itself will also deteriorate.

The workshop technique is designed not to transmit knowledge but to deploy people in contemporary corporate infrastructures and activity systems. Furthermore, it does not require students to demonstrate a uniform level of training and does not imply a hierarchical ranking using tests and examinations. The organisers of the training programme create a simulation of a problematic situation, the team members immerse themselves in it to solve any urgent practical tasks, and to build a system of activities (jobs) to overcome the problems. Every participant sees (and reflects on) their results and capabilities and is free to enter into the process and leave it at their own discretion.

Unlike the conveyor belt of the class and lesson system, the workshop technique is structured like a centrifuge. According to directives set out by the senior managers of a corporation, 'problem material' is presented to the workshop and is observed by all the participants from different angles (positions) and different speeds (depending on group dynamics and the forming and reforming of working groups). As a result, the problem is broken down or stratified into one to which a solution can be found, and the participants are stratified according to their ability to approach this solution and the extent to which they are engaged in the work. Each participant comes out of the 'game centrifuge' with their own unique result. We should once more stress that the game centrifuge, unlike the educational conveyor belt, is not an act of violence practised on the students: it works on the principle of attraction ('pull') rather than repulsion ('push'). The work of the collective takes place on a public platform in conditions of organised collective communication and participatory planning (in which all group members take part). There are no teachers or textbooks which determine the limits of the topic. Everybody can see immediately who is capable of what. People who understand what they have done are ready to take a step into the unknown, whereas people who do not want to get sucked in to the centrifuge can calmly walk by (and so maintain the status quo). In order to achieve the centrifuge effect, (see below for a typical procedure) in organisational activity games, the following must be created:

To achieve 'the centrifugal effect' (see below on standard rules of organisational activity games) the following are required:

◆ high levels of psychological and physical pressure;
◆ the simulation of actual problem situations;
◆ conditions which encourage participants to exercise self-determination;
◆ opportunities for participants to design their own actions and the actions of their team (as only designing makes people think, and only those who design have the ability to think).

In contrast to the centrifuge model of such games, the educational conveyor belt could be described as resembling the process of sowing. After the field has been ploughed, the seeds are poured into the seeding machine which is driven over the field, and every seed must be planted in the right row. For every student, teachers must find a 'way in' (plough) and plant a 'seed' of knowledge. If teachers are not able to do so, and no green shoots appear, they have not done their work properly. The centrifuge of the game separates the

Figure 7.14 The organisation of an organisational activity game

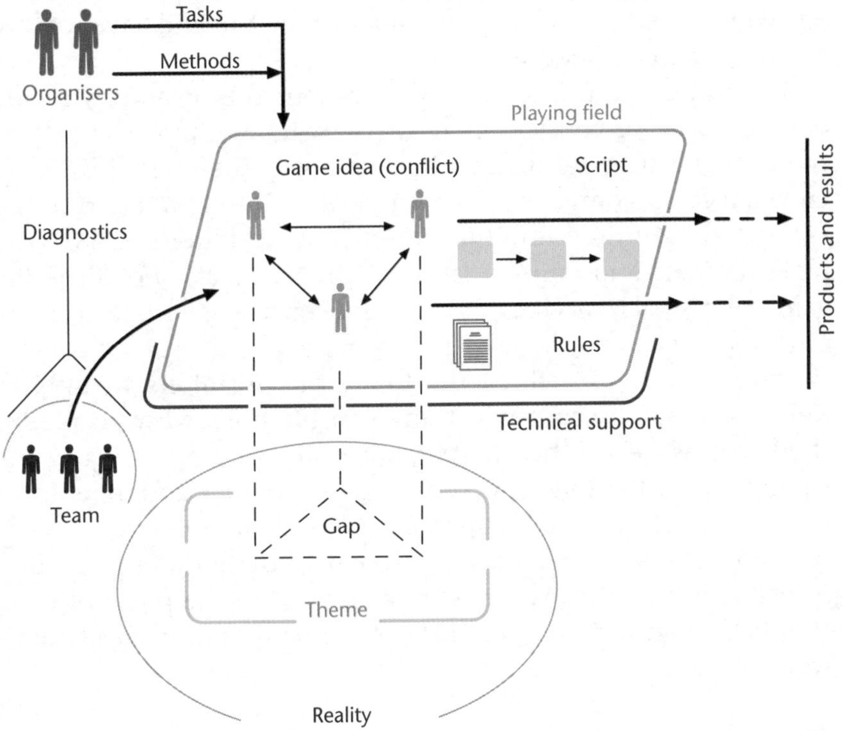

participants of the workshop into classes on the basis of their input into the solution of the problem situation. Some take on the task of finding a solution, others get involved in the work, while others throw in the towel. Some have a greater talent for reflection; some make progress in schematisation, and others show high levels of fitness. Those who are successful get the hang of it, and those who don't will not become a part of the managerial system, but will remain in a supportive capacity.

The organisational design of OAGs

Each OAG is a complex event requiring careful preparation. From the point of view of simulation, organisers should consider the event from beginning to end and put together an organisational plan describing the structure and arrangement of activities which need be collectively organised and realised.

The game is the most effective form for posing problems and

progressing in the understanding of particular topics. Since the middle of the twentieth century the world's leading corporations and educational institutions have understood this and have actively exploited game formats in their work.

In formulating the topic of the session, the organisers decide on the object of consideration for the whole group. The plot of the game must be formulated in such a way that participants are encouraged to compete to win the game. The rationale running through the entire cycle of the project-analytical session (PAS) is the main defining and limiting factor in the formulation of a specific game 'plot' – each specific PAS should be consistent with the general direction of work.[4]

Once they have defined the topic, the organisers themselves must work out its contents, using consultations with people 'in the know' as well as the Internet, books and magazines. The game should result in a product whose design is specified, and should also bring about shifts in participants' technical 'equipment', or steps forward in their development. In order to design and plan their future activities, the organisers must set out in the protocol what should happen and what should be obtained as a result of the team's work.

Construction of a PAS

To conduct a working seminar, it is quite sufficient to identify the theme, the products and the results, and to set a task for the participants. But this is not enough in order to conduct a game. The organisers need to think about how the playing field will be organised and consistently create scenarios for all the actions that will occur in this field. The game is a simulation of activities that take place in the real world. However, this simulation brings together a lot of 'fuzzy' areas from real life; it brings together people with a common interest who usually work separately, in an uncoordinated fashion. Therefore the PAS simulation must be much more eventful and more rigorous than life itself. The game needs to capture the essence of things and the key moments of reality that often pass unnoticed in day-to-day life.

Each PAS participant has to take up a particular position on the

---

4   Note: the OAG was outlined by G. P. Shchedrovitsky; the PAS is a concept by the present authors.

playing field. During the game the participants do not act on their own behalf, in accordance with their own opinions; instead they act in accordance with the principles and patterns of thought appropriate to the position they occupy in the game. The game is based on conflicts or confrontations between different gaming positions. During the communication arising from these confrontations, participants come to understand certain issues, and new content is created. Conflict is a prerequisite for the emergence of thought. Bearing in mind the structure of the playing field, the positions of the players and the technical specifications of the game, it is essential to create a scenario, to consider how events should unfold during the game. In the scenario, the organisers of the game calculate the actions that participants holding game positions may or should take.

Isolation of participants from everyday life

It is essential to isolate the participants in the workshop from daily routines as far as possible for the duration of the game so that they are able to focus on discussions of the topic and problem definition. The best way to ensure this is to accommodate the participants in an extramural centre.

Diagnostics and stratification

To allow the organisers to understand the state of each participant, there should be a continual process of evaluation. The results of this evaluation process will determine the placement of participants in game positions and changes made in the scenario during the course of the game.

Actions of the game organisers

Directive

The technical directive is an essential condition for the beginning of each new stage of the game. The directive must re-establish the picture as a whole. Before the beginning of the game (or the next stage in the game), the goals, objectives and purpose of tasks carried out during the game are re-established, and preceding stages of the work are summarised. The team needs to understand what has been done already, what needs to be done and the necessary result.

Functional breakdown.

The placement of people in working groups requires a general work plan and a list of tasks for each group in the game.

Methodology

The participants and scenarios for the work carried out by the groups on particular topics must be organised in such a way as to generate 'natural' conflicts.

Organisation of work in groups

To tackle the problems set by the directive, the team splits into groups (of ideally seven, but in any case between five and nine people). The group should discuss their own task, how to perform it, do the work and document the results. Different members of the group should be given responsibility to act as speaker at the general meeting, archivist (who records all the progress made by the group), organiser of communication, and so on.

General meetings

The group brings the results of its work to the table in a number of general meetings. At the plenary session the leading role belongs to the organiser of communication, who conducts the meeting, and to the methodologist, who is responsible for the models and concepts that the group should use. Experts, customers and others act out their positions here. The plenary session is a place for confrontation between groups representing different positions (completely opposed, contradictory or competing). The groups debate the content of the game using constructive criticism in the form of questions and comments to the speaker. The organiser of communication puts a stop to any conflict that arises.

Entering the topic of a game

If the participants do not have any idea of the subject of a forth-coming game or have no experience in working in a given area, then they may very quickly become involved in design work, as it is particularly easy to design and to change something when you are not weighed down by the old ways of doing things. However,

Figure 7.15 The techniques of staging organisational activity games

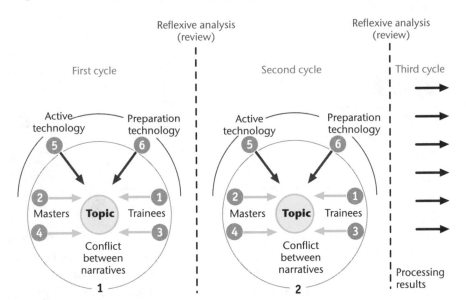

before beginning design work, the team members need to get an idea about the forthcoming object of consideration and understand the need for change (that is, project initiatives during the game). If the participants are already 'in the know' and have some experience of the work, then in order to enter into the topic of the game they need to be prepared to forget everything they already know about this topic, to question things that appear obvious. In order to ensure that the group is prepared for this approach, the game organisers usually bring in authoritative people who are convinced of the need to change and can help attune participants towards exploratory development.

Reflecting on the game

The game ends with a reflective analysis of the collective actions of both organisers and participants during the course of the game. The focus of this review can either be identified by each partici-pant independently or proposed by the organisers: reflecting is like the assembly (the fitting together) of constructive ideas which have been worked out during the game, reflection on working methods, and so on. Whatever the players are able to fully reflect on is what

Figure 7.16 The role of organisers and game designers in organisational activity games

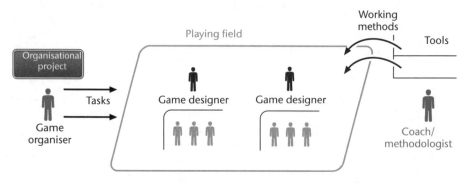

will remain with them as the result of the game. This review process is not about only the formalisation of results. Review involves the re-evaluation of everything that has happened. Its purpose is to encourage understanding and the acquisition (accumulation) of experience.

The structure and methods of the game design team

To organise such complex operations as OAGs, the group of organisers, or the game design team, must operate in a technically precise, co-ordinated fashion. Various functions and management tasks are split up among the game design team, but in performing their role, each team member must understand the idea of the game as a whole and act in accordance with the overall objectives.

Developing working methods

In order for participants to develop methods of intellectual work the organisers and business simulation team should set tasks that allow for this sort of work to take place.

Staging a situation

It is essential to stage a situation in which the participants have to solve a problem for which they do not have a ready-made solution. If participants reach a dead end in their attempts to solve the task, a working method should be suggested to them.

Figure 7.17 Task-solving in organisational activity games

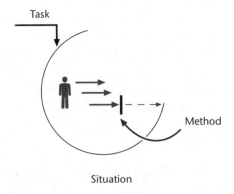

Showing by example

A specialist in business simulation must always be prepared to act as a master who can show how to use a particular method, provide an example of how work should be done, and explain the technique or the sequence of operations that need to be performed

The knowledge management game, and knowledge management training

KM is the basic work process in a corporation that has set out on the path of development. Training in KM is essential for those people who will be responsible for creating new activities based on

Figure 7.18 The role of the coach in organisational activity games

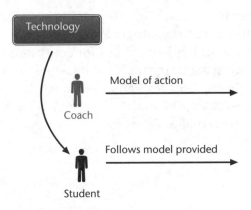

a real-life understanding of the situation, for people who are ready to change and to work on real resources. It is essential, in other words, for those people who are willing to change themselves and their work. The purpose of training in KM is to bring about a change in participants' modes of thought and actions, from an objective-ontological mode to an organisational-work mode, in the course of finding situations to organisational problems that are of current interest to the corporation.

Functions of the KM game

◆ To ensure the ability of the management system to control the work of the organisation's own executives without the use of intermediaries – consultants, advisers or competitors.
◆ To anticipate and hence forecast impending change; a continual readiness to take action in new situations.
◆ As a tool with which to combat natural inertia of thought and to get rid of or avoid '*muda*' (the term for waste in lean thinking).

The KM process

Work in the game is preceded by a preparatory course lasting at least one month. The topic is worked out by means of simulated thinking, and the appropriate organisation of work is determined. At the same time, work is carried out in selecting and setting tasks for the participants.

Work itself begins with the formulation of productive and efficient terms of reference and technical objectives from the clients – the senior management of the corporation – for the participants (see Figure 7.19). As the project teams move forward towards their targets, a process of natural selection takes place whereby people who are not ready or able to solve the tasks are weeded out. As a rule, 20 per cent of the participants get as far as stage 5 – at which point an action programme is worked out for continuing developments. These people form a group which can be relied on when organising development projects. Stages 3 and 4 are of particular importance in the process of work on KM, as they require that participants demonstrate their intellectual abilities in project design and conceptual schematisation.

Figure 7.19 Knowledge management in organisational activity games

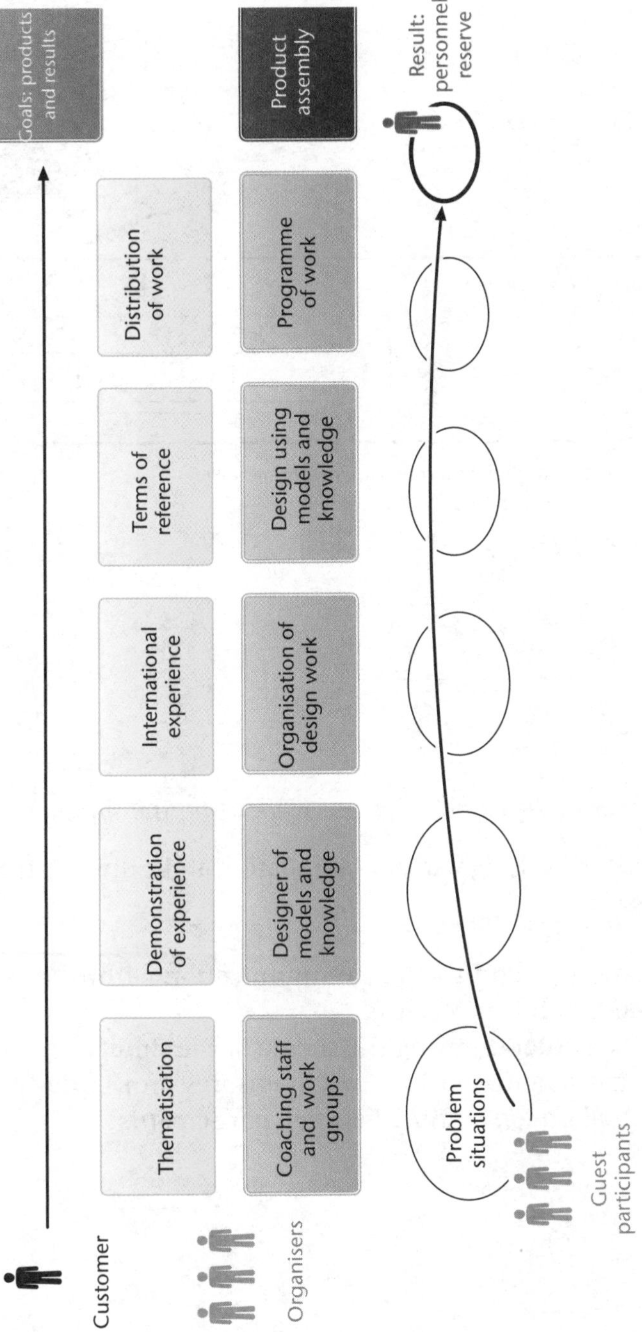

Figure 7.20 The process of work with the simulator

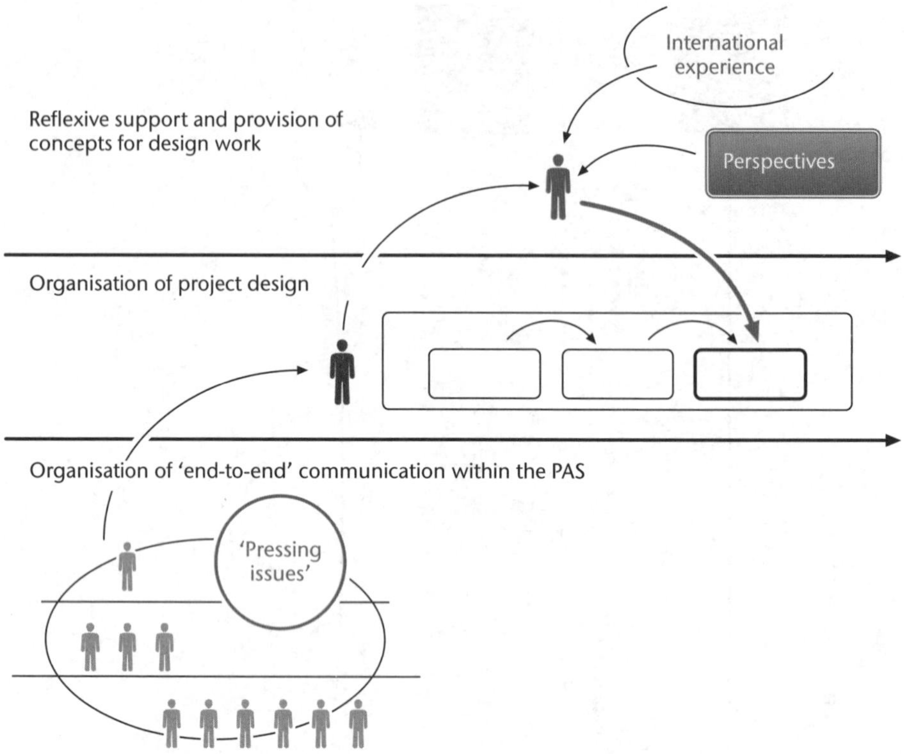

International experience

Reflexive support and provision of concepts for design work

Perspectives

Organisation of project design

Organisation of 'end-to-end' communication within the PAS

'Pressing issues'

Debriefing, or after-action review of work using the simulator

The process of working with the simulator can be divided into three subprocesses:

◆ organisation of 'end-to-end' communication within the working groups and public meetings;
◆ project construction using the theme of the simulator;
◆ conceptual schematisation, which ensures project development and mutual understanding between participants.

Tools used during workshop training of the managerial reserve

Never suffer sleep to close thy eyelids after thy going to bed, till thou hast thrice reviewed all thy actions of the day: Wherein have I done amiss? What have I done? What have I omitted that I ought to have done? If in this examination thou find that thou hast done amiss, reprimand thyself severely for it; and if thou hast done any good, rejoice.

(The Golden Verses of Pythagoras)

The attitude of the apprentice

The attitude of the apprentice is of great importance in life. This concept lies at the heart of the work in the managerial reserve workshop. An apprentice is a person who has taken another as a model and copies that other person. The apprentice needs to find a model and then try to recreate it. This is the most reliable method of learning there is. Only someone who deliberately imitates a model can be considered an apprentice.

Now we have a situation in which most people who have gone through comprehensive school are not able to take up the position of an apprentice. They see themselves as 'well-balanced personalities' and as they are not capable of copying anybody or anything, they do not want to do so.

The lower layer in Figure 7.21 shows the lifecycle of the human body, a human's instrument. This concept was first introduced by Socrates 2,000 years ago. He claimed that people use their bodies as instruments, and that we need to distinguish between subjectivity, which is the individual, and instrumentality, which is their body. The next layer shows the sequence of types of schools that people should go through, according to Comenius (nursery school, native language school, foreign language school, school of world art, school that enables the acquisition some type of skill, and so on). People here are like a composite of all the schools through which they have passed.

The third layer of Figure 7.21 represents an individual and their aims. At some point between the ages of 13 and 16, most people have the opportunity, and sometimes if they are lucky enough to have good teachers the ability, to set goals from themselves. The goals are represented as a series of 'tunnels of opportunity', and each tunnel contains the choice of one path. Goals cannot be set once

Opening a new training centre

and for all, although some historical examples of this do indeed exist. Depending on the situation, some goals may be exchanged for others, and new goals may be put forward. This process of goal-setting defines a person. If they decide at any point that they have no goals, then they are not a person, but simply an object that may be manipulated by other people.

The top layer in Figure 7.21 is a layer represents the basis on which goals can meaningfully be discussed and set. This top layer includes spheres of activity, worlds and horizons. For example, an individual can set goals that cover their entire lifetime. They can decide, for instance, what they want to have achieved by the time they die. Or they might define themselves in areas of activity and projects for which the achievement of their goal requires a much longer time than their lifespan. Therefore, during their lifetime they will need to

Figure 7.21 The trajectory of the individual in the sphere of education

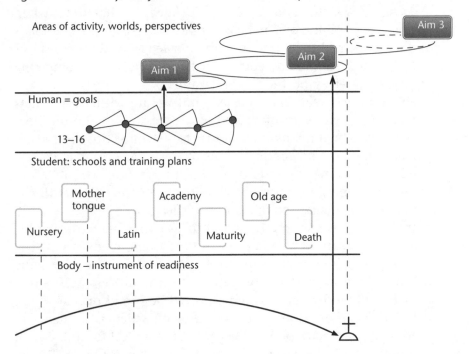

prepare successors, the next generation of people who will continue towards the goals that were set by (or for) them.

Why do we need this picture of an individual trajectory? We need it simply in order to get a detached view of ourselves. To see the limitations of our own lives, to calculate what resources we have, and what opportunities we have to acquire methods and techniques, and to set meaningful goals of our own.

The difference between the processes of learning and teaching

Teaching is an activity, the purpose of which is to raise, train and educate people. Learning consists of actions carried out by people with the purpose of growing, training and educating themselves. A mother teaches her children to watch, listen, walk, take a spoon in their hand, sit on the potty at the right time. Children try to copy their loved ones – are desperate to do everything just as they do. At first, they don't manage. Yet they try again and again.

'Teach everything to everyone' insisted Comenius in *The Great Didactic* (1658). It was a revolutionary idea for that time, when against a background of general ignorance, a small group of scholars and teachers held the monopoly on knowledge. And that idea was put into practice. Today, educational institutions are competing among themselves for students and trainees.

Five hundred years have passed, and we are witnessing a new revolution. There is an open and easy access to all the information amassed by humankind. In order to 'be competitive in today's global world' as the motto of the modern careerist has it, you need to know how to get rid of all this information. The ability to learn is becoming increasingly significant in connection with the commercial revitalisation of institutes of learning.

In order to learn something and to live your life with dignity, it is not necessary to be a hostage of the system of education. The best teacher is life itself. Hope for success and fortune may smile on you. Many successful people never went to university. The title of 'self-made individual' is something to be proud of. Life is the true arena of education, the substance of which is available to everybody. Karl Marx provided a precise theoretical formulation of this notion when he wrote, 'The essence of a man is not an abstract quality, inherent in each separate individual. It is, in effect, the totality of social relations in which a man enters over the course of his life.'

Those people in life who do not want to beg scraps from nature's table must embark on the path of meaningful learning, and they must act purposefully. For this they need a 'map' of the world of learning, complete with guidelines and directions for potential movement. It is also a good idea to have a guide. At first, together with the guide, they can trace out the necessary route on the map, and then they act, setting off in the direction indicated.

In the modern world, teaching begins at the time when a person decides (or is forced to decide) to stop being looked after and become a free agent (one who acts of their own free will and is responsible for their actions). The education provided by school through a diet of learning comes to an end, and it is time for the process of self-education to begin, although it is true that this takes a different form – that of learning in the time free from 'basic work'. The transition from scholastic training to self-education is not easy. It is not something that will come about as a matter of course at the right time and place. It means re-thinking your concept of yourself: changing yourself from a looked-after individual to a free person, and then adhering strictly to certain rules of self-organisation.

Brief instructions for those entering the world of apprenticeship

Those who do not wish to be deceived in their search for essential knowledge and skills should take the trouble to analyse the situation and plan their own activities in the learning process. Learning will be effective only if you set yourself an absolutely specific goal: to change and transform yourself, to organise your consciousness and the *modus operandi* you have mastered, as you move towards your goals and your ideals.

The activity of learning is based on the fulfilment of a few simple requirements: watch how I do it, listen to my explanations, try to do it yourself.

It can also be seen as the realisation of several requirements: act, analyse your unsuccessful actions, work out how the thing can be done, plan a new action.

A few simple principles may be used as guidelines in the world of learning.

Find a group

Whatever people might say about a level playing field, all people belong from birth to a specific social group, economic class, urban or rural civilisation, be it a gated community in the suburbs or the outskirts of a big city. Then there are two stimuli for education. The first is to retain your membership of that level of social achievement group (social class), not to fall beneath your current status. The second is to move upward through the social hierarchy. As they say, 'birds of a feather flock together'. If you end up in jail, you will get the chance to come out as a professional criminal; if you get into Oxford or the Moscow State Institute of International Relations, you will have the opportunity to belong to the ruling elite. Your environment forms you. If you want to be socially competent and financially successful, seek out the company of literate and socially successful people.

Find a school

You may get a place in an elite school (there are very few of these and they are well known), but you may also get a place in an illusory one (most schools are of this type: the teachers pretend to teach, and students pretend to learn). It is a rare case indeed, but it is the very essence of the matter of education, to find that a real, working school that has grown up on the basis of an educational institution. A school in the true sense of the word implies the presence of a special metaphysics – a body of ideas, principles, concepts, techniques and schemes, which it conveys to its students. It also presupposes bearers of that metaphysics: masters, teachers, apprentices, tutors, as well as interested students. Through this collective effort, a specific content is created. Through this collective effort, the process of education is carried out: and an attitude is formed, an attitude to life, to your colleagues, to yourself and to the common cause.

Find a teacher

It is important to occupy an 'interesting' place in society and to get into a school. But apart from this, it is essential to earn enough to make a living. In order to learn to do something useful and to learn a skill you need a model: a master. The master can pass on a way of working and a way of thinking to the student. During work with a master, what is sometimes called 'education and training content' will arise. Content should not be confused with form.

The contents of the educational process consist of the accumulated wisdom of humanity, all that has been enshrined in textbooks, curricula and teaching plans, and which is passed on by teachers and higher academic staff to students and apprentices. The definition of 'teacher' can be applied to anyone who is able to design some special organisational form – such as a training session, an exercise, a challenge, game or a test – in order to make use of their own experience and summarise and schematise this experience as knowledge. For this they need a student, one who will take on the task and reconstruct the method to try it in practice. If the student grasps how the method works and when it can be applied, a content 'event' takes place.

Master the methods of work

Only 100 years ago the content of training and education was identical to culture. (As Lenin said when he addressed Komsomol members, 'You can only become communists when you have assimilated all the culture that humankind has accumulated.')

In today's world, the role of culture has changed and the social mobility of individuals has dramatically increased. We have already become accustomed to new developments in manufacturing, following one after another in quick succession. They cause mass migrations of specialists from one area of work to another, and rapid changes in profession. Every time this happens, people are faced with the need to learn new things. Often they have neither the time nor the energy to do this. This means that people should be as well prepared as possible in advance for changing jobs and specialist professions: they should have a general education which provides the essential foundation for a wide number of jobs, reducing the process of retraining to a minimum.

In specialist professional training, the first level of specialist training is completed at the age of only 20–21, while higher-level training ends at 24–28 years. The level of training remains very low, and is often inadequate for modern production. Attempts to make learning broader and more general go down the route of mechanical integration, and as a consequence increase the quantity of knowledge presented to those undergoing retraining. The solution is to develop a 'toolkit' of universal methods of work which provides the basic essentials for life. This will allow for the efficient construction of an individual trajectory.

Learn to build the necessary knowledge on your own

There has always been a shortage of teachers who are able to set a challenge and guide students through the work in order to arrive at the necessary content. That is why it is important to learn work methods and put into use the necessary tools on your own. There is a widespread myth according to which we all have choice of education, choice of professions, academic courses, knowledge, skills and so on. The myth is underpinned by the idea of the supermarket. According to the myth, you wander down the aisles, choosing from the enormous variety on offer, according to what you want and what you can afford. But in actual fact, you have to take whatever you are palmed off with. When there are few teachers and many students, work needs to be sensibly organised and planned over the time available. It was for this purpose that the class and lesson system, school subjects and 'scholastic' knowledge, collective attendance at lectures, group training, large-scale game exercises, exams and tests were created. We might recall here Goethe's words on the subject: 'A school graduate is like a cannon which has been loaded for many years so that it could fire only once – at the exam, after which there is nothing left in it.'

You cannot just take off the shelf precisely what you need. New knowledge requires project development, then an analysis and identification of resources, without which the project cannot be implemented.

Follow disciplinary standards

You cannot achieve anything if you do not force yourself to follow strict disciplinary standards. A daily routine, a timetable and correct organisation of the interactions in the team and in the sphere of activity are all basic conditions for effective learning. When you set about learning, you must accept the standards that lie behind the concepts of 'routine', 'work', 'training' and 'responsibility'. Military drill and sports training are benchmarks for establishing discipline.

The discipline of the mind is not fundamentally different from military drill and athletic discipline. It is a set of standards and demands that people apply to themselves of their own free will in order to master and to put into practice a certain way of thinking or working. It is developed as a result of going through special training, and can be seen as the sum of attributes of an educated individual. Incidentally, where people are trained for responsible work (which carries a risk to life and health), for instance in the intelligence services, in sports and in property management (which can be a dangerous field in Russia), the only way training is regulated is through daunting punishments. At first, new recruits choose freely what they would like to do. But once they have entered a system of training, they must learn to accept the discipline of the rod. It is essential that they have a trainer who shows them the work and the way it is structured, and who gives them exercises in order to consolidate this. There should also be a tutor who can help fix the given structure within a concept and show its place and purpose in their toolkit.

Prepare yourself

In order to fulfil the standards of discipline you have taken on, you need a high level of psychological and physical preparedness. This means taking daily exercise in order to maintain good physical condition, and continually creating battle (conflict) situations to exercise stress tolerance.

Set long-term goals

Energy for work does not come from the calories in the food we eat, but from setting long-term perspectives and planning how to organise work in order to achieve them. Those who have no goals will always be vulnerable to exploitation and manipulation by other people. Sports school offers a good training in setting goals. In the process of training the sporting elite, 50 per cent of study time is dedicated to sport. This fosters a hunger for competition, a desire to compete for leadership, team spirit and systematic independent training for gruelling competitions.

Teach others what you want to learn yourself

The people who learn most quickly and effectively are those who need to organise large groups of people in order to achieve their goals. These people need to be not only organised, but motivated; this can be done by sharing your own targets. In carrying out this difficult work, you will understand for the first time the direction in which you are moving, and why. Besides, professionals are people who can show and explain their methods of work to others. Professionals not only have the ability to do a particular job, they are also in command of the rules of their business.

Turn principles into techniques

Principles are like the stars of the night sky. In the day time, when it is light and you can see where you are going, they are of no use. But in a forest at night you need them in order to go in the right direction and to come out at the right place. (The image is borrowed from Plato, and assumes knowledge of astronomy. Nowadays you can find your way in a forest at night using GPS.) Act, analyse your mistakes, check against your principles, act again, and then again. In this way, a principle can become a technique (an artificially acquired ability).

Constructive thinking: what it is and how it works

The purpose and function of constructive thinking in the process of knowledge management consists of preparing concepts and models for project design which will guarantee solutions in problematic situations. Constructive thinking is a powerful weapon in the armoury of those who command it.

It is not something that can be seen, it cannot be measured with the help of the usual tools: tests (IQ quotients), exams and so on. Thinking expresses itself in action, in the solving of practical tasks which require intellectual support. We can understand our own mental constructs when we see them reflected in other people. We see that others have heard us, taken action, reflected on their actions or moved on.

Many people are familiar with Descartes' thesis 'I think therefore I am', but few people know another of his mottos: 'the true thought is obvious'. There is a direct connection between this thought and the idea of 'visually controlling' your own thought processes and their products. In order to formulate and master the 'martial art of thinking', appropriate forms and methods of training are required. Operations and techniques should be learned in the process of putting them into practice. A coach has the right to reprimand a student if they make a mistake. Those who have gone through training to qualify them for activities that carry a certain risk to life, such as parachute jumping, diving, mountaineering and rally driving, know that such activities require strictly standardised skilled instruction, practical demonstration, insurance, and restrictions on the use of trial and error in order to receive a licence or certificate.

Working on your thought processes, however, can carry an even greater risk to your well-being and even your life than the most extreme sports. Those who have tried it understand this well.

The mechanics of constructive thinking

Let us illustrate how constructive thinking works using a historical scenario related to its origin. As is the case with many other useful concepts and practices in use today, the idea of constructive thinking was first created, practised and formulated by the ancient Greeks. Then a group of enthusiasts from the Moscow Methodological Circle under the leadership of G. P. Shchedrovitsky provided a description of this art. A fascinating piece of research on the subject was carried out by M. K. Petrov, an investigation into the history of Cretan pirates entitled *Penteconter: Or in the First Class of the European School of Thought.*

These Russian teachers reconstructed a particular method of structuring thought processes using the example of Herodotus. Herodotus wrote the history of the Greco-Persian wars. In order to collect factual material he asked veterans of these wars to provide him with details of battles and other events of days long past. As it turned out, two eyewitnesses of the same event gave Herodotus completely different accounts of what had happened. We can attempt to describe the situation Herodotus then found himself in using Figure 7.22. He had heard different stories, but in the work that he had been commissioned to do he had to give only unequivocal information. These meant that he had to try to understand the eyewitness accounts, put together, then with their help produce a reflective reconstruction of the event in question then conduct his own purely cognitive work in constructing the 'true historical fact'. This, in effect, is how every historical account is written.

Constructive thinking is essential where it is necessary, on the basis of different positions and ways of understanding a single situation – a 'problem muddle' – to find a model that explains what each of these positions is based on, and gives an integrated version of events, or preferably a 'true picture of events'.

Figure 7.22 How constructive thinking works

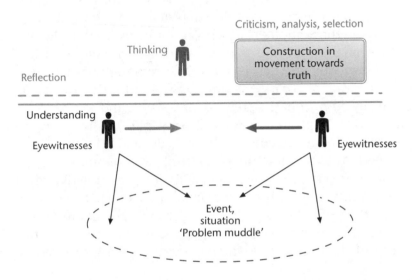

After the Cretan pirates and Herodotus, many other Europeans have since contributed to the development of constructive thinking in Europe: Aristotle, Descartes, Nicholas of Cusa, Kant and many others.

The American John Dewey attempted to apply the model of work on thinking to methods of schooling. In *How We Think* (1939) he turns Herodotus's critical model into a methodological technique. Dewey argues that an idea can only appear as a result of first formulating a thesis and then its antithesis. Dewey originated the idea of developing thought capacity by using project-based learning. This method was widely used in the Soviet school system in the 1920s, and nowadays it is used all over the world as a way of teaching 'critical thinking'.

How can constructive thinking be learned?

It is important to assess whether you really need it before you begin. Who needs constructive thinking and why?

First of all, it is essential for managers, as it allows them to deepen their understanding of the essence of a situation and reach an awareness of reality.

Second, it is a necessary tool for researchers in order to construct objects of analysis and criticism.

However, apart from this, constructive thinking is something that is rarely encountered in life and just as rarely needed. It requires special study, and even those who have gone through a good school of constructive thinking may not always, having managed to employ such thinking once or twice, be able to repeat it for a third and fourth time (so argues the Scandinavian scholar of linguistics H. J. Uldall).

So where has the rare ability to think constructively come from and how can it be mastered? There is only one answer to these questions, the ancient principle that 'It is only possible to learn how to do something by doing it in the presence of a master and role model.'

Figure 7.23 attempts to describe this principle. This is the model of apprenticeship, at the core of which is depicted the individual who knows how to do something – to think, for example – and the student who copies them. The model will function properly only if the expert wants to show how they themselves do what they do, if they allow the student to copy them and answer any questions the student has if something is not clear to them. Only then can this expert be called a teacher, one who is conveying 'living knowledge'.

Figure 7.23 The principle of 'learning by doing'

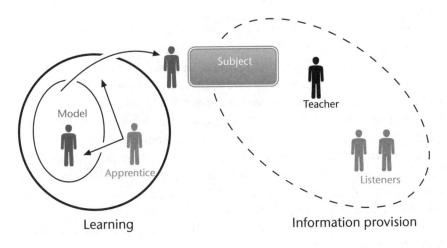

Modern methods of teaching in the class and lesson system are quite differently structured. Here, at the core is the figure of a teacher who must force the pupil to listen to, absorb and memorise some subject-related information, using whatever method it takes (the carrot or the stick, or both). In all fairness it should be observed that in the classroom situation a pupil can also learn from what a teacher does. But what teachers pass on in this way is not for the most part, that body of 'dead' subject-related knowledge they are required to transmit. The teacher informs pupils about everything that has accumulated and brought in to the subject by previous generations of thinkers and doers.

Plato made the distinction between two type of students. There is a small group of 'mathematicians' – students who are able to copy and apply the teacher's modes of thought – and the majority – the 'listeners' – who are obliged to listen and memorise. Everybody has heard of thinking, but the only ones who can try it are those who are lucky enough to find a master in life – one who can show them how to think constructively, explain to them how thinking happens and comment on their attempts.

Techniques for developing constructive thinking in KM training

Following the principles of Herodotus, Dewey and Shchedrovitsky, we have developed and now operate special forms of collective work which provide opportunities to develop constructive thinking.

The following are the basic steps and operations which must be provided by organisers and performed by participants during such work:

Step 1. Create a situation of collective 'acts of thinking' which contains substantial conflicts. For this purpose, there should be a critical mass of people and positions gathered together for an OAG.

In order to force the group to move on to design work it is essential to organise the tasks and to script (present) the situation in such a way that the members of the working group who are trying to find a solution to a problem feel that they have reached an impasse, and have no choice but to cease work on the topic. Fortunately, this does not require any particular effort: no matter where you look you will always run across dead ends. If everything is going well and you are replete with satisfaction, there is no need to think.

As the Japanese are fond of saying, 'If you don't have a problem, you have a problem.'

In practice we constantly come up against conflicts between various positions (and the corresponding knowledge that informs these positions) held by the different participants in the work. This is what we call a 'problem situation' (or 'problem muddle', according to Russell Ackoff: see Figure 7.24).

The process of 'igniting' and maintaining conflict between positions should be balanced at the point where it threatens to spill over into infighting between groups, but should always be prevented from doing so. It is essential to set the situation up in this way, or no constructive thinking will take place. Only through conflict is it possible to stop, try to understand the essence of the conflict and proceed to a debriefing – a review and analysis of the situation, and the thinking and actions of the participants. Another way of describing the process is that it aims to create a cumulative understanding.

It is better not sit on the problem for too long, as the conflict between two positions can spill over into fighting. Whenever tension reaches boiling point it is vital to suspend activities, to stop and try to understand the situation and the essence of the matter (that is to say, not the scripts but the knowledge of the other participants). It is best not to waste any time on talking and on *muda*, but to think, using the system model. This means proceeding towards ideally effective thinking and translating that understanding into a model.

Figure 7.24 Conflict between positions in the 'problem muddle'

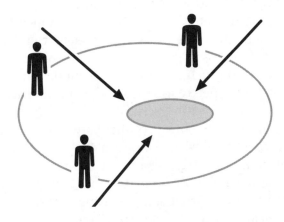

Step 2. Proceed to ideally effective thinking, and constructing models and concepts that cover the situation in its entirety. At this stage you need to move from an understanding of the situation to work on finding constructions that will remove conflict, using models and concepts. This is, without a doubt, the most difficult stage of the work. People are pragmatic nowadays, and given the need to earn a living, even senior professionals often do not consider intellectual work useful. Nevertheless, the task of the organisers at this point is to push participants towards intellectual or cognitive planning. For the participants, this means stepping right away from the conflict situation and stand-offs between individuals and

Figure 7.25 Construction of a model of ideal scenarios/objects which clarify the essence of the conflict

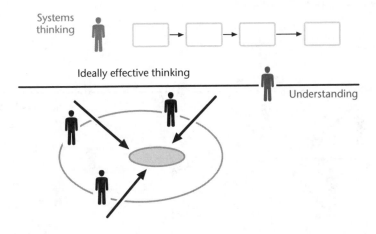

starting work on designing models of ideal objects, clarifying the essence of the conflict and showing ways out.

At this stage, participants need to be well-equipped with design and planning elements – concepts and models from the 'system' construction kit. Progress in planning these models requires several attempts or iterations in the search for a model that takes into account the positions, needs and interests of all the participants in the conflict.

How do you find a way out of conflict between different people, positions and types of knowledge; how do you resolve a problematic situation? This requires designing a new way of organising activity. Participants now need to move on to project design, creating models that will describe and 'fix' that activity, using a special 'workbench' designed specifically for this purpose (see Figure 7.25).

Constructive thinking always offers a way out of the situation in hand: that is, it enables you to design (or build) the future. People who are able to think constructively do not simply criticise or deny, nor do they dream or ponder fruitlessly, but they determine what needs to be done next, and suggest ways and solutions.

The structural and functional plan for new activity which is essential to solve the given problem is developed at the workbench (or drawing board, or sheet of paper) through several iterations (no less than three). Models can be borrowed from another context, or developed according to a prototype. They can be constructed from material available in the archive (in stock). The most difficult and interesting task is to prepare a model for the 'here and now' – for the particular case that is under consideration.

Figure 7.26 'Systems' thinking

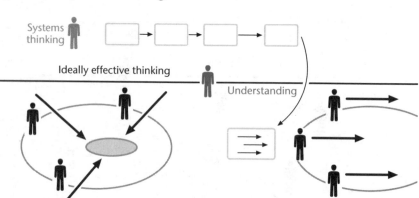

Step 3. At this stage it is essential to transform the model that has been created into a co-ordinated work plan in which every participant can see their own place and their own specific function (see Figure 7.26).

Examples of conceptual structures obtained during knowledge management training in the work of the Corporate University

These are taken from a project seminar on 'Management of the Product Lifecycle in Engine-Building and Helicopter-Building', held on 8–10 December 2011 in Yekaterinburg.

Figure 7.27 shows a model of three groups of processes in the management system, which can act as a guideline and a benchmark for the participants. Accepting and understanding this model will allow them to proceed to ideally effective thinking and to organise their own understanding in accordance with the model.

Next, Figures 7.28 and 7.29 shows models and concepts for differentiating between terms used by the participants (which include ILS: integrated logistical support; ASS: after-sales service; MRO: maintenance, repair and overhaul).

The third example (see Figure 7.30) is a plan showing the

Figure 7.27 Three groups of processes in the management system

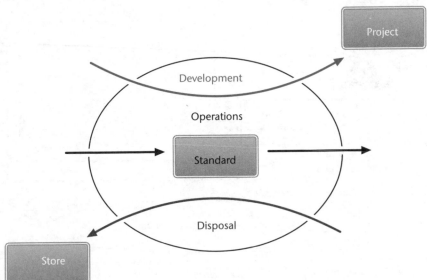

Figure 7.28 The Soviet after-sales service system

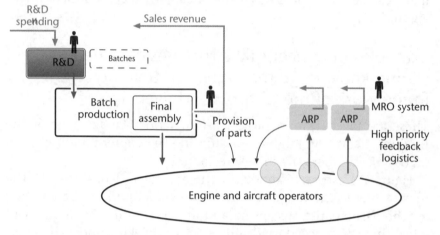

distinction between two fundamentally different financial models: sale of goods and providing services.

Finally, Figure 7.31 shows an assembly configuration – a 'road

Figure 7.29 Model of the modern system of integrated logistical support, including resources from the Soviet MRO system

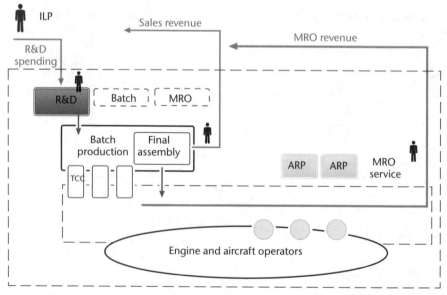

ARP: Aircraft repair plant   ILP: integrated logistics provider

Figure 7.30 The financial models of sale of goods and rendering of service

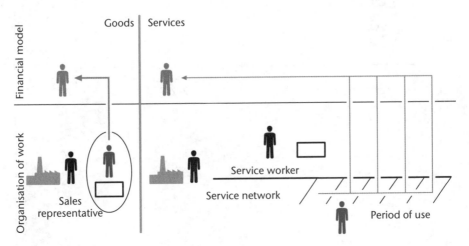

map' showing organisations and planning for creating a modern MRO service. The diagram:

◆ incorporates and distinguishes requirements for a picture of the MRO system as a whole;
◆ distinguishes different levels of the system as a whole, based on organisation and material;
◆ defines the contours of the financial models within the system as a whole;
◆ sets out the different types of activity within the organisation on the principle of aligning the basic process of value creation (adopted from the Toyota Production System).

What is meant by the 'system' of work with personnel?

The 'system' category is a set of tools for carrying out intellectual work which in our country was worked out under the leadership of G. P. Shchedrovitsky in the Moscow Methodological Circle. Nowadays, no managers would risk their reputation by declaring that they were not using the systems approach. The word 'system' is always heard in conversations about any managerial task. However, few people understand how and where to use this set of tools.

A 'system' thinker must imagine and visualise the object of control and management in five aspects or plans for consideration:

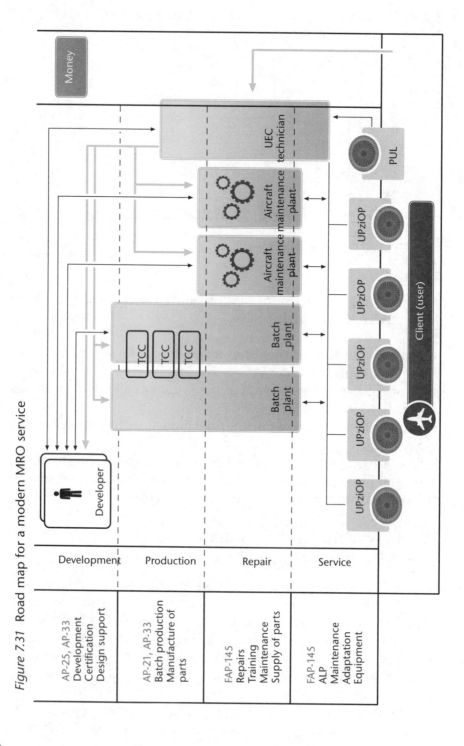

Figure 7.31 Road map for a modern MRO service

1 The 'dismantling' of the object should begin with making a list of the processes that are to be managed.

2 The task of managing a process requires designating a mechanism whose functioning leaves a 'trace' on the form of the process. Specialists with an engineering mindset, unlike specialists in the humanities, understand that the only way to describe this mechanism is to create a model of its structure. This must be a structural and functional model indicating the most important components in the structure of the mechanism which ensure its operation (for instance, in the case of a car this is the engine, the transmission, the suspension and the steering).

3 The reliable operation of the mechanism is provided for by the connections between components of the structure as a whole: in a car, mechanical and electrical connections, and in the case of an organisation, communicative, legal, social and psychological, cultural and historical connections.

4 The sites and connections are linked and their existence (or, in the case of designing a new system, their implementation) is guaranteed by a set of 'organisational entities': for instance, the fully assembled car, the organisation as a legal entity, and 'private household'. This aspect of the system, which is essentially unim-portant, has material content: it has the quality of a 'thing'. A thing, by definition, is something that is perceived using the senses, unlike the preceding three aspects which form the essence of the system, and which are perceived through the intellect or the imagination. We constantly run up against things (and people, too) and are unable to pass through them. They restrict us in our everyday life on every side. That is why we need to relate to them correctly and take into account their position, their state or (in the case of people) their opinion. Under these circumstances – the material pressure from people and things that surround them – many managers find that they are constantly busy with day-to-day control, struggling to maintain the normal functioning of their organisational entities. Organisations rarely find the time to review the three overlying aspects: the process, component structures and the functional structure of the system as a whole.

5 The fifth aspect – the *material* of the system – has a major impact on the structure of an organisation. Design features of the system depend on the capacities of the material: its durability, its resistance to wear and tear, its plasticity and so on. It is just the same

with organisations as it is with cars. A change in the structure of functions and the set of places within the system will result in new demands on the material. The restructuring of an organisation requires new people with new modes of thought. A new design of car cannot be realised using traditional materials. In general, you should not put old wine in new bottles. New systems should be created using new material.

The system of working with corporate personnel

It is essential to distinguish the 'systems' approach to working with personnel from the practical and methodical approach to work with people in a corporation.

The practical and technical approach is based on using experience of situations encountered in the past to inform the future, accumulating and systematising experience for each new situation. The best-known example of such a systematic montage is the Toyota production system. For over 30 years, the managers of this Japanese company have been collecting methods, techniques and tools for working with people from all over the world, experimenting with their use in their enterprises and design bureaux. The book *Toyota Talent: Developing your people the Toyota way* by Jeffrey Liker and David Meier[5] contains snippets of this experience. Our thanks are due to the authors.

In using the systems approach to working with personnel it is essential to proceed not from experience, but from the basic concepts and categories that make up the ontological picture (the essence of organised activity); that is to say, to move from the abstract to the concrete, and on this basis to systematise the experience, preserving and passing on what is needed and discarding what is not needed. The systems approach requires above all seeing the whole, or the managed object, rather than a set of guidelines tested by others (however good the Japanese are, it has to be remembered that we are working mainly with Russians) and often duplicating models that have already been developed. (We know the position of many leaders of enterprise in our country: they ask why we need to use the Toyota production system when our Corporate Standard from the 1970s is just as good.)

In this situation, if we understand the object of management in

---

5   New York and London: McGraw-Hill, 2007.

Figure 7.32 A 'cell' in the production process

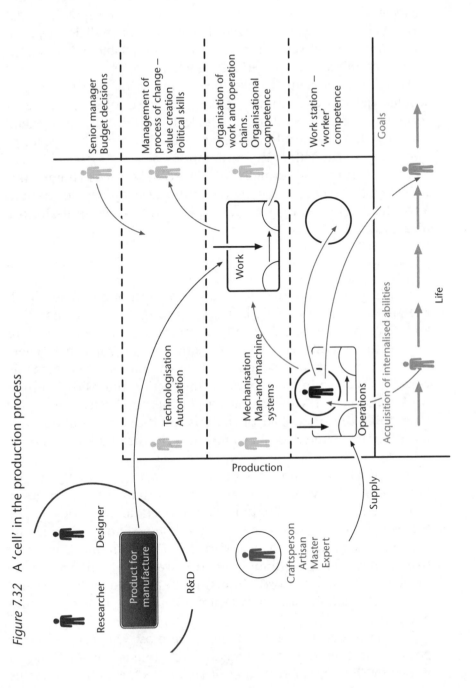

its entirety, we can work decisively to build a task typology which is easy to use, relying on the resources we have at our disposal, so that rather being in thrall to 'foreign miracles' we work judiciously, decisively and productively. In other words, use reliable old standards where possible and Toyota principles where necessary.

Therefore, a systems thinker begins by giving a picture of the whole: that is, determining the basic processes of practical transformative action (see above for logical thinking in the 'system' category) that constitute the object – in this case, the system of working with the staff of the corporation.

These practical transformative processes can be listed in nominative order as follows: production–reproduction, development–operation, and leadership–management–organisation–decommissioning (disposal).

Production

We begin to structure the places and functions of our system with the *production process*. This is a basic process for the corporation and its employees. Schematically, it can be represented as a chain of operations designed to create value for the consumer. There must be a product as the end result of the process. Those people who are involved in the process of production must take up their work stations and, adhering strictly to the norm (standard), they must fulfil the prescribed operations for that work station with regard to the material, be it at a machine, in the office, or at a daily briefing.

Individuals take time out of their lives to participate in the production process, in accordance with certain situational goals. Figure 3.32 makes a distinction between operations – performed by the worker or 'operator' – and work – designed and controlled by the 'organiser', in accordance with the norm. Around these core structures is a set of positions (and other works), which increase the capacity and productivity of the organisers and operators: mechanisation, automation, technologisation, management of change, and budgeting.

Let us once again point out the three most important types of positions in the production process (excluding engineering, represented by the upper left section of Figure 3.32, which needs to be discussed separately).

The *manager* (or 'politician') is responsible for monitoring the change that is continually taking place. Their job is to provide a framework, control the state of affairs, observe targets, and make course corrections. Their main instruments are understanding and organised communication.

The *organiser* designs activities and organises them into structures and chains of work. In the way of work they need to have a good knowledge of analytics and design, and are also responsible for the placement of people in jobs within the structure and chains of work. Their tools are schematisation (semiotic construction), anthropotechnics, regulatory description and standardisation. They must also bring in the necessary technology (not necessarily innovative technology) to strengthen the operators and increase the efficiency of their work.

The *operator* works at a pace determined by the technological system, using their hands and head. The operator's task is to act according to the norm and contemplate the improvement of the operation in order to have fun and enjoy the daily work experience. Their tool is the ability to sustain attention through continuous improvement. Out of all employees, operators are the main object of research into psycho-technics and social engineering.

Renewal, development and operation

There are obvious reasons for the *renewal* of staff: people age, equipment wears out and engineers develop new processes. There is a need to replace people and train new members of staff who are willing and able to work with new equipment. For this reason, activities have to be described in a standard manner and transformed into methods, and operations have to be standardised, as far as possible. In order to do this, appropriate services have to be created and the appropriate staff need to be trained to work in and for these services.

The next pair of processes are *development* and *operation*. Development must be understood today as a fundamental process set against the backdrop of accelerating generational change in technology, equipment and product types. If you want to keep your job, you have to run forward with the pack, not run along after it. New technologies require new people, and all of this together requires new management systems. For the development process, work on programmes of corporate and institutional development, organisational projects (project development) and production systems are of primary importance. New people will be assimilated into old forms of activity if places cannot be found for them in new organisational projects.

The development process is 'tied' to the functioning processes, which, by nature of their organisation and basic material, form the essence of the survival and lifecycle of personnel in our enterprises and design bureaux. People will respect the rules and standards of their jobs and will change to suit development programmes and new jobs, if they clearly understand how their lives will be organised in the here and now, and how they will develop in the foreseeable future. The idea 'Think first of your motherland (that is, your "own" factory) and then of yourself' is no longer applicable. Nowadays, people do not live to work, but work to live. The sphere of life-sustaining activity is shown in red in Figure 7.33.

It is clear that the period of life in which an individual is employable is relatively small. In Russia most people go through life without competing in the 'labour market' and without having a hand in 'productive labour'. They ensure their livelihood in other ways: partly at the expense of the state, partly at the expense of relatives and others. Under these circumstances, in Russia the operation of staff is now seen mainly in terms of social protection and public welfare, irrespective of how work in the corporation is organised.

The four processes regarding the practical transformation of 'human material' define the employee as an object for management. Employees must work productively within their industry. Employees should be trained up, and should follow the technological guidelines. They should be flexible, ready to become involved in new projects on work organisation. They should enjoy life and have confidence in their own future.

All of these processes must be represented in our personnel management system, which is not a practical transformation in itself, but which has to capture and include practical transformations of both material and people. It is made up of three fundamentally distinct processes: governance, management and organisation.

The processes of people management

Leadership is the process of sustaining among your staff those modes of thinking required in order to comply with the processes of practical changes listed above. 'If you are standing at the machine, think like a worker', or 'If you enter the management group, know

Figure 7.33 Processes of development and operation within the corporation

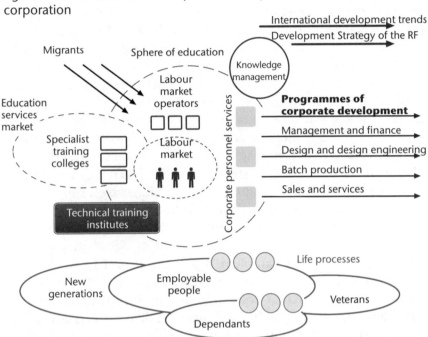

who your boss is.' Leadership keeps the organisation within certain limits and leads employees towards productive goals.

It is essential to distinguish between two different approaches towards the process of governance, 'command management' and 'continuous improvement'.

The first approach is based on the top-down principle. The work of any and every organisation begins with those at the top setting out certain principles, processes and rules – norms governing the practical implementation of change. As a rule, at the stage of establishment and development, these principles, processes and standards govern the selection and deployment of staff.

The second approach is based on the bottom-up principle. When an organisation has already been created and is able to guarantee operations, a fundamentally different approach must come into force. This approach, contrary to what you might think, is not 'motivation'. People are not machines, working consistently according to the prescribed model without a murmur of complaint. They need to make sense of what they do. Orders are the worst tool for enforcing observation of working standards and maintaining discipline in the workplace. They are only effective if they are backed up by threats of execution or dismissal (fines only irritate people). This point was understood by those managers who invented the doctrine of 'human relations' and the principle of 'continuous improvement'. (The Japanese term *kaizen* is now used widely to refer to this philosophy.) The essence of this philosophy is that employees at their work stations performing work in accordance with guidelines should think about how, and in what direction, the performance of these operations alters them, and how they can change these operations so as to become more agile, quicker and smarter than the other workers. In our organisation employees will not be given a pay rise for this, though they might, if successful, receive a small bonus. If employees become engaged in such 'improvements' – if not all of them, at least many of them – life in the workplace becomes less boring.

In our situation, the problem is to engage staff in work based on the second approach – understanding and sorting out bottlenecks within a particular company, first of all, in the company's management, and then in line managers, skilled workers and in the team as a whole. Previously, such involvement could be guaranteed by ideological means, through the Party. Today, hopes are pinned on educational initiatives. All this may be useful indeed, but our leaders know from previous experience that this will be a lengthy process requiring the efforts of many people, and that it must be properly planned and organised.

Behind the approaches outlined above, an experienced organiser should see an analogy with organisational and implementation tools, such as lean production, which is in contrast to the well-known forms and tools for implementing the 'scientific organisation of labour' (SOL). This analogy allows us how to formulate the following principles in our model:

◆ SOL is based on the idea that an expert in labour rationalisation (a rate-setter and supervisor) knows best how to carry out the work in hand. It is almost as if this supervisor were standing behind the workers' backs, inspecting their work and demanding that they fulfil their designated quotas using the traditional system of reward and punishment: the stick and the carrot.
◆ Lean production attempts to 'put the supervisor inside the employee', with the result that the employee wants to discover

Figure 7.34 Types of administration

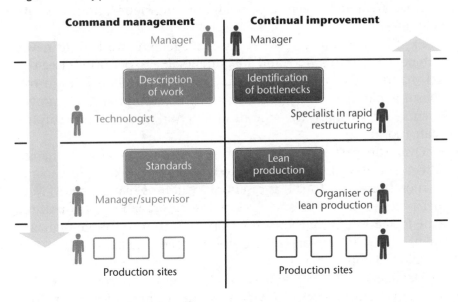

Table 7.3 Command management versus continual improvement

Demands made on personnel under 'command management'	Demands made on personnel under situation of 'continual improvement'
Controlled, predictable, accountable	Able to understand, reflect on mistakes and change
Strict adherence to the prescribed technological discipline	Willing to communicate horizontally and vertically
Employees tied to work stations	Rotation of employees in interests of (business) development
'Planned' productivity	Productivity as a side-effect

the most effective ways of organising work for themselves and come up with the most effective tools for carrying out their tasks.

The processes of personnel management

Management processes are ensured by much more complex mechanisms than those of governance. We can and must manage something that moves independently: that is, something that can change in spite of our policy directives. The massive body of the corporation undergoes change every hour of every day. Let us hope that we are able to keep track of all 'improvements', both possible and impossible.

Existing personnel services for management work were never intended to do this work and are quite unable to perform it (see the left-hand side of Figure 7.35). They work to fill free spaces in the existing manufacturing process, taking into account all its improvements and changes (increase in production, reduction in surplus staff and so on).

Over the past four years, in the race for innovation, change affecting the entire employment system has been taking place in our corporations, and thus it is essential to address management. New perspectives, set out in strategies, new forms of labour organisation (the formation of divisions, the transition to programme management, the TCC network) all require the recruitment, selection and creation of appropriate teams.

Managers must keep abreast of all these 'self-propelling' developments as they take place, and use their energy to achieve the goals that have been set. Development projects should not take on employees in the traditional manner. First, the workplace must be established, equipped and included in the new workplace structure (see the right-hand column in Figure 7.35). What is this, if not innovation? All this is not the responsibility of personnel services; it is the task of senior managers and services responsible for corporate development.

Management need to emphasise the importance of developing a proactive and ambitious personnel reserve and recruiting the future leaders of work development. These people are not being trained anywhere. They need to be raised side by side with the production which is in the process of being phased out, with all its old-timers, its masters and its hangers-on: that is, in a situation that presents some serious obstacles.

The process of organisation

The work of connecting all these processes, structures, places, relationships and organisational entities into a coherent whole, and then of maintaining that whole, constitutes the essence of the organisational process and the task of the organiser. In order to have something to manage and to be able to deploy people in the workplace, it is essential to create an organisational design, and

Figure 7.35 Personnel work in a developing corporation

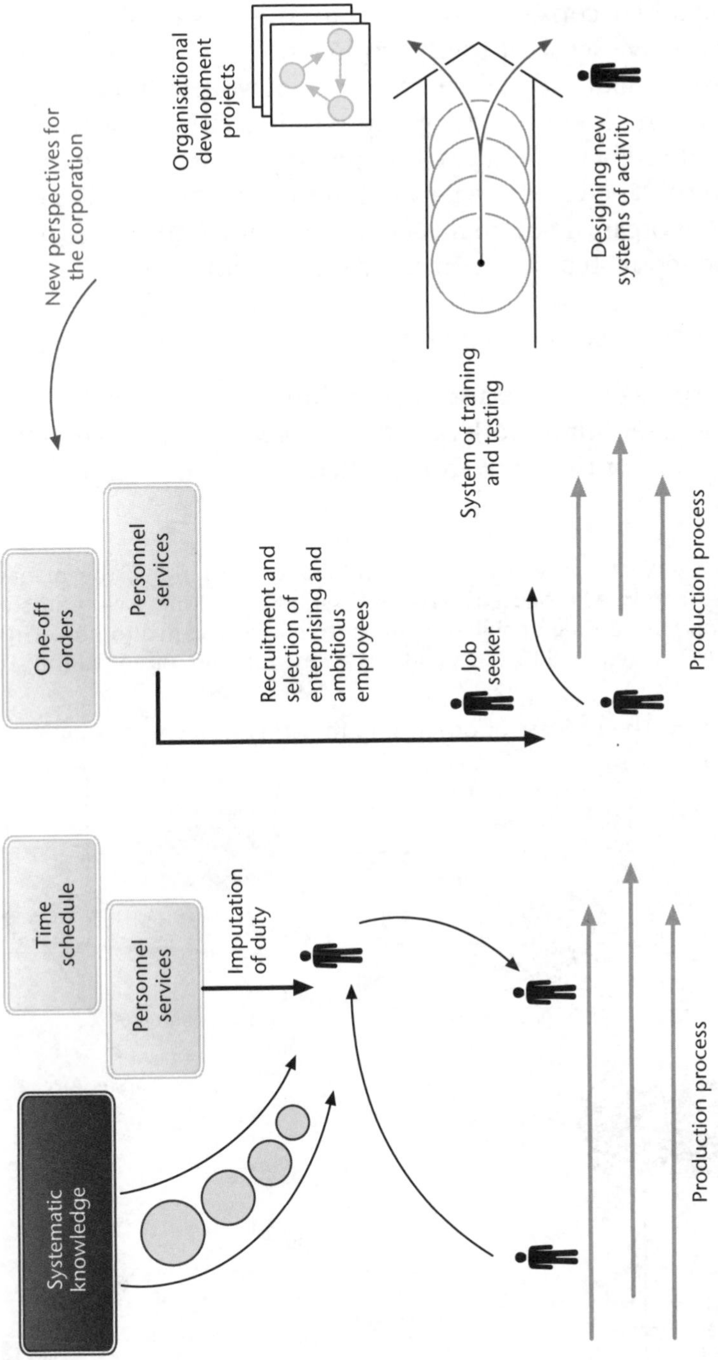

then to realise this design (or plan) using the available material. This 'material' consists of people, with their own ambitions, values, and an active sense of their own identity. We need to distinguish between organisation as a specific type of work in its own right, the tools of which are the design approach and schematisation, and which affords a view of the whole picture (or model), and the organisation that is created as a result of this work. The organiser creates a model of organisation to meet challenges inherent in the processes of production–reproduction and development–operation.

The process of phasing out personnel

The purpose of this process was beautifully described by Henri Fayol in his extraordinary work *General and Industrial Management* (1916). In a section of the book entitled 'Removal of the incapable', Fayol writes:

> To preserve the integrity and soundness of operations, the manager must remove or propose the removal of any functionary who for some reason has become unable to perform the tasks assigned to him. This is something required by duty, and it is always difficult, often painful. This

Figure 7.36 The process of organising the work of a corporation

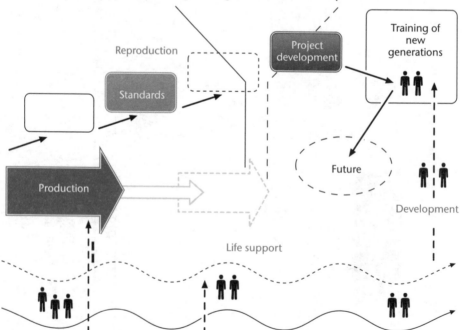

duty invokes the higher moral qualities of the manager and, in particular, that well-known quality known as civil courage, which is often more difficult to put into practice than military bravery.

Modern corporate culture is built on 'positive' principles, and therefore modern management icons use a fundamentally different formula to describe the phasing out of personnel from an operation. For example, Jack Welch, who was at the helm of General Electric from 1981–96, declared:

> I am starting to change the company. I want to raise productivity, to improve quality dramatically, to halve the number of hierarchy levels, etc. The company can survive only under such conditions, this is not my choice, it is the law of competition. I invite into my team those who are ready to build a new company. I am not dismissing anyone, but those who are lagging behind the changes and the leaders of change must leave.

Intermediate conclusions, leading to a plan of continued operations

Work on designing and starting up management companies in the field of mechanical engineering – work in which we have been engaged over the past five years – is unique according to most parameters. In both Russia and overseas, any experience that could be gleaned from others in the field is either non-existent, or is guarded by those who do not wish to share it.

The most important specific feature of this work is the particular organisation of the object of management. It is neither an enterprise, nor a distribution network, neither a financial institution, nor an experimental design bureau (EDB). But it is an object that incorporates dozens of companies, many EDBs, a set of financial institutions, and global distribution networks. In addition, and most importantly, it is a set of people: workers, engineers, managers with different skills, the products of different historical eras, organised into several levels of hierarchy.

So far, no textbooks exist and no game simulations have been developed that could teach all the aspects involved in managing entities such as this. But even now, we can clearly describe the most important features that distinguish management approaches to objects of this complexity.

First, managers of integration processes in a mechanical engineering corporation are primarily concerned with the flows of information which come in from different regions, from different types of organisations and from different levels of the management hierarchy. Without a model of the object of management, in addition to a set of models and narratives which make the entire sphere of activity that is under management or analysis clear and transparent, managers will rapidly drown in a sea of muddled information. In large, multi-tier systems, a situation of 'Chinese whispers' inevitably develops. We can stress the need for reliable information, but more important still is the need to organise, systematise and 'package' information. A special structure needs to be in place to ensure reliability of information: strain gauges, terminals, control rooms. Those 'down below' collect and arrange whatever information is necessary for those who make decisions at the top.

Second, once managers have attained a certain level in the decision-making structure, they often tend to cut back on their own intellectual efforts and rely on their 'apparatus' (deputies, advisers, assistants, consultants, aides, minions and other well-wishers). They become less exacting, less fit for the job, and begin to neglect the little things, which can lead to disastrous defeat. Typical Russian managers are strongly inclined to consolidate an 'infallible' image, emphasising their own uniqueness and fitness for the job they hold. In our opinion, such behaviour is absolutely unacceptable. Managers need to follow the Eastern principle of 'continuous improvement', to justify their status every day and in every situation, and to seek to prove to all subordinates that they do not miss a trick and that they will not slip up. Otherwise they will fall foul of the law of the jungle:

> 'Akela has missed', screamed the foul jackal Tabaqui. 'By the law of the jungle Akela cannot be the leader of the pack. He cannot!' And the old and young wolves supported him, some in an angry howl, and others in an approving silence.
>
> (*The Jungle Book*, Rudyard Kipling[6])

Third, if managers have climbed to a high level, they should not feel themselves to be above the need for methodological reflection: that is, a meticulous analysis of their own decisions and actions. As soon as they think of themselves as infallible (which is just what a hanger-on will want them to hear) and do not have the courage to

---

6   Note: this quote has been translated from the Russian, and may not reflect verbatim the English original.

admit their mistakes, nothing will stop them going downhill fast. The larger the field of activity, the higher the level of the hierarchy, the greater a manager's authority, the more rigidly they will need to stick to the rules of intellectual self-organisation.

Fourth, everything described above cannot be achieved without the right selection and deployment of personnel. Managers need people they can trust, people with acute and constructive insight, people who are willing and able to act honestly in their designated functions in a co-ordinated and accepted system of work. Every day and every hour managers are obliged to prepare people who will be able to take their place when the need arises. This is contrary to the established Russian tradition of meticulously identifying and eliminating all possible contenders for your position.

This book is an attempt to systematise certain principles, tools and experience that we have gained in order to pass all this on to the new generations of managers. However, at the same time, we understand that both our experience and our vision are severely limited by our time and available options. We are helped by the fact that 'we stand on the shoulders of giants', and we try to make the best use possible of the stepping stones left behind by great teachers of the past. We apply the principles of KM not only to the thoughts and actions of those who think and act today better than others in our production systems, but also to the thoughts and deeds of our predecessors from other historical eras. Practice – real situations of decision-making regarding management and personnel – is always unique and inimitable. But the method or path that we followed in making decisions and trying to identify using clear and simple models can, and should, be transferred not only to the new decision-making situations, but also to new generations of managers. That is, of course, if the decisions were productive (if the desired goals were achieved) and efficient (if the expected effect was obtained).

You, the reader of this book, act and take decisions in different positions, situations and circumstances. Do not try to use our models, or connect them to your own situation, without a critical look and a substantial 'upgrade'. Our final recommendation then is brief: act, understand, reflect on your actions and look for appropriate models that allow you to organise your understanding and reflection. Put together your own arsenal of models and concepts for use in business. You will not need a vast array of electronic databases and archives for this task. You do not need 'all of the culture that has been accumulated by humanity', but a personal toolkit for everyday use. You do not need to have many instruments at your command, but those you have should be readily visible and available for use.

S. B. Kravchinskaya, A. G. Reus and A. P. Zinchenko

Appendix 7.1: List of events and projects carried out by the Corporate University of OAO UIC Oboronprom

1 OAG on 'Developing terms of reference for the project of integrating the helicopter industry in Russia', Moscow, November 2007.

2 OAG on 'Developing HR policies (designing training programmes and organisational design of HR services) for UIC Oboronprom', Moscow, March 2008.

3 Cycle of OAGs, 'Training programme for project teams of Russian Helicopters (team organisation master)', Moscow, April–September 2008.

4 Conference on 'The system of manpower development for the helicopter industry', Moscow, HeliRussia Exhibition, May 2008.

5 OAG session 'Development of the Samara cluster of engine-building DB and enterprises within the United Engine Building Corporation', Samara, June 2008.

6 OAG session 'Development of staffing systems in the United Engine Building Corporation', Samara, Samara State Aerospace University, July 2008.

7 Training for senior managers of the corporation entitled 'Training in understanding, schematisation and systems thinking for managers', Moscow, August 2008.

8 OAG session 'Prospects for production development in Motorostroitel as part of UEC', Samara, August 2008.

9 OAG session 'Development of staffing systems aircraft and helicopter companies of Russia', Kazan, August 2008.

10 OAG session 'The state of the world's financial markets. Strategy and projects for OAO UIC Oboronprom', Moscow, September 2008.

11 OAG session 'The design of the UEC Training and Engineering Centre', Perm, October 2008.

12 OAG session 'Development of terms of reference for the design of a quality management system', Moscow, November 2008.

13 Working session: 'Plan for the development of the United Engine-Building Corporation', Moscow, February 2009.

14 Joint AOGH session of OAO UIC Oboronprom and Sukhoi on 'Project management in aircraft and engine building', Moscow, March 2009.

Figure 7.37 Areas of work, 2007–08

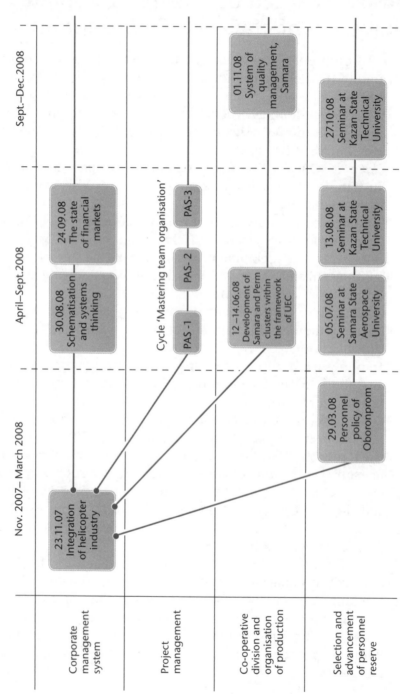

15 Training of OAO OZNA on 'The organisation of lean production', Samara, March 2009.

16 Project workshop 'Designing the educational infrastructure of the United Engine Building Corporation', Perm, April 2009.

17 Workshop together with OAO Sukhoi 'The fundamentals of lean production', Moscow, May 2009.

18 Project workshop on 'Designing a modern financial system for Russia', Moscow, June 2009.

19 Project workshop on 'Developing a preliminary design for the serial production of gas-turbine engines by a modern enterprise and the programme for its implementation at the production site', Samara, OAO Kuznetsov, July 2009.

20 Meeting on 'Current IT trends in OAO UIC Oboronprom', Moscow, July 2009.

21 Working meeting on the programme to create a personnel reserve for OAO UIC Oboronprom, Zhukovsky, MAKS Airshow, August 2009.

22 Organisational activity workshop on 'The experience of corporate management in breakthrough projects for mass production of the gas turbine engines SaM146, PAKFA, GTU110', Rybinsk, September 2009.

23 Organisational activity workshop on the 'Development of a programme for production reorganisation (incorporating lean manufacturing and co-operation in the enterprises of the corporation) for the implementation of "breakthrough projects"', Ufa, October 2009.

24 Workshop meeting on 'Organising efficient production at the batch production plant', Perm, OAO PMZ, December 2009.

25 Organisational activity workshop on 'Selecting and creating the personnel reserve', Moscow, December 2009.

26 OAG session 'The Strategy Implementation Programme for JSC Russian Helicopters', Moscow, February 2010.

27 Organisational activity workshop on 'Organisation and management of R&D in the UEC (as part of the Corporate Development Strategy)', St Petersburg, March 2010.

28 Organisational activity workshop 'Breakthrough projects of JSC Russian Helicopters as part of the Corporate Development Strategy', Kazan, April 2010.

29 Workshop meeting on 'The organisation of personnel services for the UEC strategy implementation', Moscow, May 2010.

Figure 7.38 Areas of work, 2009

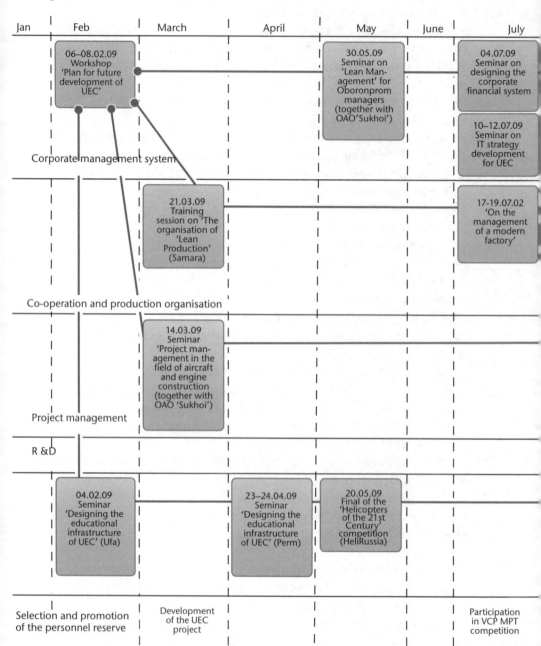

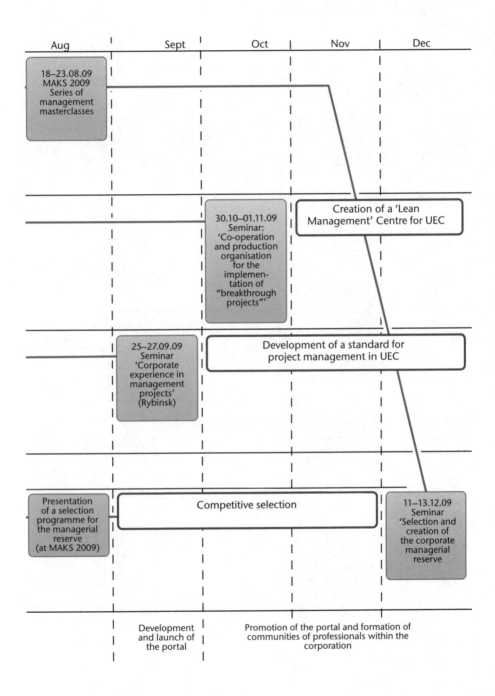

Figure 7.39 Areas of work, 2010

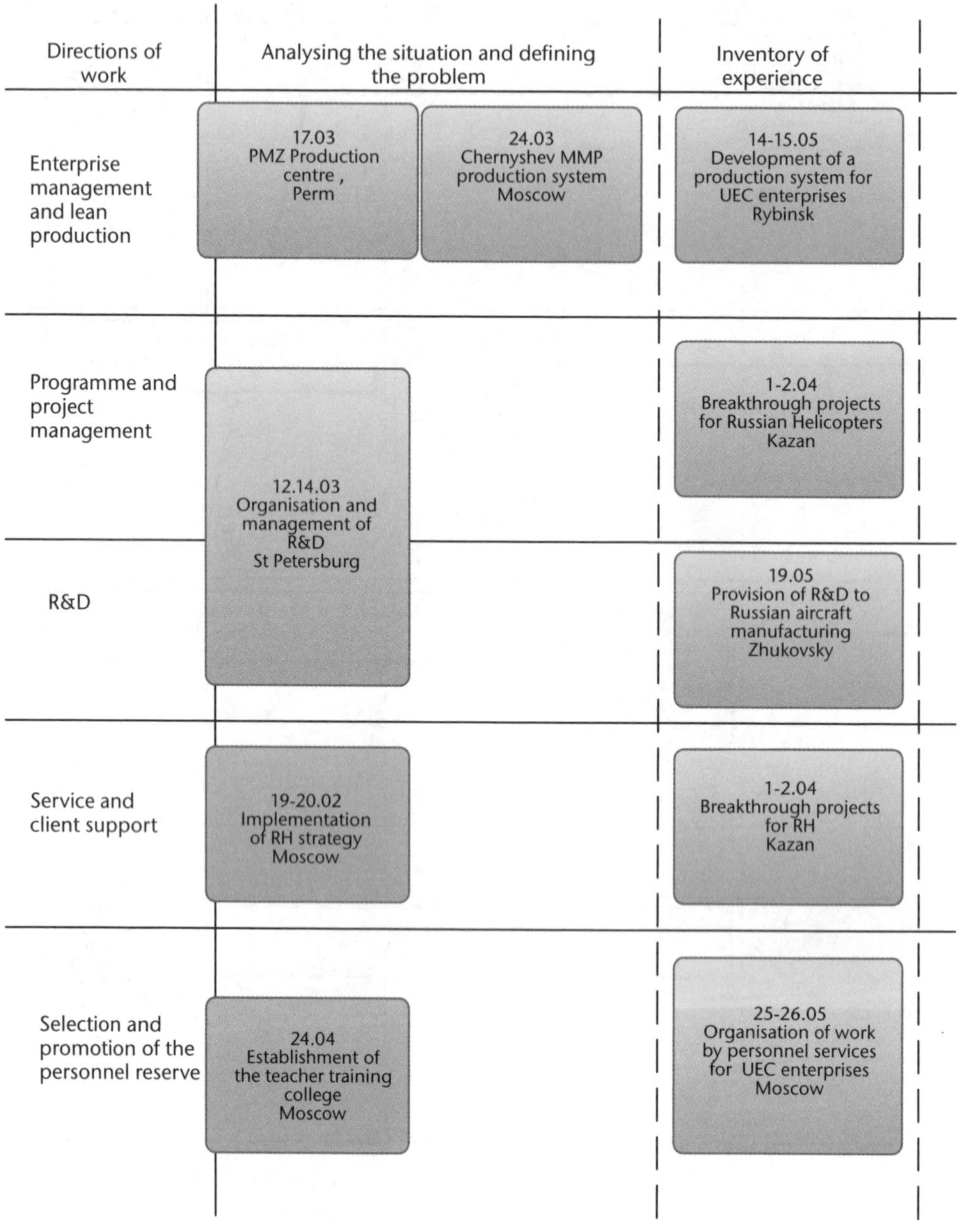

Directions of work	Analysing the situation and defining the problem		Inventory of experience
Enterprise management and lean production	17.03 PMZ Production centre , Perm	24.03 Chernyshev MMP production system Moscow	14-15.05 Development of a production system for UEC enterprises Rybinsk
Programme and project management	12.14.03 Organisation and management of R&D St Petersburg		1-2.04 Breakthrough projects for Russian Helicopters Kazan
R&D			19.05 Provision of R&D to Russian aircraft manufacturing Zhukovsky
Service and client support	19-20.02 Implementation of RH strategy Moscow		1-2.04 Breakthrough projects for RH Kazan
Selection and promotion of the personnel reserve	24.04 Establishment of the teacher training college Moscow		25-26.05 Organisation of work by personnel services for UEC enterprises Moscow

Implementing best practice

16.06
Preparation of lean
production code in
UEC
Moscow

22–25.06
Formation of a
management system for
modern enterprise
Samara

September
Development of a
production system in
RH enterprises
Kazan

11.12.06
Helicopter engines
programme
(experience from
Turbomessa)
Paris

System of
programme/project
management for UEC
Moscow

Design of a national
aircraft manufacturing
centre

Design of IC UEC
and VNTK

July
Design of a technical
support service for the
client

Jan–May
'21st Century
Helicopters'
Competition

29.06.07
Exhibition
HTTM- 2010

Perspectives in the
aircraft industry
(Seliger 2010)

December
Selection and
promotion of the
personnel reserve
2010
Moscow

February–June
'21st Century Engines'
Competition

Figure 7.40 Areas of work, 2011

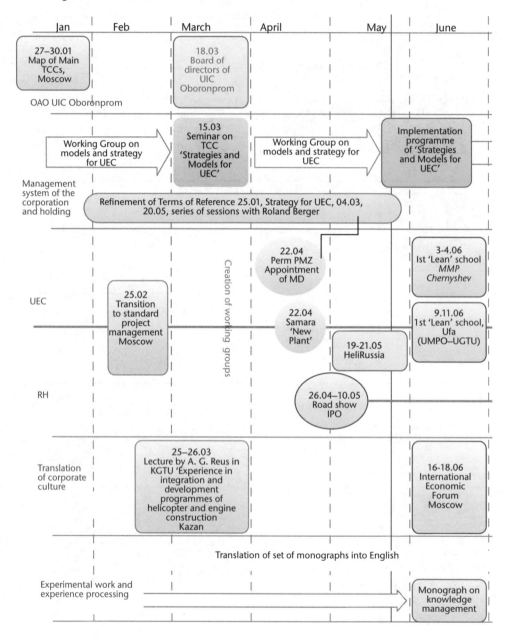

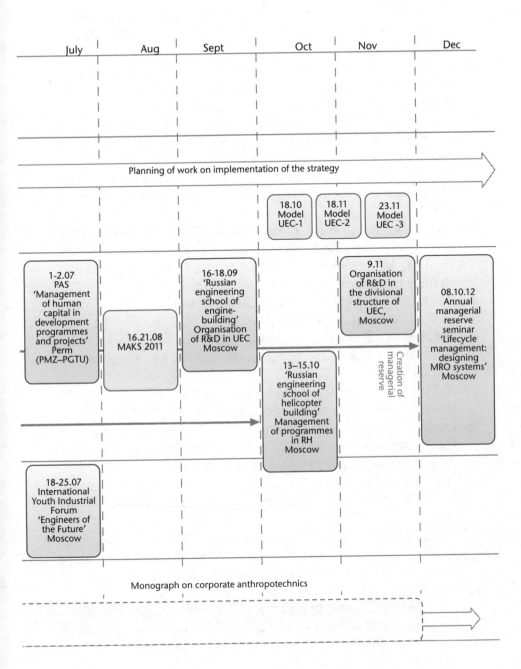

30 Project workshop on 'Providing R&D to the Russian Aircraft Construction Industry', Zhukovsky, Central Aerohydrodynamic Institute (TsAGI), May 2010.

31 Project workshop on 'The development of production systems in UEC Enterprises: experience and problems in the implementation of lean production', Rybinsk, May 2010.

32 Organisational activity workshop on 'Preparing and organising the manufacture of helicopter engines in Russia', Paris, June 2010.

33 Project workshop on 'Building management systems in modern engine-manufacturing companies', Samara, OAO Kuznetsov, July 2010.

34 Contest for the position of managing director of OAO UEC MC and organisational activity workshop: 'Organisation of work in the UEC Management System according to the programme of strategy implementation', Moscow, September 2010.

35 Workshop on 'Analysing the situation in the UEC management system', Moscow, September 2010.

36 Organisational activity workshop on 'A programme of work to "capture" a share in the world market of helicopter engineering and servicing', October 2010.

37 Meeting on 'The development of a corporate production system based on lean production', Moscow, November 2010

38 Organisational activity workshop on 'Restructuring the management companies of BP UEC in the course of programme and project management', Moscow, December 2010.

39 Organisational activity workshop on 'Map of the major technological competence centres in Russia', Moscow, January 2011.

40 Organisational activity session on 'Experience in integrating and developing the Russian helicopter and engine manufacturing complex', Kazan, March 2011.

41 The First Corporate School of Lean Production, Moscow, Chernyshev OAO MMP June 2011.

42 Organisational activity workshop on 'Developing a programme to create a corporate system of production planning and control', Ufa, OAO UMPO, June 2011.

43 Workshop on 'Corporate human capital management in the context of reform and development of the UEC', Perm, PMZ, July 2011.

44 Project workshop for the junior personnel reserve of OAO UIC Oboronprom 'Managing innovative corporate development' as part of the First International Industrial Youth Forum 'Engineers of the Future 2011', Irkutsk Region, July 2011.

45 Workshop on 'The organisation of R&D in UEC divisions and the development of a Russian School of Gas Turbine Engineering', Moscow, September 2011.

46 OAG session on 'R&D organisation in the Russian Helicopters company and the development of the Russian Helicopter Engineering School', Moscow, October 2011.

47 Workshop on 'Management of product lifecycle in the engine and helicopter manufacturing industries. designing an after-sales service system', Yekaterinburg, OAO UZGA, December 2011.

48 Workshop on 'Building a corporate staff training system. Infrastructure design and work programme of work for the educational centres of the organisation', Moscow, February 2012.

49 The Second Lean School of OAO UIC Oboronprom, 'Designing the roll-out of lean manufacturing in enterprises of the group', Rybinsk, OAO NPO Saturn, March 2012.

50 Workshop (game session on situation analysis) 'Resource status and inventory-building in Russian aggregate building', Moscow, April 2012.

51 OAG session on 'Bottlenecks and problems in creating the Combat Aircraft Engines Division', Ufa, OAO UMPO, May 2012.

52 OAG session on 'Compact cluster projects in enterprises in the group', Perm, PMZ, June 2012.

53 OAGs on 'Long-term strategy of the group', Moscow, July 2012.

Figure 7.41 Areas.of work 2012

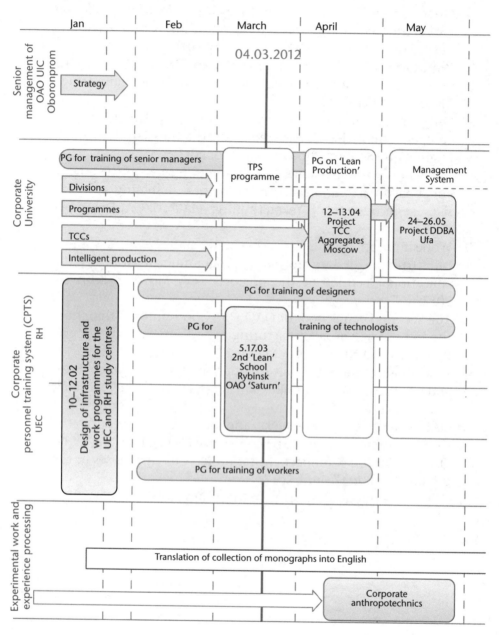

PG: project group
TPS: Toyota Production System

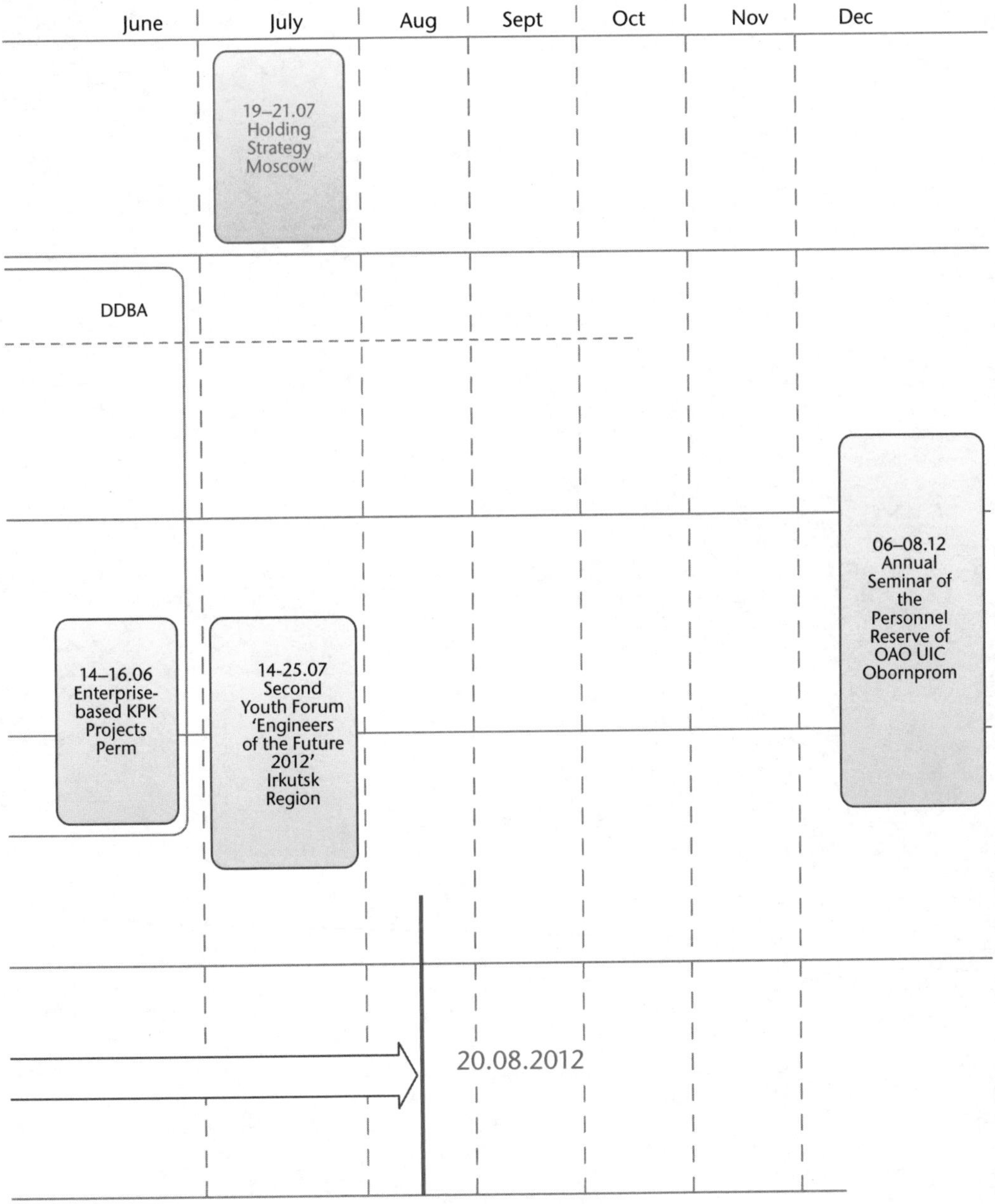
June
July
Aug
Sept
Oct
Nov
Dec
19–21.07 Holding Strategy Moscow
DDBA
06–08.12 Annual Seminar of the Personnel Reserve of OAO UIC Obornprom
14–16.06 Enterprise-based KPK Projects Perm
14-25.07 Second Youth Forum 'Engineers of the Future 2012' Irkutsk Region
20.08.2012

Index

co-ordination of reforms, 154–5, 159

composition of, 155–6, 158–64

and creation of arms'-length companies, 461–2

departmental responsibilities, delineating, 454

field of activity, 152–3

foreign relations, 226, 228, 247, 261–79, 281–98, 396–7, 426, 438–41 (*see also* G8, trade, individual countries by name)

functions of, 162–3

industrial policy *see* industrial policy

lack of system for monitoring projects, 151

legislation *see* laws

levels of local government, 193–6, 253

relation between local and national governance, 155–6, 159, 164–5, 185–6, 193, 196, 253 (*see also* budget)

state funding for industry, 151, 227, 231, 431, 465, 478–9, 645, 648, 685, 762, 764

state funding for management training, 257

state ownership of enterprises, 469, 470, 472, 476 (*see also* public–private partnerships)

state promotion of large projects, 436, 446–7, 454 (*see also under* infrastructure)

structure of public finances, 173–96

system of governance, 162–6, 317

see also Russian Federation; state, the; individual ministries, organisations and politicians by name

Russia 2050, 609

Russian Academy of Medical Sciences, 535, 544

Russian Academy of Sciences, 535, 544

Russian Electronic Industry Development Strategy up to 2025, 456

Russian Federation

economy of *see* economy

federal structure of, 143, 158–61

geographical issues, 243, 326, 334, 400

image of, 406–7

infrastructure of *see* infrastructure

as young state with developing institutions and systems, 255

see also Russia, government of

Russian Helicopters, 460, 465, 479, 567, 619, 643, 645–6, 652–4, 659–64, 679–80, 686–7, 756–64, 820

main directions and bottlenecks, 746

managing reorganisation, 739–48

mission, 747, 804

performance of, 661, 677, 679, 757–8

scope of activity, 742

strategy for, 661, 662, 741, 758

structure of, 678, 764–5

suppliers, 679–80

see also helicopters

Russian Joint Stock Power Engineering and Electrification Company, 438

Russian Light Industry Development Strategy up to 2020, 456

Russian Medical Industry Development Strategy up to 2020, 456

Russian Metals Industry Development Strategy up to 2020, 456

Russian Power Plant Engineering Development Strategy for 2010–2020 and beyond to 2030, 456

Russian Railways LLC, 529, 609

Russian Technologies, 461–2, 651–2, 645

Russian Timber Industry Development Strategy up to 2020, 456

Russian Transport Engineering Development Strategy in 2007–10 and up to 2015, 456

Russians living abroad, 287–8

RZhD OAO, 322

S

safety requirements and standards, 551–2, 558–9

see also regulation, standards

Safran, 665, 750